LEADERSHIP AND CONFLICT

THE LITTMAN LIBRARY OF
JEWISH CIVILIZATION

Dedicated to the memory of
LOUIS THOMAS SIDNEY LITTMAN
*who founded the Littman Library for the love of God
and as an act of charity in memory of his father*
JOSEPH AARON LITTMAN
and to the memory of
ROBERT JOSEPH LITTMAN
who continued what his father Louis had begun
יהא זכרם ברוך

'*Get wisdom, get understanding:
Forsake her not and she shall preserve thee*'

PROV. 4: 5

*The Littman Library of Jewish Civilization is a registered UK charity
Registered charity no.* 1000784

LEADERSHIP AND CONFLICT

◆

*Tensions in Medieval and
Early Modern Jewish History
and Culture*

◆

MARC SAPERSTEIN

Oxford · Portland, Oregon
The Littman Library of Jewish Civilization
2014

The Littman Library of Jewish Civilization
Chief Executive Officer: Ludo Craddock
Managing Editor: Connie Webber

PO Box 645, Oxford OX2 OUJ, UK
www.littman.co.uk

Published in the United States and Canada by
The Littman Library of Jewish Civilization
c/o ISBS, 920 NE 58th Avenue, Suite 300
Portland, Oregon 97213-3786

© *Marc Saperstein 2014*

All rights reserved.
No part of this publication may be reproduced,
stored in a retrieval system, or transmitted, in any form or by
any means, without the prior permission in writing of
The Littman Library of Jewish Civilization

A catalogue record for this book is available from the British Library

Library of Congress Cataloging-in-Publication Data

Saperstein, Marc.
Leadership and conflict : tensions in medieval and early modern Jewish history and culture / Marc Saperstein.
pages cm
Includes bibliographical references and index.
1. Rabbis—Office—History. 2. Jewish leadership—History. 3. Jewish law—Decision making.
4. Judaism—History—Medieval and early modern period, 425–1789.
5. Leadership in rabbinical literature. 6. Authority—Religious aspects—Judaism. I. Title.
BM652.S25 2015   296.6'1–dc23   2014010401
ISBN 978-1-906764-49-4

Publishing co-ordinator: Janet Moth
Copy-editing: Mark Newby
Indexing: Marc Saperstein
Production, design and typesetting by Pete Russell, Faringdon, Oxon.
Printed in Great Britain on acid-free paper by
TJ International Ltd., Padstow, Cornwall

For

JOSEPH SAPERSTEIN FRUG
born 21 December 2008

and

JACOB ADAM SOMEKH WINTER
born 15 November 2011

Acknowledgements

THE MATERIAL in this book is not the fruit of my most recent research, as was my previous Littman Library publication, *Jewish Preaching in Times of War, 1800–2001*. Rather, it represents almost four decades of academic study and research in various areas of medieval and early modern Jewish cultural history.

During my first two years at the New York School of Hebrew Union College–Jewish Institute of Religion, I acquired the tools that allowed me to spend the following two years earning an MA in Jewish History and Hebrew Literature at the Hebrew University in Jerusalem. The four most influential teachers there were Joseph Dan, who introduced me to the academic study of Jewish sermons as sources for Jewish history and culture (see Chapters 1, 5–7, 9), Avraham Grossman, with whom I first read the sources for the conflicts over Maimonides' philosophical writings (see Chapter 4), Dan Pagis, whose influence lingers in my interpretation of one of the most famous poems by Judah Halevi (see Chapter 11), and Haim Beinart, who guided me to a serious encounter with the literature of the final generation of Jewish life in Spain (see Chapter 7).

Upon returning to New York to complete my final year at HUC–JIR, I wrote an MA dissertation on the conflict leading to the ban proclaimed by Rashba in 1305, using the sources already studied in Jerusalem and applying the historical methodology learned from Martin A. Cohen (see Chapter 4).

Following rabbinic ordination, I entered the Ph.D. programme in Jewish studies at Harvard University. There I was privileged to have the ongoing guidance and inspiration of two towering figures of American Jewish scholarship in their generation. Isadore Twersky, for whom Maimonides was a profound influence and model, helped me appreciate an approach to Jewish intellectual and cultural history going beyond the handful of familiar intellectual giants, revealing how the work of second-tier figures writing in a variety of genres (commentaries on the Bible and the aggadah, sermons, epistles, ethical wills, encyclopaedic summaries) spread the influence of philosophical ideas to circles of Jewish society beyond a small intellectual elite (see Chapter 3). Yosef Hayim Yerushalmi's course on Jewish messianic movements led directly to a similar undergraduate course which I have offered for many years, as well as my selecting, editing, and writing an introduction to a collection of academic essays on various aspects of Jewish messianism (see Chapter 13). Jacob Katz of the Hebrew University taught two seminars at Harvard during the second year of my doctoral studies. These seminars introduced me to the academic study of responsa not only as sources for the history of halakhah but—what was for me more important—as reflections of tensions within Jewish society. Chapters 2 and 8 both began as seminar papers for his courses.

Beyond the academic inspiration of these outstanding scholars, the influence of my father, a congregational rabbi for forty-seven years, of my rabbinical training at HUC-JIR, and of my five-year tenure as Principal of Leo Baeck College in London, have all deepened my appreciation of the importance of rabbinic leadership in the medieval and early modern periods and the challenges presented to this leadership when—as is so often the case—communities of Jews and even rabbinical colleagues were deeply conflicted about issues they consider to be critically important (see Chapter 10).

All but one of the chapters in this book (Chapter 2) are reworkings of articles published in various journals, proceedings of academic conferences, anthologies, and Festschriften. A few of them have appeared quite recently. I have attempted to impose a unity of format and style on the entire text, and added a comprehensive bibliography and index. In many cases I have added references in the footnotes to more recent academic literature on the topics discussed, but for reasons of space I have not done this systematically and not all relevant recent scholarship has been incorporated into the text.

*

I was able to gather the material together and transform it into a coherent book during the spring of 2012, when I was Weinstock Visiting Professor of Jewish Studies at Harvard, teaching two courses but with ample opportunity to make full use of the extraordinary resources of Harvard's Widener Library. Despite somewhat heavier responsibilities as Horace W. Goldsmith Visiting Professor at Yale during the spring of 2013, I was still able to benefit significantly from Yale's Sterling Memorial Library in making additions, updating, and checking sources. The Leo Baeck College Library and the Cambridge University Library have also been consistently helpful resources for the material of this book since my relocation to the UK in June 2006. I am also grateful to colleagues in the Department of Theology and Religious Studies at King's College London, where I have taught during the past five years, for their encouragement and support during the final editorial work on the book.

*

Connie Webber and I communicated extensively about the technical implications of having each chapter stand on its own tub for readers who may not have access to the entire book but who will use specific sections of it. As a service to those readers, full bibliographical references are given at the first citation of a work in every chapter, as well as in the main bibliography. I am deeply grateful for the way in which Connie has worked out these details in a thoughtful dialogue with me.

Mark Newby, my copy-editor, has gone through the entire text several times with rigorous care to adapt it consistently to the details of Littman style, and to identify minor errors and infelicities of language that were not noticed in the original printing and that slipped by my own re-reading of the material before it was submitted. Ludo Craddock and Janet Moth have been extremely helpful in their quick and thorough responses to every query I have sent them.

During the period between the present book and *Jewish Preaching in Times of War* (2008), two members of a new generation in my family have enriched my life and the lives of my closest relatives. In the hope and prayer that they will come to appreciate the importance of rabbinic leadership in the past and the present experience of the Jewish people, that their lives will exemplify continuity in the chain of tradition, and that the world in which they come to full maturity will be less riddled with deadly conflict than the world in which this book is born, I dedicate this volume to them.

MS

Contents

Note on Transliteration — xiii

Introduction — 1

PART I
TWO MODES OF RABBINIC LEADERSHIP

1. The Preaching of Repentance and the Reforms in Toledo, 1281 — 13
2. Legal Decision-Making in Fourteenth-Century Toledo: The Responsa of Rabbi Judah ben Asher — 29

PART II
INTELLECTUAL CHALLENGE AND CONFLICT

3. Philosophy and Jewish Society in the Late Middle Ages — 59
4. The Conflict over the Ban on Philosophical Study, 1305: A Political Perspective — 94
5. Cultural Juxtapositions: Problematizing Scripture in Late Medieval Jewish and Christian Exegesis — 113
6. *Ein li esek banistarot*: Saul Levi Morteira's Sermons on *Parashat* 'Bereshit' — 140

PART III
LEADERS FACING COMMUNITIES IN UPHEAVAL

7. Jewish Leadership in the Generation of the Expulsion — 179
8. Rabbis, Martyrs, and Merchants: Jewish Communal Conflict as Reflected in the Responsa on the Boycott of Ancona — 204
9. Four Kinds of Weeping: Saul Levi Morteira's Application of Biblical Narrative to Contemporary Events — 221
10. Attempts to Control the Pulpit: Medieval Judaism and Beyond — 237

PART IV
CONFLICTING ATTITUDES TOWARDS EXILE, THE LAND, AND THE MESSIAH

11. 'Arab Chains' and 'The Good Things of Spain': Aspects of Jewish Exile — 253

12. The Land of Israel in Pre-Modern Jewish Thought: A History of Two Rabbinic Statements — 271

13. Messianic Leadership in Jewish History: Movements and Personalities — 291

Bibliography — 319

Index of Passages Cited — 357

General Index — 361

Note on Transliteration

THE TRANSLITERATION of Hebrew in this book reflects consideration of the type of book it is, in terms of its content, purpose, and readership. The system adopted therefore reflects a broad approach to transcription, rather than the narrower approaches found in the *Encyclopaedia Judaica* or other systems developed for text-based or linguistic studies. The aim has been to reflect the pronunciation prescribed for modern Hebrew, rather than the spelling or Hebrew word structure, and to do so using conventions that are generally familiar to the English-speaking reader.

In accordance with this approach, no attempt is made to indicate the distinctions between *alef* and *ayin*, *tet* and *taf*, *kaf* and *kuf*, *sin* and *samekh*, since these are not relevant to pronunciation; likewise, the *dagesh* is not indicated except where it affects pronunciation. Following the principle of using conventions familiar to the majority of readers, however, transcriptions that are well established have been retained even when they are not fully consistent with the transliteration system adopted. On similar grounds, the *tsadi* is rendered by 'tz' in such familiar words as barmitzvah. Likewise, the distinction between *ḥet* and *khaf* has been retained, using *ḥ* for the former and *kh* for the latter; the associated forms are generally familiar to readers, even if the distinction is not actually borne out in pronunciation, and for the same reason the final *heh* is indicated too. As in Hebrew, no capital letters are used, except that an initial capital has been retained in transliterating titles of published works (for example, *Shulḥan arukh*).

Since no distinction is made between *alef* and *ayin*, they are indicated by an apostrophe only in intervocalic positions where a failure to do so could lead an English-speaking reader to pronounce the vowel-cluster as a diphthong—as, for example, in *ha'ir*—or otherwise mispronounce the word.

The *sheva na* is indicated by an *e*—*perikat ol*, *reshut*—except, again, when established convention dictates otherwise.

The *yod* is represented by *i* when it occurs as a vowel (*bereshit*), by *y* when it occurs as a consonant (*yesodot*), and by *yi* when it occurs as both (*yisra'el*).

Names have generally been left in their familiar forms, even when this is inconsistent with the overall system.

Introduction

THROUGHOUT THE CENTURIES of diaspora history, rabbinic leadership in the Jewish community has had a Janus-like function. Facing inwards, it has sought to exercise authority in defence of unity and tradition: mediating and communicating the sacred texts, interpreting and applying them in a manner that is both rooted in the past and that refracts them with novel insight; providing guidance and making decisions to address the various internal problems that arise; speaking out or acting to secure any breach in the discipline necessary for Jewish continuity and survival under trying circumstances. Facing outwards, rabbinic leadership (sometimes the same individuals, often others) has been expected to represent the Jewish community before the Gentile world, whether in symbolic rituals that dramatize the Jewish role in the larger society or by active intervention at the highest levels of government to defend Jewish needs. Sometimes the leaders function in solidarity with their own people and the external society; frequently, however, there is tension and conflict with one group or another. There is also a very different kind of leadership usually opposed by the rabbinic establishment—one that claims messianic status—which will be discussed later in the volume.

For the analysis of rabbinic leadership and its relationship to the broader population, many familiar expressions of Jewish intellectual activity will not be of primary importance. Such products of the cultural and intellectual elite are by their very nature intended for a minuscule audience. Examples would be the legal novellae or *tosafot* of the sophisticated talmudic scholar, ingeniously solving an intellectual conundrum or apparent contradiction between one passage and another; or the probings of the philosopher-theologian evaluating the cogency of Aristotelian proofs for the eternity of the world and the relationship of such proofs to biblical texts and rabbinic traditions; or the allusive exegesis of the kabbalist, uncovering in biblical verses an array of mystical hints to the secrets of the Godhead.

The first such category—intensive dialectical talmudic study—considers issues devoid of any direct connection with contemporary Jewish life—

for example, the intricacies of the priestly rituals for Yom Kippur in the Jerusalem Temple—to be every bit as important as issues with practical consequences. There is a well-known passage in Abraham ibn Daud's *Sefer ha-kabalah* (Book of Tradition), written in the mid-twelfth century, in which an unknown Jewish captive ransomed from a Muslim privateer sat in a back corner of the synagogue study hall in Cordova. Listening to the teacher discuss a detail regarding ritual immersions by the High Priest on the Day of Atonement, the stranger—who was actually a distinguished scholar who had concealed his identity in order not to increase the ransom demanded—realized that the teacher was explaining the talmudic text incorrectly and politely indicated this by asking a question. Asked to explain the law, he did so, after which the students asked him all the questions they had, to which he responded 'out of the abundance of his wisdom'. The passage continues: 'outside the College there were litigants, who were not permitted to enter until the students had completed their lesson'; only then did the teacher turn to adjudicate the actual legal problems facing the Jews of his community.[1] The hierarchy is clear: the role of the scholar trumps the role of the judge: studies of the complexities of talmudic law take priority, even if they have been totally theoretical for a thousand years since the destruction of the Temple, and the mundane difficulties faced by contemporary Jews must wait for their solution.

Indeed, the ideal of study of Torah for its own sake led many to conclude that the most exalted form of intellectual activity was engagement with texts and exegetical problems that had absolutely no practical significance for any living Jew.[2] Through a homiletical interpretation of Ecclesiastes 4: 6, the German Jewish Pietists—contemporaries of Ibn Daud—criticized the excesses of Tosafist dialectics for being devoid of connection with the lives of contemporary Jews: '"Better is a handful with quiet": that a person will know the practical decisions of Jewish law, "than two handfuls with toil": that he knows how to pose difficult questions and give solutions and overturn passages of the Talmud, "and a chasing after wind" [*ruaḥ*]: in order to demonstrate the breadth of his spirit [*ruḥo*] and take pride in his brilliance in making hair-splitting distinctions.'[3] The kind of scholarship that the Pietists repudi-

---

[1] Abraham ibn Daud, *Sefer ha-Qabbalah: The Book of Tradition. A Critical Edition*, ed. and trans. Gerson Cohen (Philadelphia, 1967), 65–6.

[2] See Judah Galinsky, 'Halakhah, Economics and Ideology in the School of the Rosh in Toledo' (Heb.), *Zion*, 72 (2007), 388–93, nn. 5, 6, 8.

[3] *Sefer ḥasidim* [based on the Parma Manuscript], ed. Jehuda Wistinezki (Frankfurt am Main: Wahrmann Verlag, 1924; repr. Jerusalem, 1969), §648, p. 174.

ated tells us little about the mentality, the spirituality, and the practical needs of most Jews living in the vicinity of the talmudic academies.

In the case of philosophy and kabbalah, a distance from the masses is maintained overtly and explicitly, as authors warned that ordinary Jews without special preparation should stay away from material intended for an initiated elite. For philosophers like Maimonides, all Jews were expected to have an understanding of basic philosophical principles, such as the absolute unity and incorporeality of God, and these he outlined at the beginning of his monumental codification of Jewish law, *Mishneh torah*. But the essence of the philosophical enterprise was a mastery of the reasoning that led to such principles, and this was an achievement that required a prolonged and elaborate exposure to philosophical material that was beyond the ken of most Jews. Thus Maimonides states at the beginning of his *Guide for the Perplexed* that it was God's intention to conceal the deepest truths of divine apprehension from the multitude of Jews, as they were unprepared to understand them, and that only those who had already received a sound education in philosophy should undertake to study what he had written, although others might indeed derive benefit from certain passages. He further warns such readers not to teach others what they have learned from the book based on their own understanding unless it is a topic that earlier theological authorities have fully treated. This is clearly a text that reflects only an extremely limited circle of the Jewish society in which it was written.

Those who fostered the emergence of the school of Jewish mysticism we call kabbalah also explicitly discouraged the idea that the enterprise was intended for Jewish society as a whole. Many of the early kabbalists were aware that the possibilities of misunderstanding kabbalistic doctrines posed potential pitfalls more perilous than the dangers of philosophy. An early adept of kabbalah in southern France was so protective of the new doctrines that he opposed committing them to writing, insisting that they should be transmitted only by a master of the material who knew that the individual to whom he was disclosing the mysteries was ready to understand them properly. In the sixteenth century, similar opposition was expressed to the printing of the Zohar, the great classic of kabbalistic literature, because printing would make it difficult to control who had access to the material.

Nahmanides (Moses ben Nahman, Ramban) was the first to allude to esoteric interpretations in a work intended for a broader audience—his *Commentary on the Torah*—although, before printing, when texts had to be copied by scribes, only a minority within the Jewish population would have had access to an extensive biblical commentary. Like Maimonides, Nahmanides concluded his introduction with a warning: that no one should attempt to decipher the meaning of his allusions to mystical teachings independently, for they could be understood only through study with a teacher who was adept in the esoteric tradition. Readers who had no access to such a teacher should content themselves with the author's 'novel interpretations of plain meanings of Scripture and *midrashim*, and let them take moral instruction from the mouths of our holy rabbis: "Into that which is beyond you, do not seek."'[4]

Thus all three major realms of medieval Jewish intellectual enterprise—advanced talmudic study, philosophy, and kabbalah—had an elitist element. The texts they produced reveal intellectual and spiritual leaders writing for a very small circle of people like themselves and pretty much ignoring the broader circles of the society in which they lived. What such texts can tell us about Jewish society as a whole is limited and often unclear.

The two genres that will predominate in many of the following chapters—sermons and responsa—are quite different. The sermon is an address delivered in the vernacular language and intended for the entire congregation of Jews. While it may not be fully understood by everyone in the congregation, preachers facing a live audience know that however much they may want to impress by displaying their own knowledge and ingenuity, they must not speak in a manner that will be unintelligible to the majority of listeners. Occasionally, the preacher may indeed discuss technical issues of Jewish law, especially in sermons relating to the observance of holidays; or analyse a rather abstruse philosophical issue, citing the work of philosophers or theologians from outside the Jewish community (Aristotle, Averroës [Ibn Rushd], Thomas Aquinas); or even refer explicitly to complex kabbalistic doctrines. The messages from the pulpit may be challenging to some of the listeners. But the preacher knows that a significant part of the message has to reach the listeners—including Jewish men and women whose education does not rise above rudimentary literacy—if his role as leader is to be effective and enduring. Therefore, the appearance of legal, philosophical, or kabbalistic material in the texts of sermons—to the extent that these texts reflect closely the substance of the sermon as delivered orally—informs us about knowledge and concerns that spread beyond a small elite of Jewish intellectuals.

The value of the sermon as a mirror of leadership and community is also

---

[4] Nahmanides, *Commentary on the Torah*, vol. i: *Genesis*, trans. Charles Ber Chavel (New York, 1971), 15.

demonstrated by a specific genre of Jewish preaching: the sermon intended to criticize ritual, ethical, or economic behaviour, the sermon of *tokheḥah*, or rebuke. In order to meet its goal, the content has to ring true: the listeners must not respond 'What is he talking about? No one is acting that way!' Whether the speaker from the pulpit is a rabbi who has served as leader in the community for decades or an itinerant preacher who has recently arrived and will depart on Sunday morning, the listeners must recognize that the preacher is indeed referring to something that is actually being done or beliefs that people actually hold—even if their response is 'Yes, he's right, that is bad, but he is referring to other people, not to me.' While some of the behaviour criticized often represents standard topoi about the decline of standards in comparison with an idealized past, in many cases such sermons open windows into deep fissures and tension points within the contemporary society. This is the genre that will be analysed in the first chapter, reflecting the tensions in Jewish society of late thirteenth-century Toledo. Other sermons form the basis of Chapters 5, 6, 7, 9, and 10.

The second major genre—the responsum (*teshuvah*)—may be addressed to a rabbinical colleague who has sent the writer a legal query about which the local rabbi did not feel comfortable making an authoritative decision. With the exception of the unusual query that is posed merely out of intellectual curiosity about details of Jewish theology or law, the questions that stimulate the responsa literature arise from actual behaviour that has occurred and is described by the questioner in some detail. Whether the text preserved records the original wording of the question or the respondent's summary, these questions contain data about family ruptures or economic arrangements that must be accurate for the legal decision to be valid. A distortion of the facts presented or the suppression of a significant relevant fact may have undermined the validity of the decision being sought. Therefore, the queries tend to be more reliable as depictions of actual life situations than other genres such as chronicles, that tend to idealize, or ethical diatribes, that often over-emphasize the negative.

The respondent's decision about what is to be done is given not just for its theoretical value: it is intended to affect the lives or the economic interests of real people, as well as to serve as a legal precedent for similar cases in the future. Chapter 2 is based on the responsa of Rabbi Judah ben Asher, a member of one of the leading rabbinic families in early fourteenth-century Castile, whose responsa often diverge dramatically and explicitly from the principles of classical Jewish legal texts in addressing what the writer saw as the needs of his time. Responsa will also be the major source in Chapter 8 and part of Chapter 12.

Both kinds of texts, therefore, provide a window onto rabbinic leadership in action, enabling us to catch a glimpse of the diversity and conflict in a living Jewish society beyond the walls of the academy.

With regard to Jewish culture, I have been particularly fascinated by the flourishing of Jewish philosophy during the Middle Ages, and several of the chapters deal with this subject but not in the manner in which philosophically trained scholars approach it. Without diminishing the importance of the precise analysis of philosophical literature in tracing the technical terminology as it passes from one culture to another or the rigorous evaluation of the cogency of philosophical arguments, my questions are different, and they pertain not just to the highest level of intellectuals but to Jewish society as a whole.

What dynamic changes occurred when philosophical texts begin to penetrate a cultural environment where such texts had never before been studied or even accessible? What happened when philosophical ideas started to appear in forms intended for the consumption of the ordinary educated Jew? Who paid for the scholars who translated Arabic (or Latin) philosophical texts into the Hebrew language or for the scribes who copied manuscripts of lengthy, specialized, technical works? Was philosophy studied in formal Jewish academies, as part of the established curriculum of Jewish learning, or was it entirely a private arrangement between teacher and student, provider and consumer? Was there a correlation between interest in philosophy and socioeconomic status? Did philosophy undermine commitment to traditional beliefs and practices, or was it used to rationalize a flagging allegiance to Jewish distinctiveness? These questions are explored in Chapter 3.

Is there ever justification for leaders to formally ban the study of philosophical texts? The Jewish ban (*ḥerem*) is fundamentally different from the excommunication of the Catholic Church, which entails withholding from the offender the sacraments by the priest who is uniquely entitled to provide them. The *ḥerem* is a form of social ostracism which depends upon the entire Jewish community to enforce it. If it is imposed on an individual with the consensus of the community because of offences that are readily apparent (as with Spinoza in Amsterdam), it can be an extremely powerful instrument of social control. The more people placed under the ban and the vaguer the offence that leads to it (whoever does X or does not do Y), the more likely that it will create controversy and conflict and fail to achieve its purpose.

Such was the ban promulgated by the leading rabbinic authority of Aragon, Rabbi Solomon ben Adret (Rashba) in the summer of 1305, which applied to Jews who studied Hebrew translations of Greek philosophical texts—medical texts excluded—before they had reached the age of 25. The result was a deep fissure within the communities of southern France that had initiated the request for such a ban, to the point where the opposing groups each passed additional bans against the other. My own approach to this fascinating episode was to focus on the political context, which had been overlooked in the abundant scholarly literature: the efforts by the French king, Philip the Fair, to complete the incorporation of Languedoc into his royal domain and the problems raised by the French Jews apparently being regulated by a rabbi from the competing realm of Aragon.

After this article was first published, a highly esteemed Israeli historian challenged my interpretation and offered an alternative proposal. At the end of Chapter 4, I respond to this critique and explain why I consider it to be unpersuasive.

What is the proper approach of the commentator or preacher to interpreting biblical texts for the broad Jewish community? There is often a tendency to avoid texts that raise troubling problems and to focus instead on passages that will be soothing, reassuring, and inspiring for the reader or listener. Chapter 5 addresses a dramatically different approach that was apparently taken by late medieval Spanish Jewish writers under the influence of the Christian academies: the explicit articulation of problems, difficulties, or doubts raised by a biblical or rabbinic passage, bringing them to the attention even of those to whom they had never occurred, and then resolving the difficulties in what was expected to be a satisfactory and persuasive manner. It was a rather risky undertaking because of the possibility that the reader or listener would remember the doubt but not its resolution. The chapter provides evidence for widespread use of this technique especially by Spanish Jews in the late Middle Ages, along with several possible explanations as to why this exegetical technique became so popular in the generation of the Expulsion from Spain.

The following chapter focuses on Saul Levi Morteira, rabbi and preacher to the Portuguese community of Amsterdam in the first half of the seventeenth century. This community was at first composed entirely of immigrants who had been born and educated as Christians in Portugal—many of them fourth- or fifth-generation descendants of those who had been subjected to a universal forced baptism in 1497—and who decided that they wanted to leave the Iberian peninsula for somewhere they could live openly as Jews. Because of their background, they were heavily dependent on rabbinic leadership for guidance about what Jewish living meant, including the limits of acceptable dissent. Morteira's beautifully crafted sermons, delivered in Portuguese over four decades—many of which Spinoza listened to as he was growing up—provided an ongoing programme of higher Jewish learning on a sophisticated level. Chapter 6, which supplements my earlier book about Morteira and Amsterdam, follows the preacher as he systematically addresses, year after year, the many intellectual and exegetical problems arising from successive verses in the opening chapter of Genesis.

Leadership is especially challenged when external forces create unexpected tragedy or when underlying tensions burst into the open and the community is rent by conflict. The rabbinic leaders of the final generation of Jewish life on the Iberian peninsula have been criticized for mediocrity and for their failure to meet adequately the challenges posed by the Spanish Inquisition and the Edict of Expulsion. Chapter 7 explores and challenges the basis for such criticism and then reviews the work of one of the most important rabbinic figures in that perilous time, Rabbi Isaac Aboab, focusing especially on the texts of his sermons. Aboab left Spain for Portugal in the summer of 1492 and died less than a year later.

In 1556 another Inquisition—this one under the direct jurisdiction of the papacy—tried for heresy, condemned, and executed a group of New Christians, immigrants from Portugal who had joined the Italian Jewish community of Ancona, a major port on the Adriatic Sea. The result was the first attempt to mobilize international Jewish economic power to protect Jews from persecution by organizing a boycott of the port of Ancona. As reviewed in Chapter 8, the rabbinic responsa regarding this boycott written by Ottoman rabbis addressed dramatic issues of international significance that affected both the morale and the economic well-being of many Jews. These texts, grappling with legal issues on the basis of conflicting narratives of what had happened, reveal that the boycott was far more complicated than it originally appears.

Chapter 9 returns to Rabbi Saul Levi Morteira of Amsterdam and follows a single sermon as he adapted it some years after its original delivery, with explicit reference to catastrophic events that had befallen Jewish communities far away—in Lublin to the east and Recife to the west—and also a plague that had just decimated the population in Amsterdam though sparing most of its Jewish inhabitants. Chapter 10 broadens the canvas geographically and chronologically, showing the perspective of those Jewish leaders who tried to restrict the freedom of expression of preachers when delivering sermons on controversial issues. Beginning in the thirteenth century, it follows this theme into the modern period and includes the Jewish communities of the United States.

In theory, there should have been no controversy over the status of the Land of Israel in the medieval and early modern periods. There was a broad consensus that this was the homeland of the Jewish people—not only their land of origin in the past, but the land of destiny and promise for the future. Jews and their Christian neighbours alike understood that Jews were not fully at home in Spain or Italy, France, Germany or Poland—they prayed three times a day for the ingathering of the exiles that would reunite the scattered people in their ancestral homeland. Some of the most beautiful poetry written by Jews expressed their longing to return.

Yet in both theoretical and practical terms, the reality was more complex. Chapter 11 analyses three brief, powerful passages, from different environments and different literary genres, revealing an enduring ambivalence towards Jewish life in 'exile', a reluctance to concede that the centuries of Jewish life in foreign lands were devoid of any positive qualities, and even—rather surprisingly—the suggestion that life in exile might have religious advantages for Jews that were not available in the Holy Land.

Chapter 12 analyses the history of interpretation of two well-known talmudic statements about the diaspora. The first has practical, legal, and financial consequences, pertaining to the right of a husband to be freed from the financial obligation stipulated in the *ketubah* (marriage contract) if he divorced his wife because she refused to accompany him to live in the Land of Israel. The statement of the Talmud is clear, but the responsa literature reveals that in real-life cases, justifications were frequently found to protect the rights of the divorced wife against enforcement of the talmudic principle. The second statement is of powerful theological significance, addressing the relationship between God and the Land of Israel. It asserts that God may not be accessible outside the Land of Israel, implying that the possibilities for legitimate religious life in the diaspora were extremely limited. Here too exegetical literature sometimes explained the statement but frequently dissented from it, showing that diaspora Jews often refused to be bound by the more extreme anti-diaspora sentiments of their classical texts.

The most fundamental challenge to both the leaders and ordinary Jews of their communities occurred when an individual claimed to be the messiah—

the one intended by God to lead the people out of their diaspora homes and back to the land of national origin. At best such a claim was a radical threat to the existing authority structure of a traditional Jewish community; at worst it would arouse the active intervention of the host government that viewed such an individual as inciting rebellion. Chapter 13, originally the introduction to a collection of essays on messianic movements and personalities by a wide variety of Jewish scholars that I edited, is a survey of the dynamics of such movements over a period of some two millennia.

PART I

TWO MODES OF RABBINIC LEADERSHIP

CHAPTER ONE

The Preaching of Repentance and the Reforms in Toledo, 1281

ONE FORM of internal conflict in all traditional communities arises when the behaviour of the people, or certain categories of the people, or specific individuals, fails to meet the standards required by their religious leaders. To be sure, such tensions are all but guaranteed by the structure of the relationship between clergy and laity. Religious leaders are rarely content with the devotion of their flock, and there will almost invariably be shortcomings for which they judge rebuke to be in order. In some cases, these criticisms will be stylized and conventional; in others, they expose significant ideological or social fault-lines that divide a community against itself. From at least the high Middle Ages, one of the most respected media for expressing such criticism by Jewish leaders has been the sermon, which often expressed the consensus of a congregation, but occasionally articulated its divisions.[1]

Medieval Spanish Jews understood one of the central roles of the preacher to be expressed by a verse from Isaiah: 'Cry with full throat, without restraint, raise your voice like a ram's horn, declare to my people their transgression, to the House of Jacob their sin' (Isa. 58: 1).[2] Yet few extant sermons from the

---

First published in Beverly Kienzle et al. (eds.), *Models of Holiness in Medieval Preaching* (Louvain-la-Neuve, 1996), 155–72.

[1] For a general discussion of the methodological challenges in using criticism from sermons as evidence for the realities of the community being addressed, see Marc Saperstein, *'Your Voice Like a Ram's Horn': Themes and Texts in Traditional Jewish Preaching* (Cincinnati, 1996), 127–30; for the dynamics of the relationship between preacher of rebuke and congregation, see Marc Saperstein, *Jewish Preaching, 1200–1800: An Anthology* (New Haven, 1989), 46–50.

[2] See the material in the manuscript 'Ein hakore' from the mid-fifteenth century, translated in Saperstein, *Jewish Preaching, 1200–1800*, 391; and, in general, Saperstein, *'Your Voice Like a Ram's Horn'*, 83–90.

thirteenth century are devoted primarily to the task of condemning the religious and ethical shortcomings of the audience and calling upon listeners to change their behaviour.³

During the 1230s a French talmudic scholar, Moses ben Jacob of Coucy, in response (so he claimed) to a heavenly command, undertook to visit the Jewish communities of the Iberian peninsula to preach repentance.⁴ The Hebrew text of a sermon dated 1236/37 calling for repentance that may have been written by Moses of Coucy has been published.⁵ Further information about his campaign is based on references in his legal compendium, known as *Sefer mitsvot gadol*. There he informs his readers that he focused on various problems: sexual relations with Gentile women living in Jewish homes, failure to set aside time for religious study, and laxity regarding the requirements to put on ritual phylacteries (*tefilin*), to affix a parchment with specified biblical verses to the doorposts of the house (*mezuzah*), and to wear fringes upon the garment (*tsitsit*).

Moses of Coucy claimed that his preaching met with extraordinary success: 'They performed great acts of repentance; thousands and tens of thousands accepted upon themselves the commandments of *tefilin*, *mezuzot*, and *tsitsit*. And so in the other lands where I was subsequently [i.e., after being

---

³ For an example from the philosopher Jacob Anatoli, see Saperstein, *'Your Voice Like a Ram's Horn'*, 71.

⁴ Moses ben Jacob of Coucy, *Sefer mitsvot gadol* [legal compendium] (Benei Barak, 1991), positive commandment 3 (see Israel M. Ta-Shma, 'Moses ben Jacob of Coucy', *Encyclopedia Judaica*, 16 vols. [Jerusalem, 1973], xii. 418–19; Efraim Elimelech Urbach, *The Tosafists: Their History, Writings, and Methods* [Ba'alei hatosafot: toldoteihem, ḥibureihem, ushitatam] [Jerusalem, 1968], 384–95). The question of how Moses of Coucy, speaking an early French vernacular, would have made himself intelligible to Jewish listeners in the Iberian peninsula has not been addressed. He could have preached in Hebrew, but this would not have been conducive to a movement of mass repentance. For similar problems in Christian preaching, note the claim that Anthony of Padua preached with such fervour, eloquence, and clarity that even those who did not know his language were able to understand him (Francis of Assisi, *The Little Flowers of St. Francis* [Garden City, NY, 1958], 130); and the report of Vicente Ferrer in Andalusia (Alan D. Deyermond, 'The Sermon and Its Uses in Medieval Castilian Literature', *La Corónica*, 8 [1980], 127–45). In my judgement, the most likely explanation is that Moses of Coucy would have used a translator.

⁵ Israel M. Ta-Shma, 'An Epistle and a Revivalist Sermon by One of Our Early Rabbis' (Heb.), *Moriah*, 19/5–6 (1994), 7–12. Ta-Shma suggested that this revival campaign should be seen in a messianic context linked with the expectations bound up with the year 5000 in the Jewish calendar (1239/40) (see also Israel Jacob Yuval, *Two Nations in Your Womb: Perceptions of Jews and Christians in Late Antiquity and the Middle Ages* [Berkeley, 2006], 273–4).

in Spain]: my words were accepted everywhere.' 'I spoke at length, giving homiletical interpretations like these in "the Jerusalemite exile community of Sepharad" [Obad. 20], and they sent away many Gentile women in the year 1235/36.'[6] These passages are patently hyperbolic, but it would be difficult to imagine their being fabricated without some measure of at least temporary response. Unfortunately, there does not seem to be confirmation from Spanish Jewish sources of these preaching events.[7]

The dynamics of Moses of Coucy's campaign may be illuminated by a scholarly investigation of Christian revival preachers in thirteenth-century Italy.[8] Here too, the actual texts of the sermons have not survived, but extensive narrative descriptions have allowed a reconstruction of the 'sacred theatre' of the preaching event. This popular preaching of repentance swept through Italy in 1233, just three years before Moses of Coucy set off on his journey. There is no way of proving that there was any connection between the revival preaching of the Christians in Italy and that of the Jews in France and Spain, but Jews could hardly have been unaware of the excitement generated by the arrival of a powerful Christian preacher, the large crowds that gathered, and the religious fervour that often followed. The possible influence of such events upon the decision of a Jewish religious leader to undertake a similar campaign and upon the psychological readiness of the Jewish population to respond to it cannot be dismissed.

Later in the century, there was another example from Spain of a movement which combined the preaching of repentance and actual communal reform. In this case, a record of the sermon has been preserved. The events

---

[6] Moses of Coucy *Sefer mitsvot gadol*, positive commandment 3, negative commandment 112.

[7] 'But his testimony is unique and otherwise unsupported. Perhaps he wrote in an excess of preacher's fervor or in an exaggerated pride of his role as a reincarnated Ezra' (Abraham A. Neuman, *The Jews in Spain: Their Social, Political and Cultural Life during the Middle Ages*, 2 vols. [Philadelphia, 1942], ii. 11). See also the strange use of this by Salo W. Baron: 'That Mediterranean, and especially Spanish, Jews had not only Christian concubines but also Christian wives is borne out by the boast of the famous jurist Moses b. Jacob of Coucy that, on his preaching tour through Spain in 1236, he had persuaded many Jews to discharge their Christian mates' (Baron, *A Social and Religious History of the Jews*, 18 vols. [Philadelphia, 1952–83], xi. 82). The context of the passage in *Sefer mitsvot gadol* makes it clear that the author is speaking not of marriage but of a relationship akin to concubinage with a Gentile woman living in a Jewish home.

[8] Augustine Thompson, *Revival Preachers and Politics in Thirteenth-Century Italy: The Great Devotion of 1233* (New York, 1992).

occurred at Toledo in 1281, and the preacher was, almost certainly,[9] the elderly rabbi, mystic, and courtier, Todros ben Joseph Abulafia.[10]

The historical circumstances of these communal reforms have been described by the historian Yitzhak Baer, and there is no need to dwell upon them at length.[11] At the end of his glorious reign, Alfonso X the Wise of Castile faced a rebellion by his son, Sancho. Leading Jewish courtiers and tax-farmers were caught in the middle and bore the brunt of the king's fury: some of the most influential paid with their lives. In January 1281 the king had all the Jews of his realm arrested in their synagogues and held for ransom: the great Jewish community of Toledo was particularly devastated. This was a shattering blow to the morale of a community that prided itself upon the prosperity and influence of its courtiers. Abulafia was apparently one of the few Jews with standing in the court who emerged unscathed, a model of traditional, rabbinic leadership blended with prestige in the political realm, and possibly still holding an official position of authority from the Crown. With the Jewish community turning towards introspection, Abulafia was a natural figure to provide guidance.[12]

---

[9] The identification of the author was made by Gershom Scholem, based on the inclusion in the sermon of a rather lengthy passage that appears word for word in Todros ben Joseph Abulafia's *Otsar hakavod* (Satu Mare, 1926), 29b–30a (Gershom Scholem, 'Abulafia, Todros ben Josef', *Encyclopaedia Judaica*, 10 vols. [Berlin, 1928–34], i. 657). The passage in the sermon contains the phrase, 'I have already alluded to this previously; however, I have written this statement as a conclusion to this tractate' (Todros ben Joseph Abulafia, Sermon [Heb.], in Judah ben Asher, *Zikhron yehudah*, ed. Judah Rosenberg [Berlin, 1846; repr. Jerusalem, 1967], no. 91, 44b). While the first part of the phrase could conceivably refer to material in the first part of the sermon (ibid. 43b), the second part obviously fits the context of *Otsar hakavod*, which is arranged as a series of interpretations of rabbinic statements organized by talmudic tractate, whereas there is no explicit referent for 'this tractate' in the sermon passage. Part of the passage from *Otsar hakavod* is cited by Ben Zion Dinur, together with other passages complaining about the excessive influence of astrology undermining the belief in divine providence (Dinur, *Israel in the Diaspora* [Yisra'el bagolah], 2nd edn., Pt. I, 4 vols.; Pt. II, 6 vols. [Tel Aviv, 1958–72], Pt. II, vol. iv, 287). Yet Dinur, citing a long passage from the sermon in a selection of texts relating to the reform movement in Toledo, identifies it only by the name of 'Judah ben Asher', in whose fourteenth-century collection of responsa the sermon is found (ibid. 298).

[10] On Abulafia as a courtier, see Neuman, *The Jews in Spain*, ii. 243, 337 n. 136; on his outstanding personal qualities, see Hayyim (Yefim) Schirmann, 'Studies on the Poems and Letters of Abraham Bedersi' (Heb.), in Shmuel Ettinger et al. (eds.), *Yitzhak F. Baer Jubilee Volume* [Sefer yovel leyitshak baer] (Jerusalem, 1961), 164 n. 42; Yitzhak Baer, 'Todros ben Judah Halevi and His Time' (Heb.), in *Studies in the History of the Jewish People* [Mehkarim umasot betoledot yisra'el], 2 vols. (Jerusalem, 1986), ii. 279–80; id., *A History of the Jews in Christian Spain*, 2 vols. (Philadelphia, 1961–6), i. 119.

[11] Y. Baer, 'Todros ben Judah Halevi' (Heb.), 283–94; id., *A History of the Jews in Christian Spain*, i. 129–30, 257–60.

[12] The circumstances are thus not dissimilar to those surrounding the sermon of Joseph ibn Shem Tov delivered at Segovia in 1452 (see Saperstein, *Jewish Preaching, 1200–1800*, 167–79).

The sermon itself has been preserved in an anomalous way: as part of a collection of rabbinic legal responsa by a fourteenth-century rabbi of Toledo, Judah ben Asher, where it appears without explanation or even attribution.[13] The structure of the sermon leaves much to be desired. It begins with a prophetic verse but never provides an interpretation of it; it is interrupted by a long exegetical passage from another work; it contains considerable repetition—repetition so pronounced that I believe it may be an incomplete record of two separate sermons by the same preacher. What we have, therefore, is by no means a model of Jewish homiletical art. It is not easy to recognize in this text a sermon that would have inspired the listeners to change the pattern of their lives: its power must have been bound up with the circumstances of delivery and the personality of the preacher. The importance for us lies in the specificity of its criticism and its religious ideals and the evidence it provides for an occasion when these ideals became a programme for communal reform.

The contents of the sermon can be divided into three categories. First is a standard theme in medieval Jewish moralistic literature: the insistence that the harshness of Jewish life in exile is caused not by astrological forces but by divine providence and that repentance can bring the exile to an end. The arguments condemning astrological beliefs, drawn from biblical and rabbinic texts, are significant in medieval Jewish intellectual history, but they need not detain us here.[14]

The second kind of material is directly relevant to our subject. Traditional Jewish life is highly structured by a legal system that governs every aspect of behaviour. There are literally thousands of rules, rooted in the pentateuchal legislation and expanded by rabbinic interpretation, that determine how Jews in a traditional community are supposed live. A preacher who hopes to arti-

---

[13] Abulafia, Sermon (Heb.); also in Judah ben Asher, *She'elot uteshuvot zikhron yehudah lerabenu yehudah ben harosh* [responsa], ed. Avraham Yosef Havatselet (Jerusalem, 2005), no. 91, 106–12. Havatselet's introduction to the new edition states that the original printed text of Judah ben Asher's responsa, including Abulafia's sermon, was based on a manuscript written in Tunis which was copied by a Jew from Russia who sold his copy in Berlin (ibid. 42–3). The sermon has been briefly described by Michal Oron ('The Sermon of Rabbi Todros ben Joseph Halevi Abulafia on the Reform of Ethical Qualities and Behaviour' [Heb.], *Da'at*, 11 [1983], 47–51).

[14] The belief in astrological determinism was shared by the overwhelming majority of medieval Jews, but many thinkers insisted that God exercised direct providential control over the Jewish people, overruling the effects of the planets and stars. Others believed that, during the Jewish exile, God had abandoned the Jews to the control of planets and stars, suspending divine providential intervention (see e.g. Shalom Rosenberg, 'Exile and Redemption in Jewish Thought in the Sixteenth Century', in Bernard Cooperman [ed.], *Jewish Thought in the Sixteenth Century* [Cambridge, Mass., 1983], 405–7; see also below, n. 47).

culate a vision and effect change cannot possibly touch upon every infraction: he must focus on the issues he considers most important. Therefore, the criticisms that appear in a sermon such as this reflect the values and ideals of the preacher and the tension points of the society.

Some of the points raised are standard criticisms that can be found in virtually every generation from which Jewish moralistic literature has been preserved, such as complaints about conversation during public worship, failure to attend daily services,[15] or the improper use of leisure time on a day of rest: 'Also, on the sabbath and festivals, Jews should not sit in groups in the public places; they should go to their homes, or to the schools in order to hear the sermon', a recommendation not exactly surprising from a preacher.[16] Similarly: 'On the sabbath and festivals, the idlers must be prevented from gazing upon the women who pass by and indulging in other kinds of frivolity; they must adhere to every sealed ordinance passed by the seven city elders.'[17] Other standard types of criticism apply to dishonest business practices, specifying various techniques of tampering with scales to the disadvantage of the purchaser,[18] and the improper use of oaths and curses.[19]

[15] 'Concerning prayer: they must not converse between the passage beginning "Blessed is the One who spoke" and the conclusion of the Shemoneh Esreh prayer, for then the prayer will be accepted; otherwise, "Who asked that of you, to trample my courts?" [Isa. 1: 12]' (Abulafia, Sermon [Heb.], 44*b*). 'In addition, whoever is not actually at work should come to the synagogue to pray at the morning, afternoon, and evening services. For a person is forbidden to attend to his affairs before he has prayed—once having begun, he must finish all the benedictions—and each time he [interrupts] he should be fined a coin [*zahuv*] for the communal fund' (ibid. 45*b*). The final phrase is a rendering of the unusual word *lesulkiyah*, based on Dinur, *Israel in the Diaspora* (Heb.), Pt. II, vol. iv, 299. On the problem of conversation during worship, see Moses Maimonides, *Teshuvot harambam* [responsa], ed. Joshua Blau, 3 vols. (Jerusalem, 1957–61), ii. 484; Israel Bettan, *Studies in Jewish Preaching* (Cincinnati, 1939), 300.

[16] Abulafia, Sermon (Heb.), 45*b*. This indicates that the practice, at least in that community, was for the sermon to be delivered not as part of the regular morning synagogue service but in the afternoon, either in the hour before the afternoon worship or as part of the afternoon service (see Saperstein, *Jewish Preaching, 1200–1800*, 28–31).

[17] Abulafia, Sermon (Heb.), 44*b*. On the practice of gazing at women, see the passage from Azariah Figo, an early seventeenth-century Italian preacher in Bettan, *Studies in Jewish Preaching*, 237; cf. Saperstein, *'Your Voice Like a Ram's Horn'*, 99–100.

[18] Abulafia, Sermon (Heb.), 45*a*. This is an explicit violation of Lev. 19: 35–6, yet the preacher felt compelled to cite several talmudic passages emphasizing the seriousness of this transgression, as well as recommending the appointment of personnel to supervise the marketplace (see below).

[19] The actual practice specified is that of Jews who 'curse their fathers, using God's name, in order to establish their words' (Abulafia, Sermon [Heb.], 44*a*, cf. 45*b*). This apparently refers to saying: 'If this is not true, may God curse my father' (cf. Jonah Gerondi, *Sha'arei teshuvah* [Gates of Repentance] [Jerusalem, 1968], 3: 46–7). It is interesting that medieval Christian preachers sometimes berated

A high percentage of the complaints in the sermon concerned two themes—relations with women and relations with Gentiles—which overlap on the issue of Gentile servant women (primarily Muslims) living in Jewish homes. We see a concern for defending traditional standards of modesty for Jewish women and morals for Jewish men in a passage such as the following, which came at the very end of the sermon:

> There is also the matter of the bride: they may allow her [face] to be uncovered before the wedding, but they should cover her after the wedding. The law is not in accordance with the rabbi who says that it is permissible to gaze upon the bride, not even for a single hour.[20] Furthermore, people must recognize her before her marriage, so that there can be witnesses to the marriage. Also, there should always be two special witnesses there to observe the ring beforehand and ascertain whether it is worth a *perutah* [a small coin] or not, and they may hear the betrothal formula said by the husband.[21]

Here we see a tension between popular practices and the strict standards pertaining to a central institution of Jewish life.

A different issue concerned women and the laws regulating relations between Jews and Gentiles. Talmudic legislation prohibited Jews from eating bread baked by a Gentile, but the conditions of medieval Jewish communities often made it unfeasible for Jews to maintain their own bakeries, and the rabbis took a lenient stance: so long as Jewish women threw a wood chip into the oven, they would consider it as if the baking was being done jointly by

---

their congregations for blasphemous language and pointed to the Jewish abhorrence of such practices (see Saperstein, '*Your Voice Like a Ram's Horn*', 48–9).

[20] 'R. Jonathan said, "It is permissible to gaze upon the bride during the entire seven days [of the wedding festivities] in order to make her more desirable to her husband." But the halakhah is not in accordance with him' (BT *Ket.* 17*a*). Asher ben Yehiel, who came from Germany to Toledo some two decades after the sermon was delivered, wrote: 'There are those who say that for the rest of the wedding week it is prohibited, but on the first day, the day of most intense love in the husband, it is permitted, for if it were not so, who would testify that she went out with a veil and her hair uncovered? But this is not the case. It is forbidden to gaze upon the bride for even a single hour. When they see the veil that was made and say: "This belongs to such and such a bride", that counts as testimony. Also, seeing the veil when she is wearing it or the uncovering of her head is not the same as gazing at her face' (Tosafot of R. Asher on BT *Ket.* 2: 3; see also *Arba'ah turim*, 'Even ha'ezer', 21).

[21] Abulafia, Sermon (Heb.), 45*b*. The requirement of proper witnesses to testify that the betrothal ceremony has been carried out correctly is crucial in determining the marital status of the woman. Indeed, there was some effort at this time to pass communal ordinances requiring the presence of ten witnesses (see Menachem Elon, *Jewish Law: History, Sources, Principles*, 4 vols. [Philadelphia, 1994], ii. 711–12, 853–5).

a Jew and a Gentile, and the bread could be eaten.[22] But we see from this sermon that problems arose:

> Also, a woman must not bring *cazuela* or *panada*[23] to the oven of a Gentile and give it to the baker to bake along with the bread. She must herself place it in the oven, not the baker, whether he is a Muslim or a Christian. The wood chip that the women throw into the oven, or their raking of the coals under the *cazuela* or the fire in the oven under the chip does not help here. The permission of the rabbis applies only to bread.[24]

Apparently there was an attempt to push this leniency further, and the preacher protested and tried to draw a line.

Considerable attention is given to the problems arising from having Gentile servant women living in the house. There were two aspects of such problems. First was using Gentile servants to circumvent established Jewish laws, such as the prohibition on taking interest from a fellow Jew: 'They must also prevent the servant woman of a Jew from lending on interest to another Jew, for whatever the servant woman acquires is the acquisition of her master, and it is as if the Jew himself made the loan on interest'.[25] This was clearly a ruse, a legal fiction, to evade the law, and the rabbis opposed it strenuously.

Gentile servants raised a series of legal issues regarding the observance of the sabbath. We see the tension points in passages such as the following:

> Concerning the sabbath. They command their servant women to kindle lights and other such things. It is absolutely clear that this is forbidden. It is obviously forbidden to command them, for whatever a Jew may not do, he must not tell a Gentile to do. More than this: even if one does not command the Gentile, it is still forbidden to benefit from their work, as is written in the Talmud: 'If a Gentile kindles a candle, a Jew may use its light, but if it is done *for* the Jew, it is forbidden to use its light' [BT *Shab*. 122a]. Even if the Gentile does it on his own, if he is accustomed to do this, it is for-

---

[22] Mishnah *AZ* 2: 6; BT *AZ* 38b; Tosafot ad loc., *va'ata*; Moses Maimonides, *Mishneh torah*, 'Laws of Forbidden Foods', 17: 12–13; Tosafot of R. Asher on BT *AZ* 2: 33; Jacob Katz, *Exclusiveness and Tolerance: Jewish–Gentile Relations in Medieval and Modern Times* (New York, 1962), 40; Yom Tov Assis, *The Golden Age of Aragonese Jewry: Community and Society in the Crown of Aragon, 1213–1327* (London, 1997), 230–1 (where he skips over the halakhic problem by writing simply that 'ordinary bread could be baked in Christian bakeries').

[23] *Cazuela* is both a clay cooking implement and the name of a dish, made with various vegetables and meat, cooked in it (apparently related to our 'casserole') (see *Diccionario de autoridades*, 3 vols. [Madrid, 1963], i. 247–8; *Diccionario critico etimológico castellano e hispanico*, 6 vols. [Madrid, 1984–91], i. 934). *Panada* (or possibly, *panarra* or *panata*), apparently refers to some kind of breaded dish (see *Diccionario critico etimológico castellano e hispanico*, iv. 364–6).

[24] Abulafia, Sermon (Heb.), 45b.   [25] Ibid. 44a.

bidden to act shrewdly in this matter, as we see in the Talmud [BT *BM* 90*a*]. . . . This applies all the more to male and female servants of Jews, whose acts are performed with the awareness of their masters: these masters are forbidden to benefit from their work. . . .

As for those who command Christians or Muslims to write on the sabbath because of their own necessities or because of matters pertaining to leased properties—there being no lives endangered or urgent communal concern—it is obvious that this is forbidden and a profaning of the Sabbath. . . . To command a Gentile to do work for a *public* need is forbidden unless there are lives endangered, and all the more so is it forbidden for a private need. On this matter too, there is no need to speak at length.[26]

It is important to note that here, as elsewhere in the sermon, the preacher cited talmudic passages in support of his point. This suggests that he was not simply speaking as an authority to a group of ignorant listeners who felt obligated to accept whatever he said. For some, who may not have known the law and followed their own traditions, the sermon may have served an educational function: it was not unusual for legal material (of a relatively straightforward nature) to be included in sermons intended for a general Jewish audience. But the permissibility of using Gentiles for various tasks on the sabbath represented a complicated interaction of legal mandates and practical needs, and the preacher apparently felt the need not only to educate but also to substantiate his position.[27]

If one set of problems pertained to the circumvention of prohibitions that originally had nothing to do with women (loans on interest, activities on the sabbath), the other raised explicitly the issue of sexual licentiousness:

There is also the matter of the servant women, a stumbling block for the Jews. They wear embroidery, and licentiousness ensues. . . . As a result of our sins, many children have been born to female servants of Jewish fathers.

Regarding the Muslim women with whom Jews are accustomed to behave licentiously, this too is forbidden. . . . Jews, who are a holy people, must not profane their seed in the womb of a Gentile woman, thereby fathering offspring for idolatry.[28]

---

[26] Ibid. 45*a*; cf. the earlier passage: 'Concerning the sabbath. You already know that it teaches about the creation of the world, and also about the world to come. God has commanded us to rest on it. It is forbidden to *think about*, let alone to deal with, our possessions. Nor may we tell a Gentile to do something—not to write, not to light a candle, not to kindle a fire in the winter—for it is forbidden to benefit from any work done on the sabbath' (ibid. 44*a*).

[27] On this issue, see the excellent study by Jacob Katz, *The 'Shabbes Goy': A Study in Halakhic Flexibility* (Philadelphia, 1989), esp. 50–2.

[28] Abulafia, Sermon (Heb.), 44*a*, 45*b*. For the idea of sexual relations with Gentile women as a violation of Jewish holiness, see *Zohar*, 'Shemot', 2: 3*b*, 7*a*; 'Yitro' 2: 87*b*; Dinur, *Israel in the Diaspora*

Needless to say, this was strong language to be included in a sermon delivered publicly in the vernacular. The passage itself refers to one claim made by the transgressors: that compelling them to remove the Muslim servants from their homes would inflict an unendurable hardship, a claim that has a certain force in Jewish law.[29] From other contemporary sources, we know that some Jews tried to justify their behaviour with Muslim women on legal-philosophical grounds, arguing that the pure monotheistic character of Islam and its practices of circumcision and dietary laws placed its adherents in a special category, for which the prohibition of sexual relations with Gentile women did not apply.[30] The uncompromising formulation at the end— 'fathering offspring for idolatry'—appears to be a conscious repudiation of this stance, reflecting the seriousness with which Jewish leaders viewed sexual laxity and the crossing of boundary lines that would threaten Jewish distinctiveness.[31]

The third category of material in the sermon, in addition to the condemnation of astrology and the identification of sins, consisted of specific institutional reforms. Some of these reforms required that individuals be chosen for

(Heb.), Pt. II, vol. iv, 291–2; Pinchas Giller, *The Enlightened Will Shine: Symbolization and Theurgy in the Later Strata of the Zohar* (Albany: State University of New York Press, 1993), 115–16. The dominant language in this tradition speaks of taking the holy covenant (i.e. the circumcised penis) into a foreign domain (see also Marc Saperstein, *Decoding the Rabbis: A Thirteenth-Century Commentary on the Aggadah* [Cambridge, Mass., 1980], 100, 246 n. 101).

[29] 'If they are unwilling to [sell or manumit their Muslim servant women] and claim that it is a decree that they cannot endure . . .' (Abulafia, Sermon [Heb.], 45*b*). The talmudic principle is that 'no decree should be imposed on the public unless the majority can endure it' (e.g. BT *BK* 79*b*; *BB* 60*b*; see Elon, *Jewish Law*, ii. 539–41).

[30] This defence is cited by Moses de Leon in *Shekel hakodesh*, in Dinur, *Israel in the Diaspora* (Heb.), Pt. II, vol. iv, 291. The contemporary poet Todros ben Judah Abulafia (not to be confused with the preacher) defends dalliance with Muslim women on aesthetic rather than philosophical grounds (see the translation of his poem in Ross Brann, *The Compunctious Poet: Cultural Ambiguity and Hebrew Poetry in Muslim Spain* [Baltimore, 1991], 145). On Todros ben Judah Abulafia in general and especially his relationship with troubadour love poetry, see Avivah Doron, *A Poet in the Royal Court: Todros Halevi Abulafia* [Meshorer baḥatsar hamelekh: todros halevi abulafiyah] (Tel Aviv, 1989). For a general treatment of Jews and Muslim concubines in Christian Spain, including the range of rabbinic responses, see Yom Tov Assis, 'Sexual Behavior in Mediaeval Hispano-Jewish Society', in Ada Rapoport-Albert and Steven Zipperstein (eds.), *Jewish History: Essays in Honour of Chimen Abramsky* (London, 1988), 36–40.

[31] Compare the strong attack on one who has sexual relations with a servant woman by Jonah Gerondi (*Sha'arei teshuvah*, 3: 131–3; see Dinur, *Israel in the Diaspora* [Heb.], Pt. II, vol. iv, 290–1; Y. Baer, *A History of the Jews in Christian Spain*, i. 256). Several decades later, Joshua ibn Shu'eib, in a sermon discussing the zealous vigilantism of Pinhas (Num. 25: 6–8), justified its repetition for the sin of sexual relations with Gentile women 'in every generation' (Ibn Shu'eib, *Derashot hatorah* [Sermons on the Torah], 2 vols. [Jerusalem, 1992], ii. 400; see Carmi Horowitz, *The Jewish Sermon in 14th-Century*

positions of authority with responsibility to respond to lapses in behaviour. With regard to dishonesty in the marketplace, 'it is necessary to appoint as inspectors of weights and measures two respected men, of good families, who will show no favouritism or deference to [the dishonest businessmen] for there is no real repentance for this kind of robbery'.[32]

In addition to the new manpower, the preacher recommended specific procedural changes for the establishment of guilt in the Jewish courts. Ordinarily, two witnesses are necessary to confirm a fact in Jewish law, but now, 'if a single witness should come and testify under oath that he saw someone steal from a Gentile, the accused is to be punished, provided the witness is not a personal enemy of the accused'. This is an extra-legal provision, an emergency measure that Jewish authorities claimed was sanctioned in response to specific needs, as the passage continues, 'if the accusation is made by two witnesses, his punishment is prescribed *by law*'.[33]

The preacher also tried to make giving testimony about an offence into an obligation to be enforced by the whole community: 'Anyone who sees a theft committed is to be compelled, under pain of excommunication, to report it to the court immediately, so that the name of the Lord may not be publicly defamed'; 'Whoever knows that another Jew is having sexual relations with a Muslim or Christian woman must inform the judges.'[34]

Here too, the departure from ordinary judicial procedure should be noted. The mandates of the preacher stand in stark contrast with the statement in a legal responsum written fifty years later by Judah ben Asher of Toledo, in whose collection Abulafia's sermon was preserved: 'You are not

---

Spain: The Derashot of R. Joshua ibn Shu'eib [Cambridge, Mass., 1989], 46–7). Note the strong legal response to the problem of sexual relations with Christian women in the responsa of Judah ben Asher of Toledo (see Chapter 2).

[32] Abulafia, Sermon (Heb.), 45*a*; cf. Y. Baer, *A History of the Jews in Christian Spain*, i. 258. See also: 'We must appoint people with authority over the markets and other places, so that whoever swears or utters a curse will, the first and second time, pay a fine according to the judgement of the court, and if the person is unwilling to stop, he will be punished corporeally, at the court's discretion' (Abulafia, Sermon [Heb.], 44*a*). The appointing of supervisors over the markets was one of Jonah Gerondi's recommendations (*Sha'arei teshuvah*, 3: 73).

[33] Abulafia, Sermon (Heb.), 45*a*; the translation is from Y. Baer, *A History of the Jews in Christian Spain*, i. 258–9, italics added. The issue of theft from a Gentile is a controversial problem in Jewish law: although the medieval codifications prohibited it, the rabbinic sources were ambivalent, which provided grist for generations of anti-Jewish writers. Jews were accordingly quite sensitive to the matter in practice. On the legal sources, see Steven D. Fraade, *From Tradition to Commentary: Torah and Its Interpretation in the Midrash Sifre to Deuteronomy* (Albany, NY, 1991), 216 n. 148.

[34] Abulafia, Sermon (Heb.), 45*a*–*b*.

to declare an excommunicating ban in order to force witnesses to step forwards and tell what they know about any suspicion of misdeed on the part of any witness in the case—for this is a humiliating inquisitorial procedure [*pesquisa*], not to be instituted against anyone.'[35]

The distinction made by the later rabbi is clear: if a person is actually accused of a specific crime or sin, then a ban can be announced requiring everyone with knowledge of that act to testify, but the Jewish court may not compel witnesses to come forward and accuse a man about whom no accusation is made. That was the procedure of the papal Inquisition, and later the Spanish Inquisition: to proclaim a grace period for sinners to confess and for all Christians to denounce anyone they suspected of sin.[36] But this is precisely what was mandated by the preacher in Toledo, an indication of the pressing nature of the problems at hand.

Finally, there are recommendations for specific legislation by the Jewish communal leadership of Toledo,[37] also to be enforced by the threat of the ban.

You should pass a decree that [servant women] must wear only black garments made of a coarse material.[38] Their curtains should be thick, not fine [transparent]. A great ban of excommunication should be proclaimed with the ram's horns against anyone who has sexual intercourse with a Gentile woman. . . . This will remove a great obstacle.

According to our law, those who retain Muslim women and commit forbidden acts with them should be compelled to sell them or grant them their freedom. At the very least, if they are unwilling to do this and claim that it is a decree that they cannot endure,[39] a solemn ban of excommunication should be proclaimed with Torah scrolls and ram's horns, that every Jew who has sexual relations with a Muslim woman will be

---

[35] Judah ben Asher, *Zikhron yehudah*, no. 58, trans. in Jacob Bazak and Stephen M. Passamaneck, *Jewish Law and Jewish Life: Selected Rabbinic Responsa* (New York, 1979), 38; see the detailed discussion of the responsa of Judah ben Asher in Chapter 2.

[36] Henry Charles Lea, *The Inquisition of the Middle Ages* (London, 1963), 124; Nicolau Eymerich, *Le Manuel des inquisiteurs*, trans. Louis Sala-Molins (Paris, 1973), 109–13 ('If anyone knows that someone has said or done something against the faith . . . he is obliged to reveal this to the Inquisitor' [ibid. 109]); cf. Evelyn S. Procter, *The Judicial Use of Pesquisa (Inquisition) in Leon and Castile, 1157–1369*, English Historical Review Supplement, 2 (London, 1966).

[37] On legislation and especially the passing of communal ordinances in Jewish law of the Middle Ages, see Elon, *Jewish Law*, ii. 678–779; on the enactments of Toledo (though not in response to this sermon), see ibid. ii. 839–42.

[38] *Me'aprilton*, which I cannot identify; the rendering, following Dinur (*Israel in the Diaspora* [Heb.], Pt. II, vol. iv, 296), is a guess based on the context.   [39] See above, n. 29.

gripped by God's excommunication and ban and by the ban of the sacred community of Toledo. . . . Furthermore, if the head of a household in which a Muslim woman is living becomes aware of such evil behaviour on behalf of the young men or any others, he is obligated to have the guilty person imprisoned; otherwise, the specified punishment will apply to him. For the sages were strict about this matter.[40]

This was a preacher who did not content himself with abstractions: his purpose was to translate his ideals of holiness into specific measures for their implementation.

As to the impact of the sermon, a contemporary poet described a kind of spiritual 'bonfire of the vanities':

On the sabbath day, the 27th of Shevat in the year 5041 [19 Jan. 1281],[41] there was an upheaval . . . like the overturn of Sodom and Gomorrah. The entire congregation scrutinized their past behaviour with contrite heart, proclaimed a fast, called an assembly, pledged themselves to observe every commandment, and, in solemn council, over scrolls of the Law, concurred that whoever keeps a mistress will not be accepted for the quorum of ten worshippers necessary for public prayer.[42]

Yet, not surprisingly, contemporary sources undermine this idealized version. The poet who reported this sudden transformation himself wrote a poem in which he seems to be distancing himself from heavy-handed reforms imposed by fiat, arguing the need for a more gradual approach, questioning the value of the general ban, and recommending a style of sermonic rebuke that is gentle and does not embarrass the sinner in public. He also defends the legitimacy of keeping Muslim servant women in the house, against the strong denunciation of this practice by Abulafia.[43] One of the leading Aragonese rabbis of the time, Solomon ben Adret (Rashba), when consulted about the proper method of punishing miscreants, responded by counselling moderation and realism, at least on tactical grounds.[44] The stern moralist may have had his say, but it was not the final word.

[40] Abulafia, *Sermon* (Heb.), 44*a*, 45*b*.

[41] The text contains the words *im ma'os me'astanu* ('Truly, you have forsaken us' [Lam. 5: 22, the very last verse of Lamentations]) with *im* highlighted. The numerical value of *im* is 41, giving the year following 5000 in Jewish chronology. The previous verse of Lamentations, 'Take us back, O Lord, to Yourself . . . Renew our days as of old', provides a context of repentance.

[42] Todros ben Judah Abulafia, *Gan hameshalim vehaḥidot* [poetry], ed. David Yellin, 2 vols. (Jerusalem, 1932–6), i. 85; Dinur, *Israel in the Diaspora* (Heb.), Pt. II, vol. iv, 296.

[43] See Hayyim (Yefim) Schirmann, *Hebrew Poetry in Spain and Provence* [Hashirah ha'ivrit bisefarad uviprovans], 2 vols. in 4 (Jerusalem, 1960), iv. 433–4.

[44] Solomon ben Adret, *She'elot uteshuvot harashba* [responsa], 7 vols. in 4 (Benei Berak, 1958–9), v, nos. 238–43, in Y. Baer, *A History of the Jews in Christian Spain*, i. 260–1.

What general conclusions can be drawn from this sermon? First, about the nature of the sins specified, their cause, their social setting, and their significance for traditional Jewish society, the regnant view of these matters is still the one proposed by Yitzhak Baer, who described the problem as 'religious and moral nihilism', located its social nexus in the courtier class, and explained it by the 'inroad of rationalism' in an extreme form he called 'Averroism'.⁴⁵

A careful reading of the sermon provides little support for any of these conclusions. There is no indication that the problem is to be identified with Jewish courtiers: the only social marker is of Jews successful enough to have a Gentile servant living in their home, but that was not uncommon in the communities of France, where there was no courtier class at all.⁴⁶ Complaints about dishonest manipulation of weights clearly apply not to courtiers but to Jewish merchants with small shops in the market. There is also no hint that the problems can be blamed on the influence of philosophy. The preacher has nothing negative to say about the impact of philosophical study on the observance of Jewish traditions.⁴⁷

What about the nature of the infractions specified: do they represent a kind of 'religious and moral nihilism'? The sermon does not sustain such an extreme position. Some of the problems addressed—conversation during prayer, dishonesty in market practices—are likely to be found in any Jewish society, and in Christian society as well, no matter how religiously devoted. Others—gazing at the bride after the wedding, commanding or allowing servants to perform acts prohibited to Jews on the sabbath, using Gentile bakers in the preparation of certain foods, even sexual relations with Gentile servant women—represent in each case a pattern of behaviour with a problematic

---

⁴⁵ See Y. Baer, *A History of the Jews in Christian Spain*, i. 241, 250, 257; this position is followed without question by Oron, 'The Sermon by R. Todros ben Joseph Halevi Abulafia' (Heb.); for further discussion of Baer on 'Averroism', see Chapter 3.

⁴⁶ See, for example, references in letters by thirteenth-century popes (Solomon Grayzel, *The Church and the Jews in the XIIIth Century: A Study of Their Relations during the Years 1198–1254* [New York, 1966], index, s.v. servants of Jews, and esp. 107).

⁴⁷ Here we should distinguish between the material relating to the impact of astrology and that relating to behaviour. With regard to astrology, Abulafia (in the passage from *Otsar hakavod*) refers to Jews who say that 'God has abandoned the earth since the six days of Creation' (Abulafia, Sermon [Heb.], 44*b*), a view that might be related to the Aristotelian view of God as too pure to interact with the world, although it suggests those who held it still accepted the traditional biblical view of Creation that pure Aristotelians rejected. Yet these Jews are characterized as 'ignoramuses who pretend to be Jews' and are overly influenced by the views of astrologers and astronomers.

status according to Jewish law.⁴⁸ Abulafia apparently felt the need not only to condemn these acts but to cite sources and authorities to substantiate his condemnation. These are examples not of nihilism or antinomianism but of testing the flexibility of the halakhic system by individuals who demonstrate their underlying commitment to Jewish law through their use of techniques to navigate around its strictures.⁴⁹

Finally, a point about Abulafia's ideals of holiness as reflected in the sermon. It should be clear that the ideals underlying his rebuke and proposed reforms apply not to a select group of individuals uniquely talented for religious achievement but rather to the Jewish community as a whole. The behaviour expected of Jews is not the kind of ascetic renunciation attainable only by a small spiritual elite but rather conformity to the norms accepted in principle by the entire Jewish community and resistance to the social and psychological pressures to subvert these norms.⁵⁰ It is particularly in the realm of boundary lines—between men and women, masters and servants, Jews and Gentiles—that the pressures to find leniency within the halakhic system were greatest, and it was in these areas that the more conservative leaders tried to hold the line.

The result was a call for institutional mechanisms to impose conformity. But here there was a striking difference from the Christian situation. For while the preacher spoke of ban and excommunication and referred to sanctions and mechanisms of enforcement, the Jewish community had nothing analogous to the Christian excommunication by which the clergy, part of a hierarchical structure, could withhold from the deviant Christian the sacraments of the faith. The Jewish ban was primarily a form of social ostracism which depended upon the consensus of a community for its implementation. Without that consensus, in the face of a group of Jews who defiantly insisted

---

⁴⁸ See above, nn. 20, 22, 27, 30. On the legal issues pertaining to concubines, see the literature in Ephraim Kanarfogel, 'Rabbinic Attitudes toward Nonobservance in the Medieval Period', in Jacob J. Schacter (ed.), *Jewish Tradition and the Nonobservant Jew* (Northvale, NJ, 1992), 18–22.

⁴⁹ For example, throwing a chip of wood into the baker's oven when baking a casserole, asking servants to write on the sabbath, or keeping unmarried Muslim concubines are not blatant violations of dietary laws, the sabbath, or the prohibition of adultery. They are problems not at the core of the religious system but on its peripheries.

⁵⁰ The other presentations on the 'preaching of holiness' at the 30th International Congress on Medieval Studies in 1995, where a preliminary version of this chapter was delivered as a paper, made me appreciate how, in the Christian community as well, preachers in the later Middle Ages tried to extend the ideals of holiness beyond the small elite circle that had committed itself to the religious life.

on their right to follow their own practices, the most fearful expressions of anathema might have little practical effect.[51]

The sermon of Todros ben Joseph Abulafia may have inspired its listeners to change their behaviour, at least temporarily. But we can be fairly certain that it did not put an end to conversation during the worship service, the use of Gentile bakers, or the keeping of Muslim servant women in Jewish homes. Many Jews were apparently not convinced that such behaviour violated the core aspirations of Jewish life. For even the most powerful and inspiring preacher, there are limits to the permanent consequences of the spoken word.

---

[51] To be sure, the ban was pronounced in a manner that exploited the *sancta* of Jewish faith ('with Torah scrolls and rams' horns'). It could be extremely effective as an instrument of coercion when it specified a single individual, but it was less so when it referred to a group ('every Jew who has sexual relations with a Muslim woman'; 'anyone who sees a theft committed is to be compelled, under pain of excommunication, to report it'). For a discussion of the Jewish *ḥerem* in comparison with the feudal *bannum*, see Kenneth R. Stow, *Alienated Minority: The Jews of Medieval Latin Europe* (Cambridge, Mass., 1992), 183–6; on the Christian institution, see Elisabeth Vodola, *Excommunication in the Middle Ages* (Berkeley, 1986).

CHAPTER TWO

Legal Decision-Making in Fourteenth-Century Toledo: The Responsa of Rabbi Judah ben Asher

AMONG THE MOST IMPORTANT mirrors of rabbinic leadership in circumstances of conflict within the Jewish community are rabbinic responsa, answers to legal questions that local rabbis or judges did not feel fully competent to determine on their own and therefore sent to a recognized authority in the region. The approach to such texts, however, may vary.

Throughout the ages, most readers have consulted collections of responsa as a source for precedents in Jewish law (halakhah). The author, asked to render a decision on a doubtful matter, does so on the basis of his expert knowledge of earlier decisions, and his decision then becomes part of the body of authoritative precedents. Subsequent legal authorities therefore study these responsa for guidelines in determining the law under similar circumstances. Many such readers will, of course, go beyond just the decision rendered and concern themselves with the author's method in arriving at the decision, a question of considerable interest to modern scholarship as well. How did he use the talmudic sources, commentators, earlier decisors? How did he handle conflicting statements by authorities? Did he bring any novel interpretation to the traditional texts? Did he tend towards strictness or leniency? Did he allow extra-halakhic considerations to enter the decision-making process?[1] Yet another approach is that of the social historian, using the responsa (and often even more so the questions that evoked them) as sources not for Jewish

---

Previously unpublished.

[1] Such questions are characteristic of the approach of Menachem Elon (*Jewish Law: History, Sources, Principles*, 4 vols. [Philadelphia, 1994]).

law but for insight into the society in which they were produced. To what extent do they provide reflections of external events, information on Jewish economic life, communal institutions, family relations, mechanisms and problems of self-government, relations with Gentiles, and so forth?[2]

In Chapter 8, various sixteenth-century responsa will be used as sources of information about the events of a major conflict in early modern Jewish history. The present chapter focuses on a single rather small collection—the same collection that contains the sermon of 1281 analysed in Chapter 1—to examine the leadership of a rabbi facing internal conflict in fourteenth-century Toledo, Rabbi Judah ben Asher (1270–1349).[3] I will follow the second and (to a lesser extent) the third approaches indicated above, looking particularly at extra-halakhic aspects of his decision-making—the extent to which his adjudication is explicitly motivated, influenced, or guided by factors other than the interpretation of the classical sources of halakhah—and what this tells us about Jewish life in fourteenth-century Castile. Obviously the question of *takanot*, communal legislation inconsistent with the traditional law, will be relevant. So will decisions manifestly said to be not in accordance with Torah law, whether because of urgent immediate needs or

---

[2] For the methodological issues in the historical use of responsa (with examples taken from early Ashkenazi authorities and focusing extensively on textual issues), see Haym Soloveitchik, 'Can Halakhic Texts Talk History?', in id., *Collected Essays* [Oxford, 2013], i. 169–223). For some examples of its implementation, see Isidore Epstein, *Studies in the Communal Life of the Jews of Spain as Reflected in the Responsa of Rabbi Solomon ben Adreth and Rabbi Simon ben Zemach Duran*, 2 vols. in 1 (New York, 1968); Morris Goodblatt, *Jewish Life in Turkey in the XVIth Century as Reflected in the Legal Writings of Samuel di Medina* (New York, 1952); Nisson E. Shulman, *Authority and Community: Polish Jewry in the Sixteenth Century* (New York, 1986); Matt Goldish, *Jewish Questions: Responsa on Sephardic Life in the Early Modern Period* (Princeton, 2008).

[3] The original article and the research on which it was based used Judah ben Asher, *Zikhron yehudah* [responsa], ed. Judah Rosenberg (Berlin, 1846). I have now compared the new edition, based on a different manuscript: Judah ben Asher, *She'elot uteshuvot zikhron yehudah lerabenu yehudah ben harosh* [responsa], ed. Avraham Yosef Havatselet (Jerusalem, 2005). For a description of the two manuscripts, see Havatselet's introduction (ibid. 42–7). The numbers of the responsa are the same in both works.

Judah, who succeeded his father as rabbi and head of the Toledo *yeshivah*, is much less well known than his brother, Jacob ben Asher, the author of the enormously influential halakhic compendium *Arba'ah turim*. Jacob, who apparently did not hold a rabbinic position, is not known to have written responsa. Judah is mentioned only in passing in Solomon Freehof, *The Responsa Literature* (Philadelphia, 1955), 50; Neil S. Hecht et al., *An Introduction to the History and Sources of Jewish Law* (Oxford, 1966), 341; he is not mentioned at all in Louis Jacobs, *A Tree of Life: Diversity, Flexibility, and Creativity in Jewish Law* (Oxford, 1984); Elliot N. Dorff and Arthur Rosett, *A Living Tree: The Roots and Growth of Jewish Law* (Albany, NY, 1988). On Judah, see also Israel Abrahams (ed.), *Hebrew Ethical Wills*, 2 vols. (Philadelphia, 1926), i. 163–200; Judah Galinsky, 'On the Heritage of Rabbi Judah ben Asher, Rabbi of Toledo' (Heb.), *Pe'amim*, 128 (2011), 175–210.

because changing historical circumstances seemed to make the talmudic principle no longer applicable.

The halakhah itself provides the authority and rationale for such extra-halakhic procedure in such concepts as *hora'at sha'ah* (temporary teaching in response to emergencies) and *din malkhut* (law of the king or state),[4] but obviously, the extent to which such authority is employed in a collection of responsa will tell us a great deal about the respondent's philosophy of law and something about contemporary Jewish life as well. I hope to show that these extra-halakhic factors played an inordinately large role in Judah ben Asher's responsa, that they reflect a significant amount of creative adjudication and legislation—apparently deemed necessary for Jewish life—that cannot be considered consistent with the halakhah. Larger questions of external influences on the Jewish legal process—from Roman law, Spanish law, or Inquisitorial procedure—must await definitive treatment by experts in those realms.

Punishments

The most dramatic examples of decisions made not in accordance with the halakhah have to do with punishments. Divergence from talmudic law can be seen in at least three major areas: the imposition of punishments on individuals who are technically not guilty according to the halakhah, the introduction of new punishments which have no or little basis in the halakhah, and the use of non-halakhic considerations to determine precisely which punishment should be imposed. Spain was the country in which the greatest divergence seems to have taken place, under the auspices of the leading rabbinic authorities, the reason being simply that the Jewish courts in Spain were allowed a greater measure of autonomous jurisdiction than they were in any other country. Asher ben Yehiel wrote that, as far as he knew, Spain was the only country where Jewish courts were permitted by the king to try capital cases, and he registered his amazement when he learned of this upon first arriving in Spain.[5]

---

[4] See Moses Maimonides, *Mishneh torah*, 'Laws of Courts', 24: 4, 18: 6; Elon, *Jewish Law*, ii. 533–6.

[5] Asher ben Yehiel, *She'elot uteshuvot harosh* [responsa] (Vilna, 1885), no. 17: 8; Yitzhak Baer, *A History of the Jews in Christian Spain*, 2 vols. (Philadelphia, 1961–6), i. 323; cf. Elon, *Jewish Law*, ii. 802 and sources in i. 11 n. 25. Judah's attitude towards this jurisdiction is far more positive than that of his father, who wrote: 'I have let this custom stand, though I have never agreed with them on the death penalty.' He does, however, go on to recommend cutting out the tongue in a case of blasphemy (see Y. Baer, *A History of the Jews in Christian Spain*, i. 323–4). On punishments and their extra-halakhic

Using extra-halakhic corporal and capital punishment as an emergency measure to protect the Torah is sanctioned in the Talmud, and evidence that such punishments were actually imposed by medieval Jewish courts can be found in the responsa of Solomon ben Adret (Rashba) and of Judah's father, Asher ben Yehiel.[6] But Judah ben Asher's responsa provide us not only with specific examples of this phenomenon, but also with an articulate rationale for the discretionary powers of the Jewish courts. Several responsa in particular are worth discussing in some detail, both for the punishments they recommend and for the theory of law they imply.

In responsum 63, Judah drew a clear distinction between two different categories of judicial procedure. In cases of civil law, the judge does not have to know who the individuals involved are; on the contrary, it is better if he does not know, for this will ensure his objectivity. The implication is that such cases are to be decided on the basis of a fixed body of law, the halakhah. The only relevant matters of information are the facts of the dispute: the details of the original agreement, the claims of each party, the validity of the evidence. The identity and background of the contestants—whether they are rich or poor, whether one of them has been involved in many such disputes, and so forth—are irrelevant.

He goes on to say, however, that some matters were not in his time adjudicated on the basis of Torah law. The implication is that, in such cases, the discretion of the court rather than any fixed body of law was the primary factor in the decision. What justification was there for judging such cases at all? Judah gave two reasons: first, in order to keep these cases from being tried in Gentile courts. There were practical differences in the results of cases tried in the different courts: some who would be put to death by Gentile courts were saved by Jewish law; others, such as informers, were given the death

---

implications, see Simha Assaf, *Punishments after the Completion of the Talmud* [Ha'onshin aḥarei ḥatimat hatalmud] (Jerusalem, 1922).

[6] BT *Yev.* 90b; Maimonides, *Mishneh torah*, 'Laws of Courts', 24: 4–5; *Arba'ah turim*, 'Ḥoshen mishpat' 2: 1. These passages deal with flogging and not with the punitive mutilation and amputation of medieval practice. Maimonides does justify amputation (apparently without an explicit talmudic source) (*Mishneh torah*, 'Laws of Courts', 24: 9). For actual implementation, see Solomon ben Adret, *She'elot uteshuvot harashba* [responsa], 7 vols. in 4 (Benei Berak, 1958–9), iv, no. 310 (discussed in Hecht et al., *An Introduction to the History and Sources of Jewish Law*, 285). On Asher ben Yehiel, see Stephen M. Passamaneck, 'R. Judah b. Asher on Capital Penalties', *Jewish Law Association Annual*, 7 (1994), 153–72. For an example in the Iberian context, see the '*Usatges* [Law Code] of Barcelona', which gave the ruler the right to administer punishments in criminal cases including amputation of hands, feet, eyes, and women's noses, lips, ears, and breasts (in Olivia Remie Constable [ed.], *Medieval Iberia: Readings from Christian, Muslim, and Jewish Sources* [Philadelphia, 1997], 128–9).

penalty in Jewish courts but would not be liable to this penalty according to Spanish law.

At first glance, it seems that this means simply that it is good for the individuals on trial to have the greater justice of a Jewish court. But there is something a bit paradoxical about arguing that it is justifiable to adjudicate cases *not* in accordance with Torah law in order for the individuals to be judged by Jewish standards rather than by Spanish law. The real reason for the reluctance to allow important cases to be tried by default in Gentile courts was to maintain the power and hegemony of the Jewish courts, which were crucial to the autonomy that characterized medieval Jewish life.[7] What Judah seems to be saying is that Jews needed to be in control of the situation and to decide on the basis of their own needs which crimes were so serious as to warrant the death penalty and which were less critical. He did not want this decision to be made from the general perspective of Spanish society.

The second justification was the broad power of the Jewish courts to erect the 'fences' required by the particular problems of the times. This is based on the famous passage in the Talmud (BT *San.* 46*a*) in which the court metes out stricter punishments than the law requires, not because the transgressors deserve them, but because such punishments are needed as a deterrent at that particular historical moment. It is significant that the only quotation from the Talmud or any other halakhic source in the entire responsum is the passage that justifies court action inconsistent with the Torah law. The conclusion of the first part of the responsum is a clear formulation of the discretionary powers of the court: 'Every court, provided its motives are pure, and it is concerned exclusively with the pursuit of justice, has the authority to inflict corporal and other punishments in every age according to the needs of the time . . . such that others will hear [of the punishment] and be afraid [to transgress].' The word 'justice' (*tsedek*) here clearly does not mean justice for the individual who has broken the law, as we today understand the term, but rather for the society of law-abiding people.[8]

---

[7] Cf. Passamaneck's modern legal formulation: 'The court has what we might term an inherent power to exercise exigent jurisdiction, expressly provided by talmudic precedent, to take extreme measures . . . when and as the court should deem them appropriate in order to curb behaviour which in its best judgment is injurious to the Torah, that is, to the Jewish law and religion, and by implication, to the Jewish People' ('R. Judah b. Asher on Capital Penalties', 158–9; see also the extensive discussion in n. 1 [pp. 159–61]).

[8] Cf. Maimonides (in the context of civil law): 'Everything the judge does in these matters with the intention of pursuing justice only . . . he is permitted to do and will receive heavenly reward therefor, provided always that his deeds are for the sake of heaven' (*Mishneh torah*, 'Laws of Lenders and Borrowers', 2: 4; cf. 'Laws of Courts', 24: 5–10).

Judah then goes on to the particular case in hand. The problem involved a Jewish man who had sexual relations with a Gentile woman. According to the halakhah, this is not punishable by any court, and no human being has the right to do anything to the offender after the fact.[9] However, there were two important needs at the time: to prevent Jewish men from indulging in sexual licence and to guard them from the actual danger of punishment by Christian courts for illicit relations.[10] Thus both the religious and the physical well-being of the Jewish community seemed to require action on the part of the court.

The conclusion, that the courts should punish the offence, is warranted by the talmudic principle about action in response to the needs of the time, but the actual punishment is from outside the realm of halakhah entirely. Judah wrote that the punishment is left to the discretion of the courts, to be determined in accordance with the court's knowledge of the transgressor. For some, a warning that he will be handed over to the king's authorities the next time will suffice. For others, this might not work, and they should perhaps be expelled from the region.[11] The court may decide that another punishment,

---

[9] BT *San.* 81*b*–82*a*; Maimonides, *Mishneh torah*, 'Laws of Forbidden Relations', 12: 4–6; Asher ben Yehiel on BT *San.* 82*a*. Maimonides emphasizes in a homiletical manner the severity of the sin of sexual relations with a Gentile woman despite its apparent exemption from judicial punishment ('Laws of Forbidden Relations', 12: 7–8); see Isadore Twersky, *Introduction to the Code of Maimonides (Mishneh Torah)* (New Haven, 1980), 430.

[10] On relations between Jewish men and Christian women as a problem in the Spanish Jewish communities, see Yom Tov Assis, 'Sexual Behavior in Mediaeval Hispano-Jewish Society', in Ada Rapoport-Albert and Steven Zipperstein (eds.), *Jewish History: Essays in Honour of Chimen Abramsky* (London, 1988), 41–4. The punishment for such relations imposed by the Christian authorities included death by burning (ibid. 42) or castration of the Jewish male (David Nirenberg, *Communities of Violence: Persecution of Minorities in the Middle Ages* [Princeton, 1996], 131, 133). As discussed in Chapter 1, half a century earlier in Toledo sexual relations across religious boundaries primarily involved Jewish men and Muslim servant women, and the main problem was identified as the loss of the offspring to the Jewish faith.

[11] Personal banishment or exile is a complex issue in Jewish law and practice. The idea of penitential exile as atonement is rooted in the Talmud (BT *San.* 37*b*: 'Exile atones for half of men's sins') and was practised especially in Ashkenazi communities (*Sefer ḥasidim* [based on the Parma Manuscript], ed. Jehuda Wistinezki [Frankfurt am Main, 1924; repr. Jerusalem, 1969], §38, p. 40; Israel of Brunn, responsa nos. 265–6, in Hecht et al., *An Introduction to the History and Sources of Jewish Law*, 349; Israel M. Ta-Shma, 'Matters Regarding the Land of Israel' [Heb.], *Shalem*, 1 [1974], 81–2; Jacob Elbaum, *Repentance and Self-Flagellation in the Writings of the Sages of Germany and Poland, 1348–1648* [Teshuvat halev vekabalat yisurim: iyunim bashitot hateshuvah shel ḥakhmei ashkenaz] [Jerusalem, 1993], index, s.v. *galut*). This is somewhat analogous to the penitential pilgrimage imposed as a relatively minor penance by the papal Inquisition (Henry Charles Lea, *The Inquisition of the Middle Ages* [London, 1963], 219–22). Rather different is banishment as a punishment imposed by a court: according to Lea this was rarely used by the Inquisition (ibid. 216–17). Because of the difficulty in

short of capital punishment, is necessary, or the ultimate penalty may be exacted under certain conditions: if the matter is clearly proven, the danger is imminent, and the court knows that the individual will continue to offend in this way so long as he is alive. Thus, unlike the civil procedure mentioned at the beginning of the responsum, in a case such as this, knowledge of the personality and background of the individual is all-important, for this is what determines the punishment. Without such detailed knowledge, the rabbinic authority cannot give an opinion as to what the punishment should be. The level of subjectivity and discretion is extremely high: the ideal is not that the punishment should fit the crime but that it should fit the criminal. The deterrent comes from the people's knowledge that the court has the authority to inflict virtually any punishment it chooses for such an offence.

In this case, as we have seen, both the moral and the physical well-being of the Jewish community are served by strict punitive action. However, this raises the interesting question of what policy should be followed if these two goals come into conflict. Such a question was raised by Judah's nephew, Asher ben Solomon:[12] should they banish certain Jewish women of loose morals from the city?[13] Some interpreted the commandment 'There shall be no harlot of the daughters of Israel' (Deut. 23: 18) to imply that the courts had the responsibility to expel them, all the more so because these particular women did not practise ritual immersion and thus caused men to be guilty of a serious sin. On the other hand, some argued that they should be allowed to remain in the city, for otherwise the men would go to Gentile prostitutes, which would cause both a loss of 'sacred seed' and physical danger to the men.[14]

---

establishing a right of residence in a new city, such banishment could be even more catastrophic for a Jew than for a Christian (see George Horowitz, *The Spirit of Jewish Law: A Brief Account of Biblical and Rabbinic Jurisprudence* [New York, 1963], 226; cf. Salo W. Baron, *The Jewish Community*, 3 vols. [Philadelphia, 1942], ii. 9, 70–1; the sources in *Encyclopedia Judaica*, 16 vols. [Jerusalem, 1973], iv. 164–5). On Christian society, see Hanna Zaremska, *Les Bannis au Moyen Âge* (Paris: Aubier, 1996); Randolph Starn, *Contrary Commonwealth: The Theme of Exile in Medieval and Renaissance Italy* (Berkeley, 1982), esp. 31–85; for exile from the town as a common penalty for homicide or battery in Castile, see Evelyn S. Procter, *The Judicial Use of Pesquisa (Inquisition) in Leon and Castile, 1157–1369*, English Historical Review Supplement, 2 (London, 1966), 25.

[12] Judah ben Asher, *Zikhron yehudah*, no. 17, question 2. On Asher and his role in copying and gathering his uncle's responsa, see Havatselet, introduction to Judah ben Asher, *She'elot uteshuvot zikhron yehudah*, 41–2.

[13] For legislation on the banishment of prostitutes from specific cities in Languedoc in the thirteenth and early fourteenth centuries, see Leah Lydia Otis, *Prostitution in Medieval Society* (Chicago, 1985), 17, 21, 28; see also 160 n. 12; cf. the French royal ordinance of 1254: 'Expellantur autem publice meretrices, tam de campis, quam de villis' (ibid. 19, 162 n. 24).

[14] For other information about Jewish prostitution in Spain (including reference to this respon-

There was a complicated halakhic dispute over the meaning and implications of the commandment in question,[15] but Judah ignored this entirely, answering in one sentence: the Jewish prostitutes should be banished, for they cause Jewish men to transgress a negative commandment, with the punishment of excision from the people to be implemented by God, 'and it is better that [the men's] bodies be endangered than their souls'. The interesting assumptions behind this decision should be spelled out. The entire matter is viewed as an administrative procedure: the leadership of the community acts not as a court of justice but as protectors of communal welfare. Secondly, the situation is viewed from the perspective not of the women in question but of the Jewish men. It is they who are caused to sin and whose welfare is discussed.[16] The danger that the decision may raise for the women—what precisely would happen to them when they are driven out of the city—is never considered, nor are the rights of these women to judicial procedure. Intriguing also is the assumption that the men will go to prostitutes one way or another. If Jewish women are available, they prefer them, but if not, they will go to the Christians.

Finally, the question is asked not so much to determine what the law is but to resolve the conflicting interests of the spiritual and physical welfare of the community. The answer given is not that the law must be followed no matter what dangers may ensue but that spiritual welfare is, in this case, more important than physical welfare. The judgement that 'it is better that their bodies be endangered than their souls' is not a legal statement but a theological one, of the kind which would later justify the autos-da-fé of the Iberian Inquisitions. Judah's position in the two cases is consistent: the dangers that arise from sexual relations between Jewish men and Christian women must be avoided: the means for this are threatening the men with punishment and not allowing them to sin with Jewish women. The entire realm of discourse in this responsum is only tangentially related to the halakhah.

---

sum), see Assis, 'Sexual Behavior in Mediaeval Hispano-Jewish Society', 44–5. According to Israel Abrahams, 'prostitution was an unknown feature in Jewish life until quite recent times' (Abrahams, *Jewish Life in the Middle Ages* [London, 1932], 109). On the problems of sexual relations between Jews and Christian prostitutes in contemporary Aragon, see Nirenberg, *Communities of Violence*, 144–8, 152–9. Jews were sometimes specifically forbidden to consort with Christian prostitutes (see Otis, *Prostitution in Medieval Society*, 84).

[15] See Maimonides, *Mishneh torah*, negative commandment 355; Nahmanides on Deut. 23: 18.

[16] See Marc Saperstein, *Decoding the Rabbis: A Thirteenth-Century Commentary on the Aggadah* (Cambridge, Mass., 1980), 99. For a discussion of prostitutes in Christian theological literature from the previous century, see John W. Baldwin, *Masters, Princes and Merchants: The Social Views of Peter the Chanter and His Circle*, 2 vols. (Princeton, 1970), 133–7.

Responsum 58 also deals with the question of extra-halakhic punishments.[17] Here too there is an introductory section in which Judah explained that the opinion he was about to give was not a true halakhic decision, for the cases judged in his time were not true capital cases of Torah law but actions 'to close the breach of this generation', to fight the moral and religious laxity of the Jews. A modern observer might say, to ensure that the Jewish courts would continue to have control over what occurred in the Jewish communities, even though theoretically they did not have the status or powers of the courts in ancient times.

Judah thanked God that the kings of Spain had seen fit to grant such jurisdictional authority to the Jewish courts, 'for without it, Israel could not have existed in this land'. This statement, if not merely a loose exaggeration, is a rather startling evaluation of how precarious its inner tensions made Spanish Jewry, for it implies that the rabbinic leadership would have been unable to prevent the disintegration and dissolution of the Jewish communities had it not been for the broad powers of coercion granted by the secular government. However, Judah concluded, because of this and because he was acting outside the realm of Torah law, the rabbinic respondent could not respond as he would to a clearly halakhic question. What was important was not so much the rabbi's knowledge of the halakhic sources as his sense of equity and the successful practices of his own community. It was on this basis that Judah agreed to respond.

The case involved a murder. There was a quarrel: one man struck the other, who died.[18] Judah first addressed the question of the witnesses, whom the defendant had apparently challenged. Judah stated that the court may not declare a *ḥerem* on any one who knew something negative about one of the witnesses but did not come forwards. This, he said, would make the court a *pesquisa*—the Spanish word appears in the Hebrew text—and this must not be done concerning anyone. *Pesquisa* is the Spanish equivalent of *inquisitio*,[19] and

---

[17] This responsum has been translated and briefly annotated by Stephen Passamaneck in Jacob Bazak and Stephen M. Passamaneck, *Jewish Law and Jewish Life: Selected Rabbinic Responsa* (New York, 1979), 37–40.

[18] While the responsa literature, like much of the contemporary news media, presents a record of internal violence that may not reflect the experience of most members of society, in this and other responsa such violent attacks of Jews against Jews do not appear to be extremely rare. On contemporary Aragon, see Yom Tov Assis, *The Golden Age of Aragonese Jewry: Community and Society in the Crown of Aragon, 1213–1327* (London, 1997), ch. 5.5; for other references in Judah's responsa, see Havatselet, introduction to Judah ben Asher, *She'elot uteshuvot zikhron yehudah*, 31–2.

[19] See Y. Baer, *A History of the Jews in Christian Spain*, ii. 453. According to Baer, this passage is 'the sole instance in which the foreign concept of *pesquisa* is discussed in rabbinic responsa'. For the

this is apparently a reference to the Inquisitional procedure of coming to a town and declaring that whoever has information about heretical activities or beliefs on the part of anyone is required to come forward to tell the court.[20] Judah's statement that this 'must not be done concerning any man' is not justified by any halakhic source. He restricted the Jewish court from using the practice simply by identifying it with the procedure of an institution widely hated by Christians, concluding that it was the current practice to accept the testimony of every man so long as he was not explicitly disqualified by one of the impediments of Jewish law.[21]

The main section of the responsum deals with the appropriate punishment for the murderer, and here Judah gives five possibilities 'in accordance with the way we are accustomed now to judge capital cases':

1. On the evidence of two witnesses who saw him strike the blow, even though these two witnesses are first cousins: the man should be put to death.

2. On the evidence of one witness to the blow and one witness who saw the men quarrel then later saw the victim on the ground with blood rushing from his head: both hands should be cut off.

3. On the evidence of one witness to the blow, together with the general public opinion that the man is guilty: his right hand should be cut off.

4. If both witnesses to the blow are disqualified, then on the evidence of two witnesses who saw the quarrel and later the dying victim or on the evidence of one such witness together with the public repute of guilt: the left hand should be cut off.

---

pesquisa in contemporary Iberian legal procedure, see Procter, *The Judicial Use of Pesquisa*. Although she did not discuss the specific procedure repudiated by Judah, Procter showed that the *pesquisa* was the normal procedure for criminal cases in thirteenth- and early fourteenth-century Castile, and the word may have been more closely associated with the king's justice than with the ecclesiastical Inquisition, which did not function in Castile during this period.

[20] See Lea, *The Inquisition of the Middle Ages*, 123. It is the 'fishing expedition' of the inquisitorial procedure that Judah rejects, something quite different from the use of the *ḥerem* to compel witnesses known to have material knowledge of the event to appear (analogous to a subpoena), a procedure that Judah, following his father, affirms as legitimate later in this responsum. Passamaneck asserted—unconvincingly in my judgement—that there is no essential difference between the *pesquisa* method rejected by Judah and the type of ban that he endorses, which Passamaneck calls 'as much a *pesquisa* as the unacceptable procedure' (Stephen M. Passamaneck, 'Remarks on *Pesquisa* in Medieval Jewish Legal Procedure', *Jewish Law Association Annual*, 9 [1997], 159).

[21] In support of this, he cites a statement from the Talmud (BT *Ḥag.* 22a), which contrasts with the formulation of Maimonides (*Mishneh torah*, 'Laws of Witnesses', 11: 2).

5. If the evidence of all the witnesses is ruled out: the defendant should still be expelled from the city because of the public repute of guilt. In this way the city will fulfil the injunction: 'You shall sweep out evil from your midst' (Deut. 13: 6).

This entire passage is rather astonishing in its departure not only from the details but also from the entire conception of criminal justice in the halakhah. Some aspects of the traditional procedure are still maintained. The starting point is the evidence of two witnesses to the actual deed. The testimony of all the witnesses must be examined by the judges to make certain that there are no contradictions, and the standards for such testimony would seem to be those of the Talmud. But the punishments—cutting off both hands or only the right or only the left—are new. Even more important, the relationship of the punishment to the evidence is conceived in totally extra-halakhic terms.

According to classical halakhah, a man accused of murder is found by a court to be either guilty or not guilty. If the evidence, after being weighed and examined, is determined by the judges not to conform to the clearly defined requirements for conviction, the punishment for murder cannot be imposed. There is only one intermediate stage: if a man is known to have committed a murder, but the testimony is inadequate to meet the rigid standards of the halakhah, the court can imprison him for life.[22] But here we are dealing with five categories of what would be insufficient evidence by the standards of halakhah. In the previous case, we saw that the punishment was to be determined on the basis of the individual character of the defendant; here it is to be determined on the basis of the nature of the evidence against him. The death penalty is permitted where it would not be by Jewish law, as there is no mention of warning and the witnesses were relatives; the defendant is punished even if *all* of the testimony is thrown out of court. Thus there is no longer a clear distinction between innocent and guilty: in its place is a continuum along which stronger evidence proves a greater degree of guilt and hence severity of punishment.

The question of where Judah got this idea from is intriguing. The Talmud states that a court may have a man lashed for being of 'no good report', that is, for having a reputation of being a transgressor (BT *Kid.* 81a). Maimonides seems to limit this to sexual offences, and there is no indication that this principle is to be applied in a trial, where evidence is examined and rejected.[23]

---

[22] Mishnah *San.* 9: 5; Maimonides, *Mishneh torah*, 'Laws of Murderers and the Protection of Life', 4: 8.   [23] Maimonides, *Mishneh torah*, 'Laws of Courts', 24: 5.

On the other hand, the 'public repute' (*publica fama*) of guilt was an important element of Roman criminal law, which was taken over as the justification for the procedures of the Inquisition.²⁴ In the papal Inquisition, accused individuals could be punished, even if all the evidence against them was disqualified, because of the suspicion of guilt,²⁵ and there were disputes among the legal authorities about the relative force of two witnesses, one witness plus public repute of guilt, one witness without public repute, public repute alone.²⁶ All this might indicate that while some of the procedures of the Inquisition were opposed by Judah and his colleagues, others had an influence on Jewish criminal procedure.²⁷ In any case, Torah law has been frankly abandoned: Judah acknowledges this and seems rather content with the freedom of action his court is now allowed. The feelings of the judges and the community about the crime have become of primary importance.

Responsum 79 concerns a judge who was attacked.²⁸ As in other responsa, Judah began with a theoretical discussion: in this case, of the scope of judicial authority. Why were judges needed in the first place; why was a code of laws (such as the code written by his brother Judah ben Asher), to which anyone could turn and find out whether a person was innocent or guilty, liable or exempt, not sufficient? The answer was that new situations and cases constantly arise that were never dreamed of by the framers of the law. The number of different cases that could occur is infinite: no book, no matter how large, could contain laws that will cover every case.²⁹ Realizing this, the sages granted authority to all future courts to act not in accordance with

---

²⁴ Lea, *The Inquisition of the Middle Ages*, 60, 160, 179, 185; Procter, *The Judicial Use of Pesquisa*, 29.
²⁵ Lea, *The Inquisition of the Middle Ages*, 187–8.   ²⁶ Ibid. 179.
²⁷ According to Baer, 'the procedural methods used by the Jewish communities were influenced by those current at the time among the surrounding peoples, and this is true both with regard to their practical forms and their ideological basis, and especially with respect to the methods of *inquisitio*' (*History of the Jews in Christian Spain*, ii. 454). The entire question needs more detailed study.
²⁸ This is the subject of Passamaneck's detailed analysis in 'R. Judah b. Asher on Capital Penalties'.
²⁹ Cf. 'codes and statutes do not render the judge superfluous, nor his work perfunctory and mechanical. There are gaps to be filled. There are doubts and ambiguities to be cleared. There are hardships and wrongs to be mitigated if not avoided' (Benjamin Cardozo, *The Nature of the Judicial Process* [New Haven, 1963], 14). Judah's repudiation of the comprehensive code in principle is rather striking, given the monumental code, the *Arba'ah turim*, produced by his brother Jacob ben Asher. Israel Ta-Shma notes that Judah cites his father's responsa and his brother's code infrequently in his work and states that Judah's opposition to the code in favour of the individual judge was a legacy of the older German tradition, while Jacob was more open to the legal context of Spanish society that produced the magnificent thirteenth-century codification of Castilian law, *Siete partidas*. The suggestion that Judah was bound by German tradition and never became fully a part of the society in which he was living would appear to be challenged by the material cited in this chapter (see Israel M. Ta-Shma,

the classical halakhah but in accordance with their assessment of the needs of the time (BT *San.* 46*a*). However, this placed a tremendous burden of responsibility on judges. It was judges, not books of laws, who were, in the final analysis, essential to social stability and order. Whoever struck a judge threatened the very foundations of the world.

In the case at hand, a judge in Cordova ordered a man to pay a sum of taxes and to be imprisoned until they were paid. The man allegedly waited in a dark corner and, as the judge was on his way to the synagogue, attacked him with a knife. There was no witness to the act, but the man had been heard threatening the judge beforehand, had been seen waiting in ambush, and had fled after the judge was attacked. He was thus presumed to be guilty by all.

Judah was deeply impressed by the seriousness of the case. Even if the victim had been an ordinary person, he said, such a crime would warrant cutting off the hand of the guilty party. If the victim had been an emissary of the court on official business, the punishment should certainly be greater. The fact that the victim was actually a judge, who was slashed because he had given a just verdict, warranted an especially severe punishment despite the lack of witnesses. In responsum 63, Judah determined the punishment in accordance with the personality of the offender; in responsum 58, he determined it in accordance with the nature of the evidence; here, he determined it on the basis of the victim.

According to Judah, the purpose of the punishment in the present case was clear. It was to create an unmistakable deterrent to anyone else who might think of taking revenge on a judge.[30] An atmosphere must be established in which a judge could give what he considered to be the just decision without fear of the litigant, otherwise the entire legal system, and the social order, would collapse. Therefore it was permissible to hand down sentences as if there were witnesses to the act, whereas it would not be in a case where no special need was being served (such as the quarrel in responsum 58). There, the quality of the evidence had to be taken into account, although if a punishment served a special need of the moment, the court could determine it at its discretion, providing its motives were pure.[31]

'Between East and West: Rabbi Asher b. Yehi'el and His Son Rabbi Ya'aqov', in Isadore Twersky and Jay M. Harris [eds.], *Studies in Medieval Jewish History and Literature*, vol. iii [Cambridge, Mass., 2000], 193).

[30] Assis cites a case from 1281, in which the most distinguished rabbinic scholar in Aragon, Solomon ben Adret (see Chapter 4) was attacked with stones while walking in Villafranca by a group of Jews angry at his decision in their lawsuit (*The Golden Age of Aragonese Jewry*, 290–1).

[31] Compare the language from responsum 79, in Elon, *Jewish Law*, ii. 696–7.

Judah suggested one restriction in the present case: capital punishment should not be used. His reasoning was that, since there were no witnesses, the man was not subject to this punishment according to law. Thus, the only justification must be the pragmatic one of deterring others, but this was better fulfilled, Judah argued, by a severe corporal punishment such as cutting off both the culprit's hands and making him serve as a living reminder that crime does not pay.[32] 'Slay them not, lest my people forget' (Ps. 59: 12), he quoted, using the same verse Christian theologians cited to prove that the Jews should not be killed but preserved in a degraded state as a perpetual reminder of their sin,[33] surely one of the more extraordinary proof-texts against capital punishment in the legal literature. Once again the entire discussion is on an extra-halakhic plane. Judah answered the question and gave advice not in terms of what was permitted and forbidden by Jewish law but in terms of what he and the other leaders of his community found to be the most effective techniques of maintaining order and control. When his own class (judges) was threatened, he felt little inclination towards either clemency or a strict adherence to the halakhah.

Takanot

Another large area of concern in the responsa of Judah ben Asher is that of communal ordinances (*takanot*), some of which deal with punishments. He was often asked about the ordinances of his own community. The *takanot* of Toledo were well known for the innovations they made in the laws of inheritance. According to talmudic law, the husband is the sole heir of his wife. If she had come to him with a huge dowry and died a month after the wedding, he inherited it all. In the twelfth century, some of the Jewish communities of France modified this by the provision that if the wife died within one

---

[32] For another example of the judicial defence of extra-halakhic corporal punishment in the early fourteenth century, see Yom-Tov ben Abraham Ishbili (Ritva), responsum no. 138, discussed by Baer. A Jew condemned to have his tongue and hand cut off appealed to King Ferdinand IV of Castile, complaining that the Jewish judges had accepted the testimony of ineligible witnesses and failed to follow other halakhically mandated procedures. Ishbili defended the decision, arguing that the judge 'must look to the reform of the social order, extirpate wickedness from the land, and make a fence around the Torah', an argument apparently accepted by the royal court (Y. Baer, *A History of the Jews in Christian Spain*, ii. 452).

[33] e.g. Augustine, *City of God*, 18, 46 (see Jeremy Cohen, *Living Letters of the Law: Ideas of the Jew in Medieval Christianity* [Berkeley, 1999], 33, 36, 38–41, 241–2); Bernard of Clairvaux, in Robert Chazan, *Church, State, and Jew in the Middle Ages* (New York, 1980), 103, 107; Innocent III, in Solomon Grayzel, *The Church and the Jews in the XIIIth Century: A Study of Their Relations during the Years 1198–1254* (New York, 1966), 93.

year of the marriage without leaving any children the dowry was to be returned to the person who gave it.[34] But the *takanah* of Toledo overturned the law entirely, stating that whenever the wife died, her property was to be divided equally between the husband and her children, and if there were no children between the husband and her own heirs.[35] It also provided that if the husband died leaving a wife and children, and the *ketubah* represented more than half the estate, the wife could claim only half and the children were entitled to the other half. Many questions were sent to Judah ben Asher, as they had been sent to his father, about the proper interpretation and application of these *takanot* in unusual cases.[36] Judah was asked to respond to these questions not primarily as an expert in Jewish law but as the rabbi who knew more than anyone else about the famous innovation of his community and could therefore explain how it should work.

More surprising are the questions in which Judah was asked to render a decision about problems arising from the *takanot* of other communities. Here too, he was expected to respond not on the basis of Jewish law but on the basis of his interpretation of the language and intent of the ordinance.[37] Several examples will be given in order to show how large these problems—legal, administrative, quasi-governmental, but extra-halakhic—loomed in the life of Spanish Jewry in that period.

In responsum 36, Judah's nephew, Asher ben Solomon, described for his uncle a *takanah* from his community and asked questions relating to problems of interpretation in specific cases that had arisen. The *takanah* stated that whoever assaulted someone else must pay a fixed sum of money as a fine. The injured party was believed after taking an oath. Those found guilty but who did not have the money to pay the fine were to be held in prison one day for each *zahuv* they owed.[38] The purpose of this provision was to punish the

---

[34] See Louis Finkelstein, *Jewish Self-Government in the Middle Ages* (New York, 1964), 160–4; Elon, *Jewish Law*, ii. 836–8. This arrangement may derive from the old Palestinian law that half the dowry of a woman who died childless reverted to her family (see Shelomo D. Goitein, *A Mediterranean Society: The Jewish Communities of the Arab World*, 5 vols. plus index [Berkeley, 1967–93], ii. 6).

[35] For the text, see Asher ben Yehiel, *She'elot uteshuvot harosh*, 55: 1; Elon, *Jewish Law*, ii. 839.

[36] e.g. Judah ben Asher, *Zikhron yehudah*, nos. 1, 6, 22, 35, 59.

[37] On the role of the decisor as interpreter of communal ordinances, see Elon, *Jewish Law*, i. 444–73. It is understood that when doing so, the rabbi is functioning in an extra-halakhic capacity.

[38] Despite the Hebrew word meaning 'gold', Baer claims that *zahuv* refers to the silver *maravidi* in the responsa of Asher ben Yehiel (Y. Baer, *A History of the Jews in Christian Spain*, i. 424); cf. the 1281 Toledo sermon discussed in Chapter 1 above, n. 15. Judah stated that his annual salary as rabbi of Toledo ranged from 1,290 to 3,000 *zehuvim*, that his library was worth at least 3,000, and that each of his sons was guaranteed an annual stipend of 300 during his lifetime so long as they studied in Toledo

poor as well as the rich and, thereby, to deter everyone from such crimes of violence. Imprisonment for non-payment of a fine was in itself an extra-halakhic development that gained greater acceptance in the fourteenth century, as it became more common in European penal systems.[39] But, as it was still something of an innovation, many questions remained to be settled.

The ordinance in question stated that the fine to be paid by the guilty party should be divided into three parts, one-third going to the assaulted person, one-third to the court, and one-third to a *hekdesh* fund.[40] Some people argued that the court was empowered to imprison the impecunious offender only for the third belonging to the *hekdesh*, while others claimed that the intent of the *takanah* was to imprison for the entire amount owed. Without going into a discussion of the special nature and status of *hekdesh* money and obligations, Judah replied simply that since the language of the *takanah* did not specify, the man may be held for the entire amount of the fine unless those to whom money was owed—namely the plaintiff and the court—agreed to renounce their claims. A further problem arose when some offenders who had no money claimed the right to sign a document promising to pay the fine when they had enough and thereby avoiding imprisonment. Those who opposed this claim argued that if it were accepted, everyone without money would choose this option (an oblique comment on what the conditions of imprisonment must have been), and thus the entire purpose of this provision would be undermined. Judah answered that under no circumstances could individuals give a promissory note for the amount owed to the *hekdesh*—for this they must serve their time in prison—but for the other two-thirds they could give an IOU if the recipients agreed to accept it.

Another part of the *takanah* was obviously designed to protect the economic position of the local butcher, for it stated that anyone, except for the butcher, who cut meat into pieces, must pay a fine of five gold pieces. Here

(Abrahams [ed.], *Hebrew Ethical Wills*, ii. 181, 182, cf. 197). These figures seem excessive if referring to gold coins, and I therefore follow Baer.

[39] Maimonides identified imprisonment for debt as one of the characteristics of Gentile jurisprudence that was prohibited in Jewish law (*Mishneh torah*, 'Laws of Lenders and Borrowers', 2: 1). For a full discussion of the broader question of imprisonment for debt, see Menachem Elon, *Freedom of the Debtor's Person in Jewish Law* [Ḥerut haperat bedarkhei geviyat ḥov bamishpat ha'ivri] (Jerusalem, 1964).

[40] On this term, applying either to a fund supporting a hospice or hospital or to the general community fund for charity to the poor, see Baron, *The Jewish Community*, ii. 328–9; Yom Tov Assis, 'Welfare and Mutual Aid in the Spanish Jewish Communities', in Haim Beinart (ed.), *Moreshet Sepharad: The Sephardi Legacy*, 2 vols. (Jerusalem, 1992), i. 318–19, 330–2 (with reference to this responsum on p. 321).

too a problem of interpretation arose. Someone cut the udder off a cow and claimed that it was not technically meat and that he should therefore not be liable to prosecution under the terms of the ordinance. The exact status of the udder in relation to the laws of *kashrut* was a matter of some dispute;[41] however, Judah replied simply that, unless the man could prove from the language of the *takanah* that the udder was not intended to be included, it should be considered meat for the purpose of the ordinance. It is basically an administrative matter rather than a question in the realm of 'forbidden and permitted', and the answer is based more on plain common sense than on halakhah.

A second set of questions, in responsum 51, dealt with a communal agreement concerning the institutional machinery of self-government. The agreement, backed by the force of the ban, was that the community would choose two electors, who in turn would select ten trustees to manage all communal affairs. These ten men swore an oath on the Torah to fulfil their duties with pure motives ('for the sake of heaven'). The community then obligated itself to carry out the decisions of a majority of the ten for a period of ten years. Also in this agreement was the statement that at the end of the year the community should not be in debt.

The ten men were chosen. Eight of them swore the oath. Of the other two, one was outside the city and could not swear, while the other was in the city but for some reason refused to swear. Nevertheless, the newly formed council of eight trustees began to act, passing a *takanah* which related to the payment of taxes. This and other details of the council's actions seemed to conflict with the original agreement. Therefore, a majority of the community sought to nullify the actions of the trustees. They argued that until all ten swore the oath, none of them was empowered to do anything. Their opponents countered that the swearing of the majority should be considered as the swearing of all.

Although some of the principles are derived from the discourse of halakhah, this is obviously in an entirely different realm. The questions raised are of constitutional and corporate theory. What is it that brings a new corporate body into legal existence? What is the precise relationship between a community and a body of trustees to which it delegates authority? How much freedom of action does this body have in relation to its constituting charter? Under what circumstances, if any, does the community have the right to nullify the actions of the trustees or even to dissolve the entire body? Judah's answers required strict adherence to the stipulations for establishing the

---

[41] BT *Ḥul.* 109b–110a; Maimonides, *Mishneh torah*, 'Laws of Forbidden Foods', 9: 12.

council of trustees. But he gave broad scope to its powers once it had been legally constituted. So long as all ten men had not sworn the oath, the new body had not come into legal existence, and it had no authority to do anything. He might have overlooked the one man who was outside the city, as it could be argued that even if he had sworn the oath he would not have been able to enter into the council's deliberations or decisions until he returned, but the fact that one of the members in the city refused to swear the oath clearly invalidated the constitution of the body. Until this condition was fulfilled, nothing could be done.

This would have been enough to answer the question at hand, but Judah goes on to provide more information about his concept of the mandate of such a council. If it had been duly constituted through the oath of the ten members, he says, then its actions should not have been constricted by a rigid interpretation of the agreement. Even if the members had obligated the community to a debt past the end of the year, this would have been valid, for the stipulations in the agreement simply explain what the trustees were expected to do, rather than setting up iron-clad conditions to which the council must adhere. His general tendency is to give the council, as he gives the rabbinic court, a wide range of discretionary powers: the burden of proof is on those who argue that the trustees have not acted according to the agreement and that this failure nullifies their actions.

One final example of Judah being asked to solve a problem of another community arising from ambiguity in its *takanot* will be considered, for this shows clearly his method of interpretation (responsum 70). In Villareal, an ordinance was passed stating that if one judge from the court was not present, they should seat someone from the community in his place in accordance with the judgement of the other two judges, so that there would be a court of three. In the case in hand, one of the judges, though present, was apparently a relative of one of the litigants, and he therefore disqualified himself. The other two gave judgement, later defending their action on the grounds that the *takanah* said nothing about appointing a third judge when one member of the court was a relative, only when one was not present.

Judah did not accept this line of reasoning. He argued that in such cases the *takanah* should not be interpreted strictly; rather, its purpose should be fulfilled.[42] He proved this by a *reductio ad absurdum*. The *takanah* also says

---

[42] Where there is conflict between the language of the enactment and the intent of those who passed it the general principle is that the language takes precedence over the intention. Judah's decision represents an exception to this principle (see Elon, *Jewish Law*, i. 449–59).

nothing about the situation in which two of the judges are not present. If we were to follow the language of the ordinance strictly, we would conclude that where one judge is not present, a third must be chosen, but where two are not present, the sole remaining judge may try the case himself. But this would subvert the entire meaning of the *takanah*. The intention of those who passed it was obviously to have all cases tried before a court of three, and it is this intention, rather than the literal wording, that must be decisive. In the case that he himself posed, the one remaining judge must see to it that two others are appointed from the community. Thus in the case where one or two of the judges are relatives of litigants, in order to fulfil the intention of the *takanah*, appointments must be made to constitute a court of three. The action of the two judges was therefore invalid, and the case must he argued again before a full court.

These questions and answers beautifully illustrate Judah's statement that no law or book of laws can cover every case that could arise.[43] This was a period of significant legislative activity in the Spanish Jewish communities, but the leaders of these communities quickly discovered that the passing of a well-formulated law was no simple matter. A statement that seems straightforward and clear to those who wrote it may soon be shown to be ambiguous and problematic in the arena of actual legal activity. The purpose which it was intended to serve may be subverted if the ordinance is followed strictly in every case. Thus the judicial function of interpreting the law remains just as vital in a period of new legislation as it is in a period where everything is based on ancient texts. It was this function that Judah ben Asher performed.

But he did not merely interpret the *takanot* of the Spanish communities in order to apply them to individual cases. At times he argued that a specific *takanah* was a bad one and should be nullified. The reasons on which he based this kind of decision are of crucial importance for understanding Judah as a legal authority and communal leader.[44] A fine example is the long responsum 78, which is worth discussing in detail because of the wealth of information it provides about Judah's approach to law. The case concerned a rich man who died without children or brothers. His widow refused to give up his possessions, insisting on her right to be supported by his estate. The members of the community, in response, made a *takanah* that no widow may be supported

---

[43] Judah ben Asher, *Zikhron yehudah*, no. 79.

[44] For a survey of the reasons given by rabbinic authorities for restricting communal legislation, see Elon, *Jewish Law*, ii. 760–79.

from the estate of her husband for more than three months, at the end of which time she was obligated to take the value of her *ketubah* and leave.

Judah argued at length that no court had the right to make such a *takanah*. He brought forward an imposing array of arguments, some based on talmudic concepts, others derived from his philosophy of law and his pragmatic outlook on the use of law for positive social ends. The most obvious argument in justification of the ordinance was the principle of *hefker beit din hefker*, which apparently gave the court the authority to make any ordinance it wanted. Judah replied that this principle applied only to purely financial matters, but here there was the question of the honour of the deceased. It was considered an honour for a man that his widow refrain from remarrying too quickly, and there was a presumption that a man did not want his widow to be shamed by coming to the court to demand her *ketubah*. This was why the ordinance allowing widows to support themselves from their husbands' estates was originally made in talmudic times. A contemporary court had no authority to overturn such an ordinance that is explicitly stated in the Talmud and accepted by all the subsequent authorities: it cannot give to the heirs of the husband the right to force the widow to take her *ketubah*.[45] Furthermore, even if a contemporary court did have the authority to institute such a change, it could not be retroactive. It could apply only to marriages entered into from that point onwards.[46]

Up to this point, it seems that Judah was arguing on purely conservative grounds, opposing the *takanah* as an innovation that changed an important aspect of talmudic legislation, but it becomes clear that he did not really support the principle that no contemporary court has the right to overturn an ancient ordinance. The *takanah* from his own Toledo community which took away the husband's right to half the inheritance of his wife is far more revolutionary in terms of talmudic law than this one. Therefore he needed other support for his argument. Before addressing the issue itself, he discussed the possibility that a referendum of women be taken to determine their views on the matter and that the *takanah* be made in accordance with their will. He was opposed to this, but the reason for his opposition is significant.

It is well known, he wrote, that women fear their husbands, for the husband is the master of the home. Therefore, no wife would be able to vote or express her opinion as a free agent, for she is not permitted to disobey her

---

[45] See Maimonides, *Mishneh torah*, 'Laws of Marriage', 18: 1.

[46] For other responsa repudiating *takanot* intended to apply retroactively, see Elon, *Jewish Law*, ii. 772–7.

husband's will. If it turned out that the women agreed to such a *takanah* (limiting their right to be supported from the husband's estate), this would clearly be a result of compulsion and could not be considered valid. He did not reject the suggestion out of hand and claim that the opinions or desires of the women should have nothing to do with the establishment of the law, however. His opposition was based on the assumption that a wife was not free to express her own position and that therefore the results of such a poll would merely reflect the husbands' wishes—or become a source of severe domestic conflict. While it is difficult to know whether this proposal was just a rhetorical ploy rather than a serious suggestion, the idea of a referendum for women would need some plausibility to work even as rhetoric. It is an extraordinary suggestion, difficult to find a parallel for in Jewish legal literature.

Finally, Judah turned to the actual merits of the *takanah*, arguing that even if a court had the right to make it despite the Talmud, despite its being retroactive, and so forth, it should not do so, because the ordinance in question was a bad one. He introduced his argument with a passage expressing a principle of the philosophy of law: every *takanah* should 'follow the majority'. By this he did not mean that the members of the community should take a vote, but rather that only ordinances that serve beneficial ends in a majority of cases should be enacted.[47] For example, the testimony of a woman about the death of her husband is accepted. In the majority of cases, this rule serves a positive purpose, freeing women who would otherwise remain *agunot* ('chained' wives). In a few cases, women might lie for immoral purposes, and this is certainly to be deplored, but a basically good rule should not be abolished because it is abused in a few exceptional instances. No law or ordinance can be of benefit in every single case: if it is beneficial in the majority of cases it is worthwhile, and the minority of instances in which it may cause harm are overlooked.

Judah therefore refused to evaluate the *takanah* on the basis of the specific facts of the case at hand (the husband was wealthy, there were no children or brothers). He insisted on judging it by its potential impact on Jewish society as a whole, asserting that in the great majority of cases, it would be beneficial to allow the widow to be supported by the estate of her husband rather than

---

[47] For this distinction, see ibid. 997. The talmudic principle generally applies to the determination of status (e.g. the children born of a woman who has committed adultery are deemed legitimate in cases of doubt, as 'most acts of intercourse are with the husband' [BT *Sot.* 27*a*]). Maimonides used it in explaining the reasons for the commandments (Moses Maimonides, *Guide for the Perplexed*, 3: 34 [trans. and ed. M. Friedländer, 3 vols. in 1 (New York, 1946), iii. 161–3]). Judah applies the principle to the evaluation of the consequences of new legislation.

requiring her to take the amount stipulated in her *ketubah*. She would be spared the shame of coming to the court and swearing an oath in order to receive her *ketubah* and would refrain from hastily remarrying, both of which, as Judah said, concerned the honour of the deceased. Furthermore, if the widow had control over the estate, the children would honour and respect her more, even if she was only their stepmother: this was a filial obligation and another source of honour for the deceased. By contrast, if the heirs had the right to divide the inheritance among themselves, they might not honour the widow properly: they might think they were doing her a favour every day they allowed her to continue being supported from the estate. When the possessions came to be divided, quarrels would inevitably ensue, causing the children to scorn their mother, 'and this is antithetical to the purpose of religion and the Torah'.

From a strictly financial viewpoint, it is usually to the benefit of the orphans, especially if they are young and the estate is not large, to have all the money remain under the control of the widow, who can manage it more efficiently.[48] If it were to be divided up, there might not be enough to provide for the youngest children. Finally, dividing the estate among the children might split up the family. The sons might go their own way, wasting their share on expensive clothing and food. By leaving the estate under the control of the mother, the family was more likely to stay together and the children benefit from the mother's guidance. In short, Judah said that giving the widow control of the estate is beneficial on spiritual, material, and financial levels.

This is a striking passage: Judah argued for a particular legal arrangement not on halakhic grounds but rather on pragmatic, utilitarian, psychological, and sociological grounds. The stability and cohesiveness of the Jewish family was highly important in his eyes, and he was unwilling to condone any ordinance which he felt may undermine this cohesiveness. True, in a minority of cases, the widow may herself waste the money of the estate or give it to her relatives at the expense of the orphans, but such occasional abuse is not significant for the general law. Usually a mother is closer to her children than she is to her relatives, so that the arrangement would generally benefit the orphans, the widow, and the family as an institution. Furthermore, it would be a source of honour to the memory of the deceased if his family remained together.

---

[48] Note the assertion that women may be assumed to be reliable managers of financial resources. Evidence to support this assumption derives more from the Islamic environment than from Christian Europe (see Goitein, *A Mediterranean Society*, iii. 324–59).

The actual situation of the specific case, in which the deceased had no children or brothers, was very rare, and it did not justify the creation of a new *takanah*. It thus seems that Judah maintained that a law cannot be passed with one specific situation in mind: the implications of the law for society as a whole must be considered.

Judah concluded his responsum with some further reflections on innovations by contemporary courts. If a court of his time did have the authority to nullify a *takanah* of the sages, he said, it should do so only if the new ordinance was of greater benefit than the old one and if it had no negative effects. But this is clearly untrue of the *takanah* in question. All of the advantages of the original arrangement were lost by forcing the widow to take her *ketubah*. In addition, since she had to swear an oath concerning her financial state to do so, there is a further disadvantage: if she had significant financial resources, either she would swear falsely about her wealth, or she would swear truthfully, in which case the true amount of her wealth would become known to the Gentile authorities and the taxes might be increased.

Reverting to a more conservative stance, Judah maintained that even if a new *takanah* had many advantages and one great disadvantage it still should not be made: the *takanah* under consideration, with many disadvantages and little advantage, was all the more objectionable. Therefore, even if this ordinance were an existing custom, it should be nullified. The only source of support for such an ordinance that Judah could imagine was the rich courtiers and powerful leaders who were oblivious to the negative impact of the ruling on poor families where the estate was relatively small. If this is an accurate assessment of the forces supporting the passage of this *takanah*, then this responsum ends with an indication of social conflict, of tension between aristocratic interests and the rabbinic desire to structure Jewish society, through law, in accordance with different values.

Changing Conditions and the Law

Another extra-halakhic aspect of Judah ben Asher's responsa is his consideration of changes in historical circumstances and their effects on talmudic law.[49] For example, the Talmud presumes that witnesses will not sign a document unless they know that the transaction in question is valid (BT *Ket.* 19a). This was taken by most rabbis to mean that witnesses would not sign a bill of sale for a piece of land, for example, unless they knew that the land belonged to

---

[49] For a general treatment of this issue, see Jacobs, *A Tree of Life*, 122–65.

the seller. Therefore, if the signatures of the witnesses are known, the bill of sale is sufficient to convey ownership to the purchaser. In the case at hand, a man left his house and went to reside in another city.[50] Since the house was beginning to crumble, and since one of its walls constituted part of the wall between the Jewish and Christian areas, the community instructed a scribe to make the necessary repairs and to move into the house, which he did. Meanwhile the owner and his wife died. There were no children from the marriage, but the wife left a daughter from a previous marriage.

Some time later, a man came to the scribe with a document showing that he had purchased the house from the stepdaughter, but the scribe insisted that he bring additional proof that the house belonged to the stepdaughter to sell. Judah responded that, according to talmudic law, the signature of the witnesses is sufficient, and no further proof is needed to establish the legitimacy of the sale. However, he said: 'I see that witnesses in our time do not pay careful attention to this.' Therefore, anyone who sold land in Judah's own community in Toledo had to provide the purchaser with all the documents they had that established their ownership. Judah decided the case on entirely different grounds (the scribe definitely took possession without permission of the owner, whereas the other person bought it from someone who might have had the right to sell it: therefore his claim was preferable). The talmudic presumption was disregarded, because it no longer reflected the reality of the time, and the practice in Toledo had already been changed to fit the new reality.[51]

According to talmudic law, one of the implicit conditions of the *ketubah* is that sons inherit from their father the value of their mother's *ketubah* and dowry.[52] In a case posed to Judah, a son brought the *ketubah* and dowry documents before the court and claimed his due.[53] This caused problems, because the estate was small and his father had a new wife, who had borne him sons. Judah answered simply that he doubted that the principle of the '*ketubah* of the male children' was still in practice now that the community proceeded in accordance with the *takanah* of Toledo. He said he had never heard of anyone who had claimed it, and he would therefore not recognize such a claim. Here too the reality had changed, this time because of the newer inheritance

---

[50] Judah ben Asher, *Zikhron yehudah*, no. 80, question 2.

[51] For other examples of talmudic presumptions declared obsolete by medieval authorities because people could no longer be assumed to behave as they did, see Jacobs, *A Tree of Life*, 214–15.

[52] See Maimonides, *Mishneh torah*, 'Laws of Marriage', 19: 1.

[53] Judah ben Asher, *Zikhron yehudah*, no. 1, question 1.

legislation, so that—despite the absence of any explicit, authoritative legal decision invalidating it—the old talmudic law was deemed to be no longer in effect.

But Judah did not always deviate from talmudic law in order to accommodate contemporary reality. Sometimes he condemns prevailing practices, because they are in conflict with talmudic law. An example concerns the laws relating to the income from a pledge and the prohibition of interest. If someone borrows money and puts up his house as a pledge against the loan, a serious and complicated halakhic problem arises. Is the creditor allowed to live in the house or lease it to a third party and, in return, deduct an annual amount from the loan? There was a division among the authorities on this question: Rashi and Maimonides said it was forbidden; Rabbenu Tam and Isaac ben Samuel permitted it, although for different reasons.[54] Several variations of this case were posed to Judah. For example, in one, the borrower wanted to remain in his house, even though it had been placed at the disposal of the creditor. He therefore asked a third party to rent it from the creditor, and this third party in turn sublet it to the original borrower.

Judah's nephew wrote that such contracts were very common in his community, and the leaders were split as to the propriety of the arrangements.[55] Since the borrower was giving money to a third party to give to the creditor, it was argued that the third party was simply an agent for the payment of interest. In a similar arrangement, the third party actually received part of the loan, in return for which he agreed to make out the document of rental with the creditor. Judah stated that technically neither of these situations involved interest, since the creditor made a deduction from the outstanding balance of the loan for his right to lease the house (following Rabbenu Tam and Isaac ben Samuel), but it was an 'ugly' practice.[56] It used to be widespread in Toledo, he said, but after the death of Asher ben Yehiel, a *takanah* was made stating that the borrower who mortgaged his house should not continue to live in it. Judah recommended that such a *takanah* be created in his nephew's community.

Responsum 61 is the most important one on this subject. In it, Judah notes

---

[54] See BT *BM* 64*b*; Rashi ad loc., *ka mashma lan*; Maimonides, *Mishneh torah*, 'Laws of Lenders and Borrowers', 6: 2; Rabbenu Tam and Isaac ben Samuel on BT *BM* 64*b*, *velo*; cf. the discussion in *Arba'ah turim*, 'Yoreh de'ah', 172.

[55] Judah ben Asher, *Zikhron yehudah*, no. 46.

[56] Jacob ben Asher cites (and questions) a responsum of his father's in which he describes this arrangement and states that he would prohibit it, even though there is technically no direct usury (*Arba'ah turim*, 'Yoreh de'ah', 172).

the changes that have occurred in the practice of using houses as securities for loans and hypothesizes the reasons for such changes. In the past, the Jews of Toledo enjoyed economic prosperity and had plenty of money, but it was difficult for them to find houses to live in. Therefore, they were very happy to lend money on the security of a house, live in it, and deduct a fixed amount from the loan each year. The money was secure, because of the scarcity and value of houses, and they had somewhere to live. This practice, as already noted, was permitted by Rabbenu Tam and Isaac ben Samuel, although not by Maimonides. But in Judah's time, the Jews experienced an economic decline and the value of houses depreciated. Moneylenders knew that if they took possession of the houses that were mortgaged to them, they might not be able to lease them for very much. Therefore borrowers were required to find someone to rent the house for a fixed amount each year. There would be only a minimal deduction from the debt ('a *perutah* or two per year'), and no matter what the rental income of the house was, whether several times its value or nothing at all, the creditor would receive the agreed sum.

This, said Judah, is clearly forbidden. The renter is giving money to the creditor that should belong to the borrower, and he thus becomes the borrower's agent for forbidden payments. Judah explained the development of this practice on the basis of historical change, recognizing the impact of changing circumstances of supply and demand and other economic factors on the behaviour of Jews. But in this case he did not justify the practice as necessary to Jewish communal welfare. On the contrary, he tried to mobilize all the forces of the rabbinic leadership to stop it. Although the law was often moulded by rabbis and communal leaders to conform with new historical realities, there were times when reality must still be forced to conform with the law.

How are we to evaluate these decisions of the rabbi of Toledo in the second quarter of the fourteenth century? That they provide a vivid reflection of a dynamic period in the history of Jewish law is beyond question. Jewish courts exercised jurisdiction and could impose punishments that had not been granted to Jews for well over a millennium. Jewish communities passed ordinances to govern themselves and regulate their affairs in response to the perceived needs of their particular environments. Rabbis made decisions that transcended the classical texts and expressed their personal sense of justice and the needs of the Jewish community. While these responsa are technically the same genre as those written by a nineteenth-century Hungarian

Orthodox rabbi, in their initiative, their scope, and their approach to the fundamental issues of jurisprudence they seem to embody a totally different universe of discourse.

As a mirror of Jewish life, they certainly reveal a society dramatically different from the popular image of the medieval Jewish community: united in faith and cohesive in behaviour within; subjected to fierce bombardment by the Christian world without. The Jewish society of Castile appearing in Judah ben Asher's responsa was racked with inner tensions and conflict—even beyond the conflict that would normally be expected to appear in adversarial judicial literature. Most dramatically, it was an arena in which the violence frequently associated with medieval life—but not usually within the Jewish quarter—was rampant: violence of Jews against Jews, not excluding violence sanctioned by Jewish courts against Jewish defendants who could not be convicted according to the formal requirements of halakhah. Prostitution by Jewish women was a serious problem, as were illicit sexual relations across religious boundary lines. There was tension between wealthy and poor Jews and economic rivalry even between orphans and widows within the family.

A cynical reading might conclude that a figure like Judah was engaged in a rather cavalier manipulation of classical texts and precedents to maximize his own personal influence or to buttress the interests of his own class. The claim of an authority to decide in accordance with his own perception of the needs of the society, his own sense of justice, his own discretion and instinct, rather than being bound by a strict application of binding precedents, is likely to raise suspicions of self-aggrandizement and fears of abuse. It is perhaps not surprising that Judah seems most exercised by a violent attack on a member of his own special group, a fellow judge, and claimed the right—indeed the obligation—to adjudicate outside the boundaries of the law in a vindictive response.

Yet for the most part, the sense of commitment to justice (if not to tradition) evinced by the decisor seems genuine, and his courage is undeniable. While his extant written work does not reveal the profound scholarship of his father or his brother,[57] the pragmatic analysis used to strike down a

---

[57] This may be connected with the eye problems from which Judah had suffered since infancy, described in his 'Letter of Admonition' (Abrahams [ed.], *Hebrew Ethical Wills*, ii. 165–6, 169). When selected to succeed his father as rabbi of Toledo, he stated, perhaps without any undue modesty, that 'my scholarship was not sufficient for such an office' (ibid. 167; see Galinsky, 'On the Heritage of Rabbi Judah ben Asher' [Heb.], 187–95).

communal enactment because its consequences will in most cases be destructive of family values impresses me as one of the high points of medieval Jewish legal literature—an indication that the community of Toledo had at this juncture a leader of considerable stature.

PART II

INTELLECTUAL CHALLENGE AND CONFLICT

CHAPTER THREE

Philosophy and Jewish Society in the Late Middle Ages

PHILOSOPHICAL STUDY and original thought were not native enterprises for the Jews in medieval Christian Europe. As is well known, philosophy entered medieval Jewish culture in the Islamic East and spread from there to Muslim Spain and north Africa, stimulated by the achievements of Muslim philosopher-theologians and the need to defend Judaism in intellectually respectable terms. At this time, the small Jewish communities of Christian Europe cultivated an educational curriculum and a cultural agenda focused almost entirely on traditional Jewish texts: the Bible, the rabbinic classics of Talmud and Midrash, and the liturgy. The rapid penetration of philosophical study into Christian Europe—primarily southern France, Christian Spain, and Italy—thus entailed a transformation with powerful implications for Jewish culture and society.[1] As we shall see, these communities were racked more than once by fierce conflicts over the legitimacy of philosophy as a Jewish engagement, conflicts that exposed and accentuated fundamental differences between Jews even though they may have prayed the same prayers in the same synagogues.

How did this philosophical enterprise establish itself in Jewish societies that were not originally predisposed towards it, and how did it flourish?

First published in Daniel Frank and Oliver Leaman (eds.), *History of Jewish Philosophy* (London: Routledge, 1996), 294–330.

[1] The formulation of Isadore Twersky is particularly apt: 'Probably the most remarkable fact about the development of Jewish culture in [southern France] is the manner in which a Torah-centred community, widely respected throughout Jewish Europe for its wide-ranging rabbinic scholarship and deep-rooted piety . . . turned with remarkable zest and gusto to the cultivation of philosophy and other extra-talmudic disciplines. This cultural dynamism and interaction in the spheres of religious and secular learning pervades the period, producing tensions and frictions as well as substantive achievements in many areas' (Twersky, 'Aspects of the Social and Cultural History of Provençal Jewry', *Social Life and Social Values of the Jewish People*, special issue of *Journal of World History*, 11 [1968], 190–1).

Let us begin with a quick survey of the scholarly literature. The modern academic investigation of Jewish philosophy[2] produced in Christian Europe from the late twelfth to the fifteenth century (or, to use a more internal framework, between the Almohad invasion ending Jewish life in Muslim Spain and the Expulsion ending Jewish life on the Iberian peninsula) has followed several well-worn paths.

The first continues the approach used for Jewish philosophy in its classical, Islamic period. It is essentially a history of ideas, based on a rigorous philological and conceptual analysis of philosophical texts.[3] The great philosophical problems of the medieval tradition—the existence, unity, and incorporeality of God; the creation of the world and the order of being within it; the nature of the human soul; the meaning of revelation and prophecy; freedom of the will, and so forth—are traced in the works of Jewish thinkers to detect their sources and determine where innovation may be found. The impact of Maimonides and the influence of Arabic philosophers, especially Alfarabi, Avicenna (Ibn Sina), and Averroës (Ibn Rushd), are demonstrated and assessed. Evidence for the influence of Christian scholasticism is duly noted.

This approach generally focuses on the texts of those judged by modern scholars to be the most powerful minds, the most original thinkers. Gersonides (Ralbag) and Hasdai Crescas are the two giants, perhaps a dozen lesser figures are included, usually with an apologetic concession that, while not really belonging to the major league, they are the best the period can offer. Influence is traced from one writer to a colleague in the following generation, not from a thinker to the society in which he or his children lived. This is therefore a study of the thought of a tiny sub-section of the Jewish community, an analysis of disembodied texts and ideas in isolation from their historical and social milieu. In this perspective, the philosophy of the

[2] The meaning of the term 'philosophy' was broader in the medieval period than it is today, and I therefore include the natural sciences. Although attempts were made to distinguish between the status of, say, medicine and metaphysics, most recognized the existence of an encompassing philosophical curriculum in which many disciplines were included (see Harry Austryn Wolfson, 'The Classification of the Sciences in Medieval Jewish Philosophy', in id., *Studies in the History of Philosophy and Religion*, ed. Isadore Twersky and George H. Williams, 2 vols. [Cambridge, Mass., 1973, 1977], i. 493–550). According to Herbert Davidson, Gersonides 'recognized no dividing line between the natural sciences and speculative philosophy' (Davidson, 'Gersonides on the Material and Active Intellects', in Gad Freudenthal [ed.], *Studies on Gersonides* [Leiden, 1992], 195).

[3] See e.g. Harry Wolfson's classic definition of what he called the 'hypothetico-deductive method of text interpretation' as applied to philosophical works (Wolfson, *Crescas' Critique of Aristotle: Problems of Aristotle's 'Physics' in Jewish and Arabic Philosophy* [Cambridge, Mass., 1957], 248).

fifteenth century may well appear, as it did to Julius Guttmann, to contain nothing 'productive' or 'original', without a trace of 'boldness', in short, not particularly interesting.[4]

The decision to focus on a limited number of the deepest thinkers might appear to be justified by the ideology of the philosophers themselves. Many of them—most famously Maimonides—presented their own enterprise in elitist terms, emphasizing that their work was intended not for the masses of ordinary Jews but rather for the happy few who were capable, through intellectual endowment, temperament, and preparation, of comprehending the esoteric doctrine of the prophets and sages. But this common perception of Jewish philosophy as 'the privileged possession of an intellectual elite'[5] becomes increasingly inaccurate during the late Middle Ages, when a sustained effort by philosophers to communicate to wider circles of the Jewish population can be discerned. Gersonides wrote on three different levels: technical super-commentaries on Averroës, an independent theological treatise, and biblical commentaries intended for a broad readership, and there is little question about the coherence and interrelatedness of the full corpus of his work.[6] The decision to 'go public' by making accessible to the community of educated Jews what was hitherto concealed from all but a tiny elite is an important theme in the work of many of the central figures,[7] and it

---

[4] Julius Guttmann, *Philosophies of Judaism: The History of Jewish Philosophy from Biblical Times to Franz Rosenzweig* (Garden City, NY, 1933; repr. 1964), 275. See the even more extreme statement by Isaac Barzilay: 'there is indeed but little original and innovating intellectual creativity in medieval Judaism after Halevi and Maimonides' (Barzilay, *Between Faith and Reason: Anti-Rationalism in Italian Jewish Thought, 1250–1650* [The Hague, 1967], 16).

[5] Barzilay, *Between Faith and Reason*, 12.

[6] A recognition of the interconnectedness of his work underlies Charles Touati, *La Pensée philosophique et théologique de Gersonide* (Paris, 1973); H. A. Davidson, 'Gersonides on the Material and Active Intellects'; on Gersonides' rejection of esotericism, see Menachem Marc Kellner, 'Gersonides' Commentary on Song of Songs: For Whom Was It Written and Why?', in Gilbert Dahan (ed.), *Gersonide en son temps* (Louvain, 1991), 93; for the thesis that Gersonides 'was continuing the Tibbonian project of spreading philosophic erudition and sophistication among the Jews', see ibid. 104.

[7] See e.g. Aviezer Ravitzky, *History and Faith: Studies in Jewish Philosophy* (Amsterdam, 1996), 236–7, 248–9, citing Samuel ibn Tibbon and Moses Narboni on the legitimacy of transcending Maimonides' esotericism: Ravitzky's broader emphasis on the importance of the popularization of philosophy is fully articulated on pp. 3–21. A similar statement by Ibn Kaspi is in Ben Zion Dinur, *Israel in the Diaspora* [Yisra'el bagolah], 2nd edn., Pt. I, 4 vols.; Pt. II, 6 vols. (Jerusalem, 1958–72), Pt. II, vol. iv, 242. On a 'philosopher's attempt to interest the multitude in philosophy', see Steven Harvey, *Falaquera's Epistle of the Debate: An Introduction to Jewish Philosophy* (Cambridge, Mass., 1987), p. ix; on Falaquera's efforts at 'spreading philosophical learning among the Jewish people', see Raphael Jospe, *Torah and Sophia: The Life and Thought of Shem Tov ibn Falaquera* (Cincinnati, 1988), 1; Paul Fenton, 'Shem Tov Falaquera and Aristotelian Theology' (Heb.), *Da'at*, 29 (1992), 27. The deci-

suggests an approach to Jewish philosophy that takes seriously its social context and function.

The Israeli historian Yitzhak Baer has emphasized the social consequences of philosophy. Following the lead of several medieval writers[8] and reacting against the positive assessment of medieval Jewish philosophy by nineteenth-century German Jewish historians, Baer presented the enterprise of Jewish philosophy during the late medieval period in an extremely negative light.[9] He argued that philosophy, serving as the ideology of the courtier class, was fostered primarily by Jews whose loyalties to Judaism became increasingly attenuated as they rose to positions of influence in the power structure of Christian society. 'Averroism', which taught a universal truth transcending the particularistic doctrines of specific religions, corroded the foundations of traditional Judaism and sapped the willingness to sacrifice, suffer, and even die for one's faith. In times of crisis, the philosophers converted en masse, while the unsophisticated Jews who never opened a philosophical text were prepared to die as martyrs.[10] Trenchant critiques of this thesis have not succeeded in undermining its enduring influence.[11]

A similar analysis has been given to the thirteenth- and early fourteenth-century conflicts over the proper role of philosophy in Jewish culture. It was

sion to produce encyclopaedic works that would make the doctrines of the various scientific dis-ciplines accessible without the arduous task of mastering each one reflects a similar sense of mission (see, for example, Levi ben Abraham's purpose, expressed in terms strikingly analogous to Maimonides' explanation of the need for his *Mishneh torah*, in the introduction to 'Batei hanefesh vehalaḥashim' [in Israel Davidson, 'L'Introduction de Lévi ben Abraham à son encyclopédie poetique', *Revue des études juives*, 105 (1940), 86], and a similar statement by Gershon ben Solomon in his introduction to 'Sha'ar hashamayim' [Dinur, *Israel in the Diaspora* (Heb.), Pt. II, vol. iv, 184]). Views expressing contempt towards the masses as incapable of understanding philosophy were, however, still current in this period.

[8] Best known are Solomon Alami, Isaac Arama, and Joseph Yabetz.

[9] According to Baer, the external forces of political and religious oppression 'were assisted from within by a rationalism and skepticism which undermined tradition' (Yitzhak Baer, *A History of the Jews in Christian Spain*, 2 vols. [Philadelphia, 1961–6], i. 3; see also Jacob J. Schacter, 'Echoes of the Spanish Expulsion in Eighteenth Century Germany: The Baer Thesis Revisited', *Judaism*, 162 [1992], 180–2). According to Barzilay, rationalism, 'by its very nature, tended to weaken and undermine' the foundations of Judaism in the diaspora, evoking 'centrifugal tendencies of social dissolution and religious decline' (*Between Faith and Reason*, 11).

[10] On philosophy and the courtiers, see esp. Y. Baer, *A History of the Jews in Christian Spain*, i. 240–2, 263; on the links between philosophical commitments and apostasy, see ibid. ii. 137–8, 144, 148, 224, 274.

[11] Twersky, 'Aspects of the Social and Cultural History of Provençal Jewry', 189 n. 15; Haim Hillel Ben-Sasson, 'The Generation of Spanish Exiles Considers Its Fate (Heb.), in id., *Continuity and Variety* [Retsef utemurah] (Tel Aviv, 1984), 232–8.

widely assumed (though rarely demonstrated) that the upper classes were more positively disposed to philosophy than those beneath them in socio-economic status. Attempts to restrict or ban the study of philosophical works were therefore explained as efforts by the representatives of the Jewish population as a whole and its traditional rabbinic leadership to throw off the oppressive rule of an oligarchy with values diverging from the tradition.[12]

Since the 1960s scholars have attempted a more sophisticated assessment of the evidence for the role of philosophy in Jewish society and culture. Isadore Twersky, noting that 'Provence had no entrenched courtier class and yet became the seat of rationalism', succinctly suggested that the relationship between socio-economic status and cultural-ideological position was considerably more complex than Baer had posited. Joseph Shatzmiller has devoted considerable effort to probing archival collections for information on the social position of individuals involved in the philosophical enterprise, focusing particularly on physicians.[13]

Examination of the influence of philosophy within Jewish society as a whole has led to a broadening of the philosophical canon to include figures less original and profound but certainly more representative than the better known and to an understanding of the process of popularization by which philosophical assumptions, ideas, categories, and modes of reasoning penetrated widening circles of the Jewish population. This agenda required that the net be cast beyond the classical philosophical texts to include encyclopaedias, biblical and aggadic commentaries, sermons, and moralistic tracts. The introductions and colophons to the manuscripts of translators or super-

---

[12] Regarding the conflict in the early fourteenth century, Ben-Sasson wrote: 'The social tension between the middle and lower classes, which gathered round the *halakhic* scholars and the mystics, steadily increased at the sight of the opulent and, according to the moralists, dissolute way of life of the upper classes, most of whose members were inclined towards Maimonides and rationalism' (Haim Hillel Ben-Sasson, *A History of the Jewish People* [Cambridge, Mass., 1976], 543). For a more subtle attempt to link socio-political tensions in Jewish society with the conflict of the 1230s, see Bernard Septimus, 'Struggle over Public Rule in Barcelona during the Period of the Conflict over the Works of Maimonides' (Heb.), *Tarbiz*, 42 (1973), 389–97; id., 'Piety and Power in Thirteenth-Century Catalonia', in Isadore Twersky (ed.), *Studies in Medieval Jewish History and Literature*, vol. i (Cambridge, Mass., 1979), 197–230; cf. Marc Saperstein, *Decoding the Rabbis: A Thirteenth-Century Commentary on the Aggadah* (Cambridge, Mass., 1980), 263 n. 25.

[13] Twersky, 'Aspects of the Social and Cultural History of Provençal Jewry', 189; cf. however, Danielle Iancu-Agou, 'Une vente de livres hébreux à Arles en 1434', *Revue des études juives*, 146 (1987), 11; Joseph Shatzmiller, 'Livres médicaux et éducation médicale: À propos d'un contrat de Marseille en 1316', *Mediaeval Studies*, 42 (1980), 463–70; id., 'Étudiants juifs à la faculté de medecine de Montpellier, dernier quart du XIVe siècle', *Jewish History*, 6 (1992), 243–55.

commentators are often more important than the technical arguments over creation or the freedom of the will within them.[14]

Economic Bases

Like every cultural enterprise, medieval Jewish philosophy in Christian Europe had an economic foundation. Unlike contemporary Christian philosophers—predominantly celibate friars pledged to poverty whose basic needs were met within the framework of the mendicant orders[15]—Jewish philosophers had to provide not only for themselves but also for the sustenance and education of their families. Unless they were independently wealthy or supported by a reliable patron, they had to be able to derive income from their philosophical writing or from other work, whether related to philosophy (for example, medicine) or not (for example, moneylending).[16]

---

[14] See Ravitzky, 'Regarding the Path of Research on Medieval Jewish Philosophy' (Heb.), *Jerusalem Studies in Jewish Thought*, 1 (1981), 7–22; Colette Sirat, 'Le Livre hébreu en France au moyen âge', *Michael*, 12 (1991), 299–336; Danièlle Iancu-Agou, 'L'Inventaire de la bibliothèque et du mobilier d'un médicin juif d'Aix-en-Provence au milieu du XVe siècle', *Revue des études juives*, 134 (1975), 47–80; Saperstein, *Decoding the Rabbis*, 205–6, 209–10; Marc Saperstein, *'Your Voice Like a Ram's Horn': Themes and Texts in Traditional Jewish Preaching* (Cincinnati, 1996), 75–87. A striking illustration of the shift in approach is the contrast in the treatments of the thirteenth to fifteenth centuries in the surveys by Isaac Husik (first published in 1916), Julius Guttmann (first published in 1933), and Colette Sirat (1985). Husik devotes a few pages to the influence of Maimonides and one chapter each to Hillel of Verona, Gersonides, the Karaite Aaron ben Elijah, Crescas, and Albo (Isaac Husik, *A History of Medieval Jewish Philosophy* [Philadelphia, 1940]). Guttmann expands the canon a bit: in addition to lengthy treatments of Gersonides and Crescas, he discusses a dozen others—the translators, Hillel of Verona, Albalag, Abner of Burgos, Poleqar, Narboni, Duran, Albo, Abravanel, Judah Messer Leon, and del Medigo (Julius Guttmann, *Philosophies of Judaism*). Sirat treats several dozen writers from the period (Colette Sirat, *A History of Jewish Philosophy in the Middle Ages* [Cambridge, 1985]). Valuable source material for a social and cultural history of Jewish philosophy in Christian Europe was made accessible by Dinur (*Israel in the Diaspora* [Heb.], Pt. II, vol. iv, 173–257).

[15] See e.g. Richard W. Southern, *Western Society and the Church in the Middle Ages* (Harmondsworth, 1970), 292–9.

[16] Jewish philosophers were not insensitive to economic constraints. Jacob Anatoli stated that he was too 'burdened by worldly matters' to write any of his sermons. It was apparently only after his position in the court of Frederick II made his life more secure (see below) that he had the opportunity to write (Anatoli, *Malmad hatalmidim* [sermons] [Lyck, 1866; repr. Jerusalem: n.p., 1968], introduction). In the introduction to his astronomical tables, Jacob ben Makhir, writing in early 1301, asserted that the study of astronomy had been relatively neglected by Jews because its practitioners, unlike scholars of medicine and law, could not derive income from their knowledge, and the discipline had therefore been left to those who had independent means (Ernest Renan, 'Les Rabbins français du commencement du XIVe siècle', in *Histoire littéraire de la France*, vol. xxvii [Paris, 1877], 616–17). If this economic consideration was true for astronomy, how much more so would it have been for logic or metaphysics? Solomon Bonafed gives an economic explanation for the superiority of

Furthermore, they required access to books, which had to be purchased or copies commissioned from scribes. Since many crucial texts were available only in languages not intelligible to most European Jews, there was also a need for translation: first from Arabic, later from Latin. Finally, teachers were needed to help those not yet expert to master the demanding material. All of this required funding. Yet we know relatively little about the economics of the philosophical enterprise.

In the middle of the thirteenth century, philosophical texts—original books written by Jews, translations, and copies of existing works—began to proliferate in the Jewish communities of southern Europe. Writing in the first years of the fourteenth century, Abba Mari of Lunel complained that 'Aristotle and Plato succeeded in filling every nook and cranny with their books',[17] a hyperbolic formulation in a polemical context, to be sure, but reaction nevertheless to a significant cultural shift. As Harry Wolfson pointed out, the large number of extant Hebrew manuscripts of Averroian commentaries on Aristotle demonstrates a significant interest in, and demand for, such texts.[18] In the early fourteenth century, a Jewish philosopher writing his own super-commentary on Averroës' epitome of Aristotle's *Physics* had access to enough manuscripts to be able to make textual comparisons of a problematic passage, writing: 'This is the reading you find in a few manuscripts, but it is not what you find in most.'[19]

Christian scholars over Jewish ones in the various disciplines: '"They imbibe the abundance of the seas" [Deut. 33: 19]; they do not need to provide sustenance for their students or to hunt and bring game as we do today: our economic base is too small for comfort [*katsar matsa parnasatenu mehistare'a*, cf. Isa. 28: 20], and we have no true scholars among us' (in Abraham Gross, 'The Poet Solomon Bonafed and the Events of His Generation' [Heb.], in Barry Walfish [ed.], *Frank Talmage Memorial Volume*, vol. i [Haifa, 1993]: Heb. section, 36).

[17] Abba Mari ben Moses of Lunel, *Minḥat kena'ot: harbeh mikhtavim . . . el harashba umah sheheshiv lahem* [polemical letters] (Pressburg, 1838; repr. Jerusalem, 1968), 31; repeated by Ben Adret (ibid. 52). Abba Mari complains in particular about Jewish preachers using books written by Gentile authors (ibid. 3).

[18] Harry Austryn Wolfson, 'Plans for the Publication of a *Corpus Commentariorum Averrois in Aristototelem*', in id., *Studies in the History of Philosophy and Religion*, i. 431; cf. Gad Freudenthal, 'Les Sciences dans les communautés juives médiévales de Provence: Leur appropriation, leur rôle', *Revue des études juives*, 152 (1993), 93.

[19] Saperstein, *Decoding the Rabbis*, 272, n. 9, citing Yedaiah Bedersi, Annotations on Averroës' epitome of Aristotle's *Physics* (Heb.) (de Rossi Hebrew MS 1399, Palatina Library, Parma), fo. 159ᵛ. There are many similar passages, making this work a valuable resource for the textual criticism of philosophical manuscripts. The same approach characterizes Yedaiah's commentary on Avicenna's *Canon of Medicine*. For example: 'This reading is extremely corrupt, and I found it this way in all the manuscripts, and we probed after the Arabic manuscripts and it was the same. . . . In my search to remove this confusion, I found in the Baghdad recension. . . . This is the correct reading; apparently an error

Immanuel of Rome described an encounter with a Jew who had spent seven years in Toledo and brought back to Italy a collection of some 180 Hebrew and Arabic manuscripts. He left these manuscripts in sealed barrels, making the local Jews promise not to touch them while he travelled to Rome. As soon as the owner departed, Immanuel, his curiosity stimulated by the list of titles he had been shown, persuaded his friends to break the seal and copy ten of the manuscripts. A month later, the owner returned and protested, forcing Immanuel to justify his behaviour.

The identity of the texts becomes clear from Immanuel's defence. By showing the list of titles, the owner had aroused an overpowering desire 'to free them from their prison, and to show people their beauty and their splendour. . . . Our arid souls thirsted for the voice of the new learning; our thoughts cried out, "who will sate our hunger for the texts of the translations of Rabbi Moses ibn Tibbon?"' Therefore, he continued, 'if I have copied the *Physics*, that is my nature'.[20] We see here the dynamics of cultural diffusion: the philosophical works, recently translated into Hebrew, were known in Immanuel's community but not readily available. Manuscripts containing translations of Graeco-Arabic works purchased by a traveller to Spain and brought to Italy were jealously guarded. The desire for access to the 'new learning' became a cultural *force majeure*, justifying the violation of an explicit pledge.[21] These texts, Immanuel argued, were too important to be reserved for the few individuals wealthy enough to purchase them: they should be copied and made accessible to others.

This process, which forms the cultural background to the conflict over the study and dissemination of philosophy in the early years of the fourteenth century,[22] involved several categories of participants: patrons, scribes, trans-

---

crept into the Arabic text from which our translation was made' (Yedaiah Bedersi, Annotations on Avicenna's *Canon of Medicine* [Heb.] [Hebrew MS G.III.9, Escorial Library, Madrid], fos. 102^v–103^r).

[20] Immanuel of Rome, *Maḥberot*, ed. Dov Yarden, 2 vols. (Jerusalem, 1957), i. 161–5; cf. Ben-Sasson, *A History of the Jewish People*, 524–5 (where the content of the manuscripts is not revealed).

[21] Perhaps a similar impulse lay behind a case that came before the king of Aragon in 1355. The son of a deceased Jewish physician of the royal household deposed that among the books left to him by his father was 'a book called Avicenna, written on delicate calfskin parchments in a round script', which had disappeared from his house at the time of his father's death and was lately discovered 'in the hands of a Jewish surgeon of Barcelona' (Robert Burns, *Jews in the Notarial Culture: Latinate Wills in Mediterranean Spain, 1250–1350* [Berkeley, 1986], 64).

[22] While the conflicts of 1232 and 1302–5 are often lumped together as 'Maimonidean controversies', the purview had clearly changed. Ben Adret's ban applied not to Maimonides but to the philosophical works by 'the Greeks' that had been translated into Hebrew (see Chapter 4). Even in the earlier conflict, Samuel ibn Tibbon was attacked for having made Maimonides' *Guide for the Perplexed*

lators, teachers, and 'consumers', and it all required funding. Yet we know relatively little about the economics of the philosophical enterprise. For example, the extraordinary achievement of thirteenth-century Jewish translators in recasting the literature of Graeco-Arabic philosophy into Hebrew (and in some cases into Latin for Christian readers) has been extensively researched from a bibliographical perspective: the economic bases and cultural implications are less well understood.

In the Christian world, translation into Latin was situated in the institutional context of cathedral schools and royal or imperial courts.[23] Translation into Hebrew, by contrast, seems to have been considerably less structured. The classics of Jewish philosophy written in Arabic were translated by Joseph Kimhi and Judah and Samuel ibn Tibbon in southern France during the twelfth century, an undertaking endorsed and apparently subsidized by some of the pillars of Provençal Jewish society, especially Meshulam ben Jacob of Lunel and Jonathan Hakohen of Lunel.[24] This apparently whetted the desire for access to texts written by Gentiles, but the mechanisms of patronage are less well known.

The first translation of an Aristotelian text was of the *Meteorology*, completed by Samuel ibn Tibbon in 1210 at the request of Joseph ben Israel of Toledo, described as 'desirous of wisdom and enlightened in it'. Presumably this difficult work was not done merely as a favour for a friend, but no details of any financial arrangement are recorded.[25] The earliest complete translation of an Averroian commentary on Aristotle is Jacob Anatoli's translation of the middle commentary on the *Organon*, dated 1232. In his introduction, Anatoli spoke of two motivations: the need to make the discipline of logic

accessible through his translation and having 'revealed what Maimonides concealed'—perhaps in his philosophical treatise based on Genesis 1: 9, *Ma'amar yikavu hamayim* (see the letter by Judah Alfakhar in *Igerot kena'ot* [polemical letters], in *An Anthology of Maimonides' Responsa and Letters* [Kovets teshuvot harambam ve'igerotav], Pt. III, ed. Abraham Lichtenberg [Leipzig, 1859], 3b).

[23] On the translation project in Toledo under the patronage of Archbishop Raimundo, see James Kritzeck, *Peter the Venerable and Islam* (Princeton, 1964), 52–4; Étienne Gilson, *History of Christian Philosophy in the Middle Ages* (New York, 1954), 235–6. In the thirteenth century, translation shifted to royal courts: the most important figures were Emperor Frederick II, Alfonso X the Wise, and Robert of Anjou.

[24] Twersky, 'Aspects of the Social and Cultural History of Provençal Jewry', 196–202; cf. Abba Mari, *Minhat kena'ot*, 85.

[25] Moritz Steinschneider, *Die Hebraeischen Übersetzungen des Mittelalters und die Juden als Dolmetscher* (Berlin, 1893), 132–3; Dinur, *Israel in the Diaspora* (Heb.), Pt. II, vol. iv, 200. On this translation and the influence of the work, see Freudenthal, 'Les Sciences dans les communautés juives médiévales de Provence', 49–50; Aviezer Ravitzky, 'Aristotle's *Meteorology* and the Modes of Maimonidean Exegesis of Creation' (Heb.), *Jerusalem Studies in Jewish Thought*, 9 (1990), 225–50.

accessible to his fellow Jews so that they would be able to respond to the sophisticated arguments of their religious rivals and the urging of friends among the scholars and leaders of Narbonne and Béziers to undertake the task. Apparently, the interest in this text justified the translator's expectations, as there are some forty manuscripts extant, and many super-commentaries on the Hebrew text of Averroës were written.[26]

After this initial effort, the floodgates opened. Within two generations, virtually all of Aristotle in the Arabic versions was available in Hebrew, along with many other scientific and philosophical works. By the early fourteenth century, a greater proportion of scientific thought was accessible in the Hebrew language than at any other time in history: Gersonides could be at the cutting edge of contemporary scientific disciplines, and Jewish physicians could pass the most rigorous official exams without reading any other language.[27] Who subsidized the enormous investment in manpower that these translations required?[28] Some Jewish translators worked in royal courts,[29] but that was not where the bulk of the Hebrew translations was produced, nor were there well-known Jewish patrons, such as Meshulam ben Joseph, at this time. Some individuals apparently sought out texts to translate simply out of intellectual curiosity or a commitment to further the knowledge of fellow

---

[26] Steinschneider, *Die Hebraeischen Übersetzungen des Mittelalters*, 58–60, 65–94. At the end of the text, Anatoli expressed gratitude to Frederick II, 'lover of wisdom and those who seek it', who had 'generously provided [him] nourishment and sustenance' (Jacob Anatoli, *Habe'ur ha'emtsa'i shel ibn rushd al sefer hamavo leporfirius vesefer hama'amarot le'aristoteles* [Averroës' middle commentary on Porphyry's *Isagoge* and Aristotle's *Categories*], ed. Herbert A. Davidson [Cambridge, Mass., 1969], p. viii). Clearly Frederick was motivated by different goals from those described in Anatoli's introduction. On Anatoli as translator, see Freudenthal, 'Les Sciences dans les communautés juives médiévales de Provence', 50–2; James T. Robinson, 'The Ibn Tibbon Family: A Dynasty of Translators in Medieval Provence', in Jay M. Harris (ed.), *Be'erot Yitzḥak: Studies in Memory of Isadore Twersky* (Cambridge, Mass., 2005), 216–20.

[27] There remains some question about Gersonides' ability to read other languages, but Touati reports that he only cites Hebrew works (*La Pensée philosophique et théologique de Gersonide*, 39), and the inventory of his private library lists only books in Hebrew (Freudenthal [ed.], *Studies on Gersonides*, p. xv).

[28] See Joseph Shatzmiller, 'Livres médicaux et éducation médicale', 468–9; id., *Jews, Medicine and Medieval Society* 428.

[29] H. A. Davidson, introduction to Anatoli, *Habe'ur ha'emtsa'i shel ibn rushd*, p. viii. For Kalonymos ben Kalonymos translating in the service of Robert of Anjou, see Ernest Renan, 'Les Écrivains juifs français du XIVe siècle', in *Histoire littéraire de la France*, vol. xxxi (Paris, 1893), 441; Steinschneider, *Die Hebraeischen Übersetzungen des Mittelalters*, 330; Freudenthal, 'Les Sciences dans les communautés juives médiévales de Provence', 70–5. Judah Romano worked as a translator in the same court (see below). For Jewish translators in the court of Alfonso X, see Norman Roth, 'Jewish Translators at the Court of Alfonso X', *Thought*, 60 (1985), 439–55.

Jews.³⁰ But could Moses ibn Tibbon have devoted so many years to translation without deriving any income from it?³¹ There is, as yet, no satisfactory answer to this question.

The thirteenth century also saw the beginning of translation from Latin into Hebrew. Accustomed to believe that the most sophisticated expressions of secular culture were to be found in Arabic texts, it took a while for Jews to recognize that their Christian neighbours were producing philosophical and scientific work of significance. In the early fourteenth century, Judah Romano translated selections from the writings of 'the distinguished Dominican friar' Giles of Rome, Albertus Magnus, Thomas Aquinas, and others in order 'to demonstrate their wisdom' to those Jews who arrogantly thought that 'truth and insight are absent from the Gentile nations, especially from the Christians'.³² Later that century such an assumption was clearly untenable. Leon Joseph of Carcassonne studied Latin and translated Latin medical books by Christian authors, because he knew that without access to such works Jewish physicians simply could not compete with their Christian colleagues.³³

---

³⁰ Such as Samuel ben Judah (Lawrence V. Berman, 'Greek into Hebrew: Samuel ben Judah of Marseilles, Fourteenth-Century Philosopher and Translator', in Alexander Altmann [ed.], *Jewish Medieval and Renaissance Studies* [Cambridge, Mass., 1967], 307–20) and Leon Joseph of Carcassonne (Renan, 'Les Écrivains juifs français du XIVe siècle', 772–4).

³¹ For a recent list of these translations with full bibliographical references, see J. T. Robinson, 'The Ibn Tibbon Family', 221–2 n. 110.

³² Adolf Neubauer, *Catalogue of Hebrew Manuscripts in the Bodleian Library* (Oxford, 1886), 497–8. On Romano as a translator, see Steinschneider, *Die Hebraeischen Übersetzungen des Mittelalters*, 263–4; Sirat, *A History of Jewish Philosophy in the Middle Ages*, 271–2; Giuseppe Sermoneta, '"Thine Ointments have a Goodly Fragrance": Rabbi Judah Romano and the "Open Text" Method' (Heb.), *Jerusalem Studies in Jewish Thought*, 9 (1990), 106 n. 34. Just as the philosophical material translated from Arabic soon found its way into Hebrew biblical commentaries, so too did that translated from Latin (see Giuseppe Sermoneta, 'Prophecy in the Writings of Yehuda Romano', in Twersky [ed.], *Studies in Medieval Jewish History and Literature*, ii. 352–6). Immanuel of Rome praised Romano for these translations, which gathered the insights of wisdom from their dispersion among the Christians and restored them to the Jews (*Maḥberot*, i. 222).

³³ Renan, 'Les Écrivains juifs français du XIVe siècle', 772; cf. Shatzmiller, *Jews, Medicine, and Medieval Society*, 30–1. Dinur explained the translation of Latin medical works as a way to encourage Jews to seek out Jewish physicians rather than Christian ones, who give them non-kosher medicines (*Israel in the Diaspora* [Heb.], Pt. II, vol. iv, 177, 214 n. 13). See also the introduction by Meir Alguades to his early fifteenth-century translation from the Latin of Aristotle's *Nicomachean Ethics*, explaining that he had access to expert Christian scholars and a fine Latin commentary on the *Ethics* (Lawrence V. Berman, 'The Hebrew Translation from Latin of Aristotle's "Nicomachean Ethics"' [Heb.], in Moshe Idel, Warren Harvey, and Eliezer Schweid [eds.], *Shlomo Pines Jubilee Volume* [Sefer hayovel leshelomoh pines], vol. i [Jerusalem, 1988], 157–8). In 1472 Eli ben Joseph Habillo justified his translation of Joannes Versor's 'Questions' on Aristotle's *Physics* by arguing that Christian scholars, unlike their Jewish counterparts, had studied Greek philosophy in a manner consistent with religious faith,

Once the works were translated, they had to be copied. The many aspects of this enterprise have only recently begun to be studied. Who were the scribes and copyists involved? Did they specialize in philosophical and scientific texts, or did the same men work on rabbinic material as well? Did they have a special interest in the subject matter, or was it merely a technical task to be performed, perhaps without even understanding what they were copying? How long did it take to copy a text of, say, one hundred folios? Who commissioned and paid them for their work, and how much could they expect to earn?[34] Scattered through the Hebrew manuscripts of philosophical texts is abundant information pertinent to these questions that needs to be systematically gathered and analysed.

Here too, Immanuel of Rome's evidence is significant. He states that the ten philosophical works, including a commentary by Averroës on Aristotle's *Physics*, were copied within a month.[35] This sounds like a prodigious feat that would have required intensive work by a large team of copyists, probably including amateurs. The owner's anger at the copying is not explained, but it might have been because the unauthorized copying diminished the value of his manuscripts in Italy or because he had expected to charge a fee for permission to copy them. Such an arrangement is reflected in an early fourteenth-century contract whereby the owner of an important book charged a considerable fee for allowing a Jewish physician to keep it for a year and make a copy of it, stipulating that he should not allow anyone else to copy it and should limit the circulation of the copy.[36]

There is other evidence of the problems involved in copying texts. Samuel ben Judah of Marseilles, a fourteenth-century Provençal scholar, travelled with his brother from Aix to Trinquitaille to find an Arabic text of Ibn Aflah's epitome of the *Almagest*. The two of them worked feverishly for two days

---

concluding that 'whoever wants to become learned in these disciplines should study carefully these [Latin] books' (in George Margoliouth, *Catalogue of the Hebrew and Samaritan Manuscripts in the British Museum*, 4 vols. [London, 1965], iii. 185). For an example of a Jewish preacher using a technical philosophical passage from a newly completed translation of Aquinas, see Saperstein, '*Your Voice Like a Ram's Horn*', 79.

[34] For some general comments pertaining to the earlier (Islamic) period, see Salo W. Baron, *A Social and Religious History of the Jews*, 18 vols. (Philadelphia: Jewish Publication Society, 1952–83), vii. 137. [35] Immanuel of Rome, *Maḥberot*, i. 162.

[36] Shatzmiller, 'Livres médicaux et éducation médicale', 466–7; cf. Colette Sirat, 'Le Livre hébreu en France au Moyen Âge', *Michael*, 12 (1991), 332. Shatzmiller suggested that this might have been an unusual arrangement, in which the owner was related to the translator, but there is no reason why the owner of a rare and valuable manuscript would not have wanted compensation for access to it, especially if he had travelled to procure it or commissioned its copying.

copying as much as they could—less than one-eighth of the text—before they had to return it to its owner. Samuel then found a copy of the translation by Jacob ben Makhir and arranged with the owner for permission to copy it. Finally he gained access once again to the Arabic manuscript and corrected errors in the translation by comparing it with the original.[37]

Here too the cultural dynamics and economics of the enterprise need to be investigated. In some cases, such as that of Samuel ben Judah, the individual seems to have copied a text primarily for his own use.[38] The contract published by Shatzmiller required that the text be limited to the private use of the physician who was permitted to copy it.[39] On the other hand, manuscript colophons are filled with information about individuals for whom the texts were copied: sometimes the scribe's teacher,[40] but more frequently a patron or employer who seems to have commissioned the task.[41] Identification of the scribes known from the colophons of extant manuscripts and the people for whom the manuscripts were written has begun, but a systematic study of this material as a resource for the social and cultural history of the diffusion of philosophical materials is greatly to be desired.

Given the difficulties and cost of translating and copying philosophical texts,[42] it is rather impressive that Jews collected them into significant

[37] Berman, 'Greek into Hebrew', 315–16. Samuel stated that he had heard of a translation by Moses ibn Tibbon but was unable to find a copy (see Steinschneider, *Die Hebraeischen Übersetzungen des Mittelalters*, 544).

[38] See also the text described by Sirat, 'Le Livre hébreu en France au Moyen Âge', 328–30.

[39] Shatzmiller, 'Livres médicaux et éducation médicale'.

[40] e.g. 'The work [Isaac ben Shem Tov's commentary on the *Physics*] was completed by me, Abraham ibn Adret, here at Aguilar di Campaha, while I was studying this discipline from the inexhaustible fountain, the consummate scholar, Rabbi Isaac ibn Shem Tov' (in Wolfson, 'Isaac ibn Shem Tob's Unknown Commentaries on the Physics and His Other Unknown Works', in id., *Studies in the History of Philosophy and Religion*, ii. 480; see also Margoliouth, *Catalogue of the Hebrew and Samaritan Manuscripts in the British Museum*, iii. 212).

[41] For example, Asher ben Samuel of Marseilles copied a logical text by Averroës for a Spanish Jew (Berman, 'Greek into Hebrew', 301), and Abraham Farissol was employed copying manuscripts by the Norsas, prominent bankers of Mantua, a position consistent with his career as a scribe (David B. Ruderman, *The World of a Renaissance Jew: The Life and Thought of Abraham ben Mordecai Farissol* [Cincinnati, 1981], 12). Less information is available about the economics of scribes on the open market: 'there is no scribe in the world who will copy this for less than six small gulden, not counting the cost of the parchment' (1315, in Dinur, *Israel in the Diaspora* [Heb.], Pt. II, vol. iv, 420).

[42] The cost of manuscripts can be determined through the study of owners' inscriptions and notarial records. For example, a text of Maimonides' *Guide for the Perplexed* completed in 1283 and bound together with Samuel ibn Tibbon's *Yikavu hamayim* and some other texts was sold in 1378 for 50 gold florins, then resold together with a *Maḥzor* in 1461 for 100 Florentine florins (Margoliouth, *Catalogue of the Hebrew and Samaritan Manuscripts in the British Museum*, iii. 212). A Hebrew copy of an unspecified medical book brought 25 florins in 1434 (Iancu-Agou, 'Une vente de livres hébreux', 17; see also

holdings. Medieval Christian Europe had its monastic, royal, and university libraries;[43] by contrast, we know nothing of communal or institutional Jewish collections of philosophical manuscripts. Individual initiative was paramount. Judah ibn Tibbon's celebrated description of the library he made available to his son Samuel is short on details, telling us only that the books were in Hebrew and Arabic.[44] But several book lists from the fourteenth and fifteenth centuries provide a good indication of the kind of collection a reasonably wealthy Jewish intellectual could amass.

The picture emerging from the lists of Leon Masconi, a fourteenth-century Majorcan physician, Astruc of Sestiers, a fifteenth-century physician from Aix-en-Provence, and the great Jewish scientist and philosopher Gersonides is fairly consistent. The three libraries were of the same order of magnitude—between 147 and 179 books—and they were all remarkably diverse. Each contained philosophical and scientific works by Greek and Arabic writers in Hebrew translations. But they also contained numerous manuscripts of biblical texts and commentaries (Mosconi had a special affinity for Joseph ibn Kaspi, while Astruc collected works by David Kimhi [Radak]), and of rabbinic literature, including the Talmud and Midrash.[45] These libraries belie any facile generalization that a commitment to philo-

---

Shatzmiller, 'Livres médicaux et éducation médicale', 466–7; Leopold Zunz, *Zur Geschichte und Literatur* [Berlin: Veit und Comp., 1845], 211–13). The cost was determined not only by the length of the text, the aesthetic character of the writing, and the quality of the parchment or paper, but by other factors as well. In the late fourteenth century, Leon Joseph of Carcassonne reported that for twelve years he had tried in vain to acquire two new Latin medical books, as the Christians of Montpellier had banned their sale to non-Christians. He finally succeeded, paying 'twice their value', explaining: 'I bought them to benefit myself by reading them, and to benefit other [Jews] by translating them' (Renan, 'Les Écrivains juifs français du XIVe siècle', 774). The library of the wealthy Samuel Sulami must have been a powerful inducement for the impoverished Levi ben Abraham to remain in his home (Abba Mari, *Minḥat kena'ot*, 47).

[43] According to Anne-Marie Weil, in 1373 the royal library of Charles V contained 843 volumes, the pontifical library in Avignon had some 2,000, and the library of the convent of San Domenico of Bologna had 472 (Weil, 'Levi ben Gershom et sa bibliothèque privée', in Dahan [ed.], *Gersonide en son temps*, 59).

[44] Judah ibn Tibbon in Israel Abrahams (ed.), *Hebrew Ethical Wills*, 2 vols. (Philadelphia: Jewish Publication Society, 1926), i. 57, 80–2.

[45] I. Lévi, 'L'Inventaire du mobilier et de la bibliothèque d'un médicin juif de Majorque au XIVe siècle', *Revue des études juives*, 39 (1899), 242–9; Moritz Steinschneider, 'Le Bibliothèque de Leon Mosconi', *Revue des études juives*, 40 (1900), 60–73; Danièlle Iancu-Agou, 'L'Inventaire de la bibliothèque et du mobilier d'un médicin juif d'Aix-en-Provence au milieu du XVe siècle', *Revue des études juives*, 134 (1975), 47–80; Weil, 'Levi ben Gershom et sa bibliothèque privée'. In Gersonides' collection, there were 37 biblical works, 71 rabbinic texts, and 60 manuscripts of a scientific nature (ibid. 45–6).

sophical study in the fourteenth and fifteenth centuries indicated a weakening attachment to Jewish tradition.

Like translation and copying of philosophical texts, teaching also had a financial component. While it was theoretically possible for students to educate themselves in philosophy simply by reading texts, it was more common for a teacher to guide students through the curriculum. In an environment where even teachers of traditional Jewish learning were becoming professionalized, it is not surprising that philosophical teachers expected to be paid.[46]

For some it was a matter of economic necessity. In late thirteenth-century southern France, Levi ben Abraham, author of popular philosophical works that aroused the ire of his conservative opponents, was described as being so poor he had to teach Arabic to whoever would hire him, whether old or young. Yedaiah Bedersi, defending the culture of southern France against the accusation that children were taught philosophical material for which they were not prepared, conceded that in the past some men, competent in the discipline of logic, 'had fallen upon bad times and were forced to sell their expertise and reveal their views publicly'.[47]

In the fifteenth century Spanish opponents of philosophy complained that young men would pay to be taught secular sciences while slighting those who taught Torah gratis.[48] A similar complaint from contemporary Italy makes it clear that Jews were studying philosophy with Christian scholars, but here the economics were reversed: the Jews preferred to study 'wisdom' with Christian scholars, who charged lower fees (presumably because they had stipends from patrons) rather than hire rabbinic scholars who charged more.[49] The economics of higher education are revealed in the same source, as the

---

[46] On the arguments relating to financial subsidy for teaching, see Bernard Septimus, '"Kings, Angels or Beggars": Tax Law and Spirituality in a Hispano-Jewish *Responsum*', in Twersky (ed.), *Studies in Medieval Jewish History and Literature*, ii. 309–35; Ephraim Kanarfogel, *Jewish Education and Society in the High Middle Ages* (Detroit, 1992), ch. 3.

[47] Abba Mari, *Minḥat kena'ot*, 48; Yedaiah Bedersi, in Solomon ben Adret, *She'elot uteshuvot harashba* [responsa], 7 vols. in 4 (Benei Berak, 1958–9), i. 168*a*.

[48] Joseph Hacker, 'The Intellectual Activity of the Jews of the Ottoman Empire during the Sixteenth and Seventeenth Centuries', in Isadore Twersky and Bernard Septimus (eds.), *Jewish Thought in the Seventeenth Century* (Cambridge, Mass., 1987), 116; id., 'On the Spiritual Image of Spanish Jews at the End of the Fifteenth Century' (Heb.), *Sefunot* NS, 2/17 (1983), 55–6. Solomon Bonafed wrote (without complaining) that he paid 'much money' to the Christian who taught him logic in Latin for a year (Gross, 'The Poet Solomon Bonafed' [Heb.], 36).

[49] Simha Assaf, *Sources for the History of Jewish Education* [Mekorot letoledot haḥinukh beyisra'el], 4 vols. (Tel Aviv, 1925–43), ii. 101; Hava Tirosh-Rothschild, *Between Worlds: The Life and Thought of Rabbi David ben Judah Messer Leon* (Albany: State University of New York Press, 1991), 43–4.

writer complains: 'if I had said these things in distant academies in the Middle East, where the students truly desire Torah and love Talmud, they would give me at least ten ducats. . . . But these rabbis in our region do not value such things at all'.[50]

The one way in which philosophical knowledge could be widely disseminated without cost was from the pulpit. Beginning in the thirteenth century, if not before, the sermon became a vehicle through which philosophical ideas were readily popularized: simplified, integrated with traditional texts, and communicated to an audience composed of Jews at various social levels, including those without the means to purchase books or the inclination to study them. The preachers ranged from men like Jacob Anatoli, himself competent in the most technical philosophical material, to some who were accused of knowing their philosophy only at second or third hand. Many were appalled at the intrusion of what they considered to be radical, even heretical, ideas into the sermons. They protested vociferously and attempted —unsuccessfully—to exert control over what could be said from the pulpit.[51]

By the fifteenth century there is abundant evidence of philosophical material being an integral part of the sermons delivered in Spain. This included not only some rather technical discussions, but also the use of philosophical modes of reasoning—the syllogism and the scholastic 'disputed question', in which both sides of a theological or philosophical proposition were defended before the arguments for one side were refuted—which gave new forms to Jewish homiletics.[52] While the sermon was not an instrument conducive to philosophical originality or profundity, there can be no question that it served to spread many of the basic elements of philosophical thought considerably beyond the circle of serious students.

Institutional Structures

A second set of questions relates to the institutional context for philosophical study among Jews. In the contemporary Christian community, the flourish-

---

[50] Assaf, *Sources for the History of Jewish Education* (Heb.), ii. 102.

[51] Menahem Me'iri, in Simeon bar Joseph, *Ḥoshen mishpat*, in Marc Saperstein, *Jewish Preaching, 1200–1800: An Anthology* (New Haven, 1989), 383. For complaints about the use of philosophy in sermons at the beginning of the fourteenth century and attempts to regulate this through the use of the ban, see ibid. 381–3.

[52] For Leon Joseph of Carcassonne's admiration for the Scholastic disputed question in the fourteenth century, see Renan, 'Les Écrivains juifs français du XIVe siècle', 773; for the use of the disputed question in sermons, see Saperstein, *Jewish Preaching 1200–1800*, 395–6; id., *'Your Voice Like a Ram's Horn'*, 84–6, 200–7.

ing of philosophical study was intimately bound up with the emergence of the universities, which supplanted the monasteries and the cathedral schools as the centres of intellectual activity. These universities provided a standardized curriculum, a process for evaluation of progress and certification of mastery over a field, and a set of social rewards for excellence. Eventually, they acquired an identity transcending the individuals who happened to be teaching at a particular time. The very name by which this enterprise is commonly known—Scholasticism—reveals its rootedness in the new institutional context of the university.[53]

There is little evidence from the Jewish community for anything even remotely analogous as a framework for philosophical study. The educational institutions of the Jewish community were devoted almost exclusively to the study of traditional Jewish texts, primarily the Bible and the Talmud. Recently it has been questioned whether an organized system of community-sponsored elementary education or of academies for higher scholarship that were recognized as stable public institutions transcending a particularly noted individual existed in northern Europe.[54] But even in southern France and Christian Spain, where the evidence for the existence of recognized academies is considerably stronger, these do not appear to have been the context in which philosophy was studied or philosophical writings produced.[55]

Philosophical learning among Jews seems to have been transmitted predominantly through private instruction: fathers teaching their children or providing teachers for them, mature students seeking experts from whom

---

[53] On monasteries and cathedral schools as centres of learning, see Jean Leclercq, *The Love of Learning and the Desire for God: A Study of Monastic Culture* (New York, 1961), esp. 76–151; Beryl Smalley *The Study of the Bible in the Middle Ages* (New York, 1952), esp. 37–84; on universities, see Gordon Leff, *Paris and Oxford Universities in the Thirteenth and Fourteenth Centuries: An Institutional and Intellectual History* (New York, 1968).

[54] Kanarfogel, *Jewish Education and Society in the High Middle Ages*, 17–19, 55–7.

[55] A similar conclusion was reached independently by Freudenthal ('Les Sciences dans les communautés juives médiévales de Provence', 93–4 n. 238, 128–31). There are, to be sure, many curricula that incorporate the sciences alongside biblical and rabbinic texts (the most famous of which from Christian Europe is probably that of Joseph ibn Kaspi [see Abrahams (ed.), *Hebrew Ethical Wills*, i. 144–6]), but these are curricula for individual study, not for an established institution. Abraham Neuman stated it succinctly: 'One looks in vain for any institutions where these elaborate curricula could have been taught' (*The Jews in Spain*, ii. 73). Perhaps the reason was connected with the rabbinic tradition of opposition to the public teaching of philosophy (see S. Harvey, *Falaquera's Epistle of the Debate*, pp. x–xi). In a text dated 1402, Leon Joseph of Carcassonne stated that Jews 'were not permitted to expound [philosophical] wisdom in the marketplaces or the public squares . . . or to establish an academy [*yeshivah*] in public', referring apparently to opposition within the Jewish community (in Renan, 'Les Écrivains juifs français du XIVe siècle', 772).

they could learn.⁵⁶ Judah ibn Tibbon described the need to travel far to bring back a suitable teacher in the secular sciences for his son.⁵⁷ This son, the distinguished translator Samuel, in turn became the philosophical mentor of his son-in-law, Jacob Anatoli.⁵⁸ Moses Narboni was studying the *Guide for the Perplexed* with his father when he was 13 years old.⁵⁹ Autobiographical accounts written by an anonymous disciple of Abraham Abulafia, Joseph ibn Kaspi, and Kalonymos ben Kalonymos reveal a pattern of travelling to find a satisfactory teacher of philosophical texts—the Jewish equivalent of the medieval *peregrinatio academica*.⁶⁰

We also hear of individual teachers. Zerahiah ben Shealtiel Gracian of Barcelona had a considerable reputation as a teacher of philosophy in Rome, although he did not seem to have an academy of his own.⁶¹ Sen Astruc de Noves, not particularly famous as a philosopher or scientist in his own right, served as the mentor in Salon of several Jews who went on to successful careers, including Kalonymos ben Kalonymos and Samuel ben Judah of Mar-

---

⁵⁶ Compare the similar conclusion by Joseph Shatzmiller about medical education during this period (*Jews, Medicine, and Medieval Society*, 22–7).

⁵⁷ Abrahams (ed.), *Hebrew Ethical Wills*, i. 57.   ⁵⁸ Anatoli, *Malmad hatalmidim*, introduction.

⁵⁹ Moses Narboni, *Be'ur lesefer moreh nevukhim* [commentary on Maimonides' *Guide for the Perplexed*] (Vienna: K. K. Hof- und Staatsdruckere, 1852), 1a (introduction), 11b (on *Guide for the Perplexed*, 1: 63); cf. the statement by Solomon Bonafed that a Christian scholar taught him logic for a year after he had previously studied that discipline with his father (Gross, 'The Poet Solomon Bonafed' [Heb.], 36).

⁶⁰ The disciple wrote: 'I returned to my native land and God brought me together with a Jewish philosopher with whom I studied some of Maimonides' *Guide of the Perplexed*' (in Gershom Scholem, *Major Trends in Jewish Mysticism* [New York, 1941], 148). Ibn Kaspi wrote his ethical will before setting off in search of a teacher, companion, or disciple for his studies (Abrahams [ed.], *Hebrew Ethical Wills*, i. 130–1; cf. Barry Mesch, *Studies in Joseph ibn Caspi: Fourteenth Century Philosopher and Exegete* [Leiden, 1975], 46). Kalonymos complained of his inability to find an appropriate teacher in southern France and was satisfied only in Barcelona. While many of the teachers he described were talmudists, the chief attraction in Barcelona was the Ibn Hisdai brothers, 'learned in every branch of science and medicine' (see Kalonymos ben Kalonymos, *Igeret hitnatslut haketanah* [A Short Epistle of Apology], ed. Joseph Shatzmiller, *Sefunot*, 10 [1966], 21). For a discussion of the theme of wandering scholars searching for the best *yeshivah* education in medieval Christian Europe, see Mordecai Breuer 'The Wanderings of Students and Scholars: A Prologue to a Chapter in the History of the Academies' (Heb.), in Reuven Bonfil, Menahem Ben-Sasson, and Yosef Hacker (eds.), *Culture and Society in Medieval Jewish History* [Tarbut vehevrah betoledot yisra'el bimei habeinayim] (Jerusalem, 1989), 445–68.

⁶¹ 'I have already taught this book, namely the *Guide of the Perplexed*, many times to others' (in Aviezer Ravitzky, 'The Teaching of Rabbi Zerachiah ben Isaac ben Shealtiel Hen and Thirteenth-Century Maimonidean–Tibbonide Thought' [Mishnato shel r. zeraḥiyah ben yitsḥak ben she'alti'el ḥen vehahagut hamaimunit-tibonit bame'ah hashelosh-esreh] [Ph.D. diss., Hebrew University of Jerusalem, 1977], 71; see also Sirat, *A History of Jewish Philosophy in the Middle Ages*, 267–8).

seilles.⁶² Levi ben Abraham was invited by the wealthy and pious patron Samuel Sulami to live in his home and instruct him in philosophy.⁶³ The extensive literature pertaining to the conflict over philosophical study in the early fourteenth century makes no mention of formal schools: the bans promulgated by Solomon ben Adret (Rashba) in 1305 seem to be directed at individuals studying with other individuals.⁶⁴

A number of books are described as having been written for the educational needs of a particular individual. Judah ibn Tibbon speaks of the books he had made 'on all the sciences', possibly compendia, intended for his son's use.⁶⁵ Joseph ibn Kaspi claimed to have made a digest of Aristotle's *Nicomachean Ethics* (*Terumat kesef*), for his son, and hoped to do the same for the *Organon* (*Zeror hakesef*).⁶⁶ Shem Tov Falaquera described his works *Reshit ḥokhmah*, *Sefer hama'alot*, and *De'ot hapilosofim* as intended to guide a certain Jew with no background in philosophy or knowledge of Arabic through the philosophical curriculum.⁶⁷ This may have been a topos, exemplified in Maimonides' *Guide for the Perplexed* and rooted in the rabbinic tradition that certain philosophical doctrines are not to be taught to more than one at a time,⁶⁸ but it suggests the absence of established schools to which those who wanted systematic training in philosophy could turn. All of this indicates the pattern of philosophical study described by Colette Sirat: there was 'no organized teaching of the sciences, no school, but only a transmission from master to pupil'.⁶⁹

Yet there are tantalizing hints of a different picture. One text is so suggestive that it deserves to be cited at length. It appears in *Tagmulei hanefesh* (The Rewards of the Soul), a review of philosophical literature relating to the soul

---

⁶² Berman, 'Greek into Hebrew', 291, 313; Renan, 'Les Écrivains juifs français du XIVe siècle', 548–52, 419.   ⁶³ Abba Mari, *Minḥat kena'ot*, 47–8.

⁶⁴ 'No one from our community shall teach a single Jew these disciplines until they are 25 years old' (Ben Adret, *She'elot uteshuvot harashba*, i. 151*b*). In his defence of the culture of southern France, Yedaiah Bedersi conceded that some men had taught logic to children and his words could imply that this occurred in schools: 'the children returned to the houses of their mothers' without having been harmed by this exposure' (in Ben Adret, *She'elot uteshuvot harashba*, i. 168*a*). The situation is described, however, as an anomaly.   ⁶⁵ Abrahams (ed.), *Hebrew Ethical Wills*, i. 57.

⁶⁶ Ibid. i. 144; see Mesch, *Studies in Joseph ibn Caspi*, 7, 46, 51; cf. Judah ibn Tibbon, in Abrahams (ed.), *Hebrew Ethical Wills*, i. 68.   ⁶⁷ S. Harvey, *Falaquera's Epistle of the Debate*, 51, 79, 97.

⁶⁸ Mishnah *Ḥag.* 2: 1; see Moses Maimonides *Guide for the Perplexed*, introduction (trans. and ed. M. Friedländer, 3 vols. in 1 [New York: Hebrew Publishing Co., 1946], i. 7–8).

⁶⁹ Sirat, *History of Jewish Philosophy in the Middle Ages*, 243; According to Neuman, the 'amazing accomplishments [of the Jews] in the domains of science and philosophy were attained by private study rather than through a system of formal instruction' (*The Jews in Spain*, ii. 74). Joseph Shatzmiller has shown that the same pattern applied to medical studies in southern France: no formal

and the afterlife, including works by Christian authors, by Hillel of Verona:

Therefore I say that this statement of Aristotle [implying that the intellect is not immortal] does not represent his own position or his own thought, but rather the position of his predecessors that he had previously been reporting. This is what I said in my youth in the *beit hamidrash*, when I was studying in Spain with the master [*harav*] who taught me physical science, and my fellow students [*benei hayeshivah*] argued against me for a long time, and my master also would not agree with me. He disputed with me extensively, for from the commentaries of Averroës no solution was to be found to this problem.

Finally it pleased God that our master found an old text, written in an ancient hand, of a commentary by Themistius, who wrote commentaries on all the works of Aristotle. In it was written that Themistius interpreted this statement to mean that Aristotle was reporting the position of Plato and his colleagues, not his own view. Thus Themistius writes that when Aristotle said this in that chapter of the first book of *De Anima*, he was still undertaking his account of the position of his predecessors, and had not yet begun a refutation of those who hold that that there is no difference between intellect and sense. Throughout the entire chapter he speaks of the intellect as he does of the senses. . . .

This is what the master found in the commentaries of Themistius. Then he was pacified, and he accepted my position. I was delighted and thankful to God that my position agreed with that of Themistius, for he is one of the greatest of the commentators on the works of Aristotle, and all the masters [*harabanim*] rely on his commentaries as they do on the commentaries of Averroës, or even more.[70]

The substance of the debate need not concern us here. What is crucial for our purpose is the setting. The author describes youthful philosophical studies

---

schools (Christian or Jewish) but rather study with a master, who was paid for his instruction, and then submitting to official examinations ('Livres médicaux et éducation médicale', 464–5). His insistence that there is no evidence for Jews in the medical school of Montpellier before the last quarter of the fourteenth century does not, however, consider the text in Dinur, *Israel in the Diaspora* (Heb.) (Pt. II, vol. iv, 221), which indicates a Jewish presence there in the first half of the century (Joseph Shatzmiller, 'Étudiants juifs à la faculté de médecine de Montpellier, dernier quart du XIVe siècle', *Jewish History*, 6 [1992], 246).

[70] Hillel ben Samuel of Verona, *Sefer tagmulei hanefesh lehilel ben shemu'el miveronah* [The Rewards of the Soul], ed. Joseph (Giuseppe) Sermoneta (Jerusalem, 1981), 133–4. An obvious question is how this relates to Hillel's statement in his letter to 'Isaac the Physician': 'I lived in Barcelona for three years, and I studied before my teacher, Rabbi Jonah' (in *Igerot kena'ot*, 14c). Clearly, Jonah Gerondi could not have been the 'rabbi' in the above-cited passage. Hillel describes Jonah teaching halakhah with reference to Maimonides' *Mishneh torah*, and in the same letter he refers to a different mentor in philosophical studies. It is not impossible that Hillel spent periods of time in Spain studying halakhah and philosophy: the details of his early life are almost completely unknown.

in Spain, probably in the 1240s or 1250s. According to the passage, these studies occurred in the context of a school, referred to by the Hebrew terms *beit midrash* and *yeshivah*. Instruction was led by a master, called a *rav*, and a number of students were present. The subject matter included physics and psychology, investigated through the works of Aristotle with the commentaries of Averroës. Finally, the commentaries of Themistius, specifically on *De Anima*, but on other works of Aristotle as well, are described as particularly influential among 'the masters' (*harabanim*).

Were the texts studied in Hebrew or in Arabic? Hebrew translations of Averroës' commentaries on *De Anima* were being produced in precisely this period, but no Hebrew translation is known of Themistius' commentary on *De Anima*.[71] Since the Themistius text is described as old and quite rare, it is most unlikely that it could refer to an unknown thirteenth-century Hebrew translation of the text. The conclusion, therefore, is that the philosophical texts described must have been in Arabic.

If this passage is to be believed,[72] there was at least one school in Spain in the mid-thirteenth century where philosophy was being taught at a rather high level. If this was indeed a Jewish school, we are compelled to look for other evidence of a Jewish institutional structure for philosophical

---

[71] Moses ibn Tibbon's translation of Averroës' middle commentary was made in 1261; another translation, by Shem Tov ben Isaac of Tortosa, may have been completed slightly earlier. The translation of Averroës' compendium, or comprehensive summary, of *De Anima* was finished by Moses ibn Tibbon in 1244. (There is some question whether any Hebrew translation from the Arabic of the long commentary ever existed.) See Steinschneider, *Die Hebraeischen Übersetzungen des Mittelalters*, 147–50. For the Arabic translation of Themistius on *De Anima*, see Francis E. Peters, *Aristoteles Arabus: The Oriental Translations and Commentaries of the Aristotelian Corpus* (Leiden, 1968), 42. For a full record of Hebrew translations, see Mauro Zonta, 'Medieval Hebrew Translations of Philosophical and Scientific Texts', in Gad Freudenthal (ed.), *Science in Medieval Jewish Cultures* (Cambridge, 2011), 17–73.

[72] In his critical edition of the text, Sermoneta maintained that the entire story of Hillel's interpretation confirmed by his teacher's discovery of an old Themistius manuscript is a fraud. Hillel actually got the idea from a work by Thomas Aquinas written in 1270 and invented the story to take credit for the idea (Sermoneta, notes to lines 524–42, in Hillel ben Samuel, *Sefer tagmulei hanefesh*, 134). According to this view, the passage tells us nothing about the realities of philosophical study in Spain, only about the fertile imagination of Hillel. There are several reasons why I believe that the passage should not be so quickly dismissed: Hillel also refers to his philosophy mentor in a totally different text (see n. 70 above), Hillel's passage is more detailed than the passage from Aquinas on which Sermoneta maintains it was based, there is no reason why such a fabrication should have been introduced in this one place to take credit for one interpretation of an Aristotelian crux, a person who wants to be believed about a substantive issue usually does not make up a story in which the entire setting has no correspondance to reality. Space does not permit elaboration of these arguments. (Since this chapter was first written, I have discovered that Warren Harvey had questioned Sermoneta's dismissal of this passage [Harvey, 'An Edition of *The Book of the Souls Rewards*' (Heb.), *Tarbiz*, 52 (1983), 535].)

study.⁷³ For example, Isaac ben Yedaiah's description of the academy of Meshulam ben Moses in Béziers, probably during the 1230s, mentioned 'learned scholars with reputation in every discipline and branch of knowledge' and noted that students came there to learn not only the 'disputations of Abaye and Rava' but also 'the work of the chariot and the wheel of the wagon'. This suggests that something more than talmudic dialectic was being studied. As Meshulam was an opponent of kabbalah in Provence, it stands to reason that the 'work of the chariot' here is to be understood, in its Maimonidean sense, as philosophy.⁷⁴

Other material pertains to the late fourteenth and fifteenth centuries. Harry Wolfson believed that Jewish philosophy in Spain was indeed taught in a formal institutional structure. He wrote that Crescas's *Or hashem* (The Light of the Lord) 'had its origin in class-room lectures and discussions. We know of other instances where Hebrew philosophic works were the result of class-room lectures.'⁷⁵ Elsewhere he maintained that the commentaries of Averroës were intensively studied 'by individual scholars as well as by organized classes in schools',⁷⁶ and he describes Isaac ibn Shem Tov as 'a teacher actively engaged in expounding the text of the *Physics* to successive classes of students'.⁷⁷ The evidence for these statements, however, is meagre and circumstantial at best, applying just as readily to individual instruction as to formal class lectures.

In the last generation before the Expulsion from Spain, Isaac Arama complained bitterly that 'many are the teachers of alien disciplines, antagonistic to our Torah and our faith, and it is a trivial matter in their judgement to teach these disciplines in their own language'; philosophy had become the 'foundation of our *yeshivah*s, which have become devoid of Torah and Talmud'.⁷⁸ This sounds like the hyperbolic rhetoric of a polemicist. Yet, given

---

⁷³ Assaf apparently assumes that the text is reliable and refers to a Jewish school (*Sources for the History of Jewish Education* [Heb.], ii. 48). Dinur reproduces the passage without comment on its meaning or relevance to the history of Jewish education (*Israel in the Diaspora* [Heb.], Pt. II, vol. iv, 243).

⁷⁴ In Adolf Neubauer, 'Yedaya de Beziers', *Revue des études juives*, 20 (1980), 245–8; see Saperstein, *Decoding the Rabbis*, 179; Assaf, *Sources for the History of Jewish Education* (Heb.), ii. 34.

⁷⁵ Wolfson, *Crescas' Critique of Aristotle*, 29–31. Neuman states that Crescas 'discussed philosophical problems at his academy', giving as his source for this the introduction to *Or hashem* (*The Jews in Spain*, ii. 80). I can find no such evidence in this text, except for the statement that the author has investigated philosophical problems 'with the most distinguished colleagues'.

⁷⁶ Wolfson, 'Plans for the Publication of a *Corpus Commentariorum*, 431.

⁷⁷ Id., 'Isaac ibn Shem Tob's Unknown Commentaries', 488, 481.

⁷⁸ Isaac Arama, *Ḥazut Kashah*, sha'ar 12 (in *Akedat yitsḥak* [homiletical essays on the Torah], 3 vols. [Warsaw, 1882–4], iii. 24a); Assaf, *Sources for the History of Jewish Education* (Heb.), ii. 91.

the interest in philosophy on the part of leading rabbinic scholars such as Isaac Campanton and Isaac Aboab, it is not inconceivable that philosophy found its way into the curriculum as an adjunct to talmudic studies. There are references to philosophical work done in the academy of Abraham Bibago at Saragossa.[79] In the first years of the sixteenth century Joseph Garçon complained about those who 'wear themselves out beating a path to the academy [*yeshivah*] of external disciplines', yet another tantalizingly ambiguous reference to what may or may not be a Jewish institution for philosophical study.[80]

The most detailed information of a Jewish institutional base for philosophical study comes from Italy. In 1466 the king of Sicily granted a charter permitting the Jews to establish a *studium generale* and hire the experts needed to teach 'whatever approved sciences'.[81] Judah Messer Leon wrote about his academy (*yeshivah*) in Mantua, in which he gave daily instruction in the *Posterior Analytics* (on which Judah had written a super-commentary) to a 'David the Spaniard', who in turn taught, for pay, Judah's students al-Ghazali's simpler text, *Aims of the Philosophers*. While it is unclear whether any rabbinic study took place at this 'academy', it does describe a school which, though probably centred around one primary scholar, included students at different levels and instruction by different individuals.[82]

The other possibility is that the passage refers to Hillel's studies at a Christian institution. This does not at first seem likely, for the terminology used by Hillel—*beit hamidrash*, *yeshivah*, *rav*—has specifically Jewish connotations. Yet Jewish writers did use such terms to describe Christian or Muslim institutions for which there was no distinct Hebrew equivalent.[83]

---

[79] Alan Lazaroff, *The Theology of Abraham Bibago* (Tuscaloosa, 1981), 1, 52 n. 7, citing a scribe's colophon to a Hebrew commentary on a work by al-Ghazali stating that it was completed in Saragossa at the academy of R. Abraham ben Bibag. As he was not known to be a halakhist with a talmudic academy of his own, there is some questions about precisely what kind of institution is mentioned here.

[80] Hacker, 'On the Spiritual Image of Spanish Jews' (Heb.), 55; Eng. trans. in id., 'The Intellectual Activity of the Jews of the Ottoman Empire', 116. Note Hacker's conclusion, based on the same source, that kabbalah was taught in some fifteenth-century Spanish *yeshivot* ('On the Spiritual Image of Spanish Jews' [Heb.], 25–6 n. 29, 52, 54).

[81] Shatzmiller, *Jews, Medicine and Medieval Society*, 25–6; the Latin is *aprobatas sciencias quascumque*, which, as Shatzmiller notes, is far less explicit than we might like it to be.

[82] Judah ben Yehiel Messer Leon, *The Book of the Honeycomb's Flow: Sēpher Nōfeth Sūfīm*, trans. and ed. Isaac Rabinowitz (Ithaca, NY, 1983), pp. xxvii–xlii, esp. xxxvi–xxxvii, xl–xli.

[83] e.g. *hamoreh hagadol sar hayeshivah*, referring to the rector of the *studium* in Bologna, Nicolo de Fava (Neubauer, *Catalogue of Hebrew Manuscripts*, 869; cf. Shatzmiller, 'Étudiants juifs à la faculté de médecine de Montpellier', 244, 247); *ve'eshev bishivoteihem uveit iyunam*, referring to Christian institutions of higher learning (Renan, 'Les Écrivains juifs français du XIVe siècle', 773); *ushekedat*

Is it conceivable that a Jew from Italy could have studied philosophy from Arabic texts in mid-thirteenth-century Spain in a Christian institution of higher learning? Hillel of Verona's claim opens up a possibility that needs further investigation.

Social Status

What is known about the social status of those who participated in the philosophical enterprise? Do the available data substantiate the thesis that philosophy was primarily the preoccupation of the upper classes? There are several problems in addressing this issue. One is a problem of definition: who is to be included in the category of 'philosophers'? For our purposes, it will not be sufficient to limit the investigation to a few outstanding names. In order to understand the social dimensions of Jewish philosophy, it is necessary to include the less original figures, the translators, popularizers, and purveyors of philosophy alongside the intellectual giants.[84] Those who devoted a significant portion of their energy to philosophical work are as much a part of the subject as those who made a lasting contribution to the history of Jewish thought. So too are those who might be termed 'consumers': the patrons of philosophical writers, those who commissioned translations, those who purchased scientific texts. Unfortunately, in many cases little is known about certain figures beyond the texts they wrote, which contain meagre biographical information.[85] Nevertheless, enough material can be gathered to justify some preliminary conclusions.

midrasheihem, referring to Christian philosophical study in *scholae* (Solomon Bonafed, in Gross, 'The Poet Solomon Bonafed' [Heb.], 36); *kavu sham midrashoth*, referring to Islamic schools where Maimonides' *Guide for the Perplexed* was studied (Ibn Kaspi, in Abrahams [ed.], *Hebrew Ethical Wills*, i. 154).

[84] There is also a problem in classifying those who did important philosophical or scientific work yet criticized fundamental principles of philosophy or its influence in Jewish life. Crescas is the primary example in the late Middle Ages, as Judah Halevi was earlier. Members of the Ibn Hisdai family in Barcelona signed Solomon ben Adret's ban on philosophical study, yet were identified by Kalonymos ben Kalonymos as scientists (*Igeret hitnatslut haketanah*, 21–2, 49–50). Kalonymos himself sided with Abba Mari and Ben Adret, yet produced important translations of Arabic philosophical works (ibid. 16–17). Hillel ben Samuel of Verona is generally considered a philosopher, but he is classified by one scholar as 'the first anti-rationalist of Italian Jewry' (Barzilay, *Between Faith and Reason*, 14, 42).

[85] Indeed, it is something of a topos for a scholar beginning a study of a philosopher's thought to begin by noting how little is known about his life: e.g. Isaac Albalag (Georges Vajda, *Isaac Albalag: Averroïste juif, traducteur et annotateur d'al Ghazali* [Paris, 1960], 1), Nissim of Marseilles (Colette Sirat, 'Political Ideas of Nissim ben Moses of Marseilles' [Heb.], *Jerusalem Studies in Jewish Thought*, 9 [1990], 53), Abraham Bibago (Lazaroff, *The Theology of Abraham Bibago*, 1), Abraham Shalom

The most profound and original figure among the Jewish philosophers and scientists of the late Middle Ages was Gersonides. Archival research by Joseph Shatzmiller and others has elucidated the position of his family in the community of Orange.[86] Despite medieval traditions that he was a descendant of Nahmanides (Moses ben Nahman, Ramban) or Levi ben Abraham, little is definitely known about his lineage. Notarial records indicate that his family was thoroughly integrated into the life of the community, though not among its official leaders (*parnasim*: the equivalent, as Shatzmiller informs us, of the Latin *consules*). Like many contemporary Jews, Gersonides engaged in moneylending. His brother Samuel was a physician, and he may have been as well.

Shatzmiller has documented the considerable interest shown by contemporary Christian intellectuals in Gersonides' work. His reputation gave him access to the papal court in Avignon: indeed, his last piece of writing, never finished, was an astrological prediction requested by the pope. He may have used his access to the court and his prestige on behalf of his fellow Jews, although there is no evidence of specific interventions. Gersonides thus provides an example of philosophical achievements combined with court connections, but in a model quite different from that posited by Baer. He was not a wealthy, aristocratic Jewish courtier who used philosophy to rationalize his abandonment of Jewish commitments and assimilation into the society of the court but rather a Jew whose Jewish commitments were beyond reproach, who came to the attention of the Christian elite precisely because of his achievements in philosophy and science.

A figure comparable in cultural profile though certainly not of similar world-class stature is Yedaiah Bedersi. Like Gersonides, he wrote in a number of different genres, and all of his work is suffused with the philosophical ethos, though the philosophy is presented on varying levels of difficulty. There were extremely technical works, including commentaries on Averroës' epitome of Aristotle's *Physics* and Avicenna's *Canon of Medicine* and independent treatises that reveal the influence both of Islamic and scholastic

---

(Herbert A. Davidson, *The Philosophy of Abraham Shalom: A Fifteenth-Century Exposition and Defense of Maimonides* [Berkeley: University of California Press, 1964], 1).

[86] Joseph Shatzmiller, 'Gersonides and the Communities of Orange during His Lifetime' (Heb.), *Meḥkarim betoledot am yisra'el ve'erets yisra'el*, 2 (1972), 111–26; id., 'More on Gersonides and the Communities of Orange during His Lifetime' (Heb.), *Meḥkarim betoledot am yisra'el ve'erets yisra'el*, 3 (1975), 139–43; id., 'Gersonide et la société juive de son temps', in Dahan (ed.), *Gersonide en son temps*, 33–43; Seymour Feldman, introduction to Gersonides, *The Wars of the Lord*, trans. and ed. Seymour Feldman, 3 vols. (Philadelphia, 1984–99), i. 1–5.

philosophy.[87] He wrote a commentary on traditional Jewish material—selected passages from the *midrashim*—into which he incorporated specific references to a variety of technical philosophical texts,[88] and he wrote more popular literary works in which the philosophical commitment is fused with a more traditional piety.

Yedaiah's father, Abraham, was apparently from a wealthy, well-bred family, and his financial activities made him economically independent to the point that he could support other poets. In one polemical context, he expressed contempt for the lowly origins of his opponent. He was apparently related to courtiers in Béziers. At some point, however, he experienced a financial reverse: forced to flee Perpignan, he became dependent on selling poems to patrons.[89] Yedaiah was apparently a prodigy and received an expensive education in Perpignan. Yet his was not an aristocratic family: in the introduction to *Ohev nashim* (The Lover of Women), written at the age of 18, he described the two sons of Don Salomon de les Infants of Arles as above him in social prestige.[90] The economic reversals seem to have left their mark. His most popular work, *Behinat olam* (Examination of the World), reveals a deep suspicion of wealth.[91] Like Gersonides, he affirmed that Jewish philosophy could flourish without any direct connections to a courtier class and without undermining Jewish loyalties and commitments.

A different category was composed of those intimately involved in philosophy, though not original philosophers themselves. To this category belonged the Ibn Tibbon family, crucial in the process of transplanting Jewish philosophy from the Islamic to the Christian context through their ongoing project of translation. The ethical will of Judah ibn Tibbon provides considerable information about his social and economic status. In addition to

---

[87] Shlomo Pines, *Between Jewish and Gentile Thought: Studies in the History of Jewish Philosophy* [Bein maḥshevet yisra'el lemaḥshevet ha'amim: meḥkarim betoledot hafilosofiyah hayehudit] (Jerusalem, 1977), 180–2, 223–53, 263–76.

[88] Marc Saperstein, 'R. Isaac ben Yeda'ya: A Forgotten Commentator on the Aggada', *Revue des études juives*, 138 (1979), esp. pp. 32–3 for references to Bedersi's philosophical works; id., 'Selected Passages from Yedaiah Bedersi's Commentary on the Midrashim', in Twersky (ed.), *Studies in Medieval Jewish History and Literature*, ii. 423–40.

[89] Hayyim (Yefim) Schirmann, *Hebrew Poetry in Spain and Provence* [Hashirah ha'ivrit bisefarad uviprovans], 2 vols. in 4 (Jerusalem, 1960), iv. 468; id., 'Studies on the Poems and Letters of Abraham Bedersi' (Heb.), in S. Ettinger et al. (eds.), *Yitzhak Baer Jubilee Volume* [Sefer yovel leyitshak baer] (Jerusalem, 1961)', 163; Saperstein, *Decoding the Rabbis*, 166–7.

[90] Yedaiah Bedersi, *Ohev nashim* [The Lover of Women], ed. Adolf Neubauer, in *Tif'eret Seiva: Jubelschrift zum Neunzigsten Geburtstag des Dr. L. Zunz* (Berlin, 1884): Heb. section, 1; Neubauer, introduction to Bedersi, *Ohev nashim*: Germ. section, 138–9.

[91] See Schirmann, *Hebrew Poetry* (Heb.), iv. 497 lines 7–9 and frequently elsewhere in the work.

his scholarly activities, he was a merchant. He refers to an incident in Marseilles in which his son Samuel took the initiative for an unfortunate investment on behalf of the family. He travelled extensively. He took pride in the library he acquired at great expense. He was respected and honoured in the community, by Christians as well as Jews.[92]

Yet the text indicates that he was not an extremely wealthy man. While he paid 30 gold dinars a year to a teacher, he had to pledge books and borrow from friends to provide for the marriages of his two daughters. He felt impelled to remind his son that he did not arrange a marriage with an otherwise undesirable daughter of a wealthy man 'as others richer than I have done with their sons'. Samuel's wife is described as having been brought up in a good family, but having simple tastes, without a servant.[93] This is clearly a description of the middle class, not of the Jewish aristocracy.

Little is known of the social position of the other Ibn Tibbons. One scholar described them all as physicians but concedes that 'aside from their translations we know nothing of their medical activities'.[94] Judah Alfakhar, scion of an aristocratic family and one of the leaders of Toledan Jewry, referred to Samuel ibn Tibbon with little respect.[95] Moses ibn Tibbon produced such a prodigious number of translations between 1240 and 1283 that this must have been virtually a full-time occupation, yet it remains unclear how this work was financed.[96]

Connected with the Ibn Tibbon family by marriage was Jacob Anatoli.[97] While not an original philosopher, his importance as a translator and a popularizer of philosophical ideas in a homiletical context has already been noted. Anatoli referred to friends among the most learned Jews in Narbonne and Béziers, who encouraged him to translate Averroës' commentary on Aristotle's *Organon*, but he also mentioned that powerful forces in the Jewish community rebuked him for his study of logic in Arabic and forced him to

---

[92] Judah ibn Tibbon, in Abrahams (ed.), *Hebrew Ethical Wills*, i. 71–2, 57, 66–7.   [93] Ibid. 66, 78.

[94] David Romano, 'La Transmission des sciences arabes par les Juifs en Languedoc', in Marie-Humbert Vicaire and Bernhard Blumenkranz (eds.), *Juifs et judaïsme de Languedoc, XIIIe siècle–début XIVe siècle*, Cahiers de Fanjeaux, 12 (Toulouse, 1977), 369.

[95] e.g. *Igerot kena'ot*, 3b; cf. the letter by David Kimhi (ibid. 4a).

[96] He also wrote independent works in Hebrew: a super-commentary on Abraham ibn Ezra's Torah commentary, a commentary on the Song of Songs, and an interpretation of the aggadot of the Talmud. On the last work, see Sirat, *History of Jewish Philosophy in the Middle Ages*, 229–31.

[97] Anatoli spoke of having studied logic in Arabic with his father-in-law Samuel ibn Tibbon (Anatoli, *Malmad hatalmidim*, introduction), yet, in his commentary on the Song of Songs, Moses refers to Anatoli as 'my lord, my uncle'. Thus Colette Sirat identified him as the son-in-law of Samuel and the uncle of Moses (*History of Jewish Philosophy in the Middle Ages*, 226, 228): for both of these to be true, Moses would have had to have been Samuel's grandson.

discontinue his weekly sabbath preaching.⁹⁸ This is someone who had a base of supporters, but certainly not someone who wielded power in the Jewish community or outside it.

Jacob ben Makhir was part of the same distinguished family. In the first years of the fourteenth century, he led the Jews in Montpellier who opposed Abba Mari's efforts to restrict the study of philosophy. An astronomer and mathematician of some consequence, he and several Jewish colleagues had considerable interaction with Christian scholars in the University of Montpellier. It is clear, however, that this did not put him among the powerful elite of either the Jewish community or Christian society.⁹⁹ The Ibn Tibbon family was an example of ongoing philosophical commitment, sustained for at least four generations, without any links to a courtier class or any indication of an erosion of Jewish loyalties.¹⁰⁰

A third category was composed of those who did not produce philosophy at all, either by writing independent texts or by translating, but rather spread or popularized the philosophical work of others in their own writings. A good representative is David Kimhi, significant because of his incorporation of philosophical ideas into popular biblical commentaries and because of his role as a defender of Maimonides in 1232. He was apparently a teacher by

⁹⁸ See Anatoli, *Malmad hatalmidim*, introduction; see also: 'I exposed myself to their reproaches and their vilifications' (ibid. 6*b*; cf. 121*b*, 159*a*). See also Chapter 10 below.

⁹⁹ In *Minḥat kena'ot* he is identified merely as 'one of the scholars', a relative of Judah ben Moses ibn Tibbon (Abba Mari, *Minḥat kena'ot*, 62). On his career as a scientist and his contacts with Christian academics, see Shatzmiller, 'Étudiants juifs à la faculté de médecine de Montpellier', 243–4.

¹⁰⁰ In the category of those who produced philosophical works without necessarily adding much original thought are Shem Tov Falaquera, Kalonymos ben Kalonymos, Samuel ben Judah of Marseilles, and Joseph, Isaac, and Shem Tov ibn Shem Tov. Falaquera was from an aristocratic family in Tudela (Jospe, *Torah and Sophia*, 2), and his *Sefer hamevakesh* [Book of the Seeker] provides a strong statement of the ideology of the wealthy, which is, however, subjected to a withering critique (cf. Y. Baer, *A History of the Jews in Christian Spain*, i. 203–4). On his abilities as a philosopher, see Jospe, *Torah and Sophia*; Fenton, 'Shem Tov Falaquera and Aristotelian Theology'. Kalonymos also apparently came from an aristocratic family, as both he and his father are referred to by the title *nasi* (Renan, 'Les Écrivains juifs français du XIVe siècle', 417, 426; Kalonymos, *Igeret hitnatslut haketanah*, 14). However, he described himself as 'pursued by sorrows' (ibid. 35), and his writings also attack those who are overly concerned with the amassing of wealth (ibid. 31) or who boast of their lineage (Schirman, *Hebrew Poetry* [Heb.], iv. 508–10). The translator Samuel ben Judah of Marseilles presents a similar pattern: scion of an aristocratic and wealthy family (Berman, 'Greek into Hebrew', 290–1, 293), he referred to 'continuous calamities' that came upon him (ibid. 314). While Joseph ibn Shem Tov might be described as a courtier, he apparently suffered an extreme reversal of fortune, as he describes himself in the introduction to his major work as an impoverished vagrant (Saperstein, *Jewish Preaching, 1200–1800*, 167). His brother Isaac and his son Shem Tov had no known connection with court life or an aristocratic ethos.

profession, noting that 'most of my time has been spent teaching boys Talmud'. This was not a position that guaranteed particularly high status in medieval Jewish society.[101] Even at the end of his career, during his campaign in Spain to defend Maimonides, he was treated rather roughly by his opponents, informed that he was not welcome in Burgos, and addressed with what seems to be an air of condescension by Alfakhar.[102] His own writings express sympathies for the poor, and he attacked opponents for living in the lap of opulence.[103] Clearly, Kimhi's commitment to philosophy was not connected with a social status that could be described in any way as aristocratic.

Another figure in this category was Joseph ibn Kaspi. Like Kimhi, he produced no significant philosophical work of his own, devoting his energy rather to exegesis in a philosophical spirit.[104] Ibn Kaspi's ethical will indicates that he spent considerable time travelling in pursuit of knowledge, noting without undue modesty that 'wherever I go, wealth and honour are with me'.[105] In the famous description of his 'family feast', he revealed that a servant woman was in the kitchen and that not only invited guests but 'the poor' were in attendance.[106] At the same time, he disparaged wealth as unworthy of one's efforts, recommending rather attention to the insights of the traditional moralistic literature.[107] The picture seems to be of one whose economic success had given him the independence and leisure to follow his intellectual

---

[101] Frank Talmage, *David Kimhi: The Man and the Commentaries* (Cambridge, Mass., 1975), 14. Talmage's statement that 'teaching was a career which bore considerable esteem in his times' is too general. While scholars who taught Talmud at a high level to advanced students were indeed esteemed, those who introduced the subject to younger students were often treated with a notable lack of respect. For the situation in Ashkenaz at the time, see Kanarfogel, *Jewish Education and Society in the High Middle Ages*, 25–30; see also: 'the teachers seemed to have been very poor' (Ben Adret, *She'elot uteshuvot harashba*, v, no. 166, in Isidore Epstein, *Studies in the Communal Life of the Jews in Spain as Reflected in the Responsa of Rabbi Solomon ben Adreth and Rabbi Simon ben Zemach Duran*, 2 vols. in 1 [New York, 1968], i. 65); 'even Spain and Italy record complaints about the inferior status of Jewish teachers' (Salo W. Baron, *The Jewish Community*, 3 vols. [Philadelphia, 1942], ii. 184).

[102] Talmage, *David Kimhi*, 34; *Igerot kena'ot*, 2c.   [103] Talmage, *David Kimhi*, 20.

[104] Isadore Twersky, 'Joseph ibn Kaspi: Portrait of a Medieval Jewish Intellectual', in id. (ed.), *Studies in Medieval Jewish History and Literature*, 232. Ibn Kaspi wrote an epitome of Samuel ben Judah's translation of Averroës' commentary on Aristotle's *Nicomachean Ethics* and *Politics* (Steinschneider, *Die Hebraeischen Übersetzungen des Mittelalters*, 225–7), but these were intended as popularizations of the works, perhaps for his son.

[105] Ibn Kaspi, in Abrahams (ed.), *Hebrew Ethical Wills*, i. 130–1. According to Mesch, 'it appears that he had a good deal of money' (*Studies in Joseph ibn Caspi*, 47).

[106] Ibn Kaspi, in Abrahams (ed.), *Hebrew Ethical Wills*, i. 151–2.

[107] 'Pay no regard to money, for true wealth consists only of a sufficiency of bread to eat and raiment to wear. Why worry thyself to gain great riches?' (ibid. 145).

pursuits, not one whose social status predisposed him to find a philosophical rationale for assimilation to an elite circle.[108]

Courtiers and wealthy Jews were also associated with philosophy,[109] but this survey of a broad range of Jewish philosophers does not suggest that there was any special relationship between philosophy and the courtier class. On the contrary, some of the most influential Jewish courtiers were anything but enamoured of philosophy, and in some cases they actively opposed it. Meir Halevi Abulafia, who challenged Maimonides over what he thought was an overly rationalistic eschatology, was from one of the aristocratic families of Castilian Jewry, financially independent, and may have had connections with the royal court.[110] Judah Alfakhar, a physician who despite his philosophical study strongly defended an anti-Maimonidean position against David Kimhi, was from one of the most illustrious and influential families in Toledo.[111]

Todros ben Joseph Halevi Abulafia, discussed in Chapter 1, lived at the end of the thirteenth century. He was a member of an aristocratic family from Toledo, wealthy, with access to the Castilian court, and other Jewish courtiers were part of his circle. Yet he was an ascetic and a mystic, one of the leaders of the 'gnostic school' of kabbalah, with little use for philosophy.[112] Kalonymos ben Todros, the *nasi* in Narbonne, became a leader in the anti-philosophy camp of Abba Mari, and his role appears to have been decisive in preparing

---

[108] Other examples in this category would be Isaac ben Yedaiah (see Saperstein, *Decoding the Rabbis*, esp. 174), Levi ben Abraham (as noted above, extremely poor and dependent upon patrons), and Immanuel of Rome—described by Cecil Roth as 'wandering from place to place to earn his living, presumably as a house-tutor for the children of the wealthy Jewish loan-bankers' (Roth, *The Jews in the Renaissance* [Philadelphia, 1959], 90). For his reversals, see Immanuel of Rome, *Mahberot*, i. 179, 233.

[109] For example, Sheshet Benveniste, a courtier from Aragon who took a leading role in defending Maimonides during the earliest conflict while Maimonides was still alive (see Y. Baer, *A History of the Jews in Christian Spain*, i. 91, 100; Bernard Septimus, *Hispano-Jewish Culture in Transition: The Career and Controversies of Ramah* [Cambridge, Mass., 1982], 46–8), and Solomon of Lunel, a leader of the opponents to Abba Mari in 1305, royal tax collector, and extremely wealthy man. As is clear from the discussion above, the philosophical enterprise required financial backing. Meir Alguades, who translated the *Nicomachean Ethics* from Latin, described himself as 'frequenting the courts of the kings of Castile' (Berman, 'The Hebrew Translation from Latin of Aristotle's "Nicomachean Ethics"', 157, cf. 149) and stated that his work was undertaken at the request of Don Benveniste ibn Lavi of Saragossa (ibid. 158; cf. Y. Baer, *A History of the Jews in Christian Spain*, ii. 211).

[110] Septimus, *Hispano-Jewish Culture in Transition*, 5, 11, 16–17.

[111] Ibid. 17–18. The supporters of Maimonides were opposed by 'the aristocratic leadership of Castile' (ibid. 66).

[112] Y. Baer, *A History of the Jews in Christian Spain*, i. 119; Schirmann, *Hebrew Poetry* (Heb.), iii. 164–5; Gershom Scholem, *Kabbalah* (Jerusalem, 1974), 55. Baer described him as 'the very antithesis of the current tendency among Jewish courtiers to assimilate the ways of the Christian knighthood and the licentiousness of the royal court' (*A History of the Jews in Christian Spain*, i. 119).

the groundwork for Solomon ben Adret's ban.[113] Hasdai Crescas, the great critic of Aristotelian philosophy (though a profound master of the philosophical tradition) was one of the most influential Jews in Aragon because of his access to the court.[114] And of course the paradigmatic Jewish courtier at the end of the medieval period, Don Isaac Abravanel, was a trenchant critic of Jewish rationalism and its representatives.[115]

This leaves us with a final category: the 'extreme' philosophers, the 'Averroists', whose self-serving ideology was supposedly so devastating to traditional Jewish loyalties. The evidence adduced in the writings of contemporaries consists of complaints about excessive allegorization of the Bible and aggadah, claims that philosophical ideas such as *ta'amei mitsvot* (providing rational reasons for the commandments) were used to justify neglect of the commandments, and accusations that philosophers did not pray and had contempt for the sages.[116]

Several points need to be emphasized here. First, extreme care must be taken when judging views on the basis of their presentation in the polemical attacks of opponents. There is a natural tendency in polemical literature to take a position out of context and present it in its most radical form. Where the actual writings of the attacked individuals can be examined, they usually appear far more moderate and reasonable than in the descriptions of their enemies.[117] Consider, for example, a passage in one of the texts of Ben Adret's ban from 1305:

> One of them [the extreme philosophers] said when preaching publicly in the synagogue as though in surprise: 'What reason did Moses have to prohibit pork? If it is because of its poor quality, the scientists have not found its quality so bad.' And one of them said: 'The purpose of the commandment of the phylacteries is not to place them

---

[113] Abba Mari, *Minḥat kena'ot*, 120–1, 134–7, 141.

[114] Y. Baer, *A History of the Jews in Christian Spain*, ii. 84–5, 126–30.

[115] See e.g. Isaac Abravanel on Josh. 10 (*Perush al nevi'im ukhetuvim* [Commentary on the Prophets and Writings], 3 vols. [Jerusalem, 1955–60], i. 54a) and his extensive and incisive critique of sciences and philosophy (on 1 Kings 3: 6–14 [ibid. 467a–481a]).

[116] Accusations against extreme philosophers were rampant during the entire period, but especially in the literature of the conflicts of 1232 and 1305.

[117] Levi ben Abraham is a good example. Halkin concluded that 'a grave injustice has been done to Levi ben Abraham ben Hayyim in branding him a heretic, a seducer and a subverter' (Abraham Halkin, 'Why Was Levi ben Hayyim Hounded?', *Proceedings of the American Academy of Jewish Research*, 34 [1966], 76; see also Dov Schwartz, '"Greek Wisdom": A Renewed Examination of the Period of the Conflict over the Study of Philosophy' [Heb.], *Sinai*, 104 [1989], 150; id., 'Contacts between Jewish Philosophy and Mysticism at the Beginning of the Fifteenth Century' [Heb.], *Da'at*, 29 [1992], 42).

actually on the head and the arm—God has no delight in this—but only that a man should understand and remember the Lord.'[118]

The implication in this passage is that the philosophers no longer observed the prohibition of pork and no longer put on phylacteries because of their rational approach to the commandments. But, assuming that these are accurate quotes, the antinomian conclusion is by no means a necessary consequence.

The rhetorical question about pork could have been asked by a traditionalist opposed to any attempt to find reasons for the commandments, a kabbalist repudiating rational reasons in favour of mystical ones, or a rationalist rejecting Maimonides' connection of dietary restrictions with hygienic considerations in favour of a different rational explanation—for example, that pork is prohibited not because it is bad for health but as a reminder that we should avoid disgraceful and filthy personal qualities.[119] In all three cases the meat remains forbidden. As for the second statement about the phylacteries, it could mean that God does not want Jews to place them on their heads and arms, but it also could mean that God has no delight in a mechanical performance unless it is accompanied by the intellectual and emotional awareness of God represented by the heart and the brain—a purpose for the commandment quite similar to what Ben Adret himself wrote at the beginning of his commentary on the aggadot.[120] We have no evidence from their own words of even the most philosophy-intoxicated Jews at this time arguing that the performance of the commandments may be abandoned so long as their purpose is fulfilled. What we frequently find is the statement that without an inner awareness of the purpose, the mechanical unthinking act has no value in God's sight, and it might as well not have been done. It is not difficult to imagine the opponents of philosophy transforming this rhetorical assertion into a more extreme rationalization for abandoning the act.[121]

---

[118] Ben Adret, *She'elot uteshuvot harashba*, i. 153*b*, in Ben-Sasson, *A History of the Jewish People*, 544. I have corrected the translation of *haḥakhamim* in the first internal quote from 'the sages' to 'the scientists' based on Abba Mari, *Minḥat kena'ot*, 152, which reads 'the physicians'. In the second internal quote, I have substituted a better rendering of *she'ein haḥefets bazeh* than the translation: 'which serves no useful purpose'.

[119] For an example, see Menahem Me'iri, in Saperstein, *Decoding the Rabbis*, 138–9.

[120] Solomon ben Adret, *Ḥidushei harashba al agadot hashas* [novellae on the talmudic aggadot], ed. Shalom Meshulam Weinberger (Jerusalem, 1966), 5–6; cf. Levi ben Abraham, in Renan, 'Les Rabbins français du commencement du XIVe siècle', 642.

[121] According to Jacob Anatoli, the phylactery is placed upon the head 'so that one will turn his eyes to God and not turn aside to follow what one sees. . . . If one forgets all this and adorns himself

Second, the adherents of extreme philosophical positions are almost invariably presented without detailed information about their identity or their social status. They are a shadowy, anonymous group, the members of which cannot be identified with individuals whose work we know. Those philosophers whom we do know, even those who themselves were criticized by conservatives, often present their position as a moderate middle ground and attack extremists (usually called *hamitpalsefim*, 'the philosophizers') whom they reject because they misuse philosophy.[122] Descriptions of these extremists do not regularly characterize them as upper-class; in some cases, it is the opposite. The preachers who incorporated extreme allegorical interpretations into their sermons, so frequently attacked during the controversy of the early 1300s, are described as itinerants on the peripheries of Jewish society, using philosophy not to escape the Jewish community but to assert some influence within it.[123] According to Moses Narboni, the philosopher Abner of

---

with his phylacteries in order to lord it over his neighbors, what value does this commandment have for him? It would be better for him if he left his phylacteries in their bag' (*Malmad hatalmidim*, 148b–149a; cf. Saperstein, *Jewish Preaching, 1200–1800*, 126). It is all but inconceivable that anyone who identified with Judaism enough to preach regularly in the synagogue would have argued that phylacteries are unnecessary so long as one directs his heart to God. For a rare example of repudiating halakhic practice (as opposed to the performance of a mitzvah) on philosophical grounds, see Saperstein, *Decoding the Rabbis*, 141–2.

The confusion over the 'antinomianism' of Jewish philosophers continues in contemporary scholarly literature. For example, Schwartz has published striking allegorical interpretations of commandments such as the sending away of the mother bird (Deut. 22: 6) by the fourteenth-century philosopher Solomon Alconstantin (Dov Schwartz, 'The Spiritual-Religious Decline of the Spanish Jewish Community at the End of the Fourteenth Century' [Heb.], *Pe'amim*, 46–7 [1991], 108). Based on this passage, Glatzer wrote: 'Only a small step from such an allegoristic approach is liable to bring one to the claim that after the internalization of the lesson of the commandment, he no longer needs to observe it in actuality. . . . On the basis of this example, Baer's thesis [that philosophical study invariably led to laxity in traditional Jewish observance] can be substantiated' (Michael Glatzer 'Between Joshua Halorki and Solomon Halevi' [Heb.], *Pe'amim*, 54 [1993], 105). But what may seem like a 'small step' to a modern scholar may have been a gigantic step to a medieval writer. The passage in Alconstantin remains in the category of philosophical *ta'amei mitsvot*, not antinomianism, and cannot serve to substantiate Baer's thesis.

[122] See Twersky, 'Aspects of the Social and Cultural History of Provençal Jewry', 205. Examples include Anatoli, in Saperstein, *Jewish Preaching, 1200–1800*, 115, 118, 122 (and in many of his other sermons); Moses ibn Tibbon, in Sirat, *A History of Jewish Philosophy in the Middle Ages*, 230; Hillel ben Samuel of Verona, *Sefer tagmulei hanefesh*, 182; Ibn Kaspi in Abrahams (ed.), *Hebrew Ethical Wills*, i. 146–8; Mesch, *Studies in Joseph ibn Caspi*, 66; Kalonymos ben Kalonymos, 'An Ethical Epistle of Kalonymos ben Kalonymos' (Heb.), ed. Isaiah Sonne, *Kovets al-yad*, 1/11 (1936), 107; Elijah del Medigo, *Sefer behinat hadat*, ed. Jacob Ross (Tel Aviv, 1984), 33–5.

[123] Me'iri, in Simeon bar Joseph, *Hoshen mishpat*, in Saperstein, *Jewish Preaching, 1200–1800*, 383.

Burgos was driven to apostasy out of despair stemming from impoverishment.[124]

Third, we must be careful of assuming that every reference to scepticism or ritual laxness in the medieval Jewish community is the result of the influence of philosophy. The term 'Averroist' is often used quite loosely, referring not to those whose philosophical views were deeply influenced by the writings of Averroës,[125] or even to those who held a 'double truth' theory,[126] but rather as a general synonym for 'heretical' in beliefs and 'licentious' and 'immoral' in behaviour.[127] For example, Baer describes a certain Moses Faquim as a 'confirmed Averroist', who 'blasphemed against all religions', but the document providing information about Faquim says nothing about

---

[124] Y. Baer, *A History of the Jews in Christian Spain*, i. 332. These points are illustrated in an oft-cited passage from Moses de Leon's *Sefer harimon*, accusing the 'disciples of the books of the Greeks' of abandoning traditional Jewish study, casting behind them the words of Torah and the commandments, considering the sages to have spoken lies, and appearing in the synagogue on Sukkot with no palm branch or citron in their hands and with no phylacteries upon their heads on other days. When asked why, they explain their behaviour by appealing to the purpose of the commandments (rejoicing on the festival, remembering God), which they claim to observe (see Scholem, *Major Trends in Jewish Mysticism*, 397–8). Daniel Matt cites this passage as proof that 'rationalism became the vogue among the Jewish upper class. Many of these wealthy, assimilated Jews embraced a rationalistic ideology not for the pursuit of truth but in order to justify their neglect of tradition' (introduction to *Zohar: The Book of Enlightenment*, trans. and introd. Daniel Chanan Matt [New York, 1983], 6), but the passage itself says nothing that connects the objects of de Leon's attack with the upper class or with 'assimilation'. It certainly does not allow us to pass judgement on the motivation for their philosophical study, and it is suspect as a description of their practice.

[125] For example, Wolfson described Isaac, Joseph, and Shem Tov ibn Shem Tov as 'strict partisans of Averroes' (*Crescas' Critique of Aristotle*, 31). Schwartzmann claimed that although Isaac ibn Shem Tov 'dedicated his life to the interpretation of Ibn Rushd's commentaries . . . it is impossible to call him an Averroist, even though he tends to accept the positions of Averroës' (Julia Schwartzmann, 'The Commentary of Rabbi Isaac ibn Shem Tov on the *Guide for the Perplexed*' [Heb.], *Da'at*, 26 [1991], 43, 59). Harvey maintained that 'Jews turned to Averroes to learn and understand Aristotle, not—at least at first—as a source of theology' (Steven Harvey, 'Arabic into Hebrew: The Hebrew Translation Movement and the Influence of Averroes upon Medieval Jewish Thought', in Daniel H. Frank and Oliver Leaman [eds.], *The Cambridge Companion to Medieval Jewish Philosophy* [Cambridge, 2003], 270; cf. Alfred Ivry, 'Remnants of Jewish Averroism in the Renaissance', in Bernard Cooperman [ed.], *Jewish Thought in the Sixteenth Century* [Cambridge, Mass., 1983], 243–65).

[126] On the 'double truth' theory among Jewish thinkers, see Vajda, *Isaac Albalag*; Ivry, 'Remnants of Jewish Averroism'; Del Medigo, *Sefer beḥinat hadat*. Virtually nothing is known about the family or social status of Albalag, but there is absolutely no indication that he was connected with the courtier class. Del Medigo came from a respected family in Crete, and his scholarship had a certain influence among Christian intellectuals in Italy, but he was dependent on the financial support of patrons such as Pico della Mirandola. He himself attacked more extreme 'philosophizers' among the Jews (see Del Medigo, *Sefer beḥinat hadat*, 33–5).

[127] For example, Y. Baer, *A History of the Jews in Christian Spain*, esp. ii. 253–7.

philosophical study as the reason for his behaviour.[128] Averroism is posited, or rather defined, as the culprit, even where no historical connection is in evidence.

Even when a correlation between philosophical study, upper-class status, and a weakening of traditional Jewish loyalties can be established, it does not follow that philosophy was the cause. The attenuation of characteristically Jewish behaviour and beliefs perceived by conservatives may have been caused by powerful social forces; philosophy may have served to rationalize the continuation of Jewish identity as much as the abandonment of it. It is striking how many philosophical works during the period are justified by their authors as necessary for the dignity of the Jewish people faced with the charge that Jews, ignorant of philosophy and the sciences, possessed a culture inferior to that of their Christian neighbours.[129]

There is little persuasive evidence from the period immediately preceding the Expulsion to justify the conclusion that an infatuation with extreme rationalism had undermined the Jewish loyalties of the leaders and thereby demoralized the masses. There is, by contrast, abundant evidence that a moderate rationalism based on a familiarity with philosophical works written originally in Greek, Arabic, and Latin permeated the cultural life of Spanish Jewry, enriching its Hebrew language, suffusing its sermons and biblical commentaries, influencing even its talmudic scholarship. Philosophical notions, terminology, and modes of thinking are apparent even in writers like Isaac Arama and Isaac Abravanel who were ultimately suspicious of its impact. While it is impossible to determine how the experience of these communities would have differed if the attempts to ban or severely restrict philosophical study had succeeded, it is plausible to argue that without the capacity to articulate Judaism in a frame of reference intelligible to the surrounding society, and without a cadre of Jews whose scientific training rendered them useful to their Christian neighbours,[130] disaster might have befallen them even earlier.

---

[128] Ibid. ii. 52; the document is in Fritz Baer (ed.), *Die Juden im Christlichen Spanien*, 2 vols. (Berlin, 1929), i. 644–7.

[129] e.g. Anatoli, *Habe'ur ha'emtsa'i shel ibn rushd*, 1; Leon Joseph of Carcassonne, in Renan, 'Les Écrivains juifs français du XIVe siècle', 773; Abraham Bibago, in Moritz Steinschneider, 'Abraham Bibago's Schriften', *Monatsschrift für Geschichte und Wissenschaft des Judentums*, 32 (1883), 140; see the cultural defence of translation by Shem Tov Falaquera: 'it is better that we study [the branches of philosophy] in our own language than that we study them in the language of another people' (in Dinur, *Israel in the Diaspora* [Heb.], Pt. II, vol. iv, 186). See also above, n. 33.

[130] 'No one from among our nation is esteemed in their eyes except for the physician who can cure them' (Leon Joseph of Carcassonne, in Renan, 'Les Écrivains juifs français du XIVe siècle', 773).

CHAPTER FOUR

The Conflict over the Ban on Philosophical Study, 1305: A Political Perspective

FEW EVENTS of internal Jewish history during the Middle Ages more effectively exemplify diversity and conflict than the so-called 'Maimonidean conflicts', the attempts by certain Jews to control the educational curriculum and public discourse of their communities by banning various philosophical texts and those who taught or studied them. One of the best-known of these episodes, the ban restricting the study of Greek philosophy, promulgated during the summer of 1305 by Solomon ben Adret (Rashba) and his colleagues in Barcelona, has been extensively treated by historians for over a century. The bitter conflict surrounding this ban is extensively documented in *Minḥat kena'ot* (A Zealous Offering), a collection of letters edited by Abba Mari of Lunel, one of the protagonists of that conflict and an ally of Ben Adret.[1] Yet there is still no consensus among scholars about the proper interpretation of this dramatic episode, and sharp disagreement remains over what was fuelling the antagonism.[2] What follows is a suggestion of a new framework in which to evaluate the events of 1305.

First published in *Jewish History*, 1/2 (1986), 27–38. I am grateful for the help and advice of Professors Martin A. Cohen, Joseph Dan, Joseph Shatzmiller, and Kenneth Stow at early stages of the preparation of this article. Their input does not necessarily imply their endorsement of its central thesis.

[1] Abba Mari ben Moses of Lunel, *Minḥat kena'ot: harbeh mikhtavim . . . el harashba umah shebeshiv lahem* [polemical letters] (Pressburg, 1838; repr. Jerusalem, 1968). For a fine analysis of letters as a crucial vehicle of communication in this conflict, see Ram Ben-Shalom, 'Communication and Propaganda Between Provence and Spain: The Controversy over Extreme Allegorization (1303–1306)', in Sophia Menache (ed.), *Communication in the Jewish Diaspora* (Leiden, 1996), esp. 177–89.

[2] Most nineteenth- and early twentieth-century scholars, including Graetz, Renan, Gross, Schorr, and Dubnow, portrayed the conflict in purely ideological terms as a battle between progressive champions of a rational faith and fanatical obscurantist reactionaries. Yitzhak Baer, in an interesting, yet unsubstantiated, variation on this theme, maintained that Provence was used as a pretext by

The point of departure is an issue of dispute frequently mentioned but not thoroughly analysed in the secondary literature: the independence of the Jewish communities in southern France from the hegemony of Barcelona. The legal background of this question as an internal Jewish problem can be seen in the responsa of Ben Adret. Questions addressed to him from cities such as Perpignan, Montpellier, Narbonne, Carcassonne, Marseilles, and Avignon indicate that he was considered to be the outstanding halakhic authority of his time throughout southern France.[3] However, his responsa reveal a clear recognition of the principle of local self-determination and the importance of local custom in deciding the law.

The general rule is that the community may not impose its will on another, the only exceptions being a ban issued by a *nasi* or an exilarch or an emergency *gezerah* (decree) of one community that the majority of the second community are capable of obeying. When a political boundary divides the two communities, the jurisdiction of one over the other is even more strictly curtailed. Ben Adret argued that one kingdom had no jurisdiction over the subjects of another even if they were living temporarily in the first. As a legal authority, he clearly recognized the right of the local Jewish community to govern its own affairs free from the threat of outside interference by powerful neighbours.[4]

Solomon ben Adret, whose real purpose was to combat 'Averroism' in Spain (Baer, *A History of the Jews in Christian Spain*, 2 vols. [Philadelphia, 1961–6], i. 290, 293–4; see Charles Touati, 'La Controverse de 1303–1306 autour des études philosophiques et scientifiques', *Revue des études juives*, 127 [1968], 34). Joseph Sarachek and, later, Abraham Halkin argued that the Jewish conflict at the beginning of the fourteenth century reflected the triumphs of orthodoxy over rationalistic tendencies in Islam and especially in thirteenth-century Christendom (see Sarachek, *Faith and Reason: The Conflict over the Rationalism of Maimonides* [Williamsport, Pa., 1935], 2–13, 167; Halkin, 'The Ban on the Study of Philosophy' [Heb.], *Perakim*, 1 [1967], 52–5; id., 'Yedaiah Bedershi's Apology', in Alexander Altmann [ed.], *Jewish Medieval and Renaissance Studies* [Cambridge, Mass., 1967], 181–4). Some scholars have tended to view this conflict alongside that of the 1230s as a reflection of a socio-economic cleavage in Jewish society, with the lower classes spearheading the opposition to philosophy as manifest in the lifestyle of the courtier class (see Haim Hillel Ben-Sasson, *On Jewish History in the Middle Ages* [Perakim betoledot hayehudim bimei habeinayim] [Tel Aviv, 1969], 224–6, 230–2; id., *A History of the Jewish People* [Cambridge, Mass., 1976], 543). For a fuller bibliographical listing, see Gregg Stern, 'Jewish Philosophy in Southern France: Controversy over Philosophical Study and the Influence of Averroes upon Jewish Thought', in Daniel H. Frank and Oliver Leaman (eds.), *The Cambridge Companion to Medieval Jewish Philosophy* (Cambridge, 2003), 298 n. 1.

[3] See Solomon ben Adret, *She'elot uteshuvot harashba* [responsa], 7 vols. in 4 (Benei Berak, 1958–9), i, nos. 388, 1249; ii, nos. 11, 13, 49, 93, et al. (Perpignan); i, nos. 363, 395; iii, no. 237 (Montpellier); i, nos. 259, 287 (Narbonne); iii, nos. 214, 280 (Carcassonne); iii, nos. 132, 160 (Marseilles); iii, no. 350 (Avignon). For a list of the individuals mentioned, see Joseph Perles, *R. Salomo ben Abraham ben Adereth: Sein Leben und seine Schriften* (Breslau, 1863), 9–11.

[4] Ben Adret, *She'elot uteshuvot harashba*, iii, no. 394 (on local custom); iii, no. 401 (against one

Turning to the primary sources regarding the actual conflict, it is instructive to distinguish the letters Ben Adret wrote to his allies from those addressed to his opponents. Letters to the former show that from the outset Ben Adret was concerned about the charge of improper intervention. A scholar from southern France had written to ask him whether or not it was permissible to use an amulet in the form of a lion, in conjunction with certain astrological configurations, as part of a cure for kidney disease, and he had given a formal legal reply. Later, in his initial letter to Abba Mari, he asserted that when he responded to this question, he had not realized that it was the subject of controversy. Had he known this, he said, he would never have become involved, for it was not his way to give an answer where there was already strife without thoroughly investigating the situation. He was not the one to speak out publicly on this issue as Abba Mari urged him to do, for 'I know that they will say to me: "Who is this who comes to tyrannize over us in our own homes?"' During the course of the conflict leading to the ban, Ben Adret first suggested, then insisted, that the initiative must come from the leaders of the Provençal communities. In these communications with his allies, he first hesitated to intervene, and then made certain that he protected himself by receiving the original text of the ban from Provence.[5]

In letters to his opponents, Ben Adret's position was at first quite different. Writing to Levi ben Abraham, he made it clear that he would not remain silent while Jews in southern France deviated from the right path: rather, 'I will raise my voice to the holy congregations in Provence'. In his reply to Samuel ben Reuben of Béziers, he made this into a statement of principle. The boundary between Barcelona and the communities of southern France was unimportant. The Jews were one people, and all had the responsibility of reproaching others who were doing wrong.

In the final stage of the conflict, however, Ben Adret took an entirely different tack: 'We have made a ban forbidding [the study of philosophy before a certain age] in *our* place, just as you have heard. What have you found wrong in this? Have we made such a ban for *your* place? God has made a boundary

community imposing its will on another); iii, no. 440 (on jurisdiction over a subject of another kingdom living in the community).

[5] Ben Adret, in Abba Mari, Minḥat kena'ot, 22, 23, 52, 72, 104, 118, 133, 135, 137; cf. Joseph Shatzmiller, 'Between Abba Mari and Solomon ben Adret: Negotiations Preceding the Ban in Barcelona' (Heb.), *Meḥkarim betoledot am yisra'el ve'erets yisra'el*, 3 (1974), 131. Here and throughout this chapter, when speaking of the Jewish communities I have used the term 'Provence' loosely as a synonym for southern France including Languedoc. Provence and Languedoc were juridically separate, but the broad usage is consistent with that in most medieval Hebrew sources.

between us: our children are not your children. You may do what you want.' The principle of non-intervention could not be more clearly stated. After the ban was declared in Barcelona, where Ben Adret had insisted it was unnecessary since the study of philosophy had already been properly regulated, he then stated that the ban applied exclusively to his own realm, not to Provence. The other leaders of Barcelona similarly maintained that the ban applied only to them, for 'one kingdom does not infringe upon its neighbour'.[6]

Abba Mari and his colleagues in Montpellier assumed from the outset that action taken by the leadership in Barcelona would affect them in Provence. Time and again they insisted in their letters to Barcelona that Ben Adret, as the outstanding rabbinic authority of the generation, must take the initiative in combating the extreme philosophers of southern France, but as soon as the ban had been declared in Barcelona, the position of Abba Mari's faction shifted. The Barcelona leaders were severely criticized for interfering in a matter that was none of their business, and Abba Mari urgently tried to muster support from local rabbis, arguing that the proscription of philosophical study before the age of 25 was not imposed from the outside, but represented the sentiments of many authorities in southern France. As for the ban itself, even those who had requested it minimized its scope. Now they too maintained that it applied only to Barcelona and not to southern France.[7]

All this is rather strange. Abba Mari and his allies had called for initiative from Barcelona in the struggle against the extreme philosophers in Provence, and Ben Adret, despite serious reservations about interfering, had publicly affirmed the obligation of the Barcelona leaders to act. But once decisive action was taken, the supporters of the ban, both in Barcelona and in Provence, minimized its implications, conceding that it did not apply to southern France and stressing the right and the duty of Provençal Jewry to act for itself.

That is what the opponents of the ban had been arguing all along. In a dramatic clash during the summer of 1304, when Abba Mari read a letter from Barcelona urging a ban before the leaders of Montpellier, Jacob ben Makhir, the only one to oppose the idea, proclaimed: 'What do we have to do with them? God placed a boundary between us and them. We shall not listen or consent to them!' After the ban was declared, the insistence upon the

---

[6] Abba Mari, *Minḥat kena'ot*, 54, 94; Adolf Neubauer, 'Ergänzungen und Verbesserungen zu Abba Maris Minhat Kenaot aus handschriften', *Israelitische Letterbode*, 4 (1878–9), 127; 5 (1879–80), 55.

[7] Abba Mari, *Minḥat kena'ot*, 32, 167; cf. Menahem Me'iri, in Simeon bar Joseph, *Ḥoshen mishpat*, ed. David Kaufmann, in *Tif'eret Seiva: Jubelschrift zum Neunzigsten Geburtstag des Dr. L. Zunz* (Berlin, 1884): Heb. section, 149.

independence of the communities of Provence and the repudiation of outside interference intensified. Abba Mari's adversaries in Montpellier complained, 'What kind of man will go and shriek about the inhabitants of one nation before the king of another?' Such behaviour will 'tarnish the reputation of the kings of the earth', for one kingdom should not interfere in the affairs of its neighbour. A similar argument was attributed to the philosophical faction by En Duran (Simeon ben Joseph) in his letter to Barcelona, except that here the criticism is more of Ben Adret than of Abba Mari. Opponents of the ban such as Yedaiah Bedersi assumed that it did not apply to Provence, for the Barcelona rabbis had no right to legislate for Jews in a different realm.[8]

These arguments over Barcelona's right to interfere in the affairs of the Jewish communities in southern France were closely bound up with larger political issues. The reign of Philip the Fair (1285–1314) was for Languedoc a period of assimilation into the French nation. But many inhabitants of the region were unhappy about this trend, viewing the French as conquerors and Philip as a foreigner. Important forces within Languedoc society continued to oppose the incorporation of their province into the country to the north. The last insurrections against royal French rule date from this period. In Narbonne, which had intimate connections with Aragon, and especially in Montpellier, which until recently had been under Aragonese sovereignty, many still felt that their natural affinities were more with Aragon than with France.[9]

In order to bring Languedoc under his undisputed rule, Philip had to establish control over powerful potential adversaries. The Occitanian nobles and prelates cherished their traditions of independence. Confronting them was a new bureaucracy of royal officials, who served as the instruments of centralized power. Sometimes conflict ensued. The monarchy in this period claimed the exclusive right to confer knighthood on a person not already of knightly lineage, while the nobles and prelates of the seneschalcy of Beaucaire still claimed in 1298 that they alone were entitled to create knights

[8] Abba Mari, *Minḥat kena'ot*, 62; Neubauer, 'Ergänzungen und Verbesserungen zu Abba Maris Minhat Kenaot', *Israelitische Letterbode*, 4: 171; David Kaufmann, 'Deux lettres de Simeon b. Joseph', *Revue des études juives*, 29 (1894), 222; Ben Adret, *She'elot uteshuvot harashba*, i, no. 157; Mei'iri, in Simeon bar Joseph, *Ḥoshen mishpat*, 153.

[9] Paul Jean Louis Gachon, *Histoire de Languedoc* (Paris, 1921), 107; Barthélemy Hauréau, *Bernard Délicieux et l'inquisition albigeoise (1300–1320)* (Paris, 1877), 98–9. The *Chronicle of St. Denis* maintains that the south of France was on the verge of rebellion at the end of 1303 (in Joseph R. Strayer, 'Consent to Taxation under Philip the Fair', in Charles F. Taylor and Joseph R. Strayer [eds.], *Studies in Early French Taxation* [Cambridge, Mass., 1939], 66).

among the townsmen.¹⁰ In both Narbonne and Montpellier, powerful men exercising seigniorial authority jealously guarded their prerogatives against the agents of royal power.

In Narbonne, this authority was divided between Viscount Amalric II and Archbishop Gilles Aycelin. Concessions to their influence can be seen in the royal ordinances of February 1304, stating that the nobles of Narbonne who contributed to the taxes and had no fiefs were exempt from personal service in the war against Flanders and that the clergy of Narbonne was not subject to the royal tax.¹¹ In Montpellier, James of Majorca, uncle of the king of Aragon and vassal to Philip the Fair, was recognized as suzerain over the city. In 1301 and in 1312 James vigorously protested when the seneschal of Beaucaire, a high royal official, attempted to act directly in matters that required consultation with the suzerain. James of Majorca was a loyal vassal, paying homage to Philip in February 1304 when the French king visited Montpellier, but he was not one to overlook his own prerogatives.¹²

A major source of tension between the royal and the seigniorial jurisdictions was the status of the Jews. At the end of the thirteenth century, only those Jews living in royal domains were obliged to pay royal taxes. Jewish inhabitants of seigniorial domains were exempt from these arbitrary

---

¹⁰ On the royal administration in the south, see Joseph R. Strayer, 'Viscounts and Viguiers under Philip the Fair', *Speculum*, 38 (1963), 242–55; Jan Rogoziński, 'The Counsellors of the Seneschal of Beaucaire and Nîmes, 1250–1350', *Speculum*, 44 (1969), esp. 430–2; for the period immediately following the conflict, see id., *Power, Caste, and Law: Social Conflict in Fourteenth-Century Montpellier* (Cambridge, Mass., 1982), 50–83; on the conflict over knighthood, see Marc Bloch, *Feudal Society* (Chicago, 1961), 323.

¹¹ See Claude Devic and J. J. Vaissète, *Histoire générale de Languedoc, avec des notes et les pièces justificatives*, 15 vols. (Toulouse, 1872–92), ix. 263, 265; Jean Régné, *Amauri II, Viscomte de Narbonne (1260?–1328): Sa jeunesse et ses expéditions, son gouvernement, son administration* (Narbonne, 1910), esp. 99–100, 114–15; Jacqueline Caille, 'La Seigneurie temporelle de l'archevêque dans la ville de Narbonne (deuxième moitié du XIIIe siècle)', in *Les Évêques, les clercs, et le roi (1250–1300)*, Cahiers de Fanjeaux, 7 (1972), esp. 182.

¹² See Devic and Vaissète, *Histoire générale de Languedoc*, ix. 235; Hauréau, *Bernard Délicieux et l'inquisition albigeoise*, 96–7; Dominique Marie Joseph Henry, *Histoire de Rousillon: Comprenant l'histoire du royaume de Majorque*, 2 vols. (Paris, 1835), i. 189–96; Alexandre Germain, *Histoire de la commune de Montpellier*, 3 vols. (Montpellier, 1851), ii. 123–35; Albert Lecoy de la Marche, *Les Relations politiques de la France avec le Royaume de Maiorque*, 2 vols. (Paris, 1892), i. 334–7. An indication of the division in Montpellier between supporters of James, the suzerain, and of Philip the Fair can be seen in the fact that of the outstanding professors of law at Montpellier, Bremond de Montferrier worked primarily for James after 1291, defending his rights against those of the French king in conflicts with the royal functionaries, while Guillaume de Nogaret was called to Paris to serve in the central government and helped Philip to acquire the rights of the bishop of Maguelonne over Montpellieret against the claims of the king of Majorca (see Joseph R. Strayer, *Les Gens de justice du Languedoc sous Philippe le Bel* [Toulouse, 1971], 16–17).

exactions: the taxes they did pay, to their local overlord, were generally more predictable and fair. The result was a substantial migration of Jews during the second half of the thirteenth century from royal to seigniorial domains, especially to Narbonne.

This emigration, which accelerated as the pressure of royal taxes increased, generated a protracted dispute between the barons and prelates, on the one hand, and the royal administrators, on the other, over the classification of the Jews in their realm. For example, the viscount and the archbishop of Narbonne had decided in 1276 to encourage the emigration of Jews from royal domains. In the following years these men protested against the royal tax collectors, who continued to inscribe Jewish migrants to Narbonne on the royal rolls. In December 1305 the consuls of Narbonne ordered the royal judge not to inscribe on the tax rolls the names of Jews appearing on the list that they, the consuls, were about to submit.[13]

The repercussions of this struggle between the royal administration, working towards centralization, and the nobles, striving to maintain traditional prerogatives, were felt within the Jewish community. While some Jews fled royal taxation, others aided the royal administrators in investigating the status of those who had moved. Solomon of Lunel, the wealthy leader of the party opposing the ban from Barcelona, appears in a list of impost collectors for the royal tax in Carcassonne. *Minḥat kena'ot* contains a poignant letter revealing the economic pressures: caught in the squeeze of rising royal taxes, required for the king's war with Flanders, and an eroding tax base, the result of emigration from the royal domains, the Jews desperately needed to achieve a more equitable distribution of the burden.[14] The powerful tensions at the

---

[13] Gustave Saige, *Les Juifs du Languedoc antérieurement au XIVe siècle* (Paris, 1881), 31–3, 38–41, 88; Jean Régné, *Étude sur la condition des Juifs de Narbonne du Ve au XIVe siècle* (Narbonne, 1912), 117–23; Salo W. Baron, *A Social and Religious History of the Jews*, 18 vols. (Philadelphia: Jewish Publication Society, 1952–83), x. 83. Saige published more than twenty documents concerning problems arising over the taxation of 'royal Jews' (*Les Juifs du Languedoc*, 211–38; see also the abbot of Alet's complaint to the seneschal of Carcassonne about the listing on the royal tax rolls of three Jews who were under the abbot's jurisdiction [ibid. 241–2]). On general taxation of the time, see Strayer's description of the significant opposition to the taxes of Philip, especially in the years 1303–4, which failed to crystallize into permanent constitutional limitations. The nobles were unsuccessful in their attempt to preserve their independence from the royal government because there was no unifying force in France at the time that could compete with the king and his bureaucracy (Strayer, 'Consent to Taxation under Philip the Fair', 89–90, 93).

[14] Saige, *Les Juifs du Languedoc*, 90–115; Neubauer, 'Ergänzungen und Verbesserungen zu Abba Maris Minhat Kenaot', *Israelitische Letterbode*, 4: 168–9. On Jews from Languedoc connected with the royal administration in the middle of the thirteenth century, see Marc Saperstein, *Decoding the Rabbis: A Thirteenth-Century Commentary on the Aggadah* (Cambridge, Mass., 1980), 163–7; see also the

top of Christian society at the turn of the fourteenth century were thus reflected in divisions within the Jewish communities of Languedoc.

A second great power that Philip had to confront in his assimilation of Languedoc was the papal Inquisition. During the 1290s and early 1300s Philip frequently attempted to regulate its excesses. The Inquisition was controlled by the Dominicans and bitterly opposed by the Franciscans, who wanted to control it themselves. Caught in this power struggle were the inhabitants of Languedoc, especially those of Albi. Their bitterness towards the Inquisition brought the region at times to the brink of insurrection.

In 1295 there was open resistance, and the opponents of the Inquisition temporarily gained control of Carcassonne. A few years later the Inquisition prosecuted some of the most respected citizens of Albi. In the words of Henry Charles Lea, the country was 'ripe for revolt', ready to transfer its allegiance to any monarch who could protect them. To such pressure Philip had to respond. In 1301 he sent two reformers to Languedoc to curb inquisitional abuses, but, despite the introduction of certain reforms, the popular resentment in Albi began to rise again at the end of 1302. The royal reformer was excommunicated by the Inquisitor of Albi, and in October 1303, following Philip's victory over Boniface VIII, the tension over the Inquisition was heightened once again by the election of Benedict XI, a Dominican, to the papacy.[15]

At the end of 1303 Philip travelled to Languedoc, spending Christmas in Toulouse. There he heard the Franciscan leader of the opposition to the Dominican Inquisition, Bernard Délicieux, state that there had not been a single heretic among all the Albigensians for many years.[16] Others disputed this contention. The resulting edict of 13 January 1304 was a compromise

---

archival source described by Elie Szapiro, showing that Astruguet Iudeus retained a position of importance until at least 1253 (Szapiro, 'Renseignements sur les Juifs de Languedoc dans une cartulaire inédit', *Archives juives*, 5/2 [1968–9], 19–20).

[15] On the Inquisition in Albi, see Henry Charles Lea, *A History of the Inquisition of the Middle Ages*, 3 vols. (New York: Harper & Brothers, 1888), ii. 62–86; Georgine Davis, *The Inquisition at Albi, 1299–1300: Text of Register and Analysis* (New York, 1974); Charles Delpoux, 'Le Catharisme en Albigeois: La Croisade et l'inquisition au XIIIe et XIVe siècles', *Cahiers d'études cathares*, 5 (1954), 154–5; Jean-Louis Biget, 'Un procès d'inquisition à Albi en 1300', *Le Crédo, la morale, et l'inquisition*, Cahiers de Fanjeaux, 6 (1971), 319–22, 325–8; James B. Given, *Inquisition and Medieval Society: Power, Discipline, and Resistance in Languedoc* (Ithaca, NY, 1997), 131–4.

[16] He is also quoted as having said to the king: 'If the blessed Peter and Paul were alive today, and they were accused of loving heretics, and proceedings were initiated against them for this reason as certain Inquisitors have initiated proceedings in these regions against many others, they would have no way of defending themselves' (in Given, *Inquisition and Medieval Society*, 215 n. 6: my translation).

that bitterly disappointed Délicieux and many of the residents of Carcassonne. There was a plot to withdraw allegiance from Philip and offer it to Ferrand, son of the king of Majorca and cousin of James II of Aragon.

The plot was revealed to Philip before it could be implemented. During the summer of 1305 eight consuls of Carcassonne were tried for the crime of *lèse-majesté*. In September the verdict was announced at the 'royal palace' in Carcassonne, in the presence of Viscount Amalric II of Narbonne and a dozen other barons of the seneschalcy. The consuls were publicly hanged, and the city was temporarily deprived of the right to self-government.[17]

Philip's policy towards the Inquisition could not then be determined solely by his attitudes towards the heretical ideas it was supposed to be eradicating. In addition to its religious function, the Inquisition in southern France was also a political institution. Ultimately it was responsible to an external power, the papacy. So long as the papacy remained independent and beyond Philip's control—that is, until the election of the archbishop of Bordeaux as Clement V in June, 1305—Philip had to be ready to thwart the challenges posed by the Inquisition, to the extent, at least, that by doing so he would not jeopardize other important sources of support.[18]

This historical background reveals that, contemporaneous with the struggle in the Jewish community of Languedoc over the control of the educational curriculum and the preaching pulpit, there was a deep political fissure between supporters of French royal rule and those who, dependent

---

[17] For Philip's trip to Languedoc, see Devic and Vaissète, *Histoire générale de Languedoc*, ix. 257–9; Hauréau, *Bernard Délicieux et l'inquisition albigeoise*, 88–9; Thomas Bisson, *Assemblies and Representatives in Languedoc in the Thirteenth Century* (Princeton, 1964), 256–7; for the attempted revolt in Carcassonne, see Lea, *A History of the Inquisition of the Middle Ages*, ii. 87–90; Devic and Vaissète, *Histoire générale de Languedoc*, ix. 277–8; Alphonse Jacques Mahul, *Cartulaire et archives des communes de l'ancienne diocèse de Carcassonne*, 6 vols. in 7 (Paris: V. Didron, 1871), vi. 10–11; Régné, *Amauri II*, 115; Joseph Poux, *La Cité de Carcassonne: Histoire et description*, 3 vols. (Toulouse, 1922–31), ii. 176–8; Given, *Inquisition and Medieval Society*, 134–6. The operative phrase in the indictment was that the consuls *volebant facere alium regens quam Regem Franciae, et tradere Civitatem et Burgum Ferrando filio Regis Majoricarum*. The sentence was announced with great public fanfare on 29 September. According to Bernard Gui, many others would have been executed had it not been for Pope Clement V's intercession with Philip (Mahul, *Cartulaire et archives des communes de l'ancienne diocèse de Carcassonne*, vi. 10).

[18] Richard Emery argued that the explanation for the activity of the Inquisition in Narbonne in 1318–28, in contrast with the lack of activity in the thirteenth century, was the significant growth of royal power in the city beginning at the end of the century. At this time, with the papacy more or less under French control, it was in the royal interest to encourage the Inquisition, as the confiscation of property in heresy cases went to the royal officers. The archbishop therefore acquired a powerful ally against the viscount (Richard Emery, *Heresy and Inquisition in Narbonne* [New York, 1941], 145–7). Emery saw a similar situation in Montpellier (ibid. 147 n. 55).

in various ways on the old seigniorial hierarchy, felt little sympathy for the ambitions of the Capetian kings. This political fissure, insofar as it was expressed in the issue of royal taxation, had direct implications for the Jews of southern France.

The critical question, which cannot be definitively answered at present, is to what extent did these two divisions in Jewish society—the ideological and the political—overlap? Currently known source material does not yield enough information about the principals in the conflict and their relationships with the Gentile world to substantiate what would be the simplest hypothesis: that the party opposing the ban from Barcelona was composed of Jews whose sympathies lay with the royal administration rather than the more conservative opponents of French rule.[19] What is clear, however, is that the political events that also reached a climax in the summer of 1305 provided the opponents of the ban with a powerful and perhaps decisive weapon. The rhetorical question raised by Abba Mari's opponents in Montpellier—'What kind of man will go and shriek about the inhabitants of one nation before the king of another?'—is a withering insinuation of potentially treasonous behaviour that few contemporaries would have misunderstood. In the political arena of 1305, the question of outside interference escalated from an internal halakhic debate to an issue with explosive political consequences.

To the royal administration, eager to establish the claim that the king had absolute authority within his kingdom, any indication that the Jewish communities of southern France were being controlled from a foreign territory would have been repugnant.[20] In principle, an excommunication declared in

---

[19] Of the opponents to the ban, only Solomon of Lunel is known from external sources to have been associated with the royal administration. Jacob ben Makhir, another leader of the resistance to Abba Mari and Solomon ben Adret, had many contacts with physicians in Montpellier, some of whom had worked in the naval court (see Joseph Shatzmiller, 'In Search of the "Book of Figures"', *AJS Review*, 7–8 [1982–3], 383–407).

[20] For the question of the king's absolute authority in the context of the dispute between Philip and Boniface VIII, see Brian Tierney, *The Crisis of Church and State 1050–1300: With Selected Documents* (Englewood Cliffs, NJ, 1964), 173–4; for the evidence of the concern shown by political rulers when Jews in their realm appealed to authorities in the realm of their rivals, see Abraham ibn Daud, *Sefer ha-Qabbalah: The Book of Tradition. A Critical Edition*, ed. and trans. Gerson Cohen (Philadelphia, 1967), 67; Jacob Mann, *Texts and Studies in Jewish History and Literature*, 2 vols. (Cincinnati, 1931–5), i. 111–12; Myer Davis, 'An Anglo-Jewish Divorce, A.D. 1242', *Jewish Quarterly Review*, 5 (1893), 158–65. In the latter case, a contested divorce was adjudicated by a local rabbinic court, which was then overruled by royal judges. The disgruntled wife apparently then appealed to the rabbinic court of Paris, at which point she and several others were summoned to appear before justices from the King's Council 'to show cause why they sent to France [petitioning] the Jews of France to hold a chapter concerning the Jews of England' (*responsuri quarum miserunt in Francia ad Judeos Franciae pro capitulo*

Montpellier because of a directive from Barcelona would have been no more acceptable to royal policy than the Inquisition excommunicating people in Albi at the directives of Rome. For all the differences in institutional structure and legal status, Ben Adret's ban could have been seen, like the Inquisition, as a political instrument controlled from beyond the borders of the realm, and hence as an insult to the monarchy and a challenge to its aspirations. Ben Adret himself probably never dreamed that his initiative could be so construed, but that is beside the point.[21]

The political context may well explain the sudden reversal of Ben Adret and the other leaders of Barcelona, who had previously proclaimed their right to act against deviance in southern France, but then, after the ban was declared, insisted that what they did in Barcelona had nothing to do with Provence. When the ban was issued in the summer of 1305, its promulgators in Barcelona may have been unaware that eight consuls of Carcassonne were being tried for their role in a plot to transfer allegiance from Philip to the cousin of the king of Aragon. The verdict and subsequent hanging of the consuls, however, was a *cause célèbre*, known to all. Under these circumstances, the suspicion that the Jews of southern France were being governed from Barcelona was a source of grave danger. The Barcelona leadership was left with no choice but to deny publicly any implication of a claim to hegemony over the Jews of Languedoc.

The ideological and political issues converged in a critical but somewhat enigmatic episode during the final stages of the conflict. Immediately after hearing of the ban proclaimed in Barcelona, its opponents in Montpellier formulated their own counter-ban. En Duran, a Provençal ally of Ben Adret, quoted the text of this counter-ban as follows: 'The beginning of their words is: "Any man from our community who speaks insolently against his excellency [Maimonides] or his writings; anyone who slanders an author who is [Maimonides'] disciple; anyone who prevents his son from studying physics

tenendo super Judeos Angliae). In the fourteenth century, such appeals by English subjects to foreign courts were formally prohibited by statutes known as as *praemunire*. I am grateful to Kenneth Stow for this reference.

[21] In a formal epistle to the community of Montpellier urging that a ban be declared, Ben Adret and fourteen other signatories from Barcelona actually pointed to the Inquisition as a model worthy of emulation: 'Observe how the Gentiles punish their heretics, even for a single one of such heresies as these men expressed in their books. Why if any one would dare say that Abraham and Sarah represented matter and form, they would wrap him up in twigs and burn him into cinders' (in Abba Mari, *Minḥat kena'ot*, 61, in Y. Baer, *A History of the Jews in Christian Spain*, i. 295). For those who knew at first hand the potential political explosiveness of the Inquisition's activities, these words could not have been reassuring.

or metaphysics or Gentile science [*ḥokhmat ha'umot*] because of any regulation made by another community...".²²

As bans passed by the Jews had to be ratified by a royal official, the necessary approval was sought. Abba Mari reported that his adversaries sought permission 'to excommunicate the promulgators of the original ban and their allies, and any man who would prevent his son from studying physics or metaphysics or Gentile science, even if he is under 25, because of any ban made in any place'.²³ En Duran, referring to the same interview, wrote that 'the faction of the opponents [of Ben Adret] "caused men to ride over our heads", namely, the royal governor, the great minister appointed by our lord the king. They presented their case before him and recited things that may not be written, may the ears of anyone who hears them be saved!'²⁴

What did Ben Adret's opponents say to win the support of the royal governor? David Kaufmann, who published En Duran's epistle, surmised that their argument was exactly what Abba Mari reported the official himself to have said: that prohibiting the study of Greek science and philosophy and limiting the Jewish curriculum to the exclusive study of Talmud would discourage conversion to Christianity.²⁵ Irrespective of whether the official actually gave this reason for his concurrence,²⁶ it is inconceivable that any Jewish group would have used such an argument for any purpose.

---

²² In D. Kaufmann, 'Deux lettres de Simeon b. Joseph', 222; cf. Abba Mari, *Minḥat kena'ot*, 150.

²³ Abba Mari's report is from a manuscript of *Minḥat kena'ot*, in Shatzmiller, 'Between Abba Mari and Solomon ben Adret' (Heb.), 125, based on Neubauer, 'Ergänzungen und Verbesserungen zu Abba Maris Minhat Kenaot'. On the necessity of ratifications by the royal governor, see Abba Mari, *Minḥat kena'ot*, 106; Joseph Shatzmiller, 'L'Excommunication, la communauté juive et les autorités temporelles au Moyen-Âge', in Myriam Yardeni (ed.), *Les Juifs dans l'histoire de France* (Leiden: Brill, 1980), 63–9.

²⁴ In D. Kaufmann, 'Deux lettres de Simeon b. Joseph', 224. I have used the term 'royal governor' for En Duran's *moshel*. If, as seems likely, the appeal was to a royal official in Montpellier rather than to the seneschal, who had broad regional responsibilities, the proper title would have been *viguier*, or rector. According to Joseph Strayer, it was the responsibility of the *viguier* as executive agent of the royal seneschal to 'see that local administration ran smoothly, that orders were carried out, that the king's rights were preserved, that order was maintained, and that their districts were defended from attack' ('Viscounts and Viguiers under Philip the Fair', 245).

²⁵ D. Kaufmann, 'Deux lettres de Simeon b. Joseph', 217. According to Abba Mari, the royal governor spoke of the Jews restricting their study to the discipline they called *gamliel* (*Minḥat kena'ot*, 142). Scholars remain divided over whether this term was used to refer to the study of medicine or the study of rabbinic literature (see the sources given in Shatzmiller, 'Between Abba Mari and Solomon ben Adret' [Heb.], 126 n. 22). The meaning 'rabbinic literature' is probably more appropriate for the present context.

²⁶ Abba Mari's report of the governor's rationale need not be taken at face value. The fact was that the governor did endorse the section of the counter-ban that prohibited the enforcement of Ben

It makes much more sense to assume that the calumny that so horrified En Duran was the accusation that, by accepting the hegemony of the Barcelona leadership, Abba Mari and his colleagues had been disloyal to the king of France. This political charge fits the text of the counter-ban: 'anyone who prevents his son from studying physics or metaphysics or Gentile science *because of any regulation by another community*'. It is this last part of the statement, not the curriculum of Jewish education, that would have been a source of concern for the king's representative in Montpellier.

The above analysis supports the contention that the conflict at the beginning of the fourteenth century was fundamentally different from the earlier conflicts relating to philosophy. Its distinctiveness can be seen not only in the fact that the arena of communal strife was limited to southern France, with no evidence of divisiveness in Spain itself, but also in its ideological content[27] and the attendant social dynamics,[28] subjects not addressed in this essay. The delineation of a political perspective should not be taken to imply that the cultural milieu of Provençal Jewry was unimportant. Without the rapid

Adret's edict. This was certainly a defeat for Abba Mari, who may well have tried to salvage some satisfaction by inventing this anti-Jewish motivation for the governor's position.

[27] This was in no sense a battle over the works of Maimonides, and to call it one of the 'Maimonidean conflicts', as noted historians have done, is misleading. Both groups expressed such consistent adulation for Maimonides that we would be hard pressed to establish any basis for questioning their sincerity. Both groups cited him—with some justification—in support of their position. The view that Solomon ben Adret, Abba Mari, and their allies actually opposed Maimonides and really wanted to ban his philosophical works along with Aristotle is based solely on the attacks of their enemies. It is no less reasonable to conclude that the opponents of the ban manufactured the charge of concealed anti-Maimonidean goals for their own tactical reasons: in order to gain the support of those who were undecided but who resented any attack on Maimonides. In general, the case can be made that at this time, unlike in the 1230s, the broad areas of ideological agreement between the antagonistic parties concerning the role of philosophy in Jewish culture are more impressive than the tactical differences that divided the groups.

[28] Irrespective of whether the sociological analysis of a struggle between the wealthy courtier class with its philosophical leanings and the more traditional middle and lower classes is valid for the conflict of the 1230s, it clearly does not apply here. The leaders of both the proponents and the opponents of the ban represented the highest level of Jewish society in southern France. The battle seems to be not between social classes but between different elements of the Jewish aristocracy. The extreme philosophers, about whom both groups complain, are certainly not to be identified with a wealthy courtier class. The one person from this category whom we can identify, Levi ben Abraham, was so poor he was forced to teach Arabic language and literature to any who would hire him (Abba Mari, *Minḥat kena'ot*, 48; Touati, 'La Controverse de 1303–1306', 31–2). There are indications that the preachers who incorporated extreme allegorical interpretations into their sermons were itinerants whose position in Jewish society was not securely established (see Me'iri, in Simeon bar Joseph, *Ḥoshen mishpat*, 167). These extremists used philosophy not as a vehicle to justify their courtier's lifestyle, but rather as a means of gaining influence among the Jews who heard their sermons. See also the more detailed discussion in Chapter 3.

popularization of scientific and philosophical material in the second half of the thirteenth century,[29] the conflict might never have erupted. Nevertheless, given the cultural conditions, my contention is that the direction the conflict took and the configuration of forces it generated may be most readily explained in light of the larger political context: the tensions bound up with the breakdown of the old order in Languedoc and the emergence of the unified royal state of France.

APPENDIX

Ben-Shalom, 'The Ban Placed by the Community of Barcelona on the Study of Philosophy and Allegorical Preaching: A New Study'

Following the original publication of this article in 1982, my colleague Ram Ben-Shalom, a leading medievalist at the Open University in Tel Aviv, now at the Hebrew University in Jerusalem, published two articles relating to this conflict, both of which reveal his characteristic mastery of bibliography and illuminating insight. The first was 'Communication and Propaganda Between Provence and Spain: The Controversy over Extreme Allegorization (1303–1306)'. This addressed, in a stimulating manner, the role of itinerant preachers in disseminating philosophical material to broader circles of the Jewish population than would have access to written texts and especially the role of letters carried across the Pyrenees in connecting the centres of Barcelona and Montpellier and in building up momentum for the controversial bans. This article therefore focuses on one aspect of the controversy, as does mine on a very different aspect, thereby illuminating it.

The second article, 'The Ban Placed by the Community of Barcelona on the Study of Philosophy and Allegorical Preaching',[30] is different in that it contests several central components of this chapter. While I have not previously responded to this article, I believe that republication requires a clarification of why I do not find the challenges raised against my argument by Ben-Shalom's new interpretation to be persuasive.

[29] See Twersky, 'Aspects of the Social and Cultural History of Provençal Jewry', 202–6; Saperstein, *Decoding the Rabbis*, 205–6.

[30] Ram Ben-Shalom, 'The Ban Placed by the Community of Barcelona on the Study of Philosophy and Allegorical Preaching: A New Study', *Revue des études juives*, 159 (2000), 387–404.

After summarizing my argument, Ben-Shalom provides an alternative explanation of what drove Ben Adret to change his position about the second ban issued in Barcelona and to 'give up the struggle'.[31] 'Saperstein's hypothesis that this was caused by fear from the steps taken by Philip the Fair to strengthen his jurisdiction has no basis in the sources.' Instead, Ben-Shalom proposes a 'more convincing answer' which, in my judgement, not only has no basis in the sources but is considerably less convincing. This is that Ben Adret was driven by fear, said to prevail both in Aragon and Provence, that 'the division among the Jewish communities would constitute grounds for Christian intervention in the affairs of the Jewish religion',[32] specifically, that the ongoing conflict

> could be used by the mendicants as good cause for investigation, and an additional reason for the confiscation and censorship of Hebrew books. . . . It may even be assumed, if such a great authority as Ben Adret, who was well known and respected by Christians, condemned the heresy of a group of Jews, it would be hard to prevent the Church authorities from reaching a similar decision.[33]

Ben-Shalom's proposal for explaining the reversal of policy is based on the premise that 'as we know, in the course of the thirteenth century, the Church authorities had increased their attacks on the books of the Jews'.[34] This statement is true, but misleading. It is true because in the thirteenth century, the Church, through its incipient papal Inquisition, had taken unprecedented measures in subjecting the work of Maimonides and then the Talmud to scrutiny, leading—at least at Paris in 1242—to confiscation and burning. It is misleading in that in the context it implies that there had been a pattern of increasing investigation of such Jewish books throughout the century—'a growing freedom with which the Christians intervened in Jewish affairs'[35]— to the point where the possibility of intervention, confiscation, and censorship of Jewish books by the papal Inquisition would be a major fear of responsible Jewish leaders in 1305. But there was no such pattern. Indeed, although there were individuals who continued to condemn Jews for anti-Christian statements in their literature, the Church had withdrawn from active intervention.

The only 'evidence' relevant to our conflict provided by Ben-Shalom is the statement that 'in 1299, only six years before the imposition of the Barcelona ban, King Philip the Fair of France, in a reversal of his previous

---

[31] Ben-Shalom, 'The Ban Placed by the Community of Barcelona', 400.
[32] Ibid. 401.   [33] Ibid. 402–3.   [34] Ibid. 401.   [35] Ibid. 402.

policy, issued an order accusing the Jews of blasphemy and other crimes, and condemning the Talmud'.[36] But Ben-Shalom neglects to include the sentence which immediately follows: 'But in 1302, he reverted to his original stand and would not permit inquisitors to molest his Jews in matters which were of no concern of theirs, such as usury, blasphemy, or magic.'[37] There was absolutely no basis to fear that the king of France would allow the Inquisition to confiscate Jewish books within his realm or that the Inquisition was interested in doing so.

Ben-Shalom asserts that 'the explicit knowledge of a radical rationalist Jewish sect, such as that in Provence, which disqualified the simple meaning of the Torah could be used by the mendicants as good cause for investigation and an additional reason for the confiscation and censorship of Hebrew books'.[38] We should note that the evidence of such a 'radical rationalist Jewish sect' comes from the accusations of their opponents, not from their own works. All Jews influenced by philosophy 'disqualified the simple meaning' of language in the Torah that described God in anthropomorphic terms: the issue is whether their allegorical interpretation of biblical narratives and the commandments supplemented or replaced the simple meaning.[39]

---

[36] Ibid. 401–2, citing Solomon Grayzel, *The Church and the Jews in the XIIIth Century*, vol. ii: *1254–1314*, ed. Kenneth R. Stow (New York, 1989), 20. [37] Ibid.

[38] Ben-Shalom, 'The Ban Placed by the Community of Barcelona', 402.

[39] See Saperstein, *Decoding the Rabbis*, 138–9. As explained there and elsewhere in this book, the philosophers' allegorical interpretation, especially of the Bible, did not usually replace the simple meaning of a biblical statement. Here it is different: the philosophers' metaphorical interpretations of anthropomorphic descriptions of the divinity (God's hands, arms, eyes, mouth) were indeed intended to replace the literal meaning. The most common example used in the polemical literature is the charge that the extreme philosophers claimed that Abraham and Sarah were matter and form (see above, n. 21). Regarding this accusation, Ben-Shalom makes the telling point that the philosophical interpretation would have been that Abraham represents form and Sarah matter, but that the accusation was reversed to provide a simple rhyme: *avraham vesarah ḥomer vetsurah* ('Communication and Propaganda Between Provence and Spain', 181–2). Nevertheless there is no evidence at all that those who provided this philosophical interpretation denied the existence of Abraham and Sarah as historical figures or repudiated the plain meaning of the biblical narratives about their behaviour. This would have applied only where the simple meaning created a major problem, as in the assertion that Joshua made the sun stand still (Josh. 10: 12–14) or in rabbinic aggadah that a visitor to Hebron was told that Abraham was lying in the arms of Sarah, who was looking fondly at his head (BT *BB* 58a). The allegory was generally intended to add meaning rather than replace it (see Marc Saperstein, *Jewish Preaching, 1200–1800: An Anthology* [New Haven, 1989], 381–2 n. 6). This was especially true of the commandments: while extreme philosophers were accused of laxity with regard to their observance, there is no evidence that any Jewish writer or preacher claimed that a commandment had no meaning in its literal sense, only in its allegorical sense—the position held by Christians. For a fine statement of this important distinction in a contemporary source, see Menahem Me'iri, *Beit habeḥirah*

But even assuming that there were philosophers who 'disqualified the simple meaning of the Torah', why would that upset the mendicants or any other Christians? This is what Christians had been doing since the time of Paul: providing allegorical interpretations of passages from the Hebrew Scriptures that replaced their simple meaning, especially with regard to many of the commandments. The use of allegorical interpretation to make Scripture consistent with orthodox theology and with the best of the philosophical tradition has strong roots among the Church Fathers and would become one of the four valid levels of interpretation that informed the medieval tradition.[40] Why would Christians be concerned that there were Jews doing the same thing and try to prevent it? It would probably have made many think that the Jews were coming closer to the proper, Christian approach. If there are Christian sources that condemn Jews for being too philosophical in their approach to Scripture, Ben-Shalom does not cite them.[41]

The 'evidence' for such fears of intervention provided by Ben-Shalom is not at all compelling. They are statements by Ben Adret and Yedaiah Bedersi (a strong opponent of the ban) that continuing the dispute would lead Gentiles—as Bedersi put it—to 'hear of the confusion of our faith and how our Torah has been made into several teachings'.[42] But there is no reference to fear of intervention in either text. The fear seems clearly to be that this is an argument to be used in anti-Jewish polemics: 'how can you claim that your religion is true, when you can't even agree upon it yourselves?' This kind of

al masekhet avot (Jerusalem: Makhon Hatalmud, 1964), 46–8, in Saperstein, *Decoding the Rabbis*, 138–9. It should also be noted that hasidic literature in its first generations contained allegorical interpretations of biblical verses at least as radical as those attributed to the medieval philosophers: for a striking example, see Chapter 12 below.

[40] See Beryl Smalley, *The Study of the Bible in the Middle Ages* (New York, 1952), 9–12, 20–1, 28; Henri de Lubac, *Medieval Exegesis*, vol. i: *The Four Senses of Scripture* (Grand Rapids, Mich., 1998); Edward Synan, 'The Four "Senses" and Four Exegetes', in Jane Dammen McAuliffe, Barry D. Walfish, and Joseph W. Goering (eds.), *With Reverence for the Word: Medieval Scriptural Exegesis in Judaism, Christianity, and Islam* (Oxford, 2003), 225–36.

[41] In the continuation of his discussion of the purported threat posed by Jewish allegorical interpretation of Scripture, Ben-Shalom notes that the Church had 'been desperately fighting against Latin Averroism since the 1260s' ('The Ban Placed by the Community of Barcelona', 402–3). This too is misleading. 'Averroism' is based on a 'double-truth' premise—both Scripture and philosophy can be true, in different realms, even if they contradict each other. This approach eliminates the need for allegorical interpretation, which assumes that there is only one truth and that there can be no contradiction between the truth of Scripture and the truth of reason (cf. Saperstein, *Decoding the Rabbis*, 260–1 n. 128). The Church's battle against Latin Averroism, which was certainly not 'desperate', was therefore irrelevant to the issues of the Jewish conflict.

[42] Ben-Shalom, 'The Ban Placed by the Community of Barcelona', 401.

argument would conceivably enhance missionizing efforts, but that is very different from intervening in internal Jewish affairs.

The argument that Ben Adret was afraid of the papal Inquisition intervening in internal Jewish affairs seems especially misguided in that—in one of the most extraordinary passages of the conflict literature—he actually points to the Inquisition as a model for the Jews to follow.[43] Why would knowledge of the strong second ban induce the Church authorities to intervene, as Ben-Shalom asserts,[44] rather than reassure them that the Jews were taking care of the problem themselves?

Perhaps in response to Ben Adret's suggestion of the papal Inquisition as a model for emulation, Jacob ben Makhir, one of the strongest supporters of philosophical study in Montpellier, also endorsed emulation of a Christian institution, but a strikingly different one—the university:

If there is in the books of the Greeks material that tends towards heresy, we have extracted what is good in them, just as we can extract healing balm from the head of vipers. In the view of the Gentiles, our knowledge of [Greek philosophical literature] is a sign of our wisdom and insight, lest they say that our hearts are devoid of all reason and wisdom. Indeed, we should learn the ways of the Gentiles that are proper. They have translated the works of science and philosophy into their own Gentile languages; they respect these disciplines and those who have mastered them. They do not ask from which religion they emanate. Even if the conclusions and the proofs of the Greeks are in opposition to their own religion and their faith, has any Gentile converted to a pagan religion [lit.: exchanged their God] because of this? Has their faith been undermined? How much more should this apply to us, in possession of the Torah of reason, in the paths of which we walk.[45]

One final detail: in a long footnote, Ben-Shalom questions my interpretation of the encounter between the representatives of the philosophical party and the royal governor in Montpellier. Indeed he questions whether this refers to the French king at all, stating that 'it is just as reasonable to assume—based on the division of authority in Montpellier between the kingdom of France and the kingdom of Majorca—that the governor mentioned was actually . . . the representative of the king of Majorca in the city'.[46] Now neither of us is an expert on the political history of Montpellier in the first years of the fourteenth century, but the reference to 'the division of authority

---

[43] See n. 21 above.
[44] Ben-Shalom, 'The Ban Placed by the Community of Barcelona', 401.
[45] Jacob ben Makhir, in Abba Mari, *Minḥat kena'ot*, 85.
[46] Ben-Shalom, 'The Ban Placed by the Community of Barcelona', 397 n. 29.

in Montpellier' between two kingdoms is both misleading and inaccurate. According to the two scholarly works cited by Ben-Shalom at the end of the note,[47] it is clear that following 1293, there was no 'division of authority'. The king of Majorca was king in his own kingdom, but his title in the part of Montpellier in which he exercised some authority was *dominus* or *seigneur*, and he was under the suzerainty of the king of France, Philip the Fair, who was his 'immediate overlord'.[48] When it came to the expulsion of 1306, the king of Majorca had no jurisdiction that could protect the Jews: as David Abulafia puts it, 'their fate was determined by the actions of the French king as supreme overlord of the city'.[49]

Under these circumstances, it does not seem to me to be 'just as reasonable' to assume that the philosophical party, seeking official permission from the Christian authorities to issue their own ban, would turn to the representative of the king of Majorca rather than the representative of 'the supreme overlord', Philip the Fair. Ben-Shalom's suggestion that Simeon ben Joseph Duran, an ally of Abba Mari, in referring to 'the royal governor, the great prince appointed by our lord His Majesty the King' meant the representative of the king of Majorca seems incredible under these political circumstances, at a time when eight consuls in nearby Carcassonne (some 130 kilometres distant) were being tried for treason because of a plot to transfer allegiance to the king of Majorca. To use the phrase 'our lord, His Majesty the King' with reference to anyone other than Philip the Fair at this time would have been to risk condemnation for *lèse-majesté*.

Ben-Shalom's articles have indeed focused new interest in this dramatic conflict in the history of late medieval Jewish culture, but I still consider my political contextualization of the events significantly more persuasive than his reconstruction based on undocumented and implausible fear of intervention by the papal Inquisition.

---

[47] Rogoziński, 'The Counsellors of the Seneschal of Beaucaire and Nîmes'; David Abulafia, *A Mediterranean Emporium: The Catalan Kingdom of Majorca* (Cambridge, 1994).
[48] D. Abulafia, *A Mediterranean Emporium*, 46, 253.
[49] Ibid. 76, cf. 92.

CHAPTER FIVE

Cultural Juxtapositions: Problematizing Scripture in Late Medieval Jewish and Christian Exegesis

Introduction

In Chapter 4 I discussed an example of the influence of Christian politics on Jewish intellectual culture of the high and late Middle Ages. In the present chapter I would like to explore an example of cultural contact, in which the interaction would seem to be undeniable, but the actual mechanism of influence remains elusive. The prior discussion concerned issues of content; here I will focus on matters of form—which may appear to be of less significance, but which may indeed have significant ramifications.

In other contexts I have addressed this issue with regard to late medieval Jewish preaching. For example, starting from the very end of the fourteenth century, and becoming more prevalent as the fifteenth century continued, the formal 'disputed question', a hallmark of Scholastic literature, appeared in Jewish sermons. The conventions of this form required that a question be raised that had a simple yes or no answer. One position—generally the one that would ultimately be rejected—was defended, using several arguments, then the antithesis was defended, also with several arguments. Finally, the arguments supporting the first answer, which at first had seemed compelling, were refuted point by point.[1] The form was controversial among both Christians and Jews, as it required an apparently cogent defence of a position

---

First published in Jane Dammen McAuliffe, Barry D. Walfish, and Joseph W. Goering (eds.), *With Reverence for the Word: Medieval Scriptural Exegesis in Judaism, Christianity, and Islam* (Oxford, 2003), 133–56.

[1] See Marc Saperstein, *'Your Voice Like a Ram's Horn': Themes and Texts in Traditional Jewish Preaching* (Cincinnati, 1996), 17–18, 84–6, and a fine example on 200–7.

ultimately rejected, indeed even 'heretical', but it was apparently quite appealing. Similarly, I have shown how the Sephardi Jewish sermon took on a new form in the late fifteenth century, beginning with a verse from the Torah portion called by the technical term *nosé*, clearly a translation of the Latin term *thema* used in Scholastic preaching for the biblical verse on which the sermon is to be based.[2] Yet why this style of preaching was adopted by Spanish Jews just at this time remains to be explained.

I propose to raise the question here of the influence of Christian religious culture on medieval Jewish biblical exegesis. Scholars of this topic have devoted considerable energy to various matters of content.[3] Surprisingly little attention has been given to questions of form: how the content of the commentary is organized and presented; what formal innovations are discernible within the medieval tradition. Of course, the commentary genre requires special formal characteristics—primarily, the organization of material in accordance with the order of verses in the text being expounded and treatment of a relatively large percentage of the verses in that text, but, within these parameters, there is opportunity for variations in form.[4]

My focus in this chapter is on a structural model and exegetical technique widely associated with Isaac Abravanel and Isaac Arama, who flourished at the end of the fifteenth century: beginning the discussion of a textual unit by raising a series of 'doubts' (*sefekot*), 'questions' (*she'elot*), or 'difficulties' (*kushiyot*), which were resolved in the ensuing exegetical treatment. I shall refer to this hermeneutical technique as the 'method of doubts', even though the technical term *sefekot* is not always used. The origins of this form in Jewish literature, its prevalence in the generation of the Expulsion,[5] and the

---

[2] See Marc Saperstein, *Jewish Preaching, 1200–1800: An Anthology* (New Haven, 1989), 66–7.

[3] For example, the commentator's attempt to uncover the 'simple meaning' (*peshat*) of the Bible as distinct from the mode of homiletical rabbinic interpretation (*derash*); the influence of grammatical studies; criteria for the commentator's use of rabbinic midrash; the impact of philosophical rationalism in understanding the Bible; allegorical interpretation; the distinctiveness of kabbalistic symbolic exegesis; the use of biblical commentary as a vehicle for apologetical or anti-Christian polemical statements; the reflection of contemporary historical realities in the commentary. For detailed bibliographies of works on these various topics, see the articles and bibliographies in McAuliffe, Walfish, and Goering (eds.), *With Reverence for the Word*.

[4] For example, commentaries that include two, three, or even four different modes of interpretation presented one after the other (Bahya ben Asher) or, having divided the biblical material into conceptual units, provide an 'explanation of the words' followed by a series of 'beneficial lessons' (*to'aliyot*) pertaining to belief and conduct (Gersonides).

[5] For example, on Isaac Karo's commentary on the Torah, see Kalman Bland, 'Issues in Sixteenth-Century Jewish Exegesis', in David Steinmetz (ed.), *The Bible in the Sixteenth Century* (Durham, NC, 1990), 52–8.

cultural significance of this phenomenon have yet to be analysed. In 1916 Jacob Guttmann claimed that Abravanel learned the form from Christian Scholastic writers, without indicating precisely what works Abravanel might have used.[6] The possibility that Abravanel or Arama may have taken the form from earlier Jewish writers seems hardly to have been considered.[7]

I propose to explore this form of exposition in three related genres of Jewish writing: biblical exegesis, sermons, and discursive philosophical texts, beginning with the late fifteenth century and moving back as far as the evidence allows. I shall then give some examples of a similar form in the same genres of Christian writing from antiquity and the Middle Ages.[8] The challenge will be to see where these two traditions might meet. In addition to the structure, I will examine the terminology, particularly the technical term

---

[6] Jacob Guttmann, *Die Religionsphilosophischen Lehren des Isaak Abarbanel* (Breslau, 1916), 6; cf. M. Z. Segal, 'Rabbi Isaac Abravanel as Biblical Commentator' (Heb.), *Tarbiz*, 9 (1937), 266. Guttmann actually refers to the 'disputed question' so prominent in Scholastic literature, which is a related but distinct form. For an attempt to draw a parallel between the commentators on Roman law and the Tosafists in their use of 'doubt and question', see Efraim Elimelech Urbach, *The Tosafists: Their History, Writings, and Methods* [Ba'alei hatosafot: toldoteihem, ḥibureihem, ushitatam] (Jerusalem: Bialik Institute, 1968). The tosafist literature, however, does not appear to provide any basis for the method of doubts.

[7] In her full-length study of Arama, Sarah Heller Wilensky refers to 'the method of raising difficulties and solutions' in half a sentence, without any further comment on its sources or significance (Wilensky, *The Philosophy of Isaac Arama in the Framework of Philonic Philosophy* [R. yitsḥak arama umishnato] [Jerusalem, 1957], 33). It has been suggested that Abravanel derived the method from Isaac Campanton's talmudic study (Shimon Shalem, 'The Exegetical Method of Rabbi Joseph Taitatsak and His Circle' [Heb.], *Sefunot*, 11 [*Sefer Yavan*, 1] [1971–8], 120; Hayim Bentov, 'The System of Talmudic Learning in the Academies of Salonika and Turkey' [Heb.], *Sefunot*, 13 [*Sefer Yavan*, 3] [1971–8], 67). This, however, leaves unresolved the question of whether Campanton initiated this technique or derived it from another source. For an 'innovative trend in Jewish intellectual circles', which originated in Salonika after 1492 with the figure of Joseph Taitazak, see Bland, 'Issues in Sixteenth-Century Jewish Exegesis', 58. By contrast, Frank Talmage wrote: 'In Spain and Provence during the twelfth century, the *she'ilta* (*quaestio*) appears within the continuous commentary, as in Latin exegesis (the *she'ilta* reached the peaks of its development in the commentaries of Abravanel in the sixteenth century)' (Talmage, 'Medieval Christian Exegesis and Its Interaction with Jewish Exegesis' [Heb.], in Moshe Greenberg [ed.], *Jewish Bible Exegesis* [Parshanut hamikra hayehudit] [Jerusalem, 1983], 108). But this statement, which appears to blur the distinction between the 'disputed question' and the method of doubts in Abravanel, refers to twelfth-century material that is not identified, and it is not clear to me what Talmage had in mind.

[8] In this kind of investigation, it would be misleading to insist on an overly rigid differentiation between genres. Sermons, especially in the 'homily' mode (*perishah*), could be extremely close to passages from a biblical commentary. For Christian material, see Louis Bataillon, 'De la *lectio* à la *praedicatio*: Commentaires bibliques et sermons au XIIIe siècle', *Revue des sciences philosophiques et théologiques*, 70 (1986), 559–75; Phyllis Roberts, *Studies in the Sermons of Stephen Langton* (Toronto, 1968), 95–108; Beryl Smalley, *The Study of the Bible in the Middle Ages* (New York, 1952), 209–11; for Jewish material, see Saperstein, *Jewish Preaching, 1200–1800*, 14, esp. n. 23, 73–4, esp. n. 26.

sefekot, and its Latin correlatives *dubitatio* and *dubium*.⁹ Finally, I will comment on the cultural significance of this exegetical mode, what I call the 'problematizing' of the Bible by the exegete.

Generation of the Expulsion

The 'method of doubts' was far more common in the generation of the Expulsion from Spain than has been recognized: I will provide a few examples. Abravanel incorporated the form into his first biblical commentary, on the Former Prophets. In the introduction, he stated: 'I have raised fifteen questions [*she'elot*] concerning the books [of the Prophets], which have recently occurred to me, questions our ancestors did not think of.'¹⁰ After enumerating these questions, he justified the importance of his method:

[Although some of the questions will be answered in a different place] I have not refrained from mentioning them here, for the nature of the subject brought me to them, and it was necessary for the sake of thoroughness. Pay attention to everything I bring to your attention today, for the raising of doubts [*sefekot*] that I have done, and the exposition of my thoughts and opinions about their solution, is not an empty matter for you.¹¹

He then continued with the book of Joshua: 'I decided to proceed by asking at the beginning of every section six questions, based on the content of the verses and the nature of the subject to be investigated.' He did not waver from the number six, no matter how complex or straightforward the biblical passage may have been or whether the questions raised 'profound doubt' or were simple to resolve.

[This technique] facilitates complete understanding and helps in remembering. I have chosen to set out the questions before the exegesis of the verses, for that in my judgement is a beneficial way to raise the matters, to generate disputation and expand investigation. Furthermore, raising of the questions frequently leads to deeper study of the verses, and to discovery within them of matters sweeter than honey.¹²

---

⁹ I do not include here the use of this term in the classical texts of Jewish law, where *sefekot* refers to people or things the legal status of which is uncertain (e.g. Mishnah *Kid.* 4: 3; BT *Shab.* 15*b*; BM 83*b*). I see no connection between this usage and that of the authors to be analysed below. The use of *sefekot* as a technical term in talmudic study at the end of the fifteenth century is quite different: philosophical, rather than legal, in nature.

¹⁰ Isaac Abravanel, *Perush al nevi'im ukhetuvim* [Commentary on the Prophets and Writings], 3 vols. (Jerusalem: Torah Vada'at, 1955–60), i. 12*a*.   ¹¹ Ibid. i. 13*a*.   ¹² Ibid.

Abravanel did not claim to be introducing a radically new element into Jewish biblical exegesis. The novelty appears to lie in the content of at least some of the questions, the use of a fixed number of questions for each section, and the presentation of the questions as an introduction to each exegetical unit. These formal decisions are justified pedagogically: they aid in remembering and lead to deeper understanding. By the time he came to write his commentary on the Torah, he felt no need to explain his method at all. His commentary on Genesis begins by raising ten long and complex questions, ending: 'These are the questions I thought of for this first section [*parashah*], and the verses of the section should be interpreted so as to provide a solution to all of them.'[13] Similarly, after a general introduction to Deuteronomy, he continued: 'The doubts that occur in this section [*seder*], after a cursory look at the verses ... are fourteen.' After enumerating them, he concluded: 'These are the doubts I have seen fit to raise about the topics of this section [*seder*]. Their solution will come with the exegesis of the section [*parashah*] and the [proper] understanding of the verses.'[14]

The commentary on Deuteronomy used the term *sefekot* for the questions raised at the beginning of each section, whereas the other commentaries used *she'elot*, and some scholars have suggested that this may reflect the influence of Isaac Arama or Joseph Hayun.[15] But, as we shall see, the term *sefekot* was widespread in the period, as it was earlier, and it usually seems to be interchangeable with *she'elot*.[16] A sermon attributed to Abravanel also used this technique, but without any technical term for the questions at all.[17]

The same method was used in Isaac Karo's commentary on the Torah, *Toledot yitshak*.[18] Like Abravanel, Karo divided the biblical material into

---

[13] Isaac Abravanel, *Perush al hatorah* [Commentary on the Torah], 3 vols. (Jerusalem, 1964), i. 12*b*.

[14] Ibid. iii, 'Deuteronomy', 8*a*, 11*b*.

[15] For Arama's possible influence, see Segal, 'Rabbi Isaac Abravanel as Biblical Commentator' (Heb.), 266; for Hayun, see Abraham Gross, *Rabbi Joseph ben Abraham Hayun: Leader of the Lisbon Community and His Literary Work* [R. yosef ben avraham hayun: manhig kehilat lisbon vitsirato] (Ramat Gan, 1993), 146 n. 157.

[16] See e.g. Abravanel on Zech. 7: 1 (*Perush al nevi'im ukhetuvim*, iii. 219*a*). In his commentary on the Torah, Isaac Karo ordinarily used *sefekot*, but he sometimes used *she'elot* (e.g. Karo, *Toledot yitshak* [commentary on the Torah] [Trent, 1558], 38*b*, 81*b*) and sometimes *kushiyot* (e.g. ibid. 39*a*, 111*b*).

[17] Sermons by various preachers (Heb.) (MS 9856, Jewish Theological Seminary of America Library, New York), fo. 87ᵛ on the Ten Commandments. The questions bear some similarities, but are no means identical, to the questions in Abravanel's commentary on the Torah. The sermon is somewhat disappointing: a routine preaching exercise rather than a response to a special occasion. It does not provide clear evidence that Abravanel used material from sermons in his commentary as other preachers did.

[18] See Bland, 'Issues in Sixteenth-Century Jewish Exegesis'. Sha'ul Regev characterized *Toledot*

sections based on content, almost invariably introducing each one with a statement such as: 'In this section . . .' or 'In these verses, there are [a specified number of] doubts.' The solution to the doubts comes in the subsequent discussion of the verses. The absence of any explanation for this technique suggests that it was self-explanatory. Even a casual comparison reveals that many of Karo's questions were similar to those of Abravanel.[19]

The raising of problems, usually referred to as *kushiyot*, was a dominant rhetorical device in many of Karo's sermons. Sometimes they were answered immediately, sometimes after a long discussion. One sermon began with a rabbinic dictum, and then immediately continued: 'One may raise a difficulty' (*veyesh lehakshot*). Six questions followed, each one developed in some detail. Then Karo wrote: 'The answer to these difficulties [will come] when we first raise difficulties pertaining to chapter Ḥelek [of Mishnah *Sanhedrin*].' Karo then raised eleven more questions followed by: 'It seems to me that to resolve all these difficulties we must make an introductory statement, in which the resurrection of the dead will be established as true.' The eleven questions in the second set were addressed in the course of this discussion, and the original questions were addressed at the end of the discourse. Along the way, other problems were raised and resolved.[20] More intricate than the structural unit used in the biblical commentaries, this is a form that placed considerable demands upon the listeners.

The method of doubts was every bit as crucial in Joel ibn Shu'eib's collection of sermons, *Olat shabat*, where the section raising and resolving *sefekot* frequently constituted a major component of the sermon and was integral to the structure of the discourse. How these doubts were presented reveals careful attention to the intricacies of construction. Rather than the constant recurrence of a common format as in Abravanel's commentaries, Ibn Shu'eib's doubts were presented with frequent variations of form, though always

---

yitsḥak as 'a book of sermons on the Torah', recast by the editor in the form of a commentary, but unfortunately he did not compare the content of the 'commentary' with the sermons he published (see Isaac Karo, *Derashot r. yitsḥak karo* [sermons], ed. Sha'ul Regev [Ramat Gan: Bar Ilan University Press, 1995], 12).

[19] For example, six of the eight doubts raised by Karo at the beginning of the Torah portion 'Lekh lekha' can be found among Abravanel's more expansive 'questions' on the same passage (Karo, *Toledot yitsḥak*, 20b; Abravanel, *Perush al hatorah*, i. 186b–187b). After raising two doubts at the beginning of 'Ḥayei sarah', Karo continued: 'My brother, the *ḥakham* Rabbi Ephraim Karo, of blessed memory, responded to these doubts by saying . . . ', possibly reporting the content of a sermon by his brother (the father of the author of the *Shulḥan arukh*) (Karo, *Toledot yitsḥak*, 27a; cf. 40a).

[20] Karo, *Derashot*, 69–93.

with an eye to artistic balance.[21] He obviously spent considerable energy in crafting his material into what he considered to be an aesthetically appealing shape. It was not the originality of the doubts (some of which were described as 'well-known' or 'famous'), but rather the solutions he provided and the format in which he presented them that he believed to be his special contribution.

Straddling the border between a homiletical and an exegetical work is Isaac Arama's *Akedat yitsḥak*. In his introduction, Arama wrote:

And the homily [*perishah*] will proceed by first raising the doubts [*sefekot*], both new and old, that occur in the simple meaning of the verses pertaining to the subject being studied [*derush*], and also in matters that are apparent from these verses, or that have been raised by previous interpreters. I shall arrange them first in the appropriate order and then proceed to explain them so as to resolve them satisfactorily . . . consistent with what preceded it in the *derush*. In this way, I shall reconcile the verses properly, so that none of the doubts remain.[22]

This form is more complex than that of Abravanel and Karo, for the doubts appeared in the middle of the discourse, as a transition between its two main sections. Sometimes they appeared as if it were a routine procedure to 'mention the doubts that fall in this section' and 'after the mention of these [fourteen] doubts . . . proceed to an explanation'.[23] Occasionally, the project was introduced with greater fanfare:

This will be well explained when we look closely at his intent in this passage [Deut. 9: 9–10: 11]. It is truly difficult to explicate, for its words appear to be jumbled, not following the order of the events, and it also includes matters that seem to be irrelevant. I have not seen any commentator who has paid attention to this.

After specifying eight problems, Arama proceeds with a majestic sweep of his rhetorical wand: 'The solution of all these doubts, sorting out their confusion, will be based on what I shall now say.'[24]

---

[21] For examples that are formally similar to Abravanel's, see Joel ibn Shu'eib, *Olat shabat* [sermons] (Venice: Bomberg, 1577; repr. Jerusalem: Y. M. Morgenstern, 1973), 10*b*–*c* ('No'aḥ'); 73*c*–*d* ('Yitro'); for more complex forms, see ibid. 3*d*–10*a* ('Bereshit'), 13*d*–15*c* ('Lekh lekha'), 17*c*–19*a* ('Vayera'), 21*c*–24*d* ('Ḥayei sarah'), 44*b*–46*b* ('Vayeḥi'), 61*c*–62*b* ('Bo').

[22] Isaac Arama, *Akedat yitsḥak* [homiletical essays on the Torah], 3 vols. (Warsaw, 1882–4), introduction (i. 9*a*). [23] Ibid., *sha'ar* 26 (i. 155*a*–*b*).

[24] Ibid., *sha'ar* 91 (iii. 25*d*–26*a*); see also the commentary on Esther printed in the standard editions of *Akedat yitsḥak* and apparently written by Isaac's son, Meir, in which the doubts are divided into two categories, substantive and linguistic (ibid. iii). See Barry Walfish, *Esther in Medieval Garb: Jewish Interpretation of the Book of Esther in the Middle Ages* (Albany: State University of New York Press,

Another contemporary, Shem Tov ben Joseph ibn Shem Tov, began an elaborate wedding sermon based on the verse 'It is not good for the man to be alone' (Gen. 2: 18) with a formal disputed question: whether 'human perfection is achieved through solitary living, without the participation of another human being'.[25] He followed it with another discussion: 'Before we speak about the companionship of a man and his wife, which is a divine association, we shall express the relevant doubts about this association.' Specifying eight, the preacher continued: 'Now we shall respond to the first doubt.'[26] The second part of the sermon on the Torah portion 'No'aḥ' is composed of nine doubts and their answers.[27] In the sermon on 'Vayikra', a rabbinic dictum is cited and the method is applied to that: 'Now after this, we should explicate the dictum. But first, it is appropriate to express doubts about it [ra'ui lesapek bo], for whoever does not express doubts does not know, and whoever does not know remains in irremediable blindness. Now first, one may express the doubt . . .'[28] Four followed, and then their solutions. This method was one of many rhetorical options available to Shem Tov, which he used because without it, knowledge remained incomplete.

Finally, there are three manuscripts from the same period which should be mentioned. The first, titled 'Ketsat parashiyot', contains sermons by the important talmudist Isaac Aboab which differ from those in the published version of his sermons, *Nehar pishon*.[29] The sermon on 'Ḥayei sarah' began with a series of eight questions, each introduced with the same word: 'furthermore'. These were followed by the answers: after three had been discussed, the preacher stated: 'However, the rest of the questions will be resolved with the exegesis of the verses', which followed immediately.[30] We see here how close a sermon may be to a commentary.

The second manuscript is titled 'Dover meisharim', and its author is

1993), 226, although Walfish describes Isaac's commentary as also presenting questions or difficulties (ibid. 8).

[25] Shem Tov ibn Shem Tov, *Derashot* [Sermons] (Salonika, 1525; repr. Jerusalem, 1973), 5c.

[26] Ibid. 6c, 6d.

[27] Ibid. 8b–9a; see also the third part of the sermon on 'Lekh lekha', where five questions about the first ten verses were raised and answered (ibid. 9c–d). [28] Ibid. 39c.

[29] Isaac Aboab, 'Ketsat parashiyot' [sermons] (MS Hunt 342 [Neubauer 952], Bodleian Library, Oxford). The longest sermon in 'Ketsat parashiyot' has been published in Hebrew and in translation in Saperstein, '*Your Voice Like a Ram's Horn*', 293–365. For more detailed discussion of Aboab and his preaching, see Chapter 7.

[30] Aboab, 'Ketsat parashiyot', fo. 3a–b. The second and fourth questions are the same as two *sefekot* raised by Isaac Karo (*Toledot yitsḥak*, 27a). After one of his questions, Aboab states: 'Others have spoken, you may look at their explanations.'

known only by the name 'Israel'. Though most of his sermons do not use this method, he resorted to it on occasion. After a discursive introduction to a topic pertaining to the portion 'No'aḥ', he continued: 'Now we shall express doubts on this *parashah*', raising nine.[31] The following sermon, on 'Lekh lekha', had two sections each beginning *yesh lesapek*, 'one might raise a doubt'; the next one, on the same portion, used the same method: 'We shall explicate this *parashah* through the solution of these doubts.'[32] Once he explained the purpose of the technique: 'In raising doubts about a matter, it is not my intent to allow the doubt to remain in the mind of the listeners, heaven forbid, but rather that the matter become fully explicated.'[33]

The third manuscript contains sermons from several different authors, including Isaac Abravanel and Isaac Karo. We have already noted the use of questions in the sermon on Exodus 20: 2 attributed to Abravanel. The following sermon, labelled 'Another on this *parashah* ['Yitro']', began: 'My intent is to speak about the matter of the day [Shavuot] . . . but before this intent [is fulfilled], there are five difficulties to be raised . . . '. In a different sermon, on 'Toledot', the preacher began his discourse with a rabbinic dictum followed by: 'One may express four difficulties about this dictum. . . . To resolve these difficulties, it is necessary first to make an introductory statement.'[34]

Enough examples have been given to demonstrate that the method of doubts was by no means unique to Abravanel and Arama; rather, it was widely prevalent in the exegetical and homiletical literature of Jews in the generation of the Expulsion. The cultural significance of this enterprise will be discussed later, but first its sources need to be identified.

Earlier Jewish Writers

The explanation given by Shem Tov—'whoever does not express doubts does not know'—is quite similar to Isaac Campanton's justification for raising

---

[31] 'Dover meisharim' [sermons] (MS 197 [Neubauer 2447], Christ Church, Oxford), fo. 197*a–b*; see Saperstein, *Jewish Preaching, 1200–1800*, index, s.v. Israel, author of 'Dober Mesharim'; *'Your Voice Like a Ram's Horn'*, 253.   [32] 'Dover meisharim', fos. 202*a*, 206*a*.

[33] Ibid., fo. 55*a*; for Israel's defence of his use of the 'disputed question', see Saperstein, *Jewish Preaching, 1200–1800*, 395–6.

[34] Sermons by various preachers (Heb.), fos. 89ʳ, 16ʳ⁻ᵛ. The raising of doubts or difficulties about the rabbinic dictum, as opposed to the biblical passage, became increasingly common in the following century: for an example from Moses Almosnino, see Saperstein, *Jewish Preaching, 1200–1800*, 232–3; for a comparable passage, see Solomon ben Isaac Levi, *Divrei shelomoh* [sermons] (Venice, 1596; repr. Brooklyn, 1993), 126*b–c*.

doubts about the talmudic passage being studied:

> Whenever you look closely at some topic or matter, just as you must undertake to look carefully at the linguistic formulation of the matter, so should you also look for problems to raise against it [*levakesh devarim lehakshot kenegdo*], first by raising the doubts [*lehania hasefekot*] pertaining to that matter or that formulation, and by knowing the fallacies and the problems that can occur in that topic, for that is the way to reach the truth, and to understand that matter fully.[35]

It is not entirely clear whether Campanton meant the formal raising of a series of questions and then resolving them all in the course of an extended discussion or the intellectual exercise of conceiving problems, each one of which may be addressed after it is raised. The formulation he used, *lehania sefekot*, is unusual Hebrew that seems to be a technical term.[36] In a very similar passage, the Portuguese rabbi Joseph Hayun used the same phrase, and then, shifting to the apparently synonymous term *she'elot* (questions), cited Aristotle as the source for the justification:

> One should ask questions about what he is studying and raise doubts, in order to illuminate that matter, for as a result of the questions it will be fully clarified. After asking the questions, one should not leave them without an answer, but rather respond to them and set them straight. The Philosopher said: 'It is good for the truth to raise difficulties about it [*shetaksheh alav*], so that it can better endure.'[37]

Hayun used various forms of this technique. His short treatise (*ma'amar*) on Numbers 32 begins: 'There are questions on this section'—nine are provided—and ends: 'This is what I thought about the solution of these doubts, praise be to God.'[38] Similarly, a discussion of the blasphemer in Leviticus 24 begins: 'I have seen fit to raise doubts [*lehania sefekot*] about this story, and they are of two kinds.' Seven are given about the differences between this and

---

[35] Isaac Campanton, *Darkhei hagemara* [talmudic methodology] (Vilna, 1901), 13; see Gross, *Rabbi Joseph ben Abraham Hayun* (Heb.), 73.

[36] It is actually the precise equivalent of the Latin *dubitationes movere* (see below). The legacy of the Latin phrase remains in the English expression 'to move the question'.

[37] In Gross, *Rabbi Joseph ben Abraham Hayun* (Heb.), 74; cf. the later formulation by Solomon Levi in a sermon from 1573 (*Divrei shelomoh*, 205d). Solomon, however, did not use the method of doubts as an integral part of his preaching. See also the concise maxim: *mitokh havikuaḥ mitbarer ha'emet* ('from within dispute, the truth will be clarified') (Israel Davidson, *Thesaurus of Proverbs and Parables from Medieval Jewish Literature* [Otsar hameshalim vehapitgamim mesifrut yemei habeinayim] [Jerusalem: Mosad Harav Kook, 1979], 50 n. 725).

[38] In Gross, *Rabbi Joseph ben Abraham Hayun* (Heb.), 195–7. Note that not all questions in this passage are presented together: first two are given, then answers to both; other answers come immediately after their respective questions. The terms *sefekot* and *she'elot* are used interchangeably.

the account of the wood-gatherer in Numbers 15, followed by their solutions, then seven more about the passage itself, with answers after the first three, and then after each succeeding doubt. At the end Hayun stated: 'these are the two kinds of doubts that occurred to me in this story and their solution.'[39] The affinities between this and the questions in Abravanel's commentary are obvious, and some of the questions are quite similar.[40]

Joseph ibn Shem Tov, identified by Abravanel as his mentor,[41] flourished in the middle of the fifteenth century. He used the method of doubts in some, though certainly not all, of his extant sermons. The clearest example is in a discussion of the revelation at Mount Sinai, where he raised seven *sefekot*, then resolved them.[42] He began a sermon on repentance with two questions about David's sin with Bathsheba and continued: 'The sages of blessed memory already resolved these doubts [*sefekot*].'[43] After discussing several characteristics of the language of the Torah, he provided an 'answer that encompasses all these doubts'.[44] There is no indication in these passages that the author believed he was doing anything new.

A group of sermons by a disciple of Hasdai Crescas (or perhaps a circle of his disciples), dating from the first quarter of the fifteenth century, contains a fine example of the homiletical use of the disputed question.[45] Elsewhere, the preacher justified the use of this method with the statement: 'from out of intellectual give and take, the truth will sprout'.[46] In one place, the terminology of doubts is used to refer to the raising of conceptual problems crucial to the philosophical enterprise. After setting forth the position on the problem of divine attributes taken by his mentor, Crescas, the preacher expressed his own view: 'not as one who disagrees, but as one who arranges and orders

---

[39] Ibid. 198–201; cf. 222–3, raising two sets of doubts on the sin of Moses and Aaron at the waters of Meribah. The answers are given after all the doubts are raised.

[40] e.g. Abravanel, *Perush al hatorah*, ii, 'Leviticus', 149*b*, question 1, and Hayun, in Gross, *Rabbi Joseph ben Abraham Hayun* (Heb.), 200, question 1 (on Lev. 24: 10); Abravanel, *Perush al hatorah*, ii, 'Leviticus', 150*a*, question 6, and Hayun, in Gross, *Rabbi Joseph ben Abraham Hayun* (Heb.), 200, question 4 (on Lev. 24: 15). [41] Abravanel, *Perush al hatorah*, ii, 'Exodus', 253*b*.

[42] Joseph ibn Shem Tov, Sermons (Hebrew MS 1, Juynboll Family Library, Leiden), fos. 72*b*–74*a*.

[43] Joseph ibn Shem Tov, 'Sermons on Repentance' (Heb.), ed. Sha'ul Regev, *Asufot*, 5 (1991), 188; see also 207 ('the sages already resolved this doubt'). [44] Ibid. 194.

[45] See Saperstein, *'Your Voice Like a Ram's Horn'*, 183, 200–7. On a different occasion, the preacher said he would give 'the answer to this [question] in short, without points of possible argument on each of the antithetical propositions, in order to avoid the burden of excessive time' (Sermons by a disciple of Hasdai Crescas [Heb.] [Firkovitch, First Series, no. 507, Russian National Library, St Petersburg], fo. 31*a*).

[46] Ibid., fo. 13*b* (*mitokh hamasa vehamatan titsmah ha'emet*); see also Campanton, *Darkhei hagemara*, 13, cited above.

his doubts before his master, in order to learn how they can be resolved. I shall raise here six doubts'. The preacher then notes that some of his doubts had already been raised by Crescas in his philosophical-theological treatise, *Or hashem* (The Light of the Lord).⁴⁷

Crescas himself used this terminology as part of his discursive masterpiece. The discussion of God's knowledge of particulars and divine providence is filled with doubts and their resolutions. Speaking of divine providence, he noted that 'the doubts that were set forth [*hasefekot asher hinihu*] with regard to God's knowledge of things can also be set forth here'. He went on to enumerate doubts arising from empirical observation, from rational analysis, and from biblical authority, before he endeavoured to resolve them.⁴⁸ Similarly, after setting out his doctrine of prophecy, he raised a series of doubts about what he had said and then proposed his solution.⁴⁹ The formal problematizing of belief was clearly a part of Crescas's method.

Dating from the last quarter of the fourteenth century is a homiletical-exegetical work identified by its editor as written by Joseph ben David of Saragossa, a student of Nissim ben Reuben of Gerona.⁵⁰ Beginning a discussion of Isaac's blessing of Jacob, the author asserted that it contains 'matters that surprise' (*min hatemihah*):

First, when Isaac wanted to bless his son, whom he loved . . . why did he withhold the blessing until Esau had prepared a tasty dish for him to eat, in order to bless him [see Gen. 27: 4]? . . . Second, how could Rebecca advise Jacob to take the blessing deceitfully? [Gen. 27: 8–10] . . . Third, why did Jacob say: 'Perhaps he will touch me' [Gen. 27: 12], without worrying that his father might recognize him except by touch? . . . Fourth, why did God agree that Isaac should intend his blessing for a different person? . . . Fifth, after Isaac realized that he had been deceived and knew that he had not blessed Esau . . . why did he confirm his blessing? [Gen. 27: 37].⁵¹

---

⁴⁷ Sermons by a disciple of Hasdai Crescas (Heb.), fo. 14*a*.

⁴⁸ Hasdai Crescas, *Or hashem* [The Light of the Lord] (Jerusalem: Sifrei Ramot, 1990), 1.2.2 (157–62). ⁴⁹ Ibid. 2.4.3 (195–203).

⁵⁰ Leon Feldman first published this work without attributing it to anyone and then republished it as the work of Joseph ben David of Saragossa (*Perush al hatorah meyuhas letalmid rabenu nisim b. re'uven (haran)* [Commentary on the Torah], ed. Leon Feldman [Jerusalem: Makhon Shalem, 1970]). Feldman assumed that it was a commentary, but the sections have structural affinities with sermons, and there are internal indications that it was used for preaching (see e.g. ibid. 65, 132–7, 198; see also Saperstein, *Jewish Preaching, 1200–1800*, 74 n. 26).

⁵¹ Joseph ben David, *Perush al hatorah*, 18–19. These questions should be compared to those of Abravanel, for example, the first question with Abravanel's fourth, the second with Abravanel's sixth, the third with Abravanel's ninth, the fourth with Abravanel's seventh, and the fifth with Abravanel's twelfth (Abravanel, *Perush al hatorah*, i. 304*b*–305*b*).

In the course of the exegesis that provides the solutions to these problems, the author resorted several times to the technical term for doubt, *safek*: 'Now with regard to the doubt we mentioned—how could a blessing be efficacious if it was not intended for the one blessed—the answer is . . .'; 'With this the doubt we mentioned—after Isaac was "seized with violent trembling" [Gen. 27: 33], how did he confirm the blessings?—disappears'; 'As for the doubt we mentioned—why did not Rebecca and Jacob worry that Isaac would recognize him by the quality of his voice?—the likely answer is . . .'.[52] Here is evidence for the formal method of doubts more than a century before the Expulsion from Spain.

A sermon dating from the third quarter of the fourteenth century by Nissim ben Reuben of Gerona contains a passage relevant to our subject. Discussing the aftermath of the Golden Calf episode, he raised one problem about a statement by Moses (Exod. 33: 15) that seems inappropriate, ending: 'This is a great doubt that needs to be explicated. Similarly, there are many doubts pertaining to the interrelationship of [verses in] the passage that need explication. The first doubt is . . . the second doubt . . . the third doubt . . . In sum, this passage requires extensive explication.' In the ensuing discussion of the passage, the exegetical problems were addressed, providing another example of our 'method of doubts'.[53]

In the 1320s and 1330s the philosopher and exegete Gersonides (Ralbag) also used the method of doubts in its crystallized form. A good example is in the second book of *Milḥamot hashem* (The Wars of the Lord). After a preliminary discussion of knowledge about future events communicated through dreams, divinations, and prophecy, Gersonides continued: 'There are many doubts [*sefekot*] with respect to this type of communication. It is proper that we discuss them to the extent that we are able.' Eight doubts were raised, and then each one was addressed in turn: some were described as easily solvable, others as more difficult to handle.[54] This is the method of doubts applied to a conceptual problem.[55]

[52] Joseph ben David, *Perush al hatorah*, 20–1; see also 148–50, 220: 'There are also other doubts [*sefekot*] that require explication', a passage taken from Nissim ben Reuben Gerondi, *Derashot haran lerabenu nisim ben reuven gerondi* [sermons], ed. Leon Feldman (Jerusalem, 1974), 53.

[53] N. Gerondi, *Derashot*, 53. This passage is also used by his disciple Joseph ben David (*Perush al hatorah*, 220–1). See also Nissim's eighth sermon, where he raises a series of doubts, not clustered at the beginning of the discussion, but rather presented in an associative manner, the solution of one leading to the presentation of the next (N. Gerondi, *Derashot*, 136, 137, 139).

[54] Gersonides, *Milḥamot hashem* (Berlin, 1923), 2: 6 (104–11); Eng. trans. *The Wars of the Lord*, trans. and ed. Seymour Feldman, 3 vols. (Philadelphia, 1984–99), ii. 49–59. Feldman's translation has the more idiomatic 'problems'. See also ibid. 1: 13 (89–90; ed. Feldman, i. 223–4).

[55] Note also that the introduction begins by listing six 'important and difficult questions [*she'elot*]',

Gersonides' biblical commentaries also contain examples of the method of doubts that have not to my knowledge been previously noted. In his discussion of the Golden Calf episode (Exod. 31: 18–32: 35), he wrote: 'Rabbi Levi said, I have seen fit to mention a few doubts that occur in this narrative before I begin to explicate it, so that the explication, through which we shall emerge from these doubts, will be comprehensible to us. . . . Now these doubts can be resolved . . . .' After an extensive discussion of Aaron's delaying tactics, in the hope that Moses would return before the calf was made, he concluded: 'Now this is what seems proper to us in the resolution of these doubts'.[56]

Like the passage in *Milḥamot hashem*, this passage bears all the characteristics of the classic method of doubts. The problems were raised at the beginning, they were designated by the technical term *sefekot*, and they were resolved in the course of a conceptual-exegetical discussion of a series of verses (although without the marker: 'with this, the first doubt is resolved'). We should also note the unusual introduction to the section, 'Rabbi Levi said', a phrase that Gersonides ordinarily used at the beginning of a work (for example, his commentaries on the Torah and Joshua and *Milḥamot hashem*). It seems that this was a separate unit, like the *ma'amarim* by Joseph Hayun above, written in an unusual form and incorporated into the commentary. There are other examples as well in Gersonides' exegetical oeuvre.[57]

The method of doubts can be traced back in an unbroken chain to the first half of the fourteenth century, appearing in the work of some of the most influential late medieval biblical commentators and preachers. Before this, the traces become less clear. I have not found a full example of this technique in any thirteenth-century commentary or any of the very few extant collections of sermons. However, there are two other texts that should be

each one of which actually entails more than one such query (ibid., introduction [2; ed. Feldman, i. 91]). Then, 'we have also appended to these questions two religious problems, fraught with doubt [*she'elot datiyot mesupakot me'od*]' (ibid. [3; ed. Feldman, i. 92]). Gersonides also used the term *sefekot* in his technical super-commentaries on Averroës (see Ruth Glasner, 'The Early Stages in the Evolution of Gersonides' *The Wars of the Lord*', *Jewish Quarterly Review*, 87 [1996], 43–5).

[56] Gersonides, *Perush al hatorah* [Commentary on the Torah] (Venice: Bomberg, 1547; repr. New York: n.p., 1958), 112*b*–*d*. The commentary by Nissim's disciple incorporates this passage without giving credit to Ralbag, introducing it with the phrase: 'Now it is worthwhile to speak about some of the doubts that fall upon this matter' (Joseph ben David, *Perush al hatorah*, 215–16).

[57] See his discussion of the two celestial lights in the Creation story (Gersonides, *Commentary on the Torah*, 12*a*; on the first doubt and Gersonides' solution, see Joseph ben David, *Perush al hatorah*, 38); his discussion of Isaac's blessing (Levi ben Gershom, *Commentary on the Torah*, 35*d*–36*a*); his comments on the sun standing still over Gibeon (Josh. 10: 12); and on Proverbs 30: 4.

mentioned: one using the technique without the term *sefekot*, the other with the technical term but without the precise form. The first is represented by the questions with which David Kimhi (Radak) introduced his comment on the third chapter of Genesis:

One might ask [*yesh lishol*] about the matter of the serpent's speaking to the woman: how did this happen, and was it miraculous? ... Furthermore, [if it was an angel that spoke on behalf of the serpent,] how would the angel seduce the woman to transgress God's commandment? Furthermore, [if it was an angel that spoke,] what is the relevance of the snake here, and why does it say that the snake was cunning? ... And why did the angel not come to the man?[58]

These questions introduced the difficulties of the passage, which required a separate esoteric commentary, yet the questions were addressed and, for the most part, resolved in the ensuing exoteric discussion of the verses.[59] While this is not as neat as in Abravanel or Ralbag, and the technical term *sefekot* does not appear, it may be considered a rudimentary precedent for the later models.

The other example is a discursive work from the thirteenth century: Hillel of Verona's *Tagmulei hanefesh* (Retributions of the Soul). Discussing the Platonic doctrine of multiple souls, based on a passage from Thomas Aquinas, he notes:

To this, Aristotle attached doubts in the manner of questions [*sefekot bederekh she'elot*]. They are: does Plato himself hold that every one of those souls that he mentions is a unique soul in and of itself, or are they parts from one soul? And if you say that they are parts of one soul, are they all different from each other in definition alone or also spatially, that is to say, is there a special vessel for each one? He goes on to say that some of these things are not difficult to accept, and some of them raise doubts.[60]

These are not precisely the doubts of the method of doubts—problems raised to be resolved in the course of an exegesis of the text—but rather objections that cast doubt on a position taken, which are not to be resolved. Hillel serves

---

[58] David Kimhi, *Perushei rabi david kimḥi (radak) al hatorah* [commentaries on the Torah], ed. Moses Kamelhar (Jerusalem, 1970), 33. The participation of an unspecified angel in this narrative is invoked by Kimhi from Sa'adyah Gaon's comment that an angel spoke on behalf of the serpent, as an angel spoke on behalf of Balaam's ass (Num. 22: 22–35). Kimhi is raising problems here not so much with the biblical narrative as with Sa'adyah's explication of it.   [59] Ibid. 33–4.

[60] Hillel ben Samuel of Verona, *Sefer tagmulei hanefesh lehilel ben shemu'el miveronah* [The Rewards of the Soul], ed. Joseph (Giuseppe) Sermoneta (Jerusalem: Magnes Press, 1981), 116.

as a convenient transition to the Gentile material, in that he invokes both Aristotle and Thomas Aquinas, from whom the passage is taken.[61]

Gentile Writers

Aquinas wrote that Aristotle *dubitationem movet* (literally, sets a doubt in motion), and that some of Plato's views on this matter *dubitationem habent* (have or raise a doubt).[62] Aquinas was discussing Aristotle's *De Anima* 413*b* 13–26, but the origin of the method of doubts would appear to be the beginning of Book 2 of Aristotle's *Metaphysics*:

In pursuing our science, we ought first to make a careful survey of the doubts which confront us at the outset. Among them would be the diverse ways in which others have dealt with our problems and in addition any points that may have been overlooked. To have stated well the doubts is a good start for those who expect to overcome them, for what follows is, of course, the solution of those very doubts, and no one can untangle a knot which he does not see.[63]

The Greek word *aporeia*, which recurs throughout this passage, underlies the Latin *dubitatio* and the Hebrew *safek*. Aristotle set out the method of doubts

---

[61] A letter, apparently from Hillel of Verona, may provide additional information about the method of doubts. The author asks a friend to send him a copy of Maimonides' commentary on the *Aphorisms* of Hippocrates. He notes that he has 'more than one hundred great "difficulties" [*kushiyot*] pertaining to Galen's commentaries' on the *Aphorisms*, and he hopes that 'with careful study of Maimonides' commentary, all these difficulties will be resolved' (Benjamin Richler, 'An Additional Letter by Hillel ben Samuel to Isaac the Physician' [Heb.], in Abraham David [ed.], *From the Collections of the Institute of Microfilmed Hebrew Manuscripts* [Miginzei hamakhon letatselumei kitvei hayad ha'ivriyim] [Jerusalem, 1995], 12). The passage is not entirely clear, but it appears that Hillel was referring to Maimonides' 'doubts that occurred to me concerning the words of Galen' (see Moses Maimonides, *Pirkei mosheh birefuah* [medical writings], ed. Süssmann Montner [Jerusalem, 1982], 323 [I am grateful to Tzvi Langermann for this reference]). Alternatively, Hillel could be referring to his own method of studying the medical text: creating a list of the difficulties he himself found in the text and then turning to Maimonides' commentary to resolve them. This method could also be applied to biblical passages. On the works in question, see George Sarton, *A History of Science*, 2 vols. (Cambridge, Mass., 1959), i. 379–81. The quotation from Maimonides raises the issue of the method of doubts in Arabic literature, which cannot be considered here. As the Jewish writers discussed in this chapter worked in Christian Europe and few knew Arabic, it seems more fruitful to explore the Latin literature.

[62] Thomas Aquinas, *Against the Averroists: On There Being Only One Intellect*, ed. and trans. Ralph McInerny (West Lafayette, Ind., 1993), 26–7.

[63] Aristotle, *Metaphysics*, trans. Richard Hope (New York, 1952), 40. I have followed Hope's translation except I have used 'doubts' where Hope has 'difficulties', following Hope's own explication of the Greek term *aporeia* (ibid. 388).

as the soundest approach to the discovery of understanding and truth. (His commentator, Alexander of Aphrodisias, explained that it is by way of these doubts that the discoveries of the sciences occur.[64]) In the Latin text used by Aquinas, the passage read: 'Now for those who wish to investigate the truth, it is worthwhile to ponder these doubts well [*bene dubitare*]. For the subsequent study of truth is nothing else than the solution of earlier problems [*solutio dubitatorum*].' Aquinas's own paraphrase speaks of 'those subjects about which it is necessary to doubt [*dubitare*] before the truth is established'.[65] After this programmatic statement, Aristotle devotes the rest of Book 2 to formulating the numerous doubts or difficulties he will need to address.[66] The rest of his *Metaphysics* is an attempt to provide solutions.

Aquinas also commented on how the method of doubts was presented differently in the *Metaphysics*:

Aristotle was accustomed, in nearly all his works, to set forth the doubts [*praemittet dubitationes*] that emerge before investigating and establishing what is true. But while in the other works Aristotle set forth the doubts one at a time in order to establish the truth about each one, in this work he set forth all the doubts at once [*simul praemittit omnes dubitationes*], and afterwards in their proper order establishes the things that are true.[67]

This is the basis for both the intellectual approach and the literary structure of the Jewish material reviewed above. However, the Jewish material deals not merely with the difficulties that arise out of a set of ideas, but with those generated by a passage of text, and the solution comes not just from abstract argumentation, but from exegesis.

---

[64] Alexander of Aphrodisias, *On Aristotle's Metaphysics 2 & 3*, trans. William Dooley and Arthur Madigan (Ithaca, NY, 1992), 88; for the various meanings of *aporeia* in Alexander's work, see ibid. 87 n. 3.

[65] Thomas Aquinas, *Commentary on the Metaphysics of Aristotle*, trans. John Rowan, 2 vols. (Chicago, 1961), i. 141–2.

[66] For an enumeration of the fourteen problems and their solutions, see Aristotle, *Metaphysics*, 272–4.

[67] Aquinas, *Commentary on the Metaphysics of Aristotle*, i. 143. The Latin verb used in this passage is *praemittere*. Aquinas used two other phrases to characterize Aristotle's raising of conceptual problems: *ponit dubitationes* and *movet dubitationes*, the precise equivalent of the Hebrew phrases *lehaniaḥ sefekot* and *lehania sefekot* (ibid. ii. 143). Despite the distinction in the use of the verbs suggested by F. A. Blanche, the material in Thomas's commentary, especially in the passage just cited, suggests that the two terms were used by the author interchangeably (Blanche, 'Le Vocabulaire de l'argumentation et la structure de l'article dans les ouvrages de Saint Thomas', *Revue des sciences philosophiques et théologiques*, 14 [1925], 167–87; see also Thomas Aquinas, *Commentary on the Posterior Analytics of Aristotle*, trans. F. R. Larcher [Albany, 1970], 30–1).

This appears for the first time in the literature of the Church Fathers. In his *Quaestionum in Heptateuchum*, an exegetical work on the first seven books of the Bible, Augustine provided a justification of the technique and raised a series of questions about the biblical texts: How was Cain able to found a city (Gen. 4: 17), when the Bible has mentioned only his parents and the brother whom he killed? How could Methuselah have continued to live after the Flood (Gen. 5: 25)? How could the 'angels' have cohabited with the 'daughters of men' (Gen. 6: 4)?[68] and so forth. These are not simple questions with obvious answers: some of the questions are extensive, indicating apparent ways out of the conundrum that are not satisfactory. It is truly a problematizing of the biblical text. The same technique was used in his *Quaestionum in Evangeliorum*.[69]

This method, however, was not common in medieval Christian exegesis. Something similar appeared in the twelfth century in Honorius Augustodun's 'Questions and Answers' on Proverbs and Ecclesiastes,[70] and the *Quaestiones et decisiones in epistolas Pauli*, formerly attributed to Hugh of St. Victor,[71] although they differ structurally, in that the answers come immediately after each question, and conceptually, in that the questions are simplistic and the answers obvious. It is exegesis serving the purpose of catechism.[72]

---

[68] Augustine of Hippo, *Quaestionum in Heptateuchum*, Patrologiae cursus completus, Series Latina, ed. J.-P. Migne, 221 vols. (Paris, 1844–65), xxxiv, cols. 547–9.

[69] Augustine of Hippo, *Quaestionum in Evangeliorum*, Patrologiae cursus completus, Series Latina, ed. J.-P. Migne, 221 vols. (Paris, 1844–65), xxxv, cols. 1321–64. For a full discussion of problematizing Scripture in Patristic literature, see Marie-Joseph Lagrange, 'La Littérature patristique des *Quaestiones et responsiones* sur l'écriture sainte', *Revue biblique*, 41 (1932), 210–36, 341–69, 514–37; 42 (1933), 14–30, 211–29, 328–52; for more recent treatments, see Adam Kamesar, *Jerome, Greek Scholarship, and the Hebrew Bible: A Study of the Quaestiones Hebraicae in Genesim* (Oxford, 1993), esp. 82–96; C. T. R. Hayward, introduction to Jerome, *Hebrew Questions on Genesis*, trans. C. T. R. Hayward (Oxford, 1995), esp. 2–7. Kamesar notes a 'long history' of this literature before Jerome, beginning with the sixth-century BCE criticisms of Homeric poems (*Jerome, Greek Scholarship, and the Hebrew Bible*, 82).

[70] Honorius Augustodun, *Quaestiones et responsiones in Proverbia et in Ecclesiasten*, Patrologiae cursus completus, Series Latina, ed. J.-P. Migne, 221 vols. (Paris, 1844–65), clxxii, cols. 313–48.

[71] Hugh of St Victor [attrib.], *Quaestiones et decisiones in epistolas Pauli*, Patrologiae cursus completus, Series Latina, ed. J.-P. Migne, 221 vols. (Paris, 1844–65), clxxv, cols. 431–634. For the spuriousness of the attribution to Hugh, see Smalley, *The Study of the Bible in the Middle Ages*, 97 n. 1; Ceslas Spicq, *Esquisse d'une histoire de l'éxégèse latin au Moyen Âge* (Paris, 1944), 67.

[72] e.g. 'What does Solomon mean when he says: "In vain the net is spread in the eyes of every winged creature" [Prov. 1: 17]? . . . Who are the winged ones? The saints and elect of God, who have the wings of faith, hope and love, as well as the other virtues.' 'What is the wisdom about which Solomon says, "Wisdom cries aloud in the streets" [Prov. 1: 20]? Jesus Christ, who is the virtue of God and the wisdom of God.' Honorius listed twelve questions, separate from any exegetical context, and then answered them one by one (Honorius Augustodun, *Liber duodecim quaestionum*, Patrologiae cursus completus, Series Latina, ed. J.-P. Migne, 221 vols. [Paris, 1844–65], clxxii, cols. 1177–8).

Quite different was Abelard's articulation of the importance of raising problems and doubts for the pursuit of truth in the introduction to his pathbreaking *Sic et non*. After quoting Aristotle on the value of raising doubts about matters to be investigated, he continued: 'For through doubting we come to inquiry and through inquiry we perceive the truth.'[73] Abelard did not use the formal structure of raising a series of doubts in *Sic et non*.[74] Rather, the entire work can be viewed as a problematizing of the Christian tradition by juxtaposing apparently contradictory authorities on a panoply of important issues, in quest of a firm grasp on the ultimate truth.

Later in the twelfth century, the formal dialectical use of questions, including the more elaborate disputed question, made headway into scriptural study, despite considerable opposition.[75] By the thirteenth century *quaestiones* became a staple of academic instruction, and collections of such questions became a prevalent form of scholastic writing,[76] but increasingly the term *quaestio* came to mean the formal 'disputed question', in which antithetical positions were fully sustained and then the conflict was resolved. It is perhaps because of this usage that some Scholastic writers began to use the terms *dubitatio* and *dubium* for the question arising out of a problem in a text, which could be resolved without arguing its opposite.

We have seen this usage in Aquinas's commentary on Aristotle's *Metaphysics*. Bonaventure's *Commentary on the Sentences* is largely in the form of a series of disputed questions, but scattered throughout the work is a series of *dubia circa litteram magistri*, which begin with the following (or a similar) formulation: *In parte ista sunt dubitationes circa litteram. Et primo....*[77] In his com-

---

[73] *Dubitando ad inquisitionem venimus, inquirendo veritatem percipimus*, immediately following the Aristotelian quotation: *dubitare autem de singulis non erit inutile* (Peter Abelard, *Sic et non: A Critical Edition*, ed. Blanche Boyers and Richard McKeon [Chicago, 1976], 103; see Martin Grabmann, *Die Geschichte der scholastischen Methode*, 2 vols. [Berlin, 1956], i. 203, 209).

[74] Note the statement by Artur Landgraf that 'Gilbert de la Porrée and Abelard initiated this practice of introducing the *quaestio* into the scriptural commentary, a practice that would quickly become so strongly prevalent in their schools' (Landgraf, 'Collections de *Quaestiones* du XIIe siècle', *Recherches de théologie ancienne et médiévale*, 7 [1935], 124). No evidence, however, is provided for Gilbert or Abelard. The evidence for the schools is in manuscript (ibid. 124 n. 21), and I was unable to check it myself.

[75] According to Spicq, 'little by little, *quaestiones* were inserted [into biblical commentaries] in order to resolve contradictions between two biblical texts or between two exegeses of the same text; aided by the influence of Aristotelian dialectic, reasoning takes a more and more considerable place in the structure of the *quaestio*' (*Esquisse d'une histoire de l'éxégèse latin*, 68–9).

[76] See e.g. John W. Baldwin, *Masters, Princes and Merchants: The Social Views of Peter the Chanter and His Circle*, 2 vols. (Princeton, 1970), ii. 96–101.

[77] Bonaventure, *Commentary on the Sentences [of Peter Lombard]*, in *Opera theologica selecta*, 4 vols. (Florence, 1934–49). The *dubia* derived from the period of Bonaventure's studies in Paris under the

mentary on Ecclesiastes, he began with a discursive comment (postil) on the passage from the biblical text and then frequently continued with a series of questions, introduced with the phrases: *Quaeritur de hoc quod dicit* .... *Sed dubitatio est de hoc quod dicit*.... *Dubitari potest de hoc quod hic dicit*....[78] There seems to be no distinction in the terminology: *quaestio* and *dubitatio*, *quaeritare* and *dubitare* are used interchangeably, all referring to the disputed question. It should be noted, however, that where more than one question or doubt was raised, the answer almost invariably followed it immediately before the next question was discussed. Only rarely did a series of questions appear before any answers were given.[79] It is not a precise model for the fully developed method of doubts we have seen in Jewish preachers and exegetes of a later period.[80]

The Latin sermons of John Wyclif, delivered in the 1380s, provide an important example of homiletical problematizing. At the end of the preface to the published collection, he gave a succinct statement of their structure: after treating the mystical sense of the passage, 'following the custom of Augustine, I will address the doubts [*dubia*] that can be taken up from the Gospel'.[81] Wyclif regularly introduced the second part of his sermons with a phrase such as *Circa hoc evangelium dubitatur*. Many of these *dubia* are in the form of the disputed question, and they may be theological, historical, moral, or legal.[82] In some sermons only one doubt was discussed, in others, three.

---

influence of Alexander of Hales. They are from a separate manuscript and were interspersed with the text of the *Commentary on the Sentences* by the editors (see J. Guy Bougerol, *Introduction to the Works of Bonaventure* [Paterson, NJ, 1964], 100–5).

[78] Bonaventure, *Commentary on Ecclesiastes*, in *Opera omnia*, 10 vols. plus index (Florence: Quaracchi, 1882–1902), vi. 66, 57, 63. The same pattern is used in his *Commentary on John*, in *Opera omnia*, vi. 260; see Beryl Smalley, *Medieval Exegesis of Wisdom Literature* (Atlanta, Ga., 1986), 43–5; id., *The Study of the Bible in the Middle Ages*, 276. Smalley concludes that Bonaventure's purpose was 'to give the students some guidance on the type of problem which arose from the text and to sketch the lines for a solution' (*Medieval Exegesis of Wisdom Literature*, 45). For the influence of these *quaestiones* on subsequent commentators, see ibid. 49–51 (William of Tournai), 71 (William of Alton), 84–6 (John of Varzy). [79] For example, in the *Commentary on John*, 261.

[80] During the 1340s the Carmelite monk John Baconthorpe from Oxford wrote a series of biblical commentaries, of which his postil on Matthew has survived. Smalley's description indicates that it contains a series of *quaestiones*, for example: *Hec sunt tres difficultates* [another term corresponding to one in Jewish sources (*kushiyot*)]. ... *Sed tunc remanet difficultas*. ... *Sed ex hiis sequitur alia difficultas*. ... *Hic oritur quarta difficultas*. ... (Beryl Smalley, *Studies in Medieval Thought and Learning* [London, 1981], 316, 328–9).

[81] John Wyclif, *Sermones*, ed. Johann Loserth, 4 vols. (London, 1887–90), i, p. xiv.

[82] Ibid. 3, 12–13, 240, 26, 40, 236. The early sixteenth-century French preacher Michel Menot regularly devoted the second part of his sermons to a fully developed disputed question (see Étienne

Other contemporary English preachers also raised doubts as an integral part of their preaching.[83]

Jean Gerson, Chancellor of the University of Paris from 1395, was a renowned preacher. His sermons reveal the use of questions as a formal device, though not in the precise form we have sought. In a French funeral sermon, Gerson raised twelve questions about Purgatory and the fate of the soul after death. A Christmas sermon contained twelve questions about the birth of Christ, and a sermon for Pentecost contained six questions appropriate to that occasion.[84] In each case, the answer was provided immediately after the question. The questions were straightforward, and the answers fairly obvious. This was not an example of problematizing a tradition, but rather, like some of the twelfth-century commentaries, a form of catechetical teaching. Rather different were the questions in a Latin sermon on the circumcision of Christ delivered before Pope Benedict XIII. A long series of questions was placed rhetorically in the mouth of a personified *studiositas speculatrix*: each one was given a response from the speaker, with each response producing a further question. The questions were not of the sort that would have occurred to every Christian, but might have been quite troubling to many listeners.[85] This passage indeed reflects a problematizing of tradition in preaching to an elite audience.

Many of Gerson's sermons, especially those delivered before the court of Charles VI of France, contained one or more series of questions, with between two and twenty-seven questions.[86] Most often, they were about doctrinal issues, but some were about biblical passages, such as the wedding at Cana (John 2: 1–11).[87] While not a fixed part of the structure of each sermon, they were a common feature of Gerson's homiletical technique.[88]

Gilson, *Les Idées et les lettres* [Paris, 1932], 135–6; Larissa Taylor, *Soldiers of Christ: Preaching in Late Medieval and Reformation France* [Oxford, 1992], 62, 66).

[83] H. Leith Spencer, *English Preaching in the Late Middle Ages* (Oxford, 1993), 45–6.

[84] Jean Gerson, *Six sermons français inédits de Jean Gerson*, ed. Louis Mourin (Paris, 1946), 231–9, 82–4, 298–9.

[85] For example: 'What if Peter had wanted to defend his error by armed force, notwithstanding that he remained pope: would it have been permissible to repel force with force, whether by words, or by imprisonment, or finally by death itself? As Jerome and Augustine, both exceptional scholars, disagreed on this matter, must one of them be said to be a heretic?' (Jean Gerson, *L'Oeuvre oratoire*, Oeuvres complètes, 5, ed. Palem Glorieux [Paris, 1963], 72).

[86] See the many references in Louis Mourin, *Jean Gerson, prédicateur français* (Bruges, 1952), 341–2.

[87] Gerson, *L'Oeuvre oratoire*, 378–9; on the relationship between the scriptural reading and the questions in some of the sermons, see Mourin, *Jean Gerson*, 342.

[88] A different method of doubts occurs in the *Ars praedicandi* by the contemporary Catalan Franciscan friar Francesc Eiximenis of Gerona. The questions are used to introduce the theme-verse

The closest Christian model I have found is in a commentary on Peter Lombard's *Sentences* by the Augustinian friar Gregory of Rimini, who taught at the University of Paris from 1341. In this work, the author raised a series of doubts, introducing them with a phrase such as *Nunc movenda sunt quaedam dubia*. Four problems were presented. Then each one was addressed in turn, with headings: 'Solution to the first doubt . . .', 'Solution to the fourth doubt . . .'.[89] The form is the same as that used by Jewish writers, but the content of the questions is not exegetical but conceptual, indeed highly abstract. Gregory of Rimini's doubts are quite similar to those in the discursive works of Crescas or Gersonides; they are a step or two removed from the *sefekot* in the biblical commentaries and sermons.

In short, the Christian material surveyed does not reveal any obvious model for the exegetical or homiletical use of the method of doubts that could have served as the source for Jewish writers. Aristotle and Aquinas each provided a justification for raising a series of conceptual questions (called by Aquinas *dubitationes*) that fully problematized a subject and then setting out to answer them one by one, but neither Aristotle nor Aquinas used this in an exegetical work. While many Scholastic authors incorporated 'questions' into their commentaries, these were usually either simple rhetorical questions or complex disputed questions, not the series of doubts so common in Jewish literature. Indeed, the influence of Scholasticism on Christian sermons and biblical commentaries of the high and late Middle Ages appears to be less than was once assumed. Most Christian writers were quite careful to keep their genres distinct.[90] While there may indeed have been some

(which provides the answer to them) rather than arising from the verse (see P. Martí de Barcelona, 'L'Ars praedicandi de Francesc Eiximenis', *Analecta sacra tarraconensia*, 12 [1936], 335–6).

[89] Gregory of Rimini, *Gregorii Ariminensis OESA lectura super primum et secundum Sententiarum*, ed. A. Damasus Trapp and Venicio Marcolino, 6 vols. (Berlin, 1981), i. 381–8; see also: *in articulo quarto movenda sint dubia circa praedicta et solvenda* (Gabriel Biel, *Collectorium circa quattuor libros Sententiarum*, ed. Wilfred Werbeck, 4 bks. in 5 vols. [Tübingen, 1973–92], i. 22). Each of these doubts, however, is answered immediately after it is raised.

[90] This point has been made by David D'Avray, who emphasized the paucity of scholastic questions in thirteenth-century preaching (D'Avray, *The Preaching of the Friars* [Oxford, 1985], 7–8, 164–71, 242–3). See also Thomas Waley's critique of preachers who incorporated *profundae materiae theologicae* into their sermons as if they were addressing 'clerics in the schools' (a complaint that can be paralleled in Jewish sources) (in Thomas-Marie Charland, *Artes praedicandi: Contribution à l'histoire de la rhétorique au Moyen Âge* [Ottawa, 1936], 112, 344; Spencer, *English Preaching in the Late Middle Ages*, 46; L. Taylor, *Soldiers of Christ*, 33). On the important distinction between the discourse of the academic and the discourse of the preacher, see Robert of Basevorn's *Forma praedicandi* (in Charland, *Artes praedicandi*, 238) and Thomas Illyricus (L. Taylor, *Soldiers of Christ*, 83 [note her statement there that 'scholastic debates did not, for the most part, furnish material for popular preaching']).

influence from Christian writings or preaching, the precise sources of the Jewish form remain elusive.

Cultural Significance

Problematizing a tradition can be fraught with peril. When Abelard set forth apparently contradictory positions held by earlier authorities on an array of doctrinal issues, the chaotic diversity of belief may have impressed the reader more than the attempted reconciliation. When Aquinas formulated his theology through an unending series of questions and presented seemingly cogent arguments to substantiate the antithesis of every position he ultimately affirms,[91] the reader may have concluded that the arguments for the contrary position were as strong as their eventual refutation. (Indeed, Leon Modena later used the *Summa theologica* in this way, citing the first part of Thomas's questions in support of his own attacks on doctrines such as the Trinity, the Incarnation, and the Virgin Birth.[92])

The dangers of this approach in the Jewish context are expressed through a classic joke about the impact of Abravanel's biblical commentaries on a pious Jew. Each sabbath, after returning home from the synagogue, he would eat a full, leisurely sabbath meal with his family and then turn to study the weekly lesson with Abravanel's commentary. After reading the doubts that introduce each section, the man would doze off for a sabbath nap, not awakening until it was time to go to the synagogue for the afternoon prayer. Reading the doubts but never reaching the solutions, he became a heretic.[93]

I see three possible explanations for why Jews began to problematize the

---

[91] 'It seems that God does not exist' (Thomas Aquinas, *Summa theologica*, 1.2.3 [trans. Fathers of the English Dominican Province, 3 vols. (New York, 1947)]); 'It seems that to be good does not pertain to God' (ibid. 1.6.1); 'It seems that it was not fitting for God to become incarnate' (ibid. 3.1.1); 'It seems that the Mother of God was not a virgin in conceiving Christ' (ibid. 3.28.1); 'It seems that it was not necessary for Christ to suffer for the deliverance of the human race' (ibid. 3.46.1).

[92] See, for example, the long quotation from Thomas's argument that 'it seems that Christ's Mother did not remain a virgin after his birth' (ibid. 3.28.3), which Modena calls *sefekot* (Leon Modena, *Magen vaḥerev* [polemical work] [Jerusalem: Mekitsei Nirdamim, 1960], 60–1). He then goes on to rebut Thomas's answers to the doubts. It was for such reasons that Henry of Hesse warned that 'the preacher should never in the pulpit frivolously or presumptuously put any belief to the test' and that 'when the preacher brings up doubts and disputed questions in the pulpit, he should not retire without settling the point' (in Harry Caplan, *Of Eloquence: Studies in Ancient and Mediaeval Rhetoric* [Ithaca, NY, 1970], 72, 73; cf. L. Taylor, *Soldiers of Christ*, 186).

[93] See the more serious expression of the dangers of problematizing, particularly if the solution is not compelling, cogently articulated by Abraham ben David in his animadversions (*hasagot*) on Maimonides' *Mishneh torah*, 'Laws of Repentance', 5: 5.

Hebrew Scriptures in the late Middle Ages. The first is that it was a kind of duplicity, an effort by the writers to communicate an esoteric message: that the Hebrew Scriptures were indeed riddled with profound problems. In this reading, the 'resolutions' are essentially a cover that allowed the writer to express doubts without taking responsibility for them, by claiming that he had a solution for each one. The true purpose was not to provide answers, but to express grave misgivings that, given the community in which he lived, could not be presented in any other way. This interpretation might be plausible if there were just one or two authors who used the format, but it was widely prevalent in the literature of the generation of the Expulsion and not uncommon during the preceding two centuries. To assume that each of the authors who used this technique was engaging in the same subversive enterprise—that each really believed that the doubts remained despite the answers presented—strains credulity.

Assuming, then, that the authors genuinely believed that, at least in most cases, they resolved the doubts they raised, a second possibility is that they were responding to problems already present in the minds of their readers. This would suggest a broad scepticism in Spanish Jewry about the Bible, consistent with Yitzhak Baer's claim that the impact of extreme rationalism—Averroistic tendencies—had corroded and undermined the foundations of traditional Jewish belief, leaving large numbers of Spanish Jews with no effective resistance to the pressures towards apostasy.[94] According to this view, the commentators and preachers were fighting a desperate rearguard action to defend the Bible with their arguments that the doubts in the text were only apparent and could be resolved.

In addition to the problems with Baer's thesis and his promiscuous use of the term 'Averroist',[95] there is a more basic problem with this reconstruction. The doubts addressed by the commentators and preachers are not fundamental philosophical problems about the nature of God and the revelation of the Scriptures that might be generated by philosophical study. Most are problems that would not occur to the casual reader or listener; they derive from the devotion of considerable intellectual energy to a detailed and exhaustive study of the biblical text. Individuals whose commitment to traditional Jewish discourse had been subverted by immersion in philosophical texts would hardly have been likely to be bothered by the issues that are addressed by our commentators. It is therefore questionable whether the prevalence of the method of doubts in the generation of the Expulsion can

[94] See pp. 92–3 above. [95] See pp. 26, 62, 89–91, 93, above.

serve as evidence that a widespread awareness of problems required a massive effort to hold the fort.[96]

The third and most likely option is that the authors were exposing their audiences to problems in the classical texts that most of them had not thought of themselves. But why, given the risks we have noted, would they do this? Here I see two possible explanations. One is their own theoretical commitment to the proposition—going back to Aristotle's *Metaphysics*—that complete understanding of a philosophical truth, and by extension of a classical text, is impossible without exploring all the problems it raises. Jewish writers maintained this position not only in epigrammatic statements but also in developed arguments. For example, Joel ibn Shu'eib, in a confraternity sermon, cites Aristotle (apparently drawing from Aquinas's commentary on the *Metaphysics*) to justify his own use of *sefekot*:

First, in this manner, the person will come upon the way of logical demonstration. For the arguments that cast doubt upon something that is true are rhetorical, not true, as truth cannot be opposed to truth. Escape necessarily comes through knowledge of logical demonstration. This is similar to untying a knot: similarly, knowledge of logically cogent arguments comes to the perfected after knowledge of the doubts.

Second, one who does not know a matter in depth, with the doubts that can be raised about it, will come upon the truth only by chance. He will know the places that diverge from the straight path, going to a certain location, but he will not be able to guard himself from them, and he will rarely follow the straight path. . . .

Third, one who investigates speculatively should be like a judge. Just as the judge should pay attention to the contradictory arguments of the contestants, deriving the truth by investigating both sides. So the one who investigates speculatively must have the opposing arguments before him, to derive from them the truth.[97]

Ibn Shu'eib frequently justified his use of doubts with phrases suggesting that they lead to a fuller knowledge of the biblical passage: 'for when these doubts are resolved, many things in the *parashah* will be understood' or 'so that [even] the uneducated people may know'.[98] Such statements appear to indicate a

---

[96] This is not to suggest that there were no philosophical problems discussed in sermons that genuinely vexed late medieval Spanish Jews. The efficacy of repentance and its reconciliation with divine foreknowledge and justice is an example (see Saperstein, *Jewish Preaching, 1200–1800*, 395–8; id., '*Your Voice Like a Ram's Horn*', 85–6, 296–7, 317–24).

[97] Joel ibn Shu'eib, *Olat shabat*, 144*a–b*; cf. Aquinas, *Commentary on the Metaphysics of Aristotle*, i. 142. Aboab gives a similar, though more succinct, defence of this type of argument in the sermon where he cites Aquinas (see Saperstein, '*Your Voice Like a Ram's Horn*', 86–7 n. 41).

[98] Joel ibn Shu'eib, *Olat shabat*, 25*c*, 10*b*.

sincere belief in the value of the method as an educational tool for the entire people.

The second explanation is that exegetes and preachers were responding to a popular demand for this kind of discussion, that readers and listeners looked forwards to the challenge of being confronted with puzzles and problems and then seeing how they could be resolved. A hint of this may be found in the introduction to Arama's *Akedat yitshak*, where he described Jews impressed by Christian oratorical skill and demanding something similar from their own leaders.

[They] heard the [Christian] preachers and found them impressive; their appetites were whetted for similar fare. This is what they say: 'The Christian scholars and sages *raise questions and seek answers* in their academies and churches, thereby adding to the glory of the Torah and the prophets . . . Why should the divine Torah with all its narratives and pronouncements be as a veiled maiden beside the flocks of her friends and her students?'[99]

As noted above, I could find no evidence that the method of doubts was a standard part of contemporary Christian preaching, although the warnings by Christian theoreticians against exploring complex disputed questions from the pulpit indicate that it must have occurred. Nevertheless, the raising and resolving of doubts appears to have become a kind of convention among late medieval Jews. Among the various rhetorical tools at the disposal of Sephardi preachers, this method of doubting the Scriptures apparently became a favourite.

It has often been noted that many of Rashi's comments are responses to difficulties he perceived in the biblical text and that to appreciate his exegesis properly one must reconstruct the question to which his comment is an answer. That approach to the exegesis of Scripture is very different from the practice of explicitly setting forth doubts about the biblical passage before endeavouring to resolve them and constructing a form of discourse in which the exegete is required to produce problems even if they are not apparent. In this approach, no statement from the Bible is accepted as self-evident or clear. Everything is shown to be more complex than it appears. The reader or listener is expected to understand and appreciate this complexity, for only then will the eventual solution be valued.

As for the actual doubts raised, we have already noted a considerable

---

[99] Isaac Arama, *Akedat yitshak*, introduction (i. 8*a*); see Saperstein, *Jewish Preaching, 1200–1800*, 393 and n. 3.

degree of repetition and overlap, both between earlier and later writers and among contemporaries who could not have borrowed from each other. I think that correlating systematically the doubts pertaining to the Pentateuch raised by Abravanel, Isaac Karo, Isaac Arama, and Joel ibn Shu'eib would reveal a high percentage of the same *sefekot* appearing in two, three, or even all four of these works. If so, there must have been a common tradition, transmitted in the Spanish schools, of specific problems for each *parashah*, indeed for each scriptural passage, which individual writers could draw upon, supplement, and adapt to their own purpose. Originality was expressed not so much in the doubts themselves but in the formal variations through which they were presented and in the solutions that were proposed.

The prevalence of this method in the Jewish literature produced by the generation of the Expulsion and the unbroken tradition of its use for close to two centuries has no obvious parallel in Christian texts, and, even where we do find something akin to the method of doubts in Christian commentaries and sermons, this was in literature intended for an elite audience. The Jewish texts were, if not fully 'popular', intended for a wide reading public, while the sermons were appropriate for delivery to the entire congregation. There is no suggestion that this method should be restricted to the most educated and sophisticated Jews. It was not an esoteric method of discourse. All Jews were to be led through the thicket of a densely problematized scriptural tradition. Even if the solutions were not always fully satisfying, there was something of value in the very method of questioning.

CHAPTER SIX

Ein li esek banistarot: Saul Levi Morteira's Sermons on *Parashat* 'Bereshit'

IN THE SUMMER OF 2003 I sent a book-length typescript to the Hebrew Union College Press, a comprehensive study based on the massive collection of manuscript sermons by the leading rabbi of the Portuguese Jewish community in Amsterdam, Saul Levi Morteira—a project on which I had been working for more than a decade.[1] I believed that my study of these texts was completed, and I was finally free to pursue new research projects. Soon after, the invitation to contribute a chapter to the Festschrift for Joseph Dan on the general theme of 'Creation and Re-Creation in Jewish Thought' unexpectedly made me rethink this assumption.

I first met Joseph Dan at the Hebrew University in the fall of 1969, when he welcomed me into his MA seminar 'The Hasidic Story', an experience which provided a first, consciousness-expanding encounter with the academic study of Jewish mysticism and the analysis of Jewish narrative texts that negotiated the interaction of mysticism, literature, and folklore. The following year, Dan's seminar 'Homiletical Literature in Spain and Italy' whetted my interest in the conceptual and literary study of sermon texts, a topic that would later become the central focus of my academic career. His book, *Homiletical and Ethical Literature* (*Sifrut haderush vehamusar*), which appeared in 1978, provided invaluable guidance as I was beginning to move into this

---

First published in Rachel Elior and Peter Schäfer (eds.), *Creation and Re-Creation in Jewish Thought: Festschrift in Honor of Joseph Dan* (Tübingen, 2005), 209–47.

[1] Marc Saperstein, *Exile in Amsterdam: Saul Levi Morteira's Sermons to a Congregation of 'New Jews'* (Cincinnati, 2005). The manuscript collection is Saul Levi Morteira, Sermons (Heb.), 5 vols. (MS 12, Budapest Rabbinical Seminary Library). I have provided folio numbers for passages cited, as in *Exile in Amsterdam*, but readers should be aware that the manuscripts in the Budapest Library and the microfilms in the Institute for Microfilmed Hebrew Manuscripts, Jerusalem do not have them. The most effective way of finding a specific sermon in the manuscript is through the theme-verse that comes at the very beginning of each one.

new field of research. His teaching was a model for me of the master pedagogue's capacity to make any text, or any subject, spring to life. Throughout the years, he has sustained a relationship of mentor and friend. Declining the invitation to be part of his Festschrift was inconceivable to me. Yet the only way in which I could make an appropriate contribution was by returning to Morteira, immediately after having completed my book.

While *Exile in Amsterdam* contains analysis of specific themes in Morteira's preaching, including the use of history, the treatment of Christianity and 'New Christians', and the many-faceted exploration of exile and redemption, I had not discussed the theme of Creation in a systematic manner. I decided, therefore, to take Morteira's sermons on the first chapter of Genesis as a way of contributing to the theme of the Festschrift. This essay may also be considered as an addendum to *Exile in Amsterdam*, which might have been included in it had I been motivated earlier to address the topic.

For the current volume, this chapter represents a type of rabbinic leadership we have not encountered yet. At the time when Morteira first arrived in Amsterdam in 1616, the Portuguese community that had settled there was composed almost entirely of emigrants from Portugal who had been born, raised, and educated as Christians. Although the mass forced conversion of the entire Jewish population present on Portuguese soil took place in 1497, many of these migrants—great-grandchildren of those who had converted under duress—were still referred to as 'New Christians'. Many of them had had a university education in Lisbon or Coimbra, some were recognized as outstanding physicians, others were merchants engaged in international commerce. Whether because they were being harassed by the Portuguese Inquisition or because they resented the ongoing resistance to full acceptance into Portuguese society, they had made a decision to leave their familiar environment in the Iberian peninsula and find a new home. And they had made a further decision: rather than continuing to live as Christians in Bordeaux or Antwerp or other cities where there was no Inquisition but also no toleration of Jews, they had decided to find a Jewish community to join. By around 1600 Amsterdam was a possible choice.

The Portuguese congregations in Amsterdam were therefore composed of men and women who knew that they wanted to be Jews, but—with no possibility of proper Jewish study in Portugal—had little accurate concept of what the Jewish tradition contained and what Jewish life entailed. For such listeners, exposure to a weekly sermon delivered by a rabbi in their native language, which would define a specific topic and address it in impressive rhetorical style, using a full array of sources from biblical, rabbinic, and postrabbinic texts but without assuming prior knowledge beyond what had been addressed in previous sermons, was critical for the development of their new identity. Morteira provided this service for almost four decades. His weekly sermons were an ongoing programme of adult education, of life-long Jewish learning, led by a rabbi who eventually developed relationships with individuals throughout a good portion of their lives and with two or even three generations of the same family.² We will see how, during this period of his rabbinic leadership, Morteira explored one set of problems related to a specific theme that is central to both Jewish and Christian theology: Creation.

The extant manuscripts of Morteira's sermons contain thirteen different sermons on this *parashah* (all based on verses from the first chapter of Genesis), only one of which was published in the 1645 collection *Givat sha'ul*.³ I know of no collection by any other Jewish preacher that contains so many complete sermons on one chapter of the Bible.⁴ In addition, Morteira is the only preacher I know who followed a self-imposed discipline of proceeding systematically through the scriptural lessons, year after year, each sermon constructed upon a subsequent verse. The sermons on 'Bereshit' have the added advantage that—unlike many of the other texts in the manuscript collection—most of them are clearly dated, including not only the years of their original delivery, but also the dates on which some were subsequently repeated. He even included the names of the members of the congregation who were honoured by the position of *ḥatan bereshit*, the individual called to the Torah when the beginning of 'Bereshit' is read on the sabbath or Simhat Torah.⁵ Below is the list of texts, including the 'theme-verse' or *nosé*, the year in which the sermon was first delivered, the location within the five volumes of manuscripts (volume and folio number of the first page), the years in which

---

² For more detailed discussion of Morteira's sermons and his relationship to the congregation of immigrants from Portugal, see Saperstein, *Exile in Amsterdam*, esp. chs. 5, 6.

³ Saul Levi Morteira, *Givat sha'ul: ḥamishim derushim yekarim* [sermons] (Amsterdam, 1645; repr. Warsaw, 1912). Since this contains one sermon on each *parashah*, the only sermon on 'Bereshit' that was ever printed was the one on Gen. 1: 10, delivered in 1633 and again in 1639.

⁴ A comparison might be made with Samuel Saul Siriro in Fez, who left texts of 33 different sermons for Shabat Hagadol (the sabbath preceding Passover), dating from the years 1599 to 1630 (see Samuel Saul Siriro, *Derushei maharshash siriro* [sermons], ed. David Ovadiyah, 2 vols. [Jerusalem, 1989–91]).

⁵ When the sermon on Gen. 1: 6 was delivered in 1624, the *ḥatan bereshit* was Michael Espinosa, who would later become the father of Baruch Spinoza (Morteira, Sermons [Heb.], iii, fo. 317). Spinoza eventually repudiated the entire world-view that undergirded his teacher's homiletical oeuvre.

the sermon was reused, and the title Morteira gave to it:

Theme-verse	First delivered	Location in MS	Reused	Original title
Gen. 1: 2	1620	iii, fo. 1ʳ	1627, 1650	ברא בראש (Ezek. 21: 24)
Gen. 1: 3	1621	iii, fo. 87ʳ	1629, 1653	תורה אור (Prov. 6: 23)
Gen. 1: 4	1622	iii, fo. 167ʳ	1636, 1648	להבדיל בין היום (Gen. 1: 14)
Gen. 1: 5	1623	iii, fo. 243ʳ	1649	בשם יקרא (Isa. 40: 26)
Gen. 1: 6	1624	iii, fo. 316ʳ	1628	יקרא אל השמים (Ps. 50: 4)
Gen. 1: 7	1630	ii, fo. 140ʳ	1655	מעשה האלקים (Eccles. 7: 13)
Gen. 1: 8	1631	ii, fo. 206ʳ	1656	כי טוב (Gen. 1: 4)
Gen. 1: 9	1632	v, fo. 9ʳ	1638	יקוו המים (Gen. 1: 9)
Gen. 1: 10	1633	v, fo. 5ʳ	1639	אשר נקבו בשמות (Num. 1: 17)
Gen. 1: 11	1634	v, fo. 1ʳ		נפש חיה למינה (Gen. 1: 24)
Gen. 1: 12	1635	v, fo. 3ʳ		ארורה הארץ בעבורך (Gen. 3: 17)
Gen. 1: 15	1642?	v, fo. 7ʳ		להאיר על הארץ (Gen. 1: 15)
Gen. 1: 16	n.d.	v, fo. 11ʳ		מעודד ענוים (Ps. 147: 6)

From this list, we can see a clear pattern of how Morteira worked. He began his fixed responsibilities as a preacher for the Beth Jacob congregation, delivering a sermon on each sabbath, in 1619; his first sermon on 'Bereshit', for which the theme-verse was Genesis 1: 1, was delivered in the autumn of that year. The manuscript of this sermon is not extant, but the Table of Sermons in the Amsterdam 1645 edition of *Givat sha'ul* informs us that its central subject was why the first letter of the Torah is *beit* rather than *alef*. For the following five years (1620–24) Morteira moved systematically through the next five verses of Genesis 1. The sermon on the following verse, however, was not delivered until the autumn of 1630. There is no information about what he did in the years 1625 and 1626, though the sermon on Genesis 1: 1 may have been repeated in one of those years. Sermons were repeated in the late 1620s: on Genesis 1: 2 in 1627, on Genesis 1: 6 in 1628, and on Genesis 1: 3 in 1629. The regular pattern was then resumed for at least six years, from 1630 to 1635. In 1636, 1638, and 1639, earlier sermons were repeated, and the regular progression apparently began again in 1642. There is thus a pattern of systematic progression through the lesson interrupted by the occasional repetition of previous sermons.[6]

[6] On reasons for the decision to repeat sermons on occasion, see Saperstein, *Exile in Amsterdam*, 68–70.

For a preacher addressing the same congregation over a period of years, the individual sermon is different from most literary texts. On the one hand, each sermon is a self-contained unit, with its own structure and conceptual integrity. The text of the sermon, accessible for analysis long after it was delivered, is not analogous to the chapter in a philosophical book, where we expect total coherence and consistency with what precedes and succeeds it. Particularly with sermons delivered over a period of more than two decades, as is the case with those here, it should not be surprising that preachers may change their emphasis, or even their minds, on a particular exegetical or doctrinal issue.

At the same time, the individual sermon is an integral part of a larger corpus of communication by the preacher to a community of listeners. Over the years, this community changes: individuals grow old and die, newcomers arrive from other locations, children become mature enough to pay attention and process what is being said from the pulpit. This gradual change in the constituency of the congregation is one of the justifications for repeating a sermon after several years. Yet the majority of listeners from one week to the next and from one year to the next will be the same. The preacher therefore ascends the pulpit with the expectation that the listeners will remember something of what he has said in previous weeks and even in previous years: the new discourse will often build upon what has been said in the past.

Virtually every sermon by Morteira after the first few years was full of references to sermons he had delivered earlier. Sometimes these references came at the beginning; more often they came in the middle of the discussion: reminding the listeners of a previous sermon, summarizing the relevant content of that sermon, and then proceeding to develop a new point. These cross-references made the sermons like short stories by the same author involving many of the same characters: each one was complete in itself, yet each one was related to the others. The cumulative effect, as noted above, was as an ongoing programme of adult education, communicating and mediating a tradition to a congregation of listeners who knew they wanted to be Jews but knew very little about what the Jewish tradition entailed.

Yet they were not like the lectures in a university course, where each one built on what preceded it. Here the relationship of Jewish preaching to its biblical foundations contrasted with that in the Christian community. There were Christian preachers who proceeded systematically through a section of Scripture, constructing a homily on each successive verse. (An especially impressive example, not so far removed in time from Morteira, is

John Calvin's sermons on the book of Deuteronomy, delivered almost daily in 1555. Some of these began with the phrase, 'Yesterday we discussed . . .'.[7]) For the Christian audience, the continuity was obvious. For the Jewish audience, an entire year elapsed between the sermon on one verse and that on the following verse, a year in which a range of totally different topics had been addressed. Under these circumstances, the need for recapitulation and reminder becomes greater, and Morteira sometimes articulated this problem explicitly.[8]

On the other hand, the assumption that listeners will remember at least something of the sermons from the past presents a different kind of challenge to the preacher moving from verse to verse on a common topic: the need to find something new to say. Occasionally this too is explained by Morteira. In an earlier discussion of his sermons, I cited a lengthy passage in which he recapitulated the content of eleven previous sermons on the lesson 'Ḥayei sarah', in order to highlight the difficulty in finding something new to say about the subject of death and burial.[9] Here I will cite a similar passage, focusing on the first chapter of Genesis. It served as the entire introduction to the sermon on Genesis 1: 16—'God made the two great luminaries, the greater luminary to dominate the day and the lesser luminary to dominate the night, and the stars'—the latest of the sermons preserved in the manuscript, delivered in the 1640s:

I am not unaware that the listeners will be surprised at our taking for the text today our opening rabbinic dictum, the content of which focuses on the end of the verse, 'and the stars', even though the verse is filled with exalted matters and themes befitting the greatness of the subjects it speaks about, namely, 'the two great luminaries'. However, after the listeners become aware that we have already spoken and preached about every component of this verse in other places, the surprise will be abated. For first, the word 'made', beginning this verse: this raises a serious question before us . . . . However, we have investigated this matter thoroughly in connection with the first time the verb 'made' comes before us in the account of Creation, namely, 'God made the expanse' [Gen. 1: 7], about which the sages said . . . . And even though the

---

[7] See e.g. John Calvin, *Sermons on the Ten Commandments*, ed. and trans. Benjamin W. Farley (Grand Rapids, 1980), 115, 203. This is analogous to the introductory recaps in television series—'previously on *The West Wing* . . .'—which remind past viewers of what they have seen and provide new viewers with enough information to follow the programme.

[8] See Saperstein, *Exile in Amsterdam*, 79–80.

[9] Marc Saperstein, 'The Manuscript/s of Morteira's Sermons', in Joseph Dan and Klaus Herrmann (eds.), *Studies in Jewish Manuscripts* (Tübingen, 1999), 191–4; id., *Exile in Amsterdam*, 59–61.

commentators have understood this rabbinic statement in different ways, in that sermon I showed with clear proofs that . . . . There is thus no reason to return to this topic.

And if we thought of making our subject the formulation, 'the greater luminary to dominate the day and the lesser luminary to dominate the night', which would seem to imply that 'day' and 'night' are entities that exist independently of light and darkness, raising problems with the verse, 'God called the light Day and the darkness He called Night' [Gen. 1: 8], which implies that the entities are the same [i.e. day *is* light with a new name given by God]—why, we have already addressed this in connection with the verse that comes at the beginning of this section, 'God said, "Let there be luminaries in the heavenly expanse to separate day from night"' [Gen. 1: 14].

And if we wanted to investigate this dominance that belongs to the luminaries mentioned in the verse—how far does it reach, and whether the perfect human being or the luminaries is superior—why, we have already addressed this in connection with the preceding verse, 'They shall serve as luminaries in the heavenly expanse to shine upon the earth' [Gen. 1: 15], concluding that they should be compared to a candelabrum in a palace intended to provide light for those who dwell there. We further investigated all the arguments used by those who oppose this truth.

And if we wanted to investigate and explain the contradiction in this verse, in that it first says 'the two great luminaries', and then goes on to mention, 'the greater luminary . . . and the lesser luminary', and in this context it is appropriate to explain the famous and stunning rabbinic statement . . . . Why, we have already substantially addressed this matter [in a sermon] on the lection 'Aḥarei mot', on the verse, 'and the goat designated by lot for Azazel shall be left standing alive before the Eternal, to make expiation with it' [Lev. 16: 10].

If so, the only opportunity left for us is that which the sages opened for us in our dictum: the moral lesson derived from the stars accompanying the moon to teach us about the quality of humility. But how did they see this lesson, what possessed them to derive it from this verse, and what is the meaning of the three parables they brought? This will be our discourse today, as it pertains to our biblical text. We shall begin it with the help of God, 'Who guides the humble in the right path, and teaches the humble His way' [Ps. 25: 9].[10]

This introduction performs several functions for the preacher. At the outset, he flatters the listeners by a comment that presumes they are alert and attentive enough to react with surprise at his choice of a rabbinic dictum pertaining to a relatively inconsequential phrase in the theme-verse to open the sermon. Furthermore, he expresses solidarity with them by stating that he is

[10] Morteira, Sermons (Heb.), v, fo. 11ʳ (on Gen. 1: 16).

aware of and understands their surprise, even if it is based on an imperfect recollection of previous sermons. Much of the ensuing passage sets up the same topos as does the longer passage from the sermon on 'Ḥayei sarah': the preacher's difficulty in finding something new to say about biblical material that he has already discussed in many previous sermons and the triumph of overcoming this challenge and uncovering an appropriate and novel topic. Perhaps the most important function of the review of sermons on this *parashah* from previous years is to provide the listeners with just enough information to recall what was said before and to establish a background of several issues pertaining to Creation in general and the heavenly bodies in particular before moving on to the topic for the day.

Because of the nature of the genre and the temperament of the preacher, I will not attempt to reconstruct a systematic doctrine of Creation from Morteira's sermons: he was not a systematic philosopher; even less was he an adept at kabbalah. Rather, I will discuss passages where he addresses controversial issues relating to Creation in order to elucidate where he stands in the spectrum of Jewish thinkers (especially Maimonides), what he considered important to communicate to this congregation that was constantly learning about such issues, and how he employed a preacher's typical rhetorical tools—especially analogies from everyday life—to illustrate some of the abstract points in a vivid manner.

Controversies

No Mention of the Spiritual Realm

Morteira began his second sermon on the *parashah*, delivered in the autumn of 1620, with an ongoing issue in Jewish–Christian polemical literature. The Christians (identified as 'those who hate us' or 'our enemies') constantly asked why there was no mention of spiritual reward for the soul in the Torah, but only physical, this-worldly rewards, 'as if this Torah that Moses placed before the people of Israel was inadequate to provide them with this bliss until another Torah came in its place'.[11] Morteira reminded his listeners that he had already provided several cogent answers to this question in a sermon on the Torah portion 'Ekev'.[12] In the later sermon, he turned the tables by

---

[11] Cf. Joseph Albo, *Sefer ha'ikarim* [Book of Principles], 3: 25 (ed. Isaac Husik, 4 vols. in 5 [Philadelphia, 1930], iv. 40); Isaac Abravanel, *Perush al hatorah* [Commentary on the Torah], 3 vols. (Jerusalem, 1964), ii, 'Leviticus', 162a–166b, question 1 on 'Beḥukotai' and seven answers provided.

[12] This sermon, on Deut. 7: 12, the first verse of the *parashah*, delivered a few months earlier in the summer of 1620, is not extant in the manuscripts. The description at the end of the 1645 edition of

asking the Christians a different though analogous question: 'In the account of the Creation of the world, which our Torah narrates in today's lesson, why do we not find the creation of the spiritual realm and the angels?'

Christians and Jews all agreed that this spiritual realm existed, and that it existed before the creation of the physical universe, yet there is no explicit mention of it in Genesis 1. Thus the Christians must recognize that the Torah's failure to mention the spiritual realm is no proof that the Torah does not recognize such a realm, which it does mention explicitly many times in other contexts. Their use of the question about the absence of spiritual rewards in the Torah is therefore a sign not of ignorance and stupidity but of 'malice and malevolence'. For they must recognize that 'just as the Torah did not mention the creation of the world to come and the angels despite their being true . . . for a reason known to God's wisdom, so it did not mention the spiritual reward despite its being true and enduring and achieved by means of the Torah'.[13] The rest of the sermon is devoted to explicating the hints and allusions to all the other entities that had already been brought into existence by God before the account of Creation in Genesis 1 begins.

God's Continuing Influence on the World

The relationship between God and the created world was an ongoing subject of philosophical speculation. Does the world depend for its continued existence upon God's uninterrupted attention and sustenance, without which it would quickly, even immediately, cease to exist, or does it endure naturally, subject to physical laws comprehensible to human intellect, barring a special decision by God to destroy it? Maimonides' position on the issue of the world's continued existence was not entirely clear, and there is no consensus among scholars about it.[14] Morteira by contrast, was unambiguous.

He addressed this issue in a sermon on Genesis 1: 7 delivered in 1630. As this verse contains the first appearance in the Bible of the verb 'made'

Givat sha'ul states that it 'explained what all the commentators responded . . . then gave two additional new answers, then raised a problem that applies to all of them, and resolved it in different ways'. This sermon undoubtedly drew on the discussion by Abravanel cited in n. 11.

[13] Morteira, Sermons (Heb.), iii, fo. 1ʳ (on Gen. 1: 2).

[14] Kenneth Seeskin recently reviewed the antithetical positions taken by Seymour Feldman—holding that Maimonides taught that the world would wind down and cease to be without God's will to keep it in existence—and Roslyn Weiss—the world will continue permanently barring a miraculous intervention from God (Seeskin, *Maimonides on the Origin of the World* [Cambridge, 2005], ch. 6; see S. Feldman, 'The End of the Universe in Medieval Jewish Philosophy', *AJS Review*, 11 [1986], 53–77; R. Weiss, 'Maimonides on the End of the World', *Maimonidean Studies*, 3 [1992–3], 195–218).

(*vaya'as*), it provided an occasion for him to discuss divine agency (note the reference to this in the passage cited above). He begins with a rabbinic dictum, in which Ben Zoma asks how this verb is consistent with the biblical assertion that God brought these beings into existence through his word. After reviewing various discussions of Ben Zoma's statement, including Rashi, Nahmanides (Moses ben Nahman, Ramban), Abravanel, Abraham Bibago, and Samuel Jaffe (in *Yefeh to'ar*), he asserts his own view: Ben Zoma was teaching that there are two different kinds of agent. The first is represented by the builder or weaver: after their work is completed, they may depart, travel far away, or die, yet the product of their work remains unaffected until its material wears out. The second is the agent that must always be connected with the activity. An example is the lamp that illuminates a house: as soon as the lamp is removed, the light will be gone.

Which of these is the proper analogy for God's relationship with the world? Morteira insists that it is the second:

When God performs His activities, He never abandons them. If we could imagine that He would abandon them even for the briefest moment, all would immediately return to nothingness, to chaos. For the Creation that removed darkness from the world and made privation vanish is light, and the source of light must always be present, for without it darkness will return. That is why Scripture states: 'For with You is the source of light, through Your light we may see light' [Ps. 36: 10].[15]

Two years later, Morteira briefly recapitulated this theme in his sermon on Genesis 1: 9, adding two vivid illustrations of the point. Here the context is a discussion of 'individual providence'.

We must understand from this that God does not remove His providence or turn His eyes away from the earth. It is not like one who builds a house and then leaves it and goes on his way without ever paying any further attention to anything pertaining to the house. Rather, it is like one who has made a large glass sphere and suspends it from his hand; knowing that whenever it touches something it may break, he watches

---

[15] Morteira, Sermons (Heb.), ii, fo. 140ʳ (on Gen. 1: 7). The position taken by Morteira is similar to that of Thomas Aquinas, who held that 'creatures are kept in existence by God', whose role is not just like that of someone watching over a child lest it fall into a fire; rather, humans are like something 'so dependent that without the preserver it could not exist. This is the way that all creatures need God to keep them in existence. For the *esse* of all creaturely beings so depends upon God that they could not continue to exist even for a moment, but would fall away into nothingness unless they were sustained in existence by his power, as Gregory puts it.' Aquinas too uses the analogy of light: 'Every creature stands in relation to God as the air to the light of the sun' (Thomas Aquinas, *Summa theologica*, 1.104.1 [trans. Fathers of the English Dominican Province, 3 vols. (New York, 1947)]).

it constantly, lest it touch something and break. Or it is like a ship that has ruptured beneath the water line, so that large quantities of water are entering it. In order to prevent it from sinking, the sailors need to pump out the water through a pipe, never desisting from their labour. So with God, suspending the earth on the waters: it remains in place miraculously, and God's providence is always bound up with it.[16]

The first illustration is rather intriguing. The purpose of such illustrations is to explain the abstract in terms of something familiar, and the formulation seems to allude to a phenomenon known to the listeners, something that most in the audience would have recognized immediately, though it is obscure to us today. What would someone be doing walking around with a large glass sphere[17] suspended from his hand, trying to keep it from being shattered through contact with hard objects in the environment? How would that reflect the experience of the listeners?

It is not that glass spheres were entirely unknown at the time. In one of Vermeer's paintings, *The Allegory of the Faith*, a glass sphere, representing the divine world, is suspended over a woman, reflecting the rest of the room. But the painting dates from around 1670, decades after the sermon was delivered, and it is a symbolic image, not actually made and transported by a person. More to the point, perhaps, was the glass sphere used in the seventeenth century to generate electricity? There is a picture of the German engineer Otto von Guericke holding a sphere on an iron axle, which was intended to generate electricity. His first generator, created in about 1663, used a 'large sulphur ball cast inside a glass globe, mounted on a shaft'.[18] But this also was too late for Morteira's allusion. Like many allusions to contemporary ephemera, the precise resonance remains to be deciphered.

The second illustration is more straightforward, pertaining to the experiences of a community largely bound up with commerce on the seas. The sermon to which it belongs is devoted to the theological significance of the water mentioned in its theme-verse, which will be examined in greater detail below. What is striking about it is the implication of precariousness and peril for the world in which we live. In the first analogy, the most that can be lost is an

---

[16] Morteira, Sermons (Heb.), v, fo. 9ᵛ (on Gen. 1: 9).

[17] Or possibly a 'crystal ball'. This is a conceivable, though not very plausible, rendering of *kadur gadol mezekhukhit*. The crystal ball was used by the English medium (or charlatan) Edward Kelley, who had an impact on the celebrated Elizabethan John Dee, but it is unlikely that this image would have been vivid enough to Portuguese Jews in Amsterdam more than four decades later to make the analogy work.

[18] For the description and the picture, see <http://www.hp-gramatke.net/history/english/page4000.htm> (accessed 16 May 2014).

implement that can be replaced; here, the sinking of the ship endangers the lives of all on board. Furthermore, in this second analogy it is not just the need to exercise constant care against some danger in the environment. That would be like maintaining a constant watch over dikes to make sure that no water inundated cultivated land. The image of the world as a ship that has already been ruptured, into which the deadly water is already flowing, requiring not just vigilance but a continuous effort to keep it afloat, suggesting that any lapse of divine energy would allow the land to sink into the sea, is indeed both startling and disturbing.

In the sermon from 1630, Morteira took the principle that all creatures depend upon God's influence for their continued existence, for without it they would return to nothingness, and he applied it to the moral realm of reward and punishment. When it comes not to general existence but to specific actions that are matters of choice, a different calculus is in effect:

Although the existence of all creatures is contingent, such that if God removed His influence from them for one moment they would be destroyed, and it is within God's power to do so, nevertheless with regard to the righteous, it is impossible [*i-efshar*] for Him to do so. Just as it is impossible for God to sin—for it falls into the category of that which is [logically] impossible [*kat hanimna'ot*] that there be any perversion in the One Who is the Most Just of All—so it is impossible to reduce to nothingness one who has freely chosen to serve God and has earned merit in God's sight.

In this way, the righteous have a truer existence than the highest of spiritual beings, whose existence is a matter of divine grace, and there would be no perversion of justice if they were returned to their original state of nothingness. The existence of the righteous, however, is a matter of right; his annihilation would be contrary to elemental fairness.[19]

After taking a strong position on the contingent nature of all creation and its dependence upon God's constant supervision and protection for its continued existence, Morteira introduces a radical exception. God's capacity to reduce the world to primordial chaos, indeed to nothingness, is limited by God's justice. It would be no violation of this principle for God to terminate the existence of even the highest angels, all of whom serve at his pleasure and exist at his will,[20] but for righteous human beings who choose freely to serve

[19] Morteira, Sermons (Heb.), ii, fo. 140ᵛ (on Gen. 1: 7).

[20] Here too we might compare Aquinas: '*Esse* does follow per se upon form, but provided that God's causality is present, even as light results from the transparency of the atmosphere provided the sun shines. The possibility of their non-existence for spiritual beings and the heavenly bodies resides in God, who can withhold his causality, rather than in the form or matter of these creatures' (Aquinas, *Summa theologica*, 1.104.1).

God, such arbitrary annihilation would be an impossible perversion of divine justice.

Diversity from Unity

The question of how a First Cause that is the Absolute One engenders the stunning diversity of the world remained a constant challenge for medieval thinkers. It is, of course, related to the parallel question of how a material world could be engendered by a totally immaterial being, or indeed how matter can be created *ex nihilo*. Joseph Albo, whose *Sefer ha'ikarim* (Book of Principles) was frequently cited by Morteira in his sermons, formulated the problem as follows: 'Since plurality in existing things is perceived both by our intellect and by our senses, we must show how plurality can arise from the First Cause, which is one and of absolute simplicity.'[21]

In his 1635 sermon on Genesis 1: 12—'The earth brought forth vegetation, seed-bearing flora of every kind and trees of every kind'—a verse emphasizing the diversity within the sublunar realm, Morteira reviewed several solutions to the conundrum. He informed his listeners that his discussion was based on Jaffe's massive commentary on *Midrash Rabbah*, *Yefeh to'ar*.[22] a work that Morteira used extensively and praised for its value in bringing together many relevant sources. The first solution he mentions is that diversity is the result of varying kinds of underlying matter:

In accordance with the [quality of the] matter, the Simple Being effects in it changes and differences, just as fire congeals salt and melts wax, though it is the same essence.[23]

This view is null and void; it is not consistent with our Torah, but rather it is based on the premises of the pagan philosophers, or more precisely, some of them who believed in a primordial matter in which different qualities were contained, for without this premise, the explanation cannot work.[24]

The second solution is that diversity results from the intermediaries between God and the world, which were produced as a result of the emanation of supernal beings one from the other.

---

[21] Albo, *Sefer ha'ikarim*, 2: 11 (ed. Husik, ii. 59).

[22] Samuel ben Isaac Jaffe, *Yefeh to'ar* [commentary on *Midrash Rabbah*], 9 vols. (Jerusalem, 1989), i. 17*a*. The work was published in Venice between 1597 and 1608, and Morteira must have owned a copy (see Meir Benayahu, 'Rabbi Samuel Jaffe Ashkenazi' [Heb.], *Tarbiz*, 52 [1973], 419–60).

[23] Cf. Moses Maimonides, *Guide for the Perplexed*, 1: 53 (trans. and ed. M. Friedländer, 3 vols. in 1 [New York, 1946], i. 187).   [24] Morteira, Sermons (Heb.), v, fo. 3ʳ (on Gen. 1: 12 [1635]).

They said that God, who is One Simple Being, while cognizing Himself emanated a simple Intellect, and this simple Intellect in cognizing its Cause emanated another simple Intellect, and in cognizing itself—knowing that it is a simple Intellect—emanated the soul of the sphere, and in cognizing itself—knowing that it is caused and receives emanation from another source and that it is a lower level of being—emanated the matter of the sphere, which is even lower, and in this manner all of the existent beings emerged, finally reaching this lowly matter.[25]

Now in addition to this view entailing various serious difficulties, it is based on [the premise of] necessity, for—according to the philosophers—these cognitions and emanations occur out of necessity. This is not where we stand, we who follow God's Torah, which teaches [true] knowledge to human beings: that God created the world through His simple will, as He desired.[26]

When we compare the formulation of these two explanations with *Yefeh to'ar*, we see that Morteira did not mechanically reproduce his source. His account is drastically condensed, streamlined, and simplified. Jaffe identified the first position—that diversity results from different kinds of matter—as the doctrine of Plato, as explained in Averroës' *Incoherence of the Incoherence*. He then discussed a passage from Maimonides' *Guide for the Perplexed* (1: 53, on how fire congeals salt and melts wax), as interpreted by Shem Tov ibn Shem Tov, and defended Maimonides against the suggestion that he believed in primordial matter. Jaffe identified the second position as that of Avicenna (Ibn Sina). It may be understood to mean that emanation occurs through necessity, as argued by Aristotle. He explained that Maimonides, however, showed in *Guide for the Perplexed*, 2: 22 that emanation is consistent with the doctrine of Creation and that the same view was held by Joseph Albo in *Sefer ha'ikarim*, 2: 2. Morteira avoided all this complexity: in the second case, he ignores Maimonides' attempt to reconcile emanation with divine will and quickly dismisses it as a doctrine based on necessity, unworthy of serious consideration.

The third position, which he described as the correct one, denies the very legitimacy of the question, for the doctrine that from one agent there can be derived only one action applies to a natural or material agent, which affects something else from its own essence.[27] However, God, who is wise, willing, and able, is not limited regarding what he can do in heaven and on earth.

---

[25] This formulation is quite close to Albo's (*Sefer ha'ikarim*, 2: 11 [ed. Husik, ii. 60–1]; see Harry Austryn Wolfson, *The Philosophy of Spinoza: Unfolding the Latent Processes of His Reasoning*, 2 vols. [Cambridge, Mass., 1934; repr. New York, 1958], i. 218–19).

[26] Morteira, Sermons (Heb.), v, fo. 3ʳ (on Gen. 1: 12).

[27] Cf. Albo, *Sefer ha'ikarim*, 2: 2 (ed. Husik, ii. 12). Examples of this kind of 'natural agent' are fire, which heats (but cannot cool), and snow, which cools (but cannot heat).

Once again, the discussion in *Yefeh to'ar* is far more extensive and complex. Jaffe identified this position with Averroës (Ibn Rushd), and integrated into his discussion several passages by Maimonides and his commentator, Shem Tov ibn Shem Tov, including the statement that, unlike other agents who use instruments (*kelim*) as an aid to actualize the intended variety of effects, 'God does not need instruments, but He can certainly always effect even antithetical results by His will, since all have a single ultimate purpose', namely, either to preserve the existence of Creation or to benefit human beings.

After extensive discussion of the intricacies of this doctrine, Jaffe concluded:

> Not all the positions mentioned are capable of being justified by the divine Torah. It goes without saying that this applies to the position of Aristotle, based on the doctrine of necessity, for with this the entire Torah collapses, as is well known. With regard to Plato, although one [who follows him] is not called a total heretic, still this view is impossible for any believer, for our faith is in absolute Creation. This position must not be attributed to any of the sages.[28]

The other doctrines, that of Avicenna, as construed by Maimonides, and the two versions of the doctrine of Averroës, can be said to be consistent with Torah.

Here too, Morteira simplified and popularized for his listeners:

> This is the correct truth taught by the Torah and by the sages, namely, that in the Creation all was done entirely by God, Who did not act through intermediaries. As for the secondary causes, they were made by God subsequently so that through them the work of Creation would endure permanently . . . . This is the Torah truth. It has been confirmed by Rabbi Isaac Abravanel, first in his comment on the verse 'Let the waters be gathered' [Gen. 1: 9]. . . . Thus from all this it remains for us to agree that the multitude of created beings with their diversity were all created by one God, without the intermediaries that He used later on to perpetuate them.[29]

Morteira ended this part of his sermon with a reference to a body of Jewish doctrine that many listeners must have known existed, though the number of experts in the congregation would have been quite limited. How does the kabbalistic doctrine of the *sefirot* relate to Morteira's insistence that Creation, including all of the diversity of created beings, derived directly from God without intermediary implements?

---

[28] Jaffe, *Yefeh to'ar*, i. 17*a–b*.   [29] Morteira, Sermons (Heb.), v, fo. 3^{r-v} (on Gen. 1: 12).

Now if the adepts of the kabbalah have said that the *sefirot* are vessels for the creation of the world,[30] they called these *sefirot* 'radiated'[31] and not distinct from God, derived from Him as a flame is bound up with a burning coal,[32] like a man who works with his fingers,[33] so that all that was accomplished through them can be called God's work. As for me, I do not delve into esoteric doctrine [*ein li esek banistarot*] but I do agree with what is true and enduring: the statement of the prophet Isaiah, 'I, the Eternal, do it all' [Isa. 45: 7].[34]

Kabbalah, of course, had its own problems with the origins of diversity. Unlike the philosophers' problem, this extended not just to the realm of Creation but also to the very Godhead. Morteira's brief allusion shows that he was aware of this expression of Jewish spirituality and (unlike his purported mentor Leon Modena) not unsympathetic to it,[35] but it is not a topic he will discuss.

---

[30] Here Morteira states one side of the classical kabbalistic debate about the nature of the *sefirot*: whether they were identical with God's essence or ontologically distinct vessels or implements (*kelim*) (see Gershom Scholem, *Kabbalah* [Jerusalem, 1974], 101–5; Hava Tirosh-Rothschild, 'Sefirot as the Essence of God in the Writings of David Messer Leon', *AJS Review*, 7–8 [1983], 409–25).

[31] I use 'radiated' as a translation of *me'utsalim* to distinguish it from *mushpa'im*, which Morteira used in the context of the philosophical doctrine. For a discussion of the various forms from the root א-צ-ל, see Nahmanides on Num. 11: 17; Gershom Scholem, *The Origins of the Kabbalah*, ed. R. J. Zwi Werblowsky (Princeton, 1990), 447–8.

[32] A common image, originating in *Sefer yetsirah* [kabbalah] (Mantua, 1563), 1: 7.

[33] The fingers were commonly used in kabbalah as a symbol of the *sefirot* (*Sefer yetsirah* 1: 3; *Sefer habahir* [kabbalah] [Jerusalem, 1951], 1: §124; Abraham Herrera, in Gershom Scholem, *On the Mystical Shape of the Godhead: Basic Concepts in the Kabbalah* [New York, 1991], 40). It is not clear to me whether this symbol was used in kabbalistic accounts of the Creation or whether it was merely Morteira's analogy to explain the difference between the *sefirot* and intermediary instruments. Compare the philosophical-allegorical interpretation of God's fingers in Marc Saperstein, *Decoding the Rabbis: A Thirteenth-Century Commentary on the Aggadah* (Cambridge, Mass., 1980), 54. In a different sermon, Morteira referred to God's 'fingers, which are the channels that the sages of truth called *sefirot*, within which God emanates His providence'. He then proceeded to discuss each one in turn and what comes into the world through it, so that the ten *sefirot* actually provide a ten-part structure to the body of the sermon (Morteira, Sermons [Heb.], ii, fo. 73ᵛ [on Gen. 28: 16]). This wedding sermon contains Morteira's most extensive use of kabbalistic material.

[34] Morteira, Sermons (Heb.), v, fo. 3ʳ (on Gen. 1: 12). For the background of 'I do not delve into esoteric doctrine', see BT Ḥag. 13a; Maimonides, *Guide for the Perplexed*, 1: 32 (trans. and ed. M. Friedländer, i. 111–14).

[35] For fairly sympathetic references to kabbalah, including a eulogy delivered at the news of the death of Hayim Vital and Menahem Azariah of Fano in 1620, see Saperstein, *Exile in Amsterdam*, 93–6. However, Alexander Altmann has shown that in the context of the 1635 controversy over the eternality of punishment, his attitude towards kabbalah appears to have become more critical (Altmann, 'Eternality of Punishment: A Theological Controversy Within the Amsterdam Rabbinate in the Thirties of the Seventeenth Century', *Proceedings of the American Academy of Jewish Research*, 40 [1973], 11).

Humanity as the Purpose of Creation

The most sustained polemic comes in the sermon on Genesis 1: 15 pertaining to the heavenly luminaries: 'They shall serve as lights in the expanse of the sky to shine upon the earth.' The crucial exegetical-conceptual question is the relationship between these heavenly bodies and the sublunar realm. Does Scripture teach, as one reading suggests, that the sun, moon, and stars were created in order to serve a function on earth, which is the centre of Creation, with human beings as its ultimate purpose? Or do they function in their own higher realm, with the illumination provided for the earth merely one of their by-products? In the *Guide for the Perplexed*, Maimonides strongly repudiated the anthropocentric understanding of Creation, as part of a general attack against a teleology of Creation.[36] Without naming his daunting intellectual opponent or the passage which he was attempting to rebut, referring merely to a collective group of 'those who deny' the truth he espoused, Morteira proceeded to outline for his listeners a systematic rebuttal of Maimonides' discussion. His presentation isolated four separate arguments in the *Guide for the Perplexed*, providing an order to the passage that is not always apparent in the source.

The first argument focused on the theme-verse of the sermon, citing Maimonides' interpretation of it:

They said first that the verse 'They shall serve as lights in the expanse of the sky to shine upon the earth' does not mean to imply that this is the purpose of their creation. Rather the verse is intended to inform us about the nature of the heavenly luminaries, which God desired to create in such a manner that they would shine and dominate [the night and the day (Gen. 1: 16)]. [According to this view,] it is analogous to the Torah's saying with regard to the human being: 'Rule the fish of the sea' [Gen. 1: 28]. This does not mean that the human being was created for this purpose; it is only intended to inform us about the nature that God implanted within human beings.

Morteira then proceeded with his rebuttal:

Now it is indeed astonishing to compare two verses so fundamentally different. Indeed, 'Rule the fish of the sea' does refer to a special blessing that God gave to the

---

[36] Maimonides, *Guide for the Perplexed*, 3: 13 (trans. and ed. M. Friedländer, iii. 49–50); see Eliezer Goldman, 'On the Purpose of Existence in the *Guide for the Perplexed*' (Heb.), in Daniel Statman and Abraham Sagi (eds.), *Expositions and Enquiries: Jewish Thought in Past and Present* [Meḥkarim ve'iyunim: hagut yehudit ba'avar uvahoveh] (Jerusalem, 1996), 87–114; Dov Schwartz, 'Polemical and Esoteric Writing in the *Guide for the Perplexed*: The Subject of the Purpose of Existence' (Heb.), *Iyun*, 48 (1999), 129–46.

human or it is an utterance whereby God implanted this nature within the human. However, the 'to' in the infinitive 'to shine' is not like this. Its function is always synonymous with 'in order to', it invariably comes to express the purpose of something. The examples are innumerable; I do not know a single exception to this rule. 'I the Eternal am your God, Who brought you out of the land of Egypt to be [*liheyot*] your God' [Num. 15: 41], expressing the purpose of the Exodus. 'Make sacral vestments for your brother Aaron, for dignity and for adornment' [*lekhavod uletifaret*] [Exod. 28: 2], expressing the purpose of the vestments. . . . And similarly all such expressions. If the verse had said, 'Let Us make a human being in Our image . . . to rule [*liredot*] the fish of the sea', etc. that indeed would have been the true purpose. However, the phrases 'and they shall rule' or 'and rule' do not teach about the purpose. They are therefore different from 'to shine upon the earth', for that is truly the purpose.[37]

This is a clear, and—it must be confessed—rather powerful response to the scriptural argument used by Maimonides to repudiate the view that the heavenly luminaries were created for the sake of the sublunar realm. Morteira's grammatical analysis undermined the analogy made by Maimonides between Genesis 1: 15 and 1: 28. His claim that the initial *lamed* of *leha'ir* must signify purpose, as this is always its function in Hebrew, and that he does not know of any exception to this rule, must have impressed his listeners, as few would have been able to challenge him on the spot.[38]

The discussion continued with a second argument from the same chapter of the *Guide for the Perplexed*, introduced with the phrase: 'They said further. . .'. Maimonides noted a psychologically driven fallacy in human reasoning whereby the recipient of a favour concludes erroneously that the benefactor exists in order to bestow that favour. As Morteira expressed it:

Thus a certain subject of a kingdom might think that the purpose of the king is to protect his house from thieves in the night. This is true in a sense, for since the house is protected and he receives this benefit from the king, it seems as if the purpose of the king is to provide protection for the man's house. This is how we should interpret every verse that appears superficially to indicate that a superior being was made for the sake of the inferior being: we must say the meaning is that this is a necessary consequence of the nature of the superior being.

---

[37] Morteira, Sermons (Heb.), v, fo. 7ʳ (on Gen. 1: 15).

[38] Note that the Vulgate of the verse renders the Hebrew infinitive of Gen. 1: 15 with an *ut* clause of purpose, and this is how Thomas Aquinas understood it: 'the luminous heavenly bodies render service to man by aiding sight . . . *ut luceant in firmamento et illuminent terram*' (Aquinas, *Summa theologica* 1.70.2).

Protection of the individual is, according to Maimonides, a natural result of the superior being's existence, but not its *raison d'être*. Again Morteira's rebuttal was based on the assertion of a false analogy:

The following would be a proper analogy: If when the king was crowned, they said to him as a condition of his coronation or wrote in the legal books of the kingdom, that the king was crowned in order to guard the house of a specific individual, then certainly the purpose of the coronation would have been this protection. That would be analogous to the verse that proclaims on the day of the creation of the heavenly luminaries and their characteristics, 'they shall serve as lights in the expanse of the sky to shine upon the earth'. It is obvious that the king should not be named or described by a characteristic that is incidental to him, but by what is essential to him. That is why God called these heavenly bodies from the outset 'luminaries' [*me'orot*], for this is their purpose, and no one enjoys their light except for the inhabitants of earth. If there were no inhabitants of earth to enjoy their light, God would not have called them 'luminaries'.[39]

Here too, Morteira's rebuttal was made with the incisiveness of the experienced debater. Not only did he assert that the analogy is inappropriate; he proceeded to illustrate exactly how it could have been correct—if the specific conditions of the king's coronation stated a function as clearly as God's articulation of the purpose of the heavenly luminaries. Second, the argument from the Hebrew name for the heavenly bodies (*me'orot*, derived from the word *or* meaning 'light') indicates—on the assumption that words used by God to designate created beings are not arbitrary but purposeful[40]—that their primary function is to provide light for the earth.

As he continued, Morteira picked up the motif of the king and provided an analogy of his own:

Even with regard to the definition of their [lofty] place it says that was for the sake of the earth, as we see in the verse 'God set them in the expanse of the sky to shine upon the earth' [Gen. 1: 17]. Now the repetition of this purpose seems superfluous, for it was already stated in the previous verse, and it would have been enough to say: 'God set them in the expanse of the sky' [and stop there]. But God repeated it in order to teach us this lesson: do not honour these important beings because of the loftiness of their place and say that they are superior to human beings because the humans dwells

---

[39] Morteira, Sermons (Heb.), v, fo. 7ʳ (on Gen. 1: 15).

[40] Morteira discussed various problems relating to the names specifically given by God to certain created entities (day, night, land, seas, heavens, man) (Sermons [Heb.], iii, fo. 243ʳ [on Gen. 1: 5]; succinctly recapitulated in Sermons [Heb.], v, 5ʳ [on Gen. 1: 10]; see also *Givat Sha'ul* [1645 edn.], 3a; [1912 edn.], 40). Here the issue is different, however, as it refers not to a name explicitly given by God but to the Hebrew word used by God in the process of Creation.

in the nether regions, while they are on high. The reason for their lofty place is only for the sake of the human being. Not only are they not superior to human beings because of their place, the only reason God gave them this place was because of human beings. For how could they shine upon human beings if they were not stationed on high in the expanse of the sky?

Would anyone bestow honour upon a large lamp or consider it to be especially distinguished because it was placed high on the ceiling of a palace? Would anyone say that it has a place of importance above that of the inhabitants of the palace? Certainly not! For it was placed there only for the benefit of the inhabitants of the palace, and it has this position only for their sake. That is the case with regard to the heavenly luminaries; that is why the Torah says: 'God set them in the expanse of the sky to shine upon the earth.'[41]

Reading this with the leisure to ponder the analogy with the palace lamp, one might well apply the same kind of analysis that led Morteira to reject the analogies given by Maimonides. There are obvious differences, for example, between the heavenly bodies—far more numerous, far larger, and far more permanent than human beings and the sublunar realm they inhabit—and lamps that depend on human beings to keep them operative.[42] Yet it is effective in speech and perhaps defensible in the limited sense that Morteira was using it, to repudiate what has been called the 'vertical metaphor': the prevalent assumption, reflected for example in the ladder in Jacob's dream or the 'great chain of being', that height is correlated with value and goodness.[43] In this limited sense, the analogy works: the loftiness of the heavenly bodies has no implications for their value; their elevated position is purely pragmatic, enabling them to serve their function more effectively.[44]

Morteira then proceeded to a third argument from the *Guide for the Perplexed*, although he still did not explicitly attribute it to Maimonides, but to

[41] Morteira, Sermons (Heb.), v, fo. 7^{r-v} (on Gen. 1: 15).

[42] On the issue of size, compare Maimonides' formulation: 'Consider how vast are the dimensions and how great the number of these corporeal beings [the heavenly bodies]. If the whole of the earth would not constitute even the smallest part of the sphere of the fixed stars, what is the relation of the human species to all these created things, and how can one of us imagine that they exist for his sake and because of him and that they are instruments for his benefit?' (Maimonides, *Guide for the Perplexed*, 3: 14 [trans. and ed. M. Friedländer, iii. 57]).

[43] I first heard a discussion of this 'vertical metaphor' in an address by Leon Wieseltier at Congregation Kesher Israel in Georgetown.

[44] Compare Jaffe's formulation: 'An analogy is the structure of a palace, where the lower parts are the foundation for the higher parts, which would not exist without what is below; so the heavens would not exist except for the earth, for it was for the sake of the earth and for its needs that the heavens were created' (Jaffe, *Yefeh to'ar*, i. 17c). While serving a somewhat different purpose, Morteira's analogy is more concrete and effective.

'those who deny this truth'. The assumption that the heavenly bodies were created for the sake of human beings leads to a question with two possible answers, neither of which is acceptable: could the Creator make human beings without the heavenly bodies? If so, they are superfluous; if not, this limits the power of God. The only escape from this dilemma is that the assumption is false, and the heavenly bodies were not created for the sake of human beings.

Not surprisingly, Morteira challenged the validity of the conundrum. The argument is based on analogy, not substance, he insisted. To understand the problem with the analogy, we must distinguish between 'prerequisites' (*hatsa'ot*) and 'adornments' (*tikunim*).[45]

> The dilemma applies to prerequisites, not to adornments. Examples of prerequisites are a saw and an axe for cutting trees to build a house. In this case, we may ask whether the builder could make the house without them or not. If we conclude that he could, then the tools were made for no purpose, and if we conclude that he could not, then his power is limited. By contrast, examples of adornments are the decorations of the house and its artistic embellishments. Regarding them, this question is out of place. If the house were made without them, it would not be beautiful and orderly, and it is impossible to make the house beautiful and orderly without the adornments, but this does not pertain at all to the power of the worker.
>
> This is substantially what is taught by our theme-verse: 'They shall serve as lights in the expanse of the sky to shine upon the earth.' In describing the creation of the heavenly luminaries, the Torah does not state at all that they served in the creation of the human being as a saw and an axe serve in the building of a house, as we explained. Then they would be instruments and means, and we could ask the aforementioned question that poses a severe problem no matter which alternative you take. However, the verse stated that the luminaries were [like] adornments for the house, so that the human being would not dwell on earth in darkness.[46]

Although the concrete examples of a saw and an axe helped the listeners to comprehend the distinction he was making; here too, leisurely analysis reveals the problems with Morteira's response. If the heavenly luminaries are merely 'adornments' for the human being, the implication is that human life would indeed be possible without the sun, that human beings and the

---

[45] *Hatsa'ot* is used by Ibn Tibbon in his translation of the *Guide for the Perplexed*; it is rendered 'previous creations' by Friedländer and 'preliminaries' by Pines; Alharizi's translation has *tikunim*, which would undermine the terminological distinction used by Morteira. Morteira seems to use *hatsa'ot* to mean 'necessary preliminaries' or 'prerequisites'. In discussing the passage, Goldman renders it *tena'im hekhrehiyim* ('On the Purpose of Existence in the *Guide of the Perplexed*' [Heb.], 181).

[46] Morteira, Sermons (Heb.), v, fo. 7ᵛ (on Gen. 1: 15).

vegetable realm on which they depend could survive in total darkness, and—what he leaves unsaid—without any source of heat.[47] Yet once again, limiting the discussion to the biblical verse, the foundation of the sermon, he was correct in asserting that the role of the heavenly luminaries is different from, let us say, the role of the dust in the creation of man and woman. His rather elegant response may lead to problems of its own, but it served its purpose of undermining the apparent cogency of Maimonides' argument.

Morteira followed Maimonides through yet another argument denying the teleology of Creation, an attempt to show that the anthropocentric view of Creation necessarily leads to a conclusion not of purpose but of divine will:

They further said: 'Let us assume for the sake of argument that the human being is the purpose of Creation.' We must then ask: 'What is the purpose of the human being?' Let us say that his purpose is to worship God. Then we must ask further: 'What is the purpose of worshipping God? If you are righteous, what do you give Him? If your transgressions are many, how do you affect Him?' [cf. Job 35: 6–7]. We must therefore reply: 'God has willed it so; God's wisdom has decreed it this way.' If so, what I have said at the end was said at the beginning when we asked: 'What is the purpose of the world?' and we said: 'God has willed it so.' And since ultimately we came to the same conclusion, it necessarily follows that the world has no final purpose.

Now the response to this is that God is the ultimate good, as the Bible says: 'The Eternal is good to all' [or 'in the entirety'] [Ps. 145: 9]. It is the product of His totally good will to cause His beneficence to emanate to all. If so, the ultimate purpose of the creation of the human being is that some of God's beneficence be emanated upon Him, for so long as no creatures existed, there was no one to receive the divine beneficence.[48]

At this point we shall leave Morteira's detailed effort to rebut Maimonides' repudiation of the anthropocentric view of Creation, which continued with a possible challenge to his response—since *all* creatures receive God's beneficence, why not conclude that all, not just human beings, were the purpose of Creation?—and his reply defending the uniqueness of human beings. Having followed the argument in some detail, it is time to reflect briefly on its larger context. It is indeed rather difficult today to take seriously

---

[47] This conclusion is stated explicitly by Arama in his discussion of *Guide for the Perplexed*, 3: 13: 'We believe that God was capable of creating the human being without the heavens and the stars, and without the plants and animals, but the existence of the human being would not then be so fine and praiseworthy as it is, and God wanted to make the human being as perfect and praiseworthy as possible' (Isaac Arama, *Akedat yitshak* [homiletical essays on the Torah], 3 vols. [Warsaw, 1882–4], *sha'ar* 18 [i. 101*a*]).   [48] Morteira, Sermons (Heb.), v, fo. 7ᵛ (on Gen. 1: 15).

the proposition that the entire universe was created for the sake of human beings: Maimonides' view seems so much more modern. This sermon was delivered when Spinoza was still a child, but it is not hard to imagine his response if he had heard it as a mature thinker. Indeed, he alluded to this view with considerable disdain in his *Ethics*: 'It is accepted as certain that God himself directs all things to a definite goal (for it is said that God makes all things for man, and man that he might worship him). . . . Nature has no particular goal in view, and . . . final causes are mere human figments.'[49] While this is certainly not the place to trace the intellectual history of anthropocentrism in Jewish thought, some background is necessary.

In Jewish philosophy, cosmological anthropocentrism is associated most famously with Sa'adyah Gaon. Eschewing the 'vertical metaphor' mentioned above, Sa'adyah's hierarchy within the realm of creation is based on what might be called a centre-periphery metaphor. The essential part of any organic body in nature is placed not at the top but in the centre. Assuming that the earth is the centre of the universe and that the human being is pre-eminent within the sublunar realm, Sa'adyah concluded that the human being is the ultimate purpose of Creation.[50]

Gersonides (Ralbag) described the question of 'whether the stars and planets are in the spheres for their own sake or for the benefit of the sublunar world' as 'very obscure and problematical'. Accepting the axioms that the superior being cannot exist for the sake of the inferior and that the sublunar realm is inferior to the heavenly realm, he nevertheless insisted, as did Morteira, that 'the luminosity and emission of light found amongst the stars and planets are for the benefit of the sublunar world', although their essences are for themselves.[51]

Isaac Arama expressed astonishment at Maimonides' attempt to rebut the teleology of the philosophers. If the philosophers who believed in the world's eternity nevertheless hold that it must have a purpose, how much more must 'we who believe in Creation' insist that there is a purpose for the world as a whole, if not for every individual detail of it. He concluded not only that 'the

---

[49] Benedict de Spinoza, *Ethics*, Pt. I, appendix, in *Philosophy of Benedict de Spinoza*, trans. R. H. M. Elwes (New York, 1933), 70–1, 73; cf. Wolfson, *The Philosophy of Spinoza*, i. 425–6.

[50] Sa'adyah Gaon, *Emunot vede'ot* [The Book of Beliefs and Opinions], bk. 4 (trans. Samuel Rosenblatt [New Haven,1948], 180–1); see Henry Malter, *Saadia Gaon: His Life and Works* (New York, 1921; repr. 1969), 212 n. 485; Simon Rawidowicz, 'Rabbi Sa'adyah Gaon's Doctrine of the Human Being' (Heb.), *Metsudah*, 1–2 (1943), 112–25.

[51] Gersonides, *Milḥamot hashem* (Berlin, 1923), 5.2.3; Eng. trans. *The Wars of the Lord*, trans. and ed. Seymour Feldman, 3 vols. (Philadelphia, 1984–99), iii. 39–42.

world was created because of the human species', but also, taking it a step further—which Morteira certainly would have accepted but does not discuss in this context—that everything was created and endures 'for the sake of this nation', the Jewish people.[52]

Morteira's reputed mentor Leon Modena also held the anthropocentric view of Creation. In the fifth sermon in *Midbar yehudah*, Modena concluded his discussion of Psalm 8 with: 'the supernal angels and the hosts of heaven serve the earth . . . and the heavens were created for the sake of the earth'.[53] Close to Morteira's position is that of *Kol sakhal*: 'Therefore I say that man is superior to all creatures. And the whole world in its entirety and its contents, and [that which is] above and below was only created for his sake.'[54]

This brief review reveals that Morteira was certainly not alone in his anthropocentric stance, but I have not found any other text containing such a systematic effort to rebut Maimonides' arguments against it. How the audience responded to this discussion—whether with intellectual delight at an effective debater dismantling an opponent's argument or with boredom because of the demanding and abstract issue, whether at least some of them recognized that the unnamed opponent was the highly venerated Maimonides, whether they accepted the conclusion of anthropocentrism as more intellectually respectable than they had previously imagined—we cannot know.

Analogies

As emphasized above, a sermon is more than a discursive intellectual exercise. Because it is intended to be heard rather than read, and because its intended audience is a congregation with all levels of education and sophistication, preachers often use rhetorical tools to concretize the abstract arguments.[55]

---

[52] Arama, *Akedat yitshak*, *sha'ar* 18 (i. 101a–b); cf. Meir ben Ezekiel ibn Gabbai, *Avodat hakodesh* (Jerusalem: Levin Epstein, 1973), 117–18. Morteira's Judaeocentric stance is revealed, for example, at the beginning of his sermon 'Dust of the Earth': 'When Israel does God's will, everything created seems to be made for its sake' (in Saperstein, *Exile in Amsterdam*, 380).

[53] Leon Modena, *Midbar yehudah* [sermons] (Venice, 1602), 29b; new edn. Benei Berak, 2002), 101.

[54] *Kol sakhal* purports to be a treatise by an unknown Jewish author challenging Jewish tradition; many scholars believe it was actually written by Modena, who composed a rebuttal. On the specific issue of anthropocentrism, see Talya Fishman, *Shaking the Pillars of the Exile: 'Voice of a Fool', an Early Modern Jewish Critique of Rabbinic Culture* (Stanford, 1997), 84, 214 n. 60; on scholars who have noted the parallel between the passage in Modena's sermon (the date of publication for which is mis-stated as 1629) and *Kol sakhal*, see ibid. 293 n. 64.

[55] This material is part of the broader repertoire of literary devices used by the speaker to hold the interest of the listening audience (see the discussion by Joseph Dan, *Homiletical and Ethical Literature*

I will illustrate Morteira's use of one such tool, analogy, by discussing the analogies he drew between aspects of his doctrine of Creation and two things his listeners were familiar with: water and art.

Water

Water was an elemental force not only in the actual experience of the members of Morteira's community, especially the merchants whose lives and fortunes were dependent on it, but also in the consciousness of its leaders.[56] It is, perhaps, not surprising that in his sermon on Genesis 1: 9, 'Let the waters be gathered', Morteira used water as a central motif, but the treatment of water was anything but routine. Indeed, the extended homiletical exploitation of the motif in connection with various aspects of Creation is rather stunning.

Like most opponents of radical rationalism, Morteira insisted that belief in Creation *ex nihilo* as an act of divine will is a necessary antecedent to the doctrine of providential reward and punishment. This belief is incompatible with the position of 'the philosophers', that the world was generated from God out of necessity, as the rays of sunlight are generated from the sun. Since God foresaw that future generations would deny his creative act, he left a 'prototype and paradigm' (*mashal vedugma*) in the natural world from which sensitive and observant human beings could learn the truth.[57] This is the element water:

> Look first at the element water: it is by nature without any colour, without taste, without aroma, without power. Yet through it God effected the sublunar creations. It is the source of all life, and as it falls upon the earth He makes the earth generate and flourish. This is a perfect sign of God's power to make from a subject that is inferior and devoid of any perfection every kind of flawlessness and perfection, of beauty and order. . . . More and more, when we understand and take to heart the many marvellous and exemplary properties [*segulot*] that the natural scientists tell us are found in springs and rivers and other places of water, [we understand that] they all teach us of the perfection and power of the Agent, blessed be He, in His control over such inferior matter, which He makes precious.[58]

[Sifrut haderush vehamusar] [Jerusalem, 1975], 26–46, 79, *et passim*; for examples of similar analogies, see Marc Saperstein, *Jewish Preaching, 1200–1800: An Anthology* [New Haven, 1989], 93–4).

[56] See Simon Schama, *The Embarrassment of Riches: An Interpretation of Dutch Culture in the Golden Age* (Berkeley, 1988), 25–50.

[57] See the use of prototype and paradigm in a historical context in Morteira's sermon 'When They Agitated Against God' (in Saperstein, *Exile in Amsterdam*, 430–46).

[58] Morteira, Sermons (Heb.), v, fo. 9^r (on Gen. 1: 9).

This is not an altogether satisfying use of water as a paradigm for Creation. While it points to the creative power of God in bringing diversity out of simplicity and elevating inferior material to glorious products, based on the testimony of the natural scientists,[59] it might be misunderstood as a model for creation from primeval matter, a doctrine that Morteira, of course, rejected. He therefore did not linger for long on this aspect of water.

The second characteristic of water is experienced in the storm at sea.

Now after this first inspection of the nature of water, which leads to the knowledge of Creation through divine will and power, we shall inspect further the acts that God performs through water that lead to this knowledge in a manner that cannot be seen in any other of the fundamental elements. For 'those who go down to the sea in ships and ply their trade in the mighty waters have seen the works of the Eternal, His wonders in the deep' [Ps. 107: 23]. The Psalmist meant to refer to the works and wonders they have seen in the storms that passed over them, but in addition he hints that one who has seen this has been shown and has envisioned with his own eyes the Creation of the world, even though he was not present at its creation. For when he sees the storm at sea—the waves and the clamour of the winds, 'mounting to the heavens, plunging to the depths' [Ps. 107: 26], with darkness and dense clouds all around [see Ps. 97: 2], 'sun and moon are darkened, and stars withdraw their brightness' [Joel 4: 15], with much lightning, and thunder beyond measure—he sees a world destroyed, revoked, restored to its primordial chaos. Then afterwards, when the storm is reduced to a whisper and the waves are stilled [see Ps. 107: 29], the clamour of the waters [disappears] as if it had never been, he truly beholds God's works, namely the actual work of Creation, when after the chaos and the darkness over the surface of the deep, 'God said "Let there be light", and there was light' [Gen. 1: 2–3].[60]

The language of this passage is largely drawn from the Bible, especially the Psalms. Yet it evokes an experience that does not seem to be merely an application of Scripture. Simon Schama has shown that the image of a ship buffeted by a storm at sea played a significant role in contemporary Dutch moralistic literature and art.[61] Dutch ships, which were of inferior quality to

---

[59] This ambiguous passage might allude to the multitude of minute living creatures discovered in water through the microscope by Dutch scientists, but I am not certain that Morteira would have used the noun *segulot* to refer to this property of water, and whether Morteira was aware of the discovery is uncertain, as the figure most associated with it, Anthony Van Leeuwenhoek, was born in 1632, the year this sermon was delivered (see Jonathan Israel, *The Dutch Republic: Its Rise, Greatness, and Fall, 1477–1806* [Oxford, 1995], 905–7; Catherine Wilson, *The Invisible World: Early Modern Philosophy and the Invention of the Microscope* [Princeton, 1995]).

[60] Morteira, Sermons (Heb.), v, fo. 9ʳ (on Gen. 1: 9).

[61] Schama, *An Embarrassment of Riches*, 28–34 (with pictures). The purpose in the moralistic litera-

British and Flemish vessels, were particularly susceptible to disasters at sea.[62] Morteira emphasized not just the terrifying power of the storm but also the transcendent calm that follows, the appearance of blue sky and radiant light—like that evoked by the third movement of Beethoven's *Pastoral Symphony*—which makes the sailors feel as if they were witnesses to the work of Creation. Whether or not Morteira himself had experienced what he described in this passage, it is certain that many in his congregation would have known at first hand precisely what he meant.

A third characteristic of water that reveals the nature of Creation would have been accessible even to those who did not read scientific literature or travel by ship:

The sea water spreads and then is diminished in an orderly fashion, at known times, without our understanding how this occurs, in what place all this water is gathered and to what place it returns, so that there is a continuous cycle, as if God were continuously creating the water and destroying it. This is so that people will recognize that God creates everything according to His will and thereby can destroy and rebuild it according to His will. People see the land that is adjacent to the seashore: [one day] it is a coast where the ships come, and the next day it is dry, and they can walk upon it! This is for them a reminder of the manner of creation, when the entire world was water upon water, and 'God said, "Let the water below the sky be gathered into one area, that the dry land may appear", and it was so' [Gen. 1: 9]. It was about this that Job said, 'When He holds back the waters, they dry up; when He lets them loose, they transform the land' [Job 12: 15].

This was also the intention of the Psalmist when he said: 'He heaps up the ocean waters like a mound, stores the deep in vaults. Let all the earth fear the Lord, let all the inhabitants of the world dread Him. For He spoke, and it was, He commanded and it endured' [Ps. 33: 7–9]. This means, when we see the mighty waters spread over the earth, far and wide, in enormous volume, and then they are gathered and closed up as if in a bottle, after 'He heaps up the ocean waters like a mound', and as if something that was scattered was gathered in and placed within a storage container among the vaults. From that point on, 'all the earth will fear God, all inhabitants of the world will dread Him', for their fear will result from what they recognized in this marvellous act [of gathering in the sea], as the Psalmist said, 'For He spoke, and it was, He

---

ture—to teach humility and contrition in the face of a sudden catastrophe that threatened the cargo crammed into the ship's hold and the lives of the crew—was somewhat different from Morteira's point about the storm as an emblem of God's power in creation.

[62] On the quality of Dutch ships, see Israel, *The Dutch Republic*, 118; Schama, *An Embarrassment of Riches*, 31.

commanded and it endured'. Just as they see it now, so it was at the time of creation, and God left a paradigm [*dugma*] for the generations.⁶³

Where earlier he had emphasized the extraordinary event of the storm at sea, here it is the regular, rhythmic ebb and flow of the tides that reveals an aspect of the Creation: when God gathered the waters. The correlation of the tides with the moon had been noted long before, but the mechanism that controlled the displacement of vast amounts of water and the uncovering of considerable areas of the seashore remained a mystery to Morteira's contemporaries.⁶⁴ In his homiletical use of water, Morteira, beginning with the subject of the biblical verse, drew on the motif *zekher asah lenifle'otav* ('He has caused His wonders to be remembered', Ps. 111: 4), though using a different terminology. For the Jewish Pietists of Germany, the strange, inexplicable details of the world around them provided a trace of the hidden Creator.⁶⁵ Morteira also evoked the inexplicable, but the natural phenomena he used were more familiar, and his purpose was not only to provide a sense of the reality of God but to use his congregants' experience to give them some understanding of the actual process of Creation.

Art

If water was an important element of the physical environment of Jews in Morteira's Amsterdam, especially those who travelled the seas, painting was a central fixture of the cultural environment. Many of his congregants were patrons and collectors of art; some were depicted in contemporary paintings.⁶⁶ Morteira had issued a responsum permitting Jews to keep works of art

---

⁶³ Morteira, Sermons (Heb.), v, fo. 9ʳ⁻ᵛ (on Gen. 1: 9).

⁶⁴ An example of the contemporary uncertainty about the cause of the tides appears in Bernhardus Varenius's *Geographia generalis* (1650): 'Some have thought the Earth and Sea to be a living Creature, which by its Respiration, causeth this ebbing and flowing. Others imagined that it proceeds, and is provoked, from a great Whirlpool near Norway, which, for Six Hours, absorbs the Water, and afterwards, disgorges it in the same space of Time. Scaliger, and others, supposed that it is caused by the opposite Shores, especially of America, whereby the general Motion of the Sea is obstructed and reverberated. But most Philosophers, who have observed the Harmony that these Tides have with the Moon, have given their Opinion, that they are entirely owing to the Influence of that Luminary. But the Question is, what is this Influence?' (in Francis E. Wylie, *Tides and the Pull of the Moon* [Brattleboro, Vt., 1979], 20). For a review of the best scientific thought on the tides from the Middle Ages to Morteira's time, see David E. Cartwright, *Tides: A Scientific History* (Cambridge, 1999), 13–18.

⁶⁵ On this doctrine in German Pietism (*ḥasidut ashkenaz*), see Joseph Dan, *The Esoteric Doctrine of German Pietism* [Torat hasod shel ḥasidut ashkenaz] (Jerusalem, 1968), 88–94.

⁶⁶ Michael Zell, *Reframing Rembrandt* (Berkeley, 2002), 12–32, esp. 14–15 (on Venice); Steven M. Nadler, *Rembrandt's Jews* (Chicago, 2003), 72–84.

as household ornaments, at variance with the more conservative interpretation of the second commandment.[67]

In his 1657 eulogy for his younger (and more famous) colleague, Menasseh ben Israel, Morteira expanded upon a talmudic aggadah contrasting God and the human portrait artist. In his explanation, he conceded that the aesthetic appeal of the painting: 'the "drawing made upon the wall" [BT *Ber.* 10*a*] may indeed be beautiful to behold, pleasing in its colours, adorned with fine clothing and ornaments, a great delight to the eyes'. Not a few of the listeners might have envisioned some of the crowning achievements of contemporary Dutch portraiture as he spoke. Yet Morteira emphasized that these paintings, despite their external appeal, are inanimate, without breath or spirit, inferior to human beings created by God.[68] Similarly, in analogies drawn from the realm of art to illustrate aspects of the doctrine of Creation, Morteira appealed to familiar material in order to illuminate what is more distant and abstract.

Painting Details and Painting the Whole

The first example emphasizes the difference between human and divine creation. At issue, in his 1634 sermon on Genesis 1: 11, is the vast variety of vegetation brought forth from the earth at the divine bidding. Clearly vegetation in general reflects God's purpose, but is this true for every individual species of plant and flower? Morteira began by stating the opposing position:

It occurs to me to say first that an adversary, upon seeing the multitude of plants in all their varieties of appearance and colour and shape and the splendour and beauty of their leaves, might disagree and say that they could not have been made [each] for a special purpose, since human beings are ignorant of the reason for all these details, and [cannot understand] why one specific shape should be better than any other. He might therefore decide that even though this was done by the will of the agent, the shapes and the many other details were not the product of any specific intention but only of the desire to create variety and beauty in the world.[69]

At this point those members of the congregation who knew more about Judaism might have associated this position with analogous positions taken by

---

[67] H. P. Salomon, introduction to Saul Levi Morteira, *Tratado da verdad da lei de Moisés* (Coimbra, 1988), p. lxi n. 19; cf. Nadler, *Rembrandt's Jews*, 76, citing Moses d'Aguilar, a later rabbi.

[68] Marc Saperstein, *'Your Voice Like a Ram's Horn': Themes and Texts in Traditional Jewish Preaching* (Cincinnati, 1996), 415–16, 424–5. The same *midrash* and topos of God as painter was used by Morteira's purported Venetian mentor, Leon Modena (see Saperstein, *Jewish Preaching, 1200–1800*, 409, nn. 19–21).

[69] Morteira, Sermons (Heb.), v, fo. 1ᵛ (on Gen. 1: 11); cf. Arama, *Akedat yitshak*, sha'ar 18 (i. 101*b*).

Maimonides. In the Introduction to the *Guide for the Perplexed*, discussing the proper interpretation of allegorical passages in the Bible, Maimonides explained that while for some biblical figures every detail is significant, for others (the example he gives is Proverbs 7: 6–26) many of the details have no deeper significance but are present simply to make the figure more realistic. More important, however, is his explanation of the reasons for the commandments. Maimonides insisted that the general principles certainly reflect divine will and wisdom, but the details, while obligatory, may indeed have a random character. Thus while the offering of sacrifices has a significant purpose, 'no cause will ever be found for the fact that one particular sacrifice consists in a lamb and another in a ram and that the number of the offerings should be one particular number. Accordingly, in my opinion, all those who occupy themselves with finding causes for something of these particulars are stricken with a prolonged madness.'[70] This is the same attitude as the one taken by Morteira's 'adversary' to the variety of the natural world.

But before refuting this position, Morteira proceeds to make it more plausible through an analogy with a painter:

This would be like a man who paints one panel with a variety of hues, randomly making many different shapes that are intended not individually but only for the cumulative effect of variety. Think of an artist who wants to draw a depiction of [a piece of] marble that is covered with veins. He will position his tints randomly, without intending to replicate any specific detail; his intention is the picture as a whole. Even if the pattern of his hues turns out different [from the original], his purpose will be achieved, for his intention was not any one of them, but only the extreme variety of colour patterns in imitation of the natural pattern of veins. So it would be possible to think that God desired the splendour of the earth—wanting it to bring forth various kinds of grass and vegetation, of flowers and leaves, and wanting them to remain as they were at the beginning—but that precisely what the earth brought forth would be a matter of chance, even though the general purpose of the earth's production—its final cause—was the splendour and beauty of the earth.[71]

Whether or not Morteira had in mind an actual painting of veined marble,[72] it seems that he was confident that his analogy would be understood

---

[70] Maimonides, *Guide for the Perplexed*, 3: 26 (trans Shlomo Pines, in *A Maimonides Reader*, ed. Isador Twersky [New York: Behrman House, 1972], p. 313; cf. *Guide for the Perplexed*, trans. and ed. M. Friedländer, iii. 127). On the doctrine of contingency underlying this position, see Isadore Twersky, *Introduction to the Code of Maimonides (Mishneh Torah)* (New Haven, 1980), 398; on the contrast with kabbalah, see ibid. 164–5 n. 199.

[71] Morteira, Sermons (Heb.), v, fo. 1ᵛ (on Gen. 1: 11).

[72] See the 1644 painting of a figured marble column from a church in Utrecht (Nadler,

by his listeners: the painter, at least of inanimate objects, is not concerned with a photographic reproduction of precise details but with the general visual effect. Drawing again on the analogy between God and the painter, this appeal to familiar experience bestowed plausibility upon the position regarding the Creation of the natural world that he was about to rebut. After having exploited the analogy between God and the painter, he returned to the Torah to emphasize the difference.

That is why the Torah taught us that this is not the case. Rather, even the minutest detail was intended for a special purpose, for the quality and nature of that plant and its benefit in the world. The design of the various species of vegetation, their flowers, their aromas and colours, their leaves, their internal components, and all the multitude of their details—all were intended by God. 'How many are Your works, O God; You have made them all in Your wisdom; the earth is full of Your creations' [Ps. 104: 24].

This message was taught through the creation [of the various kinds of vegetation] in order, not randomly. For with one whose only intention is beauty [in general], who mixes colours together and does not care about the details of the images, you will find the colours mixed in disarray, with one colour from many places. But if the green is separate, and the red separate, and the white separate, and so on—all of them separate, without being mixed with the others—then certainly the artist intends not just the general form but also all the details.[73]

Almost to the end of the passage, it seems as if the artist analogy is so compelling that Morteira was unable to abandon it. There are indeed some artists for whom details are important as well as the general impression, and they keep their colours distinct.[74] They provide the model for what he insisted is the understanding of God's purpose in the profuse variety of vegetative life that appears in the Torah.

Rembrandt's Jews, pl. 14) and the tombstones in Jacob van Ruisdael's *The Jewish Cemetery* (ibid., pls. 8, 9). While both of these are later than the sermon, Morteira may well have seen similar examples.

[73] Morteira, Sermons (Heb.), v, fo. 1ᵛ (on Gen. 1: 11).

[74] Here Morteira seems to be making a technical point about the painter's palette, and indeed there is evidence that the dominant method at the time was to use a small number of colours on the palette for specific sections of the painting (see Ernst van de Wetering, *Rembrandt: The Painter at Work* [Amsterdam, 1997], 136–52). I do not know how much these passages reveal about Morteira's knowledge of contemporary art, especially landscape or still-life paintings of floral arrangements. Schama and Israel both speak of a 'monochromatic' style of still-life painting that prevailed in the 1620s and 1630s, which may fit Morteira's point about the palette but not his larger point about the artistic depiction of specific detail mirroring the purpose of the array of detailed differentiation in God's natural world (Schama, *An Embarrassment of Riches*, 160–1; Israel, *The Dutch Republic*, 560–1).

In order to teach this, Scripture formulated the command to the various species of vegetation in the singular: 'Let the earth sprout vegetation, seed-bearing flora' [Gen. 1: 11]. It did not say, 'Let the earth sprout plants and flowers', despite there being so many different kinds of them. This was intended to teach that God commanded the earth to sprout every individual species separately, not mixed together with the others. And the earth observed this commandment in practice: 'The earth brought forth vegetation, seed-bearing flora of every kind' [Gen. 1: 12], meaning, every kind separately, not mixed together.[75]

Morteira's use of the details of biblical language to support his point is not as compelling as in some of his other sermons. The collective singular nouns suggest that the original sprouting was indeed all vegetation mixed together.[76] Apparently Morteira interpreted the juxtaposition of the collective nouns with the phrase 'of every kind' (*lemineihu*) to mean that even with a relatively limited palette, God created a vast panoply of flora, with each detail serving a specific purpose.

Masters and Apprentices

We have seen that an important theme of Morteira's discussion of Creation, which was treated at length in his 1635 sermon on Genesis 1: 12, was the emergence of plurality and diversity from God, the Absolute One. After reviewing the various ways in which this conundrum had been solved, culminating with the view of the Torah, Morteira continued with a further refinement of the problem.

After the first Creation, performed by God as stated, when the created beings were divided into two categories—those that endure as individuals and those that endure as a species—both of these secondary groups were turned over to the power of the primary supernal beings, in order to ensure their perpetuation in their various species and to provide continuation for them as individuals, on the model of the primary beings that were created directly by the Maker of All. This is just like the apprentices of a master artist, before whom their master leaves an exemplary model [*mareh vedugma*], on the basis of which they should draw (insofar as possible),[77] without diverging in any way. Each one pursues his work day and night without rest, making copies of the original models, thereby producing thousands of copies. It is like the biblical verse 'With the bounteous yield of the sun, and the bounteous crops of the

---

[75] Morteira, Sermons (Heb.), v, fo. 1ᵛ (on Gen. 1: 11).

[76] Rashi takes the first noun *deshe* to be collective (*kulan be'arbuvia*), while the second, *esev*, refers to each plant individually (on Gen. 1: 11). Nahmanides criticizes this because of the use of the plural of *deshe* in rabbinic literature (ad loc.). [77] The words *kol ha'efshar* are inserted above the line.

moon' [Deut. 33: 14]. Such is the rule for all the other secondary created beings, which are derived in accordance with various true aspects of this analogy and illustration, as follows.[78]

Whether or not Morteira ever visited the studio of Rembrandt (who lived just a block or two away) or of one of his contemporaries cannot be established for certain.[79] However, the practice of master painters teaching apprentices in their studios was common in Dutch painting circles at the time Morteira lived. The students would begin copying prints from a drawing book or etchings by the master himself, then coloured paintings, then plaster models or casts of statues, and then finally live models in the studio.[80] Whether he observed or heard about this practice, it clearly occurred to Morteira that—like the examples from water above—it could be used to illustrate the relationship between Creation by God—the Master Artist—and the perpetuation of created beings through the influence of the heavenly bodies.

This analogy is then explored in great detail. The apprentices at work in a studio, learning their craft, cannot fully replicate the perfection of the master's creation, for various reasons that reflect the pattern of the imperfect sublunar world, a decline from the excellence of God's Creation.

First, we know that those who serve and learn from the experts,[81] as experienced as they may be, cannot hope to perform that work as perfectly and properly as the master did it, and [then?] to use what is before them to teach from it,[82] which would be the utmost perfection possible in this act. Similarly with the supernal beings. Even though they continue to follow the pattern that God made in the Creation, they cannot reach the same perfection or the exact composition [*mezeg*] that the Creator ordained in the creation of the primary beings in their full stature and their beauty,[83] for various reasons: whether because of the composition or because of the place or the

---

[78] Morteira, Sermons (Heb.), v, fo. 3ᵛ (on Gen. 1: 12).

[79] On whether there exists any authentic portrait of Morteira, see Nadler, *Rembrandt's Jews*, 120–3.

[80] See Willem Martin, 'The Life of a Dutch Artist in the Seventeenth Century', in *Seventeenth Century Art in Flanders and Holland*, Garland Library of the History of Art, 9 (New York, 1976), 85–108; Peter Schatborn, *Dutch Figure Drawings from the Seventeenth Century* (The Hague, 1981), 14–20; Jeroen Giltaij, *The Drawings by Rembrandt and His School* (Rotterdam, 1989), 13–15; Svetlana Alpers, *Rembrandt's Enterprise: The Studio and the Market* (Chicago, 1988), 69–70.

[81] The Hebrew text clearly says *hamesharetim vehamelamedim labaki'im*, but I take this to be an error that makes no sense in the context, as he has just spoken about *talmidei ha'oman habaki*.

[82] This rendering is uncertain. Again Morteira uses the verb *lelamed*, but it is unclear to me from the context whether he intends 'to teach' or 'to learn'.

[83] See BT Ḥul. 60a; my translation of *tsivyonam* reflects Maimonides' interpretation (*Guide for the Perplexed*, 2: 30 [trans. and ed. M. Friedländer, ii. 153]).

time or the intermediaries or the other accidents that ruin the perfection of the labour, so that the results will not be precisely like the originals.

Second, with these craftsmen, the coarser the materials used in their labours, the more liable they will be to deviate from perfection, for the coarseness of material prevents them from making fine engravings upon it, while the master craftsman their teacher knows how to make finely detailed engravings [see 2 Chron. 2: 6] even upon coarse materials. Similarly the supernal beings diverge more widely from the primal perfection in the products of the earth, namely, the element of dust. In these there is more change and distance from the perfection of the primal Creation than in the birds, which are the product of the air and the water, and also in the fish. Thus among the creatures made from the earth there is more change from the customary pattern, with blemishes whether in deficiency or in excess, than in those made from the water and the air. That is why the Torah does not require an unblemished state in birds as it requires in animals, in which deficiency or excess is more common.[84]

Here Morteira incorporated a halakhic principle, together with an explanation for it, into his discussion of cosmology. Describing the offerings of cattle, sheep, and goats, Scripture requires that they be without blemish (Lev. 22: 19); describing the offering of doves or pigeons, it does not specify an unblemished state (Lev. 1: 14). The conclusion in Jewish law is that minor blemishes do not exclude a bird from eligibility for the cult offerings.[85] Having stated the law, Morteira went on to provide an explanation of the different requirements: the animals, composed primarily of the coarser element of earth, are more susceptible to blemishes than the birds, composed primarily of air. (This explanation, of course, is based on the medieval theory of the four fundamental elements, which had long since been abandoned in scientific circles but remained current among Christian as well as Jewish thinkers for generations after Morteira.[86]) The purpose is to illustrate the underlying point that coarseness of matter affects the quality of the product, but along the way he has perhaps taught some of his listeners a detail of Jewish law.

The explanation above applies to what medieval philosophers would call the 'material cause' of the objects, but there is also the quality of the 'efficient cause', the agents that affect the matter:

Third, even considering their crude materials, these craftsmen vary significantly in the quality of their work due to differences in their level of knowledge and in their

---

[84] Morteira, *Sermons* (Heb.), v, fo. 1ᵛ (on Gen. 1: 11).

[85] BT *Kid.* 24*b*; Rashi on Lev. 1: 14; Moses Maimonides, *Mishneh torah*, 'Laws of Forbidden Relations', 3: 1.

[86] See e.g. the sermon by Jonathan Eybeschuetz, in Saperstein, *Jewish Preaching, 1200–1800*, 339.

diligence, for the more skilled and talented among them will produce a more perfect product, while the work of the less skilled will be deficient. Similarly with the products of the earth. With regard to the animal realm, in which the productive form is sentient, it will effect within them awe-inspiring things with the most subtle and refined results, within complex internal recesses, as we see in the arrangements of their bodies in general and in their limbs and organs in particular. However, with regard to the plants, in which the productive form is crude and coarse, namely, the vital, vegetative soul, their actions are not so sophisticated and wondrous. It has no capacity to uproot them from the place where they were spawned, but only to make them sprout and grow and to preserve them; they cannot move from the place, for they have no structural capacity to endure without it [the vegetative soul].[87]

Here too we find Morteira's vocabulary rooted in the commonplaces of the Middle Ages. After talking about matter, he talks about the 'forms' of the various levels of being on earth. These levels were characterized by different 'souls': the 'vegetative soul' that distinguishes vegetation from the inanimate realm, the 'sentient soul' that differentiates the animal from the vegetable kingdom, and the 'rational soul', unique to humanity. Following Aristotle, the soul is the 'form' of the body, since it is the agent that defines the identity of these life forms, it is the 'productive form'.[88] Yet mixed in with this antiquated language are two concepts that seem very much *au courant*: the awareness of a wide range of innate talents among the apprentices in an artist's workshop and an appreciation of the wondrously subtle details not just visible on the surface but deep within the inner recesses of animals all over the earth.

Conclusion

These sermons on the portion 'Bereshit' reveal that, in many ways, Morteira was a traditionalist. Like those of many of his rabbinic colleagues, his scientific horizons remained confined within a medieval world-view, his cosmology rooted in the Bible and the Talmud. He read the medieval Jewish philosophers and their critics—Maimonides, Albo, and Arama—used their material selectively, and vigorously repudiated positions he believed to be in conflict with the truth of the Torah. These sermons provide scant evidence of intellectual confrontation with the challenges of contemporary science, no

---

[87] Morteira, Sermons (Heb.), v, fo. 1ᵛ (on Gen. 1: 11); on the characteristics of the plant realm, see Gersonides, *Milḥamot hashem*, 5.3.6 (trans. Feldman, iii. 140).

[88] For a similar use of this somewhat unusual term, see Gersonides, *Milḥamot hashem*, 6.1.18 (trans. Feldman, iii. 335).

hint of the psychological reorientation required by the Copernican model of the universe. The young Spinoza undoubtedly heard some of the later sermons as he was growing to maturity, but at some point he concluded that this was an understanding of Creation and God's relationship with the world that he had to reject.

Morteira had an appreciation of the vast grandeur of the universe, but it apparently was derived not from contemporary science but from traditional sources. In his sermon on Genesis 1: 5 from 1623, the verse 'He counted the number of the stars, to each He gave its name' (Ps. 147: 4) in his opening rabbinic dictum drew Morteira into a discussion of the number of different stars and the much larger number of their interactions, producing the almost infinite variety of the sublunar realm. In order to illustrate this number, he cited *Sefer yetsirah*, leading his audience through a bit of mathematical calculation exploring the enormous number of permutations of the letters of the alphabet:

A similar matter is written in the fourth chapter of *Sefer yetsirah*: 'Two stones [i.e. letters] build 2 houses [words], three build 6, four [build] 24, five [build] 120, six [build] 720, seven [build] 5,040 houses. From this point on, you may calculate yourself what the mouth cannot pronounce, what the eye cannot see, and what the ears cannot hear.' Rabbi Eleazar of Worms wrote in his commentary on *Sefer yetsirah* that the eleven letters of the longest word in the Bible, והאחשדרפנים (Esther 9: 3), produce a total of 9,916,420 words. How much more is the magnitude of number of the stars, each interacting with the others with their uniquely different appearance and composition: it is truly awe-inspiring![89]

It is not clear whether Morteira consulted *Sefer yetsirah* himself or found the passage in another work. What is clear is that he had no special interest in delving into the mysteries of esoteric doctrine, either of German Jewish Pietism (*ḥasidut ashkenaz*) or of the much more accessible kabbalah. Although he respectfully referred to the kabbalists as *ḥakhmei ha'emet* ('the true sages' or 'sages of the truth'), and spoke graciously about Hayim Vital and Menahem Azariah of Fano when he learned about their deaths, his references to kabbalistic material seem largely pro forma. These sermons on 'Bereshit' reflect a totally different intellectual universe from the sophisticated effort to reconcile Lurianic kabbalah with Neoplatonic philosophy by Morteira's

---

[89] Morteira, Sermons (Heb.), iii, fo. 243ᵛ (on Gen. 1: 5). The number of combinations is 39,916,800, not 9,916,420. *Sefer yetsirah* was published with several commentaries, including that of Eleazar of Worms, at Mantua in 1563.

older contemporary in Amsterdam, Abraham Cohen Herrera.[90] 'As for me, I do not delve into esoteric doctrine', he confessed from the pulpit. It was enough for him to work through the conceptual and exegetical problems of the opening verses of Genesis with their rabbinic and medieval philosophical discussions, teaching his listeners this component of their newly discovered tradition, provoking them with an occasional polemic, engaging them with concrete illustrations of the abstract, all with the artistry of the true homiletical master.

---

[90] See Alexander Altmann, 'Lurianic Kabbalah in a Platonic Key: Abraham Cohen Herrera's *Puerta del Cielo*', in Isadore Twersky and Bernard Septimus (eds.), *Jewish Thought in the Seventeenth Century* (Cambridge, Mass., 1987), 1–37. I do not know what evidence there would be that Herrera's work was 'enthusiastically consumed by those who dominated the world in which Spinoza was educated, including . . . Saul Morteira' (Warren Montag, '"That Hebrew Word": Spinoza and the Concept of the Shekinah', in Heidi M. Ravven and Lenn Evan Goodman [eds.], *Jewish Themes in Spinoza's Philosophy* [Albany, NY, 2002], 136).

PART III

LEADERS FACING COMMUNITIES IN UPHEAVAL

CHAPTER SEVEN

Jewish Leadership in the Generation of Expulsion

THE CONVENTIONS of traditional Jewish discourse have often been overly generous in describing spiritual leadership. Sometimes it borders on hagiography, liberally bestowing superlatives to the point where all praises seem debased.[1] By contrast, modern Jewish historiography has been quite critical of Jewish leaders in the Middle Ages. Thus we learn from Graetz that after the death of Maimonides, 'the Jews stood without a leader, and Judaism without a guide', leaving the Jewish people helpless against the onslaught of the thirteenth-century papacy, spearheaded by Innocent III.[2] And if Graetz is old-hat, consider the following astonishing passage by an eminent historian of medieval Europe, Norman Cantor:

There was one courtly, rabbinical, literary, mercantile elite, and all Jews beside this immensely wealthy, prominent, fortunate, learned elite were the silent exploited masses. Exploited and repressed, I think, not only by the Gentiles, but also by the dominant court Jews. Every time I read or hear about medieval Jewry, I think of Hannah Arendt's *Eichmann in Jerusalem* and her unforgettable picture of how the Jewish masses of Hungary were sold into Nazi gas chambers by the Budapest Jewish community leaders, so many of whom survived to become American business men or indeed Israeli officials. . . . The rich, well-born and learned Jews often survived even pogroms and moved easily on to havens in other countries, while the masses in bad times sank even further into poverty, misery, and martyrdom.[3]

First published in *Anuario de studios medievales*, 42/1 (2012), 95–118.

[1] As just one example, chosen almost at random, see the salutation at the beginning of Maimonides' 'Epistle to Yemen'. Despite the hyperbolic praises, later in the epistle Maimonides gives his correspondent a rather disdainful reprimand (in Moses Maimonides, *Crisis and Leadership: Epistles of Maimonides*, trans. and ed. Abraham Halkin and David Hartman [Philadelphia, 1993], 93, 123–4).

[2] Heinrich Graetz, *History of the Jews*, 6 vols. (Philadelphia, 1893), iii. 495.

[3] Norman Cantor, 'Disputatio', in Paul Szarmach (ed.), *Aspects of Jewish Culture in the Middle Ages*

From their rhetoric and substance, one would be hard pressed to prove that these lines were written by a professional historian. But rather than linger on this overblown picture and its highly problematic use of an analogy with the Holocaust, I prefer to approach the question of Jewish leadership by focusing on a specific historical setting: the generation of the Expulsion from Spain. Norman Roth has asserted that 'an important, and hitherto little-emphasized, characteristic of fifteenth-century Spanish Jewry was the almost complete lack of leadership'.[4] Is this kind of generalization justified?

Several leading modern historians have subjected the leaders of the last generation of Spanish Jewry before the Expulsion to a two-pronged attack. The first charge impugns their perspicacity and their political judgement. Given all the warning signs, how could they not have foreseen the approaching disaster of 1492? As Benzion Netanyahu put it:

> Common sense, it would appear, should have indicated to the Jews that, with such a fierce campaign being conducted against the Marranos in the name of their Jewishness, the Jews could not possibly escape involvement. But the Jews seem not to have sensed this. . . . The blindness manifested by the Jews in the Diaspora for developments laden with mortal danger is nothing short of proverbial.[5]

In less judgemental terms, Haim Beinart wrote—whether in surprise or dismay—that 'few Jewish leaders showed any premonition of the approaching danger'.[6] These statements are fine examples of what Michael Bernstein has

---

(Albany, NY, 1979), 182. Cantor returned to this theme in his monumental compendium of misinformation, *The Sacred Chain*: 'By the second quarter of the thirteenth century the days of Ashkenaz were numbered. Anyone could see the future was gloomy, indeed hopeless. . . . The Ashkenazi rabbinate did nothing. . . . It is the syndrome of waiting quietly for the holocaust. Thus the Orthodox rabbinate failed to exercise leadership on behalf of the Jews in thirteenth-century Ashkenaz as they were to do again in twentieth-century Poland. Meanwhile the rabbinate drugged itself into comfort with the narcotic of the Cabala, an otherworldly withdrawal into astrology and demonology' (Norman Cantor, *The Sacred Chain: The History of the Jews* [New York, 1994], 180–1).

[4] Norman Roth, *Conversos, Inquisition, and the Expulsion of the Jews from Spain* (Madison, 1995), p. xvi; see also similar formulations on pp. 53, 278, 302–3.

[5] Benzion Netanyahu, *Don Isaac Abravanel* (Philadelphia, 1968), 45; Benjamin Gampel has raised this issue in the context of Navarrese Jewry (Gampel, *The Last Jews on Iberian Soil: Navarrese Jewry 1479/1498* [Berkeley, 1989], 1–2, 210 n. 40).

[6] Haim Beinart, 'Order of the Expulsion from Spain: Antecedents, Causes and Textual Analysis', in Benjamin Gampel (ed.), *Crisis and Creativity in the Sephardic World, 1391–1648* (New York, 1997), 87. Beinart goes on to note one exception, Judah ibn Verga, who 'expressed his foreboding with a symbolic act' (see Solomon ibn Verga, *Shevet yehudah* [history], ch. 62 [ed. Ezriel Shohat (Jerusalem, 1947), 127]), but Beinart's translation of the passage obscures the fact that Judah's symbolic act—involving different treatment of three pairs of doves—is said to apply to three categories of Conversos, not of Jews. Furthermore, this kind of foreknowledge claimed in a later text—'before the

called (in a literary context, particularly with regard to the Holocaust) 'backshadowing', defined as 'a kind of retroactive foreshadowing in which the shared knowledge of the outcome of a series of events by narrator and listener is used to judge the participants in those events *as though they should have known what was to come*'.[7]

Second, there is a charge of general intellectual mediocrity. According to the modern experts, this was a generation that produced no shining stars in any field of Jewish cultural endeavour.[8] The Spanish rabbis of the period made no contribution to the responsa literature, we are told by Menachem Elon, because 'the constantly deteriorating political situation and the persecutions . . . precluded the writing of responsa'.[9] Julius Guttmann reached a similar conclusion from his own perspective: 'The frightful pressure under which Spanish Jewry, the foremost bearers of Jewish philosophy, lived during the fifteenth century precluded any productive or original philosophic work.'[10] As for kabbalah, the dynamic, creative energies of earlier centuries were spent: in Gershom Scholem's words, 'the literature of the fifteenth century [in Spain] reflects an unmistakable flaccidity of religious thought and expression'.[11] The conclusion suggested by these evaluations seems unavoidable: the generation of the Expulsion, in facing its crisis, had the misfortune of being served by mediocre leaders who were simply not up to the challenge.

It is not my primary purpose either to polemicize against scholars, such as those mentioned in the previous paragraph, whose work I deeply admire or to defend the rabbinic leaders of Spanish Jewry, but rather to examine the

---

Inquisition came, he knew all it would do'—is vulnerable to the charge of creating a 'prophecy after the fact'.

[7] Michael Bernstein, *Foregone Conclusions: Against Apocalyptic History* (Berkeley, 1994), 16 (italics in original).

[8] e.g.: 'There is, therefore, no question but that the fifteenth century saw a complete breakdown and virtual collapse of the high level of Jewish learning which had characterized Spanish Jewry from the earliest days' (N. Roth, *Conversos, Inquisition, and the Expulsion*, 13; but contrast the detailed information on pp. 53–4). Yom Tov Assis recently articulated what he calls 'the view held by most scholars': 'The last century of Jewish life in Spain was on the whole a period of decline. . . . Many leaders were either dead or baptized. Inevitably, the years following the massacres were very meager in literary production. Apart from poetry and ethics, many themes of Jewish learning were almost completely neglected during the years after 1391' (Assis, 'Spanish Jewry: From Persecutions to Expulsion (1391–1492)', *Studia Hebraica*, 4 [2004], 309).

[9] Menachem Elon, *Jewish Law: History, Sources, Principles*, 4 vols. (Philadelphia, 1994), iii. 1479.

[10] Julius Guttmann, *Philosophies of Judaism: The History of Jewish Philosophy from Biblical Times to Franz Rosenzweig* (Garden City, NY, 1933; repr. 1964), 242.

[11] Gershom Scholem, *Major Trends in Jewish Mysticism* (New York, 1941), 244; cf. Yitzhak Baer, *A History of the Jews in Christian Spain*, 2 vols. (Philadelphia, 1961–6), ii. 426.

basis on which the charge of mediocrity has been levelled. For it seems to me that it is based on assumptions that are fundamentally unhistorical. Let us consider each of the charges in turn.

The accusation of political obtuseness, an inability to see the writing on the wall, a 'blindness . . . for developments laden with mortal danger', sounds more like the representation of the diaspora experience in radical Zionist ideology than a proper historical assessment. It is always easy to read history backwards—from what eventually happened to what should have been obvious. Before the fact, even the most astute and canny contemporary observers, faced with contradictory indicators and questionable precedents, confront an opaque wall. What seems so clear in retrospect appears at the time to be open-ended, ambiguous, and obscure.

Should Jewish leaders have seen the Expulsion coming? The evidence indicates that virtually everyone in Spain, including powerful courtiers and influential churchmen, was taken by surprise. At the very least, it is clear that the Catholic Monarchs carefully concealed their intentions until the last moment, permitting Jews in Granada and the surrounding conquered territories to remain in their places until 8 December 1494 and signing four-year contracts with Jewish tax farmers in January 1492. Indeed, one reconstruction suggests that the king and queen themselves decided hastily, only a couple of months before the edict was issued.[12] If, on 1 January 1492, Ferdinand and Isabella had no concrete plans to expel the Jews from Spain or deliberately disguised those plans, why should the Jewish leaders be condemned for not having foreseen it?

Was there any historical precedent? Historians neatly group the medieval expulsions from western Europe into a series: England in 1290; France in 1306, perhaps in 1322, and in 1394; Spain in 1492. The Jews of Spain knew about these earlier expulsions, but it was apparently only after their own that they began to recognize a pattern.[13] Before the fact, they understandably—

---

[12] On the Capitulations of Granada specifying the terms of surrender, see Olivia Remie Constable (ed.), *Medieval Iberia: Readings from Christian, Muslim, and Jewish Sources* (Philadelphia, 1997), 349; on the four-year contract and its possibly duplicitous intent, see Salo W. Baron, *A Social and Religious History of the Jews*, 18 vols. (Philadelphia, 1952–83), xi. 238, 403 n. 59; for the argument that the monarchs decided upon the expulsion precipitously, see Stephen Haliczer, 'The Castilian Urban Patriciate and the Jewish Expulsions of 1480–92', *American Historical Review*, 78 (1973), 35–58. There is a division among historians rather analogous to the 'intentionalist' and 'functionalist' interpretations of the Nazi Final Solution, but even from the intentionalist position it does not follow that the intentions of the rulers should have been obvious.

[13] The expulsion from France in 1322 has been called into question (see Elizabeth A. R. Brown, 'Philip V, Charles IV, and the Jews of France': The Alleged Expulsion of 1322', *Speculum*, 66/2 [1991],

and perhaps quite properly—thought of themselves as in a totally different category from their Ashkenazi colleagues. For whether we look at total population, political influence, access to the court, social integration and prestige, or longevity of presence in the land, there were ample grounds to support the claim that Spanish Jewry was uniquely rooted in the Iberian peninsula and would not suffer the fate that had befallen the communities to the north.[14]

What about the local expulsions on the Iberian peninsula? Netanyahu himself, discussing the expulsion from Andalusia in 1483, refers to 'Ferdinand's abilities at concealment and subterfuge' whereby the king and queen 'appeared as if they came to the rescue of the expelled' and supported their claims and financial interests.[15] But rather than taking this as evidence that the naive Jews were duped by Ferdinand, it may be taken to indicate that the monarchs themselves did not view this as the first step towards a general expulsion but rather as a tactical decision to solidify support in the south. When in 1486 local officials expelled the Jews from Valmaseda, Rabbi Abraham Najara wrote in protest to the monarchs, who responded with an order to permit the Jews to return.[16] There is no reason why this rabbi, or any other contemporary Jewish leader, should have seen the Crown as already plotting the end of Spanish Jewry.[17]

Should they not have seen, as Netanyahu argues, that the establishment of the Inquisition and the 'fierce campaign being conducted against the Marranos in the name of their Jewishness' pointed to a clear and present danger

294–329); concerning knowledge of earlier expulsions, see 'A Sermon on the Akedah from the Generation of the Expulsion', in Marc Saperstein, *'Your Voice Like a Ram's Horn': Themes and Texts in Traditional Jewish Preaching* (Cincinnati, 1996), 259–60; for the pattern of expulsions recognized after the fact, see Isaac Abravanel on Deut. 28 (*Perush al hatorah* [Commentary on the Torah], 3 vols. [Jerusalem, 1964], iii, 'Deuteronomy', 262b–263a); Joseph Hacker, 'New Chronicles on the Expulsion from Spain, Its Causes and Results' (Heb.), *Zion*, 44 (1979), 201 n. 1; Yosef Hayim Yerushalmi, *Zakhor: Jewish History and Jewish Memory* (Seattle, 1982), 19, 59.

[14] Note the formulation of Yosef Hayim Yerushalmi, focusing on the Jewish aristocracy: 'That the Crown could someday find it possible to dispense altogether with their services must have been inconceivable; the assumed identity of interest between king and Jews was to them axiomatic' (Yerushalmi, *The Lisbon Massacre of 1506 and the Royal Image in the Shebet Yehudah*, Hebrew Union College Annual Supplements, 1 [Cincinnati, 1976], 38–9).

[15] Netanyahu, *Don Isaac Abravanel*, 48, 277 n. 32b.

[16] Haliczer, 'The Castilian Urban Patriciate and the Jewish Expulsions of 1480–92', 55, based on Luis Suárez Fernández (ed.), *Documentos acerca de la expulsión de los Judíos* (Valladolid, 1964), 313, 317–19; see also Haim Beinart, 'The Expulsion of the Jews of Valmaseda' (Heb.), *Zion*, 46 (1981), 39–51; on the role of Abraham Seneor in reversing this expulsion, see Haim Beinart, *The Expulsion of the Jews from Spain* (Oxford, 2002), 21–2.

[17] See also Carlos Carrete Parrondo, 'Sefarad 1492: Una expulsion anunciada?', in *Movimientos migratorios y expulsiones en la diáspora occidental* (Pamplona, 2000), 49–54.

for themselves?¹⁸ It was not at all clear and present, and Spanish Jewry's regnant 'theory' of the Inquisition, which Netanyahu contemptuously dismisses, was not implausible. Whether one understands the Inquisition primarily as a religious institution or as a social and political one, it was plausible to interpret it as no direct threat to the Jewish community.[19]

Religiously, it attacked the 'Jewishness' of the Marranos only because they were defined as Christians. The 'Jewishness' of the Jews was in a totally different category, protected by long-standing Church doctrine. It was not generally argued that Judaism was by its very nature a pollution of Spanish culture, only that contact with Jews could influence the Conversos in a negative way.[20] The solution seemed to be segregation, or at worst punishment of specific communities of Jews that had encouraged Conversos to Judaize, not total expulsion. The assertion in the Edict of Expulsion that the Inquisition could never accomplish its task so long as Jews remained on Spanish soil could hardly have been anticipated.

Socially, the same is true: the Inquisition attacked Conversos accused of 'Judaizing' because, as Christians, they were theoretically entitled to advance

[18] Netanyahu, *Don Isaac Abravanel*, 45. 'Common sense', we are told, should have led the Jews to foresee the danger. It is rather extraordinary how none of the Jews then living seem to have had any 'common sense', according to Netanyahu.

[19] The scholarly dispute over the nature of the Inquisition is, of course, integrally bound up with the dispute over the nature of the Conversos. For reviews of the literature, see Bruce A. Lorence, 'The Inquisition and the New Christians in the Iberian Peninsula: Main Historiographic Issues and Controversies', in Issachar Ben-Ami (ed.), *The Sepharadi and Oriental Heritage* (Jerusalem, 1982), Eng. vol., 13–72; Joseph Kaplan, 'The Problem of the Conversos and the "New Christians" in the Historical Research of the Past Generation' (Heb.), in Mosheh Tsimerman, Menahem Stern, and Yosef Salmon (eds.), *Studies in Historiography* [Iyunim behistoriografiyah] (Jerusalem, 1988), 117–44; Jesús Martínez de Bujanda, 'Recent Historiography of the Spanish Inquisition (1977–1988): Balance and Perspective', in Mary Elizabeth Perry and Anne J. Cruz (eds.), *Cultural Encounters: The Impact of the Inquisition in Spain and the New World* (Berkeley, 1991), 221–47; for a more popular account, see Adam Gropnik, 'Inquiring Minds: The Spanish Inquisition Revisited', *New Yorker* (16 Jan. 2012), 70–6; for a political interpretation in exhaustive detail, see Benzion Netanyahu, *The Origins of the Inquisition in Fifteenth Century Spain* (New York, 1995), 918–20; see also Ellis Rivkin, 'How Jewish Were the New Christians?', *Hispania Judaica*, 1 (1980), 108; Martin A. Cohen, 'Toward a New Comprehension of the Marranos', *Hispania Judaica*, 1 (1980), 31–2.

[20] Stronger attacks against Jews and Judaism were, of course, in circulation. A blatant example is Alonso de Espina's *Fortalitium fidei* (see Y. Baer, *A History of the Jews in Christian Spain*, ii. 283–90; Netanyahu, *The Origins of the Inquisition*, 814–47). However, this book, completed in 1460, was printed in Latin only outside Spain during this period (in Strassburg by 1471, Basel *c.*1475, Nuremburg 1485, Lyons 1487). Even the most sophisticated Jewish leaders might not have known of it until quite late, if at all. Netanyahu's conclusion that for Espina, 'mass extermination' and 'annihilation' was the 'preferred solution to the Jewish problem in all the countries of Christendom' (ibid. 835) is yet another instance of his projecting back on the fifteenth century the experience of the Holocaust, not to speak of pushing sources considerably beyond what they actually say.

in Spanish society in accordance with their merits, thereby threatening the established centres of 'Old Christian' power. However, the Jews themselves did not constitute such a threat: their influence in Spanish society was not growing but waning at the time of the Expulsion.[21] It was not argued that Jews per se were taking over Spanish society and had to be stopped.

For both of these reasons, it was plausible for Jewish leaders to perceive the Inquisition as not constituting a direct threat. Just as some Conversos favoured the establishment of the Inquisition in the belief that it would separate the genuine New Christians from Judaizing heretics, so Jews were not necessarily indulging in self-delusion when they concluded that their position would not be affected by it. So long as they did not violate the ground rules of toleration by inducing conversion to Judaism and obeyed the law of the land by testifying before the Inquisition when summoned,[22] they had no obvious reason to fear that they would be the next object of attack.[23]

And what if the Jewish leaders had been able to 'foresee' the Expulsion?[24] What could they have done? Call for mass emigration in 1491 or 1480? Even in the unlikely case that they would have been heeded, the result would

---

[21] This has been persuasively argued by Stephen Haliczer ('The Expulsion of the Jews and the Economic Development of Castile', *Hispania Judaica*, 1 [1980], 39–47).

[22] On the Jewish obligation to testify before the Inquisition, see Baron, *A Social and Religious History of the Jews*, xiii. 37.

[23] Making an explicit analogy, Netanyahu similarly condemns the Jews of Germany for having 'failed to foresee Hitler's rise to power at any time during the period preceding that rise' (*Don Isaac Abravanel*, 45). It is here that the revisionist Zionist subtext becomes most apparent. Compare the following statement by Moshe Kohn: 'The blindness and stupidity of the many Jewish leaders—and of many other Jews who should have known better—before the Hitler era and in that era's early years guaranteed that there would be plenty of Jews to feed into the death machinery Hitler's Europe created and directed' (*Jerusalem Post*, international edn. [23 May 1992], 9, col. 5). One might have thought it was time to stop blaming Jewish leaders for failing to foresee unprecedented disasters they were powerless to prevent.

Note the quotations from Abravanel and Arama cited by Netanyahu (*Don Isaac Abravanel*, 276 n. 27) and used to document their 'blindness' to the approaching tidal wave. On the contrary, they may serve to indicate that there was no good reason to suspect that the position of Spanish Jewry would be imperilled (see also Gampel, *The Last Jews on Iberian Soil*, 2). Netanyahu's condemnation of Spanish Jews for not being prophets—for having 'failed to notice . . . the mountainous wave which was approaching to overwhelm them' (*Don Isaac Abravanel*, 45)—is no more convincing as metaphor than it is as history: those living by the seashore cannot see a tidal wave until it is too late.

[24] For a possible adumbration of a disaster lying ahead, see the sermon by Shem Tov ibn Shem Tov (in Saperstein *Jewish Preaching, 1200–1800*, 82–3). Ibn Shem Tov expressed deep scepticism about the ability of the Jewish courtiers to accomplish anything significant on behalf of their people. Needless to say, later accounts of 'premonitions', such as the passage from Ibn Verga in n. 6 above and the story that Isaac de Leon appeared to his widow in a dream a year before the Expulsion and ordered that the cemetery in which he was buried be ploughed over, have no evidentiary value for the period before 1492 (see Joseph Hakohen, *Emek habakhah* [history], ed. Meir Letteris [Kraków, 1895], 99).

not have been significantly different: a shift in Jewish population to new areas. Was there anything Spanish Jewish leaders could have done to prevent the Expulsion? Despite their resources, the influence of Jewish courtiers was limited. Abravanel describes his efforts to convince the Catholic Monarchs to revoke the edict, and it is difficult to imagine what more could have been attempted: Christian allies in the court were mobilized, a vast sum of money was pledged, various kinds of appeals were made.[25] At the same time, other leaders were acting to facilitate the large-scale emigration through negotiations in Portugal and Istanbul. There is little that suggests a paralysis of leadership at this crucial juncture, and if, as Haliczer has argued, the Catholic Monarchs themselves were pressed to expel the Jews by powerful social forces they could not successfully resist,[26] then the relative impotence of the Jews would have been even more pronounced.

The star witness in the case for the failure of leadership has been Abraham Seneor. One can hardly imagine a more devastating image than that of the most powerful Jewish courtier in Spain, *Rab de la corte* and 'chief judge of the *aljamas* of the Jews in Castile', accepting baptism with his illustrious son-in-law under the sponsorship of the king, queen, and a leading cardinal. Perceived as having committed the ultimate betrayal, it is not surprising that Seneor would be described by historians as 'not among the pious' and 'a man of no great stature . . . disliked by the leading Jews of Spain especially because of his religious laxity and meagre scholastic attainments'.[27]

But these negative accounts are based on post-Expulsion sources.[28] If we

---

[25] See Netanyhau, *Don Isaac Abravanel*, 54–5.

[26] Haliczer, 'The Castilian Urban Patriciate and the Jewish Expulsions of 1480–92'.

[27] For the negative evaluations of Seneor, see Y. Baer, *A History of the Jews in Christian Spain*, ii. 314; Netanyahu, *Don Isaac Abravanel*, 52; for a thorough and balanced treatment of Seneor in historical context, see Eleazar Gutwirth, 'Abraham Seneor: Social Tensions and the Court-Jew', *Michael*, 11 (1989), 169–229. The characterization of Seneor as 'chief judge', appears in a document cited ibid. 200; on the nature of this position, see ibid. 208–17.

[28] The main source states that Isaac de Leon called him *sone or* (hater of light), 'for he was a heretic, as is proven by eventual apostasy' (in Alexander Marx, 'The Expulsion of the Jews from Spain: Two New Accounts', *Jewish Quarterly Review*, 20 [1908], 250; Y. Baer, *A History of the Jews in Christian Spain*, ii. 314; Haim Hillel Ben-Sasson, 'The Generation of Spanish Exiles Considers Its Fate [Heb.], in id., *Continuity and Variety* [Retsef utemurah] [Tel Aviv, 1984], 458 n. 105); cf. the attack, made in a polemical context, by David ben Judah Messer Leon (in Hava Tirosh-Rothschild, *Between Worlds: The Life and Thought of Rabbi David ben Judah Messer Leon* [Albany, NY, 1991], 103); for an explanation of the motivation as the 'evil inclination' rather than philosophical scepticism, see Hacker, 'New Chronicles on the Expulsion from Spain', 222 n. 131. The disparity probably indicates that in the absence of solid information about the circumstances of conversion, writers used the opportunity to blame it on whatever factors they wanted to criticize. The propensity to resort to negative plays on the names Seneor and Meir (ibid. 228) also suggests a lack of substantive information.

look carefully at documents written before Seneor's conversion we find a rather different picture. He is described by his contemporaries as the enduring sceptre of Judah, 'our exilarch', who was not afraid to use his considerable influence in the court on behalf of his people. Baer concludes that 'he faithfully exercised his political functions so as to promote the welfare of his people for sixteen years, and up to the very day of his baptism . . . worked untiringly for the sake of the Jewish cause'. Together with Abravanel, he tried to persuade the monarchs to revoke their edict. One tradition, recorded by Capsali, maintains that he converted because of a threat by the queen that the alternative would be a massacre of the Jews.[29] If this is true, then the act might legitimately be understood as the ultimate self-sacrifice. If not, then the decision reflects the psychology of an 80-year-old man faced with expulsion from the only country he knew. Yet it also shows that he was not universally disliked, for if he were, how could a tradition like this have been circulated and given credence?

The only thing that might have prepared Spanish Jewry for the disaster of 1492 was a total abandonment of its historical and political traditions, an attempt to forge broader alliances with those social elements whose interests were opposed to the unification of the kingdoms, centralization of power, and the suppression of religious and political liberties. Perhaps someone might have foreseen that the strong centralized state could be a greater source of danger to the Jews than the forces from which Jews were ordinarily protected by royal authority. Some passages in the later writings of Abravanel might perhaps suggest this insight, achieved in retrospect.[30] But it was an insight

---

[29] For the letter praising Seneor from 1487, see Y. Baer, *A History of the Jews in Christian Spain*, ii. 315; Ben-Sasson, 'The Generation of Spanish Exiles Considers Its Fate' (Heb.), 205–6; cf. also the description cited ibid. 207; for Baer's positive description of Seneor's activities, see *A History of the Jews in Christian Spain*, ii. 314, 341–2, 400–2; cf. also Maurice Kriegel, 'La Prise d'une décision: L'Expulsion des juifs d'Espagne en 1492', *Revue historique*, 260 (1978), 56–7. In his comprehensive review of Seneor's career, Gutwirth gives a more nuanced assessment of Seneor's representation of Jewish issues in the political arena, suggesting that in some cases he may have been acting to defend the interests of his own economic and social class rather than the Jewish community as a whole ('Abraham Seneor', 218–19), but the main thrust of his article is to criticize the tendency to evaluate Seneor's entire career retrospectively in light of his conversion (ibid. 228). For the exculpatory interpretation of Seneor's apostasy, see Elijah Capsali, *Seder eliyahu zuta* [history], 2 vols. (Jerusalem, 1975), 210; Y. Baer, *A History of the Jews in Christian Spain*, ii. 436; Netanyahu, *Don Isaac Abravanel*, 281 n. 71; Baron, *A Social and Religious History of the Jews*, xi. 240; on Seneor's behaviour soon after the edict was proclaimed, plausibly indicating an initial intention to leave Spain, see Gutwirth, 'Abraham Seneor', 206.

[30] On the royal alliance as the axiom of Jewish political ideology and behaviour, see Yerushalmi, *The Lisbon Massacre of 1506*, esp. 38–9. Abravanel's argument is that a king is not necessary and that

that would not be fully confirmed until the twentieth century. To blame fifteenth-century Spanish Jews for not foreseeing the unprecedented is an exercise not in historiography but in polemic.[31]

Turning to the second charge, of intellectual mediocrity, we find here too a number of historical problems. First, there is an issue of selection. It is never superfluous to repeat the reminder that our evaluation of the leaders of Spanish Jewry is based almost entirely on those who wrote books. In the late fifteenth century, in the infancy of printing, no 'book' written by a contemporary Jew in Spain had widespread influence on Spanish soil.[32] The Jews of the time were influenced not by what their leaders wrote, but by what they heard them say, and this is, for the most part, lost to the historical record.[33]

---

the best government is provided by those appointed to positions of authority for limited periods of time, who make decisions in large groups, and who are divided into groups that have specialized authority and function, all of which leads to the goal of preventing the concentration of power and ensuring that it will be exercised only in the most diffuse manner. Perhaps this reflects the conclusion that the Jews had been sacrificed to the interests of centralism in Spain and that kings could be a source of danger as well as of protection. See also the passages from Shem Tov ibn Shem Tov questioning the efficacy of the 'royal alliance' and from Joel ibn Shu'eib alluding to the potential dangers of centralization (in Saperstein, *Jewish Preaching, 1200–1800*, 82–3).

[31] See Peter Gay's analysis of German antisemitism during the Wilhelmine decades, which concludes: 'To reproach Germany's Jews of that epoch with failing to see what was, after all, scarcely visible or wholly invisible is an exercise in the unhistorical' (Gay, *Freud, Jews and Other Germans: Masters and Victims in Modernist Culture* [Oxford, 1978], 169–70).

[32] The Hebrew books printed in Spain were classical texts, not the works of contemporary writers (see Perets Tishby, 'Hebrew Incunabula: Spain and Portugal (Guadalajara)' [Heb.], *Kiryat sefer*, 61 [1986–7], 522 and bibliography on p. 530). The situation was different in Italy, where Judah Messer Leon's *Nofet tsufim*, published at Mantua in 1475 or 1476, became the first Hebrew work printed during the lifetime of its author (see Isaac Rabinowitz, introduction to Judah ben Yehiel Messer Leon, *The Book of the Honeycomb's Flow: Sēpher Nōfeth Sūfīm*, trans. and ed. Isaac Rabinowitz [Ithaca, NY, 1983], p. xxx). Books written by the leaders of Spanish Jewry were printed in the sixteenth century in countries to which the Jews had emigrated. These books cannot therefore be taken as clear evidence of the influence of their authors in Spain itself. For the more limited influence of Isaac Aboab's sermons, see below.

[33] Occasionally we encounter reports in written works of what an author remembers having heard from his teacher, a preacher, and so on: 'I heard a man who thought himself to be wise and is so considered by our masses, preach to a large audience' (Isaac Abravanel, *Ateret zekenim* [Warsaw, 1894], 12*b*; I am grateful to Eric Lawee for this reference). We also find things Abravanel heard from Joseph ibn Shem Tov (Abravanel on Exod. 25: 20 [*Perush al hatorah*, ii, 'Exodus', 253*b*] [the reference in Saperstein, *Jewish Preaching 1200–1800*, 167 n. 2, should be corrected accordingly]); Isaac Karo reporting his brother Ephraim's words (Karo, *Toledot yitshak* [commentary on the Torah] [Trent, 1558], 40*a*); the words of Isaac de Leon cited by Abraham Saba on Gen. 22: 10 (*Tseror hamor . . . al hamishah humshei torah* [homiletical comments on the Torah] [New York, 1961], 'Genesis', 24*b*); Isaac Aboab reporting what he heard from 'the scholar Joseph Jeshua of blessed memory' (*Nehar pishon* [sermons] [Istanbul, 1538; repr. Zolkiew, 1806], 16*d*; cf. Y. Baer, *A History of the Jews in Christian*

In every Jewish community of Spain, sermons were delivered each sabbath during the crucial years leading to the summer of 1492. Of these thousands of sermons, many were undoubtedly uninspired, conventional, hackneyed, and devoted to standard conceptual and exegetical problems bearing no direct relevance to the period, but there were undoubtedly some that attempted to interpret the bewildering events of the times, to provide guidance, encouragement, and comfort to Jews faced with staggering uncertainties.

To mention only some of the material we know from contemporary reports: a rabbi named Levi ben Shem Tov of Saragossa delivered three sermons in 1490 exhorting his people to obey the edict compelling Jews to testify about Judaizing Conversos before the Inquisition;[34] Rabbi Solomon of Albarracin, banished from his own city because of his sermons, preached so powerfully in Teruel that he dissuaded Jews from converting and convinced them to leave Spain;[35] Abraham Saba preached a sermon on the destiny of the Jewish people and Christendom 'at a gathering of sages in Castile, and they praised it';[36] Abraham Zacuto delivered a eulogy for his teacher Isaac Aboab in Portugal, in February 1493.[37] Such material, of obvious importance in evaluating the leadership of Spanish Jewry, was never written in a form intended for future readers. Without it, assessment of the quality of leadership is bound to be precarious.

The data is limited not only by what was written but by what has been preserved. It stands to reason that a community disrupted by the cataclysm of a sudden, unexpected general expulsion will lose a greater proportion of its

---

Spain, ii. 248); Aboab recording recollections of his unnamed teacher, possibly Isaac Campanton (Isaac Aboab, *Be'ur al perush haramban latorah* [super-commentary on Nahmanides' *Commentary on the Torah*], in *Treasury of Torah Commentators* [Otsar mefarshei hatorah], 2 vols. [Jerusalem, 1973], 'Genesis', 6*b*, 12*a*, 20*b*, 36*d*; 'Exodus', 17*b*, 19*b*); Joseph ben Hayim Yabetz transmitting the words of Joseph Hayun (Yabetz, *Or haḥayim* [Ferrara, 1554], 21*a*; cf. Joseph Hacker, 'Rabbi Joseph Hayun and the Generation of the Expulsion from Portugal' [Heb.], *Zion*, 48 [1983], 275). Abraham Saba also reported a sermon delivered generations earlier by Hasdai Crescas during a drought (Eleazar Gutwirth, 'Towards Expulsion, 1391–1492', in Elie Kedourie [ed.], *Spain and the Jews* [London, 1992], 16).

[34] See Saperstein, *Jewish Preaching, 1200–1800*, 85 n. 12.

[35] Antonio Floriano, *La aljama de judios de Teruel* (Teruel, 1926), 17–18, in Y. Baer, *A History of the Jews in Christian Spain*, ii. 436.

[36] Saba, *Tseror hamor*, 'Genesis', 50*a*; cf. 'I preached this many times before the Exile' (ibid., 'Exodus', 29*b*); 'I preached this in every synagogue of the [Jewish] community in Fez after I recovered from my illness (ibid., 'Deuteronomy', 6*d*).

[37] Abraham ben Samuel Zacuto, *Sefer yuḥasin hashalem* [history of the Jews] (Jerusalem, 1963), 226*a*. Joseph ben Hayim Yabetz refers to his own sermons, none of which have been preserved, in a work written in the second year after the Expulsion (Yabetz, *Ḥasdei hashem* [Brooklyn, 1934], 22–3).

manuscripts than a community living in quiet times. Despite the concerted effort of the Spanish émigrés to save their books, the extant literature of the period is filled with references to books that have been lost, either in Spain or in Portugal.[38] How much do we know of Ephraim Karo, father of the author of the *Shulḥan arukh*? He died at a relatively young age, but his teachings are cited by his brother Isaac and his son Joseph, who apparently had access to written material, a collection of legal decisions or responsa that is not known today.[39] Indeed, there is a whole list of distinguished rabbis and heads of academies about whom hardly anything is known, either because they did not write at all or because their books have been lost.[40]

---

[38] On the effort to save books and the inevitable loss nevertheless, see Joseph Hacker, 'The Intellectual Activity of the Jews of the Ottoman Empire during the Sixteenth and Seventeenth Centuries', in Isadore Twersky and Bernard Septimus (eds.), *Jewish Thought in the Seventeenth Century* (Cambridge, Mass., 1987), 106. For material written but lost, see Meir Benayahu, introduction to Joseph ben Meir Garçon, 'The Sermons of Rabbi Joseph ben Meir Garçon' (Heb.), *Michael*, 7 (1981), 51–2 (on lost works by Garçon), 42–3 (on the lost sermons of Abraham Shamsulo and of Shem Tov Gamil [or Jamil] of Tudela); for more on Gamil, see Jacob Meir Toledano, 'From Manuscripts' (Heb.), *Hebrew Union College Annual*, 5 (1928), 403–9; Gampel, *The Last Jews on Iberian Soil*, 130–1. Abraham Saba described three of his works, including commentaries on the Torah, the Five Scrolls, and Mishnah *Avot*, which were lost in Portugal (see Dan Manor, 'On the History of Rabbi Avraham Saba' [Heb.], *Jerusalem Studies in Jewish Thought*, 2/2 [1983], 227–8; Abraham Gross, *Iberian Jewry from Twilight to Dawn: The World of Rabbi Abraham Saba* [Leiden, 1995], 8–9). Abravanel referred to his lost work *Maḥazeh shadai* (see Netanyahu, *Don Isaac Abravanel*, 85). For lost works by Joseph Isaac ibn Shem Tov, see Harry Austryn Wolfson, 'Isaac ibn Shem Tob's Unknown Commentaries on the *Physics* and His Other Unknown Works', in id., *Studies in the History of Philosophy and Religion*, ed. Isadore Twersky and George Williams, 2 vols. (Cambridge, Mass., 1973–7), ii. 490. Inquisitional documents refer to the burning of some 6,000 volumes on Judaism and sorcery at Salamanca in 1490: many of these were presumably written by Jews (Elkan Nathan Adler, 'Lea on the Inquisition of Spain and Herein of Spanish and Portuguese Jews', *Jewish Quarterly Review*, 20 [1908], 527). Abraham Saba, as noted above described the confiscation of all Jewish books in Lisbon at the time of the forced conversion of 1497. A source cited by Hacker speaks of kabbalistic manuscripts that 'sank in the sea' ('The Intellectual Activity of the Jews of the Ottoman Empire', 106).

[39] See R. J. Werblowsky, *Joseph Karo: Lawyer and Mystic* (Philadelphia, 1977), 85.

[40] See the document in Marx, 'The Expulsion of the Jews from Spain', 250, 254, 259–61 nn. 11–21. Paramount among them was Isaac de Leon, renowned as a talmudist, kabbalist, and public figure, but known primarily because of brief citations by others and mention in the celebrated Inquisitional trial of Alfonso de la Cavalleria (Isaac Hirsch Weiss, *Each Generation and Its Exegetes: A Book of the History of the Oral Law* [Dor dor vedorshav, hu sefer divrei hayamim latorah shebe'al peh], 5 pts. in 2 vols. [Vilna, 1911], v. 234–5; Marx, 'The Expulsion of the Jews from Spain', 60 n. 15; Y. Baer, *A History of the Jews in Christian Spain*, ii. 374–5, 491–2 n. 17; Moshe Idel, 'Enquiries into the Doctrine of *Sefer hameshiv*' [Heb.], *Sefunot* NS, 2/17 [1983], 262; cf. Zacuto, *Sefer yuḥasin hashalem*, 76b; Joseph Hakohen, *Emek habakhah*, 99). Some additional material about the Spanish rabbis is provided in eulogies by Joseph Garçon (see e.g. Benayahu, introduction to Garçon, 'Sermons' [Heb.], 118–20 [on Samuel Franco], 122–3 [on Jacob ibn Habib]; Joseph Hacker, 'On the Spiritual Image of Spanish Jews at the End of the Fifteenth Century' [Heb.], *Sefunot* NS, 2/17 [1983], 47–59; Abraham Gross, 'Centers

This is probably the reason why the generation of the Expulsion made little contribution to the corpus of responsa literature. One may doubt that it is, as Elon suggests, because the challenges of the times made it difficult for the rabbis to concentrate: since when have hard times, or even persecution, prevented Jews from writing *she'elot* and *teshuvot*? Nor can the problem be the ability of the rabbis. Could a generation of halakhists whom Joseph Karo spoke of with deep respect have been unable to produce responsa? It seems far more likely that the texts of responsa written by the Spanish rabbis simply did not reach the centres of Italy or the Ottoman empire where they could be collected, organized, printed, and incorporated into the recognized body of precedents.[41]

Similarly, the upheaval caused by the Expulsion is undoubtedly responsible for the loss of communal registers and minute books (*pinkasim*), which are such a valuable source of information about the leadership of communities in Italy, Poland, Amsterdam, and elsewhere. Spanish *pinkasim* are known only from occasional references in other literature—a loss of enormous historical magnitude.[42]

There is a second fundamental problem with the assessments of intellectual mediocrity cited. Modern scholars writing histories of Jewish philosophy or kabbalah can readily identify those who appear to be the truly profound, probing, and original minds, who blaze new paths for others. It does not at all follow, however, that these individuals are necessarily the most effective religious leaders of their own generation. Those who centuries later appear to be the deepest thinkers of an age may have had little to say to most of their contemporaries. Ordinary Jews need leaders who can make ideas accessible to them, relate them to traditional values and apply them to contemporary challenges. This is not an exaltation of mediocre minds; it is, rather, a suggestion that leadership in a specific historical context may require abilities and qualities different from those that impress intellectuals of a later age, and that brilliance may lie in communicating with a wide audience as well as in exploring uncharted territory.[43]

of Study and Yeshivot in Spain', in Haim Beinart (ed.), *Moreshet Sepharad: The Sephardi Legacy*, 2 vols. [Jerusalem, 1992], i, esp. 407–10).

[41] See the discussion of Aboab's responsa below.

[42] e.g.: 'It is written in the book of minutes called *registo* [*sic*]' (Isaac Aboab, responsum in *Shivah einayim: . . . she'elot uteshuvot . . . mahari abo'ab* [rabbinic miscellany] [Leghorn, 1745], 56*b*).

[43] Some combined effective leadership with profundity: Maimonides and Crescas are paramount examples. Yet their influence as leaders was not because of their technical philosophical work. It was not Crescas's critique of Aristotle that made him such an important leader for Aragonese Jewry in 1391, but rather his efforts to reconstruct the devastated *aljamas* and possibly his preaching (see

Conscious of these considerations, we can begin to evaluate the quality of leadership by criteria appropriate to the historical setting. What we should expect from religious leaders is not the ability to foresee the future or chart new intellectual paths but rather the ability to address the cultural, intellectual, ethical, and spiritual problems besetting their people in a manner that both demonstrates the relevance of the common tradition to these issues and strengthens a commitment to this tradition. By this measure, I believe there is abundant evidence that Spanish Jewry in its final generation produced figures of considerable stature.

It is hard to conceive of any definition of leadership that would exclude Isaac Abravanel from the very highest level. He is one of the handful in Jewish history who combined political influence at the pinnacle of what was possible for Jews, deep concern for the welfare of his people, and prolific writings of major cultural significance. His literary oeuvre can be seen as a summation of the entire cultural tradition of Sephardi Jewry in Spain, cutting across the lines of philosophy, kabbalah, and talmudic studies to forge a comprehensive yet accessible synthesis. Because Abravanel is so well known, detailed investigation of others is at present a more important task.[44]

The thoughts of certain figures have been investigated in monographic studies, including Isaac Arama,[45] Abraham Bibago,[46] Abraham Shalom,[47] and

---

Y. Baer, *A History of the Jews in Christian Spain*, ii. 83–5, 110–30). The power of Crescas's philosophical thought was not appreciated by Jewish philosophers even two or three generations later (see Shem Tov ibn Shem Tov, in Harry Austryn Wolfson, *Crescas' Critique of Aristotle: Problems of Aristotle's 'Physics' in Jewish and Arabic Philosophy* [Cambridge, Mass., 1957], 33; David ben Judah Messer Leon, in Tirosh-Rothschild, *Between Worlds*, 286 n. 25). Therefore the absence of a thinker of the stature of Crescas in the generation of the Expulsion does not necessarily mean that the quality of leadership was mediocre.

[44] The substantial literature on Abravanel, in addition to Netanyahu's work, need not be reviewed here, but note especially Jean-Christophe Attias, *Isaac Abravanel: La Mémoire et l'espérance* (Paris, 1992); Eric Lawee, *Isaac Abravanel's Stance Toward Tradition: Defense, Dissent, Dialogue* (Albany, NY, 2001), with references to earlier articles; Eleazar Gutwirth, 'Don Ishaq Abravanel and Vernacular Humanism in Fifteenth-Century Iberia', *Bibliothèque d'humanisme et renaissance*, 60 (1998), 641–71. On the tendency to incorporate both philosophy and kabbalah, see Sha'ul Regev, 'Rational-Mystical Jewish Thought in the Fifteenth Century' (Heb.), *Jerusalem Studies in Jewish Thought*, 5 (1986), 155–89.

[45] Sarah Heller Wilensky, *The Philosophy of Rabbi Isaac Arama within the Framework of Philonic Philosophy* [R. yitsḥak arama umishnato] (Jerusalem, 1957); Chaim Pearl, *The Medieval Jewish Mind: The Religious Philosophy of Isaac Arama* (London, 1971).

[46] Alan Lazaroff, *The Theology of Abraham Bibago* (Tuscaloosa, 1981); see also the updated bibliography in Mauro Zonta, *Hebrew Scholasticism in the Fifteenth Century: A History and Source Book* (Dordrecht, 2006), 33 n. 1.

[47] Herbert A. Davidson, *The Philosophy of Abraham Shalom: A Fifteenth-Century Exposition and Defense of Maimonides* (Berkeley, 1964).

Abraham Saba,[48] but even of those whose works survive, some—Isaac Aboab, Shem Tov ibn Shem Tov, Joel ibn Shu'eib, Isaac Karo, Joseph Yabetz, and 'Israel', the author of 'Dover meisharim'[49]—warrant more detailed and comprehensive investigation than has been given them. I will illustrate with the example of Isaac Aboab.

Aboab's stature as one of the most important talmudists of his generation is attested by many. Himself one of the outstanding disciples of Isaac Campanton, his own disciples included Jacob Berab, Joseph Fasi, Moses Danon, and Abraham Zacuto. Joseph Karo's *magid*, the mystical personification of the Mishnah whose communications Karo recorded over a period of many years, singled out Aboab's *yeshivah* as pre-eminent in the recent past, promising Karo that 'your academy will be even greater than that of My chosen one, Isaac Aboab';[50] Levi ibn Habib, rabbi of Jerusalem and fierce opponent of Berab, described Aboab as 'the greatest of his generation'.[51] Aboab's commentary on section 'Oraḥ ḥayim' of *Arba'ah turim* was an important source for Karo, who referred in his own commentary to a question disputed in the Aboab *yeshivah*. He also wrote a commentary on section 'Yoreh de'ah' and original comments (*ḥidushim*) on the talmudic tractates *Beitsah*, *Ketubot*, and *Kidushin*.[52]

In addition, we are told that he wrote responsa by the 'thousands and myriads: he made them proliferate, but we do not know who will gather them'.[53] Two of these responsa were published in the eighteenth century (at the end of

---

[48] Gross, *Iberian Jewry From Twilight to Dawn*.

[49] On the collection of his sermons in MS 197 (Neubauer 2447), Christ Church, Oxford, see Saperstein, *Jewish Preaching 1200–1800*, 19, 25, 395–8.

[50] Joseph Karo, *Magid meisharim* (Amsterdam, 1708), 2b, in Louis Jacobs, *Jewish Mystical Testimonies* (New York, 1977), 113.

[51] Levi ibn Habib, *She'elot uteshuvot haralbaḥ* [responsa] (Lemberg, 1865), 2: 24d, no. 122.

[52] Isaac Aboab, *Tur veshulḥan arukh, oraḥ ḥayim, hilkhot shabat . . . im be'ur ḥadash miketav yad mohari abo'ab* [commentary on sabbath laws in *Arba'ah turim* and *Shulḥan arukh*, 'Oraḥ ḥayim'] (Montreal, 1991); id., *Be'ur letur oraḥ ḥayim* [commentary on *Arba'ah turim*, 'Oraḥ ḥayim'] (Jerusalem, 1995); id., *Shitat hakadmonim al masekhet beitsah . . . im ḥidushei rabenu yitsḥak abo'ab* [commentary on Babylonian Talmud, *Beitsah*] (Jerusalem, 1959); see I. H. Weiss, *Each Generation and Its Exegetes* (Heb.), v. 235; Elon, *Jewish Law*, iii. 1302 n. 276, 1315 n. 17; Jacob Katz, *Halakhah and Kabbalah* [Halakhah vekabalah: meḥkarim betoledot dat yisra'el al medoreiha vezikatah haḥevratit] (Jerusalem, 1984), 41 n. 28, 61. On an important work that emerged from his academy, see Daniel Boyarin, 'Studies in the Talmudic Exegesis of the Spanish Exiles' (Heb.), *Sefunot* NS, 2/17 (1983), esp. 171 n. 31.

[53] Solomon ben Mazal Tov, introduction to Aboab, *Nehar pishon*, 2b (alluding to Ps. 39: 7). The statement may imply that unlike most collections of responsa, based on copies made by the author (or an amanuensis) before they were sent, in this case the collection of copies had been lost and all that existed were the originals sent to many different questioners who were, after the Expulsion, widely dispersed.

Shivah einayim). Both deal with a trustee who sold a portion of a house belonging to orphans who challenged the validity of the sale when they reached maturity. Aboab shows considerable independence in his decision, writing:

> The talmudic statement [BT *Git.* 52*a*] that trustees may not sell real estate applied to their time, when real estate was the basis of their livelihood, and their primary responsibility pertained to it. Today, however, when our livelihood is based primarily on moveable property, which is better than real estate in every respect, and it is well known in our time that there is no work more demeaning than [that involving] real estate [cf. BT *Yev.* 63*a*], we should change the law in accordance with the place and the time.... In this position of mine, I do not rely on anyone else, for I have not found it in any other decisor. However, together with my other arguments, this is what the law should be.[54]

Even if such independence of legal reasoning was relatively unusual in his work, if the actual number of his responsa was anywhere near a thousand, the loss of such a substantial corpus has deprived us of what would undoubtedly be a major resource for the last generation of Spanish Jews before the Expulsion.

Aboab's interests and talents were considerably broader than the world of the Talmud and Jewish law. His biblical commentary—a super-commentary on Rashi and Ramban—enters fully into the arena of biblical exegesis.[55] One could not prove from this work that the author was a distinguished halakhic authority at all, nor could one document a solid grounding in either philosophy or kabbalah. It shows little in the way of an intellectual agenda, other than to guide the reader through some of the problems in the classic commentaries of the two masters. More than anything else, it gives the impression of Torah study 'for its own sake'.

---

[54] *Shivah einayim*, 55*a*. See the use of this responsum by Gutwirth, 'Abraham Seneor', 214. On changing the law because of changed historical circumstances, see Louis Jacobs, *A Tree of Life: Diversity, Flexibility, and Creativity in Jewish Law* (Oxford, 1984), 122–65; and the discussion of Judah ben Asher in Chapter 2 above.

[55] Aboab, *Be'ur al perush haramban latorah*. *Encyclopedia Judaica* states that while the super-commentary on Nahmanides has been printed, Aboab's super-commentary on Rashi has been lost (Zvi Avneri, 'Aboab, Isaac II', *Encyclopedia Judaica*, 16 vols. [Jerusalem, 1973], ii. 93; 22 vols. [Detroit, 2007], i. 267–8). This statement seems to me to be based on a misreading of the introduction to *Nehar pishon*, in which Solomon ben Mazal Tov mentions among Aboab's works 'his commentary on the commentary of ... Rashi *z'l* on the Torah and on the commentary of ... Ramban *z'l* on the Torah'. The printed work reveals that it is as much a discussion of Rashi as of Nahmanides: it is probable therefore that the above statement does not refer to two separate works but to one.

Particularly important for our purposes are Aboab's sermons.[56] To be sure, the evidence of his preaching is less than ideal. Most of the material preserved in the book published as *Nehar pishon* is a summary, apparently written by the preacher's son from his father's notes and from notes taken by disciples, not a full transcript of anything that was said.[57] Unlike the sermons of Aboab's younger contemporary Joseph ben Meir Garçon,[58] these sermons are not identified by date or place of delivery, only by the Torah lesson or life-cycle or holiday occasion. Nevertheless, there is clear evidence that Aboab took preaching seriously, reflecting on the techniques and conventions of the art, occasionally preaching twice on the same sabbath (at Shaharit and Minhah services), delivering wedding sermons and eulogies as well as the expected sermons for Shabat Hagadol and Shabat Shuvah (the sabbaths immediately preceding Passover and Yom Kippur, respectively).[59]

Some of these sermons seem to be intended for the broadest kind of audience. For example:

There are many obstacles that hinder a person from studying God's Torah, as is known, but I will subsume them under two categories. The first is the magnitude and

---

[56] The collection of Aboab's sermons called *Nehar pishon* (see Gen. 2: 13) was first published in Istanbul in 1538 and reprinted in Zolkiew in 1806. In both editions, the sermons are arranged in what seems to be a totally random order. By contrast, in MS Or. 10701 (Gaster 1398) (British Library, London), they are arranged in the order of the Torah lessons, with the sermon on Genesis 2: 10–11, which provides the title for the collection, coming first. This manuscript contains nothing that is not in the printed edition and lacks some material that is in the printed edition (see below, n. 80). Furthermore, the manuscript contains some passages with obvious textual errors. It is not easy to imagine why a printer using a manuscript with sermons in an intelligible order would have jumbled the order to produce what we have in print. The relationship between the MS and the *editio princeps* still needs clarification. Another important manuscript of Aboab's sermons, 'Ketsat parashiyot' (MS Hunt 342 [Neubauer 952], Bodleian Library, Oxford), by contrast, contains important homiletical material that is not in the printed edition.

[57] On the sermons as copied by Aboab's disciples, see Jacob ben Isaac Aboab's statement on the final page of the Zolkiew edition; cf. Mordecai Pachter, 'The Homiletical and Ethical Literature of the Sixteenth-Century Sages in Safed, and the Array of Its Principal Ideas' [Sifrut haderush vehamusar shel ḥakhmei tsefat bame'ah hatet-zayin uma'arekhet rayonoteiha ha'ikariyim] (Ph.D. diss., Hebrew University of Jerusalem, 1976), 15. There are, however, internal indications that the abridgement was the work of the preacher himself (e.g. Aboab, *Nehar pishon*, 27c, 33a).

[58] See Joseph ben Meir Garçon, 'Sermons' (Heb.), ed. Benayahu; Hacker, 'On the Spiritual Image of Spanish Jews at the End of the Fifteenth Century' (Heb.); Saperstein, *Jewish Preaching, 1200–1800*, 199–216.

[59] Note the following themes and conventions of homiletical art: *reshut* (a formal request for permission to preach) (Aboab, *Nehar pishon*, 5b, 28a, 38d); explaining the justification for preaching when modesty would have required him to remain silent (ibid. 13b; cf. Saperstein, *Jewish Preaching, 1200–1800*, 63–4); evidence for preaching twice on the same sabbath (ibid. 31). Some indications of having addressed an actual audience remain in the written text (Aboab, *Nehar pishon*, 23c, 23d, 38d, 40d).

the extent of Torah. People say, 'How long will it take me to read every verse in the twenty-four books [of the Bible], and the entire Mishnah, and the entire Talmud, totalling sixty tractates?' This consideration keeps people from studying. God therefore said to Israel that Jews should always study Torah, for its reward is sustained and established by God even for one who reads only a single book. That is why the sages said: 'It is not incumbent upon you to finish the task' [Mishnah *Avot* 2: 16], meaning, even if you have read only a little, I will give you your reward, unlike labourers who are not paid until they finish the job.[60]

Rather than the conventional complaint about the decline in the standards of Torah study, here we find a rabbinical scholar reaching out to the simple Jew, showing empathy for the difficulties and frustrations of Torah study, and encouraging those who will never be scholars to set reasonable goals and find satisfaction in what they are able to achieve.

Or the following passage, in which Aboab discusses the actions of Jacob's sons following the rape of Dinah:

It is human nature that when people quarrel, whether over words or deeds, and come for reconciliation between themselves, if they are truly sincere, they will say: 'Even though this and that occurred between us, and such and such happened, it makes no difference.' If the reconciliation is insincere, they say: 'Never mention what happened again', while the aggrieved party holds on to his anger and bides his time until an opportunity comes for revenge. So it was with the sons of Jacob. They calculated to themselves how it would be possible to take vengeance against Shechem. When Shechem and his father Hamor came to ask for Dinah, they said: 'Even though you have done this shameful thing to our sister, we will overlook this insult and give her to you in marriage, provided that you circumcise every male.' That is why they believed them. And this is the meaning of the verse, 'The sons of Jacob answered Shechem and his father Hamor with guile' [Gen. 34: 13]. What was the guile? That they said, 'that he defiled their sister Dinah' [implying sincere reconciliation] and subsequently killed them.[61]

Here we have an insight of some psychological depth, expressed in a form that any listener can understand and identify with, used to explain a problematic verse. As in the previous passage, it is a preaching style intended to endear the preacher to a common audience.

---

[60] Isaac Aboab, 'Ketsat parashiyot', fo. 7*b* on 'Beshalaḥ'.

[61] Ibid., fo. 8*b* on 'Vayishlaḥ'. On the problems of this passage and the inadequacy of the conventional interpretations, see Abravanel on Gen. 34: 13 (*Perush al hatorah*, i. 348*b*, question 6. Like Aboab (and Saba [*Tseror hamor*, 'Genesis', 48*b*]), Abravanel interprets the last phrase of the verse not as the Torah's explanation of the reason for the 'guile', but as the content of what they spoke: his understanding of the 'guile' is different from Aboab's (Abravanel, *Perush al hatorah*, i. 352*b*–353*a*).

On the other hand, some of the printed sermons seem to have been addressed to rather sophisticated and learned audiences. The level of philosophical material in some of these was quite high, as can be seen in the following passage:

On this matter, Thomas [Aquinas] said in the commentary on the seventh book of the *Metaphysics* in the name of Averroës [Ibn Rushd] that [Aristotle] held the position that the essences of species and their definitions reside entirely in the form. Yet in many other places in the philosophical literature we find explicitly that [Aristotle] says that the essences of species and their definitions reside in both matter and form. How then could he have said the opposite?

The answer: It is known that all accidental properties have an essential aspect. They are called 'accidents' because they cannot exist without a subject. Thus, he said that the essences of species and their definitions reside entirely in the form because it is the source of accidents as accidents, which need a subject. He said that they are in both matter and form because his investigation of accidents revealed that they have an essential aspect. Whoever thinks deeply about what I have said will find that it is true, especially if he is anointed with the oil of wisdom.[62]

According to Steinschneider, the work by Aquinas was translated into Hebrew by Abraham Nahmias, apparently in 1490 in the city of Ocaña.[63] If so, it appears that Aboab, who lived not far from Ocaña in Guadalajara, acquired the translation, studied at least part of it, and incorporated a section of it into his sermon between the completion of the translation in 1490 and his death in 1493. The entire passage seems more characteristic of a lecture at the University of Paris than the conclusion of a sermon by a Spanish talmudist, a rather amazing clue to the expectations of at least one kind of Jewish audience and the intellectual breadth of an important rabbi.

More significant than the mere citation of these authors is the way they are used. Occasionally, Aboab referred to an extreme philosophical idea that could not be accepted. He argued against the 'philosophizers' (probably referring to Gersonides [Ralbag]) who denied God's knowledge of particulars,[64]

---

[62] Aboab, *Nehar pishon*, 32d; cf. Saperstein, 'Your Voice Like a Ram's Horn', 79–80; for the Hebrew original, see Marc Saperstein, 'The Sermon as Evidence for the Popularization of Philosophical Ideas' (Heb.), in Benjamin Kedar (ed.), *Studies in the History of Popular Culture* [Tarbut amamit: kovets ma'amarim] (Jerusalem, 1996), 159. For the substance of this passage, see Thomas Aquinas, *Commentary on the Metaphysics of Aristotle*, trans. John Rowan, 2 vols. (Chicago, 1961), ii. 556. See also Abraham Bibago's discussion in a sermon of the dispute between Avicenna and Averroës on the origin of forms, which he relates to a dispute in the aggadic literature over the creation of the angels (Bibago, *Zeh yenahamenu* [sermon on Creation] [Salonika, 1522], 6d).

[63] Moritz Steinschneider, *Die Hebraeischen Übersetzungen des Mittelalters und die Juden als Dolmetscher* (Berlin, 1893), 485.   [64] Aboab, *Nehar pishon*, 17a.

and referred with disdain to 'the destroyers of our religion', who teach that after death the soul will be unified with the active intellect or with God.[65] For the most part, however, Aristotle and other philosophers were cited by Aboab (and the other Spanish preachers whose works we know) not in order to refute them or to contrast their teachings with those of Torah. On the contrary, they were usually cited as established truths, self-evident principles, universally accepted doctrines, that could be used as building blocks for subsequent assertions.[66]

Where there was an apparent contradiction between the Torah and philosophical truth, Aboab often set out to resolve it: 'It is said that this Torah lesson about the creation of the world is contradicted by principles derived from reason and logical demonstration; therefore we will speak at greater length in order to show that the subject of the *parashah* agrees with the intellect and science.'[67] He realized that material in the Torah that appears to contradict reason—for example the use of anthropomorphic and anthropopathic language about God—may make it more difficult for thinking Jews to believe and that these problems must be addressed and resolved in philosophical terms.[68]

Also noteworthy is his use of philosophical tools, particularly those of philology and logic, to solve exegetical problems. For example, noting the redundancy of the extra verb 'to be' at the end of Leviticus 27: 10, Aboab said: 'To resolve this puzzle, you should know that there are two terms in the language of the Christians that the translators did not know how to render properly until recently. The first is in their language *ente* and in ours it is *nimtsa*; the second in their language is *essentia* and in ours *heyot*. In addition, you should know that things that exist [*nimtsa'im*] can exist in reality or in the imagination.'[69] This distinction enabled him to explain both the strange wording of the verse and a statement Maimonides made about it.

[65] Aboab, *Nehar pishon*, 23b.

[66] For examples, see Saperstein, *'Your Voice Like a Ram's Horn'*, 80–2.

[67] Aboab, *Nehar pishon*, 5a. Compare Abraham Bibago's sermon on Creation. After arguing that it is permissible to discuss the matter in public (Bibago, *Zeh yenaḥamenu*, 2c), he launches a strong attack against the 'Averroist' double-truth position, which he associates with 'Christian scholars': 'They state the arguments against [Creation *ex nihilo*] and resolve the problem by saying that they are true, but in the way of nature; however, faith is above nature. This is foolishness, for we cannot say: "Two is half of four in nature, but above nature two is more than four." Faith does not pertain to matters that are beyond any doubt impossible' (ibid. 4b; see also the passage from Shem Tov ibn Shem Tov, in Saperstein, *'Your Voice Like a Ram's Horn'*, 80–1).

[68] 'There are things in the Torah that may lead a man to have doubts about the existence of God, heaven forbid' (Aboab, *Nehar pishon*, 38d).

[69] Ibid. 2d. On Aquinas's *De ente et essentia*, see Joseph Bobik, *Aquinas on Being and Essence* (Notre

Philosophy influenced not just the content but also the modes of thought and forms of argument in some of Aboab's sermons. Like other contemporary preachers, he resorted to the use of syllogisms to set forth his argument, a homiletical technique about which Hayim ibn Musa had complained decades earlier.[70] This was apparently a mode of thinking that many Jews found convincing and that could be readily followed in an oral discourse. It was a development in Jewish preaching, influenced by Aristotle's works on logic that had recently been translated into Hebrew. Like other Jewish preachers of his time, Aboab also used the 'disputed question', one of the characteristic modes of medieval Scholastic discourse, in his sermons, a striking innovation in Jewish homiletics. Aboab employed the disputed question in discussing repentance, a particularly problematic doctrine in the period before the Expulsion, investigating in one sermon 'whether repentance is efficacious' and in another 'whether repentance is a root of the Torah'.[71] This form of argumentation also seems to have had a genuine appeal for many Jewish listeners, and Aboab shows how it was accommodated naturally into Spanish Jewish preaching.

Aboab was not averse to discussing kabbalistic material in his sermons. The limited evidence for the use of zoharic quotations and kabbalistic doctrines in public preaching at this time has led some scholars to conclude that, with rare exceptions, kabbalah was not incorporated into sermons before the late sixteenth century.[72] Aboab provides another example indicating that this generalization may reflect the paucity of sources rather than the realities of pulpit discourse. He cited *Midrash hane'elam* on Genesis 4: 12 (Cain's punishment) and on Leviticus 4: 22 (the sin of the *nasi*), summarized kabbalistic interpretations of Genesis 32: 26 (the wounding of Jacob) and Numbers

---

Dame, Ind., 1965). This passage is extraordinary in reflecting from the pulpit on the problems of translating Latin philosophical texts into Hebrew. For the terminology (*haheyot uvileshonam essentia . . . hanimtsa uvileshonam ens*), see Steinschneider, *Die Hebraeischen Übersetzungen des Mittelalters*, 484–5; for an alternative (Italian) tradition, in which *metsi'ut* is used as a translation for *essentia*, see Giuseppe Sermoneta, *Un glossario filosofico ebraico–italiano del xiii secolo* (Rome, 1969), 256–7; see also the example of Aboab's use of technical logic, citing Aristotle and Averroës, in a eulogy (in Saperstein, 'Your Voice Like a Ram's Horn', 81–2).

[70] For examples of syllogisms in the sermons of Aboab and contemporaries, see Saperstein, '*Your Voice Like a Ram's Horn*', 83–4; for Ibn Musa's complaint, see Saperstein, *Jewish Preaching, 1200–1800*, 83–4.

[71] On the disputed question, see Saperstein, '*Your Voice Like a Ram's Horn*', 84–6; for an example, see ibid. 311–17.

[72] See '*Your Voice Like a Ram's Horn*', 299 n. 17. Israel Bettan had already noted kabbalistic references in Arama (Betten, *Studies in Jewish Preaching* [Cincinnati, 1939], 184–5 n. 145).

12: 3 (Moses' humility), and presented a kabbalistic understanding of the sefirotic significance of repentance and a kabbalistic explanation of why the new month is not mentioned on Rosh Hashanah.[73] There is no indication that the discussion of such material from the pulpit was in any way daring. It was, rather, a way of enriching his presentation.

Despite the rather theoretical nature of the material cited so far, Aboab was by no means oblivious to the social problems faced by his community. His awareness of tensions between Christians and Jews is reflected in several passages, including: 'The Gentiles vilify us and say: "You have no share in the world to come" '—a remark that appears to cause special hurt—and the statement that they wanted Jews to be baptized.[74] Predictably, Aboab found little to praise in the Christian religion, conceding that they shared with Jews the goal of worshipping the true God, but insisting that 'they err in the means and paths they take, making light darkness and darkness light'.[75] At the same time, Jews should be careful to avoid behaviour that might engender Christian contempt for Judaism: 'Since we live among the Gentiles, we must be careful in speaking with them that our "Yes" means "Yes" and our "No", "No", careful not to trick them or to do them any injustice or wrong, for this is how our Torah and our God are forgotten in their speech.'[76]

He was not afraid to speak out about social injustice amongst Jews. Discussing the problem of loans to the poor in the context of the biblical legislation (Deut. 15: 7–9), he made a specific contemporary application:

This problem pertaining to loans has arisen many times, especially where I live. Because the Torah forbids the taking of interest when a loan is given to a Jew, no one

---

[73] Aboab, 'Ketsat parashiyot', fos. 20b, 16b; cf. Saperstein, 'Your Voice Like a Ram's Horn', 328, 315; Aboab, *Nehar pishon*, 41d, 49b–c; id., 'Ketsat parashiyot', fos. 17b, 21a; cf. Saperstein, 'Your Voice Like a Ram's Horn', 318, 329). To be sure, mere citations from the Zohar do not in themselves make the case for the dissemination of kabbalah in sermons, as the Zohar was sometimes quoted as just another work of Midrash. This cannot be said, however, about a passage such as the final one cited above: 'The answer to this, according to the masters of true doctrine [ḥakhmei ha'emet], is that Rosh Hashanah is the *sefirah* Malkhut, and on it we pray that that *sefirah* will be complete, for then it sits in judgement. That is why we do not mention the new month on Rosh Hashanah, for the new month teaches about the effluence that Malkhut receives from the *sefirot* above it, and then we do not know what will be' (Aboab, 'Ketsat parashiyot', fo. 21a). Note also the two citations of Joseph Gikatilla's *Sha'arei Orah* (Gikatilla, *Gates of Light: Sha'arei Orah*, trans. Avi Weinstein [San Francisco, 1994]; see Saperstein, 'Your Voice Like a Ram's Horn', 320, 330).

[74] Aboab, *Nehar pishon*, 45d, 34c. Elesewhere, Aboab refers to Christians as 'our enemies' or 'those who hate us' (ibid. 31b–c).   [75] Ibid. 8b.

[76] Ibid. 55a. The phrase *nishkaḥ toratenu ve'elokenu befihem* at the end is somewhat strange. It seems to suggest the idea of *ḥilul hashem*: that unethical behaviour on the part of Jews will discredit the Torah in the minds of Christians.

wants to lend to him. Since the impoverished Jew cannot get an interest-bearing loan as a Gentile can, he cannot find the money he needs, and he dies of hunger. Thus the commandment turns into a transgression. I am tempted to say that it should be considered a greater sin for someone to refuse to make the loan than it is for someone to make the loan and take interest, for in the first case there is danger and in the second there is not. . . . I have dwelt at length on this because I see wretched Jews crying out and not being answered, because of our sins, in this time of dearth.[77]

This is a rather extraordinary passage. Jewish ethical and homiletical literature is filled with denunciations by moralists of businessmen who failed to observe properly the prohibitions against loans on interest; rabbis frequently emphasized the seriousness of these laws and urged that Jews consult with competent authorities who would keep them from improper loans.[78] Rarely do we find a leading rabbinic figure saying, in effect, that the transgressions entailed in taking interest are less serious than depriving the poor of what they need to survive. While some Jewish lenders might conceivably have endorsed this position allowing them to take interest, in violation of a Torah commandment, it is extremely unlikely that the potential profit from small, risky loans to the poor would have generated support for Aboab's position from a powerful, wealthy class of Jews. This statement rather bespeaks a leader of deep social consciousness with the courage to resist possible criticism from other rabbis.

In short, the works of Aboab, and especially his sermons, provide evidence of a rabbi who could draw on all the intellectual resources of contemporary Jewish culture—halakhic expertise, biblical study, philosophy, kabbalah, and social consciousness—and bring them together in communicating with his people. But what about the great historical issues of the day? Here we are likely to be disappointed. As is characteristic of the genre, the extant texts are general and allusive rather than concrete and specific. The assertion that the present generation, 'because of our sins', cannot see God's providence as the generation of Moses did[79] may well fit the dark months of 1492, but it is too commonplace a sentiment to have historical value.

Aboab cited a parable from *Midrash tehilim*: 'A father and son were walking on a road. The son, tired and weak, asked the father if they were far from the city [their destination] or near it. The father said: "Remember this sign:

---

[77] Aboab, 'Ketsat parashiyot', fo. 16*a*; cf. Saperstein, *'Your Voice Like a Ram's Horn'*, 313–14). For possible dates of 'this time of dearth', see ibid. 295, n. 9.

[78] See examples in Saperstein, *'Your Voice Like a Ram's Horn'*, 101, 138–9.

[79] Aboab, *Nehar pishon*, 17*a*.

when you see a cemetery, that will indicate that we are near the city...". Thus when we see calamities draw near, it is a sign of the coming of the messiah.' This has been cited by historians as an example of an immediate response to the Expulsion, and indeed it may be. But the messianic dimension is almost entirely absent from these sermons. If the passage is indeed authentic and not a later interpolation, it may be nothing more than a topos of response to sorrow.[80]

There are also references to martyrdom. In one sermon, Aboab said:

The soul that does not cleave to its body does not feel it when they separate it from that body, for it is cleaving to God. That is why man has been compared to an upside-down tree with its roots above. One should therefore cleave to God, cleave to one's true root, and then he will not feel it even when they take his life.[81]

This reflects the tradition that the martyr feels no pain despite the tortures of execution, a tradition known from the somewhat later *Megilat amraphel*.[82] Yet in a different passage the preacher seemed to be clarifying his position and repudiating the radical claim:

This is like someone who accepts death as a martyr. There is no doubt that he will feel distress at the time he is being put to death, for the body is affected by it. But insofar as he imagines that by this death he attains true communion [with God], his mind will rejoice.[83]

---

[80] Aboab, *Nehar pishon*, 9a; cf. Saperstein, *Jewish Preaching, 1200–1800*, 84. The context is the response of Cain to God's pronouncement of his punishment. On the motif of Cain in this period, see ibid. 202, n. 5. The passage containing the parable is not in the London manuscript of 'Nehar pishon'. If the manuscript is primary, then those who brought the sermons to press might have added it as a response to the Expulsion. It is also possible that the manuscript was written later and the passage removed because the Expulsion did not lead to the messianic advent as anticipated.

[81] Aboab, *Nehar pishon*, 23c. The comparison of the human being with the tree, transforming the rhetorical question of Deut. 20: 19 into a proposition, is superimposed on the kabbalistic motive of the inverted tree as a symbol of the sefirotic realm and therefore related to the supernal *anthropos* (see Saperstein, *Jewish Preaching*, 371 n. 25; the source in Moshe Idel, *Kabbalah: New Perspectives* [New Haven, 1988], 57).

[82] Gershom Scholem, 'New Investigations about Rabbi R. Avraham ben Eliezer' (Heb.), *Kiryat sefer*, 7 (1930–1), 153; Y. Baer, *A History of the Jews in Christian Spain*, ii. 430–1. The idea that the martyr feels no pain is attributed to Meir of Rothenburg by his disciple Samson ben Zadok, in *Sefer tashbets* (see Scholem, 'New Investigations about Rabbi R. Avraham ben Eliezer' [Heb.], 441–2; David Tamar, 'On Rabbi Meir of Rothenburg's Statement Regarding Martyrdom' (Heb.), *Kiryat sefer*, 33 [1958], 376–7; 34 [1959], 397). Baer notes the Christian analogues of this doctrine (*A History of the Jews in Christian Spain*, ii. 508 n. 4; cf. Robin Lane Fox, *Pagans and Christians* [New York, 1987], 438, 473; Arthur J. Droge and James D. Tabor, *A Noble Death: Suicide and Martyrdom among Christians and Jews in Antiquity* [San Francisco, 1992], 138).

[83] Aboab, 'Ketsat parashiyot', fo. 20a; cf. Saperstein, '*Your Voice Like a Ram's Horn*', 325.

Without information about the date or circumstances of their delivery, it is impossible to be certain what resonance these passages about martyrdom would have had among the audience. They indicate, however, that the experience of martyrdom was being addressed as an actual issue, at a time when Jews could witness the burning of those released by the Inquisition into the hands of the secular powers.

Was the vision of a man like Isaac Aboab inadequate to the great challenges of his age? His extant writings provide little clear evidence of a profound mind or a charismatic personality.[84] He did not have the stature of Samuel ibn Nagrela or Moses Maimonides, who could both dominate their specific environment and produce work of enduring value. These writings do, however, suggest a leader of considerable talent—rooted in Spain yet capable of leaving it as an old man and preparing the groundwork for accommodation elsewhere;[85] expert in the traditional talmudic literature but fascinated by philosophy and open to the teachings of kabbalah; capable of communicating to Jews who lacked more than a rudimentary Jewish education and to the most sophisticated intellectuals; passionate about both the nuances of halakhic interpretation and the large issues of social responsibility. How many others, who are little more than names to us or whose names we do not even know, were leaders of similar calibre gracing the Spanish Jewish communities during their final decades? That is a question to which historians may never be able to give a fully adequate response.

---

[84] Note, however, the legendary account of the impression he made on the king of Portugal, reported by Moses ben Joseph di Trani (*She'elot uteshuvot mabit* [responsa], 2 vols. in 1 [New York, 1961], i, no. 16; cf. Micha Joseph Bin Gorion, *Mimekor Yisra'el: Classical Jewish Folktales*, 3 vols. [Bloomington, 1976], ii. 793–4).

[85] Our knowledge of Aboab's efforts to negotiate entry for Jewish refugees into Portugal is based on Immanuel Aboab's account of his family's traditions in his *Nomologia* (in Meier Kayserling, *Geschichte der Juden in Portugal* [Leipzig, 1867], 108–9). There does not seem to be more contemporary corroboration for this. Undoubtedly, the lost eulogy of his disciple Abraham Zacuto would have clarified matters.

CHAPTER EIGHT

Rabbis, Martyrs, and Merchants: Jewish Communal Conflict as Reflected in the Responsa on the Boycott of Ancona

THE BOYCOTT of the port of Ancona in 1556 was an unparalleled event in early modern Jewish history, the only attempt before the twentieth century to organize Jewish economic pressure and to wield it in the arena of international affairs for the benefit of Jews persecuted in other lands.[1] Powerful forces converged in this event. There were the political configurations, the towering personalities of Suleiman the Magnificent, Pope Paul IV, and Guidobaldo II, duke of Urbino, confronting and defying each other. There were the fortunes and livelihoods of merchants and traders, Gentiles as well as Jews, in Italy and throughout the Ottoman empire. There were sociological forces: the sense of solidarity among Jews transcending political boundaries and the special sense of cohesiveness among the subgroup of Portuguese Marrano exiles. There were psychological pressures generated by the outrage over the humiliation of Jews once more burned at the stake, pressures released and channelled into an expression of revenge. There were also important legal questions that had to be resolved within the framework of Jewish halakhah. Not the least fascinating aspect of this boycott is that what began as a confrontation between the Jewish and the Christian worlds —an effort to unite Jews in order to punish Christians for the persecution of

First published in *Jewish Social Studies*, 43 (1981), 215–28.

[1] See Salo W. Baron, *A Social and Religious History of the Jews*, 18 vols. (Philadelphia, 1952–83), xiv. 35–43; Solomon Freehof, *The Responsa Literature* (Philadelphia, 1955), 150–8; Joseph Nehama, *Histoire des Israélites de Salonique*, 5 vols. (Salonika, 1935–9), iv. 96–121; Cecil Roth, *The House of Nasi: Doña Gracia* (Philadelphia, 1947), 134–74; Isaiah Sonne, *From Paul IV to Pius V* [Mipaulo harevi'i ad pius haḥamishi] (Jerusalem, 1954), 146–59. On the community of Portuguese emigrants to Ancona before the persecutions that led to the boycott, see Bernard Dov Cooperman, 'Portuguese *Conversos* in Ancona: Jewish Political Activity in Early Modern Italy', in id. (ed.), *In Iberia and Beyond: Hispanic Jews between Cultures* (Newark, 1998), 297–352.

former Marranos—soon revealed deep fissures within the various Jewish communities themselves.

The most important sources for this dramatic episode are the responsa of the Ottoman rabbis.[2] These responsa contain far more than juridical arguments based on subtle distinctions in the interpretation of classical texts. Properly analysed, they yield a vivid picture of rabbinic leadership on a tumultuous issue, of rabbis subjected to fearful pressures by colleagues and other co-religionists, torn by conflicting loyalties, grappling to reconcile their understanding of traditional legal principles with their perception of immediate needs. They also reveal how competing narratives of the core events could rupture an initially unified public opinion to the point where consensus was no longer possible. It is hoped that the present study succeeds in demonstrating the value of these responsa as sources for Jewish social and communal history while reconstructing, insofar as is possible from the literary sources, the events surrounding the boycott and the forces that led to the ultimate failure of a rather noble effort.

Background

The legal questions asked of rabbis in the great cities of the Ottoman empire furnish important background material for the patterns of trade between these cities and those on the Adriatic coast of Italy, in which Jews, and especially the Marranos of the 'Portuguese diaspora', played a leading role.[3] For example, a question addressed to Rabbi Samuel de Medina of Salonika involved a Jewish businessman from Adrianople, who sent twenty-two hides to a merchant in Ancona, explicitly identified as 'one of the Marranos who came from Portugal'. With the money realized from the sale of the hides, the Anconan merchant was supposed to buy *torpini* (textiles produced in Ancona)

---

[2] Undoubtedly, archival material from Italy and Turkey would significantly supplement the picture drawn from the responsa and other literary sources. In the case of Turkey, however, most of the relevant archives are unclassified and access to them remains difficult. A definitive study, based on all extant sources including archival material, is probably still a generation off.

[3] See e.g. Asher Khananel and Eli Eškenazi (ed.), *Fontes hebraici ad res oeconomicas socialesque terrarum balcanicarum saeculo XVI pertinentes* (Sofia, 1958); Morris Goodblatt, *Jewish Life in Turkey in the XVIth Century as Reflected in the Legal Writings of Samuel di Medina* (New York, 1952); Stephen M. Passamaneck, *Insurance in Rabbinic Law* (Edinburgh, 1974). I use the word 'Marranos' to refer to Jews who had converted to Christianity under duress, but who had since left the Iberian peninsula and were living as Jews in Italy or the Ottoman empire. While not strictly accurate, it is simpler than referring to them as 'former Marranos who had returned to Judaism' or 'Portuguese Jews of Marrano background'.

and send them back to Turkey. At the same time, the Marrano sent merchandise of his own to be sold by his associate in Adrianople. However, the pope's officials seized the Marrano's property, including the money realized from the sale of the hides. In passing, the question reveals that such commercial transactions were common, for it states that 'it was their practice [in Ancona] to acquire *torpini* with the money they made from the sale of the hides or the [other] merchandise sent from Turkey'. Various sources confirm that untreated hides from Macedonia streamed into Ancona—much to the annoyance of Venetian competitors—and that *torpini* were greatly in demand because of their high quality and relatively low cost.[4] Apparently, careful records of all such transactions were kept, for the question reports that 'the sale [of the hides] was registered in the book of the municipal scribe in accordance with the law of [Ancona]'.[5]

The thriving commerce between Ancona and the Ottoman empire, in which Jews, and especially Marranos of Portuguese extraction, played a leading role, was maintained against the background of tension and hostility in the Mediterranean, where the expanding Ottoman empire collided with established European commercial powers such as Venice, Genoa, and Spain.[6] When tension erupted into open warfare, the efforts of the merchants were sometimes frustrated. Another question sent to De Medina involved a merchant from Turkey, who was stranded in Ancona and unable to draw on funds he had at home because of 'the conflicts and wars between our king [Suleiman], may his splendour be exalted, and the Christians'.[7] Despite this, trade continued and even increased.

The rabbis of the Ottoman empire were aware that the Portuguese Marranos were living as Jews in Ancona legally, with the explicit consent of previous popes. Rabbi Joseph ibn Lev wrote that according to his sources the pope had granted permission, written and sealed in the official manner, for the Marranos to 'Judaize' in Ancona because their conversion to Christianity in Portugal had been forced upon them.[8] It is a matter of historical record

---

[4] Nehama, *Histoire des Israélites de Salonique*, iv. 86–7, 48; Fernand Braudel, *The Mediterranean and the Mediterranean World in the Age of Philip II* (New York, 1972), 127 n. 88; David Abulafia, *The Great Sea: A Human History of the Mediterranean* (London, 2011), 437.

[5] Samuel de Medina, *She'elot uteshuvot maharashdam* [responsa] (Lemberg, 1862), 'Ḥoshen mishpat', no. 54; see also nos. 28, 438.

[6] 'Ancona was a "true frontier" between Islam and Christendom, where merchants from many nations met face to face' (D. Abulafia, *The Great Sea*, 438; see Braudel, *The Mediterranean and the Mediterranean World*, 904–66: Paul Coles, *The Ottoman Impact on Europe* [London, 1968], 88–105).

[7] De Medina, *She'elot uteshuvot*, 'Ḥoshen mishpat', no. 59.

[8] Joseph ibn Lev, *She'elot uteshuvot mahari ben lev* [responsa], 2 vols. (Jerusalem: Ginzei Kedem,

that in 1535, over the opposition of other Church leaders, Pope Paul III had enacted a privilege for the Jews of Ancona, including the Marranos, and that this privilege had been confirmed by Pope Julius III in 1553.[9] This was important to the rabbis, for it meant that even though the current pope, Paul IV, was the recognized ruler of Ancona, his anti-Marrano decrees were not to be considered as *dina demalkhuta*, the legitimate and binding 'law of the land' but, rather, as a capricious perversion of the established law.

According to the responsa, the new papal decrees seem to have been directed at first against specific individuals and concerned primarily with the confiscation of their property. A question addressed to De Medina states: 'The pope decreed that whoever has possession of money or its equivalent belonging to "Simon" must come, register it, and hand it over to his officials' on pain of death.[10] Even if someone had borrowed money from the designated individual, he was compelled to render it to the officials of the pope. Later, 'the pestilence spread': all those who had lived as Christians in Portugal were seized and their property confiscated for the papal treasury. In order to ensure that the confiscation was complete, the pope's officers meticulously examined the municipal registers, in which all commercial transactions were recorded.[11] The details of the imprisonment and the auto-da-fé are known from contemporary Hebrew chronicles.[12] Paul IV, the zealous spearhead of the Catholic Reformation, ordered twenty-four Marranos put to death. Others were able to escape. Some went directly to Ottoman territory, some to the nearby port of Pesaro.

Conflicting Accounts

Until this point, there is a consensus about the events that occurred; from here on, however, there is a morass of contradictory evidence, relating both to the facts and their evaluation or interpretation. From the rabbinic responsa, it

---

1960), ii, no. 115. For a detailed account of the *cambio* transaction customarily made by the Jewish merchants of Ancona in their trade with Ottoman cities, see ibid., no. 53; discussed by Passamaneck, *Insurance in Rabbinic Law*, 101–12.

[9] Baron, *A Social and Religious History of the Jews*, xiv. 36.

[10] De Medina, *She'elot uteshuvot*, 'Ḥoshen mishpat', no. 55.   [11] Ibid., nos. 54, 55.

[12] Joseph Hakohen, *Emek habakhah* [history], ed. Meir Letteris (Kraków, 1895), 134–5; the chronicle by the eyewitness Benjamin Nehemiah ben Elnathan (in Sonne, *From Paul IV to Pius V* [Heb.], 30–46). For other contemporary sources on the persecutions in Ancona, see ibid. 110–21; David Kaufmann, 'Les Martyrs d'Ancône', *Revue des études juives*, 11 (1885), 149–56; id., 'Les 24 Martyrs d'Ancône', *Revue des études juives*, 31 (1895), 222–30; Baron, *A Social and Religious History of the Jews*, xiv. 319 n. 35.

is possible to reconstruct two totally discrepant narrative accounts, describing the aftermath of the papal persecutions in Ancona from the perspectives of the advocates and the opponents of the boycott. The disparities between these accounts reveal the problems confronting the Ottoman Jews, who wanted accurate information on which to base their decision about a boycott.

The advocates' account is to be found in several letters written by the Marranos in Pesaro, and especially in the first-hand report brought by Judah Faraj to the communities of Turkey. After the seizure and execution of Marranos in Ancona, some of those who had escaped approached the duke of Urbino, Guidobaldo II, and tried to persuade him to accept the refugees in Pesaro. This would place the duke at obvious cross purposes with the pope, and the refugees' representatives realized they would have to demonstrate that he would benefit by taking such a risk. They therefore promised to organize a boycott of Ancona by the Jewish merchants of the Ottoman empire and to divert all their trade to Pesaro. This boycott was the condition of their acceptance in Pesaro by the duke.

According to this account, the acceptance of the refugees in Pesaro did indeed rupture the relationship between duke and pope. Paul IV sent his legate to Guidobaldo, demanding that the Marranos be turned over for trial by the Inquisition. The duke, eager for the economic development of his own city and relying on the promised boycott, defied the pontiff's order. Pope Paul, infuriated, immediately dismissed the duke from his position of captain general of the papal armies, for which he had received a substantial stipend. The hospitality shown to the Marranos had thus transformed the friendly relationship between duke and pope into bitter enmity. The duke had defended the refugees at great personal cost.[13]

Therefore the boycott was warranted, indeed imperative: as vengeance for the lives of the martyrs, as punishment for the city of Ancona, and as fulfilment of a commitment to reward the duke for his generosity and sacrifice. Only its implementation could guarantee the safety of the Marranos in Pesaro. If the promise was not fulfilled, the duke would accede to the pope's demands and turn the Marranos over to the Inquisition, probably resulting in death or imprisonment. The duke, meanwhile, had undertaken the renovation of the harbour of Pesaro so that it could accommodate the anticipated

---

[13] This account is based primarily on the material in Joshua Soncino, *Naḥalah lihoshua . . . she'elot uteshuvot* [responsa] (Constantinople, 1731), nos. 39, 40 (44*b*–46*b*); Soncino's responsum no. 40 is also in Yisrael Schepansky, *The Land of Israel in the Responsa Literature* [Erets yisra'el besifrut hateshuvot], 3 vols. (Jerusalem, 1966), ii. 348–53.

ships that would anchor there.[14] Thus there was no acceptable reason for not boycotting Ancona and trading exclusively with Pesaro. According to the advocates of the ban, the Jews of Ancona opposed the boycott because of their own selfish economic interests, and any Turkish Jews who opposed it proved that they valued their own money more than the lives of the refugees.

The account of the same events and the evaluation of the same situation from the other perspective yields a very different story. The opponents of the boycott, primarily the Ancona Jews, wrote to the leaders of Turkish Jewry, reminding them of an event that had occurred some time before the persecutions of Ancona. The duke's brother, together with other inhabitants of Pesaro, had committed an outrage against the local Jewish community, entering the synagogue, removing the Torah scrolls, tearing them, wrapping them around a pig, and then placing them in the ducal palace. Far-reaching conclusions were drawn from this event. First, the refugees should never have gone to Pesaro; they should have realized that it was no better than the cities of the papal states and known that they could expect to find toleration only in the Ottoman empire. Second, if there was a need for vengeance, there was as much cause for vengeance against Pesaro as there was against Ancona. What sense did it make to reward the city in which such a humiliating deed had been perpetrated?[15]

The circumstances of the refugees' acceptance in Pesaro were not at all what the refugees claimed. The duke of Urbino had made a public proclamation stating that whoever wanted to come to his territories would be welcome. It was his initiative, not that of the refugees, which led to their absorption into Pesaro. The duke was happy to receive whatever Jews decided to come, especially the Portuguese Jews, who were famed for their commercial talents. The promise of a boycott was never a condition of his acceptance of the refugees: it was devised by the Marranos after they arrived there, for their own reasons. The duke, a wise and understanding ruler, knew that it was beyond the power of the impoverished refugees to compel all the Jews of the Ottoman empire to divert their trade from one city to another. Those Jews who came to Pesaro would of course trade from there, and this would increase the prosperity of the city. There would be absolutely no danger to those Jews if the boycott did not go ahead, for by harming them, the duke would lose the commercial benefits they brought.[16]

As for the duke's relations with the pope, it was true that there had been a

---

[14] Moses ben Joseph di Trani, *She'elot uteshuvot mabit* [responsa], 2 vols. in 1 (New York, 1961), no. 237.   [15] Soncino, *Naḥalah lihoshua*, no. 39 (45a col. 2).   [16] Ibid., no. 40 (46b col. 1, 46a col. 2).

change, but for reasons unconnected with the Marranos. Guidobaldo had been captain general of the papal armies under the previous pope, whose niece he had married. When the new pope, Paul IV, was elected, he gave this coveted position to one of his own favourites: normal papal politics. As a matter of fact, the incident had occurred before the duke's defence of the Jews.[17]

Thus, according to the opponents of the boycott, it was the supporters of the boycott who were acting out of selfish economic motives. They were forbidden to travel to Ancona, the centre of trade, and therefore were trying to divert all the trade to Pesaro in order to ameliorate their own financial situation. The claim that they were in danger was only a ploy designed to fill their pockets. Furthermore, they showed themselves totally insensitive to the negative consequences of the proposed boycott. If the boycott should be effected, the leaders of Ancona would undoubtedly complain to the pope that the Jews were undermining the prestige of the papacy.[18] The pope's reaction would be easily predictable: he would intensify his persecution of all Jews living in the papal states, saying: 'Their brothers in Turkey are mocking us ... because I am a zealous Christian.'[19] As there were many more Jews in the papal states than there were in Pesaro, the implementation of the boycott posed a far greater danger than any the Jews of Pesaro might suffer if the boycott was simply forgotten about.

These are the accounts that reached the Jewish communities in Turkey. Obviously, any decision about supporting the boycott had to be based on an accurate understanding of the events which had occurred and an accurate assessment of the present and future situation. In his responsum on the validity of the boycott, Joshua Soncino gave four different answers, each appropriate to a different situation regarding the relative dangers facing the Jewish communities in Ancona and Pesaro.[20] The Ottoman rabbis were forced to play the role of modern historians, trying to reconstruct the truth from divergent and conflicting accounts of the same events, the only difference being that their reconstruction had immediate practical implications of grave import. It was not an easy task.

Many of the differences in the two accounts probably cannot be resolved without an exhaustive study of the archives of Ancona and Pesaro, but some of the issues can be illuminated by documents more readily available. As might be expected, they do not fully support either side. The outrage in

---

[17] Soncino, *Naḥalah lihoshua*, no. 39, 46*b* col. 1.
[18] Ibid. (46*a* col. 2).
[19] Ibid. no. 39 (44*b* col. 2).
[20] Ibid. (44*b* col. 2–45*b* col. 2).

Pesaro, perpetrated against the Jewish community some time before the Ancona persecutions, did indeed occur, according to contemporary Jewish chronicles. The most detailed account is in Samuel Usque's *Consolation for the Tribulations of Israel*, in which it is said to have happened in 1553.[21] The crucial element in the description recorded by Joshua Soncino, however, is missing from the chronicles: the role of the duke's brother as ringleader. Was it merely a rampage of ruffians, who may well have been punished by the duke for their civil disorder, or was it, as implied by the opponents of the boycott, performed with the tacit consent of the duke, thereby disqualifying Pesaro from being worthy of reward by the efforts and sacrifices of Ottoman Jewish merchants? The sources do not permit a definitive answer.

What about the relationship between the duke and the pope? Guidobaldo II had indeed been named captain general of the papal armies by Julius III in 1553. He was originally confirmed in his command by the newly elected Paul IV, who also restored to him the honour of prefecture of Rome, which had been denied by previous popes. Some time later, apparently in 1557, after the persecutions in Ancona and the acceptance of the refugees in Pesaro, he was relieved of his command in favour of the pope's 'favourite nephew'.[22] This would seem to confirm the account of the Marranos who favoured the boycott, but the causal nexus cannot be established. It is possible that the pope confirmed the duke at first because he needed support upon entering office and waited until he had consolidated power before transferring the position to his own man. Or might there indeed have been something to destroy the cordial relations between Guidobaldo II and Paul IV, something such as the duke's policy towards the Marranos?

The most serious difference between the accounts is their evaluation of the consequences of the alternative courses of action. How would the pope react to the boycott? How would the duke react to the failure of the boycott? Which posed the greater danger to the Jews in their respective realms? The reaction of the leaders of Ancona to threats of economic reprisal was not what the local Jews of Ancona predicted, for rather than giving vent to anti-Jewish feeling and asking the pope to intensify his persecution of Jews, they urged the pope to stop the oppression of Marranos, at least in their city. Half a year before the actual auto-da-fé, the city council of Ancona had appealed to the pope to transfer all inquisitorial proceedings away from Ancona, contending

---

[21] Samuel Usque, *Consolation for the Tribulations of Israel*, trans. and ed. Martin A. Cohen (Philadelphia, 1965), 214.

[22] James Dennistoun, *Memoirs of the Dukes of Urbino*, 3 vols. (New York, 1909), iii. 100–10.

that the public tortures were antagonizing eastern merchants and adversely affecting the city's commerce.²³ Then in August 1556, when the first effects of the boycott were being felt, the council wrote again to the pope, saying 'unless the goodness of Your Holiness will help us, this city . . . will remain abandoned and derelict'.²⁴ The Jews of Ancona surely knew about these letters, and their claim of danger initiated by the 'leaders of Ancona' seems to be either paranoid or intentionally falsified.

What of the pope himself? Could the Jews of the papal states expect retaliation from him because of the boycott? A Christian source, published by Isaiah Sonne from the autobiography of an Italian Jew who converted to Christianity in 1551, contains the threat of papal retaliation against Jews in the papal states for an unrelated incident:

Know that if our 'father' suffers death because of the accusation which you [Jews] brought against him, the injustice which you are doing to him will be considered as if you did it to the pope himself, who sent him here. And the pope, who is the head of all Christians, will arrange that all the Jews in Rome and in all the papal states will suffer persecutions. And he will command all Christian rulers to do likewise.²⁵

This independently establishes that the Jews had good reason to fear that the pope might take revenge for what he considered an insult to his dignity. Yet the Marranos' answer to this argument should not be forgotten: the pope had already shown his unquenchable hostility to the Jews long before the boycott. This is a reference to the bull *Cum nimis absurdum* of 14 July 1555, which established the ghettos of Rome and other cities in the papal states and enforced severely discriminatory economic regulations.²⁶ So powerful was his hatred of Jews that he was willing to ruin the Christian merchants of Ancona, by refusing to allow them to collect debts owed to them by the Portuguese Marranos. The advocates of the boycott concluded that with a pope so totally committed to anti-Jewish policies, it was unrealistic to assume that any action taken by Ottoman Jews would cause a further deterioration in the status of the Jews of Italy.²⁷

And what of the duke of Urbino? Contemporary writers were generally favourable about his character, and James Dennistoun notes the moderation

---

²³ Baron, *A Social and Religious History of the Jews*, xiv. 319 n. 36.
²⁴ Ibid. 39.   ²⁵ In Sonne, *From Paul IV to Pius V* (Heb.), 153–7.
²⁶ In Kenneth Stow, *Catholic Thought and Jewish Policy, 1555–1593* (New York, 1977), 294–8, see also ibid. 3–17; Baron, *A Social and Religious History of the Jews*, xiv. 345.
²⁷ David Kaufmann, 'Deux lettres nouvelles des Marranes de Pesaro aux Levantins touchant l'interruption des affaires avec Ancône', *Revue des études juives*, 31 (1895), 234.

of his reaction to a Jew who refused to make a loan necessary for the fortification of Sinigaglia in 1556.[28] However, the duke did expel the Marranos from Pesaro in 1558, an event described with characteristic pathos in the Hebrew chronicle *Emek habakhah* (The Valley of Weeping).[29] But even this, which seems to confirm the predictions of the proponents of the boycott and which has been used by modern writers to indict those who opposed it,[30] is open to interpretation. Was it indeed the duke's anger at the broken promise and his disappointment at the failure to divert significant trade to Pesaro which led him to punish the Marranos? Or was it that the exigencies of Italian politics made it impossible for him to defy the pope any longer (*Emek habakhah* says that the Marranos were expelled 'in accordance with the pope's command'), although he showed his sympathy for their plight by allowing them to depart for the Ottoman empire rather than turning them over to the Inquisition? If all of these ambiguities remain for the modern historian, who can examine the available material at leisure and with detachment, then the difficulties facing the rabbinic authorities in Turkey, with divergent and contradictory reports arriving on every ship, can well be understood.

The Ottoman Rabbis

In the Ottoman empire, the great Jewish communities heard about the events in Ancona and Pesaro and were confronted with a call to action. The emissary of the refugees in Pesaro, Judah Faraj, carrying letters from their leaders, apparently made his first stop in Salonika. His request for a boycott of Ancona evoked an enthusiastic response, and the various Jewish congregations of the city agreed that all merchants accustomed to trade with Ancona must immediately divert their business to Pesaro. One condition was appended to this agreement: that the other Jewish trading communities of the Ottoman empire—Constantinople, Adrianople, and Bursa—must agree to join the boycott.[31]

Faraj then went on to Constantinople, which held the key to the success of his mission. The communal leaders were called together to hear the emissary tell his tale and present his case. Joshua Soncino, later the outstanding rabbinic opponent of the boycott, reports he was so stirred at this meeting by the

---

[28] Dennistoun, *Memoirs of the Dukes of Urbino*, 123.
[29] Joseph Hakohen, *Emek habakhah*, 136–7.   [30] C. Roth, *The House of Nasi*, 171–2.
[31] Moses di Trani, *She'elot uteshuvot*, i, no. 237; see David Kaufmann, 'Les Marranes de Pesaro et les représailles des Juifs levantins contre la ville d'Ancône', *Revue des études juives*, 16 (1888), 61 n. 2.

plight of the martyrs and the refugees that his eyes overflowed with tears.³² The leadership of Constantinople Jewry agreed unanimously to declare a boycott, which would last for the following eight months until Passover. They, too, realized that co-operation from the majority of merchants in the other Ottoman cities—Bursa, Adrianople, Salonika, Avlona—was needed for the success of the venture. Therefore, the provision was made that if all of these communities should agree within this eight-month period, a second meeting would be called in which the boycott would be given full and permanent sanction. If the others should not agree, the boycott would lapse after Passover.

Thus the first round went to the advocates of the boycott, the Marrano refugees in Pesaro. Then problems began to emerge. Adrianople apparently supported the boycott, but only over the vociferous objections of a number of its merchants. The Jews of Bursa rejected it flatly. The reason they gave, as reported in Moses di Trani's responsum, was not concern for the welfare of Jews in the papal states, but purely economic self-interest. They felt that the losses they would sustain because of Pesaro's inadequate port facilities would be excessive. Reports arrived in Constantinople giving the impression that the other communities of Turkey were reacting unfavourably to the boycott: that it was a decree that 'the majority of the community is unable to uphold' (see BT *Hor.* 3*b*). Translated from the idiom of Jewish law, this means simply that the merchants were unwilling to risk economic ruin in order to avenge lives taken at the directive of the pope or even to protect refugees from the future wrath of the duke. At the same time, the Jews of Ancona, who were no more willing to risk economic ruin for either of these purposes, began their own propaganda campaign, exposing Turkish Jewry to an entirely different account of the events and evaluation of the situation, as described above.

As a result, even before the expiration of the original agreement at Passover 1557, the boycott was not being fully observed. Some merchants were maintaining their trade with Ancona despite the appearance of complying with the boycott. One captain, Joseph Hodara, representing the commercial house of Solomon Bonsenior, pretended to be heading for Pesaro and then, at the last moment, changed course for Ancona.³³ Others seem to have gone to Pesaro in good faith, found they were unable to unload or to sell their cargo there, and then turned to the more established port.³⁴ The Jews of

---

³² Virtually all of the subsequent material on the events in Constantinople is based on Soncino, *Naḥalah lihoshua*, no. 40.

³³ D. Kaufmann, 'Deux lettres nouvelles des marranes de Pesaro aux Levantins', 237–8.

³⁴ Moses di Trani, *She'elot uteshuvot*, i, no. 237.

Pesaro realized that the boycott was in danger of collapse and addressed new letters to the Ottoman communities. Unlike the emotionally charged original letters, which overflowed with rhetorical verbiage, these were sober responses to the arguments of their opponents, stressing the urgency of enforcing the boycott. It is at this point also that the Pesaran Jews turned to perhaps the most powerful figure in Ottoman Jewry, Doña Gracia Mendes.

This shifted the balance back in favour of the boycott. During the persecution of the Ancona Marranos, Doña Gracia had persuaded Suleiman the Magnificent to write to the pope protesting at the detainment of Ottoman Jewish citizens.[35] Now she, and her son-in-law, Don Joseph Nasi, began to exert enormous pressure for compliance with the boycott of Ancona. At her instructions, Judah Faraj went to the leading rabbis of Constantinople—Joseph ibn Lev, Abraham Yerushalmi, Solomon Bilia, and Abraham Saba—and convinced them to sign a statement requiring all Jews to heed the agreement to boycott 'because it was a matter of saving life in Pesaro'. Armed with these signatures, he went to Joshua Soncino, who refused to sign, because he was concerned by the arguments of the Ancona Jews and had already been approached for a legal decision regarding the boycott. He therefore feared that the new statement 'would be a cause of increased conflict among Jews'.

As a result of his refusal, Soncino and the leaders of his congregation were summoned to the house of Don Joseph Nasi. Soncino finally consented to sign, but only on the express condition that if the version of the Ancona Jews should be true, his signature would not imply agreement with the boycott and that he would write this to all who asked his opinion. Don Joseph concluded that it would be better for Soncino to do nothing. Soon afterwards, he was summoned by Doña Gracia, who prodded him rather more forcefully, but he continued to hold his ground. In the meantime, his further investigations only turned up more information supporting the position of the Ancona Jews. He proposed to Don Joseph and Doña Gracia that an emissary be sent to the Jews of Venice and Padua, asking them to investigate the situation and determine whose version was true. Soncino volunteered to pay the expenses of the emissary himself.

The decisive moment had come. In two of the congregations of Constantinople—the Congregation of the Expulsion and the Congregation of the Portuguese—the agreement to enforce the boycott was proclaimed. The other congregations refused to act. The result was a split in the Jewish com-

[35] Baron, *A Social and Religious History of the Jews*, xiv. 39.

munity 'such as never occurred before, for the ten Sephardi congregations here in Constantinople had never been divided among themselves on a matter of such great importance'.[36] The two factions of the Ashkenazi congregation acceded to the boycott, over the vehement protest of the one member who had commercial connections with Ancona. Their agreement was largely due to pressure from Don Joseph, who threatened to terminate his financial support of their rabbi and order his expulsion from the *yeshivah*. Finally, the Romaniot congregation of Jews native to Eastern Orthodox Christian lands was approached to declare its assent to the boycott. Soncino, who reports these events (undoubtedly in the worst possible light), stresses the fact that not a single member of this congregation had ever engaged in commercial relations with Ancona, and, thus, no one had even thought it necessary to include them in the original agreement. Now the appearance of broad support was desired. The Romaniot Jews, to whom it made absolutely no practical difference, declared for the boycott.

These activities galvanized the opposition, led by Soncino, who was saddened by the rancorous and bitter divisiveness. Asked for an official decision by 'the outstanding merchants of the land', he claimed to have proved that it was forbidden to participate in the boycott.[37] This decision was affirmed by those congregations that had refused to uphold the boycott, and Soncino sought further support for his position in the cities outside the capital. With the Ottoman communities in full conflict, the detailed information about the events comes to an end.

It should already be clear that despite all the pressure which Doña Gracia and Don Joseph could bring to bear, the opposition to the boycott was strong enough to make it unworkable. Even under optimal conditions, the boycott of Ancona would have been merely partial, for it applied only to Jewish merchants, who controlled a significant proportion of the trade but certainly not all of it. When the Jews themselves split on the issue, the economics of the boycott were radically transformed. If a significant proportion of Jews continued to trade with Ancona, the boycott would hurt the port less than it would hurt those Jews who refused to trade there and consequently lost their business to the others. This would intensify opposition to the boycott among merchants in those communities or congregations that had agreed to it and make enforcement of the boycott even more difficult. This is indeed what

---

[36] Soncino, *Naḥalah lihoshua*, no. 40 (46*b* col. 2).

[37] This is apparently the decision in Soncino, *Naḥalah lihoshua*, no. 39, which argues that the boycott is forbidden only in the case that there is real danger for the Jews of Ancona and none for those of Pesaro.

happened in the Ottoman communities. Without stringent enforcement and with infringements overlooked, it quickly became a fiction without actual economic significance. The problem was best summarized by Soncino, in what was probably intended as a thrust at the Nasi family: it can be explained to the duke of Urbino 'that because there is no king of the Jewish people, it is impossible to achieve uniformity of opinion and to compel the merchants to carry out the condition which the refugees made with him'.[38]

Even from the limited source material—and this is primarily the writings of Soncino—the major issues of the conflict emerge rather clearly. Opposition to the boycott was obviously motivated by powerful economic interests. The community of Bursa refused to accept the original agreement to the boycott, giving as their only reason 'that the merchants would suffer great loss by going to Pesaro, because of the lack of adequate harbour facilities there'. Soncino himself admits that the only significant opposition to the boycott within the Ashkenazi congregation was the one merchant who had commercial dealings with Ancona. The primary support for Soncino's censure of the boycott came from the 'outstanding merchants' of Turkey. In the legal discussions, it is assumed that the diversion of trade to Pesaro would involve considerable financial loss to the merchants, and therefore the issues raised by the rabbis are the permissibility of 'saving oneself through the money of one's neighbour' or of enforcing obedience to an ordinance which causes 'profit to one and loss to another'.[39] Soncino also pointed out several times that many of those who supported the boycott were not merchants or had no trade relations at all with Ancona. Having nothing to lose, they were free to respond to the emotional appeal of the refugees in Pesaro and were often eager to do so rather than risk the wrath or the reprisals of Dona Gracia and Don Joseph Nasi.

Economic interests alone, however, are insufficient to explain the effectiveness of the opposition. There were also other factors. Opponents were able to base their position on the alternative version of the actual events and the alternative evaluation of the boycott's impact, provided by the Jews in Ancona. They were also able to justify their refusal to co-operate by an appeal

[38] Ibid., no. 40 (46a cols. 1–2).
[39] See in particular Moses di Trani, *She'elot uteshuvot*, i, no. 237; Soncino, *Naḥalah lihoshua*, nos. 40, 39 (responsum no. 40 recounts the development of Soncino's thinking on the issue, no. 39 a more crystallized decision). The halakhic discussions of the boycott were evaluated by Sonne: 'The differences of opinion between the rabbis were based not on abstract legal minutiae, but on their different evaluation of the benefit as opposed to the harm of the boycott. The subtle halakhic distinctions do not tip the scale to one side or the other, but give a legal basis to the prior decision' (Sonne, *From Paul IV to Pius V*, 148).

to principles of Jewish law, primarily, the right of the minority not to be bound by a decision which affects it adversely when it has consistently expressed its dissent. Though this principle had not been unanimously accepted by the rabbinic authorities, it had strong roots in the writings of highly respected rabbis and in the practice of Jewish communities.[40] In short, the opposition was able to make economic interests coincide with respectable, and for some compelling, moral and legal arguments. Each side was, with some degree of plausibility, able to accuse the other of placing its material and financial interests above the welfare, or even the lives, of Jews across the sea.[41]

For the advocates of the boycott, there was no question that the emotional impact of the events—the reports of the betrayal by the pope, the martyrdom of the twenty-four Marranos, the precariousness of the plight of the refugees, the life-saving beneficence of the duke—created a powerful impetus for the original decision to boycott. Here, too, there were economic factors involved: it was not simply a case of Jewish loyalty favouring the boycott outweighed by economic interests against it. The Portuguese merchants in the Ottoman empire must have had their commercial ties in Ancona primarily with the Portuguese Marranos of that city. With the arrest, execution, and flight of the Marranos from Ancona, these ties were broken, and the only commercial links left were with the Marranos in Pesaro. Under such circumstances, it is easy to understand their enthusiasm for a boycott which would prevent other, non-Marrano, Jewish merchants (especially those of Italian origin, represented by Soncino) from continuing to profit from the lucrative Ancona trade. It is probably no accident that Bursa, the community that expressed the

---

[40] The basic talmudic source is BT *BB* 8b: 'The townspeople are at liberty to fix weights and measures, prices and wages, and to inflict penalties for the infringement of their rules.' Medieval scholars were divided over whether this meant that the minority could be compelled even if they protested against the decision from the very beginning or only if they initially agreed with the majority and later changed their minds (see Ibn Lev, *She'elot uteshuvot*, i, no. 115; ii, no 72; Moses di Trani, *She'elot uteshuvot*, i, no. 237; cf. Samuel Morell, 'The Constitutional Limits of Communal Government in Rabbinic Law', *Jewish Social Studies*, 33 [1971], 87–119; Menachem Elon, *Jewish Law: History, Sources, Principles*, 4 vols. [Philadelphia, 1994], ii. 763–71).

[41] Particularly striking is Soncino's argument that the Portuguese Marranos should never have gone to Ancona or any Christian country when they left Portugal, since experience should have taught them that no Christian country was safe for Jews. By settling in a Christian land rather than in the Ottoman empire, they placed themselves in the legal category of suicides, and there was no obligation to avenge their deaths or even to mourn for them. Furthermore, the defiling of the Torah in Pesaro was more reprehensible than what was done in Ancona (the execution of twenty-four Jews!), for the latter could at least be justified by the pope as an action against relapsed Christians, while the former was a clear insult to the Jewish people. Why then should the Ottoman Jews take vengeance against Ancona and not against Pesaro? (Soncino, *Naḥalah lihoshua*, no. 39 [45a col. 2]).

firmest and most immediate rejection of the boycott, had no congregation of Portuguese Marranos. The Portuguese newcomers to the Ottoman empire did not always see their interests as identical to those of the more established congregations.

Different cities also had different economic interests. The foremost occupation among the Jews of Turkey was the manufacture of textiles, an industry which was centred in Salonika. Ancona also produced textiles of high quality and modest price. Even before the boycott of 1556, there had been a communal ordinance prohibiting the importation by Jews of certain textiles manufactured in Ancona, because of the economic consequences.[42] Commercial links with Ancona were thus viewed by many as a threat to the vital textile industry of Salonika. This economic reality, combined with the high percentage of Portuguese Marranos living in Salonika, illuminates the background of that city's enthusiastic support for the boycott of Ancona and the diversion of trade to Pesaro.

This brings us to the position taken by the two great leaders of Ottoman Jewry, Doña Gracia and Don Joseph Nasi. Cecil Roth wrote that Doña Gracia 'risked more by the boycott scheme than anyone else', but that her 'great Jewish heart' stirred her to act so vigorously on its behalf.[43] It is no detraction from the quality of their leadership to suggest that the boycott certainly did not threaten Doña Gracia and Don Joseph with financial ruin, as it did other merchants. A full understanding of their position would require a complete study of all their commercial interests, together with a careful examination of Don Joseph's political position within the circle of courtiers surrounding Suleiman the Magnificent, especially with regard to the critical question of Ottoman policy towards the papacy and Christian Europe. This is, of course, beyond the scope of the present investigation.

---

[42] See Isaac S. Emmanuel, *Histoire de l'industrie des tissus des Israélites de Salonique* (Paris, 1935); Mark Wischnitzer, *A History of Jewish Crafts and Guilds* (New York, 1965), 127–30; Braudel, *The Mediterranean and the Mediterranean World*, 436. The protectionist regulation is recalled by De Medina: 'I remember that once here in Salonika they made an ordinance that *torpini* could not be sold in this city, because they bring about losses for the local Salonika garments, but they said that Venetian garments were not included in the prohibition because they were not of the same quality as ours' (*She'elot uteshuvot*, 'Yoreh De'ah', no. 81; see also Nehama, *Histoire des Israélites de Salonique*, iv. 48).

[43] C. Roth, *The House of Nasi*, 162. Cf. the more recent, overly simplistic, description: 'Here was a woman who would become so furious upon learning that Inquisitional officials had burned twenty-three of her people in the Italian port of Ancona that she would organize a shipping boycott that would bring the city to its knees' (Andrée Aelion Brooks, *The Woman Who Defied Kings: The Life and Times of Dona Gracia Mendes* [St. Paul, 2002], p. xix).

The conflict surrounding the boycott of Ancona was not, as the most widely read modern account would have it, that of Soncino the rabbinic scholar, a 'poor judge of current affairs', who wrote 'from the quiet of his study' a decision of 'peering legalism' totally inadequate to the burning issue at hand, versus the Nasi family with their first-hand and accurate knowledge of 'the circumstances of European politics and the mentality of European politicians'.[44] It was, on the contrary, an idea that seemed at first to be simple and compelling, economically feasible, and morally sound setting into motion such complicated economic and political forces, both in Italy and in the Ottoman empire, that it ultimately fell to the ground under its own weight.

[44] C. Roth, *The House of Nasi*, 171, 169.

CHAPTER NINE

Four Kinds of Weeping: Saul Levi Morteira's Application of Biblical Narrative to Contemporary Events

THIS CHAPTER, my contribution to an issue of *Studia Rosenthaliana* focusing on sources relating to Dutch Jewish history, is an analysis of a single sabbath morning sermon by Saul Levi Morteira. Parts of this sermon I have already discussed,[1] but I believe that it is worthy of a fuller treatment. The manuscript text—two pages front and back in the fifth volume of the Budapest manuscript collection of Morteira's sermons[2]—looks like almost all of the others, though slightly longer (most of the sermons end near the bottom of the third side), for reasons that will become clear. Yet it is an intriguingly complex text, illustrating several characteristic techniques of the master preacher, and it is unique in an important way.

The precise date of delivery of the original sermon cannot be determined, as Morteira generally did not date his sermons unless there was a special reason to do so. However, an approximate date can be estimated from Morteira's practice of preaching on successive verses of the *parashah* every year. The theme-verse (*nosé*) of this sermon is from 'Vayigash': 'He wept aloud, and the Egyptians heard, and the house of Pharaoh heard' (Gen. 45: 2). This is the eighteenth verse of the *parashah* (sermons on sixteen of the previous verses—all except for Gen. 44: 28—have been preserved). Since Morteira began his regular preaching in 1619, it could not have been delivered earlier than 1637, but since he occasionally repeated sermons—as indeed he would

First published in *Reading Texts on Jews and Judaism in the Low Countries*, special issue of *Studia Rosenthaliana*, 42–3 (2010–11), 25–42.

[1] Marc Saperstein, *Exile in Amsterdam: Saul Levi Morteira's Sermons to a Congregation of 'New Jews'* (Cincinnati, 2005), 101–6.

[2] Saul Levi Morteira, Sermons (Heb.), 5 vols. (MS 12, Budapest Rabbinical Seminary Library), v, fos. 117ʳ–118ᵛ. As mentioned in Ch. 6, n. 1 above, there are no folio numbers in the manuscript.

this one—a reasonable estimate would be that it was delivered in the mid-1640s.

The sermon, however, pointed both backwards and forwards in time. As he frequently did, Morteira used his introductory paragraph to refer to a sermon he had delivered some twenty-five years earlier on 'Vayeshev' using as his theme-verse Genesis 37: 2. Since this is the second verse of the *parashah*, the sermon was delivered at the very beginning of his Amsterdam preaching career in 1620 (the sermon on Gen. 37: 3 is dated 1621 in the manuscript). Characteristically, Morteira reviewed the contents of his earlier sermon for the benefit of those who had not heard it or had forgotten it.[3] That sermon dealt with the contrast between the righteous Joseph and the wicked Esau, based on the juxtaposition of Genesis 36 ('the generations of Esau') and Genesis 37: 2 ('the generations of Jacob: Joseph'). After recapitulating the earlier sermon, Morteira proposed a new aspect of this contrast, suggested by Joseph's weeping in Genesis 45: 2 and a rather provocative rabbinic statement on Psalm 80: 6:

Israel said before the Holy One, Blessed be He, Master of the Universe, by the merit of three tears that fell from the eyes of Esau, You gave him authority from one end of the earth to the other, and You bestowed upon him peace in this world. Should You not all the more be filled with mercy for us, whose tears flow day and night like bread? That is why the Psalmist said: 'You have fed them tears as their daily bread'.[4]

The introduction then concludes:

Now if we have found that the wicked Esau wept these three tears, the nature of which and what the sages meant by them we shall explain, we have also found that the righteous Joseph wept a number of times, and that therefore his tears of weeping compensate for the tears and weeping of his opponent.... However, what exactly are these instances of weeping [by Joseph] and what caused them? That will be the subject of our investigation today, which we shall begin with the help of God, to Whom the poet prayed and said: 'Do not be silent to my tears' [Ps. 39: 13].

---

[3] As this earlier sermon was selected by Morteira's students for incorporation into the printed collection of his sermons, *Givat sha'ul*, Morteira's summary of its contents at the beginning of the sermon on Gen. 45: 2 can be compared with the original (see Saul Levi Morteira, *Givat sha'ul: ḥamishim derushim yekarim* [sermons], no. 9 [Amsterdam, 1645], 16c–18b; [new edn. Warsaw, 1912], 85–90).

[4] Morteira, Sermons (Heb.), v, fo. 117ʳ; cf. *Midrash tehilim* 80: 4; *Midrash tanḥuma*, 'Toledot', 24; Rashi on Ps. 80: 6. Morteira's text is closest to the collection of midrashic comments on biblical verses *Yalkut shimoni* (Venice, 1566) on Ps. 80: 6 (*remez* 828). Note the rare empathetic reference to Esau, whose weeping is said to justify the material success of Christianity in this world (see Nehama Leibowitz, *Studies in the Book of Genesis* [Jerusalem, 1972], 272).

By the end of the introduction, the alert listener will know exactly what to expect: a discussion of the weeping of Joseph, triggered by the theme-verse, but recurrent as a leitmotif throughout the biblical narrative, presented in counterpoint with the weeping of Esau. Joseph amplifies the rabbinic statement, becoming a type for Jewish weeping through the centuries. A brief review of his treatment will reveal the stunning artistry of the preacher as exemplified in this ordinary sabbath sermon.

The body of the sermon makes a generalization about the occasions for weeping in the Bible. The same words may be used—'weeping', 'tears'—but the significance of the words varies dramatically. Morteira affirmed that there are four different reasons for, or functions of, 'tears that fall from the eyes', and he provided a paradigmatic example of each, none of which pertains either to Joseph or Esau:

1. weeping of supplication (*taḥanun*): 'She wept and implored him' (Esther 8: 3);

2. weeping of compassion (*raḥmanut*): 'Did I not weep for the unfortunate; did I not grieve for the needy?' (Job 30: 25);

3. weeping of pain and anguish (*tsa'ar*): 'Do not weep for the dead, do not lament for him; [weep rather for him who is leaving, for he shall never come back to the land of his birth]' (Jer. 22: 10);

4. weeping of joy (*simḥah*): 'He raised his voice and wept' (Gen. 29: 11, Jacob upon recognizing Rachel); 'They shall come with weeping, and with compassion will I guide them' (Jer. 31: 9).[5]

Turning to Esau, Morteira fleshed out the rabbinic statement about his three occasions for tears, asserting that Esau succumbed to the first three types of weeping but not the fourth, for the weeping of joy applies only to the righteous. The weeping of supplication occurred when he realized that

---

[5] While it sounds as if Morteira may be citing something of a commonplace in his statement that 'tears emerge from the eyes for four reasons', I have found no obvious source for this fourfold distinction. Compare Moses Hadarshan on Gen. 46: 29: *bekhiyah zo shel raḥamim, bekhiyah shel simḥah* (*Midrash bereshit rabati* [homiletical comments on Genesis], ed. Chanoch Albeck [Jerusalem, 1940], 229); Menahem ben Solomon on Gen. 45: 14: *zo bekhiyah shel raḥmanut* (*Midrash sekhel tov al sefer bereshit ushemot* [midrash on Genesis and Exodus], 2 vols., ed. Solomon Buber [Berlin, 1900], i. 339); Tuvyah ben Eliezer on Gen. 45: 14: *yesh bekhiyah shel raḥmanut* (citing Gen. 43: 30) (*Midrash lekaḥ tov . . . al hatorah kulah* [commentary on the Torah], ed. Solomon Buber [Vilna, 1884], 285). *Bekhiyah shel tsa'ar* is not uncommon, but I have not found the term *bekhiyah shel taḥanun*, even though it is suggested by Esther 8: 3 and Jer. 31: 8.

the blessing intended for him had already been given to his brother: 'Esau raised his voice and wept' (Gen. 27: 38), imploring his father to bless him too. Isaac saw the tears of his firstborn son and responded with a blessing. Second was the weeping of compassion: Esau took pity on his brother Jacob when he saw him humiliate himself by bowing seven times to the ground, and it was then that he ran to Jacob, embraced and kissed him, and wept (Gen. 33: 3–4). Thirdly, Esau wept out of anguish and pain at the death of his father. This—Morteira conceded—is not stated explicitly in the Torah, yet it is clear that he honoured Isaac deeply and must have wept in grief when he came to bury him (Gen. 35: 29).

The rabbinic statement asserted only that because Esau wept three times, Israel was placed in the power of Edom, and that the Jewish people had also wept. Morteira's sense of symmetry led him beyond the statement to assert that this occurred three times, and in each case the descendants of Esau were involved. The first was the attack by Amalek—a tribe descended from Esau (Gen. 36: 16) following the Exodus (Exod. 17: 8–13; Deut. 25: 17–18); the second time was the role of the Edomites in the destruction of the First Temple (Ps. 137: 7; Obad. 8–15); the third was at the destruction of the Second Temple (Lam. 4: 21).[6] These three events are what the Psalmist refers to in the verse 'You have fed them tears as their daily bread' (Ps. 80: 6). Morteira then interpreted all of Psalm 80 as pertaining to these three catastrophes for the people of Israel, each worse than the previous one.

At this point, approximately mid-way through the sermon, Morteira turned to Joseph. The alert listener would expect an example of how Joseph wept in all four categories, including the weeping for joy which is never attributed to Esau, but Morteira introduced a surprise, announcing a more complex pattern. Not only does the weeping of Joseph fit into all four categories, but within each category there is one example of weeping pertaining to the actions of God, and one pertaining to the actions of human beings. This is a challenge that the preacher set for himself, expecting that the alert listener would be eager to hear how convincingly he could fulfil the unexpected pattern. In what follows, I can merely present the examples without the full homiletical discussion.

The first weeping is weeping of supplication, exemplified shortly after the theme-verse. Jacob fell upon Benjamin's neck and wept, imploring forgive-

[6] In understanding this verse as a prophecy of the destruction of the Second Temple by the Romans, Morteira follows *Lamentations Rabbah* 4: 34; Tuvyah ben Eliezer on Lam. 4: 21 (*Perush lekah tov al megilat eikhah* [commentary on Lamentations], ed. Jacob Nacht [Berlin, 1895], 31); Rashi ad loc.

ness from his younger brother for the anguish he caused in forcing Benjamin to leave his home and in the incident of the cup (Gen. 45: 14). In the following verse, 'he kissed all his brothers, and wept over them' (Gen. 45: 15), he was not imploring their forgiveness, but rather for God to forgive his brothers for the evil they had done to him.

Second is the weeping of compassion for the suffering of others. Seeing his brothers, who have brought Benjamin from their home, grovelling before him on the ground, he withdraws to weep out of compassion for the anguish he himself has caused his brothers (Gen. 43: 26–30).[7] Earlier, hearing his brothers confess their guilt to each other and berate themselves for what they had done to him years before, he weeps out of sorrow for this punishment that God has inflicted upon them (Gen. 42: 21, 24).

Third is the weeping of pain and anguish. This is seen in Joseph's weeping at the death of his father (Gen. 49: 33–50: 1), for 'every sentient person can empathize with the sorrow felt by Joseph at that moment when his father died'. Joseph's weeping when he heard his brothers fabricate a message from their dying father requesting that he forgive their transgression against him (Gen. 50: 15–17) is related to God. He is pained that his brothers do not trust him and suspect him of planning revenge, and there is no pain greater than that of an honest man who is suspected of something. In addition, the brothers' desperate fear of punishment from Joseph, expressed in the repetition of their plea for forgiveness in Genesis 50: 17, makes Joseph feel anguish over his own imperfections in relation to the Day of Judgement: if his brothers could be so afraid of retaliation from him, how could he not weep at the thought of the possibility of punishment from God?

Finally, the weeping of joy, which Esau did not experience. Joseph's weeping for joy in relation to divine matters occurred when he met his father coming to Egypt. The Bible states that 'he appeared to him [*vayera eilav*], and fell upon his neck, and wept on his neck' (Gen. 46: 29). The sages, noting that the phrase *vayera eilav* is often used of God's sudden appearance, reached an unexpected conclusion: Joseph realized that Jacob was so engrossed in prayer that he did not at first see his son. This was the source of Joseph's overwhelming joy that brought on the tears.[8] For Joseph's weeping in joy concerning human behaviour, Morteira returned to his theme-verse, Genesis 45: 2, and

---

[7] Cf. Tuvyah ben Eliezer on Gen. 45: 14 (*Perush lekah tov*, 285).

[8] For Jacob's immersion in the recitation of the *shema* at the moment when Joseph first saw him, see Louis Ginzberg, *Legends of the Jews*, 7 vols. (Philadelphia, 1912), ii. 105 and n.; Rashi on Gen. 46: 29; Abraham ben Jacob Saba on Gen. 46: 29 (*Tseror hamor . . . al hamishah humshei torah* [homiletical comments on the Torah] [New York, 1961], 188*b*).

Joseph's joy that he can finally reveal himself to his brothers. His tears revealed that he was now appeased and had forgiven all the sins of the past. The rabbinic dictum cited at the beginning of the sermon—*Genesis Rabbah* 93: 12, which connects the theme-verse with Jeremiah 31: 8: 'With weeping they will come, with supplication I will lead them'—makes this joyous reconciliation through tears a model for the ultimate reconciliation with God. Following a characteristic recapitulation, in which all eight instances of Joseph's weeping are rehearsed, more than counterbalancing the tears of Esau, the sermon ends with a standard messianic affirmation.[9]

Several conclusions are justified at this point. One is that a lot of effort must have been invested in the preparation of this sermon, which is not fundamentally different from the hundreds of other sermons delivered week after week over a period of decades. The overriding theme of the sermon might be said to be 'Weeping in the Bible'. Ranging through all of Scripture, Morteira proposed four general categories. Joseph is certainly the biblical character most prone to weeping, and, noting that there are eight times in the Joseph narrative where the weeping is attributed to this powerful figure—all of them after he has reached a position of monumental influence—Morteira subdivided his general categories further, so that each of the four categories has divine and human components. The result is perhaps more complicated than it needed to be, and not every explanation is equally persuasive, but Morteira may well have been drawn to this subdivision by a central theme of the Joseph narrative: human activities that seem to transpire without any form of divine intervention are presented in the context of a providential world-view—reflecting both the biblical narrative and Morteira's own fundamental beliefs—that reconciles human initiative with divine planning.

In addition, there is the juxtaposition of biblical exegesis with rabbinic interpretation. The *ma'amar* is brought in only at the very end, in what may seem to be an incidental manner—it was apparently chosen after most of the sermon had been written—but the counterpoint of the weeping of Esau with the weeping of Joseph, transforming these two figures into typological prefigurations of the Jewish people in relation to Edom, Rome, and the Christians, is not at all peripheral to the sermon's message. No practical application is given, but the implication may well have been understood by the listeners: that the tears of pain and anguish they wept while still in Portugal, the tears of

---

[9] For a perceptive contemporary discussion of Joseph's weeping, obviously independent of Morteira but also noting that Joseph weeps on eight different occasions and emphasizing the diversity in the nature of such tears, see Aviad Hakohen, 'Joseph's Weeping' (Heb.), *Merkaz hayeshivot benei akiva*, <http://www.yba.org.il/show.asp?id=24152> (accessed 20 May 2014).

compassion and supplication for those left behind, and the potential tears of joy at some future reunification could have redemptive significance.

The text does not, however, end here. Near the bottom of the third side, following the concluding words, 'May it be God's will that this will occur with the coming of our righteous messiah, speedily and in our days, Amen', a new paragraph begins: 'I delivered this a second time on the 11th of Tevet in the year 5416 [8 Jan. 1656], adding all that is written below, because of the events that were happening at that time.' Thus the text of the original sermon delivered in the mid-1640s refers both back in time to a sermon from the beginning of the preacher's career and points ahead to an important message delivered some four years before his death.

Like almost all preachers, Morteira occasionally repeated sermons he had delivered earlier.[10] Most commonly, he would append to the original text a simple statement: 'And I preached this again in the year . . .'. Occasionally he would add a few words about the circumstances, or a paragraph was added for the new delivery. The addition to this sermon is extremely unusual in that it amounts to more than a third of the original text. (It is possible that Morteira shortened the original sermon, perhaps by eliminating the passage devoted to a homiletical exegesis of Psalm 80, which could be removed without any loss of continuity, although this was only about a third as long as the addition.) The only text that is comparable in terms of the amount and importance of the material added is Morteira's eulogy for his younger colleague in the Amsterdam rabbinate, Menasseh ben Israel.[11]

The addition was a response to dramatic contemporary events. This makes the discourse topical, a rare exception in the extant records of Morteira's preaching that provides an insight into how he responded to current affairs, both distant from and within his own community, and how he interpreted them within a homiletical framework.

Following is Morteira's report of the material added: 'I said that it is indeed true that at present these four kinds of weeping were occurring before us, two of them primary and two of them secondary.'

The first is the weeping of pain and anguish from the terrible events that have confronted the glorious holy community of Lublin. Cruel enemies have destroyed it, and

---

[10] On this practice, see Saperstein, *Exile in Amsterdam*, 68–70.

[11] I first published a translation of this text in Dan Cohn-Sherbock, *Traditional Quest: Essays in Honour of Louis Jacobs* (Sheffield, 1991), 133–53; for a fuller version, including the Hebrew text, see Marc Saperstein, *'Your Voice Like a Ram's Horn': Themes and Texts in Traditional Jewish Preaching* (Cincinnati, 1996), 411–44.

the weeping is profuse. It is as Jeremiah said: 'Do not weep for the dead and do not lament for him; weep, weep for the one who is leaving, for he shall never come back to see the land of his birth' [Jer. 22: 10]. This means, from this point on, weeping over the dead does not seem painful in comparison with the weeping over the captives—the men killed, their wives and small children taken into captivity. This is the greatest evil. On the biblical verse, 'Those destined for the plague, to the plague; those destined for the sword, to the sword; those destined for famine, to famine; those destined for captivity, to captivity' [Jer. 15: 2], the sages said, 'Whatever comes later in this verse is worse than what precedes it, and captivity is worst of all' [BT *BB* 8*b*].

Great emphasis has been given recently to the strong ethnic identity of the Portuguese 'nation' in Amsterdam and the tenuous solidarity felt with Ashkenazi Jews. In many ways, the members of the Portuguese community may indeed have had more of a sense of solidarity with Portuguese émigrés living as Christians in Antwerp or Bordeaux than with the Ashkenazi Jews who were their neighbours in Amsterdam.[12] However, Morteira—possibly because of his own Ashkenazi roots—felt compelled to express grief over the destruction of a glorious Jewish community in Poland and the plight of Ashkenazi Jews taken captive, possibly never to be released.[13]

But he did not stop with a description of the events in Poland and the suffering of its Jewish communities. Driven by his theological commitment to a providential world-view, he apparently felt compelled to explain these events in a traditional manner. Following an explanation of the simple meaning of Jeremiah 22: 10, he continued with a homiletical exposition: 'The prophet said "Weep, weep", meaning one weeping after another, one weeping for the punishment and one for the transgression [that caused it].' This is followed by a passage from the Torah asserting the close connection between Jewish suffering and sin (Deut. 29: 23–4) and a powerful parable from the Talmud: 'Once 400 jars of wine belonging to R. Huna turned sour. [Scholars came to

---

[12] Joseph Kaplan, 'The Attitude of Spanish and Portuguese Jews Towards Ashkenazi Jews in Seventeenth-Century Amsterdam' (Heb.), in *Transition and Change in Modern Jewish History* [Temurot bahistoriyah hayehudit haḥadashah: kovets ma'amarim, shai lishmu'el etinger] (Jerusalem, 1988), 389–412; Saperstein, *Exile in Amsterdam*, 102 n. 102.

[13] Lublin was devastated by Russians and Cossacks in 1655. Contemporary Jewish chronicles claim that thousands of Jews were killed in that year, though that may well be an exaggeration. For a German account published in 1656, see Bernard D. Weinryb, *The Jews of Poland: A Social and Economic History of the Jewish Community in Poland from 1000 to 1800* (Philadelphia, 1973), 194–5, 363 n. 32; for a quotation from this account describing the fate of the Jews, see Joel Raba, *Between Remembrance and Denial: The Fate of the Jews in the Wars of the Polish Commonwealth during the Mid-Seventeenth Century as Shown in Contemporary Writings and Historical Research*, East European Monographs, 178 (New York, 1995), 103–4.

visit and said: 'The master should examine his actions.' He said to them: 'Am I suspect in your eyes?' They replied: 'Is the Holy One, Blessed be He, suspect of punishing without justice?'] [BT *Ber.* 5*b*].'

Morteira concluded this section with a phrase that he incorporated into the end of every eulogy, applying it not to an individual but to a community:

We must assert the justice of His decrees by saying that there were two transgressions well known in that kingdom, the first the sin of taking interest on loans, which their scholars have never been capable of eradicating, and this results in the destruction of material assets.[14] The second is the sin of mentioning the divine name for an inappropriate purpose, and this results in the destruction of human lives. The sages said that there were many villages in the region of Har Hamelekh, and all of them were destroyed because of this sin.[15] Therefore weep and feel sorrow for these transgressions, and remove them from your midst, lest the evil come close to us.

The final sentence—a reminder of the type of weeping under discussion—concludes with a warning that the listeners in his own congregation are not exempt from the consequences of the specific sins mentioned.[16]

The second cause of weeping was an event that also occurred far from Amsterdam, but it brought the message somewhat closer to home:

From this is derived the second weeping, that of compassion, as Job said: 'Did I not weep for the hard-pressed; did I not grieve for the destitute?' [Job 30: 25]. This

---

[14] On moneylending with interest in Polish Jewish society, see Haim Hillel Ben-Sasson, *Deliberation and Leadership: The Social Doctrines of Polish Jews Towards the End of the Middle Ages* [Hagut vehanhagah: hashkefoteihem haḥevratiyot shel yehudei polin beshalhei yemei habeinayim] (Jerusalem, 1959), 202–4; Hillel Levine, *Economic Origins of Antisemitism: Poland and Its Jews in the Early Modern Period* (New Haven, 1991), 132–3.

[15] Cf. *Numbers Rabbah* 22: 1. This passage may have been based on Judah Leib ben Bezalel (the Maharal of Prague): 'King Jannai had 60 villages in *har hamelekh*, and all were destroyed because of true oaths, for they were accustomed to swear oaths using the Divine Name. Even though what they swore was true, nevertheless because they were accustomed to do this excessively, there was here destruction by means of the Divine Name. The general principle is that the unnecessary mention of the Divine Name, even in a true oath, causes destruction in our world' (Judah Leib ben Bezalel, *Netivot olam* [Prague, 1596], 'Netiv yirat hashem', ch. 3). The source in *Midrash tanḥuma*, does not speak of *hazkarat shem shamayim*, only of true oaths (*Midrash tanḥuma* [Buber], 'Matot', ch. 1). Morteira's use of Maharal, if indeed this was his source, may have justified his claim that this was a problem among the Jews of Poland.

[16] The rather weak warning against these two offences reveals that they were not a high priority for Morteira or the community. Morteira would occasionally refer in his sermons to illicit interest or swearing in God's name (see e.g. Saperstein, *Exile in Amsterdam*, 188), but they were not issues about which the Mahamad passed significant ordinances (Joseph Kaplan, 'The Jews in the Republic Until About 1750: Religious, Cultural, and Social Life', in J. C. H. Blom, R. G. Fuks-Mansfeld, and I. Schöffer [eds.], *History of the Jews in the Netherlands* [Oxford, 2002], 136).

applies when you think about the considerable number of notables who yesterday were wealthy, but for whom today fate has set up an ambush, when they were driven out of their domicile of pleasure, out of the land of Brazil. They are indeed hard-pressed and destitute; they are in anguish because of their previous good fortune, while now they have no covering against the cold [see Job 24: 7] as they arrive from that warm land.

As for you, living in your well-roofed houses [see Hag. 1: 4], think that God in His great strength has saved them from enemies more cruel than the first ones, and while they were travelling, with all the misfortunes they encountered, He did not give them into captivity at the hands of their enemies, who had already said they would swallow them up. All this was in order to bring them into the midst of their brothers, that they might have compassion upon them, so that God would have compassion on the compassionate, as the Bible says, 'He will show you compassion and be compassionate towards you' [Deut. 13: 18].[17]

This alludes to events that virtually everyone in the congregation would have known about. The Dutch community in Recife fell to the Portuguese in January 1654, two years before the sermon was delivered. Those who chose not to remain in Brazil were given three months to liquidate their affairs and be gone, with obvious adverse economic consequences. Today, this evacuation is associated primarily with the arrival of twenty-three refugees in New Amsterdam in September 1654, the beginning of an overt Jewish presence in North America, but others experienced significant tribulations and potential dangers before making their way back to Amsterdam, as Morteira himself described in his Portuguese magnum opus *Tratado da verdade da lei de Moisés*, written at about the same time.

The allusion to having been saved from enemies 'more cruel than the first ones' is explained in the *Tratado*: one ship containing refugees from Recife was captured by Spaniards, who intended to turn them over to the Inquisition, but they were rescued by a French battleship and eventually reached Holland. Jewish passengers on a second ship, blown off course to the island of Jamaica, under Spanish rule, were also in danger but were released because of pressure from the Dutch government instigated by the Jewish community of Amsterdam. The Spanish are therefore described here as worse than the Portuguese, who agreed to allow the inhabitants of Recife who had never lived as Catholics to remain under their rule.[18] While the destitute refugees had

---

[17] Alluding to the rabbinic comment on 'Whoever has compassion on other creatures will receive compassion from Heaven' (BT *Shab.* 151*b*).

[18] Saul Levi Morteira, *Tratado da verdade da lei de Moisés*, ed. H. P. Salomon (Coimbra, 1988), fos.

arrived in Amsterdam some time before the sermon was delivered—and it is not at all unlikely that Morteira had already spoken about these events from the pulpit in the context of divine providence months earlier—the ongoing problem occasioned a pointed lesson to the listeners about reversals of fortune, the need for compassion, and appropriate humility on the part of those listeners living 'in well-roofed houses'.[19]

The third section of the addendum applied directly to an experience shared by all of the congregation:

At this same time, we experience a third weeping: of joy. This is because of the great miracle of abundant deliverance by which God has saved us from the plague that prevailed in this city for six months. Yet among all the Jews, no one died except for two infants: they were like two lambs without blemish,[20] an atonement sacrifice for the entire community. This was while the number of dead each week was close to nine hundred! God in His mercy saved our household. Therefore, 'Cry out in joy for Jacob, shout at the crossroads of the nations' [Jer. 31: 2].... Thus we have seen that thousands and myriads have fallen from our right side, but God has not afflicted us, He has saved our homes.

Like the previous passage, this should be compared with the parallel treatment in the *Tratado*. There Morteira exemplified God's providential care for the lives of Jews by noting that during the great plague that ravaged the city of Amsterdam for six months, 'when the number of dead reached almost a thousand each week, during this entire period no Jew died'.[21] The ethical

28–9 (pp. 75–7); Arnold Wiznitzer, 'The Exodus from Brazil and Arrival in New Amsterdam of the Jewish Pilgrim Fathers, 1654', in Martin A. Cohen (ed.), *The Jewish Experience in Latin America*, 2 vols. (New York, 1971), ii. 313–30; Günter Böhm, *Los sefardíes en los dominios holandeses de América del Sur y del Caribe, 1630–1750* (Frankfurt am Main, 1992), 95–9.

[19] Compare Morteira's criticism of self-indulgently lavish housing chosen by some of the new immigrants in his community in his early sermon, 'The People's Envy' (in Marc Saperstein, *Jewish Preaching, 1200–1800: An Anthology* [New Haven, 1989], esp. 276–8).

[20] *Shetei kevasot temimot*, echoing in the feminine form Num. 28: 3, 9. The shift to the feminine indicates that those who died were baby girls.

[21] 'Hauendo hum contagio na cidade de Amstradama, e foj tão grande que durando alg s seis meses do verão cheg[a]rão a morir perto de mil cada semana, em todo este tempo naõ moreo nih judeo, com hauer na ditta cidade nuitas casas delles' (Morteira, *Tratado da verdade da lei de Moisés*, fo. 29 [p. 77]). Salomon, in his note, refers to the plague of 1635, but the passage from the sermon makes it clear that Morteira was referring to the plague of 1655 (cf. Simon Schama, *The Embarrassment of Riches: An Interpretation of Dutch Culture in the Golden Age* [Berkeley, 1988], 171, 186). An authoritative figure for the number of deaths for Amsterdam in 1655 is 16,727, suggesting that 900 per week for six months is exaggerated; in 1664, when the plague was as bad or worse, the peak figure was 1,041 burials in a week (ibid. 643 n. 64; cf. Jonathan Israel, *The Dutch Republic: Its Rise, Greatness, and Fall, 1477–1806* [Oxford, 1995], 625; Cor Snabel, 'Life in 16th and 17th Century Amsterdam Holland: Disease', *The*

question of rejoicing at a time of such massive loss of life among Gentile neighbours does not arise directly either in the sermon or in the *Tratado*, though it is clearly appropriate to the theme of different kinds of weeping. It was apparently the abatement of the plague, the beginning of the return to normal, and the realization that his own community had largely been spared that impelled the preacher to return to a sermon on Joseph's tears of joy and to bring in other examples from the recent past of the different kinds of weeping.

As in the case of weeping caused by deep sorrow or compassion, so the weeping of joy is presented with a moral message, based on the belief that all events are evidence of God's providential care for the world.

In all matters, we must judge measure for measure. Behold we have seen how our wardens and leaders during the past two years have delved deeply into the matter, and made the evil to cease from our midst [by] opposing the serious transgressions, as is well known. And God, who in His loving kindness rewards human beings according to their deeds, said, 'As you have removed what I consider evil from among you, so will I remove what you consider evil from among you.'

This is the rhetoric of allusion, so common in sermons, especially when the preacher turns to sensitive matters. Speaking to people who are part of a closely knit community, the preacher knows that everyone will understand an oblique reference without the need to provide specifics: this is expressed in the single Hebrew word, *kayadua*, 'as is well known'. Yet this is precisely the kind of passage that raises excruciating challenges for historians. I have written previously that I found no explicit reference in Morteira's sermons to the excommunications of Uriel da Costa in 1623 or Spinoza in 1656.[22] If the additional material had not been dated, we might have been tempted to conclude that this was a rare reference from the pulpit to the decisive action taken by the leaders of the Portuguese community to remove Spinoza from their midst—used in a dramatic way to explain the apparent protection of the

Olive Tree Genealogy, <http://www.olivetreegenealogy.com/nn/amst_disease.shtml> [accessed 24 Oct. 2013]). The passages about Jewish deaths in the sermon and the *Tratado* correct the assumption made by Stephen Nadler that 'there is no record of how many Jews were carried away by the epidemic, but it is reasonable to assume, once again, some proportionate contagion among them' (Nadler, *Spinoza: A Life* [Cambridge, 1999], 117). Chapter 11 of the *Tratado*, in which the references to the refugees from Brazil and the plague in Amsterdam are juxtaposed as expressions of divine providence, is quite sermonic in structure and may have been based either on the passage under discussion or on a similar sermon that has not survived.

[22] See Saperstein, *Exile in Amsterdam*, 208–10.

Jewish population from the plague. But the dates make this conclusion impossible: Morteira's sermon was delivered on 8 January 1656; Spinoza was excommunicated the following 27 July.[23]

Two events from the summer of 1654, however, suggest an alternative referent for the preacher's allusion. One was the excommunication of Jacob Moreno and his wife, together with Daniel Castiel. Castiel was said to be inappropriately visiting Moreno's wife when Moreno was travelling outside the community, despite warnings from the Mahamad.[24] Morteira himself played a role in the incident, when the rabbis and *parnasim* (wardens) of the Portuguese nation went to the Amsterdam notary to testify in proceedings against the three accused.[25] About two weeks before that formal appearance, another member of the community, Antonio Lopes Suasso, denied before the commissioner of small claims that he was the father of a child born to a New Christian woman in Antwerp, but soon afterwards agreed to pay the mother the costs of childbirth and to assume full responsibility for the cost of the child's upbringing.[26] It is unclear whether this agreement led to any further censure of Suasso by the leaders of the community.

The timing of these two incidents fits Morteira's reference to the activities of the 'past two years', and his warning against improper sexual conduct in the continuation of the passage suggests this was indeed at issue:

We too must give thanks to God for this great favour he has done for us in distinguishing us from the nations by removing the evil [of the plague] from our midst.... And we must not profane the covenant of our ancestors by having sexual relations with Gentile women[27] and becoming impure through them. For if God has distinguished us for our benefit, why should we be with them to detriment? This is indeed

---

[23] See the recent summary by Nadler, *Spinoza*, 120–38. No event involving Spinoza in the two years preceding it could have justified the language of the sermon (ibid. 118).

[24] Joseph Kaplan, 'The Social Functions of the "Ḥerem" in the Portuguese Jewish Community of Amsterdam in the 17th Century', *Dutch Jewish History*, 1 (1984), 129; Miriam Bodian, *Hebrews of the Portuguese Nation: Conversos and Community in Early Modern Amsterdam* (Bloomington, 1997), 115. According to the records reviewed by Kaplan, this was the only act of excommunication during the two years preceding the sermon (see 'The Social Functions of the "Ḥerem"'; Joseph Kaplan, 'Bans in the Sephardi Community of Late Seventeenth-Century Amsterdam' [Heb.], in Aharon Mirsky, Avraham Grossman, and Yosef Kaplan [eds.], *Exile and Diaspora* [Galut aḥar golah: meḥkarim betoledot yisra'el mugashim leḥayim beinart] [Jerusalem, 1988], 517–40).

[25] Isaac Emmanuel, 'New Information on the Portuguese Community of Amsterdam' (Heb.), *Otsar yehudei sefarad*, 6 (1963), 166; Saperstein, *Exile in Amsterdam*, 5–6 n. 7.

[26] Daniel M. Swetschinski, *Reluctant Cosmpolitans: The Portuguese Jews of Seventeenth-Century Amsterdam* (London, 2000), 217–18.

[27] The 'covenant of our ancestors' here is the covenant of circumcision, which is profaned by allowing it to enter the realm of impurity: the body of a Gentile woman.

to praise God with *Az*,²⁸ and to remain separate from the local population [*mei'amei ha'arets*], for this has always been the cause of our misfortune.

The dangers of assimilation into the surrounding population and especially of licentious behaviour or intermarriage with Gentiles were recurrent themes in Morteira's preaching.²⁹

Finally, the fourth part of the new material builds on the previous passage with an application to the audience and the institutions of their community in the wake of the plague:

From this is derived the fourth weeping, that of supplication, as it says of Esther, 'She wept and made supplication' [Esther 8: 3]. This means to weep and implore God to continue His providential beneficence with us. It is not that we must be always indebted because of the favour He has done for us, but we should always be aware of it, eternally. For several years now, the plague has been prevalent throughout this land, yet it has afflicted few from the midst of our people. As ransom for our lives, the Honen Dalim Society established the great mitzvah of lending money to the poor who were indebted.³⁰ . . . 'Then God yielded to his prayer for the land, and the plague stopped' [2 Sam. 24: 25].

Therefore, at this time, those who still have no part in it should enrol and not lose such a great merit, as this was the original reason for which it was established. Now it is God's will that we appear before Him with gifts that relate to the benefits that we seek from Him. . . . How then shall we come before the Eternal, how shall we bow down before God on high [see Mic. 6: 6] with regard to this wonder? With our gifts to the Ets Hayim Society.³¹ God has preserved our sustenance and kept us alive [see Ps. 66: 9], so shall we preserve His sustenance, for it is our life and the length of our days [see Deut. 30: 20]: life for life. As this is the banner of our community—for so it is called: the Talmud Torah Congregation—if God has raised our banner, let us raise the banner of the Torah.³²

Now every one of you should know that while some of the members of our congregation fled from the city because of the plague, I do not criticize their decision to

---

²⁸ Alluding to *Midrash tanḥuma*, which interprets *az*, the first word of Exod. 15: 1, as alluding to circumcision through its numerical value of 8, the number of days from birth to circumcision (*Midrash tanḥuma* [Buber], 'Beshalaḥ', 12).

²⁹ See e.g. Saperstein, *Exile in Amsterdam*, 185–6, 188, 198–204.

³⁰ On the Honen Dalim Society, established in 1625, see Swetschinski, *Reluctant Cosmopolitans*, 200.

³¹ On the Ets Haim Society, founded in 1616 to support needy students, see Bodian, *Hebrews of the Portuguese Nation*, 109–10.

³² Talmud Torah was the name of the congregation formed by the merger of the three separate synagogues in 1639. For another reference to the 'banner' of the congregation, see Saperstein, *Exile in Amsterdam*, 221, 432.

leave.[33] However, it is a source of shame and a serious shortcoming if they relied on this effort alone. This was the sin of Asa, as the Bible tells us: 'He did not seek the Eternal, but physicians' [2 Chron. 16: 12]. To the contrary, one must seek God first, and then the physicians. Thus God's loving kindness was with us, all of us are alive—those who left the city and those who remained. Think [. . .[34]] how much expense there would have been, how much money would have been wasted, if, God forbid, the plague had reached one small part of our academy. Our hair stands on end just to mention it! How much money was expended in their journey. And even though they did not refrain from giving charity where they went, the Ets Hayim Society became extremely impoverished during this entire period. Therefore, set your minds and eat from the Tree of Life [ets ḥayim]; soften your hearts in weeping tears of supplication to water the Tree of Life. For then God will bestow life upon you, as the Bible says: 'They shall come in weeping, and I shall bring them with supplications' [Jer. 31: 9].

In this way Morteira brought his earlier sermon up to date, beginning with events far to the east affecting Jews with whom the members of the Portuguese nation felt little natural affinity, turning to another distant location—this time in the New World—but affecting members of their own community, arriving at the recent outburst of plague that devastated their Christian neighbours but left the Jewish population relatively unscathed, and concluding with the institutions at the core of contemporary community life. Starting at the periphery, he moves closer and closer to the concerns of his neighbours. In this additional material, Esau and Joseph have been forgotten, the theme of the complexities of weeping removed from its biblical context and applied to matters at hand. From a masterful exploration of biblical narrative, the sermon has been transformed into a cogent review of critical issues engaging the Portuguese community of Amsterdam in the recent past that illustrate the preacher's compelling belief in divine providence.

It cannot of course be demonstrated that Spinoza was present when this sermon was delivered, but—six months before his excommunication and still an active member of the congregation—he might very well have been. If he had been listening, it is very likely that Morteira's typological presentation of Esau and Joseph, his insistence that tragedies occur to Jews as punishment for their sins and—conversely—that the almost total survival of Amsterdam Jews during the recent plague that ravaged the neighbouring Christian population

---

[33] For archival references to members of the Portuguese community fleeing from Amsterdam during this plague and gathering for worship in other places of refuge, see Tirtsah Levie Bernfeld, *Poverty and Welfare Among the Portuguese Jews in Early Modern Amsterdam* (Oxford, 2012), 463 n. 108.

[34] One word omitted that makes no sense to me in the context.

was God's miraculous providential reward for the initiative of the community's leadership in combating sexual licentiousness, would have impressed Spinoza as a fine paradigm of a world-view that intellectually he simply could not accept.

CHAPTER TEN

Attempts to Control the Pulpit: Medieval Judaism and Beyond

JACOB ANATOLI, son-in-law of the noted translator of Maimonides' *Guide for the Perplexed*, Samuel ibn Tibbon, was the first philosophically trained Jew who left a record of his sermons. In the second quarter of the thirteenth century, he began to present homilies at wedding ceremonies or celebrations, though he notes that he did not have time to write down even a single line of what he said: 'Then, as I got used to this discipline, I agreed to preach a little publicly each sabbath. But not long afterwards, I retreated from this path, seeing that it was considered improper by some of my companions.' The book into which he incorporated his homiletical oeuvre, *Malmad hatalmidim*, contains several references to the opposition his preaching engendered.[1]

The sermons themselves reveal an exegetical orientation, focusing on the Wisdom books of the Bible and the weekly lesson from the Pentateuch. Their philosophical content does not appear to be radical or obviously problematic, and Anatoli actually dissociates himself from extremist philosophical positions. Nevertheless, he was aware of the potential for opposition: 'Although I am aware that this novel interpretation will be regarded as overly presumptuous, some men of learning even branding it as totally fantastic, nonetheless I persist in advancing it, willingly subjecting myself to their disparagement and revilement.'[2] In another sermon:

Thus, all who would serve God must be aware of the reason for the commandment while performing it, lest it become a 'commandment learned by rote' [Isa. 29: 13]; and

First published in Katherine L. Jansen and Miri Rubin (eds.), *Charisma and Religious Authority* (Turnhout: Brepols, 2010), 93–103.

[1] Jacob Anatoli, *Malmad hatalmidim* [sermons] (Lyck, 1866; repr. Jerusalem, 1968); for an example of Anatoli's work in translation, see Marc Saperstein, *Jewish Preaching, 1200–1800: An Anthology* (New Haven, 1989), 111–23; for a general study, see Israel Bettan, *Studies in Jewish Preaching* (Cincinnati, 1939), 49–88.

[2] Anatoli, *Malmad hatalmidim*, 6b ('Bereshit'); see Bettan, *Studies in Jewish Preaching*, 53.

therefore no one should blame me for trying to explain the reason, for if I provide a sufficient reason, it is to the good, and if I fail, I may inspire someone else to come up with a sufficient reason.³

And in yet another:

Even though I know that this point of mine will not be accepted by many, because of the bad custom [that he has just criticized: excessive movement in prayer without attention of the heart], we have already said that Truth should not be bashful; she should call out at the head of busy streets [see Prov. 1: 21], on the heights of the town [see Prov. 9: 3], and if only one out of a thousand should accept her, Truth is obliged to have compassion for that one.⁴

Apparently the opposition to the philosophical orientation of Anatoli's homiletical exegesis was so strong that he decided it was not worth his while to continue the enterprise.

Anatoli's problems in the pulpit illustrate a structural problem of Jewish preaching in the Middle Ages and—to a large extent—in the modern period as well. Unlike the situation in the Catholic Church, where the authority to preach was fairly strictly regulated and preaching without authorization was by its very nature a potentially heretical activity whatever the content of the sermon might be, medieval Jewish communities had no definition of who was permitted to speak from the pulpit. In theory, any male Jew—there is no evidence of women preachers before the nineteenth century—who was respected enough to find a group of Jews willing to listen was entitled to deliver a sermon. This might be in the synagogue as an integral part of the worship service or on a sabbath afternoon before the resumption of formal worship; at a life-cycle event (circumcision, wedding, funeral) or a gathering for a special occasion or simply for study and mutual edification.⁵

In the Jewish communities of the Mediterranean basin—Spain, southern France, Italy, the Greek islands and the Ottoman empire—the common pattern was for the rabbi to deliver the sermon each week. But these rabbis were preachers not because of a sacerdotal status that restricted liturgical roles to a uniquely authorized religious cadre and certainly not because of any claim of direct inspiration from God. Such a claim was extremely unusual in medieval Judaism and generally had messianic, eschatological significance.⁶ Rather,

---

³ Anatoli, *Malmad hatalmidim*, 121*b* ('Yitro'). ⁴ Ibid. 159*a* ('Va'ethanan').

⁵ On the various occasions for traditional Jewish preaching, see Saperstein, *Jewish Preaching 1200–1800*, 26–37.

⁶ According to rabbinic doctrine, prophecy (direct verbal revelation from God) had ended with Haggai, Zechariah, and Malachi, but would be restored with the advent of the messiah. For the

the preacher's role was assumed because of the rabbi's learning and stature as teacher and moral spokesman. This, however, did not preclude others—such as Anatoli, who was not a rabbi and who claimed no expertise in Jewish law—from filling this role either in the presence or the absence of the rabbi.

Yet, as we can see from Anatoli's case, resistance to the content of some sermons occasionally crystallized into attempts to pressure the preacher to desist. There were some cases when listeners reacted negatively to what they considered to be the low level of discourse from the pulpit, claiming that the preacher was wasting their time. Maimonides was once consulted about an incident in which the 'head of the congregation' in Cairo was delivering a sermon about the fundamentals of faith when he was suddenly interrupted by a congregant, who said: 'How long will this delirium last? All you have said is nonsense; it should not be heard, it cannot be understood!'[7] Jewish preachers in early sixteenth-century Constantinople were said to deliver their sermons terrified lest a congregant should arise in the middle of the discourse and say: 'This interpretation was written by So-and-so in his book: the preacher took it from there.'[8]

More important are cases where the content of the sermon seemed to some listeners to have crossed the boundary of acceptability. To be sure, there was no formal mechanism, as there was in the European Christian Church, for investigating and determining what views would be deemed to be heretical. The process was informal and therefore often hotly contested. Such opposition might come from the established rabbinic leadership with regard to preachers such as Anatoli who were not experts in talmudic studies, or it could be initiated by lay leaders of the congregations and directed even against the rabbis themselves, particularly in their role as chastisers and rebukers of religious and social shortcomings.

---

unusual claim of divine inspiration for a preacher on a lesser level than prophecy, see Saperstein, *Jewish Preaching 1200–1800*, 420–1; id., *'Your Voice Like a Ram's Horn': Themes and Texts in Traditional Jewish Preaching* (Cincinnati, 1996), 8–9.

[7] Moses Maimonides, *Teshuvot harambam* [responsa], ed. Joshua Blau, 3 vols. (Jerusalem, 1957–61), i. 189–91, discussed in Saperstein, *Jewish Preaching 1200–1800*, 378–9. In his responsum, Maimonides criticized the public humiliation of the preacher, but declined to become involved in imposing a punishment without the opportunity of hearing the potential defendant explain his behaviour. For other examples in the Islamic environment of conflict over preachers, including a complaint about a local judge who walked out in the middle of a sermon by a visiting preacher, see Shelomo Goitein, *A Mediterranean Society: The Jewish Communities of the Arab World as Portrayed in the Documents of the Cairo Geniza*, 5 vols. plus index (Berkeley, 1967–93), ii. 217.

[8] Saperstein, *Jewish Preaching, 1200–1800*, 55 n. 31, with reference to articles by Joseph Hacker citing the source, Abraham ibn Megash.

Thus, in theory, individual Jews were free to speak from the pulpit without official approval, but, as these individuals often had no formal position, no institutionally sanctioned authority, and were often speaking to a congregation that included at least a few quite learned listeners, they were subject to various kinds of pressure from their peers. The challenge raised by the Israelite slave to Moses—'Who made you chief and ruler over us?' (Exod. 2: 14)—serves as a paradigm for this dynamic. By what right did the preacher stand before the audience and tell them what they should do or believe? This was a question that apparently bothered more than a handful of medieval and early modern Jews.

Some fifty years after Anatoli, the cultural situation of the Jews had significantly changed in southern France. By 1300 a massive project of translating Arabic texts into Hebrew had made accessible to European Jewish readers not only the philosophical works of Jews like Maimonides but also much of the corpus of Aristotle together with his Arab commentators. Such texts were read by only a limited circle of intellectuals, although there was enough demand to subsidize the translation and copying of extremely technical philosophical texts.[9] Through this technical writing, we can trace how the influence of philosophical thinking began to spread into other genres: biblical commentaries, commentaries on the non-legal components of rabbinic literature, and sermons.[10] This last was viewed by the conservatives as particularly dangerous, because sermons were accessible to the entire population of Jews who prayed regularly as part of the community on the sabbath.

Discontented listeners were not reluctant to record their complaints for others to read. The following dates from the first years of the fourteenth century:

One of the preachers, misled by the intellect, loudly proclaimed that anyone who believes that the sun actually stood still for Joshua [Josh. 10: 12–14] is simply wrong, a fool who believes in what is impossible. Concerning the voice heard at Sinai, such slander was uttered that all who heard it would have to rend their garments, and all who repeat it would need to make atonement.[11] We have heard many such things about these pernicious men who have all but stripped the Torah of its simple meaning, leaving it naked and bare.[12]

---

[9] See Chapter 3 above.

[10] See Marc Saperstein, *Decoding the Rabbis: A Thirteenth-Century Commentary on the Aggadah* (Cambridge, Mass., 1980), 205–6.   [11] The biblically based Jewish ritual of mourning.

[12] See Saperstein, *Jewish Preaching, 1200–1800*, 380–1, esp. n. 2.

Another protester referred to a sermon delivered not during the regular synagogue service but at a wedding ceremony in southern France:

One day, at the wedding of one of the leading families in the city, an important notable delivered a sermon containing things painful to hear. He said that Abraham and Sarah were [allegorical representations of] form and matter.[13] Upon the biblical section from Abraham's leaving of Haran to 'He favoured Abraham for her sake' [Gen. 12: 4–16], he built a silvery tower, which we considered pernicious. . . . He interpreted the entire episode [referring to a legendary passage in the Talmud] in a philosophical manner. All was in an uproar over this speaker. . . . Had I not seen it, I would not have believed it, but I was there, sitting next to him on the platform as he said these things.[14]

A third contemporary reported that 'we consider it disgraceful that ignorant men, with no expertise either in Bible or in the rabbinic tradition, are always getting up to preach publicly, teaching things improper, interpreting biblical verses in far-fetched, figurative ways'.[15]

In the wake of such complaints by offended listeners, it is not surprising that some community leaders tried to pass ordinances setting appropriate limits, to be enforced by the threat of a ban. But what precisely should be prohibited? On this there was no consensus. One recommendation, made by Abba Mari of Lunel, a leader of the conservative forces in Montpellier, was that 'you should ban whoever removes the stories of the Torah or the commandments from their simple meaning, whether in their sermons or in written works undermining the tradition of the sages. If certain leaders of your community should not agree to this, do it through your rabbinical court.'[16] At a later stage of the controversy, he addressed those preachers who could not be considered inadequately educated or unqualified:

You should add to your ordinance that even those who are wise and mature must not preach using material from physics or metaphysics at a wedding celebration, nor

---

[13] The allegorical tradition of associating women with 'matter' and men with 'form' goes back to Plato as reported by Moses Maimonides (*Guide for the Perplexed*, 1: 17 [trans. and ed. M. Friedländer, 3 vols. in 1 (New York, 1946), i. 68]). Most complaints by Jewish writers reverse the terms, claiming that Jews carried away by philosophy assert that Abraham and Sarah are matter and form. For a cogent explanation for this error by Ram Ben-Shalom, see Chapter 4, n. 39 above.

[14] In Saperstein, *Jewish Preaching, 1200–1800*, 381–2.   [15] Ibid. 383.

[16] Abba Mari ben Moses of Lunel, *Minḥat kena'ot: harbeh mikhtavim . . . el harashba umah sheheshiv lahem* [polemical letters] (Pressburg, 1838; repr. Jerusalem, 1968), 69; see Saperstein, *Jewish Preaching, 1200–1800*, 382–3.

speak about such matters before the masses at all, lest they praise what is a worthless coin. Let them speak of it only in the presence of those who are expert in Torah.[17]

A third suggestion, made by a rabbinic scholar with a more moderate approach, agreed on the need to control the pulpit but suggested a different strategy:

I would not repudiate these preachers completely. Rather, I would give them permission to interpret figuratively to their hearts' content verses from Job, Proverbs, Song of Songs, Ecclesiastes, and the rabbinic homilies related to their content, and certain Psalms relevant to the physical sciences. But they must not touch upon the prophetic visions [Isa. 6; Ezek. 1, 8], or the work of Creation [Gen. 1], or any of the secrets of the Torah, or prophecy, or esoteric doctrines or any of the rabbinic texts pertaining to these matters.[18]

As a result of this agitation, a solemn ban was passed at Barcelona during the summer of 1305 by Solomon ben Adret (Rashba), one of the most highly respected rabbinic authorities of the age, and his colleagues prohibiting the study of Greek philosophy by those under the age of 25—a reaction that scholars have compared to the condemnation of specific philosophical doctrines held by theologians at the University of Paris a few decades earlier.[19] But to the dismay of the conservatives the ban, the introduction to which included complaints about heretical sermons, did not attempt to impose any clear mechanism for controlling the pulpit. Philosophical material continued to appear in the sermons of preachers from southern France and Christian Spain in the fourteenth and fifteenth centuries. Indeed, these sermons are an important source for tracing the popularization and spread of philosophical material in circles of the Jewish population considerably broader than the intellectual elite that actually produced philosophical works.[20] A similar change occurred, at a somewhat later date, in the use of kabbalistic and mystical doctrines in sermons: a reluctance to divulge esoteric material not intended for the masses from the pulpit was eventually replaced by an acceptance of this material as it appeared more prominently in sermons.[21]

---

[17] Abba Mari, *Minḥat kena'ot*, 134; see Saperstein, *Jewish Preaching, 1200–1800*, 382–3.

[18] Menahem Me'iri, in Simeon bar Joseph, *Ḥoshen mishpat*, ed. David Kaufmann, in *Tif'eret Seiva: Jubelschrift zum Neunzigsten Geburtstag des Dr. L. Zunz* (Berlin, 1884): Heb. section, 166–7; see Saperstein *Jewish Preaching 1200–1800*, 383; for a discussion of Me'iri's position on this issue, see Gregg Stern, 'Philosophic Allegory in Medieval Jewish Culture: The Crisis in Languedoc (1304–6)', in Jon Whitman (ed.), *Interpretation and Allegory* (Leiden, 2000), 189–209.

[19] See Chapter 4 above. [20] See Saperstein, *'Your Voice Like a Ram's Horn'*, 75–87.

[21] For the first evidence of kabbalistic doctrines in sermons, see Carmi Horowitz, *The Jewish*

In the early modern period there is also evidence of strong resistance to preachers spreading possibly heretical doctrines, as well as other objections. One noted case arose against a young Italian preacher named David del Bene of Mantua in 1598. As with the medieval examples, the extant evidence is rather skimpy: there is a complaint from someone who did not hear the actual sermons but claimed to have heard reports from those that did, but no response from Del Bene has survived. The accusations are on the whole extremely general, indicating that the fundamental problem was the inclusion of classical material—'preaching in public empty words derived from the theatres and circuses of the Gentiles' or 'frivolity from the Gentile books'—that we would consider to be Renaissance motifs. The only specific charge recorded is that in one of his sermons, Del Bene used the phrase *quella santa Diana*, which was understood to be attributing sanctity to a goddess of the Graeco-Roman pantheon. Based on these reports, a campaign was initiated involving leading Italian rabbis and—appealing to the precedent of Ben Adret's ban—calling for decisive action to prevent Del Bene from continuing to deliver his apparently popular sermons. Under pressure from these rabbinic authorities, Del Bene withdrew from regular pulpit responsibilities and focused on his studies, eventually becoming accepted as a rabbi in Ferrara, where his subsequent sermons apparently did not spark controversy.[22]

In the Ashkenazi communities of northern and central Europe, rebukes for inappropriate behaviour were often included in sermons and were most likely to generate attempts to control the pulpit. In these communities, the common practice was for the rabbi to preach on only a few special occasions during the year: the sabbaths preceding the festival of Passover and the Day of Atonement, eulogies for important members of the community, special events in communal life. On ordinary sabbaths and in other venues, the role of the non-rabbinic preachers would be quite pronounced, and the actual records of what they said are considerably more numerous.

Ephraim Luntshitz, a celebrated preacher of the late sixteenth century, described his own experience:

Sermon in 14th Century Spain: The Derashot of R. Joshua ibn Shu'eib (Cambridge, Mass., 1989), 159–70; for later developments, see Saperstein, *'Your Voice Like a Ram's Horn'*, 299.

[22] David Kaufmann, 'The Dispute about the Sermons of David del Bene of Mantua', *Jewish Quarterly Review*, 8 (1896), 518, 519, 521. Del Bene's son, Judah Assael, also became rabbi in Ferrara and published a book of his essays at Verona in 1646; texts of fourteen of Judah's sermons and two of his father's, as recorded by an educated listener, have been preserved in manuscript (see Robert Bonfil, 'Preaching as Mediation between Elite and Popular Cultures: The Case of Judah Del Bene', in David B. Ruderman [ed.], *Preachers of the Italian Ghetto* [Berkeley, 1992], 70).

I preached in Lublin, especially during the great fairs, where Jewish leaders as well as large masses of the people gathered. There I used to express myself quite freely touching the shortcomings of the rabbis as well as of the laity, undeterred by any consideration or fear. This boldness, naturally enough, created for me numerous enemies who heaped slander upon my name and otherwise persecuted me. . . . Of course, I could have well avoided all this wrath and uproar, were I but willing to be more restrained in my utterances or were I more chary of my personal honour. But I had long resolved to put the honour of God above my own.[23]

Despite his difficulties, he refused to compromise, insisting that moral and religious rebuke was one of the primary responsibilities of the preacher.

Even rabbinic ordination did not always help. Half a century after Luntshitz, Berekhiah Berakh of Kraków complained that his colleagues were wary of expressing views from the pulpit on matters of communal leadership.

Sometimes a rabbi or talmudic scholar, accepted by the congregation as a preacher, sees that community affairs are being conducted improperly. With trepidation he rebukes the leaders, stating explicitly that they should not behave in this manner. Their response: 'Why are you bothering to concern yourself with public affairs? Confine yourself to the laws of plagues and tents, to matters of Torah.'[24]

As a result of the pressure, the preacher decided to express his criticism indirectly, by citing appropriate biblical verses that speak for themselves about the behaviour being addressed.

Itinerant preachers without official rabbinical ordination presented an acute problem in east European communities. Gatherings of community leaders—lay and rabbinical—tried to impose restrictions on the eligibility to deliver sermons through cross-communal legislation. Thus the Council of the Major Communities in Lithuania met in 1628 and announced:

No one may preach publicly without the permission of the head of the rabbinical court and the lay leaders following a gathering to deliberate on this specific issue. . . . In the surrounding communities, no one may be permitted to preach publicly unless

---

[23] Ephraim Luntshitz, *Amudei shesh* [sermons] (Warsaw, 1875), introduction, 2*a–b*, in Bettan, *Studies in Jewish Preaching*, 274. Luntshitz also refers to vicious critics of his preaching in the introduction to another collection of his homilies (*Olelot efrayim* [sermons] [Tel Aviv, 1975], 3*b*).

[24] Berekhiah Berakh, *Zera berakh* [homiletical essays on the Torah], 2 vols. in 1 (Amsterdam, 1730), 'Ki tavo, sheni', 93*b*. The attempt to limit the sphere of rabbinic influence echoes a statement in BT *San.* 38*b*, in which 'the laws of plagues and tents' refers to extremely technical legal matters with little relevance to actual life (see Haim Hillel Ben-Sasson, *Deliberation and Leadership: The Social Doctrines of Polish Jews Towards the End of the Middle Ages* [Hagut vehanhagah: hashkefoteihem haḥevratiyot shel yehudei polin beshalhei yemei habeinayim] [Jerusalem, 1959], 50–1, 194–5).

he has in hand a document signed and sealed by the head of the relevant rabbinical court. The head of the court must not issue such sealed documents giving permission to preach publicly without knowledge of the agreement of the lay leaders. Whoever disobeys this enactment must pay a fine of 5 red zlotys.[25]

Four decades later, the problem (from the perspective of the establishment) had become worse. An enactment passed in 1667 reads:

> It has recently happened that there are many individuals now travelling from place to place and preaching publicly, both in the synagogue and elsewhere, without the permission and authorization of the chief rabbi of the city and its seven elders. They claim to be public preachers of rebuke, expressing open condemnation at unnecessary length and for payment. But it appears that some of them preach primarily for their own self-glorification. We have therefore decreed that from this day forth it is absolutely forbidden for a person to assume a pious reputation for himself by travelling from place to place or to preach or to rebuke publicly, without the express permission of the chief rabbi of the city and its seven elders. If anyone has the audacity to do so, he should be removed in derision and disgrace. Furthermore, no community head or rabbi may grant permission for any man to travel from city to city to preach sermons of rebuke in public, unless all of the heads of the relevant communities and their rabbis agree.[26]

Obviously, the itinerant preachers represented a threat to the established leadership of the communities.

In contemporary Amsterdam, however, where the lay leadership exerted a decisive role in congregational governance, there is no hint that the Mahamad ever tried to impose prior censorship on the sermons of their preachers.[27] Only when the two leading rabbis of the community, Saul Levi Morteira and Menasseh ben Israel, became embroiled in a personal feud

---

[25] *Pinkas hamedinah, o pinkas va'ad hakehilot harashiyot bimedinat lita* [The Register of the State, or the Register of the Council of the Major Communities in the Duchy of Lithuania], ed. Shimon Dubnow (Berlin, 1925), 33, no. 130. The red zloty or ducat was (according to the Polish currency ordinance of 1650) equivalent to 3.5 grams of gold or 6 Polish (silver) zlotys.

[26] Ibid. 144, no. 596; Salo W. Baron, *The Jewish Community*, 3 vols. (Philadelphia, 1942), ii. 99.

[27] Morteira wrote the texts of his sermons in Hebrew each week before he delivered them in Portuguese, but it is doubtful that members of the Mahamad could even have read the Hebrew texts, much less review them for problematic content. A quite different case occurred in 1693: a Jesuit professor of theology and Hebrew at the University of Prague accused Jewish preachers of blasphemies against Christianity and instigated a campaign demanding that every sermon be submitted in writing for review by the authorities three days before its delivery. The Jews responded that this was impossible, as they did not prepare their sermons that long in advance, nor did they write out full texts (S. Schweinburg-Eibenschütz, 'Une confiscation des livres hébreux à Prague', *Revue des études juives*, 29 [1894], 268).

conducted from their respective pulpits did the lay leaders intervene, temporarily suspending both rabbis from preaching and warning that they must not offend or contradict each other in their sermons.[28]

Needless to say, the status of non-rabbinic preachers was far more precarious. In seventeenth- and eighteenth-century Poland, the burgeoning number of itinerant preachers provoked a firm response from the Jewish leaders. Intercommunal ordinances required that a person have formal authorization to preach from the chief judge of the rabbinical court of the region's main city, with the agreement of the city elders. Yet complaints abound that there were 'many now travelling from place to place and preaching publicly, both in the synagogue and elsewhere, without permission'. Those who did this were, according to the ordinance, to be 'removed in derision and disgrace'.[29] Despite such efforts, talented itinerant preachers, who developed a popular style based on the effective use of parables and exempla, often won the hearts of the masses, to the consternation of rabbis and lay leaders alike.

The effort to control the pulpit continued in western Europe and the New World, where the principle of freedom of the pulpit eventually prevailed following a prolonged struggle. In the early nineteenth century a committee of elders of London's Bevis Marks Synagogue of Spanish and Portuguese Jews, recommending that a weekly sermon be delivered in English, proposed that the text of each sermon be submitted to a committee of three elders before delivery to ensure that it contained nothing 'inimical to our religious doctrine or . . . hostile to the established institutions of the country'.[30] Although the recommendation was not approved, occasional sermons were still submitted for pre-approval by the Mahamad. Sermons published throughout the mid-nineteenth century bore the imprint of approval from the lay leaders: when one preacher published a Passover sermon in 1839 without such approval, he was reprimanded by the Mahamad.[31]

---

[28] A year later both were suspended without pay for a period of two months and warned that any further incident would lead to their 'exclusion from the service of this congregation'. Morteira, the older of the two, ended up delivering the eulogy for his illustrious younger colleague (for the text of the eulogy in Hebrew and English translation, see Saperstein, *'Your Voice Like a Ram's Horn'*, 411–44; on the relationship between the two rabbis and the wardens, see ibid. 413).

[29] Saperstein, *Jewish Preaching, 1200–1800*, 47. For a poignant and illuminating defence of the itinerant preachers of rebuke in eighteenth-century eastern Europe, see the text by Mordecai ben Samuel (ibid. 424–7).

[30] James Picciotto, *Sketches of Anglo-Jewish History* (London, 1875), 320; Albert Montefiore Hyamson, *The Sephardim of England: A History of the Spanish and Portuguese Community, 1492–1951* (London, 1951), 272.

[31] During the cholera epidemic of 1831–2, a lay member of the Bevis Marks community, David Brandon, delivered a sermon for a day of fasting after submitting the text for approval. He was urged

In Curaçao in 1825, following an open dispute with their rabbinic leader Jeosuah Piza, the regents of the oldest Jewish congregation in the New World passed the following regulation: 'In his sermons the rabbi was not to speak against the government, nor against the administration of the community by the *parnasim* [i.e. the wardens passing the regulation], nor against the members for their conduct, whether in religious or civil matters'.[32] In the United States of America, Isaac Leeser expressed a desire to preach regularly from the beginning of his tenure as *ḥazan* (cantor) of Philadelphia's Mikveh Israel Synagogue in 1829, but approval for a weekly sabbath sermon in English did not come until 1843. During the intervening years, when he preached sporadically, he was instructed by the *parnas* that he could preach only if he notified the *parnas* of his intention at least a day in advance. Here there was no question of censorship of the content, yet Leeser considered this a 'degradation of the ministry', although he abided by the decision.[33] In Cincinnati, the board of Congregation B'nai Jeshurun resolved in April 1860 'to notify the Rev. Dr. [Isaac Mayer] Wise that the Board disapprove of all political allusions in his sermons and to discontinue the same in the future'. This was despite Wise's general policy of not addressing political matters in his preaching.[34]

Italian-born and educated Sabbato Morais was elected minister of the Sephardi Mikveh Israel Congregation in Philadelphia, a position he held from his arrival in 1851 until his death in 1897. He was a preacher who expressed strong views with power and eloquence. But all was not smooth with the lay leadership of the synagogue, which passed a resolution in 1864 stating that 'henceforth all English lectures or Discourses shall be dispensed with, except by particular request of the Parnas, made in writing'. Morais gathered support from other members of the congregation, and four months

---

by the Mahamad to publish it (see Hyamson, *The Sephardim of England*, 255). On the reprimand given to Abraham Alexander Lindo for publishing the text of his 1839 Passover sermon without having sought permission from the Mahamad, see ibid. 260–1.

[32] Isaac S. Emmanuel, *History of the Jews in Netherlands Antilles*, 2 vols. (Cincinnati, 1970), 613, art. 24m. The prohibition on speaking against the government was undoubtedly connected with the granting of full citizenship to the Jews of Curaçao in the same year. But the prohibition on rebuke from the pulpit for improper behaviour of congregants in the religious realm is quite extraordinary. On later rabbis' resistance to attempts to control their preaching, see ibid. 503.

[33] Lance Sussman, *Isaac Leeser and the Making of American Judaism* (Detroit, 1995), 61–2, 103–4, 136. For an overview of the struggle for freedom of the pulpit in nineteenth-century American Jewish congregations, see Naomi Cohen, 'The Muzzled Rabbi', in ead., *What the Rabbis Said: The Public Discourse of Nineteenth-Century American Rabbis* (New York, 2008), 13–32.

[34] Sefton D. Temkin, *Isaac Mayer Wise: Shaping American Judaism* (Oxford, 1992), 173, 175–6.

later a vote of the congregation as a whole authorized him to preach on 'moral and religious subjects' at his own discretion, and 'on the subjects of the day... whenever the Synagogue may be opened by order of the Parnas'.[35]

German immigrant David Einhorn first served a congregation in Baltimore, but the abolitionist views expressed in his sermons required him flee to Philadelphia for his safety. On 13 May 1861 the trustees of the Baltimore congregation wrote that if he were to return to his position in Baltimore, 'it would be very desirable—for your own safety, as well as out of consideration for the members of your congregation—if in the future there would be no comment in the pulpit on the excitable issues of the time'. That was a proposal that Einhorn did not find especially appealing, and he accepted an invitation from Philadelphia's Keneseth Israel Congregation, offered with a promise of full freedom of the pulpit.[36]

Einhorn and others fought a courageous battle to maintain the freedom of the pulpit. In 1909, in a memorial oration on the centenary of Einhorn's birth, his son-in-law Rabbi Emil G. Hirsch of Chicago praised him as a champion of the integrity of the rabbi and preacher against the influence of wealthy laymen:

> We, who believe that the pulpit, if its message is meant to be effective and vital, must be free, owe this great preacher of ours a debt of gratitude beyond compare and computation.... He pilloried mercilessly the 'barons by the grace of the Almighty Dollar', who had attempted to inhibit their Rabbi from making allusion to the proceedings of the Philadelphia Conference.[37] He exposed pitilessly their impudence, when they arrogated to themselves influence over decisions concerning questions, for the treating of which the knowledge of the expert in theology was indispensable. Superbly did he disregard the counsel of timid souls to be cautious in the handling from the pulpit of slavery. And in asserting his right, in the name of Judaism, to protest against the iniquitous institution, he, courting the martyr's fate, rendered American Israel a service greater than any other to his credit.[38]

Hirsch said this against the background of one of the most dramatic episodes

---

[35] See Marc Saperstein, *Jewish Preaching in Times of War, 1800–2001* (Oxford, 2008), 166, with sources cited in n. 4; Naomi Cohen, 'From the Words of Sabato Morais', in ead., *What the Rabbis Said*, 33–52.

[36] Saperstein, *Jewish Preaching in Times of War, 1800–2001*, 193, with sources cited in n. 3.

[37] A conference held in November 1869 by the radical wing of American Reform rabbis (see Michael A. Meyer, *A Response to Modernity: A History of the Reform Movement in Judaism* [New York, 1988], 255–8).

[38] Emil G. Hirsch, 'Memorial Oration', in Kaufmann Kohler (ed.), *David Einhorn Memorial Volume: Selected Sermons and Addresses* (New York, 1911), 466–7.

in the battle for freedom of the Jewish pulpit, when Stephen S. Wise, under consideration for appointment as rabbi of New York's influential Congregation Emanu-El, demanded the freedom to preach without prior approval from the Board of Trustees. When this demand was refused, he established the 'Free Synagogue' of New York, where freedom of the pulpit was a fundamental principle.[39] Occasionally, congregations in the USA and Britain continued to attempt to constrain their rabbis from speaking about 'political matters' from the pulpit, especially in tense contexts such as the struggle against segregation in the American south, but with limited success.[40]

But, if there were few formal efforts to restrain the preacher's freedom, during the civil rights movement and the Vietnam war, American rabbis heard many times from individual congregants and sometimes from lay leaders the contemporary equivalent of the words reported by Berekhiah Berakh of Kraków: 'Why are you bothering to concern yourself with public affairs? Confine yourself to the laws of plagues and tents, to matters of Torah.'[41] In a sermon delivered in the early 1950s, a distinguished South African rabbi cited an article he had recently published in which he wrote: 'I am sure that the reader will be wryly amused, for instance, to hear that a member of my congregation wrote a letter to the Council asking them to forbid me from speaking on the native question, but to confine myself to Jewish ethics!'[42]

As in the Middle Ages, the conflict occasionally aroused by strong sermons was essentially one of the relationship between the preacher and his (now, or her) congregants. The respect that the rabbi had earned as a learned scholar, effective teacher, and caring pastor tended to enhance the authority as a preacher to assert and defend controversial positions from the pulpit. Personal magnetism and force of conviction conveyed through a sermon's delivery often augment the power of the ideas to persuade. The freedom of the rabbi's conscience as expressed in the sermon is now unchallenged,

---

[39] For Wise's 'Open Letter to the Members of Temple Emanu-El of New York on the Freedom of the Jewish Pulpit', see Stephen S. Wise, *Challenging Years: The Autobiography of Stephen Wise* (New York, 1949), 96–4. From January to March 1907 Wise gave a series of sermons on the topic 'Shall the Pulpit be Free?' For one example, see Stephen S. Wise, *Free Synagogue Pulpit: Sermons and Addresses*, vol. i (New York, 1908), 27–48.

[40] For Britain, see Anne J. Kershen and Jonathan A. Romain, *Tradition and Change: A History of Reform Judaism in Britain, 1840–1995* (London, 1995), 153.

[41] For one example, see Roland B. Gittelsohn, 'Answer to an Anonymous Letter', in *Fire In My Bones: Essays on Judaism in a Time of Crisis* (New York, 1969), 1–9, republished with annotation in Saperstein, *Jewish Preaching in Times of War, 1800–2001*, 500–7.

[42] Louis Rabinowitz, *Sparks from the Anvil: Sermons for Sabbaths, Holy Days and Festivals* (New York, 1955), 198.

although the question of judgement may be bitterly contested by those in the audience who pay the rabbi's salary. Anatoli stopped preaching, fashioned his discourses into a book of sermons, and continued with his philosophical studies. Today, occasionally, rabbis find that at least partly as a result of their preaching, their contract with a synagogue is not renewed, and they move on elsewhere. I suppose it means that sometimes, even today as in the Middle Ages, when a rabbi is preaching, someone out there may be listening.[43]

[43] I owe this phrase to my teacher, Rabbi Eugene Borowitz.

PART IV

CONFLICTING ATTITUDES TOWARDS EXILE, THE LAND, AND THE MESSIAH

CHAPTER ELEVEN

'Arab Chains' and the 'Good Things of Spain': Aspects of Jewish Exile

THE WORD 'exile' has unmistakably negative connotations in the English language, but its Hebrew equivalent, *galut*—or in the Ashkenazi and Yiddish pronunciations, *golus*—is even bleaker, evoking associations with a dismal reality all but devoid of redeeming characteristics. There is a geographical component: Jews forcibly displaced from their ancestral homeland, scattered, dispersed, wandering, homeless, unable to find rest. In addition, the word suggests subjugation and oppression at the hands of the Gentile nations: as a classic study formulates it, 'persecution, outrage, and injustice from which specious privileges give no relief'.[1]

There is a psychological element as well. *Galut* suggests feelings of shame; humiliation; suppressed anger before the taunting of enemies and rivals, so poignantly expressed in the mocking challenge of the Babylonian conquerors: 'Sing us one of the songs of Zion' (Ps. 137: 8); and guilt, because of the sinfulness that, in accordance with the terms of the covenant brutally enunciated in such passages as Leviticus 26 and Deuteronomy 28, initiated and prolonged the exile. There is also a theological dimension. As one celebrated Jewish preacher put it: 'the essence of our exile, that which pains our souls, is the departure of the Holy Spirit from among us, leaving us unable to sense the presence of our Creator; that is the ultimate anguish and burden of

---

First published in *AJS Review*, 26 (2002), 301–26.

[1] Yitzhak Baer, *Galut* (New York, 1948), 10 (the book, written in German, was first published in Berlin in 1936, which may to some extent explain the negativism of the description); cf. Arnold Eisen's characterization of Yehezkel Kaufmann's monumental four-volume *Golah venekhar* (Tel Aviv, 1929–32): *galut* is 'a set of interrelated processes that includes *ḥurban* (destruction of the Temple and, by extension, of the Jewish community), subjugation, wandering, confinement to ghettos, and (the most recent development) assimilation' (Arnold Eisen, *Galut: Modern Jewish Reflections on Homelessness and Homecoming* [Bloomington, 1986], 99).

exile'.² This negative ambience of *galut* in traditional Jewish literature has been highlighted and accentuated by influential Zionist writers, who used it as a foil to delineate all that they rebelled against, the antithesis of their goals and aspirations.³

While there is little question about the authenticity of such associations, the actual treatment of exile in Jewish literary texts reveals more nuanced and multivalent aspects. The familiar geography of the traditional concept—exile as forced removal from the Land of Israel and the end of exile as return to that land—is occasionally subverted in unexpected ways. Perhaps even more surprising is a revalorization of the concept, in which living in the ancestral homeland is no longer automatically identified as good, and living outside the land as bad. In this chapter, I will attempt to illustrate some of the permutations of this central concept through a literary and conceptual analysis of three pre-modern passages from Jewish literature, chosen for their range and their intrinsic interest.

---

² Jonathan Eybeschuetz, *Ya'arot devash* [sermons], 2 vols. in 1 (Jerusalem, 1968), ii. 74*a*. This is not to deny that rabbinic literature contains statements recognizing the potential advantages of demographical dispersion among the nations, whether for security reasons (e.g. *Genesis Rabbah* 76: 3 on Gen. 32: 9) or to attract proselytes (e.g. BT *Pes.* 87*b* on Hos. 2: 25), or that medieval Jews used such statements to develop theories of exile as providing opportunities for atonement or even special mission (see Shalom Rosenberg, 'Exile and Redemption in Jewish Thought in the Sixteenth Century', in Bernard Cooperman [ed.], *Jewish Thought in the Sixteenth Century* [Cambridge, Mass., 1983], 399–430; Marc Saperstein, *Exile in Amsterdam: Saul Levi Morteira's Sermons to a Congregation of 'New Jews'* [Cincinnati, 2005], 307–41, esp. 335–41). Nevertheless, such statements seem anomalous and marginal in rabbinic literature, as they are far outweighed by material such as that presented by Hayim Nahman Bialik and Yehoshua Hana Ravnitzky (*The Book of Legends: Sefer ha-Aggadah: Legends from the Talmud and Midrash*, trans. William G. Braude [New York, 1992], 377–86). Note the conclusion of Isaiah Gafni, after reviewing all the rabbinic sources: 'Despite the statements we have cited, and especially the tradition in BT *Pes.* 87*b* attributed to R. Eliezer, it does not seem that the idea of a mission to the Gentiles acquired primary standing in the totality of what the sages said about the reasons for the dispersion' (Gafni, 'Punishment, Blessing, or Mission?' [Heb.], in Aharon Oppenheimer, Isaiah Gafni, and Daniel Schwartz [eds.], *Jews in the Hellenistic-Roman World* [Hayehudim ba'olam ha-helenisti veharomi: meḥkarim lezikhro shel menaḥem stern] [Jerusalem, 1996], 246–7).

³ e.g. A. B. Yehoshua's characterization of *galut* as 'a national disaster, a temporary situation, a fall, and the root of all evil' (Yehoshua, 'Exile as a Neurotic Solution', in Etan Levine [ed.], *Diaspora: Exile and the Contemporary Jewish Condition* [New York, 1986], 22). For examples of other Zionist writers on exile, see Joseph Brenner, 'Self-Criticism', in Arthur Hertzberg (ed.), *The Zionist Idea: A Historical Analysis and Reader* (New York, 1971), esp. 310; Jacob Klatzkin, 'Boundaries', in Hertzberg (ed.), *The Zionist Idea*, esp. 322–3; and the position taken by the character Yudka in Haim Hazaz's 'The Sermon' (trans. I. M. Lask, in Robert Alter [ed.], *Modern Hebrew Literature* [New York, 1975], esp. 279–82). It has been noted that some extreme Zionist characterizations of Jewish life in the diaspora have much in common with the literature of late nineteenth- and twentieth-century antisemites. This case was made in 1934 (in a Zionist context) by Yehezkel Kaufmann ('The Ruin of the Soul', in Michael Selzer [ed.], *Zionism Reconsidered: The Rejection of Jewish Normalcy* [New York, 1970], 117–29) and has been further developed by contemporary scholars.

The first text is one of the most famous poetic creations of Judah Halevi:

> My heart is in the east, and I at the edge of the west—
> How can I taste what I eat? How can I enjoy it?
> How can I fulfil my vows and my bonds, while yet
> Zion is in the fetters of Edom, and I in Arab chains?
> It would be easy for me to leave behind all the good things of Spain, as
> It would be precious for me to behold the dust of the desolate Shrine.[4]

The six lines of the poem (actually three long lines, each composed of two hemistiches) can be divided into two sections. The first, containing the first four lines, is constructed in a syntactic chiasmus. Lines 1 and 4 both express situations of contrast, disjunction, and distance: east versus west is paralleled in line 4 by Edom (the realm of Christendom) versus Arab (the world of Islam). The poet's heart versus 'I'—his physical body—is paralleled in line 4 by Zion versus 'I'. Lines 2 and 3 express the poet's reaction to this situation in the form of three rhetorical questions, each beginning with a form of the Hebrew word 'how?' The first two, *eikh*, evoke an analogous rhetorical question to 'How can we sing the Lord's song in a foreign land?' (Ps. 137: 4): the response to the Babylonian captors' mockery. The third, *eikhah*, resonates with the opening word of the book of Lamentations, the paradigmatic response to the catastrophe of the conquest of Jerusalem.

In Halevi's poem, the tension is more internal: between the expectations of normal life—that the taste of good food will be enjoyed, that serious obligations freely undertaken will be fulfilled—and the poet's assertion that these expectations of normalcy are confounded under present circumstances. Like the question in Psalm 137, the rhetorical questions are ambiguous. They could refer to an objective condition, meaning: 'Even good food tastes bland to me, and I am unable to fulfil my vows.' Or they could reflect the poet's inner conflict, meaning: 'The food actually does taste good, but I *should not* be enjoying it; I *should not* be fulfilling my normal obligations, although I do.'

---

[4] The translation is based on Judah Halevi, *Selected Poems*, trans. Nina Salaman (Philadelphia, 1928), 2; T. Carmi (ed. and trans.), *The Penguin Book of Hebrew Verse* (New York: Viking Press, 1981), 347, with modifications. Note the much freer translation by David Aberbach, which loses some of the nuances of the Hebrew, especially in the last two lines: 'I'd lightly leave the good of Spain / to see the Temple's dust again' (Aberbach, *Revolutionary Hebrew, Empire and Crisis* [New York, 1998], 111). The first line of the poem is one of the best known in Hebrew poetry by Israelis. Note the ironic misappropriation of it in a modern Israeli drama, when a survivor of the Holocaust eking out his existence in the newly established Jewish state misquotes: ' "I sleep in the East. My heart is in the West." Rabbi Judah Halevi, if I'm not mistaken' (Ben-Zion Tomer, 'Children of the Shadows', in Michael Taub [ed.], *Israeli Holocaust Drama* [Syracuse, NY, 1996], 175).

Both readings of the first line contradict the 'wine poems' that were a common genre in the writings of Halevi's colleagues and of Halevi himself, poems that celebrate the pleasures of good food and drink. The second reading, which in my judgement produces a stronger poem, echoes the conclusion of an early wine poem by Dunash ibn Labrat: 'Even as you rejoice, jackals run wild in Zion; then how can we drink wine?'[5] The third question is more serious. 'Vows and bonds', a biblical phrase (Num. 30: 5–6), possibly intended to evoke the beginning of the Yom Kippur formula *kol nidrei* ('All vows and bonds . . .'), conveys both religious obligations to God and the contractual obligations of economic exchange. The implication is that in exile all normal life is insipid, paralysed, or hypocritical.[6]

The assertion in line 4 requires consideration of the historical context. 'Zion is in the fetters of Edom', the standard medieval Jewish name for Christendom, applies to the period following 1099 (and ending in 1187, though Halevi died in 1141), when the Crusaders controlled Jerusalem. 'I in Arab chains' together with 'I at the edge of the west' show that the poet is writing in Muslim Spain. It is significant that Halevi used this phrase to describe his situation before the Almohad invasion of the 1140s devastated the Jewish communities of Andalusia. This poem was written during a period of relative tolerance, in which Jewish communities flourished and Jewish culture thrived under Islamic auspices. While this was by no means an idyllic environment, Halevi's own success in so many realms—professionally (as a physician), economically, and culturally (as poet, theologian, and teacher)[7]—

---

[5] Dunash ibn Labrat, 'The Poet Refuses an Invitation to Drink' (in Carmi [ed. and trans.], *Hebrew Verse*, 280). There seems to be a lot more ambivalence in this poem towards the pleasures of life in exile than the final lines would suggest. See also Halevi's wine poem *Bekha a'ir zemirot*, in Hayyim (Yefim) Schirmann, *Hebrew Poetry in Spain and Provence* [Hashirah ha'ivrit bisefarad uviprovans], 2 vols. in 4 (Jerusalem, 1960), i. 443: 'from [the bottle's] mouth I taste the goodness of fine fruits'.

[6] Schirmann explains this as 'the vow he made to emigrate to the land of Israel' (*Hebrew Poetry in Spain and Provence* [Heb.], i. 489; followed by Carmi, *Hebrew Verse*, 347), but this seems implausible for several reasons. First, the phrase, with both nouns in the plural, is more likely to refer to many obligations than to a single vow. Second, the parallelism between lines 2 and 3 suggests that line 3 also applies to life in Spain, not to the possibility of leaving Spain. Finally, 'Arab chains' could not have prevented him from leaving Spain, for Jewish merchants travelled across the Mediterranean all the time. As for Crusader control over the Holy Land, why would he have made such a vow if the Crusader conquest had already made it impossible for him to fulfil it? (See Raymond P. Scheindlin, *The Song of the Distant Dove: Judah Halevi's Pilgrimage* [Oxford, 2008], 170.)

[7] For the success and pre-eminent reputation of Halevi, see Shelomo D. Goitein, *A Mediterranean Society: The Jewish Communities of the Arab World as Portrayed in the Documents of the Cairo Geniza*, 5 vols. plus index (Berkeley, 1967–93), v. 448, 467; cf. Ross Brann, *The Compunctious Poet: Cultural Ambiguity and Hebrew Poetry in Muslim Spain* (Baltimore, 1991), 85.

underlies what must have been a surprise for his readers in the formulation: 'I in Arab chains'.

This surprise is heightened by the very next line with its evocation of 'all the good things of Spain', suggesting a characterization of Andalusian Jewish life in strong tension with 'Arab chains'. That tension is never fully resolved. The second unit of the poem, comprising the final two lines, seems more like a wistful fantasy than a resolute plan. We note again the parallelism at the beginning of the two hemistiches, linked by the conjunction *kemo* ('like') and reinforced by the assonance of the Hebrew verbs *yekal* and *yekar*, setting up a comparison that is not reproduced in the published translations. 'It would be easy' just as 'it would be precious'. But the endings of the lines bring the reader back to the contrasts established in lines 1 and 4: 'all the good things of Spain' versus 'the dust of the desolate Shrine'. The power of the statement lies in the reversal of expectation: 'all the good things of Spain' had little value for the poet; 'dust' and 'desolation' were somehow precious.[8]

How does this poem relate to the conception of exile as an unmitigated disaster, as uncompromisingly bleak? What is the poet's personal stance with regard to the continuation of his life in exile? This cannot unambiguously be determined from the poem itself: additional information is necessary. If 'I in Arab chains' means that Halevi was actually writing from prison,[9] and if 'Zion in the fetters of Edom' suggests that the Christian Crusaders prohibited Jews from setting foot in the Holy Land, the poem would be a lament for the constraints that made it impossible for him to undertake the journey to Jerusalem. But, while this reading cannot be excluded on strictly internal grounds, abundant external data confirm that neither Halevi personally, nor Jews in general, were physically or legally prevented from leaving Spain to journey eastwards. This suggests a possible reading close to what A. B. Yehoshua characterized as a 'neurotic choice':[10] the poet yearns for Jerusalem, theoretically rejects life in *galut*, yet remains where he is, perhaps despising himself for continuing to enjoy the 'good things' that he claims it would be so easy to abandon. There is in this poem no obvious manifesto for a personal

---

[8] Cf. Moses ibn Ezra: 'O lend him thy wings / That he may fly unto his loved ones and rejoice in the dust of their land [Andalusia]' (in Schirmann, *Hebrew Poetry in Spain and Provence* [Heb.], i. 380).

[9] As, for example, was Menahem ibn Saruk, who wrote a lengthy poetic epistle from his prison cell (ibid. i. 8–30).

[10] See Yehoshua, 'Exile as a Neurotic Solution'; compare the statement by the character Otto Weininger: 'the Jew prefers to live in exile because exile is his natural habitat, he chooses it voluntarily' (Joshua Sobol, 'Jewish Soul: The Last Night of Otto Weininger', *Modern International Drama*, 22/2 [Spring 1989], 58 col. 1).

aliyah ('ascent' to the Land of Israel), and certainly not for a mass movement; on the contrary, it appears like an anguished description of resignation to a conflicted status quo.

Yet we know that Halevi did indeed leave Spain with the intention of reaching Jerusalem. Should the poem be read in the context of the poet's decision to seek out the 'desolate Shrine' in the east? Such a reading ordinarily takes the poem to express both a yearning for home and a forceful repudiation of an accommodation to *galut*, even when conditions are relatively benign. The poet lived in a period of cultural flourishing in Muslim Spain, in which he, personally, reached a pinnacle of success, yet he rejected it all, refusing in this poem to recognize anything of value in his Andalusian environment. In this reading, life in exile is indeed a disaster, the Jew in the Gentile environment is an outsider, an alien, incapable of finding fulfilment on the most significant level. At least one Jew was able to draw the consequences and act accordingly, revealing what was possible if only other Jews had chosen similarly.[11]

But this paradigmatic rejection of *galut* is not so simple. First, it is important to note that the poet concedes there were indeed 'good things' in exile. Food and wine generally did taste good, even in Muslim Spain; vows and bonds were made all the time, and most Jews did (and indeed should) fulfil them. The presentation of *galut* in this poem is not totally bleak. Furthermore, if we incorporate Halevi's later decision into our reading of the poem, we must include also the poems written while he was on board ship on his journey eastwards. These poems give the lie to the rhetorical claim 'It would be easy . . .' and suggest that its syntax may hint at ambivalence and uncertainty. Some of the sea poems echo, in greater detail, the willingness or even eagerness to abandon good food, possessions, and wealth,[12] but others express

---

[11] Thus Halevi becomes a kind of proto-Zionist, whose decision to abandon the diaspora has messianic significance and prefigures the *aliyah* of Zionists in the late nineteenth century (see Ben Zion Dinur, 'Rabbi Judah Halevi's *Aliyah* to the Land of Israel' [Heb.], in id., *Historical Writings*, vol. ii: *In the Struggle of the Generations* [Ketavim historiyim, 2: bema'avaq hadorot] [Jerusalem, 1975], 202–31). Franz Rosenzweig, commenting on this poem, wrote that 'the lonely yearning of Halevi's soul is the first beacon of the new movement, a movement that carries into the present day' (Rosenzweig, *Ninety-Two Poems and Hymns of Yehuda Halevi* [Albany, NY, 2000], 235). This view tends to overlook the strong quietistic attitude towards messianism—that bearing exile and degradation with patience and humility is the key to redemption—evidenced in much of Halevi's writings: 'to suffer humbly and be patient is the mission of the Jews in the Galut' (Y. Baer, *Galut*, 31). For this theme in Halevi's works, see Judah Halevi, *The Kuzari: An Argument for the Faith of Israel*, trans. Hartwig Hirschfield (New York, 1964), 5: 115; Halevi, *Me'az me'on ha'ahavah hayitah*, in Schirmann, *Hebrew Poetry in Spain and Provence* (Heb.), i. 467.

[12] e.g. Halevi, *Lekha nafshi betuḥah*, in Schirmann, *Hebrew Poetry in Spain and Provence* (Heb.), i.

a deep sense of loss: of home, family, friends, disciples, an ordered religious life with synagogue and academy that was not only comfortable but rather attractive.[13] What is being abandoned in these poems does not at all seem to be 'exile'. Indeed, in a climactic passage of *The Kuzari*, Halevi used the term 'exile' to characterize the decision to leave behind a comfortable life in the diaspora and to brave the dangers of a journey to the Holy Land.[14] Leaving Spain for Jerusalem was a self-imposed exile, a pilgrimage of suffering sacrifice with atoning power—an idea more commonly associated with Christian than with Jewish thought (although Halevi was not unique in this regard).[15] One might argue that this decision could be considered at least as 'neurotic' as the decision to remain.

There is one other element of Halevi's ambivalence. While his poem was written in Hebrew, like the other Andalusian Jewish poets of his own and previous generations, he followed an Arabic rhyme scheme and an Arabic metrical system. Not only this, but the very content of the poem appears to be influenced by Arabic poetry of nostalgia and longing for distant places. In some of these poems, the site of fond memories—often a caravanserai—is now abandoned and in ruins; in others it is beautiful yet unattainable. A striking application of this topos to a personal situation in Muslim Spain

503, lines 9–10; on the ambivalence of such passages in Halevi's poetry, see Sidra DeKoven Ezrahi, *Booking Passage: Exile and Homecoming in the Modern Jewish Imagination* (Berkeley, 1999), 41.

[13] e.g. Halevi, *Hetsiktani teshukati*, in Schirmann, *Hebrew Poetry in Spain and Provence* (Heb.), i. 501, lines 2–9: the proclamations 'I will not weep over . . . I will not remember . . . I will almost forget . . .' are clearly protesting too much; see also Halevi, *Lekha nafshi betuḥah*, ibid. 503, lines 11–12. According to Goitein, in Spain 'he found rest in the houses of study and prayer, enjoyed his Sabbaths, festive holidays, and glorious Passovers; he loved his family; cultivated an endless circle of worthy friends; and, last but not least, was succcessful within his medical profession and, consequently, enjoyed a satisfactory economic situation' (Goitein, *A Mediterranean Society*, v. 467). Hillel Halkin characterizes the poem as 'a miniature marvel of balance in which opposites tug in different directions while remaining musically joined' (Halkin, *Yehudah Halevi* [New York, 2010], 117).

[14] 'He is supported by the saying of the sages, "Exile atones for sins" [BT *Mak.* 2*b*], especially if his exile brings him into the place of God's choice' (Halevi, *The Kuzari*, 5: 23).

[15] Joshua Prawer notes the anomalous use of 'exile' and suggests parallels with the Christian doctrine of atoning pilgrimage as articulated by Bernard of Clairvaux (Prawer, *The History of the Jews in the Latin Kingdom of Jerusalem* [Oxford, 1988], 145–6). Elhanan Reiner has shown that many subsequent Jewish 'pilgrims' to the land of Israel thought of their dangerous journey as having atoning power (see Haviva Pedaya, 'The Spiritual Versus the Concrete Land of Israel in the Geronese School of Kabbalah' [Heb.], in Moshe Hallamish and Aviezer Ravitzky [eds.], *The Land of Israel in Medieval Jewish Thought* [Erets yisra'el bahagut hayehudit bimei habeinayim] [Jerusalem, 1991], 246). Other contemporaries of Halevi, including Moses ibn Ezra, Abraham ibn Daud, and Moses Maimonides, also used the word *galut* to refer to the forced abandonment of Muslim Spain, but the use of this word for a journey from Spain to the land of Israel is quite an extraordinary reversal.

was written by Abd ar-Rahman I, survivor of the Umayyad dynasty, who established himself in Andalusia after the Abbasid seizure of power in the east:

> A palm tree I beheld in Ar-Rusāfa,
> Far in the west, far from the palm-tree land.
> I said: 'You, like myself, are far away, in a strange land;
> How long have I been far away from my people!
> You grew up in a land where you are a stranger,
> And like myself, are living in the farthest corner of the earth.'[16]

Indeed, the sense of exile and alienation is considerably stronger in this than in Halevi's poem, for the Arab refugee ruler recognized no 'good things' in Spain and did not have the option of returning to the east. In short, Halevi's poetic repudiation of the 'golden age' is formulated in ways that reflect the Arabic ambience he claimed he would readily abandon. Perhaps this, rather than any legal subservience or oppression, is the meaning of the 'Arab chains' he bemoaned, but as he continued to write this style of poetry even on his journey, it is not clear that he would have maintained that he had left all of the 'Arab chains' behind.[17] Halevi's poem shows no way to leave exile at present. At best, he might substitute one form for another.

*

The second passage comes from a text that has been the subject of considerable scholarly investigation: Nahmanides' account of his 'Disputation at Barcelona' with the apostate Paul Christian.

> I said, 'My lord king, bear with me [a little]. The essence of our judgement, truth, and justice does not depend upon the messiah. You are worth more to me than the messiah. You are king, and he is king. You are a Gentile king, and he is a Jewish king, for the messiah is but a king of flesh and blood like you. When I worship my Creator in

---

[16] Abd ar-Rahman, in Alois Richard Nykl, *Hispano-Arabic Poetry, and Its Relations with the Old Provençal Troubadours* (Baltimore, 1946), 18; on Ar-Rusāfa, see Jaroslav Stetkevych, *The Zephyrs of Najd: The Poetics of Nostalgia in the Classical Arabic Nasīb* (Chicago, 1993), 109, 269–70 n. 13; cf. 117, 189. In the nineteenth and twentieth centuries this geography of nostalgia is reversed, with Middle Eastern Arab poets writing longingly about Andalusia (see Reuven Snir, '"Al-Andalus Arising from Damascus": Al-Andalus in Modern Arabic Poetry', in Stacy N. Beckwith [ed.], *Charting Memory: Recalling Medieval Spain* [New York, 1999], 263–93).

[17] For a discussion, and rejection, of the view that Halevi repudiated Arabic-style Hebrew poetry late in his life, see Brann, *The Compunctious Poet*, 88–92. As Brann argues, Halevi seems to have maintained a complex and ambivalent attitude towards this kind of poetry to the end (ibid. 96). Aberbach's claim that in this poem Halevi 'breaks out of the shackles of Arabic ornamentation' (*Revolutionary Hebrew*, 111) does not seem persuasive.

your dominion, exiled, suffering, and under subjugation, 'the shame of the nations' [Ezek. 36: 15], who taunt me always, my reward is abundant, for I bring a whole offering to God from my physical being. Because of that, I shall increasingly merit life in the world to come. However, when a king of Israel, of my own faith, will rule over all the nations, and I have no choice but to abide by the law of the Jews, my reward will not be as abundant.[18]

In this passage, Nahmanides (Moses ben Nahman, Ramban) set out to diminish the significance of messianic belief for Judaism. Even if the current exile were to continue forever, he maintained, even if there should never be a messiah, never an ingathering of the exiles, never a rebuilding of the Temple or a restoration of the Davidic line of kings, the essence of Judaism would not be affected, its foundation would not be undermined. The contrast with Christianity is not explicit, but it is clearly implied: Christianity cannot stand without its doctrine of the messiah; Judaism can.

This position was expressed through what appears to be a shocking hyperbole: James I, the king of Aragon, was worth more to this rabbi than the messiah. So unexpected is this formulation that the reader instinctively tends to turn to various hermeneutic options. Is this the fawning of an insecure courtier? Was Nahmanides expressing himself with irony? Is it conventional flattery not intended to be taken seriously by Jews? Is it the discourse of the persecuted, compelled to speak in a way that did not reflect what he truly believed?

This last option has a certain plausibility in the context of the entire report. The passage comes from Nahmanides' account of the second day of the disputation. On the first day, he had been exposed to the new style of Christian argumentation rooted in rabbinic literature. The first question to be disputed was 'whether the messiah had already come'. In support of this proposition, Paul Christian had cited rabbinic texts affirming that the messiah was born on the day the Temple was destroyed. Nahmanides first replied that he did not believe that statement, then that it must have an esoteric meaning, but this opened him to the charge of rejecting the authority of the talmudic sages—a precarious position for a medieval Jewish leader to defend.

---

[18] Nahmanides, 'Disputation', in id., *Ramban: Writings and Discourses*, ed. and trans. Charles Ber Chavel, 2 vols. (New York, 1978), ii. 672–3; Robert Chazan, *Barcelona and Beyond: The Disputation of 1263 and Its Aftermath* (Berkeley, 1992), bibliography, 244. The complex questions of the relationship of Nahmanides' text to the Latin account of the disputation and to what he actually said before the king in Barcelona are not important here. On these issues, which have been studied extensively for more than a century, see ibid. 39–79; on the literary character of Nahmanides' account, see ibid. 100–41.

Finally, he resorted to a technicality: even if the messiah was born in the year 70, that did not prove that he had 'come'; that is, actually begun his public career. To this the king made the obvious point that this messiah would have to be well over 1,000 years old.

Despite Nahmanides' effort to put the best possible spin on his performance in the text for Jewish readers, he was clearly in a difficult position by the end of the first day.[19] He must have given extensive thought that night to various strategies for the resumption of the debate, for at the beginning of the second day he made two dramatically new points. First, unlike the legal component of rabbinic literature, the non-legal component, aggadah, is not authoritative and binding upon Jews; it is, rather, analogous to the sermons delivered by a bishop: to be taken seriously, but not to be considered infallible. Second, even if the messiah had come and gone and the exile should continue forever without any hope for a messiah in the future, the Jewish religion would not be substantively affected.

Whether indeed this marginalization of the messianic age was merely a tactical ploy or reflects what Nahmanides really believed continues to be debated.[20] Yet setting Nahmanides' sincerity aside, the plausibility and internal coherence of the position do not seem open to doubt. That the messiah would be a human being and therefore in the same category as a Gentile king was the normative Jewish position throughout the ages. That Judaism does not depend upon the messianic belief is considerably more controversial, for well-known Jewish thinkers, including Maimonides, made it a fundamental principle of Jewish faith. Yet Nahmanides reiterated this in another, non-polemical context, and other Jewish thinkers also maintained a similar position.[21]

---

[19] The difficulty of Nahmanides' position is emphasized in Martin Cohen, 'Reflections on the Text and Context of the Disputation of Barcelona', *Hebrew Union College Annual*, 35 (1964), 172.

[20] One obvious problem is that Nahmanides claims to have insisted at the very outset that the disputation be focused not on peripheral issues of Jewish practice but on 'matters upon which the entire controversy is contingent', and therefore they 'agreed to discuss first of all the subject of the messiah' ('Disputation', 658). His position on the second day seems to contradict this. Yitzhak Baer thus maintains that this position was taken 'against his own convictions' (Baer, *A History of the Jews in Christian Spain*, 2 vols. [Philadelphia, 1961–6], i. 153; cf. Chazan, *Barcelona and Beyond*, 65, 128 [where this inconsistency is noted without drawing a direct conclusion about Nahmanides' sincerity]).

[21] Nahmanides, 'The Book of Redemption', in id., *Ramban: Writings and Discourses*, ii. 606–7; cf. Y. Baer, *A History of the Jews in Christian Spain*, i. 248. Solomon Schechter took this parallel, in a context 'where there was no occasion to be over polite to the Government', as evidence that it reflects Nahmanides' genuine view (Schechter, *Studies in Judaism* [Philadelphia, 1896], 106; cf. Isaac Polgar, *Ezer hadat*, ed. Jacob Levinger [Tel Aviv, 1984]; Dov Schwartz, *The Messianic Idea in Medieval Jewish Thought* [Harayon hameshiḥi bahagut hayehudit bimei habeinayim] [Ramat Gan, 1997], 192).

How could Nahmanides and the others make this surprising claim? There are several unspoken assumptions from various sources which may lead to this conclusion. First, the essence of Judaism is not living in the messianic age, but observing the commandments of the Torah.[22] Second, the value of observing the commandments is directly proportionate to the difficulty of the observance. This view, with roots in the rabbinic literature ('the reward is proportional to the pain' [Mishnah *Avot* 5: 22]), reiterated by Maimonides in his *Epistle on Apostasy*, is commonly associated with the doctrine of medieval German Jewish Pietism (*ḥasidut ashkenaz*).[23] Third, the conditions of life in exile make the observance of the commandments extremely difficult for Jews: there are powerful pressures to abandon their faith, and those who cling to it are subjected to taunting and humiliation from their Christian neighbours.[24] Fourth, while some of the most important commandments could not be observed—especially the offering of sacrifices in the Temple—this was more than compensated for when Jews offered themselves as a sacrifice to God through their willingness to remain Jews, rather than follow the easier path of conversion.[25] Finally, the essential reward, the desired end of all life, was

---

[22] For the tension (or contradiction) between this principle and the position, taken by Nahmanides in his commentary on the Torah, that even those commandments applicable outside the land of Israel cannot be *fully* observed in exile, see Chapter 12.

[23] Maimonides maintained that those Jews compelled to remain in a place where Judaism was not tolerated would be rewarded doubly for each commandment observed because of the devotion necessary to overlook the danger (Moses Maimonides, 'Epistle on Apostasy', in *Crisis and Leadership: Epistles of Maimonides*, trans. and ed. Abraham Halkin and David Hartman [Philadelphia, 1993], 33). Halkin notes a parallel with Halevi's *The Kuzari*, I: 114. On German Pietism and its doctrine of rewards proportionate to the difficulty (or the apparent senselessness) of the commandment, the pressures to transgress it, and the humiliation endured for its performance (at the hands not only of Christians but of other Jews), see Yitzhak Baer, 'The Religious-Social Tendency of *Sefer Ḥasidim*' (Heb.), *Zion*, 3 (1937), 9; Joseph Dan, *The Esoteric Doctrine of German Pietism* [Torat hasod shel ḥasidut ashkenaz] (Jerusalem, 1968), 239; Haym Soloveitchik, 'Three Themes in *Sefer Ḥasidim*', *AJS Review*, 1 (1976), 336–7; Ivan Marcus, *Piety and Society: The Jewish Pietists of Medieval Germany* (Leiden, 1981), 32.

[24] Since every Jew could 'become the friend and equal of his oppressor by uttering one word, and without any difficulty' (i.e. through conversion to the majority faith, in Halevi's case Islam), those who bear humiliation and degradation and remain loyal to Judaism earn a rich reward from God (Halevi, *The Kuzari*, I: 115).

[25] This motif is present in the chronicles and liturgies written in the wake of the massacres during the First Crusade (see e.g. Alan Mintz, *Ḥurban: Responses to Catastrophe in Hebrew Literature* [New York, 1984], 94–7, 101; Robert Chazan, *European Jewry and the First Crusade* [Berkeley, 1987], 126–31). Compare the formulation by Ezra of Gerona: 'Nowadays the Jews are already released from the obligation [to dwell in] the land of Israel. Their suffering—out of love of God—the [vicissitudes of] the dispersion, and their afflictions and subjugation are like an atoning altar for them, as it is written: "For Thy sake are we killed all day long" [Ps. 44: 23]' (in Moshe Idel, 'The Land of Israel in Medieval

immortality of the soul in the world to come. The messianic age, physical rather than spiritual, in time rather than eternity, was far less important than this.

Putting all these assumptions together, Nahmanides' conclusion makes sense. Maimonides had earlier argued that the messianic age is a means to the ultimate goal of a purely spiritual reward in the world to come, in that it will make it easier for the Jews to devote themselves to 'the Law and its wisdom', namely the attainment of philosophical enlightenment.[26] Nahmanides accepted the premise that the spiritual reward, not life in this world, is the ultimate good. But, resorting to the pietistic notion that the more difficult the challenge—the greater the temptation to opt out—the greater the reward will be, he drew the opposite conclusion: because the messianic age will make observing the commandments easier, it is precisely the current life in exile that is more conducive to achieving the reward in the world to come.[27]

Even more than Halevi, Nahmanides presents *galut* as an arena of suffering. Jews in exile, mocked and scorned by their neighbours, were subjected to fearsome pressures to abandon a distinctive religious identity and accept the ways of the majority. At best they could rely on sympathetic kings to guarantee their physical safety and the possibility of observing their traditions. Yet even under such relatively benign conditions, remaining a Jew in *galut* entailed a struggle. Loyalty to Jewish demands and worship of the Creator through performance of the commandments required a sacrificial effort,

---

Kabbalah', in Lawrence Hoffman [ed.], *The Land of Israel: Jewish Perspectives* [Notre Dame, Ind., 1986], 177). Haviva Pedaya arrives at the 'paradoxical conclusion that it is obligatory to live in exile [at present]' ('The Spiritual Versus the Concrete Land of Israel' [Heb.], 248). Abraham Shalom wrote that 'Rav Sheshet used to sacrifice the blood of his own body in place of the [Temple] sacrifice (*Neveh shalom* [Venice, 1575], 193a, in Hava Tirosh-Rothschild, 'The Political Philosophy of Abraham Shalom: The Platonic Tradition' [Heb.], *Jerusalem Studies in Jewish Thought*, 9/2 [1991], 439). This is apparently based on R. Sheshet's prayer while fasting: 'May it be Your will that my diminished fat and blood be deemed as though I had presented them on the altar as an offering before You' (BT *Ber.* 17a).

[26] Moses Maimonides, *Mishneh torah*, 'Laws of Kings and Their Wars', 12: 4; cf. his formulation in the introduction to his comment on Mishnah San. 10: in the days of the messiah, 'perfection will be widespread, with the result that men will merit the life of the world to come' (in *A Maimonides Reader*, ed. Isadore Twersky [New York, 1972], 415).

[27] Compare the later formulation by the eighteenth-century hasidic writer Jacob Joseph of Polonnoye: 'What the experts in ethics have written is well known: that the reward for one who serves God truly and devotedly in the time of exile is many times greater than [the reward for] one who served God in the earlier period' (in Mendel Piekarz, *Ideological Trends in Polish Hasidism during the Interwar Period and the Holocaust* [Ḥasidut polin: megamot rayoniyot bein shetei hamilḥamot uvigezerot 1939–1945 ('ha-Sho'ah')] [Jerusalem, 1990], 219 n. 28; cf. the formulation of later hasidic masters, including Judah Leib of Gur [ibid. 214–15, 225–6]).

tantamount to a form of ongoing martyrdom. To be a Jew in exile was to transform one's own body into a sacrifice to God.

Nevertheless, this negative depiction of life in exile, though apparently similar in some ways to Halevi's 'Arab chains', functioned differently for Nahmanides. Halevi contrasted exile in the far west to the site of the Temple Mount at the time—desolate, controlled by the forces of Christendom, empty of Jews. Yet this depressing alternative is Halevi's goal. It can be achieved only through a total repudiation of the present geographical exile for a different form of exile in the Holy Land, superficially far more dismal, yet to the poet more desirable. Nahmanides sets up a triad. Exile, with all its present bleakness, is contrasted with a future return to Jewish sovereignty under the messianic king, but the expected valence of this dichotomy—*galut*: bad, messianic age: good—is subverted through the introduction of a third element: life in the world to come, which is understood to be more important than the messianic age.

This ultimate goal could be achieved not through sacrificing the 'good things' of the contemporary *galut* but by sacrificial loyalty despite the adverse pressures of *galut*, for this is what enabled Jews to reach the ultimate reward. While Halevi's poem articulates a negation of the exile despite its 'good things', Nahmanides' statement suggests a surprising affirmation of the exile, for its very difficulties and challenges make it instrumental for a higher purpose. Exile, with all its pain and oppression, is therefore the key to spiritual immortality, and—paradoxically—life under a messianic king who will compel all Jews to observe the commandments may be more perilous for the future of the soul in eternity.

*

The third text is from a homiletical composition by the early hasidic master Dov Baer, the Maggid of Mezhirech. It begins with the apparently simple statement from Mishnah *Avot* 1: 7 *harḥek mishakhen ra*, usually translated as 'draw away from an evil neighbour':

Harḥek mishakhen ra: This means that it is easier to achieve the Holy Spirit in our time, a time of exile, than it was in the days when the Temple was still standing. To understand this, consider how difficult it would be to approach a king in his royal palace, as compared to when he is travelling through the countryside. While he is on the road or at an inn, anyone can approach him, even a simple farm lad who would never be permitted to enter the palace. In the same way, God will immediately inspire and dwell within someone who thinks about communion with God now, in our time of exile. For this reason, it is important to remove ourselves from evil desires and evil thoughts, so that God will not be separated from us. Rather, whatever we do should be for the sake of God's name. Thus *harḥek mishakhen* 'remove from the neighbour', namely from the One who dwells by (or within) you, *harḥek hara* 'remove the evil'.[28]

The passage is framed by a novel piece of homiletical exegesis. In typical hasidic style, the preacher took a simple, familiar phrase from the classical literature and gave it a twist that is novel yet firmly rooted in the language of the text, for 'draw away from an evil neighbour' should have used not the *hiphil*, *harḥek*, but the *hitpa'el*, *hitraḥek*.[29] The homilist therefore broke down the traditional syntax of the three words and constructed it anew. There is no 'evil neighbour'. The *shakhen* is the indwelling presence of God (*shekhinah*). 'Evil' becomes the direct object of the transitive verb *harḥek*, 'remove', meaning 'set at a distance'. Though 'evil' is directly juxtaposed to 'neighbour' in the sentence, the goal is to set distance between them. Evil thoughts must be set at a distance, lest they cause God to be separated from us.

If this new insight into the familiar words from Mishnah *Avot* comes at the end of the paragraph, the reader (or listener) was confronted with a stunning and challenging novelty at the very beginning: 'it is easier to achieve the Holy Spirit in our time, a time of exile, than it was in the days when the Temple was still standing'. Such an assertion would appear to violate much of what Jews 'knew' about *galut*, as expressed in so many statements indicating that God was more accessible in the Holy Land, in the Holy City, in the Temple, than in the 'lands of idolatry'. One tradition was that with the destruction of the Temple, the divine presence withdrew entirely from the earth, that even God's providential protection terminated completely with the exile, leaving the Jewish people to the fate determined by the stars, the brutalities of cynical politics and military might, or chance.[30] A stunning expression of this, written

---

[28] Dov Baer of Mezhirech, *Magid devarav leya'akov*, ed. Rivka Schatz Uffenheimer (Jerusalem: Magnes Press, 1990), 70; translation based on Joseph Dan (ed.), *The Teachings of Hasidism* (New York, 1983), 132–3; Martin Buber introduces the element of the king's being 'driven from his realm' without any basis in sources I could find (Buber, *Tales of the Hasidim*, 2 vols. [New York, 1964], i. 103).

[29] This problem is not addressed by most of the commentators, who apparently assume the meaning is *harḥek [et atsmekha]*, 'set [yourself] at a distance'. Judah Lerma, noting the use of *hifil* rather than *hitpa'el*, suggested that the meaning is that one should warn a newcomer about an evil neighbour and thereby remove him from the neighbour's influence (in Samuel de Uçeda, *Midrash shemu'el* [commentary on *Pirkei avot*] [Benei Berak, 1992], 33).

[30] On the withdrawal of the Shekhinah, see Ephraim Elimelech Urbach, *The Sages: Their Concepts and Beliefs*, trans. Israel Abrahams (Cambridge, Mass., 1987), 61–5. On the removal of providence, see, for example, the sources cited in Chapter 12 as interpretations of the talmudic statement 'Whoever dwells outside the land is as one who has no God' (BT *Ket.* 110b). The most extreme

not long after the Maggid's homily, represents the more common, pessimistic view of distance and inaccessibility:

> During the time of the Temple, no man dwelled in permanent sin, for the sacrificial offerings would atone . . . and nothing stood in the way and prevented our prayers from rising to our Father in heaven. Today, however, that is not the case. For due to the multitude of our sins . . . there is an iron wall that separates us [from God] and stops [our prayers]. And there is no direct route for the ascent of our prayers . . . and our worship is like a barren woman, for it does not give birth and it yields no fruit, for the gates of prayer have been locked.[31]

The more comforting affirmation was that the divine presence went into exile with the Jewish people,[32] or, in the words of the Khazar king in Judah Halevi's *The Kuzari*, 'one can draw near to God in any place with a pure heart and strong desire'[33]—a position close to that of Dov Baer. But even this does not maintain that God is *more* accessible in exile than in the ancient Temple of Jerusalem. That appears to be a revolutionary claim,[34] and it was substantiated not by a complex conceptual or exegetical argument, but by recourse to a simple analogy.

---

expression of this is that 'even when he prays to God, God does not hear his prayer, as he is under [the jurisdiction of] princes and constellations'.

[31] Hillel ben Zev Wolf of Kovno, *Heilel ben shaḥar* (Warsaw, 1804), in Allan Nadler, *The Faith of the Mithnagdim: Rabbinic Responses to Hasidic Rapture* (Baltimore, 1997), 76. The images of the intervening 'wall of iron' and the locking of the gates of prayer come from the Talmud (BT *Ber.* 32*b*), but the expression of the barrenness of Jewish worship in exile goes beyond the familiar sources.

[32] BT *Meg.* 29*a* and parallels; cf. Shalom Rosenberg, 'The Link to the Land of Israel in Jewish Thought: A Clash of Perspectives', in Hoffman (ed.), *The Land of Israel*, 155; Rivka Schatz Uffenheimer, *Hasidism as Mysticism: Quietistic Elements in Eighteenth Century Hasidic Thought* (Princeton, 1993), 337.

[33] Halevi, *The Kuzari*, 5: 22. The Jewish spokesman does not deny this, but counters that 'heart and soul are perfectly pure and immaculate only in the place which is known to be specially selected by God' (ibid. 5: 23).

[34] Scholem characterized it as 'a rather astounding idea' (Gershom Scholem, *Major Trends in Jewish Mysticism* [New York, 1941], 330), and 'a statement for which one would look in vain in any other place' (id., *The Messianic Idea in Judaism and Other Essays on Jewish Spirituality* [New York, 1971], 201). While there may be no clear precedent for this statement, other hasidim repeated it with approval. See the expanded version of Elimelekh of Lyzhansk, *No'am elimelekh* (in Schatz Uffenheimer, *Hasidism as Mysticism*, 338–9) and the briefer summary of Uziel Meisels (ibid. 336). For subsequent uses of this parable by late nineteenth- and early twentieth-century hasidic masters—some of whom attributed it to the Ba'al Shem Tov—see Piekarz, *Ideological Trends in Polish Hasidism* (Heb.), 218–19 (with bibliography in n. 28), 227. Piekarz devotes an entire chapter to 'Acceptance of Exile and Emphasis of Its Advantages' containing abundant material in the tradition both on the Nahmanides passage and the Maggid's parable (ibid. 205–31).

As in so many traditional Jewish analogies and parables, this one involves a king, who clearly represents God. Usually, it is a member of the king's family who goes out from the palace into a foreign realm: his wife or son, representing the Jewish people. Sometimes a messenger is sent out of the palace by the king. In *The Kuzari*, Judah Halevi spoke of a man who became so close to the king that he was invited to the king's table and could enter the king's presence whenever he wished. Unlike the other subjects, when he went on a dangerous journey, far away from the palace, he was fully confident that he would continue to enjoy the king's protection, even at a distance.[35] Maimonides' celebrated 'parable of the castle' focuses on the efforts of various categories of human being to find the palace, enter its gates, and thereby come into the presence of the king.[36]

In all of these analogies, the king remains in his palace: only rarely do we find a king journeying forth.[37] This passage, therefore, subverts a literary tradition as well as a theological commonplace. What is particularly striking is that while we might expect the parable and its application to apply exclusively to the *tsadik* and his unique access to God, substituting a new *axis mundi* for the sacred geography of Jerusalem and Temple, it instead applied to the ordinary Jews being addressed.[38] Despite reference to the 'Holy Spirit', this was not a validation of the *rebbe*'s unique role, but a call for the hasidim to take advantage of their spiritual opportunities. Perhaps there was an appeal to actual experience: a Jew in the late eighteenth century, who would never get

---

[35] Halevi, *The Kuzari*, 3: 21.

[36] Moses Maimonides, *Guide for the Perplexed*, 3: 51 (trans. and ed. M. Friedländer, 3 vols. in 1 [New York, 1946], iii. 279–81); cf. David Stern, *Parables in Midrash: Narrative and Exegesis in Rabbinic Literature* (Cambridge, Mass., 1991), 226–7. Compare the more active and eroticized king, still in his palace, who reveals himself by removing some of his garments to his intimates and all of his garments to the queen (Joseph Gikatilla, *Gates of Light: Sha'arei Orah*, trans. Avi Weinstein [San Francisco, 1994], 166). There is nothing in this passage, however, about venturing outside the palace and thereby revealing himself to ordinary subjects.

[37] For example, *Exodus Rabbah* 33: 1 on Exod. 25: 2; *Lamentations Rabbah, Petiḥta* 25; see also Benno Heinemann, *The Maggid of Dubno and His Parables* (New York, 1967), 205. One hasidic writer cited *Leviticus Rabbah* 7: 2, which involves a king travelling in the wilderness, as a source for the present parable (see Norman Lamm, *The Religious Thought of Hasidism: Text and Commentary* [New York, 1999], 539), but that parable emphasizes the superiority of the Temple over the wilderness and is therefore quite different.

[38] On the *tsadik* as substitute for the holiness of the land of Israel in other hasidic writers, see Arthur Green, 'Zaddiq as *Axis Mundi* in Later Judaism', *Journal of the American Academy of Religion*, 45/3 (1977), 327–47; Moshe Idel, *Hasidism: Between Ecstasy and Magic* (Albany, NY, 1995), 205–6; on the question of whether the Maggid recognized such a fundamental distinction in essence between the *tsadik* and the ordinary Jew, see Ada Rapaport-Albert, 'God and the Zaddik as the Two Focal Points of Hasidic Worship', *History of Religions*, 18/4 (1979), 319–20.

through the doors of the imperial palace, might conceivably catch a glimpse of the tsar travelling through the countryside. But this just validates the theological insight; it is unlikely that it would generate such a dramatic reversal of traditional assumptions. There must be a deeper rationale.

The passage works through the implications of the concept that God dwells within the pure and devoted human being—an idea that is neither biblical nor rabbinic but apparently first appeared in Judaism, probably influenced by Sufism, in the poetry of the Spanish 'golden age'.[39] It may also reflect the influence of the popular Lurianic notion of the *nitsotsot*, sparks of the divine essence, scattered throughout the world, and therefore accessible even to ordinary human beings, a doctrine developed into a full immanentist theology by the Maggid of Mezhirech.[40] Whatever the source of this idea, the implications for the nature of exile are dramatic. What separates the Jew from God is not *galut*—detachment from the Holy Land, destruction of the Temple, immersion in a Gentile environment—but the evil desires of the human heart, which can be mastered. If indeed it is easier to encounter God in exile than in the Temple of Jerusalem, exile is not a total catastrophe, devoid of any meaningful religious life. It is, rather, an opportunity and a challenge.

While the passages from Nahmanides and the Maggid of Mezhirech reflect a much more positive attitude towards the function of exile in the religious life than Halevi's poem, the difference between them should also be clear. Although the Maggid was living in late eighteenth-century eastern Europe under conditions generally considered to be harsher than those in Muslim Spain, in the Maggid's homily there was no suggestion of 'Arab chains' nor was there any hint of a sacrificial offering of the Jew's body as in Nahmanides. The essential characteristic of exile is access to God, who may

---

[39] *Hanimtsah vakeravim*, 'Who is found in the innermost places' (Halevi, *Yah anah emtsa'akha*, line 3, in Schirmann, *Hebrew Poetry in Spain and Provence* [Heb.], i. 524). In *The Kuzari*, the Jewish spokesman maintains (somewhat more ambiguously than the poem) that in the spiritual giants of the Jewish past, 'the Shekhinah found a worthy abode [*mahal*]' (Halevi, *The Kuzari*, 3: 65; cf. 5: 23; on this passage and its probable Sufi background, see Diane Lobel, 'A Dwelling Place for the Shekhinah', *Jewish Quarterly Review*, 90 [1999], 103–25). See also the Sufi tradition: 'heaven and earth contain Me not, but the heart of My faithful servant contains Me' (in Annemarie Schimmel, *Mystical Dimensions of Islam* [Chapel Hill, 1975], 190). For somewhat later Jewish mystical expressions, see Scholem, *Major Trends in Jewish Mysticism*, 110; Lamm, *The Religious Thought of Hasidism*, 538; for the idea of God dwelling within the human being in Dov Baer, the Maggid of Mezhirech, see Schatz Uffenheimer, *Hasidism as Mysticism*, 192, 213; Idel, *Hasidism*, 114; cf. Lamm, *The Religious Thought of Hasidism*, 307.

[40] On the Lurianic sparks in the teachings of the Ba'al Shem Tov and the Maggid, see Gershom Scholem, *On the Mystical Shape of the Godhead: Basic Concepts in the Kabbalah* (New York, 1991), 246–7; on the Maggid's immanentist theology, see Schatz Uffenheimer, *Hasidism as Mysticism*, 177, 192, 269.

also be suffering in exile. Of course, conditions are better in the palace than 'on the road or at an inn', but this applies to the king, not to the 'simple farm lad'—the ordinary Jew—who would never be allowed into the palace. Homelessness, uprootedness, powerlessness, all the common characteristics associated with *galut* are, at least temporarily, forgotten. The surprising suggestion is that in spiritual terms, the situation of the Jews has actually improved with the exile in comparison with the period when the Temple was still standing. The conclusion is similar to that of Nahmanides—that Judaism does not depend upon a messianic age, that attention should be focused on the present rather than on the future—but for a very different reason. In the statement of this hasidic *rebbe*, we find something that might be termed an 'affirmation of the exile'. Such an attitude would certainly lead one to expect that any messianic tension, any urgency of expectation for radical change on a national level, any activism to bring about the messiah, would be dissipated or neutralized.

These three texts suggest an unexpected complexity of 'authentic' Jewish attitudes towards exile and the diaspora in the pre-Emancipation era, illustrating how the valences of an apparently straightforward passage can often be uncovered only through a careful investigation of its literary, historical, and conceptual dimensions. (In Chapter 12, I examine a similar complexity with regard to attitudes towards the Land of Israel.) As for the material in the modern period, texts produced against the background of the debates over Emancipation, the emergence of the Reform movement, Zionism, the Holocaust, and the establishment of the State of Israel reveal an array of attitudes towards 'exile' even more diverse and provocative.

CHAPTER TWELVE

The Land of Israel in Pre-Modern Jewish Thought: A History of Two Rabbinic Statements

> The Jewish people ... forced to leave their ancient country,
> has never abandoned, never forsaken, the Holy Land; the Jewish people
> has never ceased to be passionate about Zion.
> It has always lived in a dialogue with the Holy Land.[1]

THESE WORDS, written by Abraham Joshua Heschel, express a sentiment reiterated by dozens of Jewish thinkers of the past three generations.[2] The passionate attachment of diaspora Jewry to *erets yisra'el*, the Land of Israel, from the destruction of the Temple at least until the Emancipation, is an ideological axiom shared by the vast majority of contemporary Jews. Why this is so widely assumed to be true might be worthy of a study in itself: it was certainly not the case at the beginning of the twentieth century, when anti-Zionists sought to temper the passion of the attachment through quietistic and universalistic teachings, and Zionist writers berated medieval and

First published in Lawrence Hoffman (ed.), *The Land of Israel: Jewish Perspectives* (Notre Dame, Ind., 1986), 188–209.

[1] Abraham Joshua Heschel, *Israel: An Echo of Eternity* (New York, 1969), 58–9.

[2] Two other examples, by distinguished historians: 'Throughout the long generations of the Dispersion every Jew firmly believed that "the Land is Israel's everlasting possession, which only they shall inherit and in which only they shall settle, and if perchance they are exiled from it they will return to it again, for it is theirs in perpetuity and no other nation's" [Bahya ben Asher, *Be'ur al hatorah* (Commentary on the Torah), ed. Charles Chavel, 3 vols. (Jerusalem, 1966), 'Lekh lekha']. This was not merely an ideological slogan, nor the messianic dream of unworldly visionaries, but a vividly felt and living attachment which found expression in deeds no less than in words' (Ben Zion Dinur, *Israel and the Diaspora* [Philadelphia, 1969], 7); 'In every generation of its protracted exile, longings for Zion and yearnings for redemption in its land have filled the hearts of the people. The idea of a return to Zion was the animating spirit of its cultural creativity and the essential direction of all its social and spiritual currents' (Raphael Mahler, in Michael A. Meyer [ed.], *Ideas of Jewish History* [Detroit, 1987], 311).

contemporary Jews for having made peace with life in *galut* (exile).[3] This chapter, however, will look at different questions: To what degree does a statement like that of Heschel reflect a demonstrable historical reality? What kinds of source material would be relevant for testing such a statement? How might the statement be documented or proven? How is the role of the Land of Israel in Jewish thought and consciousness from 70 to 1800 to be evaluated?

The technique most frequently employed for this purpose is not especially fruitful. It is the method of anthology, the collection of sources from all periods and genres of Hebrew literature which praise the merits of the Land of Israel, emphasize the importance of living there, articulate yearnings for its holy places, and so forth. Such collections[4] generally remove the passages from their historical and literary context and present them without any indication of opposing viewpoints or analysis of what they might really mean: they are at best a starting point, and at worst they are biased distortions. It is not enough merely to collect rabbinic pronouncements—'Whoever dwells in the Land of Israel lives without sin' (BT *Ket.* 111*a*), 'Whoever walks four cubits in the Land of Israel is assured of a place in the world to come' (BT *Ket.* 111*a*), 'Dwelling in the Land of Israel counterbalances all of the divine commandments' (*Sifrei* on Deut. 12: 29)—as if they were self-explanatory and sufficient as evidence for the view of 'the Jewish tradition'. Questions fundamental to any historical investigation must be raised: Whose view does this represent? Why was it said? To what extent does it typify Jewish attitudes and conduct? How does the sentiment relate to other statements concerned with Jewish values and obligations?

---

[3] e.g. Joseph Brenner, 'Self-Criticism', in Arthur Hertzberg (ed.), *The Zionist Idea: A Historical Analysis and Reader* (New York, 1971), 310. Pre-Emancipation Jews, when in the mood for self-criticism, would also have dissented from a generalization such as that of Professor Heschel. See the retrospective characterization of Spanish Jewry by Jacob Emden: 'Misfortune befell us when Israel enjoyed honours in countries like Spain and assimilated with the people among whom they lived. No one at all yearned for Zion; it was abandoned and forgotten' (introduction to *Amudei shamayim*, in Philip Birnbaum [ed.], *A Treasury of Judaism* [New York, 1962], 405). Jacob J. Schacter shows that Emden attributed to the Spanish Jews the statement: 'We already found another Land of Israel and Jerusalem just like it' (Schacter, 'Echoes of the Spanish Expulsion in Eighteenth Century Germany: The Baer Thesis Revisited', *Judaism*, 162 [1992], 188 n. 39).

[4] A representative, but certainly not exhaustive, list would include Michael Guttmann, *The Land of Israel in the Midrash and Talmud* [Erets yisra'el bemidrash vetalmud] (Breslau, 1929); Yosef Zahavi, *Erets Israel in Rabbinic Lore* (Jerusalem, 1962); Avraham Holtz, *The Holy City: Jews on Jerusalem* (New York, 1971); Yitzhak Raphael, *Hasidism and the Land of Israel* [Haḥasidut ve'erets yisra'el] (Jerusalem, 1940); Simon Federbusch, *Hasidism and Zion* [Haḥasidut vetsiyon] (Jerusalem, 1963); Moshe Hayim Tiberg, *From the Praises of the Land: A Collection of Praises of the Land of Israel According to the Sources*

In this chapter, I am therefore concerned with the substantive matters and methodological issues relating to the use of sources bearing on the Land of Israel. The following principles might be suggested at the outset. First, religious leaders usually do not bother denouncing sins that are not being committed; preachers generally emphasize values that are challenged and problematic. As historical evidence, a rabbinic statement warning against leaving the Land of Israel or underlining the importance of living there is therefore double-edged: it reveals not only the commitment to the land of at least one (and possibly many) religious leaders, but also a weakness of commitment among the Jews such leaders were trying to convince.[5] Second, a statement from either Talmud or Midrash cannot be assumed to be equally valid for all periods of subsequent Jewish history. For legal statements, one must attempt to determine to what extent they were actually enforced in Jewish courts throughout the ages. For aggadic statements, it is important to trace the history of their use: whether a particular statement had significant repercussions or was consigned to virtual oblivion, who quoted it and for what purpose, how it was interpreted and applied. Finally, more can be learned about the role of the Land of Israel from discussions that reveal tension or conflict between loyalty to the land and other values in Jewish life than from hyperbolic praise. I shall attempt to apply these principles to a well-known halakhic and aggadic statement from the most important locus of rabbinic views on the land, the end of tractate *Ketubot* of the Babylonian Talmud.

'She must be compelled to go up to the Land of Israel, and if she does not consent, she may be divorced without her *ketubah*'

The following text, from the period of the Mishnah, probably datable before the year 200 CE, raised legal dilemmas for generations of rabbinic judges:

[Mishivḥei ha'arets: osef shivḥei erets yisra'el lefi hamekorot] (Tel Aviv, 1975); Hen-Melekh Merhavyah, *Voices Calling to Zion* [Kolot korim letsiyon] (Jerusalem, 1980).

[5] Consider, for example, R. Simeon b. Yoḥai's comment: 'Elimelech, Mahlon, and Chilion were great men and leaders of their generation. Why then were they punished? Because they left the Land of Israel for a foreign country' (BT *BB* 91a). As historical evidence, this probably tells us little about the theological underpinnings of the book of Ruth. It may indeed serve as evidence for the emigration of Jews in the wake of devastating economic conditions following the disastrous Bar Kokhba revolt in the middle of the second century. A late thirteenth-century author, faced with a quite different problem in his environment, concluded that Elimelech and his sons were punished because they married alien women (*Zohar ḥadash: rut* [Livorno, 1866], 99a).

Our rabbis taught: if the husband desires to go up [to the Land of Israel] but his wife refuses she must be compelled to go up, and if she does not consent, she may be divorced without a *ketubah* [marriage settlement]. If she desires to go up and he refuses, he must be compelled to go up, and if he does not consent, he must divorce her and pay her *ketubah*. (BT *Ket.* 110a)[6]

This passage concerns a conflict between two important Jewish values: encouraging settlement of the Land of Israel and protecting the contractual rights of a wife. The law unambiguously states that the settlement of the land takes priority. While a husband cannot ordinarily compel his wife to move with him to a different country,[7] he may do so if he wants to settle in the Land of Israel, even if it means moving from a fine dwelling to an inferior one. If the wife refuses, the husband may divorce her and be freed of the obligation to pay the amount specified in her marriage contract.

Was this law enforced in the diaspora? Based on actual cases recorded in the rabbinic responsa literature, the answer would appear to be 'sometimes, but often not'. For example, the following problem was presented to Maimonides in Egypt near the end of the twelfth century. A young man married the daughter of a leading Jewish family in Alexandria. When their first son was three months old, the husband quarrelled with his in-laws and tried to pressure his wife to renounce certain contractual rights. The court determined in favour of the wife, leaving the husband bound to all stipulations of the marriage agreement. A friend suggested that the husband ask his wife to settle with him in Israel: she would certainly refuse to leave her entire family and move with an infant to a strange country, and then he could divorce her without any financial obligation whatsoever. This time the court, following the clear dictum of the Talmud, ruled that the wife was obligated to accompany her husband or she would lose her rights to the stipulated payment upon divorce. The dumbfounded leaders of the community complained: 'From now on, everyone who dislikes his wife and wants to divorce her without paying will fabricate this claim. Many women will consequently be divorced by their husbands.'

---

[6] According to a different version of this statement, preserved in a manuscript of the Tosefta and in the Jerusalem Talmud, the husband who refuses to accompany his wife to the Land of Israel is *not* compelled to do so (see Saul Lieberman, *Tosefta Ki-Feshutah: A Comprehensive Commentary on the Tosefta, Ketubot* [New York, 1967], 386). The Palestinian text would appear to reflect the view that this technique of fostering the settlement of the Land of Israel was not worth undermining the husband's supremacy in the marital relationship.

[7] BT *Ket.* 110b; Moses Maimonides, *Mishneh torah*, 'Laws of Marriage', 13: 17.

In response, Maimonides reported the practice of many Jewish courts of pronouncing a general ban of excommunication upon anyone who claimed to want to settle in Palestine for any reason other than the pure motivation of enjoying the blessing of the Holy Land: only after the husband answers 'Amen' to such a ban do they enforce the rule in his case, permitting him to go. Maimonides himself went even farther in restricting its enforcement, despite the absence of talmudic support: the husband must have a general reputation for honesty, and there must be no known strife between husband and wife, for 'it is a light matter for most men to cause grief to their wives and to free themselves from the obligation of paying their *ketubah*, and we must guard against such a sin'.[8] In other words, in the case at hand, he would have dissented from the court and refused to enforce the talmudic law.

The noted thirteenth-century German authority Meir of Rothenburg suggested a different provision, also apparently intended to protect the wife against the machinations of a husband not sincerely committed to living in the Land of Israel. The wife may be divorced without her *ketubah* 'provided that he goes to the Land of Israel and does not return. But if he should come back to settle outside the land, even after many years, if she is still alive she may demand [the money stipulated in the *ketubah*] and if, God forbid, she has previously died, her heirs may claim it.' Meir was also careful to limit enforcement to precisely what is stated by the Talmud so that the woman would not be excessively penalized. The wife may lose her right to the amount stipulated in the *ketubah* as compensation for divorce, but dowry property she had brought to the marriage was certainly to be protected for her.[9] Neither Maimonides nor Meir of Rothenburg was prepared to go so far as to change the principle of the law or to reverse the theoretical hierarchy of values, but the potential for abuse generated an effort to ensure greater protection for wives and an obligation for judges to investigate closely the circumstances and motivations of the proclaimed desire to settle in the Holy Land.

---

[8] Moses Maimonides, *Teshuvot harambam* [responsa], ed. Joshua Blau, 3 vols. (Jerusalem, 1957–61), ii. 639–41. For other examples of husbands who may have used the Holy Land as a pretext for desertion of wives whom they knew would not agree to the turbulent conditions of Palestine, see Shelomo D. Goitein, *A Mediterranean Society: The Jewish Communities of the Arab World as Portrayed in the Documents of the Cairo Geniza*, 5 vols. plus index (Berkeley, 1967–93), iii. 198–9.

[9] Meir of Rothenburg, in Yisrael Schepansky, *The Land of Israel in the Responsa Literature* [Erets yisra'el bisfrut hateshuvot], 3 vols. (Jerusalem, 1966), i. 156. Meir's decision about the obligation of the husband to pay his former wife if he subsequently left the Land of Israel was accepted by later codifiers (see Moses Isserles, *Darkhei mosheh* [commentary on *Arba'ah turim*] [Zhitomir, 1858] on *Arba'ah turim*, 'Even ha'ezer', 75; id., *Mapah perusah* [glosses on *Shulḥan arukh*] [Halberstadt, 1861] on *Shulḥan arukh*, 'Even ha'ezer', 75).

An even more radical view was recorded in the Tosafot to the talmudic passage: 'This law does not apply at the present time, because of the dangers of the journey.'[10] The talmudic legislation made sense to the early Palestinian rabbis, who wanted to attract immigration from the relatively nearby countries of the second-century diaspora, but for twelfth- and thirteenth-century French rabbis, it was not so simple. Factoring in all the hazards of travel between northern Europe and Palestine during the period of the Crusades, when even armed nobles knew they might not reach their destination safely, the French rabbis decided that the balance had shifted and that the value of settlement in the war-torn Land of Israel could no longer justify compelling a wife to undertake the venture against her will. The result they recommended was a benign neglect of what the Talmud clearly mandated.

Later rabbis, especially those living in Mediterranean countries, generally agreed in principle that the law should not be enforced under conditions of serious danger, and the question shifted to whether or not such danger actually existed in their time. The matter was never finally resolved: problems relating to this rule continued to appear in the responsa literature of almost every generation. In the fifteenth century Solomon ben Simeon Duran (Rashbash) maintained that a full discussion of the law was necessary, despite its unambiguous formulation in the Talmud, 'because times change, so that novel circumstances that have not occurred in a thousand years can arise very quickly; in our times we see new misfortunes and new dangers constantly arising for those who travel by sea and on land'. His conclusion, cited as binding in *Shulḥan arukh*, is that the wife is not compelled to accompany her husband to Israel by land if she lives anywhere west of Alexandria, but that she may he compelled to travel by sea in the summer 'provided there are no pirates'—a provision leaving the door ajar for subsequent litigation. As for his own personal experience: 'This case has already come before me, and I have adjudicated several times that we do not enforce going up.'[11]

In the sixteenth century Samuel de Medina used the danger principle as the basis for an a fortiori argument relating to a different issue. Asked whether

---

[10] Tosafot *Ket.* 110b, *hu*; for other examples of tosafistic determinations that talmudic rulings were not applicable in their time, see Efraim Elimelech Urbach, *The Tosafists: Their History, Writings, and Methods* [Ba'alei hatosafot: toldoteihem, ḥibureihem, ushitatam] (Jerusalem, 1968), 50, 79, 151–2, 203, 290, 320–1; Jacob Katz, 'Alterations in the Time of the Evening Service (Ma'ariv): An Example of the Interrelationship between Religious Customs and their Social Background', in id., *Divine Law in Human Hands: Case Studies in Halakhic Flexibility* (Jerusalem, 1998), 88–127; id., *Exclusiveness and Tolerance: Jewish–Gentile Relations in Medieval and Modern Times* (New York, 1962), 30.

[11] Solomon ben Simeon Duran, in Schepansky, *The Land of Israel in the Responsa Literature*, i. 129–32; cf. Joseph Karo, *Beit yosef* and *Shulḥan arukh*, 'Even ha'ezer', 75.

a mother's deathbed command to transfer her body for burial in Palestine should be enforced, he replied: 'If in the matter of settling in the land, the hazard of travel is sufficient to nullify the law so that we do not compel either the husband or wife . . . how much more in regard to the present matter of burial is the fact of danger to the living and the dead sufficient to justify refraining from any action.'[12]

But this was not all. One of the Tosafists, Hayim ben Hananel Hakohen, went considerably beyond the rationale of 'dangers of the journey' in arguing for the unenforceability of the talmudic law. He stated that in his own time, the late twelfth century, 'living in the Land of Israel is not a religious obligation at all, owing to the difficulty or impossibility of fulfilling many of the precepts attached to the soil'.[13] Here is an unmistakable reversal of the tannaitic hierarchy of values: according to Hayim ben Hananel, the importance of living in the Land of Israel had diminished to the point where it was outweighed by other considerations. The talmudic rule was abrogated not because of conditions that might readily be changed, such as the geographical location of the couple or the peacefulness of the region, but because of the very nature of Jewish life itself.

Hayim ben Hananel's statement caused considerable consternation among later authorities, and the majority did not accept it as normative.[14]

[12] Samuel de Medina, in Schepansky, *The Land of Israel in the Responsa Literature*, i. 439. In this responsum, Medina reviewed the widely differing positions recorded in the rabbinic literature on the value of burial in the Land of Israel for one who lived and died outside the land. This remained a matter of controversy in post-talmudic times. While the halakhah recognized burial in the Land of Israel as important enough to justify disinterment (*Shulḥan arukh*, 'Yoreh de'ah', 363), opposition in principle to the burial in the Land of Israel of someone who had never lived there continued throughout the Middle Ages and can be seen both in the Zohar (e.g. 'Terumah', 2: 141*b*) and in philosophical sources (see Marc Saperstein, 'Selected Passages from Yedaiah Bedersi's Commentary on the Midrashim', in Isadore Twersky [ed.], *Studies in Medieval Jewish History and Literature*, vol. ii [Cambridge, Mass., 1984], 428–9, esp. n. 13).

[13] Tosafot *Ket.* 110*b*, *ḥu*; on Hayim ben Hananel, see Urbach, *The Tosafists* (Heb.), 107–10. Hayim's point, recorded rather elliptically, appears to be that those who lived in the Land of Israel would be liable to punishment for transgression of the commandments that are incumbent on those living in the land, yet were difficult or impossible to observe at the time. Under such circumstances it should not be considered a religious obligation to live there. This is how his words were understood by Hayim Ya'ir Bachrach (*Ḥavot ya'ir* [responsa] [Lemberg: Salat, 1896], no. 210 [110*a*]). Bachrach used the example of going to live in the Land of Israel to clarify his position on the values and perils of studying kabbalah: the analogy *ba lelamed venimtsa lamed* ('it comes to teach, and itself is illuminated [by the item it was intended to explain]'). I am grateful to Professor Isadore Twersky for directing me to this source.

[14] According to Isaiah Horowitz, Hayim ben Hananel's statement is 'the view of an individual, his reason is illogical . . . we need pay no attention to his words' (Horowitz, *Shenei luḥot haberit* [Warsaw, 1852], 'Sha'ar ha'otiyot', *kof*, 1: 234*b*).

Joseph ben Moses of Trani, noting Meir of Rothenburg's repudiation of any distinction between the religious significance of the Land of Israel in the time of the Temple and after the destruction of the Temple, concluded that Meir, the outstanding expert on the Tosafists, did not consider Hayim's statement to be part of the Tosafot, for Meir would surely not have ignored such an important authority as Hayim ben Hananel. Joseph ben Moses concluded that Hayim ben Hananel, like the other Tosafists, recognized only the argument based on danger: the statement was 'the marginal note of a student, bearing no authority at all'.[15]

In short, Joseph ben Moses insisted that it was indeed a mitzvah to live in the Land of Israel, even at the time in which he lived. But this insistence impelled him to formulate the central question in a manner that could not be more lucid and succinct: 'Which mitzvah takes precedence, sustaining one's wife and children or going to live in the Land of Israel and thereby leaving them in hunger and thirst? . . . When you sit and weigh the obligations of these mitzvot, you find that it is more obligatory to remain with one's wife and children and provide for their needs and guide them in the right way and raise them to the study of Torah than to go physically to the Land of Israel.'[16] Again we see the talmudic law not being enforced in a vacuum but weighed in the balance with other vital needs.

The following early sixteenth-century responsum provides another fine example of the dynamic issues impinging upon the decision of whether to implement the rule about the wife's *ketubah*. In this case, a woman went to the court claiming that she wanted to settle in the Land of Israel in order to escape from her sick husband, who was mistreating her and giving away his property to relatives so that there would be nothing left to pay the *ketubah* obligation at his death. It might appear that the situation provided good grounds for enforcing the talmudic law. While the woman's motivation for living in the land was apparently not the purest, all she was asking was that the court grant her the money stipulated in her *ketubah*, to which she would certainly be entitled at the husband's death, before he could succeed in his devious attempt to deprive her. Tam ibn Yahya refused to enforce the law. The husband's sickness meant that he was not unwilling but unable to go, and the rule of compulsion therefore did not apply.

All the more so since he can claim that food is extremely scarce in the Land of Israel and there is not enough to earn a livelihood, and [this is why] he does not want to go

---

[15] Joseph ben Moses of Trani, in Schepansky, *The Land of Israel in the Responsa Literature*, i. 318.
[16] Ibid. 319.

there: this is certainly a legitimate claim. . . . Especially if he is knowledgeable in Torah, we do not compel him, because there is a scarcity of food. One who lives in Israel may leave it in order to study Torah,[17] therefore one who is able to study outside the land is obviously not to be compelled to go there. All the great rabbis of France and Germany relied upon this reason, in addition to the danger of the journey, in not going to Israel. I have a tradition that this is why the rabbis of Babylonia did not go. And perhaps this is why Maimonides did not, even though he was close to Israel and safe caravans were readily available to travel there from Egypt [where Maimonides was living] . . . . He would not have been able to provide for himself in accordance with his dignity in the Land of Israel and also to study Torah.[18]

This passage goes beyond the immediate case at hand, not only justifying the refusal to enforce the talmudic law but explaining the historical reality of great centres of Jewish learning led by pious scholars who theoretically could have moved to the Holy Land but chose not to. Ibn Yahya then cited one final reason for his unwillingness to act in the present case. After a detailed discussion of the Tosafot, including the statement of Hayim ben Hananel, he concluded: 'since there is a dispute among the giants, we will not act to compel the husband to divorce her and pay'.[19]

In short, the undisputed tannaitic ruling intended to promote settlement of the Land of Israel cannot be assumed to have governed Jewish life in all ages. While it was indeed sometimes enforced,[20] other interests relating to

---

[17] See BT *AZ* 13*a* (a priest may incur ritual impurity by leaving the Land of Israel in order to study Torah); Maimonides, *Mishneh torah*, 'Laws of Kings and Their Wars', 5: 9. Meir of Rothenburg, asked why a group of French rabbis who had emigrated to Palestine later commanded their sons to return to Europe, replied that 'they were unable to engage in Torah because they were compelled to work so hard to provide physical sustenance, and, as there was no learning, the Jews there were not expert in the details of the commandments' (in Schepansky, *The Land of Israel in the Responsa Literature*, i. 120).

[18] Tam ibn Yahya, in Schepansky, *The Land of Israel in the Responsa Literature*, i. 363. Compare Solomon ben Simeon Duran's listing of all the values that, in his view, outweigh the precept of living in the Holy Land: 'One is not obligated to emigrate to Israel if there are serious obstacles, for those who live there are permitted to leave in order to marry or to study Torah. . . . This is all the more true if a husband wants to go and his wife does not, and he would have to divorce her, and perhaps he would not find a wife there, or would find one demanding too much money, as is fashionable these days; or if the man has children and cannot bring them and would leave them orphans. Or if he cannot study Torah there on an appropriate level, while he can outside the land. Similarly, if he can support himself outside Israel but not there, or if he would have to borrow money to pay the expenses of his voyage. Neither the Torah nor the sages have obligated a man to become a beggar in order to go to the land of Israel. . . . All of these reasons have prevented many great Jews from moving there' (in Schepansky, *The Land of Israel in the Responsa Literature*, i. 133; cf. iii. 43).   [19] Ibid. i. 363.

[20] For a literary example, see Shmuel Yosef Agnon, *In the Heart of the Seas*, trans. I. M. Lask (New York, 1948).

the institution of marriage and its contractual obligations, intellectual aspirations, economic realities, and a judicial reluctance to intervene in a highly controversial and problematic matter, often made the talmudic law a dead letter.[21]

'Whoever dwells outside the land is as one who has no God'

The second statement, also from *Ketubot* 110*b*, raises completely different problems. This statement has no halakhic significance, yet it is quoted in virtually every discussion of the Land of Israel in medieval and early modern Hebrew literature: 'Whoever dwells in the land of Israel is as one who has a God, and whoever dwells outside the land is as one who has no God.' Here too, a tension is generated between important values. On the one hand, there is the centrality of the Land of Israel for Jewish religious experience; on the other hand, there is the universality of God and the danger of implying that access to God is limited to one geographical location. This is compounded by the problems of undermining the religious status of pious Jews who were born, lived, and died in the diaspora. Indeed, the statement is challenged immediately in the Talmud itself: 'Does one who lives outside the land really have no God?' It is as if some later Babylonian rabbi argued that the original formulation was too extreme, that the second-century rabbis had been carried away with their own rhetoric. It is appropriate to assert that God has a special relationship with the Land of Israel, but it is not appropriate to say that God has no relationship with other lands.[22] Therefore a more moderate form was suggested: 'Whoever dwells outside the land is as one who worships

---

[21] There were also cases in which a husband who decided to live in the Land of Israel and leave his reluctant wife behind decided to pay the amount of his wife's *ketubah*, apparently without rabbinical mandate, because he felt it was the right thing to do: see the letter written from Safed by Shlomel of Dresnitz, Moravia: 'I divorced my wife, because she did not want to go with me, and I gave her everything that was due to her according to the Ketubah' (in Franz Kobler [ed.], *Letters of Jews Through the Ages*, 2 vols. [New York, 1978], ii. 394 [I owe this reference to an anonymous reviewer of this book for the Littman Library]).

[22] This is how Samuel Edeles (Maharsha) understood the objection (see Edeles, *Ḥidushei agadot al kol shitat hatalmud* [novellae on talmudic aggadot] [Lublin, 1627] on BT *Ket.* 110*b*). According to the preacher Joseph ben Hayim Zarfati of Adrianople, the objection came from one who understood the statement literally to mean that those who live outside the land have no God, and protested that 'this is something that reason cannot tolerate'. Zarfati's own interpretation of the statement, influenced by Nahmanides, was that God immediately punishes the sins of those who dwell in the land of Israel because of the holiness of the land, whereas the sins performed on impure soil are not immediately punished: 'This is why those who dwell in the land appear to have a God watching over them, while those outside the land do not' (Joseph ben Hayim Zarfati, *Yad yosef* [sermons] [Amsterdam, 1700], 'Vayeḥi', 86*d*).

idols.' This way, at least the possibility of a relationship with God in the diaspora is not denied.

Modifications were occasionally made in quoting these statements. Commenting on Genesis 17: 8, Rashi wrote 'and *there* I will be to them as God, but an *Israelite* who dwells outside the land is as one who has no God'. In the context of God's promise to Abraham, 'whoever' has been changed to 'Israelite' without any obvious justification. In this formulation, it is clear that the statement did not apply to Rashi's Christian neighbours. But what about contemporary Jews? Commenting on Leviticus 25: 38, the verse that the Talmud adduced as the basis for its aggadic statement, Rashi ignored the talmudic exegesis and followed the halakhic *midrash Sifra*: 'To whoever dwells in the land, I am as God, but whoever departs from it is as one who worships idols.' In this view, it is emigrating from the Holy Land, not being born and living one's life in the diaspora, that is presented as sinful.

Maimonides also followed the *Sifra* formulation in *Mishneh torah*: 'Whoever departs from the land [of Israel] is as one who worships idols.'[23] In the sixteenth century Yom Tov ben Moses Zahalon defended this alteration not on textual but on logical, or one might say ideological, grounds:

> Maimonides' intent was to defend the merit of those who dwell outside the land. He did not want to say that all who lived outside the land are, as it were, Godless; he therefore wrote that the talmudic statement was not intended to apply to one who lived [in the diaspora] as his ancestors had since the time they were expelled from holy soil and compelled through divine decree to live outside the land. What was he to do? Of such a person it is not said: 'He must not live outside the land'; if it were, what should we say about all the Jews, and especially our sainted rabbis, who have lived in the diaspora?[24]

In other words, Maimonides chose the *Sifra* formulation because the implications of the talmudic statement were distasteful: how could he possibly codify the assertion that all the great diaspora rabbis were like idolaters? But there is more than this in Zahalon's comment; indeed, he seems to be attributing a critical historical sense to Maimonides' halakhic technique. The original talmudic statement had been made by a Palestinian rabbi to a Palestinian audience. The problem it addressed had actually been as Maimonides under-

---

[23] Maimonides, *Mishneh torah*, 'Laws of Kings and Their Wars', 5: 12; cf. Bezalel ben Abraham Ashkenazi, who combines both formulations: 'whoever dwells outside the land—who leaves the land of Israel to live outside it—is as one who has no God' (*Shitah mekubetset: asefat zekenim, vehu ḥidushei masekhet ketubot* [novellae on Babylonian Talmud *Ketubot*] [Constantinople, 1738], on BT *Ket.* 110*b*).

[24] Zahalon, in Schepansky, *The Land of Israel in the Responsa Literature*, i. 403.

stood it: leaving the Land of Israel. Simply to have reproduced verbatim the original wording in his medieval diaspora context would have been to falsify its intent, by equating a Jew born in the diaspora who decided to remain there with a Jew born in the Land of Israel who decided to leave it. What Zahalon appears to be arguing is that Maimonides abandoned the wording of the talmudic statement in order to convey its original intent most effectively—and accurately—to the audience he was addressing.

Despite Maimonides however, it was in its original form that the statement was most frequently cited in subsequent literature: 'Whoever *dwells* outside the land is as one who has no God.' This was generally associated with the doctrine that God has a special providential relationship with the Land of Israel. This assertion, with strong roots in the classical texts of the tradition—'a land which the Lord your God looks after; on which the Lord your God always keeps His eye' (Deut. 11: 12); 'the Land of Israel is watered by the Holy One praised be He Himself, the rest of the world through an emissary' (BT *Ta'an.* 10a)—was not particularly controversial, but the conclusions drawn from this premise could point in markedly different directions, depending on the theory of divine providence being used.

Some Jews writing in the philosophical tradition applied the Maimonidean doctrine that God's providential protection of any individual is directly proportional to that individual's intellectual apprehension of God.[25] This was combined with the assumption—unquestioned by medieval Jews—that the Land of Israel possessed a climate and air quality uniquely conducive to intellectual activity.[26] Its inhabitants were therefore likely to have reached a higher level of intellectual perfection than the inhabitants of other lands, and consequently there would be greater providential attention directed to the Land of Israel. The difference, however, was not absolute but relative. A clear expression of this view is given in the early fourteenth century by Yedaiah Bedersi, in his discussion of a passage from *Sifrei* on Deuteronomy 11: 12. According to Yedaiah:

---

[25] Moses Maimonides, *Guide for the Perplexed*, 3: 51 (trans. and ed. M. Friedländer, 3 vols. in 1 [New York, 1946], iii. 288–91). On this rather controversial doctrine, see Zevi Diesendruck, 'Samuel and Moses ibn Tibbon on Maimonides' Theory of Providence', *Hebrew Union College Annual*, 11 (1936), 341–66; Alvin Reines, 'Maimonides' Concepts of Providence and Theodicy', *Hebrew Union College Annual*, 43 (1972), esp. 188–94.

[26] This view, supported by the talmudic statement 'The air of the land of Israel makes one wise' (BT *BB* 158b), was integrated into a general theory of the relationship between climate and national character (see Shalom Rosenberg, 'The Link to the Land of Israel in Jewish Thought: A Clash of Perspectives', in Lawrence Hoffman [ed.], *The Land of Israel: Jewish Perspectives* [Notre Dame, Ind., 1986], 150–3).

[The Bible and the rabbis speak] as if to indicate that the part of the world most providentially supervised is the Land of Israel, but the reason for this degree of providence is the high status of its inhabitants, who are watched over by God more than any other nation . . . for the degree of providence is proportional to the degree of knowledge and guidance.[27]

The combination of appropriate conditions for intellectual activity (climate and air) and proper guidance for this activity (the Torah) makes Jews living in the Land of Israel capable of perfecting their souls and attaining a direct providential relationship with God.

It is against this background that the talmudic statement is to be understood. In a different context, Yedaiah himself made the connection: 'the superior status of that land and its air is well known, as the rabbis said: "The air of the Land of Israel makes one wise", and "Whoever lives outside the land is as one who has no God", and it is therefore called "the place which the Lord has chosen".'[28] This formulation is rather laconic, omitting the critical doctrine of intellectual apprehension and divine providence, as if it could be assumed that the reader was already familiar with the argument linking the two statements. A fuller statement of the entire theory was given by Abraham Bibago in the fifteenth century:

The reason why they said that whoever lives outside the land is as one who has no God is that such a person will not have a balanced temperament, and consequently his intellect will not be settled, as it would be with a proper corporeal environment. If a person's temperament is not appropriate, he will resist philosophical enlightenment. . . . This is why one who dwells outside the land is as one who has no God. . . . For the Land of Israel is moderate for its inhabitants, situated in the fourth climate, in the centre of the inhabited world; those who are born there and live there will not be frozen by cold nor scorched by heat; their temperament will therefore be perfect for rational speculation, and their intellect clean and pure.[29]

This does not imply that it is impossible for anyone outside the Land of Israel

[27] Yedaiah Bedersi, Commentary on the midrashim (Heb.) (De Rossi Hebrew MS 222, Palatina Library, Parma) on *Sifrei* on Deut. 11: 12; see also: 'His eyes roam throughout the entire world, but His providence is revealed and seen in the Land of Israel, because of the degree of preparation the air affords to its inhabitants' (Joel ibn Shu'eib, *Olat shabat* [sermons] [Venice, 1577; repr. Jerusalem, 1973], 129*a*).

[28] Yedaiah Bedersi, Commentary on the midrashim (Heb.) (Hebrew MS 738.3, National Library of France, Paris), on *Genesis Rabbah* 96: 5 (fos. 208ᵛ–209ʳ); see Saperstein, 'Selected Passages from Yedaiah Bedersi's Commentary on the Midrashim', 424–5, 428–9.

[29] Abraham Bibago, *Derekh emunah* [The Way of Faith] (Constantinople, 1522; offprint edn. Jerusalem, 1970), 94*c–d*.

to attain philosophical enlightenment and thereby merit God's providential attention. Rather, the conditions outside the land are more difficult, fewer will reach the aspired level, and therefore, in general, those living in the diaspora will be more likely to be 'as one who has no God'.

A very different explanation of the uniqueness of the Land of Israel, not dependent on the controversial Maimonidean doctrine of providence, was widely accepted. In the rabbinic formulation, the other lands were under the jurisdiction of heavenly 'princes' (*sarim*) while the Land of Israel was governed directly by God. A medieval reformulation of this idea taught that the events occurring outside the Land of Israel were part of the ordinary pattern of nature, the end result of a long chain of intermediate causes in which the stars were generally considered to have a dominant role. The Land of Israel was different: there God acted directly, not through the stars.

Solomon ben Adret (Rashba) of Barcelona was asked for a formal responsum on 'Whoever dwells outside the land is as one who has no God'.[30] Following his teacher Nahmanides (Moses ben Nahman, Ramban), he formulated the fundamental, metaphysical difference between the Land of Israel and the other lands in this manner: '[God] did not give the land [of Israel] and the people [of Israel] to [the jurisdiction of] a star or to one of the heavenly princes whom He apportioned to all the [other] nations.... Our land is perpetually chosen, for it is not handed over to an emissary, but to God's own providence.'[31] For some writers, therefore, merely living in a foreign land under the dominion of 'princes' or stars was enough to explain the rabbinic comparison with Godlessness.[32]

Others carried the implications even further. Living under the intermediaries which God ordained to govern the affairs of the world might be viewed

---

[30] Solomon ben Adret, *She'elot uteshuvot harashba* [responsa], 7 vols. in 4 (Benei Berak, 1958–9), i, no. 134.

[31] Solomon ben Adret, *Ḥidushei harashba al agadot hashas* [novellae on the talmudic aggadot], ed. Shalom Meshulam Weinberger (Jerusalem, 1966), 67; cf. Nahmanides on Lev. 18: 25; id., 'Discourse on Rosh Hashanah', in id., *Ramban: Writings and Discourses*, ed. and trans. Charles Ber Chavel, 2 vols. (New York, 1978), i. 350–51; *Zohar*, 'Lekh lekha', 1: 78a.

[32] See e.g. Isaiah Pinto, in Jacob ibn Habib, *Ein ya'akov ... im kol hamefarshim* [anthology of talmudic aggadot], 5 vols. in 3 (Vilna, 1883–90; repr. Jerusalem, 1964–72), on BT *Ket.* 110b; Abraham Bornstein, in Schepansky, *The Land of Israel in the Responsa Literature*, iii. 42. According to the Maharal of Prague, 'it means that he has no God to aid and to help him through a divine act, for the Land of Israel is especially sought out, while the other lands are the portion of the angels, and whoever dwells outside the land, it is as if he had departed from the dominion of the Holy One, God forbid!' (Judah Leib ben Bezalel of Prague, *Gur aryeh* [super-commentary on Rashi's *Commentary on the Torah*], on Gen. 17: 8, in *Treasury of Torah Commentators* [Otsar mefarshei hatorah], 2 vols. [Jerusalem, 1973], i. 48a).

as diminishing the efficacy of prayer. This was the conclusion of Nissim ben Reuben Gerondi in a sermon:

'Whoever dwells outside the land is as one who has no God.' This is because the other lands of the idolaters are given over to the government of the heavenly princes, which cannot be changed except through a miracle . . . . Consequently, the prayer of one who dwells outside the land and is under [the jurisdiction of] a constellation or star is not heard as much [*ein tefilato nishma'at kol kakh*] as if he were in the Land of Israel, which is not under the governance of any ruler but God Himself.[33]

An even more extreme formulation, is attributed by a later author to 'the Yalkut':

'Whoever dwells in the Land of Israel is as one who has a God', for he prays to God and God hears his prayer; he is not under [the jurisdiction of] a constellation, but under the power of the Holy One Himself. But 'whoever dwells outside the land is as one who has no God', for even when he prays to God, God does not hear his prayer, as he is under [the jurisdiction of] princes and constellations.[34]

It would be hard to find a more radical theological negation of the diaspora in post-talmudic literature.

The statement could be extended beyond prayer to all the commandments. It was not merely that certain commandments applied exclusively to the Land of Israel, although certain commentators did, in fact, use this fact in their interpretations.[35] The more powerful doctrine held that even those commandments not dependent on the land, those that could be observed in the diaspora, were somehow incomplete when performed outside the Land of Israel. Based on statements of the rabbinic literature, this doctrine was given classical formulation by Nahmanides in two important passages.

In commenting on Leviticus 18: 25, Nahmanides addressed the notion that the Land of Israel expels its inhabitants because of sexual misconduct. He began by discussing the distinctiveness of the Land of Israel in familiar terms: the other nations are assigned to their own constellations, which in turn are overseen by special angels, but the Land of Israel is 'the Estate of the Eternal', subject to no intermediate power but only to God. This is why

---

[33] Nissim ben Reuben Gerondi, *Derashot haran lerabenu nisim ben reuven gerondi* [sermons], ed. Leon Feldman (Jerusalem, 1974), 54.

[34] Samuel Shalem, in Schepansky, *The Land of Israel in the Responsa Literature*, iii. 609. Shalem referred to his source simply as 'the Yalkut', probably but not explicitly *Yalkut shimoni* (a late collection of rabbinic statements arranged according to biblical verses). Schepansky wrote: 'I have not found his source in the Yalkut' (*The Land of Israel in the Responsa Literature*, iii. 609, n. 36).

[35] e.g. Isaiah Pinto, in Ibn Habib, *Ein ya'akov*, on BT Ket. 110b.

the land is unable to tolerate idolatry, the worship of intermediate beings, or the sexual immorality so often associated with it. Even nations that practise idolatry with impunity outside the land are punished for the very same actions when they dwell within it (2 Kings 17: 26). After quoting several additional rabbinic statements to this effect, he continued:

This is the meaning of the saying of the rabbis: 'Whoever dwells outside the land is as one who has no God.' In the Tosefta of tractate *Avodah zarah*, the rabbis said: 'When you are in the land of Canaan, I am your God; when you are not in the land of Canaan, I am, so to speak [*kiveyakhol*], not your God.' . . . On this basis the rabbis said in *Sifrei*: 'And you perish quickly from off the good land' (Deut. 11: 17). Although I banish you from the land to outside the land, you should make yourselves distinct [*metsuyanim*] by the commandments, so that when you return they shall not be novelties to you. . . . And so did the prophet Jeremiah say: 'Erect markers' [*tsiyunim*] (Jer. 31: 21). These are the commandments, by which Israel is made distinct. . . . For the essence of the commandments [*ikar hamitsvot*] is for those dwelling in the land of God. Therefore the Rabbis said in *Sifrei* . . . 'Dwelling in the Land of Israel is of equal importance to all the commandments of the Torah.'

There is much in this passage that Nahmanides left unexplained.[36] Most important for our purposes is the conclusion drawn from the premise of

---

[36] In particular, the kabbalistic assumptions with which Nahmanides seems to be working here are not made explicit. Jerohom Perelmann noted Nahmanides' doctrine, but left it without further comment because 'we do not deal with esoteric teachings [*ein lanu esek banistarot*]' (Perelmann, in Schepansky, *The Land of Israel in the Responsa Literature*, iii. 61). There seems to be a reluctance among certain authors to explore the implications of this doctrine fully (see Judah ben Samuel Rosanes, *Parashat derakhim* [sermons] [Warsaw, 1871], no. 22 [91*b*]). On the other hand, note the rhapsodic praise of Nahmanides' teaching by the sixteenth-century Salonika preacher Solomon ben Isaac Levi: 'Woe to the eyes that see this and the ears that hear this and do not make for themselves wings like a dove to fly and dwell in the Holy Land as he himself [Nahmanides] did; not only did he preach beautifully, he fulfilled what he preached. leaving his home and his portion [in Spain] and making his way to Jerusalem' (Solomon ben Isaac Levi, *Divrei shelomoh* [sermons] [Venice, 1596; repr. Brooklyn, 1993], 73*a*).

For modern treatments of this important aspect of Nahmanides' thought (which he reiterated in a climactic passage in his 'Sermon for Rosh Hashanah'), see Dov Rappel, 'Nahmanides on Exile and Redemption' (Heb.), *Ma'ayanot*, 7 (1960), 107. According to Newman, 'his thesis is that none of the laws of Judaism have any intrinsic validity outside *Erets Yisra'el*' (Aryeh Newman, 'The Centrality of Erets Yisra'el in Nachmanides', *Tradition*, 10 [1968–9], 24). No discussion that I am aware of has noted the conflict between this and another striking Nahmanidean doctrine, discussed in detail in Chapter 11: that Judaism does not depend upon the future advent of the messiah or the restoration of the Jewish people to the Land of Israel, that the essence of the Torah would be unaffected if the Jewish people were to remain permanently in its exile, and that indeed the ultimate reward of immortality for the soul may be greater when the commandments are observed in *galut* than would be the case when they are observed in Israel under the messianic kingdom (see Nahmanides, 'Disputation', in id.,

God's special providential relationship with the land. The commandments performed in exile have little intrinsic importance: they have an instrumental value, preserving Jewish distinctiveness and keeping those who perform them in practice for when they return to the land and perform them as they were intended to be. In short, the very same actions have a totally different significance when they are performed upon the 'Estate of the Eternal'. A Jew outside the land is as one who has no God, because the commandments he performs, mediated through the long chain of intermediate causes, have little direct effect upon the Godhead.

Such conclusions, which appear to make the efficacy of prayer or the value of the mitzvot dependent upon geographical location rather than on inner, spiritual factors, were abhorrent to other Jewish thinkers. The problems inherent in the talmudic assertion are evident in hasidic literature, where several striking reinterpretations use various rhetorical techniques to nullify the simple meaning and to make the highest spiritual status available to Jews outside the land. For example, the following was attributed to the Ba'al Shem Tov by his disciple, Jacob Joseph of Polonnoye:

> I heard from my teacher that wherever a person is in his thought, there he is indeed. If he dwells outside the land, but yearns and thinks of the Land of Israel constantly, he is similar [*domeh*] to one who has no God, but he actually has one. . . . This is not the case if he is in the Land of Israel, but his status and livelihood are outside the land, for he will always be thinking of such matters. . . . Such a person is similar to one who has a God, but in reality, he has none, for his thought is outside the land.[37]

This interpretation focuses on the use of the word *domeh*. The rabbis did not say, 'Whoever dwells outside the land has no God', but 'is as one' or 'appears like one who has no God'. According to the Ba'al Shem Tov, the similarity is one only of appearance.

A similar interpretation is given by Elimelekh of Lyzhansk:

> A person who wants his prayer to be heard must focus his thought as if he were praying in the Land of Israel, with the Temple rebuilt and the altar set in its proper place. . . . This is the meaning of 'whoever dwells in the Land of Israel', namely,

---

Ramban: Writings and Discourses, ii. 672–3; id., 'The Book of Redemption', ibid. 606–7). Both doctrines are presented without any indication of the tension between them in Yitzhak Baer, *A History of the Jews in Christian Spain*, 2 vols. (Philadelphia, 1961–6), i. 248.

[37] Jacob Joseph of Polonnoye, *Ben porat yosef* [homiletical comments on the Torah] (Piotrków Trybunalski, 1883; repr. New York, 1970), 87b; cf. Louis Jacobs, *Hasidic Thought* (New York, 1976), 209.

whoever imagines to himself that he is standing in the Land of Israel: through this exercise, he attains clarity in prayer. 'Is as one who has a God' means he is like one who investigates God's exaltedness in order to apprehend the Creator through His works, namely, the heavenly bodies in their courses. And 'whoever dwells outside the land', who does not conduct himself during his prayer in this manner, 'is as one who has no God', meaning, he is like one who does not investigate the world around him in order to know that there is a God.[38]

In both these interpretations, the Land of Israel remains central—as an ideal—but the distinction between physically living in the land and living outside it has been abandoned for a spiritual distinction. It is the ability to think of the Land of Israel and to imagine oneself praying in the reconstructed Temple, no matter where one happens to be living, that is now critical.

A more radical spiritualization of the Land of Israel, not explicitly applied to this statement but clearly in the same tradition, was proposed by Menahem Nahum of Chernobyl in his homiletical interpretations of selected aggadot:

Even though the physical Land of Israel exists, its essence is a spiritual matter, namely, the life force coming from God. Although we are outside the land, we nevertheless have an aspect of the Land of Israel. . . . for in every house of worship and study, the life force of the Land of Israel is emanated from God. Therefore the sages said: 'Houses of study and worship are destined to stand in the Land of Israel' [BT *Meg.* 29*a*], for they themselves are an aspect of the vitality of the Land of Israel. Understand this. If so, one who stands in the house of worship or study and prays in words suffused with thought is indeed in the Land of Israel, that is, in the life force of the creator. But if a person thinks vain thoughts . . . then even though his body is in the house of worship, his essential part, which is his thought, is not in 'the Land of Israel', namely the house of worship.[39]

---

[38] Elimelekh of Lyzhansk, *No'am elimelekh* [homilies on the Torah], ed. Gedalyah Nigal (Jerusalem, 1978), 32–3.

[39] Menahem Nahum of Chernobyl, *Yesamaḥ lev: ḥidushei agadot hashas* [novellae on talmudic aggadot] (Slavuta, 1798), 20*b*–*c* (on BT *Ket.*) (I am grateful to Professor Arthur Green for bringing this source to my attention); cf. Ephraim Luntshitz, *Keli yakar* (Lemberg, 1864), on Deut. 11: 21, which may be the source of this passage. Joseph Perl referred to this passage in his parody *Megaleh temirin* [The Revealer of Secrets] (Vienna, 1819), letter 128 (p. 46*b* n. 2); see Dov Taylor, *Joseph Perl's Revealer of Secrets: The First Hebrew Novel* (Boulder, Colo., 1997), 211. For Perl's critique of the hasidic spiritualization of the Land of Israel, see Tovah Cohen, 'Hasidism and the Land of Israel: An Additional Aspect of the Satire in *The Revealer of Secrets*' (Heb.), *Tarbiz*, 48 (1979), 332–40. The same passage can also seem to be in the background of Shmuel Yosef Agnon's story 'The Emissary from the Land of Israel' (Heb.), where, to the amazement of everyone, the magnificent *beit midrash* of an arrogant Polish community flies away in literal fulfilment of the aggadah that had been spiritualized by Menahem Nahum of Chernobyl (Agnon, *The Complete Stories of Shmuel Yosef Agnon* [Kol sipurav shel

Here a further step has been taken. It is not even necessary to imagine oneself being in the Land of Israel or to yearn for it, but merely to be in the synagogue and to pray with devotion and purity of thought. This in itself constitutes 'being in the Land of Israel'.

Perhaps the most astonishing reinterpretation of the statement is attributed to the Ba'al Shem Tov by Benjamin ben Aaron of Zalosce. According to this view, the rabbis were not referring to the Land of Israel at all, but rather to two spiritual levels to be found in different Jews. First, there is the Jew who is bound by his terrestrial nature (*artsiyut*), by his corporeality: this is the one who 'dwells in the land'. He thinks that he worships God fully and completely, that there is nothing lacking in his service. But he thinks this only because he fails to recognize the greatness of the Creator. In this way, 'one who lives in the land—that is, ensconced in his corporeality—imagines himself [another interpretation of *domeh*, based on the Hebrew word for 'imagination', *dimayon*] to have a God', but in reality he has no God at all and has not even begun the appropriate service of God.

The opposite is true of the Jew who lives 'outside his terrestrial nature' (*ḥuts la'arets*).[40] He understands the greatness of God and realizes that he has not even begun to serve him properly. As his thought cleaves to God's exalted nature, he is constantly abashed by the shortcomings of his own service measured against the standard of perfect love and awe. This man, who lives 'outside the land', imagines that he has no God, but in reality he does have God within him.[41] In this interpretation, the physical Land of Israel has totally disappeared, even as an ideal. Dwelling 'in the land' has become a negative characterization, dwelling 'outside the land' a positive one. The statement is transformed into a paradox emphasizing the distance between appearance

shemu'el yosef agnon] [Berlin, 1931], ii. 212–23). Another example of hasidic de-emphasis of the geographical Land of Israel is Nahman of Bratslav's claim that 'a Jew may purify the atmosphere of a place by praying there, and he may then breathe holy air just as he does in the Land of Israel' (Nahman of Bratslav, *Likutei moharan*, 2 vols in 1 [Benei Berak, 1965], i. 44; see also ii. 40).

[40] This striking reinterpretation of the phrase is also found in the thirteenth-century kabbalist Abraham Abulafia (see Moshe Idel, 'The Land of Israel in Medieval Kabbalah', in Hoffman [ed.], *The Land of Israel*, 179).

[41] Benjamin ben Aaron of Zalosce, *Amtaḥat binyamin: be'ur kohelet* [commentary on Ecclesiastes] (Minkowitz, 1796), 3c (on Eccles. 1: 5). According to this report, the Ba'al Shem Tov cited the aggadah as if the word 'Israel' did not appear and it read simply: 'Whoever dwells in the land is as one who has a God'. With this interpretation of *erets*, compare the striking allegory by Elimelekh of Lyzhansk: God's command to send forth men to scout out the land of Canaan (*erets kena'an*) means that the proper way to serve the Creator is for man to look carefully at his own corporeality and earthiness (*artsiyut*) and thereby to subdue (*lehakhnia*, from the same root as *kena'an*) it (*No'am elimelekh*, 215).

and reality: the ultimate value has nothing to do with one's geographical location, but lies rather in the humble recognition that the human being can never hope to worship God in accordance with his true greatness.

I have traced some of the vicissitudes of two early rabbinic statements affirming the absolute centrality of the Land of Israel and denigrating the value of life in the diaspora and shown how these statements, reverberating in many different contexts of Jewish life and thought, have been used to draw a panoply of conclusions.[42] While some have reaffirmed the centrality of the Land of Israel with all its implications in accordance with the straightforward meaning of the rabbinic pronouncements, others have in effect repudiated the simple meaning, de-emphasizing the significance of the Land of Israel (at least in pre-messianic times) in favour of other important Jewish values.

This is not to suggest that the millennial Jewish attachment to the Land of Israel had little basis in reality. It is, rather, to suggest that beginning with the talmudic period, intellectual and spiritual leaders of the Jewish people had to walk a treacherous tightrope, balancing diverse and sometimes conflicting goals, all of which were in some sense critical to Jewish survival. They had to maintain the importance, indeed the centrality, of the Land of Israel, Jerusalem, and the Temple Mount, without undermining the possibility of continued and creative Jewish life in the diaspora. They had to instil the consciousness that Jewish religious life was somehow incomplete without land and Temple, yet make certain it would remain full and rich enough to merit the loyalties of adherents tempted by powerful rivals. They had to foster yearnings for the land of the Bible, the land that God had chosen, without cultivating the idolatrous worship of soil and stones. While occasionally one element or another got out of balance, the full history of interpretation of rabbinic statements about the land reveals a rather impressive harmonization of these goals.

---

[42] At least three other statements in the same talmudic passage have been similarly controversial and repercussive, and a study of the history of their interpretation and use would reveal other dynamics of the Jewish link with the Land of Israel: 'Israel shall not go up [to the Land of Israel] all together as if surrounded by a wall'; 'The dead outside the land will not be resurrected'; and 'Whoever walks four cubits in the Land of Israel is assured of a place in the world to come' (BT *Ket.* 111a).

CHAPTER THIRTEEN

Messianic Leadership in Jewish History: Movements and Personalities

THE MOST DRAMATIC TESTS of leadership in the history of the Jewish diaspora have come when an individual presented himself as playing a central role in the process that would bring an end to the exile of the diaspora. The messianic figure—whether claiming to be the actual messiah from the line of David or a prophet or forerunner of the messiah—transcended the accepted categories by which authority has been asserted and expressed in post-biblical Jewish life. However rooted in traditional texts and expectations the ideology of the incipient movement may have been, for the individual at its core this claim was by its very nature a radical departure from the norms, a revolutionary challenge to the status quo. This placed the more traditional Jewish leadership, especially the rabbinic authorities, who were structurally bound to a conservative position in society, in a difficult situation.

On the one hand, they wanted to preserve and even strengthen the hope for national redemption through the messiah, the belief that deliverance was on its way, which enabled Jews to persevere in holding the fortress of faith despite the battering rams of oppression and the alluring rewards promised for surrender. On the other hand, established leaders naturally viewed with suspicion any actual figure who by the very nature of his claim would be likely to undermine their own authority and—what was perhaps even more worrying—endanger Jewish status and perhaps even lives by provoking the secular authorities, who almost invariably viewed Jewish messianic claims as political revolt and suppressed them violently and ruthlessly.[1] The appearance of a

---

First published in Marc Saperstein (ed.), *Essential Papers on Messianic Movements and Personalities in Jewish History* (New York: New York University Press, 1992), 1–31, with an extended passage taken from 'A "Ritual Dance of Destruction?"' [review of Harris Lenowitz, *The Jewish Messiahs: From the Galilee to Crown Heights*], *Jewish Quarterly Review*, 90 (1999), 151–8.

[1] Encouraging belief in the imminent advent of the messiah while vehemently condemning belief in an actual messianic figure is powerfully expressed in Maimonides' 'Epistle to Yemen' (in Moses

messianic figure was thus guaranteed to create a situation of deep conflict within the Jewish community and a confrontation of leadership modes, with enormously interesting, if sometimes tragic, implications.

The analysis of messianic movements as a category of Jewish historical experience requires some definition of terms. A 'movement', among other things, requires a programme that will lead to significant change and a group of people prepared to act on the basis of that programme.[2] The subject of this chapter is thus to be distinguished from 'the messianic idea', or 'messianic doctrine', or 'messianic speculation'.[3] Jewish thinkers from antiquity to the present have wrestled with various theoretical questions about the messiah and the messianic age. Was the date of the coming of the messiah programmed into history and encoded in classical texts? If so, what was that date? Could human actions influence the coming of the messiah? If so, what actions? Could the signs of imminent advent be detected in historical events? Was suffering and bloodshed an integral part of the messianic scenario? How could the true messiah be recognized? What effect would the messianic advent have on the Gentile nations of the world? Would history and the natural order be fundamentally different after the messiah came? What was the relationship between the messianic age, the resurrection, and the spiritual reward (or punishment) of the soul?[4]

Such questions have produced a considerable body of literature, but these

Maimonides, *Crisis and Leadership: Epistles of Maimonides*, trans. and ed. Abraham Halkin and David Hartman [Philadelphia, 1993], 96, 123–7).

[2] See Rudolph Heberle and Joseph Gusfield, 'Social Movements', in David L. Sills and Robert K. Merton (eds.), *International Encyclopedia of the Social Sciences*, 17 vols. (New York, 1968), xiv, esp. 438–9; cf. Bernard D. Weinryb, *The Jews of Poland: A Social and Economic History of the Jewish Community in Poland from 1000 to 1800* (Philadelphia, 1973), 366 n. 1 (a corrective statement on this point which pushes it too far); Moshe Idel, introduction to Aaron Ze'ev Aescoly, *Jewish Messianic Movements: Sources and Documents on Messianism in Jewish History* [Hatenuot hameshiḥiyot beyisra'el: otsar hamekorot vehate'udot] (Jerusalem, 1988), 11.

[3] Many of the best-known general treatments of Jewish messianism available in English have focused on these dimensions (e.g. Abba Hillel Silver, *A History of Messianic Speculation in Israel* [New York, 1927]; Joseph Sarachek, *The Doctrine of the Messiah in Medieval Jewish Literature* [New York, 1932]; Joseph Klausner, *The Messianic Idea in Israel from its Beginnings to the Completion of the Mishnah* [New York, 1955]; Gershom Scholem, *The Messianic Idea in Judaism and Other Essays on Jewish Spirituality* [New York, 1971]). Collections of textual materials in English, such as Raphael Patai (ed.), *The Messiah Texts* (New York, 1979), also tend to focus on ideas rather than movements or personalities. An exception is Harris Lenowitz, *The Jewish Messiahs: From the Galilee to Crown Heights* (Oxford, 1998).

[4] For a fuller discussion of some of these questions, see Eliezer Schweid, 'Jewish Messianism', in Marc Saperstein (ed.), *Essential Papers on Messianic Movements and Personalities in Jewish History* (New York, 1992), 53–70.

speculations, the indulgence of thinkers pondering their books in serenity and solitude, were often devoid of direct, practical social, political, or even religious consequences. The answers may have been influenced by earlier expressions of messianic activism, and they may in turn have influenced the course of subsequent movements, but unless these doctrines were expounded in connection with a call to act, functioning as the ideology of a movement, they are beyond the purview of the present discussion. Thus the voluminous scholarly literature concerning teachings about the messiah and the messianic age in the Pseudepigrapha, the Dead Sea Scrolls, the Talmud, and other works of rabbinic literature; Sa'adyah Gaon, Maimonides, Abravanel, the Maharal of Prague, and other medieval thinkers; apocalyptic works that interpret historical events as part of some eschatological scenario, literary works that express a longing for the messiah to put an end to the exile—all of these will figure only indirectly in the present chapter.

In addition to a programme for action, a movement requires a response from within the broader society, a group of people who attempt to reorient their behaviour in accordance with the programme. When an exotic individual made messianic claims or announced that the messiah would soon come, we must look for evidence of his impact, evidence of Jews who committed themselves to implement the leader's instructions. The broader the segment of the population that supported the programme and acted on it and the longer the group defined itself by its loyalty to those who enunciated the programme, the stronger the case for considering it a true social movement.

It is often difficult to reach a definitive judgement about the responses to a messianic claim because of the limited extant sources. The thirteenth-century mystic Abraham Abulafia may be considered a messianic personality. His own writings show that he thought of himself in (rather unconventional) messianic terms, but we know little about the possibility of an incipient Abulafian 'movement' beyond the concession by a leading contemporary rabbi, Solomon ben Adret (Rashba), that Abulafia 'seduced some Jews with his lies', making it necessary for the rabbi to act.[5] Another messianic

---

[5] See Abraham Berger, 'The Messianic Self-Consciousness of Abraham Abulafia: A Tentative Evaluation', in Saperstein (ed.), *Essential Papers on Messianic Movements*, 250–5; cf. Moshe Idel, *The Mystical Experience in Abraham Abulafia* (Albany, NY, 1988), 3; id., *Messianic Mystics* (New Haven, 1998), 73–4, 295–302. Unlike Berger, some scholars see Abulafia's journey to Rome and his attempt to meet the pope as an aspect of his messianic self-conception (see Moshe Idel, 'Abraham Abulafia and the Pope: An Account of an Abortive Mission' [Heb.], *AJS Review*, 7–8 [1982–3]: Heb. section, 1–17).

Not long after, there occurred what Baer called 'the messianic movement of 1295', which 'shook the Castilian Jewish communities to their very foundations', but although there was a prophetic figure who apparently announced that the messiah would appear in 1295, reports of Jewish responses

personality, Nahman of Bratslav, is the subject of a fascinating study by Arthur Green. Unlike that of Abulafia, Nahman's circle of devoted followers is well documented. His messianic mission included political dimensions (liberation of the Jews of Russia, return to the Land of Israel, conversion of Gentiles), and concrete tasks were imposed on his hasidim to prepare for the messianic event. While not a broad social movement, there is considerably more here than mere speculation by scholars, as is the case with Abulafia.[6]

As for the term 'messianic', it implies, among other things, the expectation of fundamental changes in Jewish life: an end of the Jews' dispersion and oppression by foreign powers; an ingathering to the Land of Israel; a re-establishment of the classical institutions of ancient Judaism (Temple, Sanhedrin, prophecy, the Davidic line); and—perhaps—the reformation of Jewish society in accordance with the highest ideals of social justice and of international relations in accordance with the dream of universal peace. For a movement to be considered 'messianic', it need not have a programme oriented towards the direct attainment of all these goals, but its leaders and adherents must understand its programme as necessary to produce the context in which these goals will be fulfilled.[7]

Our sources do not always allow us to determine with confidence whether or not certain expressions of group behaviour were understood to be the beginning of this kind of radical transformation of the status quo. A movement of religious reform, calling on the people to abandon undesirable patterns of behaviour, undertake penitential acts, and return to the way of the Torah, may be bound up with expectation of imminent redemption, but it need not have any explicitly messianic component.[8] A movement of migra-

to this are limited to an apostate's later, hostile, and self-justifying account, intended to demonstrate the naivety of the Jews and the pathetic absurdity of their messianic hope. This is a slim foundation for speaking of a messianic movement (see Yitzhak Baer, *A History of the Jews in Christian Spain*, 2 vols. [Philadelphia, 1961–6], i. 277–81).

[6] Arthur Green, *Tormented Master: A Life of Rabbi Nahman of Bratslav* (New York, 1981), 182–220.

[7] See R. J. Zvi Werblowsky, 'Messianism in Jewish History', in Saperstein (ed.), *Essential Papers on Messianic Movements*, esp. 36–8. Scholars have recently questioned whether the concept of Jewish messianism has been unduly restricted by insisting on the presence of the political-historical dimension (see Marc Saperstein, *Decoding the Rabbis: A Thirteenth-Century Commentary on the Aggadah* [Cambridge, Mass., 1980], 112–20; Moshe Idel, 'Types of Redemptive Activism in the Middle Ages' [Heb.], in Zvi Baras [ed.], *Messianism and Eschatology: A Collection of Essays* [Meshihiyut ve'eskhatologiyah: kovets ma'amarim] [Jerusalem, 1983], 254–63; Yehuda Liebes, 'Sabbatian Messianism' [Heb.], *Pe'amim*, 40 [1989], 4–20; Idel, introduction to Aescoly, *Jewish Messianic Movements* [Heb.], 12–14; id., *Messianic Mystics*, 29–35). In the present discussion, I retain the more traditional, restrictive notions, which focus on history rather than spirituality.

[8] For example, none of the evidence about the reforms in Toledo in 1281 indicates a messianic dimension (see Y. Baer, *A History of the Jews in Christian Spain*, i. 257–61; Chapter 1 above).

tion to the Land of Israel is conceivable on the basis of motivations other than the attempt to bring about the coming of the messiah.[9] A military uprising by Jews against an oppressive power may be of a purely political nature without claiming any messianic significance.[10] The assumption that any movement challenging the established order must necessarily be messianic is certainly one that needs to be tested. On the other hand, it is certainly likely that the leaders of such movements would be tempted to mobilize the energies bound up with the messianic claim. Even in the absence of direct evidence for such a claim, the hope for redemption may have served as a powerful motivation for both the leaders and those they led.

An additional element implied by the term 'messianic' is, of course, the figure of the messiah. All of the traditional expectations enumerated above may theoretically be fulfilled through the direct intrusion of divine power, without the appearance of any special human leader. Indeed, many of the biblical passages most frequently thought of as 'messianic', whether prophecies of ingathering and resettlement of the land (Deut. 30: 1–10; Amos 9: 9–15) or of universal peace (Isa. 2: 2–4) do not mention a messiah figure at all. They might be considered visions of a messianic age without a messiah.

Perhaps it is preferable to distinguish such eschatological visions by calling them 'redemptive' rather than 'messianic'.[11] Although less common after

---

[9] See e.g. Ephraim Kanarfogel, 'The *'Aliyah* of "Three Hundred Rabbis" in 1211: Tosafist Attitudes Toward Settling in the Land of Israel', *Jewish Quarterly Review*, 76 (1986), 191–215; cf. Gerson D. Cohen, 'Messianic Postures of Ashkenazim and Sephardim', in Saperstein (ed.), *Essential Papers on Messianic Movements*, 207; Alexandra Cuffel, 'Call and Response: European Jewish Emigration to Egypt and Palestine in the Middle Ages', *Jewish Quarterly Review*, 90 (1999), 62 n. 2. On the messianic motivations and expectations of later movements of *aliyah*, see Joseph Hacker, 'Links between Spanish Jewry and Palestine, 1391–1492', in Richard I. Cohen (ed.), *Vision and Conflict in the Holy Land* (Jerusalem, 1985), 111–39; Ben Zion Dinur, 'The New Era in Jewish History' (Heb.), in id., *Historical Writings*, vol. i: *In the Turning of the Generations* [Ketavim historiyim, 1: bemifneh hadorot] (Jerusalem, 1955), 26–7; id., 'Ideological Foundations of Jewish Immigration to the Land of Israel, 1740–1840' (Heb.), in id., *Historical Writings*, i. 75–8; Arie Morgenstern, 'Messianic Concepts and Settlement in the Land of Israel', in Saperstein (ed.), *Essential Papers on Messianic Movements*, 433–55.

[10] For example, the best historiographical accounts of the Hasmonean revolt of 168–165 BCE provide no indication of any messianic dimension (see Jonathan A. Goldstein, *I Maccabees: A New Translation with Introduction and Commentary* [Garden City, NY, 1976], 241). Werblowsky, however, points out that the book of Daniel indicates that at least some contemporaries saw messianic implications in the revolt ('Messianism in Jewish History', 38; cf. Joseph Klausner, 'Daniel', in Leo Landman [ed.], *Messianism in the Talmudic Era* [New York, 1979], 212–13). John J. Collins' claim that the apocalyptic vision of Daniel 'provides a basis for nonviolent resistance to Hellenistic rule, even in the throes of the Maccabean rebellion' is more widely accepted (Collins, *The Apocalyptic Imagination: An Introduction to Jewish Apocalyptic Literature* [Grand Rapids, Mich., 1998], 114).

[11] General discussions of this phenomenon often distinguish between 'millenarism' (a term

the biblical period, this approach by no means disappeared from Jewish history. The puzzling statement of the third-century Rabbi Hillel, 'There is no messiah for Israel, for they already enjoyed him in the days of Hezekiah' (BT *San.* 99*a*), may be a repudiation of the hope not for redemption but only for *messianic* redemption as opposed to redemption directly by God: at least this is how some later commentators understood him.[12] In Lurianic kabbalah, the messiah played an almost insignificant role in the cosmic drama of exile and redemption.[13] The modern-day Gush Emunim, while it existed, spearheaded a movement energized by the expectation of imminent redemption and its political demands, but no individual was identified as a messianic figure, and little speculation was devoted to questions about the messiah himself.[14]

A full messianic movement must therefore have some active role for a messiah in the achievement of redemption. Here an additional distinction may be useful. In some movements, the leader was clearly understood to be the messiah (or more properly, *a* messiah, for much Jewish speculation from the rabbinic period on assumed that there would be two, with different roles, who would come in sequence).[15] In others, the central figure claimed to be playing an introductory role—as prophet or immediate forerunner. We might call the first type 'messiah movements'—Sabbatianism would be the paradigm—and the second 'messianic'—expecting the imminent arrival

derived from Christian eschatology and not appropriate for Jewish material) and 'messianism' to express this difference. 'Millenarism usually involves messianism, but the two do not necessarily coincide. Expectation of a human–divine savior is not always accompanied by expectation of total and final redemption. Conversely, expectation of the millennium does not always involve the mediation of a messiah. Redemption is in certain cases brought about directly by the divine' (Yonina Talmon, 'Millenarism', in David L. Sills and Robert K. Merton [eds.], *International Encyclopedia of the Social Sciences*, 17 vols. [New York, 1968], x. 353).

[12] See A. H. Silver, *A History of Messianic Speculation*, 13–14; Morton Smith, 'Messiahs: Robbers, Jurists, Prophets, and Magicians', in Saperstein (ed.), *Essential Papers on Messianic Movements*, 74; for a philosophical reinterpretation, see Saperstein, *Decoding the Rabbis*, 110–11.

[13] On the messianic tension in Lurianic kabbalah, see Gershom Scholem, *Sabbatai Sevi: The Mystical Messiah* (Princeton, 1973), esp. 46–55, 67. Scholem's view of the inevitable messianic tension accompanying the spread of Lurianic kabbalah has been challenged (see Moshe Idel, *Kabbalah: New Perspectives* [New Haven, 1988], 258–9).

[14] See Uriel Tal, 'Foundations of a Political Messianic Trend in Israel', in Saperstein (ed.), *Essential Papers on Messianic Movements*, 492–503; Menachem Kellner, 'Messianic Postures in Israel Today', ibid. 504–18.

[15] See Joseph Heinemann, 'The Messiah of Ephraim and the Premature Exodus of the Tribe of Ephraim', *Harvard Theological Review*, 68 (1975), 1–16; David Berger, 'Three Typological Themes in Early Jewish Messianism: Messiah Son of Joseph, Rabbinic Calculations, and the Figure of Armilus', *AJS Review*, 10 (1985), 141–64.

of a figure who is not identified with any historical person. It is often impossible to determine in which category a movement should be classified, because the limited sources available usually do not permit an unambiguous understanding of how the central figure understood his own role, what claims he made to his circle of followers and to the world beyond that circle, or how his position was understood while the movement still flourished. The ongoing debate over the messianic claim of Jesus illustrates the difficulties faced.

There is one kind of terminology, however, that has no place in a proper historical treatment: 'false messiah' or 'pseudo-messiah'.[16] To characterize a figure such as Sabbatai Zevi as a 'false messiah' (or even worse, a 'messianic pretender', implying a conscious deception) is to destroy any possibility of understanding the historical dynamics of the movement that coalesced around him. After all, what kind of people would follow a 'false messiah'? Only by recognizing the importance of the messianic belief in the self-understanding of Jews, the power of the messianic hope in their experience of exile, and the believer's genuine conviction that the time had finally come and the figure at hand was really the fulfilment of the age-old dream, thereby justifying whatever risks commitment to the cause entailed, can the movement be made intelligible. In the moment when crucial choices must be made, there are no 'true' and 'false' messiahs, only followers and opponents of an individual who claims a certain role. The 'falsity' of the messianic figure, like the 'falsity' of a particular biblical prophet, can be discerned only in retrospect and only on the understanding that it reflects the perspective of a particular tradition.

A related issue is raised in the most extensive presentation in English of primary texts pertaining to messianic movements and personalities, Harris Lenowitz's *The Jewish Messiahs*. The book is framed by an introduction and a conclusion, in which Lenowitz provides a rather idiosyncratic interpretative phenomenology of Jewish messianic movements. All of them share one characteristic: 'the messiah's failure to achieve his stated promises'.[17] Every 'messiah' will die, every movement will eventually collapse. The author maintains that this ineluctable reality is reflected in the sources: 'from the beginning of every account, disaster is present and only awaiting its turn to appear', 'the texts have known all along the immanence [*sic*] and proximate emergence of

---

[16] Note H. G. Friedmann, 'Pseudo-Messiahs', *Jewish Encyclopedia*, 12 vols. (New York, 1901–6), x. 251–5; in contrast, the index to *Encyclopaedia Judaica* reads 'Pseudo-Messiahs, see Messianic Movements' (*Encyclopaedia Judaica*, 16 vols. [New York, 1973], i. 703).

[17] Lenowitz, *The Jewish Messiahs*, 264.

doom', they 'do not believe in the messiah because they allow reality to check their freedom'.[18]

These assertions appear to be based on accounts of messianic figures and movements included in *The Jewish Messiahs*, accounts that were written after the denouements of the movements they describe. When Josephus portrayed first-century charismatic leaders, Kirkisani the Persian messiahs,[19] Benjamin of Tudela (not to mention Samau'el ibn Abbas) David Alroy, it was indeed impossible for the authors not to be influenced by their knowledge of how these figures ended: in violent deaths at the hands of the authorities. But other accounts were written in the midst of the movements, indeed at high points of enthusiasm. It is difficult to detect in Nathan of Gaza's letter to Raphael ben Joseph a knowledge of 'the immanence [or imminence] and proximate emergence of doom'.[20] Nor do the Christian texts cited, written after the death of their messiah, concede disaster or ratify the claim that 'every movement will eventually collapse'. The emphatic generalizations about the sources are skewed by the fact that most of the extant accounts derive from outside the movements.

But Lenowitz goes beyond this to make a claim about the messianic figures and their followers as well. The messianic figure, fully aware of the history of his predecessors, 'knows he can't do it and will probably die in the attempt. Again, the reality of the situation is observable and reputably recorded and predictable.'[21] And the followers, 'having all the messiah' knowledge of their own traditions and texts, know what they are doing. They have come into the relationship to betray the messiah. . . . They know, and so does the messiah, that they will revert to marginality, abandoning their new society under stress.'[22] Thus 'both the messiah and his followers strive to destroy themselves and the world. Their awareness of what they are doing makes them desperate to drive their movement on to the rocks.'[23] The entire enterprise is a 'ritual dance of destruction'.

As already indicated, I believe that this presentation is misguided and misleading. Using the tools of anthropology, Lenowitz presents the messianic movement as a Sisyphean ritual, in which all the protagonists know from the outset how the drama will end. I would argue that ritual is the wrong trope for messianism. History, for the participants, if not always for the historians, is

---

[18] Lenowitz, *The Jewish Messiahs*, 264.

[19] For reasons that are unclear to me, Lenowitz characterizes this Karaite's rather detached and neutral accounts of Abu Isa and Yudghan as 'anti-hagiographies' (ibid. 14–15), the same rubric used for the strongly anti-Christian counter-Gospel, *Toledot yeshu*.

[20] Ibid. 154–6.   [21] Ibid. 274.   [22] Ibid. 275.   [23] Ibid. 263.

very different from Greek tragedy. The analysis of behaviour, knowledge, and motivation from the perspective of what occurs at a later date is (to use Michael Bernstein's felicitous term) illegitimate 'backshadowing'.[24] It is hard to imagine that the protagonists of a messianic movement genuinely believe that they are following a script with a tragic ending. For them there is an alternative script in which the ending is luminous.

Whatever knowledge of past movements the messianic figure and his followers may have (and here I believe Lenowitz exaggerates, writing as if not only the leader but the followers all had access to Aescoly's *Jewish Messianic Movements* [*Hatenuot hameshiḥiyot beyisra'el*]), the messianic movement is comprehensible only on the assumption that both leader and follower believe that *this time it will be different*. They genuinely believe that the *others* were 'false messiahs', but *this* one is the real thing; that now the time for redemption is *truly* at hand. To the extent that we already 'know' that a messianic movement is doomed to failure, we show ourselves alienated from the very people we try to understand and explain. Only through the effort to recapture the power of the belief in an imminent redemption and the exhilarating intoxication of a historical moment when the future, open-ended, is holding unprecedented promise—when, for example, pious Jews throughout the world made kiddush on Tishah Be'av 1666[25]—can we hope to penetrate somewhere near the core of the messianic impulse. Any interpretative framework based on knowledge that the movement would ultimately fail blocks us from meaningful access to such a moment.[26]

Messianic movements are not evenly distributed chronologically or geographically in Jewish history. There were periods when considerable messianic activity crystallized into diverse movements and others when no such turbulence is discernible. Similarly, messianic activism is significantly more

---

[24] Michael Bernstein, *Foregone Conclusions: Against Apocalyptic History* (Berkeley, 1994), 16. Rather than condemning participants in the events for not knowing what was to come, Lenowitz attributes to them a knowledge of the future which they could not have had.

[25] See Scholem, *Sabbatai Sevi*, 628–31 (with the text of the kiddush on p. 628). In normal Jewish life, the kiddush, which proclaims the sanctity of the holy day beginning with a blessing over wine, is inconceivable for a day of fasting such as the Ninth of Av. Sabbatai drew on a biblical tradition that the fast days linked with the destruction of the First Temple would be transformed into days of rejoicing with restoration and rebuilding and a medieval understanding of a rabbinic tradition that the messiah would be born on the Ninth of Av (Sabbatai's own birthday). By sending advance instructions for all Jews to begin Tishah Be'av in 1666 with kiddush culminating in the drinking of wine, he required Jews throughout the world to take an unambiguous stance about his messianic status, with 'let's wait and see' no longer an option.

[26] For a fuller discussion of Lenowitz's book, see Saperstein, 'A "Ritual Dance of Destruction?"'.

prevalent among Jews living in Islamic environments than among those living under Christian rule, more around the Mediterranean basin than in northern Europe.[27] These empirical realities suggest certain factors that may explain when and where a Jewish messianic movement is more likely.

Major social and political upheavals resulting in dramatic changes in the established power arrangement of nations and empires often stimulated messianic movements. Jews, who believed that God was the sovereign master of all history, found it difficult to concede that such epic events were without any transcendent significance. Convinced that the relationship between the Jewish people and God was the principal drama of history, yet painfully aware that they appeared to be consigned to a minor role far from centre-stage, they felt a natural tendency to interpret mass movements, major military confrontations, or the breakdown of long-established institutions as part of a messianic scenario in which the Jewish people would be the ultimate beneficiaries.

The rapid defeat of Babylonia by Cyrus and the establishment of a new Persian empire was viewed by one of the great biblical prophets as God's redemptive act, with clear implications for Jewish behaviour (see Isa. 40–66, esp. 45: 1–8). The Muslim conquest in the seventh century, when a new religious-political force erupted from the Arabian peninsula and quickly mastered the enormous territory that for centuries had been divided between Sassanians and Byzantines, appeared to some contemporary Jews not as the start of a long new era but as the beginning of the end of history. The Crusades could readily be interpreted as a divinely arranged conflict in which the armed forces of Christendom and Islam would destroy each other so that the Jews could return to their proper position of glory. The fall of Constantinople, capital of the eastern Roman empire, to the Ottoman Turks followed by the defection of a substantial body of Christians from the Church of Rome during the Reformation was perceived as portending the collapse of the old order. The expulsion of the great Jewish community from Spain, which occurred between these two events, looked like the beginning of a mass movement of Jews back to the Land of Israel. Such events provided fertile ground for messianic speculation and activity.[28]

---

[27] This phenomenon is demonstrated and explained by G. D. Cohen ('Messianic Postures'). For a penetrating re-evaluation of the thesis, see Elisheva Carlebach, *Between History and Hope: Jewish Messianism Between Ashkenaz and Sepharad*, Annual Lecture of the Selmanowitz Chair of Jewish History (New York, 1998). There is some question whether the operative distinction should be between Ashkenazi and Sephardi Jews, rather than between those living in a Christian and those living in an Islamic environment.

[28] Sometimes such events produced intense speculation among Christians as well (see David B.

A second factor was the expectation that particular dates were fraught with redemptive significance. Here too, the underlying assumption was God's sovereign mastery of history, with the corollary that historical events affecting the Jewish people occurred in accordance with patterns encoded in the texts of God's revelation. After the catastrophic destruction of the Temple by the Romans in 70 CE, Jews naturally attempted to make sense of their plight by appealing to paradigms from the past: the belief that it all fitted into a divine scheme was more comforting than the fear that history was lurching out of control. According to the Bible, the exile following the destruction of the First Temple by the Babylonians was to last for seventy years (Jer. 25: 11–12): the seventh decade following the destruction of the Second Temple saw a new revolt with messianic dimensions.[29]

When this failed, different paradigms were sought. The sojourn in Egypt had lasted 400 years (Gen. 15: 13): as the fourth century after the destruction of the Temple by the Romans drew near to an end, expectations of redemption again became more intense, and there are indications of messianic uprisings in Babylonia and Crete.[30] Other possible dates were derived from interpretations of enigmatic verses in the book of Daniel, numerical decodings of key words in prophecies of redemption, and speculations about the larger patterns of historical chronology.[31] In many cases, there was a correlation between a particular date and an eruption of messianic fervour.

A third factor was the quality of Jewish life. It seems obvious that social humiliation, economic oppression, and violent persecution would intensify the forces in Jewish society impelling Jews to abandon the familiar status quo for the risks of a redemptive movement. Conversely, conditions of relative

---

Ruderman, 'Hope Against Hope: Jewish and Christian Messianic Expectations in the Late Middle Ages', in Aharon Mirsky, Avraham Grossman, and Yosef Kaplan [eds.], *Exile and Diaspora: Studies in the History of the Jewish People Presented to Professor Haim Beinart* [Jerusalem, 1991], esp. 190–2).

[29] See the views of Elazar ben Azariah (BT *San.* 99a), in A. H. Silver, *A History of Messianic Speculation*, 19–20.

[30] See R. Hanina (BT *AZ* 9b); on Crete, see Salo W. Baron, *A Social and Religious History of the Jews*, 18 vols. (Philadelphia, 1952–83), v. 167–8; Lenowitz, *The Jewish Messiahs*, 63–4; on Babylonia, see Jacob Neusner, *A History of the Jews in Babylonia*, 5 vols. (Leiden, 1965–70), v. 65–8. In Babylonia, the messianic date coincided with severe persecutions by Yazdagird II.

[31] See A. H. Silver, *A History of Messianic Speculation*, 243–59; Ruderman, 'Hope Against Hope', 188–90. Striking examples of biblical exegesis producing messianic dates, many based on the numerical values of words (gematria) can be found in Isaiah Tishby, *Messianism in the Generation of the Expulsions from Spain and Portugal* [Meshiḥiyut bador gerushei sefarad ufortugal] (Jerusalem, 1985), parts of which are translated in id., 'Acute Apocalyptic Messianism', in Saperstein (ed.), *Essential Papers on Messianic Movements*, 259–86.

prosperity and tranquillity should make it less likely that Jews would want to opt for a radical change. Similarly, it seems reasonable that those on the margins of Jewish society, who have the least stake in the established order and the least to lose by transforming it, would be more likely to support a messianic movement than those possessing economic power, political influence, or religious authority.[32]

Related to this is the stability of the political environment in which Jews were living. By its nature a messianic movement is a challenge to the Gentile political order, and it stands to reason that it would have a greater chance of success during a period of general upheaval and turbulence than during a period in which a strong central government enjoyed widespread support and controlled powerful resources for keeping the peace. Messianic activity was therefore more likely during periods of general political turmoil, which were usually dangerous for Jews in themselves.[33]

Plausible as they may seem, none of these conditions is necessary, and even together they are not sufficient, to inspire messianic activism. They are not necessary, because the greatest Jewish messianic movement of the past 2,000 years—that of Sabbatai Zevi in the 1660s—had no such background. It was not a period of distinctive world conflict; the date 1666 had messianic significance for Christians but not for Jews; the movement had considerable appeal among wealthy Jewish merchants as well as among the poor, among lay and rabbinic leaders as well as among the disenfranchised; and the Turkish government at the time was relatively stable and strong.[34] They are not sufficient, because none of the factors need entail the conclusion that Jews should do anything other than wait until God sends an unmistakable sign, an unambiguous instruction. They may heighten expectation, increase tension, stimulate speculation, but they do not necessarily produce an actual messianic

---

[32] This is the theory of deprivation, or relative deprivation (the gulf between expectations and the available means for their satisfaction), as a primary factor in messianism (see Norman Cohn, *The Pursuit of the Millennium: Revolutionary Millenarians and Mystical Anarchists of the Middle Ages*, 3rd edn. [New York, 1970], esp. 53–61; Peter Worsley, *The Trumpet Shall Sound: A Study of the 'Cargo Cults' in Melanesia*, 2nd edn. [New York, 1968], 243; David Aberle, 'A Note on Relative Deprivation Theory as Applied to Millenarian and Other Cult Movements', in Sylvia Thrupp [ed.], *Millennial Dreams in Action* [The Hague, 1962], 209–14; Stephen Sharot, *Messianism, Mysticism, and Magic: A Sociological Analysis of Jewish Religious Movements* [Chapel Hill, 1982], 241–4).

[33] For a clear example of this principle, see Friedländer's discussion of the Jewish messianic movements in the tumultuous Umayyad period (Israel Friedländer, 'Shiitic Influences in Jewish Sectarianism', in Saperstein [ed.], *Essential Papers on Messianic Movements*, 113–61, esp. 115–17; originally published in *Jewish Quarterly Review* NS, 1 (1910–11), 183–215; 2 (1911–12), 481–516; 3 (1912–13), 235–300).

[34] See Scholem, *Sabbatai Sevi*, 1–6, 101–2.

movement. The relative significance of these factors, therefore, will have to be assessed in relation to each of the movements analysed in the following pages.

The paradigm for a fully developed messianic movement in Jewish history is Sabbatianism. It is documented in a multitude of contemporary sources from various perspectives; its central figure made explicit claims to messianic status and its intellectuals articulated a doctrine relating the claims to traditional Jewish texts;[35] it inspired a significant following at all levels of Jewish society and opposition both from Jewish leaders and Gentile authorities; it culminated in the shocking ambiguities of unexpected events and ingenious attempts to explain them; its influence continued among 'believers' after all the original protagonists had disappeared from the stage. No other messianic movement in Jewish history fulfils all these criteria. In many cases the decision about whether to consider a particular historical phenomenon in this category will necessarily involve an element of subjectivity, as becomes obvious in even a superficial chronological review.

Scholars have noted that the actual doctrine of the messiah did not crystallize in Judaism until after the biblical period.[36] The Hebrew Bible articulated the idea of redemption—a re-establishment of the proper relationship between God and the Jewish people, situated once again in its land, after a period of disruption. It provided descriptions of an ideal political ruler (some of which may originally have been intended to express the hope for an actual figure born into the royal line or newly crowned), visions of an ideal age in the future (which may not have been intended to suggest a rupture in history or an eschatological 'end of time'), and prophecies of divine intervention in history to balance the scales of justice.[37] It furnished characters—especially Moses and David—who could serve as paradigms or types for a redeeming messiah,[38] and it suggested motifs, such as the 'suffering servant',

---

[35] Liebes argued that the essence of the Sabbatian ideology, as formulated by its leading figures, was not concerned with the traditional political-territorial redemption of the people but rather with the spiritual-mystical redemption of the Jewish faith ('Sabbatian Messianism' [Heb.], esp. 10–11). However, the appeal of Sabbatianism that made it a mass movement before the apostasy was indeed bound up with traditional Jewish messianic aspirations, as Liebes concedes (although he hesitates to call those Jews who were motivated merely by these elements true 'Sabbatians').

[36] See Solomon Zeitlin, 'The Origin of the Idea of the Messiah', in Landman (ed.), *Messianism in the Talmudic Era*, 102–4.

[37] For a helpful recent review of these themes, see Shemaryhu Talmon, 'Biblical Visions of the Future Ideal Age', in id., *King, Cult and Calendar in Ancient Israel: Collected Studies* (Jerusalem, 1986), 140–64.

[38] See Joseph Klausner, 'The Source and Beginnings of the Messianic Idea', in Landman (ed.),

that originally had no messianic significance at all but could later be incorporated into messianic doctrines. These were the threads from which coherent messianic doctrines and eschatological scenarios could be woven in later times.

It is arguable, furthermore, that although the term 'messianic' is anachronistic in this context, the first actual messianic movements in Jewish history occurred in biblical times. Although the biblical narratives allow us little confidence that we can reconstruct how the Exodus from Egypt was perceived by contemporaries, it certainly contains many of the elements that characterize 'messianic movements': liberation of the people from oppression through the instrumentality of a human leader who claimed to be working in concert with divine power, significant opposition to the movement not only by the Gentile authorities but also within the people itself, promise of a future life of prosperity ('a land flowing with milk and honey'), and a close, secure relationship with God. Unquestionably, the Exodus served as the central paradigm for the rhetoric and sometimes even the game-plan of messianic redemption throughout subsequent Jewish history.[39] The one factor that makes it anomalous is its almost total success.

A second candidate for a biblical 'messianic movement' is the return from exile following the Persian conquest of Babylonia. Our sketchy knowledge of this movement is essentially limited to the writings of its theorist and propagandist, the prophet whose writings are preserved in the book of Isaiah from chapter 40 onwards. Cyrus himself is the 'messianic' figure, God's 'anointed' (Isa. 45: 1): not the only time in Jewish history when a Gentile ruler would be presented in this role.[40] The prophet's practical message, couched in some of

---

Messianism in the Talmudic Era, 25–28 (Moses), 31–3 (David). Despite the centrality of Moses in early biblical history and his use as a prototype of the messiah ('the last redeemer will be like the first' [*Numbers Rabbah* 11: 2]), it is striking that Jewish messianic speculation did not grant him any role in the eschatological scenario, as it did to Elijah (see Daniel Jeremy Silver, *Images of Moses* [New York, 1982], 152–5).

[39] For the power of the Exodus as redemptive paradigm—'Messianism comes late in Jewish history, and it comes, I think, by way of Exodus thinking'—see Michael Walzer, *Exodus and Revolution* (New York, 1985), 16.

[40] For example, there seems to have been considerable speculation in the late fifteenth century that the Ottoman sultan was a messianic figure (see Charles Berlin, 'A Sixteenth-Century Hebrew Chronicle of the Ottoman Empire', in id. [ed.], *Studies in Jewish Bibliography, History and Literature in Honor of I. Edward Kiev* [New York, 1971], 27–8; Benzion Netanyahu, *Don Isaac Abravanel* [Philadelphia, 1968], 323 n. 161; I. Tishby, 'Acute Apocalyptic Messianism', 281–3 n. 34). According to a contemporary Christian writer, some Jews viewed the French king Charles VIII, who led a dramatic invasion of Italy in 1494, as an eschatological figure (Amnon Linder, 'L'Expédition italienne de

the most glorious rhetoric of biblical literature, is essentially simple: God had shown, by sending this messianic figure, that the redemption had arrived; it was now time for Jews to respond by re-enacting the Exodus, journeying once again through the wilderness, and returning to their land.[41]

This movement reveals some of the problems characteristic of later Jewish messianism. Many in the Babylonian Jewish community refused to heed the prophet's call to leave their homes and return to Zion.[42] No sources produced by the opponents of the movement have survived, but it is not difficult to imagine their arguments. Jeremiah had urged an accommodation to life outside the Holy Land, insisting that it was possible to worship the one true God in Babylonia and warning against those who promised an early end to the exile. The time had not yet come; barely two-thirds of the seventy-year period he mentioned had elapsed. This new prophet therefore called upon the people to disregard Jeremiah, whose dire predictions had been proven correct, and he dared to affirm that a pagan king was God's anointed ruler.

As for those who responded to the prophet's call to return, reality must have dampened some of their enthusiasm. Certainly no 'way paved in the wilderness' lay before them. After a long and arduous journey, they would have found a devastated city, a demoralized people, the Temple still in ruins. The lavish promises of the prophet may well have begun to sound hollow to those confronted with the slow and difficult task of rebuilding. In messianism, even more than in ordinary politics, the rhetoric of inspiration may easily lead to discouragement and disillusion even if some of the goals are achieved. The Second Commonwealth was thus born in the ambiguities of the messianic claim, a claim that can mobilize tremendous energy, but can also become an enormous burden when historical reality falls short of exaggerated hopes.[43]

Charles VIII et les espérances messianiques des Juifs', *Revue des études juives*, 137 [1978], 179–86; Ruderman, 'Hope Against Hope', 191–2).

[41] What makes this atypical of 'messianic movements' is that it was a call not to challenge the Gentile ruler but to act on instructions given by the ruler.

[42] Later Jewish thinkers referred to this with a mixture of anger and irony: 'many of them stayed in Babylon, not willing to leave their possessions' (Josephus, *Antiquities of the Jews*, 11.1.3); 'the majority and the aristocracy remained in Babylon, preferring dependence and slavery, and unwilling to leave their houses and their affairs' (Judah Halevi, *The Kuzari: An Argument for the Faith of Israel*, trans. Hartwig Hirschfield [New York, 1964], 2: 24). Their intuition is confirmed by archaeological evidence of Jewish prominence in Babylonian business transactions in the fifth century BCE (see Michael Coogan, 'Life in the Diaspora: Jews at Nippur in the Fifth Century BCE', *Biblical Archaeologist*, 37 [1974], 6–12).

[43] The uprising of 522 BCE against Persian rule in Judea may also be considered a messianic

Like the sixth century BCE, the first century of the Christian era was a period of instability that produced radical challenges to the status quo. The most influential, the movement surrounding Jesus of Nazareth, is one of the very few for which the literature of the movement itself has been preserved: only the Sabbatian movement is more extensively documented. During the life of its central figure and the first generation or two of his followers after his death, it was very much a part of Jewish history: its protagonists were Jews, it appealed to Jews, and its claims were justified with reference to traditional Jewish sources.

It is now universally recognized that the 'Jesus movement' must be understood in the context of Jewish messianic speculation (as evidenced in various works of the Pseudepigrapha and the Dead Sea Scrolls) and of political-religious activity.[44] The historian Josephus has provided a series of hostile yet tantalizing glimpses of figures who, apparently claiming prophetic inspiration, gathered groups of followers in the wilderness to march across the Jordan river or ascend the Mount of Olives in some kind of symbolic expression of independence from the ruling authorities. At least this was how the Romans perceived their activities, for each uprising was summarily suppressed by Roman military might, its central figure put to death.[45] We know virtually nothing of the internal dynamics of these events, and whether they deserve to be considered either 'messianic' or 'movements' cannot be clearly established with the limited sources available, but they provide a fascinating point of comparison with the 'Jesus movement'.

---

movement. During a time of severe problems for the central authorities (there were rebellions all over the Persian empire), the 'messianic' hope for a genuine restoration of Davidic sovereignty, focused on the figure of Zerubbabel, was articulated by the prophets Haggai and Zechariah. The results remain a mystery, except that nothing more is heard about Zerubbabel, or any of his descendants, throughout the Persian period. The Persians probably suppressed this movement ruthlessly, a paradigm for the reaction of Gentile rulers to Jewish messianism (see John Bright, *A History of Israel* [Philadelphia, 1959], 351–5; Frank Moore Cross, 'A Reconstruction of the Judean Restoration', *Journal of Biblical Literature*, 94/4 [1975], 4–18; Joachim Schaper, 'The Persian Period', in Markus Bockmuehl and James Carleton Paget [eds.], *Redemption and Resistance: The Messianic Hopes of Jews and Christians in Antiquity* [London, 2007], 5–8).

[44] For fine collections of essays on this subject, see Jacob Neusner, William Scott Green, and Ernest S. Frerichs (eds.), *Judaisms and Their Messiahs at the Turn of the Christian Era* (Cambridge, 1987); Craig Evans and Peter Flint (eds.), *Eschatology, Messianism, and the Dead Sea Scrolls* (Grand Rapids, Mich., 1997).

[45] Josephus, *Antiquities of the Jews*, 18.1.1, 20.5.1–2, 20.8.6; id., *The Jewish War*, 2.13.4–6; see Richard Horsley, 'Popular Messianic Movements Around the Time of Jesus', in Saperstein (ed.), *Essential Papers on Messianic Movements*, esp. 95–8; Richard Horsley and John Hanson, *Bandits, Prophets, and Messiahs: Popular Movements at the Time of Jesus* (Minneapolis, 1985).

Should the 'Great Revolt', launched against Rome in 66 CE and culminating in the fall of Jerusalem and the destruction of the Temple four years later, be considered a redemptive movement? It is unlikely that the leaders of the revolt would have risked so much without believing that their initiative would produce God's intervention to liberate the Land of Israel from the pagan rule that forced Jews to compromise their commitment to Torah. Yet no extant literature articulates the leaders' own ideology of revolution, and there is little relevant direct evidence in the hostile accounts of Josephus or the talmudic sages. The most intriguing is Josephus's statement that Jews were inspired to revolt because of an 'ambiguous oracle found also in their sacred writings that "about that time, one from their country should become governor of the habitable earth"'. The Jews understood this to be a prediction of the messiah, whereas the oracle really referred to Vespasian, who was named emperor while he was in the Land of Israel. Josephus was apparently content to concede the 'messianic' role in his time to Rome.[46]

The revolt of the years 132–135 CE, led by the man who signed his name Simeon ben Kosiba, but who is better known under the name preserved in Christian sources, Bar Kokhba, had a clearer messianic component. Jewish sources report that Rabbi Akiva, the most respected scholar of his generation, publicly identified Ben Kosiba as the messiah, an assertion so embarrassing after the failure of the revolt that it could not plausibly have been fabricated. Eusebius records what appears to be a messianic claim on the part of the leader himself, and coins and letters from the period, discovered only recently, are dated according to a new, seemingly messianic, calendar: the year 'of the redemption of Israel'.[47] Subsequent Jewish sources are ambivalent about this military figure who achieved spectacular successes before suffering

---

[46] Josephus, *The Jewish War*, 6.5.4. This passage has received considerable attention in the scholarly literature (see Louis Feldman, 'Selective Critical Bibliography', in Louis Feldman and Cohei Hata [eds.], *Josephus, the Bible and History* [Detroit, 1989], 410–11; Tessa Rajak, *Josephus: The Historian and His Society* [Philadelphia, 1984], 192–3; Martin Goodman, 'Messianism and Politics in the Land of Israel, 66–135 CE', in Bockmuehl and Carletone Paget [eds.], *Redemption and Resistance*, 151–3). On possible messianic elements accompanying the Great Revolt, see Horsley, 'Popular Messianic Movements Around the Time of Jesus', 98–103; for the argument that there is no evidence for any significant messianic component, see Yisrael L. Levin, 'Messianic Tendencies at the End of the Second Commonwealth' (Heb.), in Baras (ed.), *Messianism and Eschatology*, 138–9, 147–52.

[47] For accessible translations of the literary sources and the dramatic numismatic and epistolary discoveries, see Yigael Yadin, *Bar Kokhba* (New York, 1971), 255–9; for a general review of the scholarly literature, see Benjamin H. Isaac and Aharon Oppenheimer, 'The Revolt of Bar Kokhba: Ideology and Modern Scholarship', *Journal of Jewish Studies*, 36 (1985), 33–60; on the messianic dimension, see Aharon Oppenheimer, 'The Messianism of Bar Kokhba' (Heb.), in Baras (ed.), *Messianism and Eschatology*, 153–65.

devastating defeat, and it has been argued that this experience led to the development of a new messianic persona: the messiah descended from Joseph, who would be killed in battle before the advent of the messiah from the Davidic line.[48]

The ruthless Roman suppression of the revolt destroyed the taste for open defiance of imperial power; during the Pax Romana, Jewish leaders developed a quietistic, anti-militaristic messianic ideology, prohibiting all rebellion.[49] Nevertheless, dramatic external challenges to the established order occasioned sporadic movements. Rabbinic sources are all but silent about the stunning decision by the pagan emperor Julian to permit the Jews to return to Jerusalem and rebuild the Temple, but we can imagine the excitement this must have engendered in Jews who saw clear parallels with Cyrus the Great. The impact of this heady but short-lived reversal is documented as far away as Iran.[50] Other messianic claims surfaced against the background of the barbarian invasions of the fifth century and the Islamic conquest of the seventh. Little is known about the individuals involved, although the seventh-century figure apparently appealed to an element of social discontent, as we are told that he 'gathered around him weavers, carpetmakers, and launderers'.[51] In both cases, their influence was local and brief.

---

[48] See J. Heinemann, 'The Messiah of Ephraim'. On the polyvalent image of Ben Kosiba in subsequent Jewish literature, see Richard Marks, *The Image of Bar Kokhba in Traditional Jewish Literature: False Messiah and National Hero* (University Park, 1994). As has recently been shown by Ram Ben-Shalom, Vicente Ferrer, the charismatic revivalist preacher of the early fifteenth century, using material in Raymond Martini's *Pugio Fidei*, incorporated accounts of Ben Kosiba (*Barcován, que quiere dezir fijo de mentira* [*Bar Koziva*]) and Rabbi Akiva to argue that Jews have historically jumped from one false messiah to another while refusing to accept the true messiah (Ben-Shalom, *Facing Christian Culture: Historical Consciousness and Images of the Past among the Jews of Spain and Southern France during the Middle Ages* [Mul tarbut notsrit: toda'ah historit vedimuyei avar bekerev yehudei sefarad uprovans bimei habeinayim] [Jerusalem, 2006], 269–71).

[49] See the classical rabbinic statement of quietism, according to which God made the Jewish people swear an oath not to immigrate en masse to the land of Israel or to rebel against the nations of the world before the proper time (BT *Ket.* 111*a*). See also Nahum Glatzer, 'The Attitude Toward Rome in Third-Century Judaism', in Alois Dempf (ed.), *Politische Ordnung und Menschliche Existenz* (Munich, 1962), 243–57. For a more recent statement, see Philip S. Alexander, 'The Rabbis and Messianism', in Bockmuehl and Carletone Paget (eds.), *Redemption and Resistance*, 238.

[50] Geo Widengren, 'The Status of the Jews in the Sassanian Empire', *Iranica Antiqua*, 1 (1961), 133 (text in n. 2); Neusner, *A History of the Jews in Babylonia*, iv. 32–4; on Julian's Jewish policy and possible Jewish responses, see Baron, *A Social and Religious History of the Jews*, ii. 160–1, 392; Glen Warren Bowersock, *Julian the Apostate* (Cambridge, Mass., 1978), 88–90; Jacob Neusner, *Midrash in Context: Exegesis in Formative Judaism* (Philadelphia, 1983), 113–17; Michael Avi-Yonah, *The Jews under Roman and Byzantine Rule: A Political History of Palestine from the Bar Kokhba War to the Arab Conquest* (New York, 1984), 185–207, esp. 193–8.

[51] See Baron, *A Social and Religious History of the Jews*, v. 184; Lenowitz, *The Jewish Messiahs*, 64.

The turbulent period of the Islamic Umayyad caliphate, based in Damascus and challenged militarily and ideologically by powerful forces from the east, was the next environment in which Jewish messianic activism flourished. Despite the relatively late provenance of the sources, more is known about Abu Isa of Isfahan and his movement than about any other messianic movement between the second century and the twelfth. The provocative study by Israel Friedländer, still invaluable more than a century after publication, shows the profound influence of Islamic doctrines—particularly those of the Shia—on the ideology of the Jewish movement.[52] Messianism thus provided an instance of a dialectical relationship between the two traditions: Jewish messianic expectation helped mould the contours of the Shi'ite historical world-view and eschatology, while the movements of Abu Isa and his follower Yudghan are the first major example of Islamic influence within Judaism that would produce the great flourishings of medieval Jewish culture in Baghdad and Muslim Spain. Those who believed in Abu Isa, known as the *'Isawiyya*, maintained their collective identity and were present as a distinct group in Damascus some 200 to 250 years after his death.[53] They must have developed their own theology, liturgy, legends, and law in order to maintain continuity over time. Nothing of this has survived, a disastrous loss for the historical record of Jewish diversity.[54]

The establishment of the Abbasid caliphate in Baghdad stabilized the political environment, and strong central Jewish institutions, dependent upon and loyal to the caliphate, left little space for active messianic challenges. This stability was rocked by the Crusades. A series of twelfth-century messianic personalities and uprisings, from Yemen and Iraq to Morocco and Andalusia, challenged the ingenuity of Jewish leaders such as Maimonides, who wrote to strengthen the hope of ordinary Jews that deliverance from their suffering would come soon, yet, at the same time, to discredit concrete manifestations of messianic activity and dissuade Jews from involvement.[55]

Steven M. Wasserstrom provides important contextual material about the extent to which workers on cloth and skins were treated as a despised underclass in Roman, Jewish, Muslim, and Christian sources and appear in accounts of various challenges to the established order (Wasserstrom, *Between Muslim and Jew: The Problem of Symbiosis under Early Islam* [Princeton, 1995], 20–3).

[52] Friedländer, 'Shiitic Influences in Jewish Sectarianism'.

[53] This is reported by the Karaite historian Jacob al-Kirkisani, in Leon Nemoy (ed.), *Karaite Anthology: Excerpts from the Early Literature* (New Haven, 1952), 51.

[54] For a fine review of what is known about the *'Isawiyya*, which treats them appropriately as the second most important sectarian Jewish movement (after the Karaites) between the second and seventeenth centuries, see Wasserstrom, *Between Muslim and Jew*, 68–89, esp. 68, 71.

[55] This is one of the purposes of Maimonides' 'Epistle to Yemen', which also provides an

One of the most attractive messianic figures was David Alroy, whose intellectual attainments and appealing personality are conceded even in a sarcastically hostile Islamic account. The temporary success of his movement, the opposition by the established Jewish leadership, and the ultimate betrayal that led to his death are recounted with surprising sympathy by the perceptive traveller Benjamin of Tudela.[56]

The upheavals in European and in Jewish history of the late fifteenth and sixteenth centuries produced a dazzling array of activities with messianic significance, although no full-blown movement. Various expressions of prophecy and messianic agitation among Conversos, speculation about the eschatological significance of contemporary events, intense expectation focused on particular years, prayer vigils to promote the confession and repentance that would bring the messiah, even the printing of the Zohar as a vehicle for the dissemination of mystical doctrine, all testify to the messianic tension in the generations following the Expulsion from Spain.[57]

Particularly intriguing is the programme of the enigmatic eastern Jew David Reubeni. He came to Rome in 1524 claiming to be the emissary of a kingdom of 300,000 Jews in northern Arabia, and succeeded in getting an audience with Pope Clement VII and receiving papal endorsement for his mission to King John III of Portugal. In his memoir, Reubeni eschews any messianic claims for himself, but he apparently promised the Portuguese Conversos that he would soon return to bring them to the Land of Israel, and his secret goal may well have been to initiate an eschatological world war between Christian Europe and the Ottoman empire.[58]

important review of messianic movements in the twelfth century (*Crisis and Leadership*, 96, 123–30). For other expressions of Jewish messianic speculation and activism against the background of the Crusades, see Shelomo D. Goitein, 'A Report on Messianic Troubles in Baghdad in 1120–21', in Saperstein (ed.), *Essential Papers on Messianic Movements*, 189–201; Cuffel, 'Call and Response', 86–9.

[56] See Baron, *A Social and Religious History of the Jews*, v. 202–5. In addition to the account by Benjamin, the other major source is by a hostile and contemptuous Jewish convert to Islam (see Jacob Rader Marcus, *The Jew in the Medieval World*, rev. edn. [Cincinnati, 1999], document 50 [278–81]; all accounts are reviewed by Lenowitz, *The Jewish Messiahs*, 81–91).

[57] See I. Tishby, *Messianism in the Generations of the Expulsions* (Heb.); for other expressions of messianism in this period, see Netanyahu, *Don Isaac Abravanel*, 195–247; Yosef Hayim Yerushalmi, 'Messianic Impulses in Joseph ha-Kohen', in Bernard Cooperman (ed.), *Jewish Thought in the Sixteenth Century* (Cambridge, Mass., 1983), 460–87; Ira Robinson, 'Messianic Prayer Vigils in Jerusalem in the Early-Sixteenth Century', *Jewish Quarterly Review*, 72 (1981–2), 32–42; Isaiah Tishby, 'The Controversy over the Zohar in Sixteenth-Century Italy' (Heb.), in id., *Studies in Kabbalah and Its Branches* [Ḥikrei kabalah usheluḥoteiha], 3 vols. (Jerusalem, 1982–93), i. 102–6.

[58] I know of no adequate monograph study in English of the activities of David Reubeni. Baron's discussion is, as always, a fine starting point (*A Social and Religious History of the Jews*, xiii. 109–15).

One of the focal points of messianic speculation and activity was the Land of Israel, particularly the city of Safed, which attracted an extraordinary cadre of outstanding personalities. As Jacob Katz has argued, the attempt to renew the traditional ordination of rabbinical judges and thereby establish courts with authority to adjudicate areas of Jewish law that had remained purely theoretical for almost 1,500 years was an attempt to prepare the necessary conditions for the messianic advent—and therefore qualifies as a kind of redemptive movement even without a messianic personality at its core.[59] The new kabbalistic mythos divulged by Isaac Luria in Safed, a mythos in which the categories of exile and redemption (thought not the messiah) played a central role, was capable of creating a messianic tension absent from classical kabbalah. Together with more traditional and popular sources of eschatological ideas, Lurianic kabbalah would serve as the matrix for the ideology of the Sabbatian movement, helping to explain its paradoxical quirks in familiar terms, as can be seen in Gershom Scholem's magisterial study.[60]

Despite the collective psychological trauma of Sabbatianism, expressions of traditional messianic activity continued into the nineteenth century. Two examples are the movement of large-scale re-settlement of the Land of Israel in preparation for the expected advent of the messiah in 1840, and the movement surrounding the Yemenite messianic figure Shukr Kuhayl II.[61] While these were rather marginal phenomena, four major movements of modern Jewish history have a complex and ambiguous relationship to the tradition of Jewish messianism, each raising special conceptual problems.

Reubeni's memoir, written after the events, has been reissued in Hebrew with substantial introductions by Aescoly, Moshe Idel, and Eliyahu Lipiner (David Reubeni, *Sipur david hare'uveni al pi ketav yad oksford* [The Story of David Reubeni Copied from the Oxford Manuscript], ed. Aaron Ze'ev Aescoly [Jerusalem, 1993]; Eng. trans. in Elkan Nathan Adler [ed.], *Jewish Travellers* [New York, 1931], 251–328). Extensive passages from it, together with other relevant texts, are presented in Lenowitz, *The Jewish Messiahs*, 103–23. There is considerable scholarly material in Hebrew on the subject (see the bibliographical review in Azriel Shochat, 'On The Matter of David Reubeni' [Heb.], *Zion*, 35 [1970], 96 n. 1).

[59] Jacob Katz, 'The Dispute Between Jacob Berab and Levi ben Habib over Renewing Ordination', in id., *Divine Law in Human Hands: Case Studies in Halakhic Flexibility* (Jerusalem, 1998), 146–70.   [60] Scholem, *Sabbatai Sevi*; Idel, *Kabbalah*, 258–9.

[61] See Morgenstern, 'Messianic Concepts and Settlement in the Land of Israel'; Bat-Zion Eraqi Klorman, 'The Messiah Shukr Kuhayl II (1868–75) and his Tithe (Ma'aser): Ideology and Practice as a Means to Hasten Redemption', in Saperstein (ed.), *Essential Papers on Messianic Movements*, 456–72; for fuller studies, see Arie Morgenstern, *Messianism and the Return to the Land of Israel in the First Half of the Nineteenth Century* [Meshiḥiyut veyishuv erets yisra'el bamaḥatsit harishonah shel hame'ah hatesha-esreh] (Jerusalem, 1985); Bat-Zion Eraqi Klorman, *The Jews of Yemen in the Nineteenth Century: A Portrait of a Messianic Community* (Leiden, 1993); for English texts on the two Shukr Kuhayls, see Lenowitz, *The Jewish Messiahs*, 235–56.

Scholars continue to debate whether Polish hasidism should be considered a messianic movement. The historian Ben Zion Dinur argued the case for the messianic character of hasidism; his interpretation has been vigorously rejected by Gershom Scholem and other respected historians.[62] But whether the founders intended their movement as a way to bring about the advent of the messiah or as a way to neutralize the dangers of messianic activism, it cannot be doubted that a powerful messianic tension has informed certain expressions of hasidism, including the coterie of Nahman of Bratslav in the early nineteenth century and the Lubavitcher hasidim today.[63]

Three nineteenth-century movements raise a different problem. Reform Judaism called for fundamental changes in the religious and political structures of traditional Jewish life to accompany an end to the experience of life in 'exile'. Its central aspiration was the messianic age envisioned by the prophets, which some of its leaders believed to be imminent. Yet while it claimed to be continuing the genuine messianic tradition of Judaism and often indulged in its rhetoric, Reform severed the connection with much of traditional messianism by abandoning the figure of the personal messiah and

---

[62] Ben Zion Dinur, 'The Beginnings of Hasidism and Its Social and Messianic Foundations' (Heb.), in *Historical Writings*, i. 83–227; the key section on messianism is translated in Ben Zion Dinur, 'The Messianic-Prophetic Role of the Baal Shem Tov', in Saperstein (ed.), *Essential Papers on Messianic Movements*, 377–88; see Gershom Scholem, 'The Neutralization of the Messianic Element in Early Hasidism', in id., *The Messianic Idea in Judaism*, 176–202. Crucial to the dispute is the proper interpretation of the letter by the Ba'al Shem Tov to his brother-in-law Gershon of Kuty (ibid. 182–4); see also Isaiah Tishby, 'The Messianic Idea and Messianic Trends at the Beginning of Hasidism' (Heb.), *Zion*, 32 (1967), 1–45; Rivka Schatz Uffenheimer, *Hasidism as Mysticism: Quietistic Elements in Eighteenth Century Hasidic Thought* (Princeton, 1993), 330–9.

[63] On messianic activism among the Bratslaver hasidim during the past generation, see Mendel Piekarz, 'The Transition in the History of the Messianism of Bratslaver Hasidism' (Heb.), in Baras (ed.), *Messianism and Eschatology*, 325–42; for academic analyses of the messianic activism in contemporary Habad, see Aviezer Ravitzky, 'The Contemporary Lubavitch Hasidic Movement: Between Conservatism and Messianism', in Martin Marty and R. Scott Appleby (eds.), *Accounting for Fundamentalisms: The Dynamic Character of Movements* (Chicago, 1994), 303–27; Menachem Friedman, 'Habad as Messianic Fundamentalism: From Local Particularism to Universal Jewish Mission', in Marty and Scott Appleby (eds.), *Accounting for Fundamentalisms*, 328–57; Joseph Dan, 'The Two Meanings of Hasidic Messianism', in Jodi Magness and Seymour Gitin (eds.), *Ḥesed ve-Emet: Studies in Honor of Ernest S. Frerichs* (Providence, RI, 1998), 391–407; David Berger, *The Rebbe, the Messiah, and the Scandal of Orthodox Indifference* (London, 2001); M. Avrum Ehrlich, *The Messiah of Brooklyn: Understanding Lubavitch Hasidism, Past and Present* (Jersey City, 2004), esp. ch. 9; Yitshak Kraus, *The Seventh: Messianism in the Last Generation of Habad* [Hashevi'i: meshiḥiyut bador hashevi'i shel ḥabad] (Tel Aviv, 2007). Unfortunately, no such academic study was available at the time I was selecting material for *Essential Papers on Messianic Movements*. Lenowitz's treatment of Habad messianism strikes me as rather disappointing (*The Jewish Messiahs*, 215–23; see Saperstein, 'A "Ritual Dance of Destruction?"', 156).

renouncing the national components of the redemption ideal—ingathering of the exiles in the Land of Israel, restoration of the Davidic kingdom, rebuilding of the Temple, and re-establishment of the sacrificial cult.[64] The elements of continuity with earlier expressions of Jewish messianism are outweighed by the decisive changes.

Socialism championed the principle of radical change in the social order that would bring about the fulfilment of the messianic hopes for an end of oppression of the downtrodden and the beginning of a new age of universal brotherhood. Yet even more than Reform Judaism, Socialism emptied the messianic ideal of any specifically Jewish content. The Socialist ideology required that bonds of solidarity between workers throughout the world take precedence over solidarity between Jews of different economic classes. Unlike Reform, Socialism also abandoned the religious dimensions of the messianic hope. Even those Jews who opted for a Socialist commitment under specifically Jewish auspices saw their position as a transvaluation of antiquated ideas, as is evident in the following song of the Jewish Socialist Bund:

> The messiah and Judaism are dying, expiring,
> A new messiah is appearing,
> The Jewish worker whom the rich man exploits
> Is raising the banner of rebellion.[65]

Socialism may have roots in the world-view that informed the messianic tradition, but it is a mutation that cannot be considered part of that tradition.

Like Reform Judaism and Socialism, Zionism crystallized as a movement to realize certain traditional messianic goals, in this case the ingathering of the exiles to the Land of Israel and the re-establishment of Jewish sovereignty as a means to bring an end to the exile. However, most Zionist thinkers

---

[64] On the attitudes towards messianic doctrine in the early Reform movement, see David Philipson, *The Reform Movement in Judaism* (New York, 1931), 173–80; W. Gunther Plaut (ed.), *The Rise of Reform Judaism* (New York, 1963), 133–45; Steven Schwarzschild, 'The Personal Messiah: Toward the Restoration of a Discarded Doctrine', *Judaism*, 5 (1956), 123–35; Michael A. Meyer, *Response to Modernity: A History of the Reform Movement in Judaism* (New York, 1988), 122, 137–8.

[65] In Sharot, *Messianism, Mysticism, and Magic*, 217. Sharot questions the interpretation that Jewish Socialists, including Marx, were motivated by a secularized form of traditional Jewish messianism (ibid. 214–15). According to Irving Howe, messianic fervour 'would flame in the immigrant world, a blazing secular passion appearing first as socialism. . . . The Messiah would be replaced by the messianic principle, the grandiose solitary figure by a collective upheaval' (Howe, *World of Our Fathers* [New York, 1976], 223; see also Richard Wolin, 'Reflections on Jewish Secular Messianism', in Jonathan Frankel [ed.], *Jews and Messianism in the Modern Era*, Studies in Contemporary Jewry, 7 [New York, 1991], 186–96).

thought of their enterprise as a repudiation of traditional messianism, which they identified with a passive, quietistic reliance upon God and an unwillingness to take any human initiative towards the fulfilment of the desired goals until the messiah actually arrived. It is therefore problematic to conceive of Zionism as a redemptive movement: certainly the Zionist ideal of 'normalization' of Jewish life would seem to be almost the antithesis of most traditional messianic visions.

Yet the relationship between Zionism and messianism remains in more of a state of ongoing tension than is the case with the other movements mentioned.[66] First, a minority of 'proto-Zionist' and Zionist thinkers insisted on seeing their goals as an integral part of the traditional messianic scenario.[67] Second, this conception has been concretized in authoritative liturgical formulations, including the description of the state of Israel as *reshit tsemiḥat ge'ulateinu*, literally 'the beginning of the sprouting of our redemption'.[68] Most importantly, some of the most interesting developments in Zionist thought and practice, especially in movements committed for eschatological reasons to settling the entire Land of Israel and actively preparing for a rebuilding of the Temple, have had an explicit messianic character. If it is not accurate to describe Zionism as a messianic movement, it is impossible to avoid confronting the messianic stream within Zionism.[69]

This chronological review of the major expressions of messianic activism in the light of the Sabbatian paradigm suggests a number questions that could be asked of each movement. How do we know about the movement; what is

[66] On this complex dialectic, see Jody Elizabeth Myers, 'The Messianic Idea and Zionist Ideologies', in Frankel (ed.), *Jews and Messianism in the Modern Era*, 3–13; Eli Lederhendler, 'Interpreting Messianic Rhetoric in the Russian Haskalah and Early Zionism', ibid. 14–33; Aviezer Ravitzky, '"Forcing the End": Zionism and the State of Israel as Antimessianic Undertakings', ibid. 34–67.

[67] See Jacob Katz, 'Israel and the Messiah', in Saperstein (ed.), *Essential Papers on Messianic Movements*, esp. 480–2; Arthur Hertzberg (ed.), *The Zionist Idea: A Historical Analysis and Reader* (New York, 1971), 105–7, 111–14, 403–5.

[68] This is the formulation of the prayer for the state of Israel incorporated into the liturgy of most Orthodox congregations in Israel and the diaspora. It is also used in the most recent prayer book of the American Conservative movement, *Sim shalom*, and—at least in Hebrew—of the American Reform movement, *Mishkan tefillah*. The English version of the prayer in the Reform seder states: 'Bless the State of Israel, which marks the dawning of hope for all who seek peace', a far more universalistic formulation than the Hebrew.

[69] See Tal, 'Foundations of a Political Messianic Trend in Israel'; Kellner 'Messianic Postures in Israel Today'; Janet Aviad, 'The Messianism of Gush Emunim', in Frankel (ed.), *Jews and Messianism in the Modern Era*, 197–213; Aviezer Ravitzky, *Messianism, Zionism, and Jewish Religious Radicalism*, trans. Michael Swirsky and Jonathan Chipman (Chicago, 1996), 79–145. Ravitzky characterizes messianic religious Zionism as ' "messianism" without a messiah' (ibid. 81).

the nature of the source material? Is it contemporary with the events? If not, how much later, and how reliable is the author's own knowledge? Were the sources produced inside the movement or outside; if outside? Was the author sympathetic, hostile, or more or less neutral? The 'Jesus movement' would certainly look quite different if all that had been preserved about it were a few lines by a hostile outsider, similar to Josephus's descriptions of other first-century charismatic figures and their followers. Similarly, those movements known only from terse descriptions by Josephus or Maimonides might look quite different if texts produced by their members had been preserved.

What was the role of the messianic figure around whom the movement crystallized? Can we be certain about the precise nature of his claims: messenger of the messiah, Ephraimite messiah, Davidic messiah? Did he function as a military leader, a charismatic, inspirational preacher of repentance, the bearer of a new teaching? Was he a learned Jew? Were miraculous powers attributed to him? Did he act in a way that violated Jewish traditions or norms? Was the ideology of the movement taught *by* the messianic figure or *about* him by others? Was there an identifiable theoretician or propagandist of the movement? If so, what was his relationship with the messianic figure?

To what extent did the ideology of the movement draw from existing doctrine? To what extent did it generate its own doctrine in response to the specific contours of the situation? How much influence from surrounding Christian or Muslim cultures can be detected in its ideology? Did a revolutionary social doctrine—the redistribution of wealth or the promise of a greater role for women—have a significant impact? Are the poor or women particularly discernible among the followers?

One of the underlying regularities of Jewish historical experience is that traditional Jewish leaders oppose messianic movements and Gentile governments suppress them. What are the arguments used by Jewish leaders that enable them both to reassert the fundamental validity of messianic belief and to repudiate the particular manifestation of it promising the most immediate fulfilment? Did the Gentile authorities pressure the Jewish leadership to act against the messianic claimant? What is the explanation for the blatant exception to the rule: the impressive number of rabbis and other Jewish leaders who supported the claims of Sabbatai Zevi?

What happened to the movement after the death of the central figure? Where information comes from external sources, the narrative usually ends when the messianic figure died (usually, was killed) and his followers became disillusioned. Yet occasionally there is evidence of a group of followers continuing to exist long after the career of the central figure ended without his promises being fulfilled. How did a group accommodate itself to shattering disappointment yet manage to maintain its coherence? How were an unusual belief and a potentially dangerous commitment transmitted from those who had personal contact with the charismatic figure to those who did not?

A final set of questions bears upon the role of messianic doctrine within Judaism and of messianic activity within Jewish history. Discussions of Jewish messianism frequently overemphasize its importance, giving the impression that it was an integral component of diaspora Jewish life. Did ordinary Jews living between the late first century and the nineteenth feel a sense of acute messianic expectation and urgency? Did praying three times a day for the coming of the messiah mean that they were predisposed to respond enthusiastically to an individual who claimed to be the awaited redeemer, that they eagerly anticipated the opportunity of leaving their homes to return to the Land of Israel?

It is, of course, almost impossible to answer such questions with confidence, for the 'ordinary Jews' did not leave us much evidence of their *mentalité*. Nevertheless, it should be noted that, with the exception of the Sabbatian movement, messianic uprisings do not appear to have been mass movements. There are many decades, even centuries, when no messianic activism can be documented anywhere in the world, and there are large regions—particularly, as Gerson Cohen has shown, northern Europe—where hardly any messianic movements occurred. The accusation made by certain Zionist writers that medieval Jews prayed for the messiah but, on the whole, were not really eager to leave the diaspora may be a polemical exaggeration, but it is probably not without some measure of truth.[70]

---

[70] Joseph Brenner, 'Self-Criticism', in Hertzberg (ed.), *The Zionist Idea*, 310; Haim Hazaz, 'The Sermon', trans. I. M. Lask, in Robert Alter (ed.), *Modern Hebrew Literature* (New York, 1975), 278–81. The charge of insincerity in the traditional messianic prayers was also a theme raised by spokesmen of the Reform movement (though with a very different purpose) (see Jakob Josef Petuchowski, *Prayerbook Reform in Europe: The Liturgy of European Liberal and Reform Judaism* [New York, 1968], 278; Paul Mendes-Flohr and Jehuda Reinharz [eds.], *The Jew in the Modern World: A Documentary History*, 2nd edn. [New York, 1995], 184a). Note the trenchant comments of the Haskalah poet Judah Leib Gordon (*Igerot yehudah leib gordon*, ed. Y. Y. Weisberg, 4 vols. in 2 [Warsaw, 1894], ii. 172–4), in Michael Stanislawski, *For Whom Do I Toil? Judah Leib Gordon and the Crisis of Russian Jewry* (New York, 1988), 100–1. The accusation that many Jews did not really want to leave their homes for the eschatological ingathering in the Land of Israel was made in traditional ethical literature (see e.g. Ephraim Luntshitz's attack on those Jews who live prosperously in the lands of the Gentiles and 'never sincerely beseech God to bring them to their own land' (*Keli yakar* [homiletical commentary on the Torah] [Lemberg, 1864], on Gen. 47: 28). David Reubeni recorded meeting a wealthy Italian Jew who told him: 'I have no desire in Jerusalem, but only in Siena' (Reubeni, *Sipur david hare'uveni*, 51 [trans.

Furthermore, we need to take seriously what might be called the peripheralizing of the messianic dimension in certain respectable understandings of Judaism. Many have noted how relatively minor a role the messianic doctrine plays in some of the most important texts of the Jewish tradition: the Torah and Hagiographa in the Bible, the Mishnah, Maimonides' *Guide for the Perplexed*, and that masterpiece of medieval German Jewish Pietism *Sefer ḥasidim*. Some rabbis whose views are recorded in the Talmud were apparently so fearful of the sufferings to come during the turbulent prelude to the messianic advent that they hoped the messiah would not come in their lifetimes (BT *San.* 98*b*). Medieval Jewish philosophers were convinced that they could achieve the ultimate purpose of human life—cultivation of the intellect leading to spiritual immortality—under their present conditions of diaspora life, and some drew the conclusion that the messiah would not benefit them at all.[71]

There is also the claim that Judaism does not depend upon a messianic doctrine because the basic structure of the commandments, the true foundation of Judaism, could remain intact indefinitely in the diaspora. Articulated most famously as a defensive ploy in a thirteenth-century polemical context by Nahmanides (Moses ben Nahman, Ramban), this idea has an intellectual integrity of its own. Jews may reveal devotion to the covenant more powerfully by observing the commandments under the difficult conditions of exile than in the messianic kingdom when obedience will be enforced. Therefore, even if it were certain that the messiah will never come, that the present (medieval) structure of Jewish life would continue forever, the heart of Judaism would not be affected.[72] This position was reasserted not a few times in the years after Nahmanides.[73] It was also repudiated by those who maintained that the messianic impulse lies at the core of Jewish identity.

Adler, 281]), and Abner of Burgos reported the popular contentment with diaspora life of contemporary Jews (in Y. Baer, *A History of the Jews in Christian Spain*, i. 352).

[71] See e.g. the idea expressed by Isaac ben Yedaiah in the thirteenth century that the Jewish intellectual elite would not benefit from the messiah's arrival at all (Saperstein, *Decoding the Rabbis*, 109–11).

[72] Nahmanides, 'The Book of Redemption', in id., *Ramban: Writings and Discourses*, ed. Charles Ber Chavel, 2 vols. (New York, 1978), i. 606–7; Nahmanides, 'Disputation', ibid. i. 672–3. See the detailed discussion of the key passage in Chapter 11.

[73] The view that Judaism can stand without the hope for the coming of the messiah was repeated by many, including Isaac Polgar: 'No enlightened person should believe that our faith depends upon the coming of the messiah' (Polgar, *Ezer hadat*, ed. Jacob Levinger [Tel Aviv, 1984], 57; see Dov Schwartz, *The Messianic Idea in Medieval Jewish Thought* [Harayon hameshiḥi bahagut hayehudit bimei habeinayim] [Ramat Gan, 1997], 192–3; Saul Levi Morteira, in Marc Saperstein, *Exile in Amsterdam: Saul Levi Morteira's Sermons to a Congregation of 'New Jews'* [Cincinnati, 2005], 342–5).

Distinct from the question of the importance of messianism in Jewish history and doctrine is an evaluation of its impact. Has messianism, on the whole, been a positive or negative force in Jewish experience? Have Jewish messianic movements been essentially energizing and inspiring or disillusioning and destructive?[74] What kind of 'price' does messianism exact of those who give it their commitment?[75] Despite the abundant historical investigation of recent decades, there are still many unanswered questions.

Writers and preachers such as Nahmanides, Polgar, and Morteira certainly did not question the coming of the messiah, but were contrasting the function of the messianic doctrine in Judaism and Christianity. There is also evidence of Jews who doubted that the messiah would ever come yet remained Jews, such as Hayim Galipappa (see Joseph Albo, *Sefer ha'ikarim* [Book of Principles], 4: 42 [ed. Isaac Husik, 4 vols. in 5 (Philadelphia, 1930), iv. 418]).

[74] For a provocative yet overly extreme and polemical assessment of messianism as a negative, idolatrous force in Jewish history, see Lionel Kochan, *Jews, Idols and Messiahs: The Challenge from History* (Oxford, 1990), 160–91.

[75] See Jacob Taubes, 'The Price of Messianism', in Saperstein (ed.), *Essential Papers on Messianic Movements*, 551–7.

Bibliography

Primary Sources

ABBA MARI BEN MOSES OF LUNEL, *Minḥat kena'ot: harbeh mikhtavim . . . el harashba umah sheheshiv lahem* [polemical letters] (Pressburg: Anton Edlen von Schmid, 1838; repr. Jerusalem: n.p., 1968).

ABELARD, PETER, *Sic et non: A Critical Edition*, ed. Blanche Boyers and Richard McKeon (Chicago: University of Chicago Press, 1976).

ABOAB, ISAAC, *Be'ur al perush haramban latorah* [super-commentary on Nahmanides' Commentary on the Torah], in *Treasury of Torah Commentators* [Otsar mefarshei hatorah], 2 vols. (Jerusalem: n.p., 1973).

—— *Be'ur letur oraḥ ḥayim* [commentary on *Arba'ah turim*, 'Oraḥ ḥayim'] (Jerusalem: Makhon Yerushalayim, 1995).

—— 'Ketsat parashiyot' [sermons] (MS Hunt 342 [Neubauer 952], Bodleian Library, Oxford).

—— 'Nehar pishon' [sermons] (MS Or. 10701 [Gaster 1398], British Library, London).

—— *Nehar pishon* [sermons] (Istanbul: Eliezer Soncino, 1538; repr. Zolkiew, 1806).

—— *Shitat hakadmonim al masekhet beitsah . . . im ḥidushei rabenu yitsḥak abo'ab* [commentary on Babylonian Talmud, *Beitsah*] (Jerusalem: Oraita, 1959).

—— *Tur veshulḥan arukh, oraḥ ḥayim, hilkhot shabat . . . im be'ur ḥadash miketav yad mohari abo'ab* [commentary on sabbath laws in *Arba'ah turim* and *Shulḥan arukh*, 'Oraḥ ḥayim'] (Montreal: Hadrat Kodesh, 1991).

ABRAHAMS, ISRAEL (ed), *Hebrew Ethical Wills*, 2 vols. (Philadelphia: Jewish Publication Society, 1926).

ABRAVANEL, ISAAC, *Ateret zekenim* (Warsaw: Dubersh ben Alexander Toresh, 1894).

—— *Perush al hatorah* [Commentary on the Torah], 3 vols. (Jerusalem: Benei Arbel, 1964).

—— *Perush al nevi'im ukhetuvim* [Commentary on the Prophets and Writings], 3 vols. (Jerusalem: Torah Vada'at, 1955–60).

ABULAFIA, TODROS BEN JOSEPH, *Otsar hakavod* (Satu Mare: M. L. Hirsch, 1926).

—— Sermon (Heb.), in Judah ben Asher, *Zikhron yehudah* [responsa], ed. Judah Rosenberg (Berlin: D. Frindlender, 1846; repr. Jerusalem: n.p., 1967), no. 91, 43*a*–45*b*; also in Judah ben Asher, *She'elot uteshuvot zikhron yehudah lerabenu yehudah ben harosh* [responsa], ed. Avraham Yosef Havatselet (Jerusalem: Makhon Yerushalayim, 2005), no. 91, 106–12.

ABULAFIA, TODROS BEN JUDAH, *Gan hameshalim vehaḥidot* [poetry], ed. David Yellin, 2 vols. (Jerusalem: n.p., 1932–6).

AESCOLY, AARON ZE'EV (ed.), *Jewish Messianic Movements: Sources and Documents on Messianism in Jewish History* [Hatenu'ot hameshiḥiyot beyisra'el: otsar hamekorot vehate'udot] (Jerusalem: Bialik Institute, 1988).

AGNON, SHMUEL YOSEF, 'The Emissary from the Land of Israel' (Heb.), in *The Complete Stories of Shmuel Yosef Agnon* [Kol sipurav shel shemu'el yosef agnon] (Berlin: Schocken Books, 1931), ii. 212–23.

—— *In the Heart of the Seas*, trans. I. M. Lask (New York: Schocken Books, 1948).

ALBO, JOSEPH, *Sefer ha'ikarim* [Book of Principles], ed. Isaac Husik, 4 vols. in 5 (Philadelphia: Jewish Publication Society, 1930).

ALEXANDER OF APHRODISIAS, *On Aristotle's Metaphysics 2 & 3*, trans. William Dooley and Arthur Madigan (Ithaca, NY: Cornell University Press, 1992).

ANATOLI, JACOB, *Habe'ur ha'emtsa'i shel ibn rushd al sefer hamavo leporfirius vesefer hama'amarot le'aristoteles* [Averroës' middle commentary on Porphyry's *Isagoge* and Aristotle's *Categories*], ed. Herbert Davidson (Cambridge, Mass.: Medieval Academy of America, 1969).

—— *Malmad hatalmidim* [sermons] (Lyck: Mekitsei Nirdamim, 1866; repr. Jerusalem: n.p., 1968).

AQUINAS, THOMAS, *Against the Averroists: On There Being Only One Intellect*, ed. and trans. Ralph McInerny (West Lafayette, Ind.: Purdue University Press, 1993).

—— *Commentary on the Metaphysics of Aristotle*, trans. John Rowan, 2 vols. (Chicago: H. Regnery, 1961).

—— *Commentary on the Posterior Analytics of Aristotle*, trans. F. R. Larcher (Albany: Magi Books, 1970).

—— *Summa theologica*, trans. Fathers of the English Dominican Province, 3 vols. (New York: Benziger Brothers, 1947).

ARAMA, ISAAC, *Akedat yitshak* [homiletical essays on the Torah], 3 vols. (Warsaw, 1882–4).

ARISTOTLE, *Metaphysics*, trans. Richard Hope (New York: Columbia University Press, 1952).

ASHER BEN YEHIEL, *She'elot uteshuvot harosh* [responsa] (Vilna: Y. L. Mets, 1885).

ASHKENAZI, BEZALEL BEN ABRAHAM, *Shitah mekubetset: asefat zekenim, vehu ḥidushei masekhet ketubot* [novellae on Babylonian Talmud *Ketubot*] (Constantinople: Jonah ben Jacob, 1738).

ASSAF, SIMHA, *Sources for the History of Jewish Education* [Mekorot letoledot haḥinukh beyisra'el], 4 vols. (Tel Aviv: Dvir, 1925–43).

AUGUSTINE OF HIPPO, *Quaestionum in Evangeliorum*, Patrologiae cursus completus, Series Latina, ed. J.-P. Migne, 221 vols. (Paris: Migne, 1844–65), xxxv, cols. 1321–64.

—— *Quaestionum in Heptateuchum*, Patrologiae cursus completus, Series Latina, ed. J.-P. Migne, 221 vols. (Paris: Migne, 1844–65), xxxiv, cols. 547–823.

BACHRACH, YA'IR HAYIM, *Ḥavot ya'ir* [responsa] (Lemberg: Salat, 1896).

BAER, FRITZ (ed.), *Die Juden im Christlichen Spanien*, 2 vols. (Berlin: Akademie Verlag, 1929).

BAZAK, JACOB, and STEPHEN M. PASSAMANECK, *Jewish Law and Jewish Life: Selected Rabbinic Responsa* (New York: Union of American Hebrew Congregations, 1979).

BEDERSI, YEDAIAH, Annotations on Avicenna's *Canon of Medicine* (Heb.) (Hebrew MS G.III.9, Escorial Library, Madrid).

—— Annotations on Averroës' epitome of Aristotle's *Physics* (Heb.) (De Rossi Hebrew MS 1399, Palatina Library, Parma).

—— Commentary on the midrashim (Heb.) (De Rossi Hebrew MS 222, Palatina Library, Parma).

—— Commentary on the midrashim (Heb.) (Hebrew MS 738.3, National Library of France, Paris).

—— *Ohev nashim* [The Lover of Women], ed. Adolf Neubauer, in *Tif'eret Seiva: Jubelschrift zum Neunzigsten Geburtstag des Dr. L. Zunz* (Berlin: L. Gershel, 1884), Germ. section, 138–40 (introduction); Heb. section, 1–19 (text).

BEN ADRET, SOLOMON (RASHBA), *Ḥidushei harashba al agadot hashas* [novellae on the talmudic aggadot], ed. Shalom Meshulam Weinberger (Jerusalem: n.p., 1966).

—— *She'elot uteshuvot harashba* [responsa], 7 vols. in 4 (Benei Berak: n.p., 1958–9).

BENJAMIN BEN AARON OF ZALOZCE, *Amtaḥat binyamin: be'ur kohelet* [commentary on Ecclesiastes] (Minkowitz, 1796).

BEREKHIAH BERAKH, *Zera berakh* [homiletical essays on the Torah], 2 vols. in 1 (Amsterdam: Solomon ben Joseph Props, 1730).

BIALIK, HAYIM NAHMAN, and YEHOSHUA HANA RAVNITZKY (eds.), *The Book of Legends: Sefer ha-Aggadah: Legends from the Talmud and Midrash*, trans. William G. Braude (New York: Schocken Books, 1992).

BIBAGO, ABRAHAM, *Derekh emunah* [The Way of Faith] (Constantinople, 1522; offprint edn. Jerusalem: Sifriyat Mekorot, 1970).

—— *Zeh yenaḥamenu* [sermon on Creation] (Salonika, 1522).

BIEL, GABRIEL, *Collectorium circa quattuor libros Sententiarum*, ed. Wilfred Werbeck, 4 bks. in 5 vols. (Tübingen: Mohr, 1973–92).

BIN GORION, MICHA JOSEPH, *Mimekor Yisrael: Classical Jewish Folktales*, ed. Emanuel bin Gorion, 3 vols. (Bloomington: Indiana University Press, 1976).

BIRNBAUM, PHILIP (ed.), *A Treasury of Judaism* (New York: Hebrew Publishing Co., 1962).

BONAVENTURE, *Opera omnia*, 10 vols. plus index (Florence: Quaracchi, 1882–1902).

—— *Opera theologica selecta*, 4 vols. (Florence: Quaracchi, 1934–49).

BUBER, MARTIN, *Tales of the Hasidim*, 2 vols. (New York: Schocken Books, 1964).

CALVIN, JOHN, *Sermons on the Ten Commandments*, ed. and trans. Benjamin W. Farley (Grand Rapids: Baker Books, 1980).

CAMPANTON, ISAAC, *Darkhei hagemara* [talmudic methodology] (Vilna: n.p., 1901).

CAPSALI, ELIJAH, *Seder eliyahu zuta* [history], 2 vols. (Jerusalem: Makhon Ben-Tsevi, 1975).

CARMI, T. (ed. and trans.), *The Penguin Book of Hebrew Verse* (New York: Viking Press, 1981).

CONSTABLE, OLIVIA REMIE (ed.), *Medieval Iberia: Readings from Christian, Muslim, and Jewish Sources* (Philadelphia: University of Pennsylvania Press, 1997).

CRESCAS, HASDAI, *Or hashem* [The Light of the Lord] (Jerusalem: Sifrei Ramot, 1990).

DAN, JOSEPH (ed.), *The Teachings of Hasidism* (New York: Behrman House, 1983).

DAVIDSON, ISRAEL, *Thesaurus of Proverbs and Parables from Medieval Jewish Literature* [Otsar hameshalim vehapitgamim mesifrut yemei habeinayim] (Jerusalem: Mosad Harav Kook, 1979).

DEL MEDIGO, ELIJAH, *Sefer beḥinat hadat*, ed. Jacob Ross (Tel Aviv: Chaim Rosenberg School of Jewish Studies, 1984).

Diccionario de autoridades, 3 vols. (Madrid: Gredos, 1963).

Diccionario critico etimológico castellano e hispanico, 6 vols. (Madrid: Gredos, 1984–91).

DOV BAER OF MEZHIRECH, *Magid devarav leya'akov*, ed. Rivka Schatz Uffenheimer (Jerusalem: Magnes Press, 1990).

'Dover meisharim' [sermons] (MS 197 [Neubauer 2447], Christ Church, Oxford).

EDELES, SAMUEL, *Ḥidushei agadot al kol shitat hatalmud* [novellae on talmudic aggadot] (Lublin: Tsevi bar Abraham Kalonimo Yafeh, 1627).

ELIMELEKH OF LYZHANSK, *No'am elimelekh* [homilies on the Torah], ed. Gedalyah Nigal (Jerusalem: Mosad Harav Kook, 1978).

EYBESCHUETZ, JONATHAN, *Ya'arot devash* [sermons], 2 vols. in 1 (Jerusalem: Lewin-Epstein, 1968).

EYMERICH, NICOLAU, *Le Manuel des inquisiteurs*, trans. Louis Sala-Molins (Paris: Mouton, 1973).

FRANCIS OF ASSISI, *The Little Flowers of St. Francis* (Garden City, NY: Image Books, 1958).

GARÇON, JOSEPH BEN MEIR, 'The Sermons of Rabbi Joseph ben Meir Garçon' (Heb.), ed. Meir Benayahu, *Michael*, 7 (1981), 42–205.

GERONDI, JONAH, *Sha'arei teshuvah* [Gates of Repentance] (Jerusalem: Lewin-Epstein, 1968).

GERONDI, NISSIM BEN REUBEN, *Derashot haran lerabenu nisim ben reuven gerondi* [sermons], ed. Leon Feldman (Jerusalem: Makhon Shalem, 1974).

GERSON, JOHN, *L'Oeuvre oratoire*, Oeuvres complètes, 5, ed. Palem Glorieux (Paris: Desclée & Cie, 1963).

—— *Six sermons français inédits de Jean Gerson*, ed. Louis Mourin (Paris: J. Vrin, 1946).

GERSONIDES (RALBAG), *Milḥamot hashem* (Berlin: L. Lames, 1923); Eng. trans.: *The Wars of the Lord*, trans. and ed. Seymour Feldman, 3 vols. (Philadelphia: Jewish Publication Society, 1984–99).

—— *Perush al hatorah* [Commentary on the Torah] (Venice: Bomberg, 1547; repr. New York: n.p., 1958).

GIKATILLA, JOSEPH, *Gates of Light: Sha'arei Orah*, trans. Avi Weinstein (San Francisco: HarperCollins, 1994).

GITTELSOHN, ROLAND B., *Fire in My Bones: Essays on Judaism in a Time of Crisis* (New York: Bloch, 1969).

GOLDSTEIN, JONATHAN A., *I Maccabees: A New Translation with Introduction and Commentary* (Garden City, NY: Doubleday, 1976).

GRAYZEL, SOLOMON, *The Church and the Jews in the XIIIth Century: A Study of Their Relations during the Years 1198–1254* (New York: Hermon Press, 1966).

—— *The Church and the Jews in the XIIIth Century*, vol. ii: *1254–1314*, ed. Kenneth R. Stow (New York: Jewish Theological Seminary of America, 1989).

GREGORY OF RIMINI, *Gregorii Ariminensis OESA lectura super primum et secundum Sententiarum*, ed. A. Damasus Trapp and Venicio Marcolino, 6 vols. (Berlin: Walter de Gruyter, 1981).

HALEVI, JUDAH, *The Kuzari: An Argument for the Faith of Israel*, trans. Hartwig Hirschfield (New York: Schocken Books, 1964).

—— *Selected Poems of Jehudah Halevi*, trans. Nina Salaman (Philadelphia: Jewish Publication Society, 1928).

HAZAZ, HAIM, 'The Sermon', trans. I. M. Lask, in Robert Alter (ed.), *Modern Hebrew Literature* (New York: Behrman House, 1975), 271–87.

HILLEL BEN SAMUEL OF VERONA, *Sefer tagmulei hanefesh lehilel ben shemu'el miveronah* [The Rewards of the Soul], ed. Joseph (Giuseppe) Sermoneta (Jerusalem: Magnes Press, 1981).

HIRSCH, EMIL G., 'Memorial Oration', in Kaufmann Kohler (ed.), *David Einhorn Memorial Volume: Selected Sermons and Addresses* (New York: Bloch, 1911), 457–82.

HONORIUS AUGUSTODUN, *Liber duodecim quaestionum*, Patrologiae cursus completus, Series Latina, ed. J.-P. Migne, 221 vols. (Paris: Migne, 1844–65), clxxii, cols. 1177–86.

—— *Quaestiones et responsiones in Proverbia et in Ecclesiasten*, Patrologiae cursus completus, Series Latina, ed. J.-P. Migne, 221 vols. (Paris: Migne, 1844–65), clxxii, cols. 313–48.

HOROWITZ, ISAIAH, *Shenei luḥot haberit* (Warsaw, 1852).

HUGH OF ST VICTOR [attrib.], *Quaestiones et decisiones in epistolas Pauli*, Patrologiae cursus completus, Series Latina, ed. J.-P. Migne, 221 vols. (Paris: Migne, 1844–65), clxxv, cols. 431–634.

IBN DAUD, ABRAHAM, *Sefer ha-Qabbalah: The Book of Tradition. A Critical Edition*, ed. and trans. Gerson Cohen (Philadelphia: Jewish Publication Society, 1967).

IBN GABBAI, MEIR BEN EZEKIEL, *Avodat hakodesh* (Jerusalem: Levin Epstein, 1973).

IBN HABIB, JACOB, *Ein ya'akov . . . im kol hamefarshim* [anthology of talmudic aggadot], 5 vols. in 3 (Vilna: Romm, 1883–90; repr. Jerusalem: Keren Hotsa'at Sifrei Rabbanei Bavel, 1964–72).

IBN LEV, JOSEPH, *She'elot uteshuvot mahari ben lev* [responsa], 2 vols. (Jerusalem: Ginzei Kedem, 1960).

IBN SHEM TOV, JOSEPH, Sermons (Hebrew MS 1, Juynboll Family Library, Leiden).

—— 'Sermons on Repentance' (Heb.), ed. Sha'ul Regev, *Asufot*, 5 (1991), 183–211.

IBN SHEM TOV, SHEM TOV, *Derashot* [Sermons] (Salonika, 1525; repr. Jerusalem: Hebrew University, 1973).

IBN SHU'EIB, JOEL, *Olat shabat* [sermons] (Venice: Bomberg, 1577; repr. Jerusalem: Y. M. Morgenstern, 1973).

IBN SHU'EIB, JOSHUA, *Derashot hatorah* [Sermons on the Torah], 2 vols. (Jerusalem: Vagshal Publishing, 1992).

IBN VERGA, SOLOMON, *Shevet yehudah* [history], ed. Ezriel Shohat (Jerusalem: Bialik Institute, 1947).

Igerot kena'ot [polemical letters], in *An Anthology of Maimonides' Responsa and Letters* [Kovets teshuvot harambam ve'igerotav], Pt. III, ed. Abraham Lichtenberg (Leipzig: H. L. Shnoys, 1859).

IMMANUEL OF ROME, *Maḥberot*, ed. Dov Yarden, 2 vols. (Jerusalem: Bialik Institute, 1957).

ISSERLES, MOSES, *Darkhei mosheh* [commentary on *Arba'ah turim*] (Zhitomir: Heschel, 1858).

—— *Mapah perusah* [glosses on *Shulḥan arukh*] (Halberstadt: Yeruham Hirsch, 1861).

JACOB JOSEPH OF POLONNOYE, *Ben porat yosef* [homiletical comments on the Torah] (Piotrków Trybunalski, 1883; repr. New York: n.p., 1970).

JAFFE, SAMUEL BEN ISAAC, *Yefeh to'ar* [commentary on *Midrash Rabbah*], 9 vols. (Jerusalem: H. Wagschal, 1989).

JEROME, *Hebrew Questions on Genesis*, trans. C. T. R. Hayward (Oxford: Clarendon Press, 1995).

JOSEPH BEN DAVID OF SARAGOSSA, *Perush al hatorah meyuḥas letalmid rabenu nisim b. re'uven (haran)* [Commentary on the Torah], ed. Leon Feldman (Jerusalem: Makhon Shalem, 1970).

JOSEPH HAKOHEN, *Emek habakhah* [history], ed. Meir Letteris (Kraków: Faust's Buchhandlung, 1895).

JUDAH BEN ASHER, *She'elot uteshuvot zikhron yehudah lerabenu yehudah ben harosh* [responsa], ed. Avraham Yosef Havatselet (Jerusalem: Makhon Yerushalayim, 2005).

—— *Zikhron yehudah* [responsa], ed. Judah Rosenberg (Berlin: D. Frindlender, 1846).

JUDAH LEIB BEN BEZALEL OF PRAGUE (MAHARAL), *Gur aryeh* [super-commentary on Rashi's *Commentary on the Torah*], in *Treasury of Torah Commentators* [Otsar mefarshei hatorah], 2 vols. (Jerusalem: n.p. 1973).

—— *Netivot olam* (Prague: Gershom ben Bezalel Katz, 1596).

KALONYMOS BEN KALONYMOS, 'An Ethical Epistle of Kalonymos ben Kalonymos' (Heb.), ed. Isaiah Sonne, *Kovets al-yad*, 1/11 (1936), 93–110.

—— *Igeret hitnatslut haketanah* [A Short Epistle of Apology], ed. Joseph Shatzmiller, *Sefunot*, 10 (1966), 7–52.

KARO, ISAAC, *Derashot r. yitsḥak karo* [sermons], ed. Sha'ul Regev (Ramat Gan: Bar Ilan University Press, 1995).

—— *Toledot yitsḥak* [commentary on the Torah] (Trent: Riva di Trento, 1558).

KHANANEL, ASHER, and ELI EŠKENAZI (eds.), *Fontes hebraici ad res oeconomicas socialesque terrarum balcanicarum: Saeculo XVI pertinentes* (Sofia: Bulgarian Academy, 1958).

KIMḤI, DAVID (RADAK), *Perushei rabi david kimḥi (radak) al hatorah* [commentaries on the Torah], ed. Moses Kamelhar (Jerusalem: Mosad Harav Kook, 1970).

KOBLER, FRANZ (ed.), *Letters of Jews through the Ages*, 2 vols. (New York: East and West Library, 1978).

LAMM, NORMAN, *The Religious Thought of Hasidism: Text and Commentary* (New York: Yeshiva University Press, 1999).

LEVI IBN ḤABIB, *She'elot uteshuvot haralbaḥ* [responsa] (Lemberg, 1865).

LUNTSHITZ, EPHRAIM, *Amudei shesh* [sermons] (Warsaw: N. Shriftgisser, 1875).
—— *Keli yakar* [homiletical commentary on the Torah] (Lemberg: B. L. Necheles, 1864).
—— *Olelot efrayim* [sermons] (Tel Aviv: Offset Brody-Katz, 1975).
MAIMONIDES, MOSES, *Crisis and Leadership: Epistles of Maimonides*, trans. and ed. Abraham Halkin and David Hartman (Philadelphia: Jewish Publication Society, 1993).
—— *Guide for the Perplexed*, trans. and ed. M. Friedländer, 3 vols. in 1 (New York: Hebrew Publishing Co., 1946).
—— *A Maimonides Reader*, ed. Isador Twersky (New York: Behrman House, 1972).
—— *Pirkei mosheh birefuah* [medical writings], ed. Süssmann Montner (Jerusalem: Mosad Harav Kook, 1982).
—— *Teshuvot harambam* [responsa], ed. Joshua Blau, 3 vols. (Jerusalem: Mekitsei Nirdamim, 1957–61).
MEDINA, SAMUEL DE, *She'elot uteshuvot maharashdam* [responsa] (Lemberg: P. M. Balaban, 1862).
MENAHEM BEN SOLOMON, *Midrash sekhel tov al sefer bereshit ushemot* [midrash on Genesis and Exodus], ed. Solomon Buber, 2 vols. (Berlin: Ittskovsky, 1900).
MENAHEM NAHUM OF CHERNOBYL, *Yesamah lev: ḥidushei agadot hashas* [novellae on talmudic aggadot] (Slavuta, 1798).
MENDES-FLOHR, PAUL, and JEHUDA REINHARZ (eds.), *The Jew in the Modern World: A Documentary History*, 2nd edn. (New York: Oxford University Press, 1995).
MESSER LEON, JUDAH BEN YEHIEL, *The Book of the Honeycomb's Flow: Sēpher Nōfeth Sūfim*, trans. and ed. Isaac Rabinowitz (Ithaca, NY: Cornell University Press, 1983).
MEYER, MICHAEL A. (ed.), *Ideas of Jewish History* (Detroit: Wayne State University Press, 1987).
MODENA, LEON, *Magen vaḥerev* [polemical work] (Jerusalem: Mekitsei Nirdamim, 1960).
—— *Midbar yehudah* [sermons] (Venice: Daniel Zaniti, 1602; new edn. Benei Berak: Mishor, 2002).
MORTEIRA, SAUL LEVI, *Givat sha'ul: ḥamishim derushim yekarim* [sermons] (Amsterdam: Immanuel Benvenisti, 1645; new edn. Warsaw: Israel Alafin, 1912).
—— Sermons (Heb.), 5 vols (MS 12, Budapest Rabbinical Seminary Library).
—— *Tratado da verdad da lei de Moisés*, ed. H. P. Salomon (Coimbra: Por Ordem da Universidade, 1988).
MOSES HADARSHAN, *Midrash bereshit rabati* [homiletical comments on Genesis], ed. Chanoch Albeck (Jerusalem: Mekitsei Nirdamim, 1940).
MOSES BEN JACOB OF COUCY, *Sefer mitsvot gadol* [legal compendium] (Benei Berak: n.p., 1991).
MOSES BEN JOSEPH DI TRANI, *She'elot uteshuvot mabit* [responsa], 2 vols. in 1 (New York: n.p., 1961).
NAHMAN OF BRATSLAV, *Likutei moharan*, 2 vols. in 1 (Benei Berak: Yeshivat Breslav, 1965).

NAHMANIDES (MOSES BEN NAHMAN, RAMBAN), *Commentary on the Torah*, vol. i: *Genesis*, trans. Charles Ber Chavel (New York: Shilo, 1971).

—— *Writings and Discourses*, ed. and trans. Charles Ber Chavel, 2 vols. (New York: Shilo, 1978).

NARBONI, MOSES, *Be'ur lesefer moreh nevukhim* [commentary on Maimonides' *Guide for the Perplexed*] (Vienna: K. K. Hof- und Staatsdruckere, 1852).

NEMOY, LEON (ed.), *Karaite Anthology: Excerpts from the Early Literature* (New Haven: Yale University Press, 1952).

PATAI, RAPHAEL (ed.), *The Messiah Texts* (New York: Avon, 1979).

PERL, JOSEPH, *Megaleh temirin* [The Revealer of Secrets] (Vienna: Anton Strauss, 1819).

Pinkas hamedinah, o pinkas va'ad hakehilot harashiyot bimedinat lita [The Register of the State, or the Register of the Council of the Major Communities in the Duchy of Lithuania], ed. Shimon Dubnow (Berlin: Ayanot, 1925).

PLAUT, W. GUNTHER (ed.), *The Rise of Reform Judaism: A Sourcebook of Its European Origins* (New York: World Union for Progressive Judaism, 1963).

POLGAR, ISAAC, *Ezer hadat*, ed. Jacob Levinger (Tel Aviv: Tel Aviv University Press, 1984).

RABINOWITZ, LOUIS, *Sparks from the Anvil: Sermons for Sabbaths, Holy Days and Festivals* (New York: Bloch, 1955).

REUBENI, DAVID, *Sipur david hare'uveni al pi ketav yad oksford* [The Story of David Reubeni Copied from the Oxford Manuscript], ed. Aaron Ze'ev Aescoly (Jerusalem: Bialik Institute, 1993); Eng. trans. in Elkan Nathan Adler (ed.), *Jewish Travellers* (New York: Bloch, 1931), 251–328.

ROSANES, JUDAH BEN SAMUEL, *Parashat derakhim* [sermons] (Warsaw, 1871).

SA'ADYAH GAON, *Emunot vede'ot* [The Book of Beliefs and Opinions], trans. Samuel Rosenblatt (New Haven: Yale University Press, 1948).

SABA, ABRAHAM BEN JACOB, *Tseror hamor . . . al hamishah humshei torah* [homiletical comments on the Torah] (New York: Y. Ze'ev, 1961).

SCHEPANSKY, YISRAEL, *The Land of Israel in the Responsa Literature* [Erets yisra'el besifrut hateshuvot], 3 vols. (Jerusalem: Mosad Harav Kook, 1966).

SCHIRMANN, HAYYIM (YEFIM), *Hebrew Poetry in Spain and Provence* [Hashirah ha'ivrit bisefarad uviprovans], 2 vols. in 4 (Jerusalem: Bialik Institute, 1960).

Sefer habahir [kabbalah] (Jerusalem: Mosad Harav Kook, 1951).

Sefer hasidim [based on the Parma Manuscript], ed. Jehuda Wistinezki (Frankfurt am Main: Wahrmann Verlag, 1924; repr. Jerusalem: Wahrmann Books, 1969).

Sefer yetsirah [kabbalah] (Mantua: Jacob Cohen of Gazulo, 1563).

Sermons by a disciple of Hasdai Crescas (Heb.) (Firkovitch, First Series no. 507, Russian National Library, St Petersburg).

Sermons by various preachers (Heb.) (MS 9856, Jewish Theological Seminary of America Library, New York).

Shivah einayim: . . . she'elot uteshuvot . . . mahari abo'ab [rabbinic miscellany] (Leghorn, 1745).

SIMEON BAR JOSEPH (EN DURAN), *Hoshen mishpat* [polemical letters], ed. David Kaufmann, in *Tif'eret Seiva: Jubelschrift zum Neunzigsten Geburtstag des Dr. L. Zunz* (Berlin: Louis Gerschel, 1884): Germ. section, 143–51 (introduction); Heb. section, 142–74 (text).

SIRIRO, SAMUEL SAUL, *Derushei maharshash siriro* [sermons], ed. David Ovadiyah, 2 vols. (Jerusalem: David Ovadiyah, 1989–91).

SOBOL, JOSHUA, 'Jewish Soul: The Last Night of Otto Weininger', *Modern International Drama*, 22/2 (Spring 1989), 45–84.

SOLOMON BEN ISAAC LEVI, *Divrei shelomoh* [sermons] (Venice: Zaniti and Prizinain, 1596; repr. Brooklyn: Goldenberg Brothers, 1993).

SONCINO, JOSHUA, *Naḥalah liyhoshua . . . she'elot uteshuvot* [responsa] (Constantinople, 1731).

SPINOZA, BENEDICT DE, *Ethics*, in *Philosophy of Benedict de Spinoza*, trans. R. H. M. Elwes (New York: Tudor Publishing Co., 1933), 39–278.

SUÁREZ FERNÁNDEZ, LUIS (ed.), *Documentos acerca de la expulsión de los Judios* (Valladolid: Consejo Superior de Investigaciones Científicas, Patronato Menéndez Pelayo, 1964).

TIBERG, MOSHE HAYIM, *From the Praises of the Land: A Collection of Praises of the Land of Israel According to the Sources* [Mishivḥei ha'arets: osef shivḥei erets yisra'el lefi hamekorot] (Tel Aviv: n.p., 1975).

TOMER, BEN-ZION, 'Children of the Shadows', in Michael Taub (ed.), *Israeli Holocaust Drama* (Syracuse, NY: Syracuse University Press, 1996), 127–85.

TUVYAH BEN ELIEZER, *Midrash lekaḥ tov . . . al hatorah kulah* [commentary on the Torah], ed. Solomon Buber (Vilna, 1884).

—— *Perush lekaḥ tov al megilat eikhah* [commentary on Lamentations], ed. Jacob Nacht (Berlin, 1895).

UÇEDA, SAMUEL DE, *Midrash shemu'el* [commentary on *Pirkei avot*] (Benei Berak: S. L. A., 1992).

USQUE, SAMUEL, *Consolation for the Tribulations of Israel*, trans. and ed. Martin A. Cohen (Philadelphia: Jewish Publication Society, 1965).

WISE, STEPHEN S., *Challenging Years: The Autobiography of Stephen Wise* (New York: Putnam's Sons, 1949).

—— *Free Synagogue Pulpit: Sermons and Addresses*, vol. i (New York, Bloch, 1908).

WYCLIF, JOHN, *Sermones*, ed. Johann Loserth, 4 vols. (London: Wyclif Society, 1887–90).

Yalkut shimoni [midrashic comments on biblical verses] (Venice, 1566).

YABETZ, JOSEPH BEN HAYIM, *Ḥasdei hashem* (Brooklyn: Moineshter, 1934).

—— *Or haḥayim* (Ferrara: Abraham Usque, 1554).

ZACUTO, ABRAHAM BEN SAMUEL, *Sefer yuḥasin hashalem* [history of the Jews], ed. Hirschell Filipovski (Jerusalem: n.p., 1963).

ZARFATI, JOSEPH BEN HAYIM, *Yad yosef* [sermons] (Amsterdam: n.p., 1700).

Zohar: The Book of Enlightenment, trans. and introd. Daniel Chanan Matt (New York: Paulist Press, 1983).

Zohar ḥadash: rut (Livorno: Yisra'el Kushta, 1866).

Studies

ABERBACH, DAVID, *Revolutionary Hebrew, Empire and Crisis* (New York: New York University Press, 1998).

ABERLE, DAVID, 'A Note on Relative Deprivation Theory as Applied to Millenarian and Other Cult Movements', in Sylvia Thrupp (ed.), *Millennial Dreams in Action* (The Hague: Mouton, 1962), 209–14.

ABRAHAMS, ISRAEL, *Jewish Life in the Middle Ages* (London: Edward Goldston, 1932).

ABULAFIA, DAVID, *The Great Sea: A Human History of the Mediterranean* (London: Allen Lane, 2011).

—— *A Mediterranean Emporium: The Catalan Kingdom of Majorca* (Cambridge: Cambridge University Press, 1994).

ADLER, ELKAN NATHAN, 'Lea on the Inquisition of Spain and Herein of Spanish and Portuguese Jews and Marranos', *Jewish Quarterly Review*, 20 (1908), 509–71.

AELION BROOKS, ANDRÉE, *The Woman Who Defied Kings: The Life and Times of Dona Gracia Mendes* (St. Paul: Paragon House, 2002).

ALEXANDER, PHILIP S., 'The Rabbis and Messianism', in Markus Bockmuehl and James Carletone Paget (eds.), *Redemption and Resistance: The Messianic Hopes of Jews and Christians in Antiquity* (London: Continuum, 2007), 227–44.

ALPERS, SVETLANA, *Rembrandt's Enterprise: The Studio and the Market* (Chicago: University of Chicago Press, 1988).

ALTMANN, ALEXANDER, 'Eternality of Punishment: A Theological Controversy Within the Amsterdam Rabbinate in the Thirties of the Seventeenth Century', *Proceedings of the American Academy of Jewish Research*, 40 (1973), 1–88.

—— 'Lurianic Kabbalah in a Platonic Key: Abraham Cohen Herrera's *Puerta del Cielo*', in Isadore Twersky and Bernard Septimus (eds.), *Jewish Thought in the Seventeenth Century* (Cambridge, Mass.: Harvard University Press, 1987), 1–37.

ASSAF, SIMHAH, *Punishments after the Completion of the Talmud* [Ha'onshin aḥarei ḥatimat hatalmud] (Jerusalem, n.p., 1922).

ASSIS, YOM TOV, *The Golden Age of Aragonese Jewry: Community and Society in the Crown of Aragon, 1213–1327* (London: Littman Library, 1997).

—— 'Sexual Behavior in Mediaeval Hispano-Jewish Society', in Ada Rapoport-Albert and Steven Zipperstein (eds.), *Jewish History: Essays in Honour of Chimen Abramsky* (London: Peter Halben, 1988), 25–59.

—— 'Spanish Jewry: From Persecutions to Expulsion (1391–1492)', *Studia Hebraica*, 4 (2004), 307–19.

—— 'Welfare and Mutual Aid in the Spanish Jewish Communities', in Haim Beinart (ed.), *Moreshet Sepharad: The Sephardi Legacy*, 2 vols. (Jerusalem: Magnes Press, 1992), i. 318–45.

ATTIAS, JEAN-CHRISTOPHE, *Isaac Abravanel: La Mémoire et l'espérance* (Paris: Cerf, 1992).

AVI-YONAH, MICHAEL, *The Jews under Roman and Byzantine Rule: A Political History of Palestine from the Bar Kokhba War to the Arab Conquest* (New York: Schocken Books, 1984).

AVIAD, JANET, 'The Messianism of Gush Emunim', in Jonathan Frankel (ed.), *Jews and Messianism in the Modern Era*, Studies in Contemporary Jewry, 7 (New York: Oxford University Press, 1991), 197–213.

AVNERI, ZVI, 'Aboab, Isaac II', *Encyclopedia Judaica*, 16 vols. (Jerusalem: Keter, 1973), ii. 93; 22 vols. (Detroit: Macmillan Reference, 2007), i. 267–8.

BAER, YITZHAK, *Galut* (New York: Schocken Books, 1948).

—— *A History of the Jews in Christian Spain*, 2 vols. (Philadelphia: Jewish Publication Society, 1961–6).

—— 'The Religious–Social Tendency of *Sefer Ḥasidim*' (Heb.), *Zion*, 3 (1937), 1–50.

—— 'Todros ben Judah Halevi and His Time' (Heb.), in *Studies in the History of the Jewish People* [Meḥkarim umasot betoledot yisra'el], 2 vols. (Jerusalem: Israel Historical Society, 1986), ii. 269–305.

BALDWIN, JOHN W., *Masters, Princes and Merchants: The Social Views of Peter the Chanter and His Circle*, 2 vols. (Princeton: Princeton University Press, 1970).

BARCELONA, P. MARTÍ DE, 'L'Ars praedicandi de Francesc Eiximenis', *Analecta sacra tarraconensia*, 12 (1936), 301–40.

BARON, SALO W., *The Jewish Community*, 3 vols. (Philadelphia: Jewish Publication Society, 1942).

—— *A Social and Religious History of the Jews*, 18 vols. (Philadelphia: Jewish Publication Society, 1952–83).

BARZILAY, ISAAC, *Between Faith and Reason: Anti-Rationalism in Italian Jewish Thought, 1250–1650* (The Hague: Mouton, 1967).

BATAILLON, LOUIS, 'De la *lectio* à la *praedicatio*: Commentaires bibliques et sermons au XIIIe siècle', *Revue des sciences philosophiques et théologiques*, 70 (1986), 559–75.

BEINART, HAIM, *The Expulsion of the Jews from Spain* (Oxford: Littman Library, 2002).

—— 'The Expulsion of the Jews of Valmaseda' (Heb.), *Zion*, 46 (1981), 39–51.

—— 'Order of the Expulsion from Spain: Antecedents, Causes and Textual Analysis', in Benjamin Gampel (ed.), *Crisis and Creativity in the Sephardic World, 1391–1648* (New York: Columbia University Press, 1997), 79–94.

BEN-SASSON, HAIM HILLEL, *Continuity and Variety* [Retsef utemurah: iyunim betoledot yisra'el bimei habeinayim uva'et haḥadashah], ed. Joseph Hacker (Tel Aviv: Am Oved: 1984).

—— *Deliberation and Leadership: The Social Doctrines of Polish Jews towards the End of the Middle Ages* [Hagut vehanhagah: hashkefoteihem haḥevratiyot shel yehudei polin beshalhei yemei habeinayim] (Jerusalem: Bialik Institute, 1959).

—— *A History of the Jewish People* (Cambridge, Mass.: Harvard University Press, 1976).

—— *On Jewish History in the Middle Ages* [Perakim betoledot hayehudim bimei habeinayim] (Tel Aviv: Am Oved, 1969).

BEN-SHALOM, RAM, 'The Ban Placed by the Community of Barcelona on the Study of Philosophy and Allegorical Preaching: A New Study', *Revue des études juives*, 159 (2000), 387–404.

—— 'Communication and Propaganda Between Provence and Spain: The Controversy over Extreme Allegorization (1303–1306)', in Sophia Menache (ed.), *Communication in the Jewish Diaspora* (Leiden: Brill, 1996), 171–224.

BEN-SHALOM, RAM, *Facing Christian Culture: Historical Consciousness and Images of the Past among the Jews of Spain and Southern France during the Middle Ages* [Mul tarbut notsrit: toda'ah historit vedimuyei avar bekerev yehudei sefarad uprovans bimei habeinayim] (Jerusalem: Ben-Zvi Institute, 2006).

BENAYAHU, MEIR, 'Rabbi Samuel Jaffe Ashkenazi' (Heb.), *Tarbiz*, 52 (1973), 419–60.

BENTOV, HAYIM, 'The System of Talmudic Learning in the Academies of Salonika and Turkey' (Heb.), *Sefunot*, 13 [*Sefer Yavan*, 3] (1971–8), 5–102.

BERGER, ABRAHAM, 'The Messianic Self-Consciousness of Abraham Abulafia: A Tentative Evaluation', in Marc Saperstein (ed.), *Essential Papers on Messianic Movements and Personalities in Jewish History* (New York: New York University Press, 1992), 250–5.

BERGER, DAVID, *The Rebbe, the Messiah, and the Scandal of Orthodox Indifference* (London: Littman Library, 2001).

—— 'Three Typological Themes in Early Jewish Messianism: Messiah Son of Joseph, Rabbinic Calculations, and the Figure of Armilus', *AJS Review*, 10 (1985), 141–64.

BERLIN, CHARLES, 'A Sixteenth-Century Hebrew Chronicle of the Ottoman Empire', in id. (ed.), *Studies in Jewish Bibliography, History and Literature in Honor of I. Edward Kiev* (New York: Ktav, 1971), 21–44.

BERMAN, LAWRENCE V., 'Greek into Hebrew: Samuel ben Judah of Marseilles, Fourteenth-Century Philosopher and Translator', in Alexander Altmann (ed.), *Jewish Medieval and Renaissance Studies* (Cambridge, Mass.: Harvard University Press, 1967), 289–320.

—— 'The Hebrew Translation from Latin of Aristotle's "Nicomachean Ethics" ' (Heb.), in Moshe Idel, Warren Harvey, and Eliezer Schweid (eds.), *Shlomo Pines Jubilee Volume* [Sefer hayovel lishelomoh pines], 2 vols. (Jerusalem: Daf Noi Press, 1988), i. 147–68.

BERNSTEIN, MICHAEL, *Foregone Conclusions: Against Apocalyptic History* (Berkeley: University of California Press, 1994).

BETTAN, ISRAEL, *Studies in Jewish Preaching* (Cincinnati: Hebrew Union College Press, 1939).

BIGET, JEAN-LOUIS, 'Un procès d'inquisition à Albi en 1300', in *Le Crédo, la morale, et l'inquisition*, Cahiers de Fanjeaux, 6 (1971), 273–341.

BISSON, THOMAS, *Assemblies and Representatives in Languedoc in the Thirteenth Century* (Princeton: Princeton University Press, 1964).

BLANCHE, F. A., 'Le Vocabulaire de l'argumentation et la structure de l'article dans les ouvrages de Saint Thomas', *Revue des sciences philosophiques et théologiques*, 14 (1925), 167–87.

BLAND, KALMAN, 'Issues in Sixteenth-Century Jewish Exegesis', in David Steinmetz (ed.), *The Bible in the Sixteenth Century* (Durham, NC: Duke University Press, 1990), 50–67.

BLOCH, MARC, *Feudal Society* (Chicago: University of Chicago Press, 1961).

BOBIK, JOSEPH, *Aquinas on Being and Essence* (Notre Dame, Ind.: University of Notre Dame Press, 1965).

BODIAN, MIRIAM, *Hebrews of the Portuguese Nation: Conversos and Community in Early Modern Amsterdam* (Bloomington: Indiana University Press, 1997).

BÖHM, GÜNTER, *Los sefardíes en los dominios holandeses de América del Sur y del Caribe, 1630–1750* (Frankfurt am Main: Vervuert, 1992).

BONFIL, ROBERT, 'Preaching as Mediation between Elite and Popular Cultures: The Case of Judah Del Bene', in David B. Ruderman (ed.), *Preachers of the Italian Ghetto* (Berkeley: University of California Press, 1992), 67–88.

BOUGEROL, J. GUY, *Introduction to the Works of Bonaventure* (Paterson, NJ: St Anthony Guild Press, 1964).

BOWERSOCK, GLEN WARREN, *Julian the Apostate* (Cambridge, Mass.: Harvard University Press, 1978).

BOYARIN, DANIEL, 'Studies in the Talmudic Exegesis of the Spanish Exiles' (Heb.), *Sefunot* NS, 2/17 (1983), 165–84.

BRANN, ROSS, *The Compunctious Poet: Cultural Ambiguity and Hebrew Poetry in Muslim Spain* (Baltimore: Johns Hopkins University Press, 1991).

BRAUDEL, FERNAND, *The Mediterranean and the Mediterranean World in the Age of Philip II* (New York: Harper & Row, 1972).

BRENNER, JOSEPH, 'Self-Criticism', in Arthur Hertzberg (ed.), *The Zionist Idea: A Historical Analysis and Reader* (New York: Atheneum, 1971), 307–12.

BREUER, MORDECAI, 'The Wanderings of Students and Scholars: A Prologue to a Chapter in the History of the Academies' (Heb.), in Reuven Bonfil, Menahem Ben-Sasson, and Yosef Hacker (eds.), *Culture and Society in Medieval Jewish History* [Tarbut veḥevrah betoledot yisra'el bimei habeinayim] (Jerusalem: Merkaz Zalman Shazar, 1989), 445–68.

BRIGHT, JOHN, *A History of Israel* (Philadelphia: Westminster Press, 1959).

BROWN, ELIZABETH A. R., 'Philip V, Charles IV, and the Jews of France: The Alleged Expulsion of 1322', *Speculum*, 66/2 (1991), 294–329.

BUJANDA, JESÚS MARTÍNEZ DE, 'Recent Historiography of the Spanish Inquisition (1977–1988): Balance and Perspective', in Mary Elizabeth Perry and Anne J. Cruz (eds.), *Cultural Encounters: The Impact of the Inquisition in Spain and the New World* (Berkeley: University of California Press, 1991), 221–47.

BURNS, ROBERT, *Jews in the Notarial Culture: Latinate Wills in Mediterranean Spain, 1250–1350* (Berkeley: University of California Press, 1986).

CAILLE, JACQUELINE, 'La Seigneurie temporelle de l'archevêque dans la ville de Narbonne (deuxième moitié du XIIIe siècle)', in *Les Évêques, les clercs, et le roi (1250–1300)*, Cahiers de Fanjeaux, 7 (1972), 165–209.

CANTOR, NORMAN, 'Disputatio', in Paul Szarmach (ed.), *Aspects of Jewish Culture in the Middle Ages* (Albany: State University of New York Press, 1979), 181–6.

—— *The Sacred Chain: The History of the Jews* (New York: HarperPerennial, 1994).

CAPLAN, HARRY, *Of Eloquence: Studies in Ancient and Mediaeval Rhetoric* (Ithaca, NY: Cornell University Press, 1970).

CARDOZO, BENJAMIN, *The Nature of the Judicial Process* (New Haven: Yale University Press, 1963).

CARLEBACH, ELISHEVA, *Between History and Hope: Jewish Messianism Between Ashkenaz and Sepharad*, Annual Lecture of the Selmanowitz Chair of Jewish History (New York: Graduate School of Jewish Studies, Touro College, 1998).

CARTWRIGHT, DAVID E., *Tides: A Scientific History* (Cambridge: Cambridge University Press, 1999).

CHARLAND, THOMAS-MARIE, *Artes praedicandi: Contribution à l'histoire de la rhétorique au Moyen Âge* (Ottawa: Institut d'études médiévales d'Ottawa, 1936).

CHAZAN, ROBERT, *Barcelona and Beyond: The Disputation of 1263 and Its Aftermath* (Berkeley: University of California Press, 1992).

—— *Church, State and Jew in the Middle Ages* (New York: Behrman House, 1980).

—— *European Jewry and the First Crusade* (Berkeley: University of California Press, 1987).

COHEN, GERSON D., 'Messianic Postures of Ashkenazim and Sephardim', in Marc Saperstein (ed.), *Essential Papers on Messianic Movements and Personalities in Jewish History* (New York: New York University Press, 1992), 202–33.

COHEN, JEREMY, *Living Letters of the Law: Ideas of the Jew in Medieval Christianity* (Berkeley: University of California Press, 1999).

COHEN, MARTIN A., 'Reflections on the Text and Context of the Disputation of Barcelona', *Hebrew Union College Annual*, 35 (1964), 157–92.

—— 'Toward a New Comprehension of the Marranos', *Hispania Judaica*, 1 (1980), 21–36.

COHEN, NAOMI, *What the Rabbis Said: The Public Discourse of Nineteenth-Century American Rabbis* (New York: New York University Press, 2008).

COHEN, TOVAH, 'Hasidism and the Land of Israel: An Additional Aspect of the Satire in *The Revealer of Secrets*' (Heb.), *Tarbiz*, 48 (1979), 332–40.

COHN, NORMAN, *The Pursuit of the Millennium: Revolutionary Millenarians and Mystical Anarchists of the Middle Ages*, 3rd edn. (New York: Oxford University Press, 1970).

COHN-SHERBOCK, DAN (ed.), *Traditional Quest: Essays in Honour of Louis Jacobs* (Sheffield: Journal for the Study of the Old Testament Press, 1991).

COLES, PAUL, *The Ottoman Impact on Europe* (London: Thames & Hudson, 1968).

COLLINS, JOHN J., *The Apocalyptic Imagination: An Introduction to Jewish Apocalyptic Literature* (Grand Rapids, Mich.: Eerdmans, 1998).

COOGAN, MICHAEL, 'Life in the Diaspora: Jews at Nippur in the Fifth Century B.C.', *Biblical Archaeologist*, 37 (1974), 6–12.

COOPERMAN, BERNARD DOV, 'Portuguese *Conversos* in Ancona: Jewish Political Activity in Early Modern Italy', in id. (ed.), *In Iberia and Beyond: Hispanic Jews between Cultures* (Newark: University of Delaware Press, 1998), 297–352.

CROSS, FRANK MOORE, 'A Reconstruction of the Judean Restoration', *Journal of Biblical Literature*, 94/4 (1975), 4–18.

CUFFEL, ALEXANDRA, 'Call and Response: European Jewish Emigration to Egypt and Palestine in the Middle Ages', *Jewish Quarterly Review*, 90 (1999), 61–101.

DAN, JOSEPH, *The Esoteric Doctrine of German Pietism* [Torat hasod shel ḥasidut ashkenaz] (Jerusalem: Bialik Institute, 1968).

—— *Homiletical and Ethical Literature* [Sifrut haderush vehamusar] (Jerusalem: Keter, 1975).

—— 'The Two Meanings of Hasidic Messianism', in Jodi Magness and Seymour Gitin (eds.), *Ḥesed ve-Emet: Studies in Honor of Ernest S. Frerichs* (Providence, RI: Brown University Press, 1998), 391–407.

DAVIDSON, HERBERT A., 'Gersonides on the Material and Active Intellects', in Gad Freudenthal (ed.), *Studies on Gersonides* (Leiden: Brill, 1992), 195–265.

—— *The Philosophy of Abraham Shalom: A Fifteenth-Century Exposition and Defense of Maimonides* (Berkeley: University of California Press, 1964).

DAVIDSON, ISRAEL, 'L'Introduction de Lévi ben Abraham à son encyclopédie poétique', *Revue des études juives*, 105 (1940), 80–94.

DAVIS, GEORGINE, *The Inquisition at Albi, 1299–1300: Text of Register and Analysis* (New York: Octagon, 1974).

DAVIS, MYER, 'An Anglo-Jewish Divorce, A.D. 1242', *Jewish Quarterly Review*, 5 (1893), 158–65.

D'AVRAY, DAVID, *The Preaching of the Friars* (Oxford: Oxford University Press, 1985).

DELPOUX, CHARLES, 'Le Catharisme en Albigeois: La Croisade et l'inquisition au XIIIe et XIVe siècles', *Cahiers d'études cathares*, 5 (1954), 81–91, 145–56.

DENNISTOUN, JAMES, *Memoirs of the Dukes of Urbino*, 3 vols. (New York: John Lane, 1909).

DEVIC, CLAUDE, and J. J. VAISSÈTE, *Histoire générale de Languedoc, avec des notes et les pièces justificatives*, 15 vols. (Toulouse: E. Privat, 1872–92).

DEYERMOND, ALAN D., 'The Sermon and Its Uses in Medieval Castilian Literature', *La Corónica*, 8 (1980), 127–45.

DIESENDRUCK, ZEVI, 'Samuel and Moses ibn Tibbon on Maimonides' Theory of Providence', *Hebrew Union College Annual*, 11 (1936), 341–66.

DINUR, BEN ZION, *Historical Writings*, vol. i: *In the Turning of the Generations* [Ketavim historiyim, 1: bemifneh hadorot] (Jerusalem: Bialik Institute, 1955).

—— *Historical Writings*, vol. ii: *In the Struggle of the Generations* [Ketavim historiyim, 2: bema'avaq hadorot] (Jerusalem: Bialik Institute, 1975).

—— *Israel and the Diaspora* (Philadelphia: Jewish Publishing Society, 1969).

—— *Israel in the Diaspora* [Yisra'el bagolah], 2nd edn., Pt. I, 4 vols.; Pt. II, 6 vols. (Tel Aviv: Dvir, 1958–72).

—— 'The Messianic-Prophetic Role of the Baal Shem Tov', in Marc Saperstein (ed.), *Essential Papers on Messianic Movements and Personalities in Jewish History* (New York: New York University Press, 1992), 377–88.

DORFF, ELLIOTT N., and ARTHUR ROSETT, *A Living Tree: The Roots and Growth of Jewish Law* (Albany: State University of New York Press, 1988).

DORON, AVIVAH, *A Poet in the Royal Court: Todros Halevi Abulafia* [Meshorer baḥatsar hamelekh: todros halevi abulafiyah] (Tel Aviv: Dvir, 1989).

DROGE, ARTHUR J., and JAMES D. TABOR, *A Noble Death: Suicide and Martyrdom among Christians and Jews in Antiquity* (San Francisco: HarperSanFrancisco, 1992).

EHRLICH, M. AVRUM, *The Messiah of Brooklyn: Understanding Lubavitch Hasidism, Past and Present* (Jersey City: Ktav, 2004).

EISEN, ARNOLD, *Galut: Modern Jewish Reflections on Homelessness and Homecoming* (Bloomington: Indiana University Press, 1986).

ELBAUM, JACOB, *Repentance and Self-Flagellation in the Writings of the Sages of Germany and Poland, 1348–1648* [Teshuvat halev vekabalat yisurim: iyunim bashitot hateshuvah shel ḥakhmei ashkenaz] (Jerusalem: Magnes Press, 1993).

ELON, MENACHEM, *Freedom of the Debtor's Person in Jewish Law* [Ḥerut haperat bedarkhei geviyat ḥov bamishpat ha'ivri] (Jerusalem: Magnes Press, 1964).

—— *Jewish Law: History, Sources, Principles*, 4 vols. (Philadelphia: Jewish Publication Society, 1994).

EMERY, RICHARD, *Heresy and Inquisition in Narbonne* (New York: Columbia University Press, 1941).

EMMANUEL, ISAAC S., *Histoire de l'industrie des tissus des Israélites de Salonique* (Paris: Lipschutz, 1935).

—— *History of the Jews in Netherlands Antilles*, 2 vols. (Cincinnati: American Jewish Archives, 1970).

—— 'New Information on the Portuguese Community of Amsterdam' (Heb.), *Otsar yehudei sefarad*, 6 (1963), 160–82.

EPSTEIN, ISIDORE, *Studies in the Communal Life of the Jews in Spain as Reflected in the Responsa of Rabbi Solomon ben Adreth and Rabbi Simon ben Zemach Duran*, 2 vols. in 1 (New York: Hermon Press, 1968).

EVANS, CRAIG, and PETER FLINT (eds.), *Eschatology, Messianism, and the Dead Sea Scrolls* (Grand Rapids, Mich.: Eerdmans, 1997).

EZRAHI, SIDRA DEKOVEN, *Booking Passage: Exile and Homecoming in the Modern Jewish Imagination* (Berkeley: University of California Press, 1999).

FEDERBUSCH, SIMON, *Hasidism and Zion* [Haḥasidut vetsiyon] (Jerusalem: Mosad Harav Kook, 1963).

FELDMAN, LOUIS, and GOHEI HATA (eds.), *Josephus, the Bible and History* (Detroit: Wayne State University Press, 1989).

FELDMAN, SEYMOUR, 'The End of the Universe in Medieval Jewish Philosophy', *AJS Review*, 11 (1986), 53–77.

FENTON, PAUL, 'Shem Tov Falaquera and Aristotelian Theology' (Heb.), *Da'at*, 29 (1992), 27–39.

FINKELSTEIN, LOUIS, *Jewish Self-Government in the Middle Ages* (New York: Feldheim, 1964).

FISHMAN, TALYA, *Shaking the Pillars of the Exile: 'Voice of a Fool', an Early Modern Jewish Critique of Rabbinic Culture* (Stanford: Stanford University Press, 1997).

FRAADE, STEVEN D., *From Tradition to Commentary: Torah and Its Interpretation in the Midrash Sifre to Deuteronomy* (Albany: State University of New York Press, 1991).

FRANKEL, JONATHAN (ed.), *Jews and Messianism in the Modern Era: Metaphor and Meaning*, Studies in Contemporary Jewry, 7 (New York: Oxford University Press, 1991).

FREEHOF, SOLOMON, *The Responsa Literature* (Philadelphia: Jewish Publication Society, 1955).

FREUDENTHAL, GAD, 'Les Sciences dans les communautés juives médiévales de Provence: Leur appropriation, leur rôle', *Revue des études juives*, 152 (1993), 29–136.

—— (ed.), *Studies on Gersonides* (Leiden: Brill, 1992).

FRIEDLÄNDER, ISRAEL, 'Shiitic Influences in Jewish Sectarianism', in Marc Saperstein (ed.), *Essential Papers on Messianic Movements and Personalities in Jewish History* (New York: New York University Press, 1992), 113–61; originally published in *Jewish Quarterly Review* NS, 1 (1910–11), 183–215; 2 (1911–12), 481–516; 3 (1912–13), 235–300.

FRIEDMAN, MENACHEM, 'Habad as Messianic Fundamentalism: From Local Particularism to Universal Jewish Mission', in Martin Marty and R. Scott Appleby (eds.), *Accounting for Fundamentalisms: The Dynamic Character of Movements* (Chicago: University of Chicago Press, 1994), 328–57.

FRIEDMANN, H. G., 'Pseudo-Messiahs', in *Jewish Encyclopedia*, 12 vols. (New York: Funk & Wagnalls, 1901–6), x. 251–5.

GACHON, PAUL JEAN LOUIS, *Histoire de Languedoc* (Paris: Boivin, 1921).

GAFNI, ISAIAH, 'Punishment, Blessing, or Mission?' (Heb.), in Aharon Oppenheimer, Isaiah Gafni, and Daniel Schwartz (eds.), *Jews in the Hellenistic-Roman World* [Hayehudim ba'olam haheleniti veharomi: meḥkarim lezikhro shel menaḥem stern] (Jerusalem: Merkaz Zalman Shazar, 1996), 229–50.

GALINSKY, JUDAH, 'Halakhah, Economics, and Ideology in the School of the Rosh in Toledo' (Heb.), *Zion*, 72 (2007), 387–419.

—— 'On the Heritage of Rabbi Judah ben Asher, Rabbi of Toledo' (Heb.), *Pe'amim*, 128 (2011), 175–210.

GAMPEL, BENJAMIN, *The Last Jews on Iberian Soil: Navarrese Jewry 1479/1498* (Berkeley: University of California Press, 1989).

GAY, PETER, *Freud, Jews and Other Germans: Masters and Victims in Modernist Culture* (Oxford: Oxford University Press, 1978).

GERMAIN, ALEXANDRE, *Histoire de la commune de Montpellier*, 3 vols. (Montpellier: J. Martel, 1851).

GILLER, PINCHAS, *The Enlightened Will Shine: Symbolization and Theurgy in the Later Strata of the Zohar* (Albany: State University of New York Press, 1993).

GILSON, ÉTIENNE, *History of Christian Philosophy in the Middle Ages* (New York: Random House, 1954).

—— *Les Idées et les lettres* (Paris: J. Vrin, 1932).

GILTAIJ, JEROEN, *The Drawings by Rembrandt and His School* (Rotterdam: Museum Boijmans Van Beuningen, 1989).

GINZBERG, LOUIS, *Legends of the Jews*, 7 vols. (Philadelphia: Jewish Publication Society, 1912).

GIVEN, JAMES B., *Inquisition and Medieval Society: Power, Discipline, and Resistance in Languedoc* (Ithaca, NY: Cornell University Press, 1997).

GLASNER, RUTH, 'The Early Stages in the Evolution of Gersonides' *The Wars of the Lord*', *Jewish Quarterly Review*, 87 (1996), 1–46.

GLATZER, MICHAEL, 'Between Joshua Halorki and Solomon Halevi' (Heb.), *Pe'amim*, 54 (1993), 103–16.

GLATZER, NAHUM, 'The Attitude toward Rome in Third-Century Judaism', in Alois Dempf (ed.), *Politische Ordnung und Menschliche Existenz* (Munich: Beck, 1962), 243–57.

GOITEIN, SHELOMO D., *A Mediterranean Society: The Jewish Communities of the Arab World as Portrayed in the Documents of the Cairo Geniza*, 5 vols. plus index (Berkeley: University of California Press, 1967–93).

—— 'A Report on Messianic Troubles in Baghdad in 1120–21', in Marc Saperstein (ed.), *Essential Papers on Messianic Movements and Personalities in Jewish History* (New York: New York University Press, 1992), 189–201.

GOLDISH, MATT, *Jewish Questions: Responsa on Sephardic Life in the Early Modern Period* (Princeton: Princeton University Press, 2008).

GOLDMAN, ELIEZER, 'On the Purpose of Existence in the *Guide for the Perplexed*' (Heb.), in Daniel Statman and Abraham Sagi (eds.), *Expositions and Enquiries: Jewish Thought in Past and Present* [Meḥkarim ve'iyunim: hagut yehudit ba'avar uvahoveh] (Jerusalem: Magnes Press, 1996), 87–114.

GOODBLATT, MORRIS, *Jewish Life in Turkey in the XVIth Century as Reflected in the Legal Writings of Samuel di Medina* (New York: Jewish Theological Seminary of America, 1952).

GOODMAN, MARTIN, 'Messianism and Politics in the Land of Israel, 66–135 C.E.', in Markus Bockmuehl and James Carletone Paget (eds.), *Redemption and Resistance: The Messianic Hopes of Jews and Christians in Antiquity* (London: Continuum, 2007), 149–57.

GRABMANN, MARTIN, *Die Geschichte der scholastischen Methode*, 2 vols. (Berlin: Akademie-Verlag, 1956).

GRAETZ, HEINRICH, *History of the Jews*, 6 vols. (Philadelphia: Jewish Publication Society, 1893).

GREEN, ARTHUR, *Tormented Master: A Life of Rabbi Nahman of Bratslav* (New York: Schocken Books, 1981).

—— '*Zaddiq* as *Axis Mundi* in Later Judaism', *Journal of the American Academy of Religion*, 45/3 (1977), 327–47.

GROPNIK, ADAM, 'Inquiring Minds: The Spanish Inquisition Revisited', *New Yorker* (16 Jan. 2012), 70–6.

GROSS, ABRAHAM, 'Centers of Study and Yeshivot in Spain', in Haim Beinart (ed.), *Moreshet Sepharad: The Sephardi Legacy*, 2 vols. (Jerusalem: Magnes Press, 1992), i. 399–410.

—— *Iberian Jewry from Twilight to Dawn: The World of Rabbi Abraham Saba* (Leiden: Brill, 1995).

—— 'The Poet Solomon Bonafed and the Events of His Generation' (Heb.), in Barry Walfish (ed.), *Frank Talmage Memorial Volume*, vol. i (Haifa: Haifa University Press, 1993), Heb. section, 35–61.

—— *Rabbi Joseph ben Abraham Hayun: Leader of the Lisbon Community and His Literary Work* [R. yosef ben avraham ḥayun: manhig kehilat lisbon vitsirato] (Ramat Gan: Bar Ilan University Press, 1993).

GUTTMANN, JACOB, *Die Religionsphilosophischen Lehren des Isaak Abravanel* (Breslau: Verlag von M. & H. Marcus, 1916).

GUTTMANN, JULIUS, *Philosophies of Judaism: The History of Jewish Philosophy from Biblical Times to Franz Rosenzweig* (Garden City, NY: Doubleday, 1933; repr. 1964).

GUTTMANN, MICHAEL, *The Land of Israel in the Midrash and Talmud* [Erets yisra'el bemidrash vetalmud] (Breslau: R. Mas, 1929).

GUTWIRTH, ELEAZAR, 'Abraham Seneor: Social Tensions and the Court-Jew', *Michael*, 11 (1989), 169–229.

—— 'Don Ishaq Abravanel and Vernacular Humanism in Fifteenth-Century Iberia', *Bibliothèque d'humanisme et Renaissance*, 60 (1998), 641–71.

—— 'Towards Expulsion, 1391–1492', in Elie Kedourie (ed.), *Spain and the Jews* (London: Thames & Hudson, 1992), 51–73.

HACKER, JOSEPH, 'The Intellectual Activity of the Jews of the Ottoman Empire during the Sixteenth and Seventeenth Centuries', in Isadore Twersky and Bernard Septimus (eds.), *Jewish Thought in the Seventeenth Century* (Cambridge, Mass.: Harvard University Press, 1987), 95–135.

—— 'Links between Spanish Jewry and Palestine, 1391–1492', in Richard I. Cohen (ed.), *Vision and Conflict in the Holy Land* (Jerusalem: Ben-Zvi Institute, 1985), 111–39.

—— 'New Chronicles on the Expulsion from Spain, Its Causes and Results' (Heb.), *Zion*, 44 (1979), 201–28.

—— 'On the Spiritual Image of Spanish Jews at the End of the Fifteenth Century' (Heb.), *Sefunot* NS, 2/17 (1983), 21–95.

—— 'Rabbi Joseph Hayun and the Generation of the Expulsion from Portugal' (Heb.), *Zion*, 48 (1983), 273–80.

HAKOHEN, AVIAD, 'Joseph's Weeping' (Heb.), *Merkaz hayeshivot benei akiva*, <http://www.yba.org.il/show.asp?id=24152> (accessed 11 Aug. 2014).

HALICZER, STEPHEN, 'The Castilian Urban Patriciate and the Jewish Expulsions of 1480–92', *American Historical Review*, 78 (1973), 35–58.

—— 'The Expulsion of the Jews and the Economic Development of Castile', *Hispania Judaica*, 1 (1980), 39–47.

HALKIN, ABRAHAM, 'The Ban on the Study of Philosophy' (Heb.), *Perakim*, 1 (1967), 35–55.

—— 'Why Was Levi ben Hayyim Hounded?', *Proceedings of the American Academy of Jewish Research*, 34 (1966), 65–76.

—— 'Yedaiah Bedershi's Apology', in Alexander Altmann (ed.), *Jewish Medieval and Renaissance Studies* (Cambridge, Mass.: Harvard University Press, 1967), 165–84.

HALKIN, HILLEL, *Yehudah Halevi* (New York: Schocken Nextbook, 2010).

HARVEY, STEVEN, 'Arabic into Hebrew: The Hebrew Translation Movement and the Influence of Averroes upon Medieval Jewish Thought', in Daniel H. Frank and Oliver Leaman (eds.), *The Cambridge Companion to Medieval Jewish Philosophy* (Cambridge: Cambridge University Press, 2003), 258–80.

—— *Falaquera's Epistle of the Debate: An Introduction to Jewish Philosophy* (Cambridge, Mass.: Harvard University Press, 1987).

HARVEY, WARREN, 'An Edition of *The Book of the Soul's Rewards*' (Heb.), *Tarbiz*, 52 (1983), 529–37.

HAURÉAU, BARTHÉLEMY, *Bernard Délicieux et l'inquisition albigeoise (1300–1320)* (Paris: Hachette, 1877).

HEBERLE, RUDOLPH, and JOSEPH GUSFIELD, 'Social Movements', in David L. Sills and Robert K. Merton (eds.), *International Encyclopedia of the Social Sciences*, 17 vols. (New York: Macmillan, 1968), xiv. 438–52.

HECHT, NEIL S., et al., *An Introduction to the History and Sources of Jewish Law* (Oxford: Clarendon Press, 1966).

HEINEMANN, BENNO, *The Maggid of Dubno and His Parables* (New York: Philipp Feldheim, 1967).

HEINEMANN, JOSEPH, 'The Messiah of Ephraim and the Premature Exodus of the Tribe of Ephraim', *Harvard Theological Review*, 68 (1975), 1–16.

HENRY, DOMINIQUE MARIE JOSEPH, *Histoire de Rousillon: Comprenant l'histoire du royaume de Majorque*, 2 vols. (Paris: À l'imprimerie royale, 1835).

HERTZBERG, ARTHUR (ed.), *The Zionist Idea: A Historical Analysis and Reader* (New York: Atheneum, 1971).

HESCHEL, ABRAHAM JOSHUA, *Israel: An Echo of Eternity* (New York: Farrar, Straus & Giroux, 1969).

HOLTZ, AVRAHAM, *The Holy City: Jews on Jerusalem* (New York: Norton, 1971).

HOROWITZ, CARMI, *The Jewish Sermon in 14th Century Spain: The Derashot of R. Joshua ibn Shu'eib* (Cambridge, Mass.: Harvard University Press, 1989).

HOROWITZ, GEORGE, *The Spirit of Jewish Law: A Brief Account of Biblical and Rabbinic Jurisprudence, with Special Note on Jewish Law and the State of Israel* (New York: Central Book Company, 1963).

HORSLEY, RICHARD, 'Popular Messianic Movements Around the Time of Jesus', in Marc Saperstein (ed.), *Essential Papers on Messianic Movements and Personalities in Jewish History* (New York: New York University Press, 1992), 83–110.

—— and JOHN HANSON, *Bandits, Prophets, and Messiahs: Popular Movements at the Time of Jesus* (Minneapolis: Winston, 1985).

HOWE, IRVING, *World of Our Fathers* (New York: Harcourt Brace Jovanovich, 1976).

HUSIK, ISAAC, *A History of Medieval Jewish Philosophy* (Philadelphia: Jewish Publication Society, 1940).

HYAMSON, ALBERT MONTEFIORE, *The Sephardim of England: A History of the Spanish and Portuguese Community, 1492–1951* (London: Methuen, 1951).

IANCU-AGOU, DANIÈLLE, 'L'Inventaire de la bibliothèque et du mobilier d'un médicin juif d'Aix-en-Provence au milieu du XVe siècle', *Revue des études juives*, 134 (1975), 47–80.

—— 'Une vente de livres hébreux à Arles en 1434', *Revue des études juives*, 146 (1987), 5–62.

IDEL, MOSHE, 'Abraham Abulafia and the Pope: An Account of an Abortive Mission' (Heb.), *AJS Review*, 7–8 (1982–3), Heb. section, 1–17.

—— 'Enquiries into the Doctrine of *Sefer hameshiv*' (Heb.), *Sefunot* NS, 2/17 (1983), 185–266.

—— *Hasidism: Between Ecstasy and Magic* (Albany: State University of New York Press, 1995).

—— *Kabbalah: New Perspectives* (New Haven: Yale University Press, 1988).

—— 'The Land of Israel in Medieval Kabbalah', in Lawrence Hoffman (ed.), *The Land of Israel: Jewish Perspectives* (Notre Dame, Ind.: University of Notre Dame Press, 1986), 170–87.

—— *Messianic Mystics* (New Haven: Yale University Press, 1998).

—— *The Mystical Experience in Abraham Abulafia* (Albany: State University of New York Press, 1988).

—— 'Types of Redemptive Activism in the Middle Ages' (Heb.), in Zvi Baras (ed.), *Messianism and Eschatology: A Collection of Essays* [Meshiḥiyut ve'eskhatologiyah: kovets ma'amarim] (Jerusalem: Merkaz Zalman Shazar, 1983), 254–63.

ISAAC, BENJAMIN H., and AHARON OPPENHEIMER, 'The Revolt of Bar Kokhba: Ideology and Modern Scholarship', *Journal of Jewish Studies*, 36 (1985), 33–60.

ISRAEL, JONATHAN, *The Dutch Republic: Its Rise, Greatness, and Fall, 1477–1806* (Oxford: Clarendon Press, 1995).

IVRY, ALFRED, 'Remnants of Jewish Averroism in the Renaissance', in Bernard Cooperman (ed.), *Jewish Thought in the Sixteenth Century* (Cambridge, Mass.: Harvard University Press, 1983), 243–65.

JACOBS, LOUIS, *Hasidic Thought* (New York: Behrman House, 1976).

—— *Jewish Mystical Testimonies* (New York: Schocken Books, 1977).

—— *A Tree of Life: Diversity, Flexibility, and Creativity in Jewish Law* (Oxford: Oxford University Press, 1984).

JOSPE, RAPHAEL, *Torah and Sophia: The Life and Thought of Shem Tov ibn Falaquera* (Cincinnati: Hebrew Union College Press, 1988).

KAMESAR, ADAM, *Jerome, Greek Scholarship, and the Hebrew Bible: A Study of the Quaestiones Hebraicae in Genesim* (Oxford: Clarendon Press, 1993).

KANARFOGEL, EPHRAIM, 'The *'Aliyah* of "Three Hundred Rabbis" in 1211: Tosafist Attitudes toward Settling in the Land of Israel', *Jewish Quarterly Review*, 76 (1986), 191–215.

—— *Jewish Education and Society in the High Middle Ages* (Detroit: Wayne State University Press, 1992).

—— 'Rabbinic Attitudes toward Nonobservance in the Medieval Period', in Jacob J. Schacter (ed.), *Jewish Tradition and the Nonobservant Jew* (Northvale, NJ: Jason Aronson, 1992), 3–35.

KAPLAN, JOSEPH, 'The Attitude of Spanish and Portuguese Jews towards Ashkenazi Jews in Seventeenth-Century Amsterdam' (Heb.), in *Transition and Change in Modern Jewish History* [Temurot bahistoriyah hayehudit haḥadashah: kovets ma'amarim, shai lishmu'el etinger] (Jerusalem: Merkaz Zalman Shazar, 1988), 389–412.

—— 'Bans in the Sephardi Community of Late Seventeenth-Century Amsterdam' (Heb.), in Aharon Mirsky, Avraham Grossman, and Yosef Kaplan (eds.), *Exile and Diaspora* [Galut aḥar golah: meḥkarim betoledot yisra'el mugashim leḥayim beinart] (Jerusalem: Ben-Zvi Institute, 1988), 517–40.

KAPLAN, JOSEPH, 'The Jews in the Republic Until About 1750: Religious, Cultural, and Social Life', in J. C. H. Blom, R. G. Fuks-Mansfield, and I. Schöffer (eds.), *History of the Jews in the Netherlands* (Oxford: Littman Library, 2002), 116–63.

—— 'The Problem of the Conversos and the "New Christians" in the Historical Research of the Past Generation' (Heb.), in Mosheh Tsimerman, Menahem Stern, and Yosef Salmon (eds.), *Studies in Historiography* [Iyunim behistoriografiyah] (Jerusalem: Merkaz Zalman Shazar, 1988), 117–44.

—— 'The Social Functions of the "Ḥerem" in the Portuguese Jewish Community of Amsterdam in the 17th Century', *Dutch Jewish History*, 1 (1984), 111–55.

KATZ, JACOB, *Divine Law in Human Hands: Case Studies in Halakhic Flexibility* (Jerusalem: Magnes Press, 1998).

—— *Exclusiveness and Tolerance: Jewish–Gentile Relations in Medieval and Modern Times* (New York: Schocken Books, 1962).

—— *Halakhah and Kabbalah* [Halakhah vekabalah: meḥkarim betoledot dat yisra'el al medoreiha vezikatah haḥevratit] (Jerusalem: Magnes Press, 1984).

—— 'Israel and the Messiah', in Marc Saperstein (ed.), *Essential Papers on Messianic Movements and Personalities in Jewish History* (New York: New York University Press, 1992), 475–91.

—— *The 'Shabbes Goy': A Study in Halakhic Flexibility* (Philadelphia: Jewish Publication Society, 1989).

KAUFMANN, DAVID, 'Les 24 martyrs d'Ancône', *Revue des études juives*, 31 (1895), 222–30.

—— 'Deux lettres de Simeon b. Joseph', *Revue des études juives*, 29 (1894), 214–28.

—— 'Deux lettres nouvelles des Marranes de Pesaro aux Levantins touchant l'interruption des affaires avec Ancône', *Revue des études juives*, 31 (1895), 231–9.

—— 'The Dispute about the Sermons of David del Bene of Mantua', *Jewish Quarterly Review*, 8 (1896), 513–24.

—— 'Les Marranes de Pesaro et les représailles des Juifs levantins contre la ville d'Ancône', *Revue des études juives*, 16 (1888), 61–72.

—— 'Les Martyrs d'Ancône', *Revue des études juives*, 11 (1885), 149–56.

KAUFMANN, YEHEZKEL, 'The Ruin of the Soul', in Michael Selzer (ed.), *Zionism Reconsidered: The Rejection of Jewish Normalcy* (New York: Macmillan, 1970), 117–29.

KAYSERLING, MEIER, *Geschichte der Juden in Portugal* (Leipzig: J. Springer, 1867).

KELLNER, MENACHEM MARC, 'Gersonides' Commentary on Song of Songs: For Whom Was It Written and Why?', in Gilbert Dahan (ed.), *Gersonide en son temps* (Louvain: E. Peeters, 1991), 81–107.

—— 'Messianic Postures in Israel Today', in Marc Saperstein (ed.), *Essential Papers on Messianic Movements and Personalities in Jewish History* (New York: New York University Press, 1992), 504–18.

KERSHEN, ANNE J., and JONATHAN A. ROMAIN, *Tradition and Change: A History of Reform Judaism in Britain, 1840–1995* (London: Vallentine Mitchell, 1995).

KLATZKIN, JACOB, 'Boundaries', in Arthur Hertzberg (ed.), *The Zionist Idea: A Historical Analysis and Reader* (New York: Atheneum, 1971), 316–27.

KLAUSNER, JOSEPH, 'Daniel', in Leo Landman (ed.), *Messianism in the Talmudic Era* (New York: Ktav, 1979), 200–14.

—— *The Messianic Idea in Israel from Its Beginnings to the Completion of the Mishnah* (New York: Macmillan, 1955).

—— 'The Source and Beginnings of the Messianic Idea', in Leo Landman (ed.), *Messianism in the Talmudic Era* (New York: Ktav, 1979), 25–37.

KLORMAN, BAT-ZION ERAQI, *The Jews of Yemen in the Nineteenth Century: A Portrait of a Messianic Community* (Leiden: Brill, 1993).

—— 'The Messiah Shukr Kuhayl II (1868–75) and his Tithe (Ma'aśer): Ideology and Practice as a Means to Hasten Redemption', in Marc Saperstein (ed.), *Essential Papers on Messianic Movements and Personalities in Jewish History* (New York: New York University Press, 1992), 456–72.

KOCHAN, LIONEL, *Jews, Idols and Messiahs: The Challenge from History* (Oxford: Blackwell, 1990).

KRAUS, YITSHAK, *The Seventh: Messianism in the Last Generation of Habad* [Hashevi'i: meshiḥiyut bador hashevi'i shel ḥabad] (Tel Aviv: Miskal, 2007).

KRIEGEL, MAURICE, 'La Prise d'une décision: L'Expulsion des juifs d'Espagne en 1492', *Revue historique*, 260 (1978), 49–90.

KRITZECK, JAMES, *Peter the Venerable and Islam* (Princeton: Princeton University Press, 1964).

LAGRANGE, MARIE-JOSEPH, 'La Littérature patristique des *Quaestiones et responsiones* sur l'écriture sainte', *Revue biblique*, 41 (1932), 210–36, 341–69, 514–37; 42 (1933), 14–30, 211–29, 328–52.

LANDGRAF, ARTUR, 'Collections de *Quaestiones* du XIIe siècle', *Recherches de théologie ancienne et médiévale*, 7 (1935), 113–28.

LANE FOX, ROBIN, *Pagans and Christians* (New York: Knopf, 1987).

LAWEE, ERIC, *Isaac Abravanel's Stance toward Tradition: Defense, Dissent, Dialogue* (Albany: State University of New York Press, 2001).

LAZAROFF, ALAN, *The Theology of Abraham Bibago* (Tuscaloosa: University of Alabama Press, 1981).

LEA, HENRY CHARLES, *A History of the Inquisition of the Middle Ages*, 3 vols. (New York: Harper & Brothers, 1888).

—— *The Inquisition of the Middle Ages* (London: Eyre & Spottiswoode, 1963).

LECLERCQ, JEAN, *The Love of Learning and the Desire for God: A Study of Monastic Culture* (New York: Fordham University Press, 1961).

LECOY DE LA MARCHE, ALBERT, *Les Relations politiques de la France avec le Royaume de Maiorque*, 2 vols. (Paris: E. Leroux, 1892).

LEDERHENDLER, ELI, 'Interpreting Messianic Rhetoric in the Russian Haskalah and Early Zionism', in Jonathan Frankel (ed.), *Jews and Messianism in the Modern Era: Metaphor and Meaning*, Studies in Contemporary Jewry, 7 (New York: Oxford University Press, 1991), 14–33.

LEFF, GORDON, *Paris and Oxford Universities in the Thirteenth and Fourteenth Centuries: An Institutional and Intellectual History* (New York: John Wiley & Sons, 1968).

LEIBOWITZ, NEHAMA, *Studies in the Book of Genesis* (Jerusalem: World Zionist Organization, 1972).

LENOWITZ, HARRIS, *The Jewish Messiahs: From the Galilee to Crown Heights* (Oxford: Oxford University Press, 1998).

LÉVI, I., 'L'Inventaire du mobilier et de la bibliothèque d'un médicin juif de Majorque au XIVe siècle', *Revue des études juives*, 39 (1899), 242–9.

LEVIE BERNFELD, TIRTSAH, *Poverty and Welfare Among the Portuguese Jews in Early Modern Amsterdam* (Oxford: Littman Library, 2012).

LEVIN, YISRAEL L., 'Messianic Tendencies at the End of the Second Commonwealth' (Heb.), in Zvi Baras (ed.), *Messianism and Eschatology: A Collection of Essays* [Meshiḥiyut ve'eskhatologiyah: kovets ma'amarim] (Jerusalem: Merkaz Zalman Shazar, 1983), 135–52.

LEVINE, HILLEL, *Economic Origins of Antisemitism: Poland and Its Jews in the Early Modern Period* (New Haven: Yale University Press, 1991).

LIEBERMAN, SAUL, *Tosefta Ki-Feshutah: A Comprehensive Commentary on the Tosefta, Ketubot* (New York: Jewish Theological Seminary of America, 1967).

LIEBES, YEHUDA, 'Sabbatian Messianism' (Heb.), *Pe'amim*, 40 (1989), 4–20.

LINDER, AMNON, 'L'Expédition italienne de Charles VIII et les espérances messianiques des Juifs', *Revue des études juives*, 137 (1978), 179–86.

LOBEL, DIANE, 'A Dwelling Place for the Shekhinah', *Jewish Quarterly Review*, 90 (1999), 103–25.

LORENCE, BRUCE A., 'The Inquisition and the New Christians in the Iberian Peninsula: Main Historiographic Issues and Controversies', in Issachar Ben-Ami (ed.), *The Sepharadi and Oriental Heritage* (Jerusalem: Magnes Press, 1982), Eng. vol., 13–72.

LUBAC, HENRI DE, *Medieval Exegesis*, vol. i: *The Four Senses of Scripture* (Grand Rapids, Mich.: Eerdmans, 1998).

MCAULIFFE, JANE DAMMEN, BARRY D. WALFISH, and JOSEPH W. GOERING (eds.), *With Reverence for the Word: Medieval Scriptural Exegesis in Judaism, Christianity, and Islam* (Oxford: Oxford University Press, 2003).

MAHUL, ALPHONSE JACQUES, *Cartulaire et archives des communes de l'ancienne diocèse de Carcassonne*, 6 vols. in 7 (Paris: V. Didron, 1871).

MALTER, HENRY, *Saadia Gaon: His Life and Works* (New York: Hermon Press, 1921; repr. 1969).

MANN, JACOB, *Texts and Studies in Jewish History and Literature*, 2 vols. (Cincinnati: Hebrew Union College Press, 1931–5).

MANOR, DAN, 'On the History of Rabbi Abraham Saba' (Heb.), *Jerusalem Studies in Jewish Thought*, 2/2 (1983), 208–31.

MARCUS, IVAN, *Piety and Society: The Jewish Pietists of Medieval Germany* (Leiden: Brill, 1981).

MARCUS, JACOB RADER, *The Jew in the Medieval World*, rev. edn. (Cincinnati: Hebrew Union College Press, 1999).

MARGOLIOUTH, GEORGE, *Catalogue of the Hebrew and Samaritan Manuscripts in the British Museum*, 4 vols. (London: Trustees of the British Museum, 1965).

MARKS, RICHARD, *The Image of Bar Kokhba in Traditional Jewish Literature: False Messiah and National Hero* (University Park: Pennsylvania State University Press, 1994).

MARTIN, WILLEM, 'The Life of a Dutch Artist in the Seventeenth Century', in *Seventeenth Century Art in Flanders and Holland*, Garland Library of the History of Art, 9 (New York: Garland Publishing, 1976), 85–108.

MARX, ALEXANDER, 'The Expulsion of the Jews from Spain: Two New Accounts', *Jewish Quarterly Review*, 20 (1908), 240–71.

MERHAVYAH, HEN-MELEKH, *Voices Calling to Zion* [Kolot korim letsiyon] (Jerusalem: Merkaz Zalman Shazar, 1980).

MESCH, BARRY, *Studies in Joseph ibn Caspi: Fourteenth Century Philosopher and Exegete* (Leiden: Brill, 1975).

MEYER, MICHAEL A., *Response to Modernity: A History of the Reform Movement in Judaism* (New York: Oxford University Press, 1988).

MINTZ, ALAN, *Ḥurban: Responses to Catastrophe in Hebrew Literature* (New York: Columbia University Press, 1984).

MONTAG, WARREN, ' "That Hebrew Word": Spinoza and the Concept of the Shekinah', in Heidi M. Ravven and Lenn Evan Goodman (eds.), *Jewish Themes in Spinoza's Philosophy* (Albany: State University of New York Press, 2002), 131–44.

MORELL, SAMUEL, 'The Constitutional Limits of Communal Government in Rabbinic Law', *Jewish Social Studies*, 33 (1971), 87–119.

MORGENSTERN, ARIE, 'Messianic Concepts and Settlement in the Land of Israel', in Marc Saperstein (ed.), *Essential Papers on Messianic Movements and Personalities in Jewish History* (New York: New York University Press, 1992), 433–55.

—— *Messianism and the Return to the Land of Israel in the First Half of the Nineteenth Century* [Meshiḥiyut veyishuv erets yisra'el bamaḥatsit harishonah shel hame'ah hatesha-esreh] (Jerusalem: Ben-Zvi Institute, 1985).

MOURIN, LOUIS, *Jean Gerson, prédicateur français* (Bruges: De Temple, 1952).

MYERS, JODY ELIZABETH, 'The Messianic Idea and Zionist Ideologies', in Jonathan Frankel (ed.), *Jews and Messianism in the Modern Era: Metaphor and Meaning*, Studies in Contemporary Jewry, 7 (New York: Oxford University Press, 1991), 3–13.

NADLER, ALLAN, *The Faith of the Mithnagdim: Rabbinic Responses to Hasidic Rapture* (Baltimore: Johns Hopkins University Press, 1997).

NADLER, STEVEN M., *Rembrandt's Jews* (Chicago: University of Chicago Press, 2003).

—— *Spinoza: A Life* (Cambridge: Cambridge University Press, 1999).

NEHAMA, JOSEPH, *Histoire des Israélites de Salonique*, 5 vols. (Salonika: Molho, 1935–9).

NETANYAHU, BENZION, *Don Isaac Abravanel* (Philadelphia: Jewish Publication Society, 1968).

—— *The Origins of the Inquisition in Fifteenth Century Spain* (New York: Random House, 1995).

NEUBAUER, ADOLF, *Catalogue of Hebrew Manuscripts in the Bodleian Library* (Oxford: Clarendon Press, 1886).

—— 'Ergänzungen und Verbesserungen zu Abba Maris Minḥat Kenaot aus handschriften', *Israelitische Letterbode*, 4 (1878–9), 122–32, 160–73; 5 (1879–80), 53–8.

NEUBAUER, ADOLF, 'Yedaya de Béziers', *Revue des études juives*, 20 (1980), 244–8.

NEUMAN, ABRAHAM A., *The Jews in Spain: Their Social, Political and Cultural Life during the Middle Ages*, 2 vols. (Philadelphia: Jewish Publication Society, 1942).

NEUSNER, JACOB, *A History of the Jews in Babylonia*, 5 vols. (Leiden: Brill, 1965–70).

—— *Midrash in Context: Exegesis in Formative Judaism* (Philadelphia: Fortress Press, 1983).

—— William Scott Green, and Ernest S. Frerichs (eds.), *Judaisms and Their Messiahs at the Turn of the Christian Era* (Cambridge: Cambridge University Press, 1987).

NEWMAN, ARYEH, 'The Centrality of Erets Yisra'el in Nachmanides', *Tradition*, 10 (1968–9), 21–30.

NIRENBERG, DAVID, *Communities of Violence: Persecution of Minorities in the Middle Ages* (Princeton: Princeton University Press, 1996).

NYKL, ALOIS RICHARD, *Hispano-Arabic Poetry, and Its Relations with the Old Provençal Troubadours* (Baltimore: J. H. Furst Co., 1946).

OPPENHEIMER, AHARON, 'The Messianism of Bar Kokhba' (Heb.), in Zvi Baras (ed.), *Messianism and Eschatology: A Collection of Essays* [Meshiḥiyut ve'eskhatologiyah: kovets ma'amarim] (Jerusalem: Merkaz Zalman Shazar, 1983), 153–65.

ORON, MICHAL, 'The Sermon of Rabbi Todros ben Joseph Halevi Abulafia on the Reform of Ethical Qualities and Behaviour' (Heb.), *Da'at*, 11 (1983), 47–51.

OTIS, LEAH LYDIA, *Prostitution in Medieval Society* (Chicago: University of Chicago Press, 1985).

PACHTER, MORDECHAI, 'The Homiletical and Ethical Literature of the Sixteenth-Century Sages in Safed and the Array of Its Principal Ideas' [Sifrut haderush vehamusar shel ḥakhmei tsefat bame'ah hatet-zayin uma'arekhet rayonoteiha ha'ikariyim] (Ph.D. diss., Hebrew University of Jerusalem, 1976).

PARRONDO, CARLOS CARRETE, 'Sefarad 1492: Una expulsion anunciada?', in *Movimientos migratorios y expulsiones en la diáspora occidental* (Pamplona: Universidad Pública de Navarra, 2000), 49–54.

PASSAMANECK, STEPHEN M., *Insurance in Rabbinic Law* (Edinburgh: University of Edinburgh Press, 1974).

—— 'R. Judah b. Asher on Capital Penalties', *Jewish Law Association Annual*, 7 (1994), 153–72.

—— 'Remarks on *Pesquisa* in Medieval Jewish Legal Procedure', *Jewish Law Association Annual*, 9 (1997), 143–59.

PEARL, CHAIM, *The Medieval Jewish Mind: The Religious Philosophy of Isaac Arama* (London: Vallentine Mitchell, 1971).

PEDAYA, HAVIVA, 'The Spiritual Versus the Concrete Land of Israel in the Geronese School of Kabbalah' (Heb.), in Moshe Hallamish and Aviezer Ravitzky (eds.), *The Land of Israel in Medieval Jewish Thought* [Erets yisra'el bahagut hayehudit bimei habeinayim] (Jerusalem: Ben-Zvi Institute, 1991), 233–89.

PERLES, JOSEPH, *R. Salomo ben Abraham ben Adereth: Sein Leben und seine Schriften* (Breslau: Schretter, 1863).

PETERS, FRANCIS E., *Aristoteles Arabus: The Oriental Translations and Commentaries of the Aristotelian Corpus* (Leiden: Brill, 1968).

PETUCHOWSKI, JAKOB JOSEF, *Prayerbook Reform in Europe: The Liturgy of European Liberal and Reform Judaism* (New York: World Union for Progressive Judaism, 1968).

PHILIPSON, DAVID, *The Reform Movement in Judaism* (New York: Macmillan, 1931).

PICCIOTTO, JAMES, *Sketches of Anglo-Jewish History* (London: Trübner, 1875).

PIEKARZ, MENDEL, *Ideological Trends in Polish Hasidism during the Interwar Period and the Holocaust* [Ḥasidut polin: megamot rayoniyot bein shetei hamilḥamot uvigezerot 1939–1945 ('hasho'ah')] (Jerusalem: Bialik Institute, 1990).

—— 'The Transition in the History of the Messianism of Bratslaver Hasidism' (Heb.), in Zvi Baras (ed.), *Messianism and Eschatology: A Collection of Essays* [Meshiḥiyut ve'eskhatologiyah: kovets ma'amarim] (Jerusalem: Merkaz Zalman Shazar, 1983), 325–42.

PINES, SHLOMO, *Between Jewish and Gentile Thought: Studies in the History of Jewish Philosophy* [Bein maḥshevet yisra'el lemaḥshevet ha'amim: meḥkarim betoledot hafilosofiyah hayehudit] (Jerusalem: Bialik Institute, 1977).

POUX, JOSEPH, *La Cité de Carcassonne: Histoire et description*, 3 vols. (Toulouse: E. Privat, 1922–31).

PRAWER, JOSHUA, *The History of the Jews in the Latin Kingdom of Jerusalem* (Oxford: Clarendon Press, 1988).

PROCTER, EVELYN S., *The Judicial Use of Pesquisa (Inquisition) in Leon and Castile, 1157–1369*, English Historical Review Supplement, 2 (London: Longmans, 1966).

RABA, JOEL, *Between Remembrance and Denial: The Fate of the Jews in the Wars of the Polish Commonwealth during the Mid-Seventeenth Century as Shown in Contemporary Writings and Historical Research*, East European Monographs, 178 (New York: Columbia University Press, 1995).

RAJAK, TESSA, *Josephus: The Historian and His Society* (Philadelphia: Fortress Press, 1984).

RAPAPORT-ALBERT, ADA, 'God and the Zaddik as the Two Focal Points of Hasidic Worship', *History of Religions*, 18/4 (1979), 296–325.

RAPHAEL, YITZHAK, *Hasidism and the Land of Israel* [Haḥasidut ve'erets yisra'el] (Jerusalem: Hotsa'at Hasefarim Ha'erets Yisra'elit, 1940).

RAPPEL, DOV, 'Nahmanides on Exile and Redemption' (Heb.), *Ma'ayanot*, 7 (1960), 79–109.

RAVITZKY, AVIEZER, 'Aristotle's *Meteorology* and the Modes of Maimonidean Exegesis of Creation' (Heb.), *Jerusalem Studies in Jewish Thought*, 9 (1990), 225–50.

—— 'The Contemporary Lubavitch Hasidic Movement: Between Conservatism and Messianism', in Martin Marty and R. Scott Appleby (eds.), *Accounting for Fundamentalisms: The Dynamic Character of Movements* (Chicago: University of Chicago Press, 1994), 303–27.

—— '"Forcing the End": Zionism and the State of Israel as Antimessianic Undertakings', in Jonathan Frankel (ed.), *Jews and Messianism in the Modern Era: Metaphor and Meaning*, Studies in Contemporary Jewry, 7 (New York: Oxford University Press, 1991), 34–67.

—— *History and Faith: Studies in Jewish Philosophy* (Amsterdam: J. C. Gieben, 1996).

—— *Messianism, Zionism, and Jewish Religious Radicalism*, trans. Michael Swirsky and Jonathan Chipman (Chicago: University of Chicago Press, 1996).

RAVITZKY, AVIEZER, 'Regarding the Path of Research on Medieval Jewish Philosophy' (Heb.), *Jerusalem Studies in Jewish Thought*, 1 (1981), 7–22.

—— 'The Teaching of Rabbi Zerachiah ben Isaac ben Shealtiel Hen and Thirteenth-Century Maimonidean–Tibbonide Thought' [Mishnato shel r. zeraḥiyah ben yitsḥak ben she'alti'el ḥen vehahagut hamaimunit–tibonit bame'ah hashelosh-esreh] (Ph.D. diss., Hebrew University of Jerusalem, 1977).

RAWIDOWICZ, SIMON, 'Rabbi Sa'adyah Gaon's Doctrine of the Human Being' (Heb.), *Metsudah*, 1–2 (1943), 112–25.

REGEV, SHA'UL, 'Rational-Mystical Jewish Thought in the Fifteenth Century' (Heb.), *Jerusalem Studies in Jewish Thought*, 5 (1986), 155–89.

RÉGNÉ, JEAN, *Amauri II, Viscomte de Narbonne (1260?–1328): Sa jeunesse et ses expéditions, son gouvernement, son administration* (Narbonne: F. Caillard, 1910).

—— *Étude sur la condition des Juifs de Narbonne du Ve au XIVe siècle* (Narbonne: F. Caillard, 1912).

REINES, ALVIN, 'Maimonides' Concepts of Providence and Theodicy', *Hebrew Union College Annual*, 43 (1972), 169–206.

RENAN, ERNEST, 'Les Écrivains juifs français du XIVe siècle', in *Histoire littéraire de la France*, vol. xxxi (Paris: Imprimerie Nationale, 1893), 351–789.

—— 'Les Rabbins français du commencement du XIVe siècle', in *Histoire littéraire de la France*, vol. xxvii (Paris: Imprimerie Nationale, 1877), 431–734.

RICHLER, BENJAMIN, 'An Additional Letter by Hillel ben Samuel to Isaac the Physician' (Heb.), in Abraham David (ed.), *From the Collections of the Institute of Microfilmed Hebrew Manuscripts* [Miginzei hamakhon letatselumei kitvei hayad ha'ivriyim] (Jerusalem: National and University Library, 1995), 11–13.

RIVKIN, ELLIS, 'How Jewish Were the New Christians?', *Hispania Judaica*, 1 (1980), 103–15.

ROBERTS, PHYLLIS, *Studies in the Sermons of Stephen Langton* (Toronto: Pontifical Institute of Medieval Studies, 1968).

ROBINSON, IRA, 'Messianic Prayer Vigils in Jerusalem in the Early-Sixteenth Century', *Jewish Quarterly Review*, 72 (1981–2), 32–42.

ROBINSON, JAMES T., 'The Ibn Tibbon Family: A Dynasty of Translators in Medieval Provence', in Jay M. Harris (ed.), *Be'erot Yitzḥak: Studies in Memory of Isadore Twersky* (Cambridge, Mass.: Harvard University Press, 2005), 193–224.

ROGOZIŃSKI, JAN, 'The Counsellors of the Seneschal of Beaucaire and Nîmes, 1250–1350', *Speculum*, 44 (1969), 421–39.

—— *Power, Caste, and Law: Social Conflict in Fourteenth-Century Montpellier* (Cambridge, Mass.: Medieval Academy of America, 1982).

ROMANO, DAVID, 'La Transmission des sciences arabes par les Juifs en Languedoc', in Marie-Humbert Vicaire and Bernhard Blumenkranz (eds.), *Juifs et judaïsme de Languedoc, XIIIe siècle–début XIVe siècle*, Cahiers de Fanjeaux, 12 (Toulouse: Edouard Privat, 1977), 363–86.

ROSENBERG, SHALOM, 'Exile and Redemption in Jewish Thought in the Sixteenth Century', in Bernard Cooperman (ed.), *Jewish Thought in the Sixteenth Century* (Cambridge, Mass.: Harvard University Press, 1983), 399–430.

—— 'The Link to the Land of Israel in Jewish Thought: A Clash of Perspectives', in Lawrence Hoffman (ed.), *The Land of Israel: Jewish Perspectives* (Notre Dame, Ind.: University of Notre Dame Press, 1986), 139–69.

ROSENZWEIG, FRANZ, *Ninety-Two Poems and Hymns of Yehuda Halevi* (Albany: State University of New York Press, 2000).

ROTH, CECIL, *The House of Nasi: Doña Gracia* (Philadelphia: Jewish Publication Society, 1947).

—— *The Jews in the Renaissance* (Philadelphia: Jewish Publication Society, 1959).

ROTH, NORMAN, *Conversos, Inquisition, and the Expulsion of the Jews from Spain* (Madison: University of Wisconsin Press, 1995).

—— 'Jewish Translators at the Court of Alfonso X', *Thought*, 60 (1985), 439–55.

RUDERMAN, DAVID B., 'Hope Against Hope: Jewish and Christian Messianic Expectations in the Late Middle Ages', in Aharon Mirsky, Avraham Grossman, and Yosef Kaplan (eds.), *Exile and Diaspora: Studies in the History of the Jewish People Presented to Professor Haim Beinart* (Jerusalem: Ben-Zvi Institute, 1991), 185–202.

—— *The World of a Renaissance Jew: The Life and Thought of Abraham ben Mordecai Farissol* (Cincinnati: Hebrew Union College Press, 1981).

SAIGE, GUSTAVE, *Les Juifs du Languedoc antérieurement au XIVe siècle* (Paris: A. Picard, 1881).

SAPERSTEIN, MARC, *Decoding the Rabbis: A Thirteenth-Century Commentary on the Aggadah* (Cambridge, Mass.: Harvard University Press, 1980).

—— *Exile in Amsterdam: Saul Levi Morteira's Sermons to a Congregation of 'New Jews'* (Cincinnati: Hebrew Union College Press, 2005).

—— *Jewish Preaching, 1200–1800: An Anthology* (New Haven: Yale University Press, 1989).

—— *Jewish Preaching in Times of War, 1800–2001* (Oxford: Littman Library, 2008).

—— 'The Manuscript/s of Morteira's Sermons', in Joseph Dan and Klaus Herrmann (eds.), *Studies in Jewish Manuscripts* (Tübingen: Mohr Siebeck, 1999), 171–98.

—— 'R. Isaac ben Yeda'ya: A Forgotten Commentator on the Aggada', *Revue des études juives*, 138 (1979), 17–45.

—— 'A "Ritual Dance of Destruction?" ', *Jewish Quarterly Review*, 90 (1999), 151–8.

—— 'Selected Passages from Yedaiah Bedersi's Commentary on the Midrashim', in Isadore Twersky (ed.), *Studies in Medieval Jewish History and Literature*, vol. ii (Cambridge, Mass.: Harvard University Press, 1984), 423–40.

—— 'The Sermon as Evidence for the Popularization of Philosophical Ideas' (Heb.), in Benjamin Kedar (ed.), *Studies in the History of Popular Culture* [Tarbut amamit: kovets ma'amarim] (Jerusalem: Merkaz Zalman Shazar, 1996), 155–6.

—— *'Your Voice Like a Ram's Horn': Themes and Texts in Traditional Jewish Preaching* (Cincinnati: Hebrew Union College Press, 1996).

—— (ed.), *Essential Papers on Messianic Movements and Personalities in Jewish History* (New York: New York University Press, 1992).

SARACHEK, JOSEPH, *The Doctrine of the Messiah in Medieval Jewish Literature* (New York: Jewish Theological Seminary of America, 1932).

SARACHEK, JOSEPH, *Faith and Reason: The Conflict over the Rationalism of Maimonides* (Williamsport, Pa.: Bayard Press, 1935).
SARTON, GEORGE, *A History of Science*, 2 vols. (Cambridge, Mass.: Harvard University Press, 1959).
SCHACTER, JACOB J., 'Echoes of the Spanish Expulsion in Eighteenth Century Germany: The Baer Thesis Revisited', *Judaism*, 162 (1992), 180–9.
SCHAMA, SIMON, *The Embarrassment of Riches: An Interpretation of Dutch Culture in the Golden Age* (Berkeley: University of California Press, 1988).
SCHAPER, JOACHIM, 'The Persian Period', in Markus Bockmuehl and James Carletone Paget (eds.), *Redemption and Resistance: The Messianic Hopes of Jews and Christians in Antiquity* (London: Continuum, 2007), 3–14.
SCHATBORN, PETER, *Dutch Figure Drawings from the Seventeenth Century* (The Hague: Government Publishing Office, 1981).
SCHATZ UFFENHEIMER, RIVKA, *Hasidism as Mysticism: Quietistic Elements in Eighteenth Century Hasidic Thought* (Princeton: Princeton University Press, 1993).
SCHECHTER, SOLOMON, *Studies in Judaism* (Philadelphia: Jewish Publishing Society, 1896).
SCHEINDLIN, RAYMOND P., *The Song of the Distant Dove: Judah Halevi's Pilgrimage* (Oxford: Oxford University Press, 2008).
SCHIMMEL, ANNEMARIE, *Mystical Dimensions of Islam* (Chapel Hill: University of North Carolina Press, 1975).
SCHIRMANN, HAYYIM (YEFIM), 'Studies on the Poems and Letters of Abraham Bedersi' (Heb.), in Shmuel Ettinger et al. (eds.), *Yitzhak Baer Jubilee Volume* [Sefer yovel leyitsḥak baer] (Jerusalem: Israel Historical Society, 1961), 154–73.
SCHOLEM, GERSHOM, 'Abulafia, Todros ben Josef', *Encyclopaedia Judaica*, 10 vols. (Berlin: Eshkol, 1928–34), i. 657.
—— *Kabbalah* (Jerusalem: Keter, 1974).
—— *Major Trends in Jewish Mysticism* (New York: Schocken Books, 1941).
—— *The Messianic Idea in Judaism and Other Essays on Jewish Spirituality* (New York: Schocken Books, 1971).
—— 'New Investigations about Rabbi Abraham ben Eliezer Halevi' (Heb.), *Kiryat sefer*, 7 (1930–1), 149–65, 440–56.
—— *On the Mystical Shape of the Godhead: Basic Concepts in the Kabbalah* (New York: Schocken Books, 1991).
—— *The Origins of the Kabbalah*, ed. R. J. Zwi Werblowsky (Princeton: Princeton University Press, 1990).
—— *Sabbatai Sevi: The Mystical Messiah* (Princeton: Princeton University Press, 1973).
SCHWARTZ, DOV, 'Contacts between Jewish Philosophy and Mysticism at the Beginning of the Fifteenth Century' (Heb.), *Da'at*, 29 (1992), 41–67.
—— ' "Greek Wisdom": A Renewed Examination of the Period of the Conflict over the Study of Philosophy' (Heb.), *Sinai*, 104 (1989), 148–53.
—— *The Messianic Idea in Medieval Jewish Thought* [Harayon hameshiḥi bahagut hayehudit bimei habeinayim] (Ramat Gan: Bar-Ilan University Press, 1997).

—— 'Polemical and Esoteric Writing in the *Guide for the Perplexed*: The Subject of the Purpose of Existence' (Heb.), *Iyun*, 48 (1999), 129–46.

—— 'The Spiritual-Religious Decline of the Spanish Jewish Community at the End of the Fourteenth Century' (Heb.), *Pe'amim*, 46–7 (1991), 92–114.

SCHWARTZMANN, JULIA, 'The Commentary of Rabbi Isaac ibn Shem Tov on the *Guide for the Perplexed*' (Heb.), *Da'at*, 26 (1991), 43–56.

SCHWARZSCHILD, STEVEN, 'The Personal Messiah: Toward the Restoration of a Discarded Doctrine', *Judaism*, 5 (1956), 123–35.

SCHWEID, ELIEZER, 'Jewish Messianism', in Marc Saperstein (ed.), *Essential Papers on Messianic Movements and Personalities in Jewish History* (New York: New York University Press, 1992), 53–70.

SCHWEINBURG-EIBENSCHITZ, S., 'Une confiscation des livres hébreux à Prague', *Revue des études juives*, 29 (1894), 266–71.

SEESKIN, KENNETH, *Maimonides on the Origin of the World* (Cambridge: Cambridge University Press, 2005).

SEGAL, M. Z., 'Rabbi Isaac Abravanel as Biblical Commentator' (Heb.), *Tarbiz*, 9 (1937), 260–99.

SEPTIMUS, BERNARD, *Hispano-Jewish Culture in Transition: The Career and Controversies of Ramah* (Cambridge, Mass.: Harvard University Press, 1982).

—— '"Kings, Angels or Beggars": Tax Law and Spirituality in a Hispano-Jewish *Responsum*', in Isadore Twersky (ed.), *Studies in Medieval Jewish History and Literature*, vol. ii (Cambridge, Mass.: Harvard University Press, 1984), 309–35.

—— 'Piety and Power in Thirteenth-Century Catalonia', in Isadore Twersky (ed.), *Studies in Medieval Jewish History and Literature*, vol. i (Cambridge, Mass.: Harvard University Press, 1979), 197–230.

—— 'Struggle over Public Rule in Barcelona during the Period of the Conflict over the Works of Maimonides' (Heb.), *Tarbiz*, 42 (1973), 389–97.

SERMONETA, GIUSEPPE, *Un glossario filosofico ebraico–italiano del xiii secolo* (Rome: Edizioni dell'Ateneo, 1969).

—— 'Prophecy in the Writings of Yehuda Romano', in Isadore Twersky (ed.), *Studies in Medieval Jewish History and Literature*, vol. ii (Cambridge, Mass.: Harvard University Press, 1984), 337–74.

—— ' "Thine Ointments have a Goodly Fragrance": Rabbi Judah Romano and the "Open Text" Method' (Heb.), *Jerusalem Studies in Jewish Thought*, 9 (1990), 77–113.

SHALEM, SHIMON, 'The Exegetical Method of Rabbi Joseph Taitatsak and His Circle' (Heb.), *Sefunot*, 11 [*Sefer Yavan*, 1] (1971–8), 113–34.

SHAROT, STEPHEN, *Messianism, Mysticism, and Magic: A Sociological Analysis of Jewish Religious Movements* (Chapel Hill: University of North Carolina Press, 1982).

SHATZMILLER, JOSEPH, 'Between Abba Mari and Solomon ben Adret: Negotiations Preceding the Ban in Barcelona' (Heb.), *Meḥkarim betoledot am yisra'el ve'erets yisra'el*, 3 (1974), 121–37.

—— 'Étudiants juifs à la faculté de médecine de Montpellier, dernier quart du XIVe siècle', *Jewish History*, 6 (1992), 243–55.

SHATZMILLER, JOSEPH, 'L'Excommunication, la communauté juive et les autorités temporelles au Moyen-Âge', in Myriam Yardeni (ed.), *Les Juifs dans l'histoire de France* (Leiden: Brill, 1980), 63–9.

—— 'Gersonide et la société juive de son temps', in Gilbert Dahan (ed.), *Gersonide en son temps* (Louvain: E. Peeters, 1991), 33–43.

—— 'Gersonides and the Communities of Orange during His Lifetime' (Heb.), *Meḥkarim betoledot am yisra'el ve'erets yisra'el*, 2 (1972), 111–26.

—— 'In Search of the "Book of Figures"', *AJS Review*, 7–8 (1982–3), 383–407.

—— *Jews, Medicine, and Medieval Society* (Berkeley: University of California Press, 1994).

—— 'Livres médicaux et éducation médicale: À propos d'un contrat de Marseille en 1316', *Mediaeval Studies*, 42 (1980), 463–70.

—— 'More on Gersonides and the Communities of Orange during His Lifetime' (Heb.), *Meḥkarim betoledot am yisra'el ve'erets yisra'el*, 3 (1975), 139–43.

SHOCHAT, AZRIEL, 'On the Matter of David Reubeni' (Heb.), *Zion*, 35 (1970), 96–116.

SHULMAN, NISSON E., *Authority and Community: Polish Jewry in the Sixteenth Century* (New York: Ktav, 1986).

SILVER, ABBA HILLEL, *A History of Messianic Speculation in Israel* (New York: Macmillan, 1927).

SILVER, DANIEL JEREMY, *Images of Moses* (New York: Basic Books, 1982).

SIRAT, COLETTE, *A History of Jewish Philosophy in the Middle Ages* (Cambridge: Cambridge University Press, 1985).

—— 'Le Livre hébreu en France au Moyen Âge', *Michael*, 12 (1991), 299–336.

—— 'Political Ideas of Nissim ben Moses of Marseilles' (Heb.), *Jerusalem Studies in Jewish Thought*, 9 (1990), 53–76.

SMALLEY, BERYL, *Medieval Exegesis of Wisdom Literature* (Atlanta, Ga.: Scholars Press, 1986).

—— *Studies in Medieval Thought and Learning* (London: Hambledon Press, 1981).

—— *The Study of the Bible in the Middle Ages* (New York: Philosophical Library, 1952).

SMITH, MORTON, 'Messiahs: Robbers, Jurists, Prophets, and Magicians', in Marc Saperstein (ed.), *Essential Papers on Messianic Movements and Personalities in Jewish History* (New York: New York University Press, 1992), 73–83.

SNABEL, COR, 'Life in 16th and 17th Century Amsterdam Holland: Disease', *The Olive Tree Genealogy*, <http://www.olivetreegenealogy.com/nn/amst_disease.shtml> (accessed 11 Aug. 2014).

SNIR, REUVEN, ' "Al-Andalus Arising from Damascus": Al-Andalus in Modern Arabic Poetry', in Stacy N. Beckwith (ed.), *Charting Memory: Recalling Medieval Spain* (New York: Garland, 1999), 263–93.

SOLOVEITCHIK, HAYM, *Collected Essays*, vol. i (Oxford: Littman Library, 2013).

—— 'Three Themes in *Sefer Ḥasidim*', *AJS Review*, 1 (1976), 311–57.

SONNE, ISAIAH, *From Paul IV to Pius V* [Mipaulo harevi'i ad pius haḥamishi] (Jerusalem: Bialik Institute, 1954).

SOUTHERN, RICHARD W., *Western Society and the Church in the Middle Ages* (Harmondsworth: Penguin, 1970).

SPENCER, H. LEITH, *English Preaching in the Late Middle Ages* (Oxford: Clarendon Press, 1993).

SPICQ, CESLAS, *Esquisse d'une histoire de l'éxégèse latin au Moyen Âge* (Paris: J. Vrin, 1944).

STANISLAWSKI, MICHAEL, *For Whom Do I Toil? Judah Leib Gordon and the Crisis of Russian Jewry* (New York: Oxford University Press, 1988).

STARN, RANDOLPH, *Contrary Commonwealth: The Theme of Exile in Medieval and Renaissance Italy* (Berkeley: University of California Press, 1982).

STEINSCHNEIDER, MORITZ, 'Abraham Bibago's Schriften', *Monatschrift für Geschichte und Wissenschaft des Judentums*, 32 (1883), 79–96, 125–44, 239–40.

—— 'Le Bibliothèque de Leon Mosconi', *Revue des études juives*, 40 (1900), 60–73.

—— *Die Hebraeischen Übersetzungen des Mittelalters und die Juden als Dolmetscher* (Berlin: Kommisionsverlag des Bibliographischen Bureaus, 1893).

STERN, DAVID, *Parables in Midrash: Narrative and Exegesis in Rabbinic Literature* (Cambridge, Mass.: Harvard University Press, 1991).

STERN, GREGG, 'Jewish Philosophy in Southern France: Controversy over Philosophical Study and the Influence of Averroes upon Jewish Thought', in Daniel H. Frank and Oliver Leaman (eds.), *The Cambridge Companion to Medieval Jewish Philosophy* (Cambridge: Cambridge University Press, 2003), 280–303.

—— 'Philosophic Allegory in Medieval Jewish Culture: The Crisis in Languedoc (1304–6)', in Jon Whitman (ed.), *Interpretation and Allegory* (Leiden: Brill, 2000), 189–209.

STETKEVYCH, JAROSLAV, *The Zephyrs of Najd: The Poetics of Nostalgia in the Classical Arabic Nasīb* (Chicago: University of Chicago Press, 1993).

STOW, KENNETH R., *Alienated Minority: The Jews of Medieval Latin Europe* (Cambridge, Mass.: Harvard University Press, 1992).

—— *Catholic Thought and Jewish Policy, 1555–1593* (New York: Jewish Theological Seminary of America, 1977).

STRAYER, JOSEPH R., 'Consent to Taxation under Philip the Fair', in Charles F. Taylor and Joseph R. Strayer (eds.), *Studies in Early French Taxation* (Cambridge, Mass.: Harvard University Press, 1939), 3–108.

—— *Les Gens de justice du Languedoc sous Philippe le Bel* (Toulouse: Association Marc Bloch, 1971).

—— 'Viscounts and Viguiers under Philip the Fair', *Speculum*, 38 (1963), 242–55.

SUSSMAN, LANCE, *Isaac Leeser and the Making of American Judaism* (Detroit: Wayne State University Press, 1995).

SWETSCHINSKI, DANIEL M., *Reluctant Cosmpolitans: The Portuguese Jews of Seventeenth-Century Amsterdam* (London: Littman Library, 2000).

SYNAN, EDWARD, 'The Four "Senses" and Four Exegetes', in Jane Dammen McAuliffe, Barry D. Walfish, and Joseph W. Goering (eds.), *With Reverence for the Word: Medieval Scriptural Exegesis in Judaism, Christianity, and Islam* (Oxford: Oxford University Press, 2003), 225–36.

SZAPIRO, ELIE, 'Renseignements sur les juifs de Languedoc dans une cartulaire inédit', *Archives juives*, 5/2 (1968–9), 19–20.

SZARMACH, PAUL (ed.), *Aspects of Jewish Culture in the Middle Ages* (Albany: State University of New York Press, 1979).

TA-SHMA, ISRAEL M., 'Between East and West: Rabbi Asher b. Yehi'el and His Son Rabbi Ya'aqov', in Isadore Twersky and Jay M. Harris (eds.), *Studies in Medieval Jewish History and Literature*, vol. iii (Cambridge, Mass.: Harvard University Press, 2000), 179–96.

—— 'An Epistle and a Revivalist Sermon by One of Our Early Rabbis' (Heb.), *Moriah*, 19/5–6 (1994), 7–12.

—— 'Matters Regarding the Land of Israel' (Heb.), *Shalem*, 1 (1974), 81–95.

—— 'Moses ben Jacob of Coucy', *Encyclopedia Judaica*, 16 vols. (Jerusalem: Keter, 1973), xii. 418–19

TAL, URIEL, 'Foundations of a Political Messianic Trend in Israel', in Marc Saperstein (ed.), *Essential Papers on Messianic Movements and Personalities in Jewish History* (New York: New York University Press, 1992), 492–503.

TALMAGE, FRANK, *David Kimhi: The Man and the Commentaries* (Cambridge, Mass.: Harvard University Press, 1975).

—— 'Medieval Christian Exegesis and Its Interaction with Jewish Exegesis' (Heb.), in Moshe Greenberg (ed.), *Jewish Bible Exegesis* [Parshanut hamikra hayehudit] (Jerusalem: Bialik Institute, 1983), 101–12.

TALMON, SHEMARYAHU, *King, Cult and Calendar in Ancient Israel: Collected Studies* (Jerusalem: Magnes Press, 1986).

TALMON, YONINA, 'Millenarism', in David L. Sills and Robert K. Merton (eds.), *International Encyclopedia of the Social Sciences*, 17 vols. (New York: Macmillan, 1968), x. 353.

TAMAR, DAVID, 'On Rabbi Meir of Rothenburg's Statement Regarding Martyrdom' (Heb.), *Kiryat sefer*, 33 (1958), 376–7; 34 (1959), 397.

TAUBES, JACOB, 'The Price of Messianism', in Marc Saperstein (ed.), *Essential Papers on Messianic Movements and Personalities in Jewish History* (New York: New York University Press, 1992), 551–7.

TAYLOR, DOV, *Joseph Perl's Revealer of Secrets: The First Hebrew Novel* (Boulder, Colo.: Westview Press, 1997).

TAYLOR, LARISSA, *Soldiers of Christ: Preaching in Late Medieval and Reformation France* (Oxford: Oxford University Press, 1992).

TEMKIN, SEFTON D., *Isaac Mayer Wise: Shaping American Judaism* (Oxford: Oxford University Press, 1992).

THOMPSON, AUGUSTINE, *Revival Preachers and Politics in Thirteenth-Century Italy: The Great Devotion of 1233* (New York: Oxford University Press, 1992).

TIERNEY, BRIAN, *The Crisis of Church and State 1050–1300: With Selected Documents* (Englewood Cliffs, NJ: Prentice Hall, 1964).

TIROSH-ROTHSCHILD, HAVA, *Between Worlds: The Life and Thought of Rabbi David ben Judah Messer Leon* (Albany: State University of New York Press, 1991).

—— 'The Political Philosophy of Abraham Shalom: The Platonic Tradition' (Heb.), *Jerusalem Studies in Jewish Thought*, 9/2 (1991), 409–40.

—— 'Sefirot as the Essence of God in the Writings of David Messer Leon', *AJS Review*, 7–8 (1982–3), 409–25.

TISHBY, ISAIAH, 'Acute Apocalyptic Messianism', in Marc Saperstein (ed.), *Essential Papers on Messianic Movements and Personalities in Jewish History* (New York: New York University Press, 1992), 259–86.

—— 'The Messianic Idea and Messianic Trends at the Beginning of Hasidism' (Heb.), *Zion*, 32 (1967), 1–45.

—— *Messianism in the Generation of the Expulsions from Spain and Portugal* [Meshiḥiyut bador gerushei sefarad ufortugal] (Jerusalem: Merkaz Zalman Shazar, 1985).

—— *Studies in Kabbalah and Its Branches* [Ḥikrei kabalah usheluḥoteiha], 3 vols. (Jerusalem: Magnes Press, 1982–93).

TISHBY, PERETS, 'Hebrew Incunabula: Spain and Portugal (Guadalajara)' (Heb.), *Kiryat sefer*, 61 (1986–7), 521–46.

TOLEDANO, JACOB MEIR, 'From Manuscripts' (Heb.), *Hebrew Union College Annual*, 5 (1928), 403–9.

TOUATI, CHARLES, 'La Controverse de 1303–1306 autour des études philosophiques et scientifiques', *Revue des études juives*, 127 (1968), 21–37.

—— *La Pensée philosophique et théologique de Gersonide* (Paris: Éditions de Minuit, 1973).

TWERSKY, ISADORE, 'Aspects of the Social and Cultural History of Provençal Jewry', *Social Life and Social Values of the Jewish People*, special issue of *Journal of World History*, 11 (1968), 185–207.

—— *Introduction to the Code of Maimonides (Mishneh Torah)* (New Haven: Yale University Press, 1980).

—— 'Joseph ibn Kaspi: Portrait of a Medieval Jewish Intellectual', in id. (ed.), *Studies in Medieval Jewish History and Literature* (Cambridge, Mass.: Harvard University Press, 1979), 231–57.

URBACH, EFRAIM ELIMELECH, *The Sages: Their Concepts and Beliefs*, trans. Israel Abrahams (Cambridge, Mass.: Harvard University Press, 1987).

—— *The Tosafists: Their History, Writings, and Methods* [Ba'alei hatosafot: toldoteihem, ḥibureihem, ushitatam] (Jerusalem: Bialik Institute, 1968).

VAJDA, GEORGES, *Isaac Albalag: Averroïste juif, traducteur et annotateur d'al Ghazali* (Paris: Librarie Philosophique J. Vrin, 1960).

VODOLA, ELISABETH, *Excommunication in the Middle Ages* (Berkeley: University of California Press, 1986).

WALFISH, BARRY, *Esther in Medieval Garb: Jewish Interpretation of the Book of Esther in the Middle Ages* (Albany: State University of New York Press, 1993).

WALZER, MICHAEL, *Exodus and Revolution* (New York: Basic Books, 1985).

WASSERSTROM, STEVEN M., *Between Muslim and Jew: The Problem of Symbiosis under Early Islam* (Princeton: Princeton University Press, 1995).

WEIL, ANNE-MARIE, 'Levi ben Gershom et sa bibliothèque privée', in Gilbert Dahan (ed.), *Gersonide en son temps* (Louvain: E. Peeters, 1991), 45–59.

WEINRYB, BERNARD D., *The Jews of Poland: A Social and Economic History of the Jewish Community in Poland from 1000 to 1800* (Philadelphia: Jewish Publication Society, 1973).

WEISS, ISAAC HIRSCH, *Each Generation and Its Exegetes: A Book of the History of the Oral Law* [Dor dor vedorshav, hu sefer divrei hayamim latorah shebe'al peh], 5 pts. in 2 vols. (Vilna: Romm, 1911).

WEISS, ROSLYN, 'Maimonides on the End of the World', *Maimonidean Studies*, 3 (1992–3), 195–218.

WERBLOWSKY, R. J. ZWI, *Joseph Karo: Lawyer and Mystic* (Philadelphia: Jewish Publication Society, 1977).

—— 'Messianism in Jewish History', in Marc Saperstein (ed.), *Essential Papers on Messianic Movements and Personalities in Jewish History* (New York: New York University Press, 1992), 35–52.

WETERING, ERNST VAN DE, *Rembrandt: The Painter at Work* (Amsterdam: Amsterdam University Press, 1997).

WIDENGREN, GEO, 'The Status of the Jews in the Sassanian Empire', *Iranica Antiqua*, 1 (1961), 117–62.

WILENSKY, SARAH HELLER, *The Philosophy of Rabbi Isaac Arama within the Framework of Philonic Philosophy* [R. yitsḥak arama umishnato] (Jerusalem: Bialik Institute, 1957).

WILSON, CATHERINE, *The Invisible World: Early Modern Philosophy and the Invention of the Microscope* (Princeton: Princeton University Press, 1995).

WISCHNITZER, MARK, *A History of Jewish Crafts and Guilds* (New York: Jonathan David, 1965).

WIZNITZER, ARNOLD, 'The Exodus from Brazil and Arrival in New Amsterdam of the Jewish Pilgrim Fathers, 1654', in Martin A. Cohen (ed.), *The Jewish Experience in Latin America*, 2 vols. (New York: Ktav, 1971), ii. 313–30.

WOLFSON, HARRY AUSTRYN, *Crescas' Critique of Aristotle: Problems of Aristotle's 'Physics' in Jewish and Arabic Philosophy* (Cambridge, Mass.: Harvard University Press, 1957).

—— *The Philosophy of Spinoza, Unfolding the Latent Processes of His Reasoning*, 2 vols. (Cambridge, Mass.: Harvard University Press, 1934; repr. New York: Meridian Books, 1958).

—— *Studies in the History of Philosophy and Religion*, ed. Isadore Twersky and George Williams, 2 vols. (Cambridge, Mass.: Harvard University Press, 1973–7).

WOLIN, RICHARD, 'Reflections on Jewish Secular Messianism', in Jonathan Frankel (ed.), *Jews and Messianism in the Modern Era*, Studies in Contemporary Jewry, 7 (New York: Oxford University Press, 1991), 186–96.

WORSLEY, PETER, *The Trumpet Shall Sound: A Study of the 'Cargo Cults' in Melanesia*, 2nd edn. (New York: Schocken Books, 1968).

WYLIE, FRANCIS E., *Tides and the Pull of the Moon* (Brattleboro, Vt.: Stephen Greene Press, 1979).

YADIN, YIGAEL, *Bar Kokhba* (New York: Random House, 1971).

YEHOSHUA, A. B [ABRAHAM B.], 'Exile as a Neurotic Solution', in Etan Levine (ed.), *Diaspora: Exile and the Contemporary Jewish Condition* (New York: Steimatzky, 1986), 15–35.

YERUSHALMI, YOSEF HAYIM, *The Lisbon Massacre of 1506 and the Royal Image in the Shebet Yehudah*, Hebrew Union College Annual Supplements, 1 (Cincinnati: Hebrew Union College Press, 1976).

—— 'Messianic Impulses in Joseph ha-Kohen', in Bernard Cooperman (ed.), *Jewish Thought in the Sixteenth Century* (Cambridge, Mass.: Harvard University Press, 1983), 460–87.

—— *Zakhor: Jewish History and Jewish Memory* (Seattle: University of Washington Press, 1982).

YUVAL, ISRAEL JACOB, *Two Nations in Your Womb: Perceptions of Jews and Christians in Late Antiquity and the Middle Ages* (Berkeley: University of California Press, 2006).

ZAHAVI, YOSEF, *Erets Israel in Rabbinic Lore* (Jerusalem: Tehilla Institute, 1962).

ZAREMSKA, HANNA, *Les Bannis au Moyen Âge* (Paris: Aubier, 1996).

ZEITLIN, SOLOMON, 'The Origin of the Idea of the Messiah', in Leo Landman (ed.), *Messianism in the Talmudic Era* (New York: Ktav, 1979), 99–111.

ZELL, MICHAEL, *Reframing Rembrandt* (Berkeley: University of California Press, 2002).

ZONTA, MAURO, *Hebrew Scholasticism in the Fifteenth Century: A History and Source Book* (Dordrecht: Springer, 2006).

—— 'Medieval Hebrew Translations of Philosophical and Scientific Texts', in Gad Freudenthal (ed.), *Science in Medieval Jewish Cultures* (Cambridge: Cambridge University Press, 2011), 17–73.

ZUNZ, LEOPOLD, *Zur Geschichte und Literatur* (Berlin: Veit und Comp., 1845).

Index of Passages Cited

HEBREW SCRIPTURES

Genesis
- 1   242
- 1:1   143
- 1:2   143
- 1:2–3   165
- 1:3   143
- 1:5   175
- 1:6   142–3
- 1:7   145, 148–9
- 1:8   146
- 1:9   67, 149, 154, 164, 166
- 1:10   142
- 1:11   168, 171
- 1:12   152, 171
- 1:14   146
- 1:15   146, 156–7
- 1:16   145, 156
- 1:17   158
- 1:28   156–7
- 2:10–11   195
- 2:18   120
- 4:12   199
- 4:17   130
- 5:25   130
- 6:4   130
- 12:4–16   241
- 15:13   301
- 17:8   281, 284
- 22:10   188
- 27:4   124
- 27:8–10   124
- 27:12   124
- 27:33   125
- 27:37   124
- 27:38   224
- 29:11   223
- 32:9   254
- 32:26   199
- 33:3–4   224
- 34:13   196
- 35:29   224
- 36:16   224
- 37:2   222
- 37:3   222
- 42:21   225
- 42:24   225
- 43:26–30   225
- 45:2   221, 222, 225–6
- 45:14   223, 225
- 45:15   225
- 46:29   223, 225
- 47:28   316
- 49:33–50:1   225
- 50:15–17   225
- 50:17   225

Exodus
- 2:14   240
- 15:1   234
- 17:8–13   224
- 20:2   121
- 25:2   268
- 25:20   188
- 28:2   157
- 31:18–32:35   126
- 33:15   125

Leviticus
- 1:14   173
- 4:22   199
- 16:10   156
- 18:25   284–5
- 19:35–6   18
- 22:19   173
- 24   122
- 24:10   123
- 24:15   123
- 25:38   281
- 26   253
- 27:10   198

Numbers
- 11:17   155
- 12:3   199–200
- 15   123
- 15:41   157
- 22:22–35   127
- 28:3   231
- 28:9   231
- 30:5–6   256
- 32   122

Deuteronomy
- 9:9–10:11   119
- 11:12   282–3
- 11:17   286
- 11:21   288
- 12:29   272
- 13:6   39
- 13:18   230
- 15:7–9   200
- 20:19   202
- 22:6   91
- 23:18   35, 36
- 25:17–18   224
- 28   183, 253
- 29:23–4   228
- 30:1–10   295
- 30:20   234
- 33:14   171–2
- 33:19   65

Joshua
- 10   89
- 10:12   126
- 10:12–14   109, 240

2 Samuel
- 24:25   234

1 Kings
- 3:6–14   89

2 Kings
- 17:26   286

Isaiah
- 1:12   18
- 2:2–4   295
- 6   242

Isaiah (cont.):
   28:20 65
   29:13 237
   45:1–8 300
   45:1 304
   45:7 155
   58:1 13

Jeremiah
   15:2 228
   22:10 223, 228
   25:11–12 301
   31:2 231
   31:8 223, 226
   31:9 223, 235
   31:21 286

Ezekiel
   1 242
   8 242
   36:15 261

Hosea
   2:25 254

Joel
   4:15 165

Amos
   9:9–15 295

Obadiah
   8–15 224
   20 15

Micah
   6:6 234

Haggai
   1:4 230

Zechariah
   7:1 117

Psalms
   25:9 146
   33:7–9 166
   36:10 149
   39:7 193
   39:13 222
   44:23 263
   59:12 42
   66:9 234
   80 227
   80:6 222, 224
   97:2 165
   104:24 170
   107:23 165
   107:26 165
   107:29 165
   111:4 167
   137:4 255
   137:7 224
   137:8 253
   145:9 161
   147:4 175

Proverbs
   1:17 130
   1:20 130
   1:21 238
   7:6–26 169
   9:3 238
   30:4 126

Job
   12:15 166
   24:7 230
   30:25 223, 229
   35:6–7 161

Lamentations
   1:1 255
   4:21 224
   5:22 25

Ecclesiastes
   1:5 289
   4:6 2

Esther
   8:3 223, 234
   9:3 175

2 Chronicles
   2:6 173
   16:12 235

MISHNAH
Ḥagigah
   2:1 77

Kidushin
   4:3 116

Sanhedrin
   9:5 39
   10 ('Ḥelek') 118, 264

Avodah zarah
   2:6 20

Avot
   1:7 265
   2:16 196
   5:22 263

BABYLONIAN TALMUD
Berakhot
   5b 229
   10a 168
   17a 264
   32b 267

Shabat
   15b 116
   122a 20
   151b 230

Pesaḥim
   87b 254

Ta'anit
   10a 282

Megilah
   29a 267, 288

Ḥagigah
   13a 155
   22a 38

Yevamot
   63a 194
   90b 32

Ketubot
   17a 19
   19a 51
   110a 274
   110b 266, 274, 276–7, 280–1, 284–5
   111a 272, 290, 308

Sotah
   27a 49

Gitin
    52*a* 194

Kidushin
    24*b* 173
    81*a* 39

Bava kama
    79*b* 22

Bava metsia
    64*b* 53
    83*b* 116
    90*a* 21

Bava batra
    8*b* 218, 228
    58*a* 109
    60*b* 22
    91*a* 273, 301
    158*b* 282

Sanhedrin
    37*b* 34
    38*b* 244
    46*a* 33, 41
    81*b*–82*a* 34
    98*b* 317
    99*a* 296, 301

Makot
    2*b* 259

Avodah zarah
    9*b* 301
    13*a* 279
    38*b* 20

Horayot
    3*b* 214

Ḥulin
    60*a* 172
    109*b*–110*a* 45

MIDRASHIM

Genesis Rabbah
    76:3 254
    93:12 226
    96:5 283

Exodus Rabbah
    33:1 268

Leviticus Rabbah
    7:2 268

Numbers Rabbah
    11:2 304
    22:1 229

Lamentations Rabbah
    Petiḥta 25 268
    4:34 224

Sifrei, Deuteronomy
    11:12 282–3
    11:17 286
    12:29 272

Midrash tanḥuma
    'Toledot' 24 222

Midrash tanḥuma [Buber]
    'Beshalaḥ' 12 234
    'Matot' 1 229

Midrash tehilim
    20 201–2
    80:4 222

Yalkut shimoni
    on Ps. 80:6 222

MISHNEH TORAH

Introduction: *Book of Commandments*
    neg. comm. 355 36

Laws of Courts
    18:6 31
    24:4 31
    24:4–5 32
    24:5 39
    24:5–10 33
    24:9 32

Laws of Forbidden Foods
    9:12 45
    17:12–13 20

Laws of Forbidden Relations
    3:1 173
    12:4–6 34
    12:7–8 34

Laws of Kings and Their Wars
    5:9 279
    5:12 281
    12:4 264

Laws of Lenders and Borrowers
    2:1 44
    2:4 33
    6:2 53

Laws of Marriage
    13:17 274
    18:1 48
    19:1 52

Laws of Murderers and the Protection of Life
    4:8 39

Laws of Repentance
    5:5 135

Laws of Witnesses
    11:2 38

GUIDE FOR THE PERPLEXED

Introduction 3, 77, 169
    1:17 241
    1:32 155
    1:53 152–3
    1:63 76
    2:22 153
    2:30 172
    3:13 156, 161
    3:14 159
    3:26 169
    3:34 49
    3:51 268, 282

KUZARI
    1:114 263
    1:115 263
    2:24 305
    3:21 268
    3:65 269
    5:22–3 267

KUZARI (cont.):
    5:23 259, 269
    5:115 258

ZOHAR
Lekh lekha
    1:78*a* 284

Shemot
    2:3*b* 21
    2:7*a* 21

Yitro
    2:87*b* 21

Terumah
    2:141*b* 277

Zohar ḥadash: rut
    99*a* 273

General Index

A
Aaron ben Elijah 66
Abba Mari of Lunel 82
  anti-philosophy camp of 88
  attempt by to control preaching 241–2
  attempt by to restrict study of philosophy 86, 96–8, 103, 105–6, 112
  collection of letters by 94
  complaint by about Aristotle and Plato 65
Abbasid caliphate 309
Abd ar-Rahman I 260
Abelard, Peter 131, 135
Aberbach, David 255, 260
Abner of Burgos 64, 91–2, 317
Aboab, Immanuel 203
Aboab, Isaac 81, 137, 188
  biblical exegesis of 194
  on Christians in sermon of 200
  citation of Latin terms by 198
  citation of philosophers by 197–8
  citation of unnamed teacher by 189
  efforts for entry into Portugal 203
  eulogy by 199
  eulogy for 189, 203
  homiletical conventions in sermons of 197
  as Jewish leader 203
  kabbalistic material in sermons of 199–200
  left Spain for Portugal 8
  on martyrdom 202–3
  references to current events by 202
  responsa by 191, 194
  on response to rape of Dinah 196
  sermons by 120, 195
  on social injustice among Jews 200–1
  as talmudist 193
  use of disputed questions by 199
  use of syllogisms by 199
Aboab, Jacob ben Isaac 195
Abraham ben David (Rabad) of Posquières 135
Abravanel, Isaac 127, 139, 149, 196, 293
  on absence of spiritual reward in Torah 147–8
  against centralized royal power 187–8
  biblical commentaries of 138
  as courtier critic of philosophy 89
  on Creation 154
  on diversity from unity 154
  efforts to revoke Edict of Expulsion 186–7
  on Jewish expulsions 183
  as Jewish leader 185, 192
  joke about 135
  lost work of 190
  and 'method of doubts' 114–19, 123, 124
  philosophical concepts used by 93
  on response to rape of Dinah 196
  sermon attributed to 117
  sermons by 121
Abu Isa of Isfahan ('Isawiyya) 298, 309
Abulafia, Abraham 76
  on 'Land of Israel' 293
  as messianic personality 293
Abulafia, David 112
Abulafia, Meir Halevi 88
Abulafia, Todros ben Joseph Halevi 16–28, 88
Abulafia, Todros ben Judah 22, 25
Adret, Solomon ben (Rashba) 65, 115
  on Abraham Abulafia 293
  attacked by angry Jews 41
  ban on philosophical study by 7, 66, 77, 82, 89–90, 94–111, 242
  commentary on aggadot by 90, 97, 284
  on Land of Israel 284
  and papal Inquisition 104, 111
  on political boundaries 95, 96
  on punishing miscreants 25
  responsa of 25, 32, 95, 284
Adrianople 205, 206, 213
  objections to boycott in 214
Aescoly, Aaron Zeev 299
aggadah:
  not binding upon Jews 262
  see also Talmud: aggadot of
Agnon, S. Y. 279, 288
Alami, Solomon 62
Albalag, Isaac 64, 86, 92
Albertus Magnus 69

General Index

Albi, Albigensians 101
Albo, Joseph 64, 152, 153, 174
Alconstantin, Solomon 91
Alexander of Aphrodisias 129
Alexandria 274
Alfakhar, Judah 67, 85, 87, 88
Alfarabi 60
Alfonso X of Castile ('el Sabio/the Wise') 16, 67, 68
al-Ghazali 81
Alguades, Meir 69, 88
Alharizi, Judah 160
al-Kirkisani, Jacob 298, 309
allegorization:
   of Bible and aggadah 89, 91, 106, 109, 114
   in Christianity 110
   of commandments 91
   in hasidism 110
Almagest (Ptolemy) 70–1
Almaric, Viscount 99
Almohad invasion 60
Almosnino, Moses 121
Alonso de Espina 184
Alroy, David 298, 310
Altmann, Alexander 155
Amalric II, Viscount 99, 102
Amsterdam 6–8, 140, 176, 191, 247
   Ashkenazi Jews in 228
   Jewish confraternities in 234–5
   Menasseh ben Israel in 227
   Morteira's arrival in 141
   Morteira's preaching career in 222
   painting in 167
   plague in 231–2, 235
   Portuguese 'nation' in 140–1, 150, 228, 235
   return of Recife refugees to 230–1
   testimony before notary of 233
Anatoli, Jacob 76, 93, 240, 250
   on Emperor Frederick II 68
   financial circumstances of 64
   Malmad hatalmidim of 237
   as preacher 14, 74, 86, 89, 237–9
   on reasons for commandments 90–1
   translations by 67–8, 85
Ancona 8, 204–20
   boycott as punishment for 211
   boycott's danger to Jews in 214
   local reaction to boycott of 209, 211
   opposition to boycott by Jews in 208, 212
   papal persecutions in 207–8, 215
   papal privilege for 207
   Portuguese immigrants in 204, 218
   PR campaign by Jews of 214
   textile industry in 219
   trade with Ottoman empire 205–6, 208
Andalusia 14, 256–9, 309
   Arab nostalgia for 260
   expulsion from 183
Anthony of Padua 14
anthropocentrism, cosmic 162
antinomianism 27, 90
Antwerp 141, 228, 233
aporeia (doubt), *see* 'method of doubts'
Aquinas, Thomas 4, 69, 135, 157
   cited in sermon by Aboab 70, 197
   commentary on *Metaphysics* by 128–9, 131, 137, 197
   on God's relationship to the world 149, 151
   and Hillel of Verona 79, 127
   and 'method of doubts' in antiquity 128–9, 134
   Summa theologica of 135, 151, 157
Aragon 7, 66, 88–9, 108, 191
   James I of 261
   James II of 99, 102, 104
   Jewish violence in 37, 41
   Jews and Christian prostitutes in 36
   relations with Narbonne and Montpellier 98
Arama, Isaac 185, 192
   on anthropocentric Creation 161–3
   as critic of Jewish philosophy 62, 80
   on influence of Christian preachers 138
   kabbalistic material in sermons by 201
   and 'method of doubts' 114–15, 117, 119, 121, 139
   philosophical concepts used by 93
   possible influence on Abravanel by 117
   used by Morteira 174
Arama, Meir 119
   archival material 205
Arendt, Hannah 179
Aristotle ('the Philosopher') 4, 79, 92, 154, 198, 199
   ban of works by 106
   Crescas's critique of 191

De Anima 78, 128
 on diversity from unity 154
 on emanation 153
 Hebrew translation of works by 68, 74, 199, 240
 and Hillel of Verona 78
 influence of 65
 Metaphysics 128–9, 131, 137, 197
 and multiple souls 128
 Nicomachean Ethics 69, 77, 87–8
 Organon 67, 77, 85, 199
 Physics 65, 69–70, 83
 Politics 87
 Posterior Analytics 81
 on raising difficulties/doubts 122, 127–9, 131, 134
 on soul as 'form' of body 174
Asher ben Samuel of Marseilles (scribe) 71
Asher ben Solomon 35, 43
Asher ben Yehiel 32, 53
 on gazing upon bride 19
 on Jewish courts and capital cases 31
 and *takanah* of Toledo 43
Ashkenaz, *see* Germany
Assaf, Simcha 80
Assis, Yom Tov 41, 181
astrological determinism 19
astrology 180
 and Adret 96
 condemnation of 22
 and Gersonides 83
 influence of 16, 26
 and Jewish exile 17
Astruc of Sestiers 72
Augustine, St 42, 130, 132, 133
auto-da-fé in Ancona 207, 211
Averroës (ibn Rushd) 4, 60–1, 80, 92, 126, 154
 on Aristotle's *De Anima* 78–9
 on Aristotle's *Ethics* 87
 on Aristotle's *Organon* 67–8, 85
 on Aristotle's *Physics* 65, 70, 83
 on Aristotle's *Politics* 87
 cited by Aquinas and Aboab 197, 199
 Hebrew translations of 84
 Incoherence of the Incoherence by 153
 Logic text by 71
'Averroism', 'Averroist' 26, 62, 93, 95, 136
 Latin 110

 see also 'double truth' theory
Avicenna (Ibn Sina) 60, 153–4, 197
 Canon of Medicine by 65–6, 83
Avignon:
 legal questions to Adret from 95
 papal court in 83
 pontifical library in 72
Aycelin, Archbishop Gilles 103

B
Ba'al Shem Tov, *see* Israel Ba'al Shem Tov
Babylonia 253, 255
 defeat by Cyrus of 300, 304
 Jeremiah on life in 305
 messianic uprising in 301
 rabbis of 279, 280
Bachrach, Hayim Ya'ir 277
'backshadowing' 181, 299
Baconthorpe, John 132
Baer, Yitzhak:
 on Abraham Seneor 187
 on 'Averroism' 26, 62, 92–4, 136
 on communal reforms in Toledo 16
 on conflict over philosophical study 94–5
 on *galut* (exile) 253
 on Jewish coinage 43
 on Jewish criminal procedure 40
 on martyr feeling no pain 202
 on medieval Jewish philosophy 63, 83, 91
 on 'messianic movement' of 1295 293–4
 on Nahmanides and messianic age 262, 287
 on *pesquisa* 37
Bahya ben Asher 114
 on Land of Israel 271
ban (*ḥerem*) 6–7, 28, 37, 38
 in community affairs 45
 in Jewish criminal law 24–5, 27–8
 on philosophical study 63, 66, 77, 82, 89, 93, 94–112
 see also excommunication
Bar Kokhba revolt 273, 307
Barcelona 285
 conflict over philosophical study in 94–112, 242
 Disputation of 260–5
 Hillel of Verona in 78
 ibn Hisdai brothers in 76, 82
 Jewish surgeon of 66

Barcelona (*cont.*):
  respected teachers in 76
  Usatges (Law Code) of 32
Barzilay, Isaac 61, 62
Beaucaire, seneschalcy of 98–9
Bedersi, Abraham 84
Bedersi, Yedaiah:
  commentary on *midrashim* by 84
  comparison of philosophical manuscripts by 65–6
  on Land of Israel 277, 282–3
  as opponent of Adret's ban 73, 98, 110
  philosophical writings of 65–6, 83–4
  on teachers of philosophy 73, 77
Beinart, Haim 180
Benedict XI, Pope 101
Benedict XIII, Pope 133
Benjamin ben Aaron of Zalosce 289
Benjamin of Tudela 298, 310
Ben-Sasson, Haim Hillel 63
Ben-Shalom, Ram 111–15, 308
Benveniste ibn Lavi of Saragossa, Don 88
Benveniste, Sheshet 88
Berab, Jacob 193
Berekhiah Berakh 244, 249
Bernard of Clairvaux, St 42, 259
Bernstein, Michael 180–1, 299
Bettan, Israel 199
Bevis Marks Synagogue, London 246
Bezalel ben Abraham Ashkenazi 281
Béziers 68, 80, 84, 85
Bibago, Abraham 149, 192, 197
  Saragossa academy of 81
  sermon on Creation by 198
biblical exegesis 113–39
Bilia, Solomon 215
Bonafed, Solomon:
  studies logic with Christian scholar 73, 76
  on superiority of Christian scholars 64–5
Bonaventure 131–2
Boniface VIII, Pope 101, 103
Bonsenior, Solomon 214
Bordeaux 102, 141, 228
Borowitz, Eugene 250
Brandon, David 246–7
Brann, Ross 260
Brazil 230, 232
Buber, Martin 266
Budapest 140, 179, 221

Bund, Jewish socialist 313
Burgos 87
Bursa 213
  rejection of boycott in 214, 217, 218–19

C
Cairo 239
Calvin, John 145
Campanton, Isaac 81, 189
  disciples of 193
  raises 'doubts' on talmudic passages 115, 121–2
Cantor, Norman 179
Capsali, Elijah 187
Carcassonne:
  attempted revolt in 102
  collectors of royal tax in 100
  consuls on trial in 102, 104, 112
  Inquisition in control of 101
  legal questions to Adret from 95
Castiel, Daniel 233
Castile 5, 88, 186, 189
  exile as judicial penalty in 35
  gathering of sages in 189
  Jewish society of 30, 55
  judicial procedure in 38
  rebellion in 16
Catholic Monarchs 182, 186
  see also Ferdinand; Isabella
Charles VI of France 133
Charles VIII of France 304–5
Christian, Paul, *see* Paul Christian
Christians 9, 24, 38, 93, 141
  academies of 7, 86
  allegorical interpretations of 109–10
  attitude towards commandments of 114
  bakeries of 20
  biblical exegesis of 130–2
  as concubines 15, 22, 23, 34
  and Esau 226
  and excommunication 27–8
  interest in Gersonides 83
  language of (Latin) 198
  as philosophers 64–5, 67, 69, 92
  polemical literature of 147–8, 260–1
  preaching of 14–15, 18–19, 132–3, 138, 144–5
  prostitutes among 35–6
  and Reformation 300

respect for Adret by 108
as scholastic writers 60, 115, 134
in sermons of Aboab 200
as servants to Jews 21
as teachers for Jews 73, 76, 81–2
as theologians 42
universities of 111
vilification of Jews by 200
see also Gentiles
Church Fathers 115, 130
see also Augustine; Jerome
Clement V, Pope 102
Clement VII, Pope 310
Cohen, Gerson 316
Cohen, Martin A. 94
Collins, John J. 295
communities:
  Ashkenazi 34
  educational curriculum of 59
  fissure within 7, 59, 215–16
  local self-determination of 95
community ordinance/s (*takanah/takanot*) 24, 30, 42–51, 54
Congregation B'nai Jeshurun, Cincinnati 247
Congregation Emanu-El, New York 249
Constantinople:
  call for boycott in 213
  challenge to preachers in 239
  division among congregations of 215–16
  fall of 300
  proclamation of boycott in 214–15
  rabbis of 215
Conversos:
  attitude towards Inquisition of 185
  and David Reubeni 312
  messianic activism among 312
  religious nature of 184
  see also Marranos
Cordova 2, 41
Council of the Major Communities in Lithuania 244
counter-ban:
  against ban on philosophical study 107–9
courtiers, Jewish 16, 26, 51, 84, 185
  Abraham Seneor as 183, 186–7
  Abravanel as 89, 186–7, 192
  Crescas as 89
  Joseph ibn Shem Tov as 86

Joseph Nasi as 219
philosophy and 62, 88
Todros Abulafia as 16
courts, Gentile 32–4
courts, Jewish 23, 37, 40–1, 51
  discretionary powers of 32–4
  jurisdiction of 31–2, 54–5
Creation 126, 140–64
Crescas, Hasdai 60, 64, 82, 134
  as communal leader 191
  as courtier 89
  critique of Aristotle by 89, 191–2
  disciple of 123–4
  on doubts 124
  Harry Wolfson on 80
  sermon in time of drought by 189
Crete 92
  messianic uprising in 301
Crusades 276
  messianic activism during 309–10
  messianic significance of 300
Cum nimis absurdum, *see* Paul IV, Pope
Curaçao 247
curriculum for Jewish education 6, 75, 81
  control of 94, 102, 106
  of Falaquera 77
  limited to traditional texts 59, 105–6
  philosophical study in 60, 73
Cyrus 'the Great' 300, 308
  as 'messianic' figure 305

D

Damascus 309
Dan, Joseph 94, 140, 141
Danon, Moses 193
D'Avray, David 134
Dead Sea Scrolls 293, 306
Dee, John 150
Del Bene, David 243
Del Bene, Judah 243
Délicieux, Bernard 101, 102
Dennistoun, James 212–13
deprivation, theory of 302
diaspora 1, 9–10, 62, 291, 314, 316–17
  all commandments incomplete in 285–6
  alleged 'blindness' of Jews in 180, 182
  complexity of attitudes towards 270
  denigration of life in 290
  efficacy of prayer in 284–5
  enforcement of talmudic law in 274–6

diaspora (cont.):
    and Halevi 258–9
    and Land of Israel 271
    Portuguese 205
    radical negation of 285
    religious status of Jews in 280–7
    Zionist characterizations of 254
    see also exile
din malkhut (law of the king or state) 31
Dinur, Ben Zion 16, 69, 80
    on hasidic messianism 312
Disputation at Barcelona 260–5
'disputed question' 113, 115
    and Christian scriptural study 131
    in Jewish sermons 74, 120, 121, 123
divine providence 16, 17
    Aboab on 201
    Crescas on 124
    and exile 268
    and Land of Israel 282–4
    Morteira on 149–50, 155, 231–2, 235
Dominicans 101
'double truth' theory 92, 110
    see also 'Averroism'
Dov Baer (Maggid of Mezhirech) 265–70
    immanentist theology of 269
dubitatio, dubium (doubt) 116, 122, 128–9, 131–2, 134
    in Christian exegesis 118
    see also 'method of doubts'
Dunash ibn Labrat 256
Duran, Profiat 64
Duran, Simeon ben Joseph (En Duran) 98, 104–6, 112
Duran, Solomon ben Simeon (Rashbash) 278, 279

E
Edeles, Samuel (Maharsha) 280
Edom (as Christendom) 224, 226, 255–6
Einhorn, David 248
Eisen, Arnold 253
Eiximenis, Francesc 133–4
Eleazar of Worms 175
Elijah del Medigo 64, 92
Elimelekh of Lyzhansk 267, 287–8, 289
Elon, Menachem 29, 181, 191
Emden, Jacob 272
Emek habakhah (The Valley of Weeping), see
    Joseph Hakohen

Emery, Richard 102
'Epistle on Apostasy', see Maimonides
eschatology:
    Christian 296
    Maimonidean 88
    Shi'ite 309
Espinosa, Michael 142
'Estate of the Eternal' 285, 287
Ets Hayim Society (Amsterdam) 234, 235
Eusebius 307
excommunication 6, 23–5, 27–8, 103–4, 233
    general ban of 275
    see also ban; Spinoza; Uriel da Costa
exegesis 1
    Christian biblical 130–2
    hasidic homiletical 266
    medieval Jewish biblical 114–28
    see also Abravanel; allegorization;
        Nahmanides; Rashi
exile 141, 241–70, 272
    achieving Holy Spirit during 265–6
    all commandments incomplete in 290
    ambivalence towards 9, 270
    in Arabic poem 260
    and atonement 259
    connotations of the word 253–4
    as court-imposed punishment 34–5
    disparate attitudes towards 273
    divine presence in 267
    divine providence and 17
    Dunash ibn Labrat on 256
    following Babylonian conquest 301, 304–5
    God suffering in 270
    'good things' in 258
    Halevi and Nahmanides on 264–5
    hasidic conception of 272
    iron wall blocks prayer in 267
    Jewish life as disaster in 256–8, 259
    and Jewish mission 254
    as leaving home in Spain 259
    longing of Jews for Israel during 274
    and Lurianic kabbalah 311
    messiah will end 291, 293
    might continue forever 261–2, 286
    in Morteira's sermons 141
    negation versus affirmation of 267
    observance of commandments in 263–5, 287, 317
    pleasures of life in 256

prolonged by Jewish sins 253
and Reform Judaism 312–13
repentance will end 17
return from Babylonian 304–5
and world to come 264
Zionism to end Jewish 313–14
Zionist writers on 254
see also diaspora
Exodus from Egypt:
as paradigm for redemption 304
expulsion:
from Andalusia 183
from England 182
from France 112, 182
from Valmaseda 183
Expulsion from Spain 60, 80, 93, 125, 202, 300
difficulty of foreseeing 182
Edict of 8, 184
generation of 7, 114, 116–21, 136, 139, 179–203
messianic tension following 300, 310
Eybeschuetz, Jonathan 173
Ezra of Gerona 263

F
Falaquera, Shem Tov 61, 77, 86, 93
Faquim, Moses 92
Faraj, Judah 208, 213, 315
Farissol, Abraham 71
Fasi, Joseph 193
Feldman, Leon 124
Feldman, Seymour 148
Ferdinand 'the Catholic' 182, 183
see also Catholic Monarchs
Ferrand of Majorca 102
Ferrer, Vicente 14, 308
Fez 142
Flanders 99, 100
Fortalitium fidei, see Alonso de Espina
France 9, 98, 103–4, 107
disloyalty to king of 106, 112
expulsion of Jews from 182
Jewish legislation in 42–3
no Jewish courtier class in 26
power of royal government in 100
rabbis of 279
revival preaching in 15
see also Languedoc; Provence; southern France

Franciscans 101
Franco, Samuel 190
Frederick II, Emperor 64, 67, 68
Free Synagogue, New York 249
Friedländer, Israel 302, 309

G
Gafni, Isaiah 254
Galen 128
Galipappa, Hayim 318
galut, see exile
Gamil, Shem Tov 190
Garçon, Joseph 81
eulogies by 190
sermons by 195
Gay, Peter 188
Genoa 206
Gentiles:
bread baked by 19–20
courts of 32–4
emulating ways of the 111, 243
interaction with 19
Jew stealing from 23
prostitutes among 35–6
punishment for heretics by 104
sabbath work by 21
servants living in Jewish homes 20
sexual relations with 21, 24–5, 34, 234
texts written by 67
see also Christians
Germany 9, 19, 185, 188
Jewish Pietists of (*ḥasidei ashkenaz*) 2, 167, 263
legal tradition of 40
rabbis of 279
Gerondi, Jonah 22, 23, 78
Gershon of Kuty 312
Gershon ben Solomon 62
Gerson, Jean 133
Gersonides (Levi ben Gershon, Ralbag) 60, 64, 72, 84
access to papal court by 83
biblical commentaries of 114, 126
on God's knowledge 197–8
on heavenly bodies 162
library of 72
'method of doubts' in 125–6, 134
supercommentaries on Averroës by 126
uses only Hebrew texts 68
writings on different levels by 61

gezerah (emergency decree) 95
Gikatilla, Joseph 200, 268
Gilbert de la Porrée 131
Giles of Rome 69
Givat sha'ul 142, 143, 222
　see also Morteira, Saul Levi
Glatzer, Michael 91
Goitein, S. D. 259
Gordon, Judah Leib 316
Gracian, Zerahiah ben Shealtiel 76
Graetz, Heinrich 94, 179
'great chain of being' 159
'Great Revolt' of 66–70 CE 307
Green, Arthur 288, 294
Gregory of Rimini 134
Guadalajara 197
Guericke, Otto von 150
Guide for the Perplexed 77, 237, 241
　1283 manuscript of 71
　on allegory in Bible 169
　conceals deepest truths 3, 67
　discussed in Morteira sermon 153, 156–61
　Hebrew translation of 66–7, 160, 237
　parable of the castle in 268
　paucity of messianism in 317
　repudiates anthropocentric Creation 156–61
　studied by 13-year-old 76
　studied in Islamic schools 82
　see also Maimonides; Index of Passages Cited
Guidobaldo II, duke of Urbino 204, 218
　acceptance of refugee Marranos by 208, 209
　attitude towards Jews of 212–13
　as captain of papal armies 208, 210, 211
　expulsion of Marranos from Pesaro by 213
　rupture with pope over Marranos 208, 211
Gush Emunim 296
Guttmann, Jacob 115
Guttmann, Julius 61, 64, 181
Gutwirth, Eleazar 187

H

Habillo, Eli ben Joseph 69–70
Hacker, Joseph 81
halakhah (traditional Jewish law) 29, 45, 204
　on bride at wedding 19
　on burial in the Land of Israel 277
　decisions departing from 30–42, 55
　Hillel of Verona studying 78
　on murder conviction 39
Halevi, Judah 61, 83, 255–60, 264
　ambivalence of 260
　compared with Nahmanides 267
　on God's accessibility anywhere 269
　influence of Arabic poetry on 260, 262
　Kuzari of 267–8
　as proto-Zionist 259
　sea poems of 259
　success in Muslim Spain of 256
　wine poems of 256
　see also Index of Passages Cited
Haliczer, Stephen 188
Halkin, Abraham 95–6, 263
Halkin, Hillel 259
Harvey, Steven 92
Harvey, Warren 79
hasidism (Polish):
　on access to God in exile 267–8, 287
　homiletical exegesis in 266
　and messianism 294, 312
　rebbe/tsadik in 268, 270
　on serving God in exile 264
　spiritualization of Land of Israel in 287–9
Hasmonean revolt 295
Havatselet, Avraham 17
Hayim ben Hananel Hakohen 277–9
Hayun, Joseph 117, 122–3, 126, 189
Hebron 109
hefker beit din hefker (the court's authority is decisive) 48
hekdesh 44
Henry of Hesse 138
herem, see ban; excommunication
Herrera, Abraham Cohen 175–6
Heschel, Abraham Joshua 271, 272
Hillel ben Samuel of Verona 64
　and 'method of doubts' 128
　philosophical study in Spain by 78–9, 81–2
　sefekot terminology by 127
　Tagmulei hanefesh of 77–8
Hirsch, Emil G. 248
Hodara, Joseph 214
Holocaust:
　analogy with 180
　and 'backshadowing' 181
Honen Dalim Society (Amsterdam) 234

Honorius Augustodun 132
hora'at sha'ah (temporary teaching) 31
Horowitz, Isaiah 277
Howe, Irving 313

I

Iberian peninsula 8, 14, 60, 141, 183, 205
   see also Portugal; Spain
ibn Abbas, Samau'el 298
ibn Adret, Abraham (scribe) 71
Ibn Aflah, Jabir 70
ibn Daud, Abraham 2, 259
ibn Ezra, Moses 259
ibn Habib, Jacob 190
ibn Habib, Levi 193
ibn Hisdai brothers 76, 82
ibn Kaspi, Joseph 61, 72, 76, 91
   digest of Aristotle's *Nicomachean Ethics* by 77
   educational curriculum of 75
   as popularizer of philosophy 87
ibn Lev, Joseph 206, 215
ibn Musa, Hayim 201
ibn Nagrela, Samuel 203
ibn Shem Tov, Isaac 71, 80, 86, 92
ibn Shem Tov, Joseph 86, 92
   lost works of 190
   sermons of 16, 123
ibn Shem Tov, Shem Tov ben Joseph 86, 92, 193
   commentary on Maimonides' *Guide* by 153–4
   on Crescas 192
   questioning of royal alliance by 188
   scepticism about Jewish courtiers of 185
   sermons by 120, 185, 198
ibn Shu'eib, Joel 139, 193, 283
   on dangers of centralized power 188
   and 'method of doubts' 118–19, 137
ibn Shu'eib, Joshua 22
ibn Tibbon family 84–6
ibn Tibbon, Judah 80, 86, 87
   education of son by 76, 77
   library of 72
   socio-economic status of 84–5
ibn Tibbon, Judah ben Moses 86
ibn Tibbon, Moses 66, 69, 71, 85, 91
   translation of Averroës by 79
ibn Tibbon, Samuel 61, 72, 76, 87, 160, 237

   attacked for translating the *Guide* 66–7
   as mentor of Anatoli 76
   Yikavu hamayim by 71
ibn Verga, Judah 180, 185
ibn Verga, Solomon 180
Immanuel of Rome 66, 69–70, 88
ingathering of the exiles 9, 261, 294, 295, 313, 316
inheritance, laws of 42, 48, 50, 52–3
Innocent III, Pope 42, 179
Inquisition, papal 112, 213
   and burning of Talmud 108
   as model for Solomon ben Adret 104, 111
   penitential pilgrimage imposed by 34
   and Philip the Fair 101–2, 104, 109
   and Pope Paul IV 208
   procedure of 24, 38, 40
Inquisition, Portuguese 141
Inquisition, Spanish 8, 24, 180–1, 189, 203, 230
   establishment of 183
   purpose of 184–5
   regnant theory of 184
Isaac de Leon 185, 186, 188, 190
Isaac ben Samuel 53, 54
Isaac ben Yedaiah 80, 88, 317
Isabella 'the Catholic' 182
   see also Catholic Monarchs
'Isawiyya, *see* Abu Isa of Isfahan
Ishbili, Yom Tov ben Abraham (Ritva) 42
Islamic conquest 308
Islamic East 59
Israel, author of 'Dover meisharim' 120–1, 193
Israel Ba'al Shem Tov 269, 287, 289, 312
Istanbul 186, 195
Italy 9, 191, 220, 238
   Adriatic coast of 205
   Christian intellectuals in 92
   Christian revival preachers in 15
   copying of manuscripts in 70
   Hebrew books printed in 188
   homiletical literature in 140
   invasion of in 1494 305
   manuscripts brought from Toledo to 66
   merchants and traders in 204
   papal anti-Jewish policy in 212
   philosophical study in 59, 73, 81–2, 87

J

Jacob ben Asher 30, 40, 53
Jacob ben Makhir:
  and Christian universities 86, 111
  opposes ban on philosophical study 97, 103
  on study of astronomy 64
  translation of *Almagest* by 70–1
Jacob Joseph of Polonnoye 264, 287
Jaffe, Samuel 149, 152–4, 159
James I of Aragon 261
James II of Aragon 99, 102, 104
James of Majorca 99, 102, 111, 112
Jerome, St 133
Jerusalem 267, 269, 290
  Babylonian conquest of 255
  controlled by Crusaders 256
  fall of in 70 CE 307
  Halevi's intention to reach 257–9
  Nahmanides reaches 286
  'no desire in' 316
  permission from Julian to return to 308
  sacred geography of 268
Jeshua, Joseph 191
'Jesus movement' 307, 315
John III, of Portugal 310
John of Varzy 132
Jonathan Hakohen of Lunel 67
Joseph ben David of Saragossa 124–5
Joseph ben Israel of Toledo 67
Joseph ben Moses of Trani 278
Joseph Hakohen 185, 213
Joseph Nasi, Don 215, 217, 219
Josephus 298, 306, 307, 315
Judah ben Asher 16
  on changing historical circumstances 51–4
  on community legislation (*takanot*) 42–51
  on excommunicating ban 23–4, 37–8
  on extra-halakhic punishments 31–42
  eye problems of 55
  'Letter of Admonition' (ethical will) by 55
  on prostitutes 35–6
  responsa of 5, 17, 30–56
Judah Leib ben Bezalel (Maharal of Prague) 229, 284, 293
Judah Leib of Gur 264
Julian, Emperor 308
Julius III, Pope 207, 211

K

kabbalah 3, 4, 169, 191, 201
  Aboab and 194, 199–201, 203
  Abravanel and 192
  absence of messianic tension in 311
  elitist element of 4
  in fifteenth-century Spain 81, 181
  'gnostic school' of 88
  modern histories of 191
  Morteira and 147, 155, 175–6
  opposition to in Provence 3, 80
  in sermons 200, 203, 242
  values and perils of studying 277
  see also Lurianic kabbalah
Kalonymos ben Kalonymos 76, 86
  seeking teacher of philosophy 76
  as translator 68, 82
Kalonymos ben Todros 88
Kaplan, Joseph 233
Karo, Ephraim 118, 188, 190
Karo, Isaac 119, 121, 139, 188, 193
  sermons of 118, 120
  Torah commentary of 114, 117–18
Karo, Joseph 190–1, 193
Katz, Jacob 311
Kaufmann, David 105
Kaufmann, Yehezkel 253
Kelley, Edward 150
Keneseth Israel Congregation, Philadelphia 248
ketubah (marriage contract) 9, 52, 280
  divorce without payment of 273–9
  takanah concerning 43, 47–52
Kimhi, David (Radak) 72, 85
  biblical commentaries of 127
  as defender of Maimonides 87–8
  as popularizer of philosophy 86
Kimhi, Joseph 67
Kohn, Moshe 185
Kol nidrei 256
Kol sakhal 163
kushiyot (difficulties) 114
  in Isaac Karo 117, 118
  see also 'method of doubts'
Kuzari, see Halevi, Judah

L

Land of Israel 9, 254, 270, 271–90, 300, 307–8, 313, 316

General Index

air of conducive to intellectual activity 282–3
attachment of diaspora Jews to 271
burial in 277
centrality of 280, 293
commandments properly observed only there 263, 285
and David Reubeni 310
essence of commandments only there 287
focusing thought on 287–8
in Jewish thought 272
Judah Halevi and 255–8
large-scale resettlement in 311
leaving to live elsewhere 281–2
and marital conflict 274–80
messianic return to 294, 311
methodology for sources on 273
mitzvah to live there at present 278
movement of migration to 254–9
no longer an obligation to live there 277
not controlled by stars 284–5
pilgrims atone by visiting 259
poor living conditions there 278
praises of 272
prayers more efficacious in 285
and sexual misconduct 286
special providential relationship with 282–5, 287
spiritualization of 288–9
Zionism and 314
Landgraf, Artur 131
Langermann, Tzvi 128
Languedoc 7, 35, 96, 98, 104, 107, 111
papal Inquisition in 101–2, 109
royal policy towards 98–103
see also Provence; southern France
Lawee, Eric 188
Lea, Henry Charles 101
leadership:
alleged intellectual mediocrity of 181, 188–91
aristocratic 88
in Barcelona 97, 104, 106
communal 24, 36, 191
condemnations of Spanish Jewish 179–80, 186
evaluation of 192–203
rabbinic 6, 8, 16, 29–30, 37, 54, 63, 141–2, 206

Leeser, Isaac 247
Leeuwenhoek, Anthony van 165
Lenowitz, Harris 291, 297–9
Leon Joseph of Carcassonne 72, 74–5
Lerma, Judah 268
Levi ben Abraham of Villefranche 83, 96
accusations against 89
on need for encyclopedic works 62
as popularizer 73
poverty of 72–3, 88, 106
wealthy patron of 72, 77
Levi ben Gershon (Ralbag), *see* Gersonides
Levi ben Shem Tov of Saragossa 189
libraries:
Christian 72
of individual Jews 43, 68, 72, 85
Lisbon 141, 190
Lombard, Peter 134
Lubavitcher messianism 312
Lublin 8, 244
oppression of Jews in 227–8
Luntshitz, Ephraim 243, 244, 288, 316
Lurianic kabbalah 269
exile and redemption in 296, 311
and Neoplatonic philosophy 175–6
see also kabbalah

M

Macedonia 208
Mahamad 229, 233
in Amsterdam 245
in London 246–7
Maharal of Prague, *see* Judah Leib ben Bezalel
'Maimonidean conflicts' 94, 106
Maimonides, Moses (Rambam) 3–4, 53–4, 147, 174, 179, 198, 240, 259, 293
allows corporal punishment 32
and anthropocentric view of Creation 158–9, 161–3
on biblical allegory 169, 241
commentary on Hippocrates by 128
as communal leader 191, 203, 309
on conversation during worship 18
decision not to live in Land of Israel by 279
defence of wife's *ketubah* by 274–5
description of messianic movements by 315
on dietary laws 90
disputes over writings of 86–8, 104, 106

Maimonides, Moses (*cont.*):
  on diversity from unity 153–4
  'Epistle on Apostasy' by 263
  'Epistle to Yemen' by 179, 291–2, 309–10, 315
  on heavenly bodies 161
  on imprisonment for debt 44
  on insult to preacher 239
  on judicial discretion 33
  leadership following death of 179
  on leaving Muslim Spain 259
  on living outside the Land of Israel 281–2
  on messiah as fundamental belief 262
  on messianic age as means to an end 264
  Mishneh torah of 3, 62, 78, 281
  Morteira's challenge to 156–63
  and papal Inquisition 108
  parable of the castle by 268
  as philosopher 60–1, 63–4, 66–7
  on reasons for commandments 49, 90, 169
  responsa of 18, 239, 274–5
  revision of talmudic text by 282
  on sexual relations with Gentiles 34, 39
  on world's continued existence 148
  see also Guide for the Perplexed; Index of Passages Cited
Majorca 111
  King James of 99, 102, 112
Mantua 71, 81, 190, 243
manuscripts:
  of Anatoli's translation 68
  collection of 180, 66
  colophons of 63, 71
  cost of 72
  scribal copying of 6, 70, 78
  of sermons 120–1
  of technical philosophical works 65, 66, 70
Marranos:
  campaign against 180, 183–4
  former in Italy 205–16
  former in Salonika 219
  martyrdom in Ancona of 207–8, 218
  thriving commerce of 206
  see also Conversos
Marseilles 85
  legal questions to Adret from 95
Martini, Raymond 308
martyrdom, Jewish 62, 179, 218, 264–5
  in sermons of Aboab 202–3

Masconi, Leon 73
Matt, Daniel 93
medical studies 72, 76, 77–8
Medigo, Elijah del 66
Medina, Samuel de (Maharashdam):
  on bringing body for burial in Land of Israel 276–7
  legal questions to 205–7
  on protectionist ordinance in Salonika 219
Meir of Rothenburg 275
  on Land of Israel 278, 279
  on martyrdom 202
Me'iri, Menahem 91, 106
  on reasons for commandments 90, 109–10
  restricting of preachers by 74, 242
Menahem Azariah of Fano 155, 175
Menahem Nahum of Chernobyl 288
Menahem ben Solomon 223
Menahem ibn Saruk 257
Menasseh ben Israel 245–6
  Morteira's eulogy for 168, 227
Mendes, Doña Gracia 215, 219
  fear of reprisals from 217
mendicants 108, 109–10
  see also Dominicans; Franciscans
Menot, Michel 132–3
Meshulam ben Jacob of Lunel 67
Meshulam ben Joseph 68
Meshulam ben Moses 80
Messer Leon, David 155, 186
  on Crescas 192
Messer Leon, Judah 64, 81, 188
messiah 9–10, 227, 291–318
  activism to bring 270, 292, 293, 312
  born in 70 CE(?) 261, 262
  Christian doctrine of 261
  and current calamities 202
  denial of future 296
  descended from Joseph 308
  doctrine of 304
  at end of Morteira's sermons 229
  Gentile king more important than 260–1
  as human king 260, 262
  improper terminology regarding 297
  Judaism not dependent upon 261, 286, 317
  prophecy renewed with advent of 238
  socialist transformation of 313
  as threat to established leadership 10, 291–2

General Index

to be born on Ninth of Av 299
messianic doctrine 303-4
  questions relating to 261, 292, 316
  quietistic component of 258, 308
  and Shi'ite doctrines 310
messianic figures and personalities, *see* Abu Isa; Abulafia, Abraham; Alroy; Bar Kokhba revolt; Nahman of Bratslav; Reubeni; Zevi
messianic movements 292-303, 314-16
  in biblical times 304-5
  and calculated dates 301
  fundamental questions about 315-18
  Gentile governments and 291, 302
  hasidism as 312
  and messianic personalities 293-4, 298
  as positive or negative force 318
  as threat to established leadership 10, 291-2
'method of doubts' 114-39
  see also *sefekot*
mezuzah 14
Middle East academies 74
Midrash, *see* Index of Passages Cited
Midrash hane'elam 199
Mikveh Israel Synagogue, Philadelphia 247
'millenarism' 295-6
Minḥat kena'ot (A Zealous Offering) 94, 100
  see also Abba Mari of Lunel
Mishneh torah 3, 78, 281
  Maimonides on need for 62
  see also Maimonides; Index of Passages Cited
Modena, Leon 155, 163, 168
  use of *Summa theologica* by 135
Montpellier 72, 97, 107, 111-12
  attempts to control pulpit in 241
  legal questions to Adret from 95
  links with Aragon in 98
  medical school of 78
  opposition to Abba Mari in 86, 98, 103-4
  resistance to French royal power in 99
  royal official in 105-6, 111
  university of 86, 111
Morais, Sabato 247
Mordecai ben Samuel 246
Moreno, Jacob 233
Morteira, Saul Levi 7-8, 140-71, 176, 221-36

  and anthropocentric Creation 156-63
  and Aquinas 149, 151
  and creation *ex nihilo* 164
  on dangers of assimilation 234
  dating of his sermons 143, 221
  on diversity from unity 152-4, 171
  on divine providence 164, 231, 232, 235
  educational role of 141-2, 144-5
  effort of in preparing sermons 226
  and esoteric doctrine 176
  eulogy for kabbalists by 156
  eulogy for Menasseh ben Israel by 168, 247
  and grandeur of universe 175
  on halakhic principle and cosmology 173
  and Jewish-Christian polemic 147
  Judaeocentric stance of 163
  on kabbalah 147, 154-5, 175-6
  on large glass sphere 149-50
  medieval vocabulary of 174
  and microscope 165
  occasional repetition of sermons by 229
  on painting and Creation 168, 170
  quarrel of with Menasseh ben Israel 245
  rebuttal of Maimonides by 156-61
  and Rembrandt 172
  responsum on art by 167-8
  rhetorical use of analogies by 164
  and Samuel Jaffe 152-4, 159
  on sea as emblem of Creation 164-8
  sense of symmetry of 224
  sermons of, as adult education 142
  sermons on *parashat Bereshit* by 140-76
  Tratado da verdade da lei de Moisés by 230-2
Moses Hadarshan 223
Moses ben Jacob of Coucy 14-15
Moses ben Joseph di Trani 203
  responsum of 214
Moses de Leon 22, 92
Muslim conquest:
  messianic significance of 300
Muslim Spain, *see* Spain, Muslim

N

Nadler, Stephen 232
Nahman of Bratslav 289, 312
  as messianic personality 293-4
Nahmanides (Moses ben Nahman, Ramban) 83, 149, 269-70, 280, 317

Nahmanides (cont.):
  Aboab's supercommentary on 189, 194
  account of Disputation by 260–5
  allusions to kabbalah by 3–4
  on commandments in diaspora 285–6
  compared with Halevi 264–5
  on exile as suffering 263
  on God outside the Land of Israel 284–7
  and messianic belief in Judaism 260–1, 317
  Torah commentary of 3, 155, 171, 285–6
  true beliefs of about messiah 261–4
Nahmias, Abraham 197
Najara, Abraham 183
Narboni, Moses 61, 64, 76, 91
Narbonne:
  Anatoli's colleagues in 68, 85
  Jewish migration to 100
  legal questions to Adret from 95
  nasi in 88
  papal Inquisition in 102
  seigniorial authority in 99–100
  ties to Aragon of 98
Nathan of Gaza 298
Netanyahu, Benzion 180, 184, 185
Neuman, Abraham 75, 77, 80
New Amsterdam 230
'New Christians' 8, 141, 185
  see also Conversos; Marranos
Newman, Aryeh 286
Nissim ben Reuben Gerondi 124, 285
  'method of doubts' in 125
Norsas, of Mantua 71

O

oath:
  by community leaders 45–6
  improper use of 18
  by injured party 43
  of messianic quietism 308
  by single witness 23
  using divine Name 229
  by widow 50–1
Orange (south-eastern France) 83
Ottoman empire 191, 219–20, 238, 310
  merchants and traders in 204, 206, 208, 218
  rabbis in 205–6, 215–27
  toleration of Jews in 209, 213

P

Padua 217
Paris:
  burning of Talmud in 108
  rabbinic court of 103
  University of 133, 134
Passamaneck, Stephen 33, 37, 38, 40
Paul (apostle) 101, 110
Paul III, Pope 207
Paul IV, Pope 204, 207, 208, 210–11, 213–14
Paul Christian (Pablo Christiani) 260–1
Pedaya, Haviva 265
peregrinatio academica (travelling to find good teachers) 76
Perelmann, Jerohman 288
Perl, Joseph 291
Perpignan 86, 96
Pesaro 207–19
  acceptance of Marranos in 208
  anti-Jewish outrage in 209, 210–11, 213, 218
  diversion of trade to 210, 213, 219
  port of 207, 208–9
  as problematic trade destination 217
pesquisa 24, 39
Philadelphia 249, 250
Philip the Fair:
  conflict with Pope Boniface VIII 101, 103
  and Jews 99, 101, 108–9
  and Languedoc 98–104, 112
  and papal Inquisition 101–2, 104, 108–9
  war with Flanders of 100
'philosophizers' 91, 92, 97
philosophy:
  ban on study of 6, 94, 96–8, 103–6, 108
  and commandments 89–90
  conflict over 59, 61, 63, 66, 77, 88–9, 94–112
  economic foundations of 64–74
  entering medieval Jewish culture 59
  in fifteenth-century Spain 73–4, 181
  flourishing of Jewish 6
  intended for intellectual elite 3–4, 61
  and Jewish courtiers 88–9, 95, 106
  of law 31, 48, 49
  learning from Christian scholars 69, 73, 86
  misuse of 91, 241
  Neoplatonic 175
  opponents of 73, 89, 90, 109, 164

patrons of 71, 64–8, 71, 73, 77, 82, 88
popularization of 61, 63, 74, 82, 85–7
role of in Jewish culture 106
scholarship on Jewish 60–3, 181, 191
scholastic 75, 86, 113
in sermons 74, 91, 106, 199
social context of 62, 63–4, 74–5, 82–92
study by Christians, of 67, 69–70, 111
study of Greek 7, 66, 69–70, 92–4, 105, 242
teachers of 65, 67, 73, 75–80, 85–7
and upper classes 63, 82, 92–3
see also 'Averroism'; Baer; Maimonides; translation
Pico della Mirandola 92
Piekarz, Mendel 267
Pietism, German Jewish (*hasidut ashkenaz*) 175, 263, 317
pilgrimage 34, 259
pinkasim (communal registers) 191
Piza, Joshua 249
Plato 78, 128, 241
on diversity from unity 153–4
influence of 65
on multiple souls 127
Poland 9, 180, 191, 228–9
non-rabbinic preachers in 246
sins of Jews in 229
Polgar (Pollegar), Isaac 64, 262, 317
Portugal:
1492 negotiations in 186, 203
Aboab's death in 189
books destroyed in 190
David Reubeni in 310
emigrants from in Amsterdam 7–8, 141–2, 226–7
emigrants from in Ancona 205, 218
forced conversion in 141, 206–7
Portuguese 'nation' 228
Prawer, Joshua 259
preachers:
allegorization in sermons of 109
Christian 15, 18, 27, 144–5
disseminating philosophical ideas 70, 74, 89–91, 109–10
itinerant 5, 91, 106–7, 244–5
see also Aboab; Abulafia; Morteira
preaching:
Christian 14
control over 102, 237–50

of repentance 16
see also rebuke, sermons of; sermons
prostitution 35–6, 55
Provence:
efforts to ban philosophical study in 94, 96–8, 104, 108–9
no Jewish courtier class in 63
opposition to kabbalah in 80
see also Languedoc; southern France
publica fama 40
punishment 23, 25
banishment as 33, 36
capital 37, 38, 42
by Christian courts 34
corporal 32–3, 39, 42
depending on evidence 41
as deterrent 33
extra-halakhic 32, 27, 39, 42
imprisonment as 44
responsa on 31–42

R
Rabbenu (Jacob ben Meir) Tam 53, 55
Rabinowitz, Louis 251
Raimundo, archbishop of Toledo 72
Ralbag, *see* Gersonides
Rambam, *see* Maimonides
Ramban, *see* Nahmanides
Raphael ben Joseph 298
Rashi 53, 138, 149, 284
Aboab's supercommentary on 194
on Gen. 1: 11 171
on Gen. 17: 8 281
on Gen. 46: 29 225
on Lam. 4: 21 224
on Lev. 1: 14 173
on Lev. 25: 38 281
on Ps. 80: 6 222
Ravitzky, Aviezer 314
rebuke, sermons of 5, 13–14, 18–24, 27, 239, 243–7
Recife 24, 232
redemption 141
and Bar Kokhba movement 307
dates calculated for 301
in Hebrew Bible 303–5
imminent 294, 299
in Lurianic kabbalah 311
and the messiah 291, 295–6

redemption (cont.):
  quietism as key to 258
  in Reform Judaism 313
  and the State of Israel 314
  yearnings for 271
reductio ad absurdum 46–7
Reform Judaism 248–9, 270
  and prayers for messiah 316
  and prayers for State of Israel 314
  rejection of traditional messianism by 312–13
Reformation:
  Catholic 207
  Protestant 300
Regev, Sha'ul 117–18
Reiner, Elhanan 260
Rembrandt 172
repentance:
  brings end to exile 17, 310
  preaching of 14–15, 123
  as problematic doctrine 199–200
responsa 29–56, 196, 214, 281, 319–21, 323–5, 327
  on enforcement of talmudic law 274–5
  of Ephraim Karo 190
  extra-halakhic factors in 29–32, 37, 39, 42, 43, 51
  in fifteenth-century Spain 181
  in generation of the Expulsion 191
  of Hayim Ya'ir Bachrach 277
  of Isaac Aboab 193–4
  of Joseph ibn Lev 206
  of Joshua Soncino 208–11, 214, 216–18
  of Judah ben Asher 17, 23–4, 30–56
  of Maimonides 18, 239, 277–5
  of Moses di Trani 214, 217
  of Ottoman rabbis 205, 213–18
  as reflection of society 29–30
  responding to papal persecutions 207, 208
  of Samuel de Medina 205–7, 278–9
  of Saul Levi Morteira 167–8
  of Solomon ben Adret 25, 95, 284
  of Solomon ben Simeon Duran 276, 279
  as sources for Jewish history 5–6, 205
Reubeni, David 310
Robert of Anjou 67, 68
Roman law 31, 115
Romano, Judah 68, 69
Rome 66, 76

Abulafia's journey to 293
David Reubeni in 310
establishment of ghetto in 212
Rosenzweig, Franz 258
Roth, Cecil 88, 219
Roth, Norman 180

S

Sa'adyah Ga'on 127, 162, 293
Saba, Abraham 188, 193, 215
  on Genesis 188, 225
  lost works of 190
  on response to rape of Dinah 196
  sermon by 189
Saba, Abraham (rabbi in Constantinople) 215
Sabbatai Zevi 297, 302
  supported by many Jewish leaders 315
sabbath, and Gentile servants 20
Sabbatianism 302–3, 304, 307
  collective trauma of 311
  as 'messiah movement' 296
Safed 280, 311
Salomon de les Infants of Arles, Don 84
Salomon, H. P. 231
Salonika 115, 214, 286
  as centre of textile industry 219
  request for boycott in 213
Samson ben Zadok 202
Samuel ben Judah of Marseilles 69, 70, 71, 76–7, 86, 87
Samuel ben Reuben of Béziers 96
Sancho IV of Castile 16
Sarachek, Joseph 95
Saragossa 81
Scaliger, Joseph 167
Schacter, Jacob J. 272
Schama, Simon 165
Schirmann, Hayyim 256
scholasticism 60, 75, 115
  and Christian sermons 114, 134
  and 'disputed question' 74, 113, 131, 134, 199
  philosophy of 114, 134
Scholem, Gershom 16, 181, 267, 296, 311
  on hasidic messianism 312
Schwartz, Dov 91
Schwartzmann, Julia 92
scribes 3, 6, 65, 66

colophons of 63, 71, 81
  in legal case 52
  of philosophical manuscripts 70, 71
Second Commonwealth 306
Seeskin, Kenneth 149
sefekot (doubts) 114–20, 123–7, 129
  in Abravanel 116–17
  in Isaac Arama 119
  in talmudic study 116, 122
Sefer hakabalah (Book of Tradition) 2
Sefer hasidim (Book of the Pious) 3, 317
  see also Pietism, German Jewish
Sefer yetsirah (Book of Creation) 175
sefirot (kabbalah) 154, 155, 200, 202
Segovia 16
Sen Astruc de Noves 76
Seneor, Abraham 183, 186–7
Sermoneta, Giuseppe 79
sermons 4–5, 9, 13
  addressed to entire community 20
  attempts to restrict 9, 237–50
  by Christian preachers 15, 138
  by disciple(s) of Crescas 123
  by Isaac Aboab 120, 195–201
  by Isaac Karo 118
  by Jean Gerson 133
  by Joel ibn Shu'eib 118–19, 137
  by John Calvin 144–5
  by John Wyclif 132
  by Joseph ibn Shem Tov 16, 123
  legal material in 21
  by Moses of Coucy 14
  by Nissim ben Reuben 124–5
  rebuke in 5, 16–28, 239, 243–4
  by Samuel Siriro 142
  by Saul Levi Morteira 8, 140–75, 221–36
  by Shem Tov ibn Shem Tov 120, 185
  by Spanish Jewish preachers 114–25, 189
  by Todros Abulafia 16–28
  at weddings 120, 155, 195, 237, 241
sexual licentiousness 21–2, 35–6, 56
Shabbat Hagadol 142
Shalom, Abraham 193, 265
Shamsulo, Abraham 194
Sharot, Stephen 313
Shatzmiller, Joseph 70, 71, 81, 79, 94
  on Gersonides 83
  on Jewish physicians 63, 76–7

Shekhinah (divine presence) 266, 269
Shem Tov ben Isaac of Tortosa 79
Shlomel of Dresnitz 280
Shukr Kuhayl II 311
Sicily 81
Siete partidas (Castilian law code) 40
Simeon ben Kosiba (Bar Kokhba) 307
Sinigaglia 213
Sirat, Colette 64, 77, 85
Siriro, Samuel 142
Smalley, Beryl 132
socialism, Jewish 313
Solomon ben Isaac Levi 121, 286
Solomon ben Mazal Tov 192
Solomon of Albarracin 189
Solomon of Lunel 88, 100, 103
Soncino, Joshua 208, 215–17
  on anti-Jewish outrage in Pesaro 211
  condemns Marranos for settling in Italy 218
  and Doña Gracia Mendes 215
  first response to Marrano persecution by 213–14
  leads opposition to boycott 216
  negative presentation of 220
  responsum on validity of boycott 210
Sonne, Isaiah 212, 217
southern France 59, 96, 103, 238
  attempts to control pulpit in 240–2
  conflict over philosophy in 7, 77, 94–112
  controversial wedding sermon in 241
  culture of 59, 73, 75, 77, 240
  early kabbalah in 3
  independence from Barcelona of 95, 97–8, 103–4
  Jewish aristocracy in 106
  Jewish society in 106
  medical studies in 77–8
  papal Inquisition in 101–2, 104, 108–9, 111–12
  philosophical sermons in 242
  philosophical teachers in 73, 75–6, 78
  question to Adret from 96
  translation into Hebrew in 67, 240
  see also Languedoc; Provence
Spain 106, 203, 206, 238, 257–9, 286
  'Averroism' in 95
  biblical exegesis in 115–21
  books destroyed in 190

Spain (cont.):
  David Kimhi in 87
  Expulsion from 7, 80, 115, 180, 182, 202, 300, 310
  'good things' of 253, 255, 258
  Hebrew books published in 188
  Hillel of Verona in 78–9, 82
  Jewish assimilation in 272
  Jewish courtiers in 182, 186–7
  Jewish courts in 31, 37
  Jewish cultural tradition in 181, 192–3
  Jewish leadership in 179–203
  Jewish philosophy in 59, 66, 78–80, 181
  Jewish prostitutes in 35–6
  Jews not fully at home in 9
  kabbalah in 181
  Moses of Coucy in 14–15
  Muslim concubines in 22
  sermons in 74, 189, 242
  see also Aragon; Castile; Expulsion from Spain; Iberian peninsula
Spain, Muslim 6, 256, 310
  Abd ar-Rahman I in 260
  Almohad invasion of 60
  cultural flourishing in 258, 309
  Jewish philosophy in 59
  leaving as *galut* 259
Spicq, Ceslas 131
Spinoza, Baruch (Benedict) 6, 8, 142, 175, 176
  Ethics of 162
  excommunication of 232, 233
  rejection of Morteira's theology by 235–6
Steinschneider, Moritz 197
Stow, Kenneth 94, 104
Suasso, Antonio Lopes 233
Sufism 269
Sulami, Samuel 72, 77
Suleiman the Magnificent 204, 206, 219
Summa theologica, see Aquinas

T
ta'amei mitsvot (rational reasons for commandments) 49, 89–90, 91, 169
Taitazak, Joseph 115
takanah/takanot, see community ordinance/s
Talmage, Frank 115
Talmud 9, 16, 18, 22, 42, 48–9, 72, 196, 273–90

Aboab's novellae on 193
  aggadot of 85, 90, 168, 262, 288
  allegorical interpretation of 241
  on bread baked by Gentile 19
  burning of in Paris 108
  Campanton's study of 115, 121–2
  on candle lit by Gentile 20–1
  challenge for ordinary Jews of 196
  and community *takanah* 48–9
  in Disputation of Barcelona 261–2
  on emergency measures 32–4
  intensive study of 1–3, 80, 105, 116
  in Jewish curriculum 59, 75, 80–1, 105
  on messianic age 293, 317
  and minority rights 218
  Morteira's parable from 228–9
  and new circumstances 31, 51–3, 194
  on penitential exile 34
  and Philip the Fair 108–9
  in responsa literature 29
  teaching of 76, 86–7
  see also Index of Passages Cited
Talmud Torah Congregation (Amsterdam) 234
Tam ibn Yahya 281
Ta-Shma, Israel 14, 40
taxes:
  in Languedoc 99–100
  in legal case 41, 51
  takanah on 45
tefilin (phylacteries) 14
Temple 290, 294
  destruction by Babylonians of 299, 301
  destruction by Romans of 224, 261, 266, 301
  pilgrimage to site of 255, 265
  possible rebuilding of 287–8, 308
  sacrifices in 263–4, 267, 269, 271, 278
Themistius 78, 79
to'aliyot (beneficial lessons) 114
tokehah, see rebuke, sermons of
Toledo 5, 11–56, 66, 88, 294
  takanot of 42–3
  translation project in 67
Tosafists 2, 115
  refusal to apply talmudic rule 276–8
Touati, Charles 68
Toulouse 101
translation 7, 72–3, 82, 93

by Christians 67, 111
from Latin into Hebrew 69–70, 199
by Moses ibn Tibbon 66, 69–71, 79
of philosophical texts 65–8, 71, 79, 84–5
tsadik, rebbe 268, 270
tsitsit (fringes) 14
Tudela 86
Turkey 205–19
Tuvyah ben Eliezer 223–5
Twersky, Isadore 59, 63, 277

U
Umayyad caliphate 260
  messianic activism during 302, 309
universities:
  and Christian philosophical study 75
  libraries of 72
  Montpellier 86
  Paris 133, 134, 197, 242
  Prague 245
  as worthy of emulation 111
uprising of 522 BCE 305–6
Uriel da Costa 232
Usque, Samuel 211

V
Valmaseda 183
Varenius, Bernhardus 167
Venice 206, 215
Vermeer, Johannes 150
'vertical metaphor' 159
Vespasian, Emperor 307
violence, among Jews 37, 44, 55
Vital, Hayim 155, 175

W
Waley, Thomas 134
wandering scholars 76
Wasserstrom, Steven M. 309

wedding 19, 26, 120
  at Cana 133
  sermons delivered at 120, 155, 195, 237, 241
Weiss, Roslyn 149
Werblowsky, R. J. Zvi 295
Wieseltier, Leon 161
Wilensky, Sarah Heller 115
Wise, Isaac Mayer 247
Wise, Stephen S. 249
Wolfson, Harry 60, 65, 80, 92
Wyclif, John 132–3

Y
Yabetz, Joseph 62, 189, 193
Yazdagird II, of Persia 301
Yehoshua. A. B. 254, 257
Yemen 311
  messianic uprising in 309
Yerushalmi, Abraham 215
Yerushalmi, Yosef Hayim 183
  on royal alliance 187
Yudghan 298, 309

Z
Zacuto, Abraham 189, 193, 203
Zahalon, Yom Tov ben Moses 281–2
Zarfati, Joseph ben Hayim of Adrianople 280
Zionism:
  and messianism 313–14
  and 'normalization' of Jewish life 314
Zohar:
  on burial in Land of Israel 277
  on marrying alien women 273
  printing of 3, 310
  quotations from in sermons 199–200
  on sexual relations with Gentiles 21–2
  as text of Midrash 200
  see also Index of Passages Cited